Management Accounting Change

Management Accounting Change: Approaches and perspectives, an important new management accounting text, bridges the gap between technical, managerial and theoretical perspectives in management accounting. The book discusses technical developments in management accounting from conventional cost accounting to contemporary strategic management accounting and beyond. Part I shows how conventional cost accounting techniques and management control models evolved in line with the development of mass production and bureaucracy. Part II discusses how recent developments such as customer and strategic orientations in business, flexible manufacturing, post-bureaucracy, network and virtual organizational technologies implicate in management accounting. The book also provides a number of alternative theories through which the transition of management accounting from mechanistic to post-mechanistic approaches can be explained. Parts III and IV elaborate rational theories and interpretive/critical theories, respectively.

This exciting text meets a desperate need for an advanced management accounting textbook that incorporates theory with practice that is accessible and engaging for all those studying in this challenging area.

Danture Wickramasinghe (B.Sc., M.Com, M.Sc., Ph.D.) obtained his Ph.D. from the University of Manchester where he also teaches management accounting and control. He has taught management accounting in a number of universities over 20 years and has been published in *Accounting, Auditing and Accountability Journal*, *Critical Perspectives on Accounting*, *Financial Management* (UK), *Advances in Public Interest Accounting* and the *Journal of Accounting and Organizational Change*.

Chandana Alawattage (B.Sc., MBA, Ph.D.) obtained his Ph.D. from Keele University and teaches management accounting at the University of Aberdeen Business School. He has taught management accounting and related subjects in various other universities over 10 years and has been published in *Critical Perspectives on Accounting, Journal of Accounting and Organizational Change* and a number of conference proceedings in critical accounting.

Management Accounting Change

Approaches and perspectives

Danture Wickramasinghe
and Chandana Alawattage

Routledge
Taylor & Francis Group

LONDON AND NEW YORK

First published 2007
by Routledge
2 Park Square, Milton Park, Abingdon, Oxon OX14 4RN

Simultaneously published in the USA and Canada
by Routledge
270 Madison Ave, New York, NY 10016

Routledge is an imprint of the Taylor & Francis Group, an informa business

© 2007 Danture Wickramasinghe and Chandana Alawattage

Typeset in Perpetua by
Keystroke, 28 High Street, Tettenhall, Wolverhampton
Printed and bound in Great Britain by
The Cromwell Press, Trowbridge, Wiltshire

British Library Cataloguing in Publication Data
A catalogue record for this book is available from the British Library

Library of Congress Cataloging in Publication Data
Wickramasinghe, Danture.
Management accounting change : approaches and perspectives /
Danture Wickramasinghe and Chandana Alawattage.
p. cm.
Includes bibliographical references and index.
1. Managerial accounting. I. Alawattage, Chandana. II. Title.
HF5657.4.W522 2007
658.15′11—dc22
2006039487

ISBN10: 0–415–39331–0 (hbk)
ISBN10: 0–415–39332–9 (pbk)

ISBN13: 978–0–415–39331–7 (hbk)
ISBN13: 978–0–415–39332–4 (pbk)

To our families

Contents

Part III Rational perspectives on management accounting change   **347**

Part IV Interpretive and critical perspectives on management accounting change 409

Illustrations

FIGURES

TABLES

BOXES

EXHIBITS

CASE EXTRACTS

Preface

Welcome to the changing world of management accounting! In this book, we will take you through this world of management accounting and show you how this particular discipline originated and has changed. We will meet key authorities in the discipline to inquire into why and how this change has occurred. At some points, we will have a break to think about the fascination as well as the complexity of this change. At other points, we will debate whether we have to accept different perspectives on management accounting change. Let us start the journey at the beginning.

THE BEGINNING

The idea of writing this book was generated, thanks to a 'free' telephone package, during hour-long intellectual discussions. One day, we were talking about the selection of journal articles for teaching advanced management accounting to third-year undergraduates. We focused on the fact that students at this level often struggle to understand and contextualize these 'hard-going' articles. Our conclusion was that there is no bridge between these academic articles and technical textbooks. Even though a lot of excitement occurs in this academic world, nothing is effectively conveyed to these undergraduates. The 'remedial measure' which emerged from our discussion was to write this book! But the genesis of this idea goes far back to our own undergraduate learning. In those good old days, we thought management accounting was merely a technical subject. The ability to deal with more 'complex' calculative problems would constitute the supremacy of knowledge. After decades of research and teaching, we have now realized that management accounting knowledge lies in a wider spectrum. It lies not only in techniques but also in the changing context in which such techniques evolve; not only in the implementation of techniques, but also in the effects of such implementation; not only in one-sided but also in multiple aspects. A boost came from this realization to write a book on management accounting embracing such a wider spectrum. This is it. It is about the change in management accounting from a mechanistic to a post-mechanistic approach. This is also about multiple perspectives on this change.

The rationale

Change is a pervasive reality. Everything changes everywhere. Management gurus talk about change. There has been a flood of management fads such as 'change management', 'managing change', 'incremental change' and 'radical change'. Simultaneously, best practices for change are now emerging. Attempts have been made for popularizing management strategies, such as 'continuous improvement', 'learning organization', 'TQM' and 'business process re-engineering'. Change has come to be the religion in the field of management. Everybody admires change. Management accounting is not an exception. Since the 1980s the status quo of both theory and practice of management accounting has been questioned. Change has come to the top of management accounting's agenda. It has become one of the most popular topics among hundreds of Ph.D. students around the world. Some explore how management accounting changed in the last century. Others look into how it is changing now. Some attempt to discern whether there is a real change beyond discourse and slogan. Others try to see whether it changes incrementally or radically. Some question whether change is possible in the first place. Others question whether change is even necessary. Some attempt to explore the issue of resistance to all this change.

Unfortunately, the change agenda has been compartmentalized within academia. Even though 'new' techniques are being poured into technical texts, an understanding of change has been far from the territory of undergraduate education. Is this fair to undergraduates and M.Sc./MBA students? Would it be a good idea to add a text covering the change agenda? If so, how could we explain change? How could we produce a complete text? We found answers to these questions through our telephone conversations. The undergraduates and M.Sc./MBA students must embrace the change agenda if they want to know about both the theory and practice of management accounting. As long as there is no such a text, the compilation of a complete text on management accounting is the demand of the day. As long as we are experiencing a rapid change that we have never seen before, it is an immediate necessity. Management accounting change is a response to the external pressures as well as internal transformations. That said, it is due to the interaction between technological/environmental changes and changing management/organizational ideologies. Such changes are fundamentally linked to the nature of economy and society. Once, economy and society were based on craft production. Later, following the industrial revolution, this transformed into mass production within a mechanistic and monopolistic environment. This context gave rise to product costing methods, the ancestor of management accounting. The approach to this accounting came into congruence with mechanization and monopolization: the 'mechanistic approach' to management accounting. Now, following the IT revolution in the factory, customer orientation in the market and globalization of the world, 'good old' management accounting has become subject to serious attacks from both academics and practitioners. People are now busy discovering a post-mechanistic approach to management accounting to be implemented in new factories within a new market and a new world. A number of new management accounting techniques as well as practices have now emerged.

How do we explain the change? Obviously, there is no definitive answer. The answers depend upon our perspective. Different perspectives produce different views of change. We therefore present all possible perspectives, allowing the reader to choose one or several. You may recognize different perspectives, argue for and against them, and be interested in adopting one or some. It is up to you. We do not believe that there is any absolute truth in the field of management accounting. All we can do is engage in speculation and interpretation. Moreover, we can explain what we see through some frameworks which we think suitable. Our aim is not to provide definitive answers to the issues of management accounting change. Rather, we want to raise issues for thought, discussion and reflection. Perspectives which we unfold in the second half of this book will provide an alternative framework for this intellectual exercise. These perspectives range from fashionable economic ideas to critical political debates, from economic theories to political thoughts, and from well-established models to emerging theorizations.

STRUCTURE AND CONTENT

This book contains fifteen chapters. In Chapter 1, we introduce a framework of views, approaches and perspectives. The rest of the book is divided into four parts. In the first two parts, we concentrate on technical development in management accounting from mechanistic to post-mechanistic approaches.

On mechanistic approaches, Part I discusses the emergence of management accounting in relation to:

- mass production and bureaucracy (Chapter 2)
- product costing (Chapter 3)
- profit planning through budgeting (Chapter 4)
- management control through budgeting (Chapter 5)
- economic models of decision-making (Chapter 6)

On post-mechanistic approaches, Part II covers recent modifications and innovations in management accounting concerning:

- customer orientation and flexible manufacturing (Chapter 7)
- strategic management accounting (Chapter 8)
- cost management (Chapter 9)
- new organizations and management control (Chapter 10)

Parts III and IV introduce perspectives – the rational, the interpretive and the critical. Within the rational perspective, two chapters introduce:

- neoclassical economic theories of MACh (Chapter 11)
- contingency theory of MACh (Chapter 12)

The interpretive and critical perspectives are unfolded in three chapters that address:

- interpretations, institutions and networks in MACh (Chapter 13)
- political economy of MACh (Chapter 14)
- beyond political economy of MACh (Chapter 15)

GUIDE

This book has been written for advanced students in management accounting. By 'advanced students' we mean those taking third- or fourth-year management accounting courses at undergraduate level, and those on M.Sc. and MBA programmes. Perhaps the last two parts will be more useful for these students in choosing an appropriate theoretical framework for data analysis.

This book can be read in a tailored manner. If you want to know about management accounting history, you may concentrate on Part I, with a general understanding of Parts II, III and IV. If you want to know about how management accounting change occurs, you may concentrate on both Parts I and II, with an overview of Parts III and IV. If you want to advance your understanding of why management accounting emerged in a particular manner, then you may concentrate on

Parts I, III and IV, with an understanding of Part II. If you need to know about the whole gamut of management accounting change, then you should give all parts your careful and questioning attention. In addition, this book can be used as a reference guide, when academic needs arise, and we have made every attempt to include the most up-to-date references and resources.

However you use this book, it is important to test your understanding. For this, we have included two types of chapter-end questions. First, under 'Have you understood the chapter?', there are questions to test your understanding as well as memory. Second, under 'Beyond the chapter', there are open-ended critical questions that will broaden your understanding beyond the mere content of the chapter. When you deal with these questions, you may consult additional resources listed at the end of each chapter in the 'Further reading' sections. If you intend to probe into 'unseen issues and perspectives', these additional resources will be more helpful.

We hope you enjoy reading this book, and that it will provoke divergent thoughts, theoretical debates and multiple reflections.

KEY TO BOXES

Learning objectives: Presented at the start of each chapter, these boxes carry the highlights of core coverage in terms of learning objectives/outcomes you should achieve/acquire after studying each chapter.

Key terms: Presented between necessary paragraphs throughout the text, these boxes entail relevant definitions of key concepts, techniques and methods covered in respective sections of each chapter.

Point in focus: Inserted in respective sub-sections throughout the text, these boxes summarise the main point being discussed, which will be a useful guide for revising each chapter.

Acknowledgements

This book is a product of the help and blessings of a number of people. From the inception, Professor Trevor Hopper at the University of Manchester encouraged us by providing stimulating comments and guidance. His specific comments on the shape of a book of this nature resulted in meaningful changes and modifications. Equally, Professor Robert Scapens at Manchester was instrumental in providing further encouragement. In particular, one of us had the opportunity to share a final-year course on advanced management accounting with Professor Scapens from which this book began and developed. The students at Manchester who took this course provided formal and *ad hoc* comments collectively and individually on most of the early versions of the chapters. We were glad to see that the students were excited to know that there is some knowledge of accounting behind numbers which they had inadvertently ignored.

We wish to acknowledge the professional and friendly support given by Jaqueline Curthoys, Francesca Heslop and Emma Joyes at Routledge and their understanding of the pains of putting this book together. While producing it, we received much encouragement and support from the staff in the production department at Routledge. Above all, Emma made all this possible.

We would like to thank the following publishers whose materials have been included in the text: ASQ, Cornell University, USA; Blackwell Publishers Ltd., UK; Elsevier Ltd., UK; Harvard Business School Publishing, USA; Oxford University Press, UK; Palgrave Macmillan Ltd., UK; Sage Publications, UK; Simon & Schuster Inc., USA; Thompson Publishing Services, UK; and University of Alabama Press, USA.

Every effort has been made to contact copyright holders for their permission to reprint selections of this book. The publishers would be grateful to hear from any copyright holder who is not here acknowledged and will undertake to rectify any errors or omissions in future editions of this book.

Over the past twenty years or so, we have discussed much of the material contained in this book with undergraduate students from a technical perspective. During the past fifteen years or so, we have discussed the same material with postgraduate and MBA students from a managerial perspective, believing that management accounting textbook materials are universal solutions for organizational problems. It was our studies at Manchester (with Professor Trevor Hopper) and at Keele (with Professor Peter Armstrong and Dr Darren McCabe) that began to provide us with a set of critical perspectives from which those technical and managerial prescriptions of management accounting could be seen differently. We wish to acknowledge those students with whom we enjoyed the 'wonderful world of management accounting', and Trevor, Peter and Darren for their critical insights which led us to question the state of that world of management accounting. This book is a product of this long journey.

We are so grateful to Sanjeevanie Cooray, a PhD student at the University of Manchester, and Tharusha Goonaratne, a lecturer at the University of Colombo, for their comments and corrections on technical aspects of the entire book. Mr John Kitching read the whole manuscript in draft and took great care in making comments on the expression and presentation. We benefited greatly from his comments for changes and recommendations. Manoj, Kasun and Shamanie Wickramasinghe provided immense help in 'correcting' early drafts and giving all secretarial support.

Our families lived with this book for several years. We are grateful for their forbearance and encouragements during this time which was far too long for all of us. Our wives, Lalanie and Shamanie should have the credit for providing the stimulating academic and social environment in which the book materialized. It was delightful to have our children Imesha and Sajan Alawattage and Kasun and Manoj Wickramasinghe 'disturb' the daily writing process.

Chapter 1

Learning management accounting change

A STARTING POINT: THE RELEVANCE LOST

Writing in the 1980s, Johnson and Kaplan (1987: xi–xii) argued for a 'relevance lost' in management accounting. By this, what they had in mind was the issue of inappropriateness of current management accounting which offered, they believe, little capacity for providing useful and timely information for better decisions and control in the areas of product costing and managerial performance. Moreover, they pointed to the contemporary environment of rapid technological change, vigorous global and domestic competition, and enormously expanding information-processing capabilities. Conventional management accounting which developed from a stable and monopolistic environment had been 'subservient to financial reporting' rather than facilitating internal processes for better management of resources.

Johnson and Kaplan contended that the period between 1825 and 1925 represented the heyday of management accounting, during which cost management practices were well developed. However, after 1925, virtually nothing was developed, yet the same practices were used by firms even in the 1980s. If management accounting systems in organizations were to respond to environmental changes and to be shaped into meaningful managerial devices, then there was a simple question as to how the century-old knowledge of management accounting could be suitable for the contemporary world of management. To put it another way, as Johnson and Kaplan illustrated from the case of General Motors, the inadequacy of current systems arose from a lag in replacing pre-war cost accounting systems, designed for financial reporting and tax purposes, with modern information and accounting systems.

The Japanese counterparts of General Motors, Johnson and Kaplan pointed out, were using different methods and techniques detached from external financial reporting and were becoming more competitive in the global market. Emerging management 'philosophies' such as total quality management (TQM) and continuous improvement have come to be parts of management accounting systems which provide both financial and non-financial information. Management accountants in such contexts have become business analysts and internal consultants rather than a type of support staff providing auxiliary services to line managers. In Japan, practices of management accounting systems in different organizations vary, depending upon the nature of market they cater to, rather than relying on a set of prescriptions developed outside the organization.

SETTING THE SCENE

What you have seen above is a non-changing nature of management accounting in a changing environment. It summarizes why management accounting has not been responding to this change. In response to this, several new techniques of management accounting have been developed in the last two decades. In this book, we categorize these techniques under three major titles: cost management, strategic management and management accounting in new organizations. This development is now commonly known as management accounting change (hereafter MACh). To learn about MACh, some would tend to concentrate only on these new developments. Does this make sense of MACh? Were there any early changes in management accounting at all? What is management accounting in the first place? How do we learn about MACh in a sensible manner? Is there only one way of learning about change? These questions have motivated us to write this chapter. Let us first talk about your previous management accounting courses.

> MACh can be reflected in recent developments in three major areas: cost management, strategic management and management accounting in new organizations.

> Basic questions which motivated us:
>
> ■ Does this make sense of MACh?
> ■ Were there any early changes in management accounting at all?
> ■ What is management accounting in the first place?
> ■ How do we learn about MACh in a sensible manner?
> ■ Is there only one way of learning about change?

The introductory management accounting courses that you have taken emphasized the technical aspects of management accounting. They introduced you to various management accounting techniques. They also guided you to rehearse and practise those techniques through examples and chapter-end exercises. Moreover, from advanced management accounting texts, you learned about new developments in those techniques. Thereby, you may believe that MACh means those additions to the existing stock of techniques. Further, you might tend to think that these techniques emerge on their own. This is partly correct, in that changes in management accounting are reflected in the emergence of new techniques. However, you inadvertently neglect external factors which underlie such developments. To capture the total picture of change, we believe, one should understand not only those technical developments but also their underlying socio-economic factors. One of the main themes around which this book is organized is that technical developments in management accounting take place in correspondence with evolutions in socio-economic systems as a whole. That said, management accounting evolves to serve certain managerial rationales in evolving socio-economic systems.

The purpose of this chapter is to provide a framework which aligns technical developments in management accounting with the major phases in the evolution of socio-economic systems.

To begin with, we will first define management accounting in terms of three different views: technical–managerial, pragmatic–interpretive and critical–socio-economic. These views tell us that the definitions of management accounting can be an interpretive and ideological project rather than an ultimate conclusion of a 'science of management accounting'. This will also point to an interesting comparison between the three views which blur the widespread conception that management accounting belongs to a single world view dominated by a global project of professionalization.

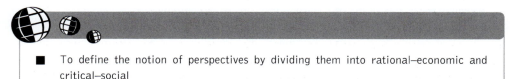

- To define management accounting in terms of three views: technical–managerial, pragmatic–interpretive and critical–socio-economic
- To compare and contrast the three views which may blur the conception that management accounting belongs to one single world view

The second set of learning objectives has been specified for the examination of the notion of MACh. After raising the issue of understanding this term, a section will define MACh as a movement from mechanistic to post-mechanistic forms of management accounting. In this, references will be given to respective chapters to specify the working definitions of the terms 'mechanistic' and 'post-mechanistic'.

- To examine the phenomenon of MACh
- To view MACh as a movement from mechanistic to post-mechanistic forms

The last section of the chapter will define the notion of perspectives, the second theme of the book. Two perspectives will be teased out: rational–economic and critical–social. As will be shown, the perspectives provide not only a meaning system for understanding MACh, but also a guide for evaluating alternative research paradigms which have been debated in management accounting research.

- To define the notion of perspectives by dividing them into rational–economic and critical–social
- To highlight the academic significance of understanding alternative perspectives on MACh

WHAT IS MANAGEMENT ACCOUNTING?

This question has been repeatedly asked by almost all management accounting texts. They rely largely on some popular definitions developed by accounting professional bodies. Accordingly, the commonly held view is that management accounting is a unitary and universal practice, independent of the time and space in which it operates. For this, management accounting has a specific set of functions based on perfectly defined techniques which have been developed from both theory and practice. It is hoped that wherever and whenever these techniques are used, the same outcomes are expected, and their fullest original forms are adopted. While this view has to be respected, we can move beyond this point, to study the subject broadly and realistically.

> The commonly held view is that management accounting is a unitary and universal practice, but we move beyond this point, to study the subject broadly and realistically.

Instead of providing a firm definition of what management accounting is, it might be better to look at different world views of the subject. In some sense, we can consider three different views of management accounting, and sets of its functions. The first set is related to the technical–managerial view, which is widely held by practising management accountants and most textbook writers. The second set is related to the pragmatic–interpretive view, which is promoted by a group of accounting researchers who attempt to understand management accounting practice. The third set is related to a critical–socio-economic view, which offers critical evaluations of the functioning of management accounting within its broader socio-economic context. A brief account of those views is presented below.

> There can be three world views of management accounting:
>
> ■ technical–managerial view
> ■ pragmatic–interpretive view
> ■ critical–socio-economic view

Technical–managerial view

According to the technical–managerial view, management accounting is:

1. A set of calculative practices. In support of decision-making and control, management accountants use various techniques, such as product costing, budgeting, variance analysis, cost–volume–profit analysis, investment appraisal and so on. All these calculative practices are collectively known as management accounting.
2. A managerial function or a sub-system of the overall organizational information system. In an organization, there are certain managerial functions, such as production, marketing, HRM,

R&D, etc. Management accounting, which is often under the purview of finance, is such a managerial function. The role of that management accounting function is to support decision-making and control by providing financial and non-financial information.

> According to the technical–managerial view, management accounting constitutes a set of calculative practices and a managerial function or a sub-system of the overall organizational information system.

To maintain management accounting as a set of calculative practices and a distinct managerial function within organizations, the necessary infrastructure is provided by professional bodies and academia. They develop, disseminate and diffuse management accounting knowledge and techniques, and they train and qualify necessary personnel to practise management accounting. Box 1.1 shows two definitions of management accounting from two professional bodies.

BOX 1.1 VIEWS OF PRACTITIONERS

American Accounting Association, 1958

The application of appropriate concepts and techniques in processing the historical and projected economic data of an entity to assist management in establishing plans for reasonable economic objectives and in the making of rational decisions with a view toward achieving these objectives.

Chartered Institute of Management Accountants (UK), 2000

Management accounting is an integral part of management. It requires the identification, generation, presentation, interpretation and use of information relevant to:

- formulating business strategy;
- planning and controlling activities;
- decision-making;
- efficient resource usage;
- performance improvement and value enhancement.

The technical–managerial view represents the conventional wisdom of management accounting which is presented in most textbooks. Students using these textbooks reproduce the underlying techniques in the form of calculative and prescriptive answers to their exam questions. Graduates and professionals, those who have passed these exams, reproduce the management accounting techniques as part of management accounting practices within organizations. Consultants who believe that these techniques provide solutions to managerial problems reproduce those techniques as applicable models. In this way, the conventional wisdom of management accounting is sustained generation after generation, with some modifications and changes offered by textbooks, universities, professionals and consultants. Being a powerful organizational practice, this conventional view has now succeeded in influencing the daily programmes of organizational and individual lives: we cannot find any organization which avoids the use of accounting information for a variety of purposes. Chapters 3, 4, 5 and 6 introduce this sustained wisdom of the subject matter of management accounting.

> The technical–managerial view represents the conventional wisdom of management accounting, with some modifications and changes offered by textbooks, universities, professionals and consultants. This has now become a powerful organizational practice.

Pragmatic–interpretive view

The pragmatic–interpretive view is concerned with management accounting practice. By 'practice', we mean the ways in which it is applied and the organizational consequences of such applications. These concerns are usually raised by researchers rather than practitioners. However, as research efforts in this regard are fragmented, it is difficult to synthesize these concerns into a single phrase. Some researchers – for example, Robert Kaplan and his followers – provide descriptive accounts of practices, identify prevailing problems and formulate solutions. Other researchers – for example, Birkett and Poullaos (2001) – study practices, identify changing features and define the subject in more pragmatic terms. Some interpretive researchers – for example, Robert Scapens – study the practice more closely and explain the same theoretically. A brief sketch of the contributions of Kaplan, Birkett and Poullaos and Scapens is presented below.

> Some researchers provide descriptive accounts of practices, identify prevailing problems and formulate solutions. Others study practices, identify changing features and define the subject in more pragmatic terms. A third group study the practice more closely and explain it theoretically.

According to Johnson and Kaplan (see p. 1 above), management accounting is a corporate information system that is subservient to external financial reporting rather than providing useful and timely information for product costing and managerial performance. Thus, it is important, as implied by Johnson and Kaplan, to develop more appropriate management accounting systems for better decision-making and management control. Following this recognition of 'irrelevance', Harvard Business School academics led by Robert Kaplan developed/introduced more 'relevant' management accounting techniques such as the balanced scorecard (BSC) and activity-based costing (ABC). The former argued for a connection of management accounting with strategy and the role of non-financial performance. The latter introduced an alternative cost allocation method along with a methodology for 'activity-based management'. Chapters 8 and 9 will explore these two developments and their managerial consequences. The chapters highlight that, despite these consequences, the 'new' techniques tend to be popular and influential.

> To Johnson and Kaplan, today's management accounting is irrelevant to today's environment. The balanced scorecard (BSC) and activity-based costing (ABC) have been introduced as more 'relevant' techniques. Chapters 8 and 9 will explore these developments.

According to Birkett and Poullaos (2001), the current state of management accounting is an outcome of a historical evolution from the 1950s. In that decade, the emphasis was on the term 'management accounting' in which costing and budgeting techniques became the central subject matter. (This existed even earlier as separated organizational practice.) From the mid-1960s, management accounting was a support or staff role which concentrated on planning and control, while early budgeting and costing became organizational routines. From the mid-1980s, it was about 'resource management', which invaded the 'provinces' of others, such as waste management, continuous improvement and business process re-engineering (BPR). From the 1990s, the 'resource management' perspective on management accounting became more focused on risk management and value creation. Consequently, Birkett defines management accounting in more pragmatic terms:

> Management accounting is part of the management process which is focused on organizational resource use. Thus, it refers to managerial processes and technologies that are focused on adding values to organisations by attaining the effective use of resources, in dynamic and competitive context.
>
> (IMPAS1, section 28, cited in Baxter and Chua, 2006)

> To Birkett and Poullaos, management accounting is an outcome of a historical evolution: in the 1950s it was conventional 'management accounting'; from the mid-1960s, it was a support or staff role; from the mid-1980s, it was about 'resource management'; from the 1990s, the 'resource management' perspective became more focused on risk management and value creation.

Moreover, Birkett (as a single author) articulated that management accounting practice is a product of four interrelated factors: social institutions (e.g., professions and the state), organizational context, technologies and research contributions. By configuring these factors, Birkett believed, the 'resource-based perspective' on management accounting can be furthered by establishing certain organizational practices, such as 'direction setting', 'structuring', 'commitment', 'change' and 'control'. Management accounting (that is, accountants) is a facilitator in materializing these practices. Birkett also highlighted the fact that, as a distinct professional practice, management accounting is under 'threat', as its current trend is to invade 'other provinces' of organizational practice. As we will see in Chapters 12 and 13, as a result of this boundary clash, management accounting tends to produce both intended and unintended organizational consequences, such as resistance.

Management accounting practice is a product of four interrelated factors: social institutions, organizational context, technologies and research contributions. The 'resource-based perspective' can be furthered through 'direction setting', 'structuring', 'commitment', 'change' and 'control'. However, management accounting is under 'threat' as it invades 'other provinces'.

Departing into more analytical and academic views, Robert Scapens (1984, 1994, 2006) points to a gap between management accounting 'theory' (as developed in major textbooks) and management accounting 'practices' (being prevalent in the Anglo-Saxon world). As will be explained in Chapter 13, this view represents a broader interpretive project by which management accounting is seen as social and institutional practice rather than the direct application of textbook techniques. For Scapens, management accounting practices must be studied and interpreted through what is actually happening, rather than being much concerned about a 'gap' between theory and practice. More importantly, management accounting is a set of 'rules' that could be 'routinized' and 'institutionalized' as accepted practices, and if necessary social and cultural imperatives support such a process of 'routinization' and 'institutionalization'. By specifying these terms and providing sociological meanings, Scapens and his followers have developed a theoretical framework called institutional theory, which is now widely used as a tool for explaining the status quo of management accounting in action. The followers tend to study management accounting practices and identify numerous factors that enable or constrain the institutionalization of management accounting within certain organizational settings.

Robert Scapens pointed to a gap between 'theory' and 'practices'. He has recently said that 'practices' must be studied and interpreted rather than being much concerned about the 'gap'. When looking at practices, management accounting is a set of 'rules' that could be 'routinized' and 'institutionalized': an institutional theory view. Scapens' followers study 'practices' and identify numerous factors that enable or constrain the process of institutionalization.

Critical–socio-economic view

In contrast to the above views, there is a school of academia which engages in a critical evaluation of management accounting practices in relation to the interplay between organizations and their wider socio-economic contexts. They are critical about the confinement of the meanings of management accounting to technical and managerial aspects of economic organizations. They take the meanings and functions of management accounting beyond the organizational boundaries, and argue that management accounting practices play certain roles in the reproduction of wider socio-political systems of domination and exploitation. For example, Puxty (1993: 4) argues:

> management accounting is a set of social practices that delineate the space within which the activity of the workforce might be made visible and susceptible to rational calculations . . . [It is] an instrument within an enterprise that facilitates the exploitation of, and extraction of surplus value from, its employees by the capitalist interests that, through management, control the accounting systems.

This is about a critical evaluation of management accounting practices in relation to the interplay between organizations and their wider socio-economic contexts.

Thus, critical views cannot contain a set of widely accepted definitions. They are debatable, arguable and divergent. As we will show later, these views are derived from certain social theories. A commonly shared feature of these views is that they are sceptical about the technical–managerial views and look to social theories to understand practices: the proponents believe that the practices are theoretical as long as they can be explained in a social theory. As we will show in Chapters 14 and 15, by using social theories, critical researchers address the issues of management control systems in organizations which are reflected in broader structural dimensions, such as politics, class struggle, gender, ethnicity, patronage and the like.

Critical researchers are sceptical about the technical–managerial views and look to social theories, believing that the practices are theoretical as long as they can be explained in a social theory.

The three views compared

The three views above can be summarized by comparing their aims, focuses, orientations and theoretical foundations. Box 1.2 provides a snapshot of this.

The above comparison points to a movement of management accounting research from a technical–managerial to a sociological orientation. Even though the future of management accounting seems to be uncertain and unpredictable, the present is an interesting contestable terrain in that the opening up of the research agenda to a sociological paradigm results in unlimited avenues of analysis and debate. One vibrant area of interest is MACh, which has brought in new techniques and managerial philosophies. We shall look at this phenomenon of change.

The future of management accounting seems to be uncertain and unpredictable, but the present is a contestable terrain. 'Change' can be considered under these circumstances.

BOX 1.2 THREE VIEWS COMPARED

	Technical–managerial	Pragmatic–interpretive	Critical–socio-economic
Aims	To develop management accounting tools and techniques to ensure efficient and effective management of organizations	To describe, interpret and theorize what is being practised	To highlight social problems and issues in the use of management accounting techniques and tools
Focus	Organizational/technical	Human consciousness	Social
Orientation	Prescriptive	Interpretive	Interpretive
Theoretical foundation	Neoclassical economics, systems theory, industrial psychology and the like	Sociological analysis of human behaviour (e.g., symbolic interactionism, institutional theory and the like)	Sociological theories (e.g., Marxism, neo-Marxism, postmodernism and the like)

WHY 'CHANGE'?

We suggest that change is a learning methodology. It guides us to understand how environmental factors shape internal processes within organizations. The environmental factors include technology, competition, globalization effects, economic uncertainty, social and cultural influences, political initiatives and also effects of management accounting research and consultancy. The internal processes include all interrelated functions of R&D, accounting, finance, HRM, marketing, production, etc. Change occurs, we believe, as a result of the interaction between the environmental factors and internal processes. When focusing on change, we can learn how this interaction happens, what factors are more influential, why change is fast or slow, how organizational members react to such change, and how change impacts on the social and economic well-being of a society.

Change is a learning methodology to understand how environmental factors shape internal processes within organizations. Important questions concern how this interaction happens, what factors are more influential, why change is fast or slow, how organizational members react to such change and how change impacts on the social and economic well-being of a society.

As a learning methodology, change can broaden our understanding of management accounting. It leads us to realize that management accounting is a social science rather than a mere set of technical tools available for practice. The notion of change shows how management accounting relates to social systems, within which dynamic (changing) relations are maintained. Among these relations, old techniques of management accounting tend to be replaced by new ones, and new techniques become evaluated and condemned when new demands from the changing environment are in place. Such a process of change reflects on the question of how techniques emerged, evolved and were transformed. This means both management accounting techniques and interactive social and organizational context cannot be learned together unless we focus on the change dimension. However, change cannot be understood through straightforward definition. This is because there are different perspectives that can explain change. We will introduce these perspectives later in this chapter.

WHAT HAS CHANGED IN MANAGEMENT ACCOUNTING?

Changes might occur deliberately or accidentally. The deliberate and the accidental have links to the time (history) and the space (geography) in which they occur. Understanding changes along with historical and geographical concerns would constitute a realistic knowledge of management accounting. With regard to linking technical changes with history and geography, the technical–managerial view of management accounting has little to offer. But a combination of all three views mentioned above would give a complete pedagogical approach to understanding MACh. This would enable us to explore the questions of why some techniques and practices came to be prominent, and how these techniques could be reflected in the interaction between the contextual factors and internal processes.

Understanding changes with historical and geographical concerns would constitute realistic knowledge. All three views will enable this understanding to explore the questions of why some techniques and practices came to be prominent, and how these techniques could be reflected in the interaction between the contextual factors and internal processes.

Change places much onus on technological innovations which are linked to customer-orientation and globalization effects. These factors are considered to be the most dominant environmental forces affecting businesses today. Highly dynamic and volatile markets are the resultant immediate business context: firms soon find new customer needs to satisfy and new forms of competition to beat. Markets are fragmenting and 'mass production' and 'mass marketing' are no longer valid business strategies. Instead, S–T–P marketing[1] has become the generic mode of marketing. Fordism[2] as an organizational form became more or less outdated, and management gurus soon launched into the discovery of organizational forms of greater flexibility and adaptability, such as the 'learning organization' (Senge, 1990) and even 'effective organization' (Mintzberg, 1983). Visionary leadership, organizational culture, teamwork and networking became the structural apparatuses of the expected organizational form. Continuous improvement, total quality management, business process re-engineering, lean production and so on became the buzz-words in various management discourses. Change management evolved into a popular course in business schools and in-house company training programmes. As a result of all these dynamics, the notion of 'change' is now projected not only as a means for various other ends, but also as an end in itself.

11

> Technological innovations, customer-orientation and globalization effects are considered to be the most dominant environmental forces. Firms find new customer needs and new forms of competition. S–T–P marketing has become generic. Organizational forms of greater flexibility and adaptability are discovered. 'Change' is not only a means for various other ends, but also an end in itself.

The concern for 'change' in other disciplines of management had certain knock-on effects on management accounting. Management accountants had to face the challenge of changing their techniques and procedures to meet this overall agenda of change. It is said that traditional management accounting techniques of budgeting and control were no longer sufficient to meet the demands of emerging strategic dimensions of organizations. More specifically, management accounting was faced with the problem of moving beyond the traditional administrative mode of control (responsible accounting) to integrate itself with the emerging strategic and marketing aspects of businesses. It can be argued that balanced scorecards (BSC) and activity-based management (ABM) were reactions to this problem. This drive for integrating strategic and other non-accounting business dimensions with management accounting was quite explanatory in the nature of change taking place in the professional management accounting syllabi: for example, those of the Chartered Institute of Management Accountants (UK).

> Management accountants had the challenge of changing their techniques and procedures to meet this overall agenda of change. Balanced scorecards (BSC) and activity-based management (ABM) are reactions. Professional management accounting syllabi are also being changed accordingly.

MACh AS A MOVEMENT FROM ONE APPROACH TO ANOTHER

Now we see that change is inevitable and challenging, this book offers a learning methodology for reflection on this important phenomenon. The methodology we unfold is a movement from the mechanistic to the post-mechanistic approach. Mechanistic approach is a broad term we use to define the conventional wisdom of management accounting which persisted until the 1980s. The defining principles are: mechanization in production technology; and production-orientation in management. By 'mechanization', we mean the technology used for mass production, one dedicated to produce similar products on a large scale. The engineering character of this technology is semi-automatic and inflexible. Once the investments in such technologies have been made, the recovery of the cost of capital has to be achieved by large-scale production over a long period of time, a production conception which leads to economies of scale. Thus, orientation is essentially centred on production rather than customer needs. Once the firm has identified a large segment of customers, investment is made in technologies to produce for that market. Profit is made by forcing customers to buy the products. This was indeed possible when most firms operated in industries where there was the potential for monopoly or oligopoly. In Chapter 2, this broad context is defined and explained in terms of a systematic shift of craft production to mass production.

> The methodology we unfold is a movement from the mechanistic to the post-mechanistic form.

> The defining principles of the mechanistic approach are: mechanization in production technology; and production-orientation in management.

The mechanistic approach to management accounting emerged to facilitate this mechanistic form of enterprise. As the investment decisions were made very occasionally, much more flexible and dynamic capital budgeting techniques were not a necessity. Methods such as NPV, IRR and payback period were sufficient for evaluating financial feasibility. As production processes were standardized and put through dedicated machines, standard costing and associated budgetary control systems were appropriate to facilitate the process of standardization. Thus, those management accounting practices became easily routinized and institutionalized within their organizational settings characterized by rigid bureaucratic rules. Consequently, responsibility accounting and performance evaluation methodologies became pervasive among large-scale business enterprises, and most textbooks and university and professional programmes built their educational materials on the examples and procedures of these developments. These are the contextual accounts of the emergence of the conventional wisdom of management accounting, and we term this development the mechanistic form of management accounting. Chapters 3, 4, 5 and 6 introduce the accounting techniques and organizational procedures of this form. The topics covered in these chapters are costing, budgeting and profit planning, budgeting and management control, and economic models of decision-making, respectively.

> Responsibility accounting and performance evaluation methodologies became pervasive among large-scale business enterprises, and most textbooks and university and professional programmes built their educational materials on the examples and procedures of these developments.

As is shown in Figure 1.1, the mechanistic approach to management accounting moved to a post-mechanistic form from the late 1980s. Production systems are now governed by digital technologies with a manufacturing flexibility. Flexible manufacturing environments are now capable of creating a variety of product designs and functionalities which can satisfy the divergent needs of customers. Possibilities have also been created for the production-orientation of management to shift to a customer-orientation. The marriage between the digitalization in technology and the customer-orientation in management has given rise to new ways of doing business, and new

13

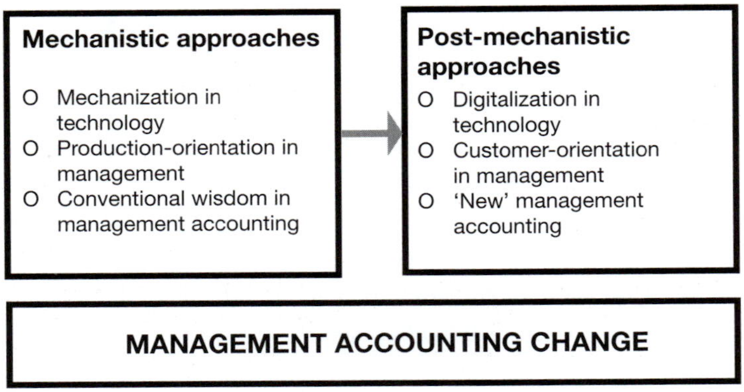

Mechanistic approaches	Post-mechanistic approaches
O Mechanization in technology O Production-orientation in management O Conventional wisdom in management accounting	O Digitalization in technology O Customer-orientation in management O 'New' management accounting

MANAGEMENT ACCOUNTING CHANGE

Figure 1.1 *MACh from mechanistic to post-mechanistic approaches*

business enterprises through which competitive advantage is achieved by exploring 'economies of scope', as opposed to 'economies of scale'. The form of organization which serves this change has also now changed into a post-bureaucratic form where we can find new features, such as organizational flexibility and functional integration. Chapter 7 will elaborate on this broad context of post-mechanistic form of the business enterprise, and reading that chapter is a prerequisite for locating new management accounting in its proper context.

The mechanistic approach to management accounting moved to a post-mechanistic form from the late 1980s. Now digital technologies can satisfy divergent needs of customers, giving rise to 'economies of scope', as opposed to 'economies of scale'.

Chapters 8, 9 and 10 will reveal the heart of the subject matter of what we call the post-mechanistic form of management accounting. The respective topics covered in these chapters are 'strategic management accounting', 'cost management' and 'management accounting and control practices in new organizations'. Following the reconfiguration of production technology and its orientation into a digital and customer-oriented form, the function of management accounting has now become integrated with strategic dimensions of business and management which you will learn about in Chapter 8. As opposed to the conventional methods, costing techniques now have changed to 'activity-based' methods which are linked to 'activity-based management'. You will learn about these developments in Chapter 9. Moreover, due to the deconstruction of organizational form into a more flexible and post-bureaucratic one, management accounting and control systems have also taken a new shape. By reading Chapter 10, you will learn that organizational consequences such as lateral relations, teamwork, inter-organizational–network relations and hybridization of work, including management accounting, have produced new forms of management accounting and control systems.

PERSPECTIVES ON MACh

We have now explained that management accounting has changed from a mechanistic to a post-mechanistic form. The fundamental question before us is why this change has occurred in this particular manner. No answer is straightforward, but we have used the term 'perspectives' to provide some explanations. By 'perspectives' we mean alternative theories which are capable of explaining the practices of management accounting. As one theory can vary from another, we cannot find one universal explanation for the existence and persistence of such practices: different 'perspectives' would give us different answers, together with distinct interpretations. These different 'perspectives' should be consulted with a view to interpreting the changes in different ways. This will not only broaden our understanding of management accounting practices, but also guide us to design appropriate management accounting systems for respective economic organizations. A theoretical perspective gives you a lens to see something more clearly, in greater detail. A single perspective may lock you into one unitary view. In contrast, divergent theoretical perspectives provide you with different lenses that can change your world view. Different views can broaden your understanding, by making you think that 'there are other things as well'. For seeing MACh in this way, we categorize these 'perspectives' into three main camps: rational, interpretive and critical.

'Perspectives' are alternative theories which may explain the practices. Different perspectives would give different interpretations/explanations and make you think that 'there are other things as well'. Three 'perspectives' will be discussed: rational, interpretive and critical.

Rational perspective

The rational perspective represents the mainstream of management accounting research. Its theoretical stance is built upon neoclassical economics and theory of organization. While neoclassical economics[3] provides frameworks for seeing management accounting as a set of calculative practices which help decision-makers to maximize their utility, organization theory comes to understand the relationships between management accounting systems and contingencies. Rational theories of management accounting which developed from both neoclassical economics and organization theory can be threefold, as is shown below.

Rational theories of management accounting which developed from both neoclassical economics and organization theory can be threefold: transaction cost theory, agency theory and contingency theory.

Transaction cost theory of management accounting

This is an extension of neoclassical economics and is presented in historical analysis of MACh (Williamson, 1970, 1975). The proponents of this approach (e.g., Johnson and Kaplan, 1987) take the view that managerial co-ordination within organizations rather than market transactions is key to achieve economies and, in turn, efficiency. The role of management accounting is to reduce the cost of this managerial co-ordination.[4] It is assumed that by reducing the 'transaction costs', profits can be increased and that by enhancing the managerial co-ordination, developments of the capitalist enterprise can be made. According to the proponents of this theory, this explains why and how management accounting came to be an inevitable technical development in the history of business. Johnson and Kaplan (1987) argue that management accounting was developed in response to managerial actions in a search for efficiency. In this way, MACh occurs when existing techniques are no longer effective in the preservation of effective managerial co-ordination, together with reduced transaction costs.

> As an extension of neoclassical economics, this theory takes the view that managerial co-ordination within organizations, rather than market transactions, is key to achieve economies and, in turn, efficiency. The role of management accounting is to reduce the cost of this managerial co-ordination.

Agency theory of management accounting

This is also derived from neoclassical economics. It aims to formulate the relationship between principals (owners and senior managers) and agents (managers and their subordinates), whereby agents are appropriately motivated (or de-motivated) to act in the interest of the principal: that is, maximizing the wealth (Baiman, 1982, 1990; Spicer and Ballew, 1983). The role of management accounting in this relational context is to develop the models of performance evaluation, management control, decision-making, etc. It is believed that these models are embedded in organizations through persistent relationships between the agents and principals. In other words, management accounting is presented to resolve the problems of divergent interests between agents and principals (Wilson and Chua, 1993). When the principals realize that present management accounting techniques tend to be invalid in resolving the agency problem, they search for new techniques.

> Agency theory aims to formulate the relationship between principals and agents, whereby agents are appropriately motivated to act in the interest of the principal. The role of management accounting is to develop models of performance evaluation, management control, decision-making, etc.

Contingency theory of management accounting

This draws on systems theory and organizational and behavioural decision theories. The researchers in this school tend to understand the relationship between environmental and organizational variables. The included environmental variables are technology, uncertainty and complexity; and organizational variables are structure, ownership, size, task complexity, decentralization, etc. By adding more variables, management accounting studies have focused on the relationships between environmental and accounting variables (such as types of budgeting, participation in budgeting, control models and performance evaluation systems) as well as between organizational designs and accounting variables. The aim of this type of study is to generate possible generalization about the above relationships and to prescribe how management accounting can be best used in different situations. In respect of MACh, the position of contingency theory is that as long as present techniques do not match the changing environmental demands, new techniques must be developed in conformity with new demands.

> The aim is to generate possible generalization about the above relationships and to prescribe how management accounting can be best used in different situations. If present techniques do not match the changing environmental demands, new techniques must be developed in conformity with new demands.

As economic-rational perspectives on MACh, transaction cost theory and agency theory can be read about in Chapter 11. There you will learn the fundamental assumptions of these theories and their applications to management accounting research, with a brief evaluation of such research. Contingency theory is something of a deviation of the economic perspective, but it still maintains a kind of rationality by providing the prescription that management accounting systems can be understood by an examination of the relationships between accounting systems and contingent factors. You will learn more about this perspective in Chapter 12.

Interpretive perspective

This provides us with a particular methodology for doing management accounting research. The main thrust of this methodology concerns the belief that practices of management accounting are not artificial. Rather, they are the outcomes of shared meanings (perceptions) of organizational actors. For instance, organizational goals cannot be rationally developed instruments for achieving organizational effectiveness. Instead, they are regarded as symbolic resources drawn upon to guide and legitimize a variety of potentially contestable actions. Thus, MACh is not an objective phenomenon: it is an outcome of those contestable actions guided and legitimized by shared meanings. Rather than relying on deliberate actions by outside consultants, MACh occurs through natural organizational processes fortified with intersubjective meanings and competing actions. A foremost exemplar for an interpretive perspective on MACh is Berry *et al.* (1985), which shows how a particular production culture became prominent through shared meanings leading to the control of labour.

17

The interpretive perspective is a particular methodology for doing management accounting research, a belief that practices of management accounting are the outcomes of shared meanings of organizational actors. For example, Berry *et al.* (1985) show how a particular production culture became prominent through shared meanings leading to the control of labour.

Thus, the interpretive perspective is a research tool which is used to explain management accounting practices. Unlike rational theorists, interpretive researchers believe that 'rationality' can be articulated through subjective interpretations of organizational participants, such as managers and employees. Thus, 'rationality' is an interpretive project rather than a universal reality that can be seen in every organization. By doing case studies of individual organizations, such interpretations can be documented. As you will see in Chapter 13 interpretive researchers began to conduct such case studies from the 1980s and reported on how management accounting systems produce different consequences which are not seen by rational-economic theorists. You will read some summaries of such case studies in that chapter.

'Rationality' is an interpretive project rather than a universal reality that can be seen in every organization. Interpretive researchers conducting case studies report on how management accounting systems produce different consequences which are not seen by rational-economic theorists.

Moving much further, interpretive researchers developed their perspective by using particular social theories. Again, you will see that development in Chapter 13. We have highlighted three such theories: institutional theory derived from old institutional economics and evolutionary economics; new institutional sociology; and actor–network theory. We will not describe these theories here, but we want to emphasize that the interpretive project has developed along with the development of theoretical stances, and has enriched the interpretations of management account-ing practices by providing case study evidence. Researchers use these theories, on the one hand, to explain the data (about management accounting practices) and, on the other hand, to explain and modify the theories. Thus, the interpretive perspective is involved in both theory application and theory development.

Interpretive researchers also use such social theories as institutional theory, new institutional sociology and actor–network theory, and enrich the interpretations of management account-ing practices.

Critical perspective

As is explained in Chapters 14 and 15, a critical perspective on MACh emerged in response to the problems of rational perspectives and also to resolve some problems of interpretive perspectives. The proponents of this perspective examine the interplay between the organization and the broader socio-economic and historical context by consulting other social sciences, such as sociology, history, political science, anthropology, etc. This disciplinary shift leads critical management accounting researchers to identify a number of limitations of the rational perspective. Puxty (1993) outlines these limitations.

> Critical perspective examines the interplay between the organization and the broader socio-economic and historical context by consulting other social sciences, such as sociology, history, political science, anthropology, etc.

- It is framed from the perspective of the organization. Thus, management accounting has nothing to do with the broader socio-economic and social context.
- It treats the organization effectively as a closed system. So, except for contingency theory of management accounting, most mathematical models of decision-making and control ignore the existence of the environment of organizations.
- It has a technical orientation. This is because management accounting is specifically geared towards evaluating only the technical efficiency of the process of producing something, rather than evaluating the totality.
- It is prescriptive, in that it provides better methods of doing things. The management accounting textbook writers are not sure if these techniques are used in practice, but they feel that they should be.
- It is ahistorical. Rational perspectives usually tend to ignore historical evolutions of management accounting techniques. Instead, they believe that they are static methods to be used for ever. But, in practice, this is not the case.
- It is apolitical. Even though political issues such as the question of power (and interest) are naturally presented in management accounting practices, the rational researchers implicitly avoid them. This is far more difficult than in any social science.
- It is rationalistic. Management accounting is based on rational behaviour: rational calculations, rational decision-making and rational controls. However, rationality is, to some extent, insubstantial and bounded.
- It is functionalist. Management accounting techniques are said to be beneficial to the organization – there are no dysfunctional effects. This is why techniques such as standard costing have survived for half a century.
- It is reductionist. The use of management accounting is reduced to two domains. One is that management accounting is about a mere economic phenomenon. The second is that social effects of management accounting can be reduced to individual effects and individual actions. The practices beyond economic phenomena and effects on broader organizations and society are then ignored.
- It is positivist. There are two assumptions about management accounting research. The first is

that management accounting phenomena are measurable practices and principles. The second is that these practices and principles can be tested through mathematical/statistical models for proving or disproving predetermined propositions (hypotheses). Thus, the practices that are unmeasurable (such as social and political) keep out of the domain of research.

■ It is problem-centred. Management accounting is meant to solve problems rather than see how it is implicated in organizational problems. Some organizational problems develop from management accounting initiatives, and these problems are often linked with social problems.

The limitations of rational and interpretive perspectives have stimulated a critical perspective that has developed a number of alternative theoretical frameworks. The commonality of these frameworks is that they see the practices of management accounting beyond technical boundaries and articulate how and why they are organizationally and socially embedded. You will become acquainted with these frameworks in a two-way categorization.

> The limitations of rational and interpretive perspectives have stimulated a critical perspective that has developed a number of alternative theoretical frameworks.

Political economy

This branch of scholarship developed from an identification of limitations of the interpretive perspective. Studies such as Cooper (1980), Hopper *et al.* (1987) and Cooper and Hopper (2006) show that there are broader structural factors which pre-empt the meanings and actions persistent in organizations. The political economy of accounting considers such structural factors as family, state, accounting profession, culture, political ideologies, industry, commerce, international relations, trade unions, etc. It is argued that these structural factors permeate a 'historical totality': that is, a political economy of capitalism which aims to search for a means of yielding a profitable surplus. MACh is presented in a context of political economy, and the purpose of change is to provide such a means. Specifically, MACh can be understood by referring to the labour process theory – one widely known political economy framework. According to that theory, MACh is seen as a consequence of the class structuring of production relations: struggles between labour and capital, between one group of professionals and another, between managers and workers, etc. For the purpose of appropriating surplus, new surveillance and control systems (embedded in management accounting and control systems) need to be instituted within such class-based organizational settings. To the extent that the existing management accounting and control systems become inappropriate, more 'appropriate' systems need to be introduced, diffused and adopted. In relation to MACh and professional rivalry, similar arguments can be found in works such as Armstrong (1985).

> According to the critical perspective, broader structural factors permeate a political economy. MACh is seen as a consequence of the class struggle. For the purpose of appropriating surplus, new surveillance and control systems need to be instituted.

Post-structuralism/postmodernism

The structuralism fostered in the political economy of MACh has now been questioned for its deterministic nature. The ensuing scholarship overcoming this problem is now known as post-structuralism/postmodernism (PS/PM). Despite the difficulty in differentiating post-structuralism from postmodernism,[5] there is a common goal of this trend. While structuralists attempt to develop a unitary framework about the ways in which MACh occurs, PS/PM offer indeterminacy rather than determinism, diversity rather than unity, difference rather than synthesis and complexity rather than simplification. Hence, MACh can be understood by referring to a variety of factors, such as power, knowledge, language, meanings, discourses, gender, ethnicity, etc. Two foremost figures used in management accounting research are Michel Foucault and Jürgen Habermas, French and German philosophers, respectively. The Foucauldian view of MACh is that the emergence and development of controls (such as management accounting controls) are due to the imposition of discipline on to and punishment of individuals, making them governable and controllable (Hopwood, 1987; Miller and O'Leary, 1987; Hopper and Macintosh, 1993). The Harbermasian view of MACh is that management accounting provides 'steering media' for the decisions of managers and 'colonizes' the 'life-world' of people (Laughlin, 1987). PS/PM views do not reject that management accounting is implicated in class structure. However, the researchers in this school clarify how it happens within and outside the organization.

> PS/PM offer indeterminacy rather than determinism, diversity rather than unity, difference rather than synthesis and complexity rather than simplification. Hence, MACh can be understood by referring to a variety of factors, such as power, knowledge, language, meanings, discourses, gender, ethnicity, etc.

BOX 1.3 THREE PERSPECTIVES COMPARED

Essential aspects	Rational	Interpretive	Critical
Organizational goals	A congruence of interests of organizational participants	Symbolic resources that guide and legitimize a variety of actions	A set of negotiations and reified devices that channel and legitimate sectional interests
Focus of analysis	Individuals, sub-units and systems	Human consciousness/ interpretation	Social interaction and institutionalized subordination of labour

continued

Essential aspects	Rational	Interpretive	Critical
Image of organizational reality	Rational and co-operative behaviour	A shared meaning system	A set of individuals worried about others' actions, and a site of class (and power) struggle, domination, disciples and colonization
State of management accounting	A technical and neutral information service for decision-making	Interpretive project subject to changes under articulations by members of the organization	A process whereby certain designated actors negotiate shared meanings and a set of control devices shaped by and reinforcing the dominant mode of production
Contribution of management accounting	A mirror-like objective depiction of reality	Subjective and/or theoretical explanations	A language subjectively created and modified inter-subjectively or a partial and interested language of accounting information
MACh	As a result of technical and organizational progress	No historical analysis as depicted by naturalism. In response to crises and opportunities presented by unfolding contradictions, as depicted by PE and PS/PM	

Source: adapted from Hopper *et al.* (1987)

HAVE YOU UNDERSTOOD THE CHAPTER?

1. Distinguish between the technical–managerial, pragmatic–interpretive and critical views of management accounting.
2. What is the difference between management accounting practice and management accounting theory?
3. Why is an emphasis on MACh important?
4. Describe briefly two different approaches to the practices of management accounting.
5. Distinguish between rational, interpretive and critical perspectives on MACh.

BEYOND THE CHAPTER

1. Is management accounting a branch of accounting?
2. Why does management accounting represent multiple views as opposed to a unitary and universal view?

3. Why is management accounting governed by some professional bodies?
4. If we ignore the MACh perspective, then what do you think are the problems of studying the subject properly?
5. To what extent are the perspectives covered in this chapter appropriate for studying change in any other discipline in management?

FURTHER READING

1. Johnson and Kaplan (1987) will give you a thorough understanding of the historical development of management accounting in the USA and the issue of 'irrelevance'.
2. Loft (1986) will give another angle for seeing cost accounting developments in the UK. This contains rich data about how costing was used in the early twentieth century.
3. Puxty (1993) will provide a brief theoretical introduction to the social and organizational dimension of management accounting theory. This starts with a critical evaluation of the conventional wisdom of management accounting.
4. Scapens (2006) will help you understand the recent development of management accounting. The subject matter of management accounting can be traced by reading this.
5. Hopper *et al*. (1987) and Cooper and Hopper (2006) are seminal papers for an understanding of the three major theoretical perspectives on management accounting. Limits of postmodernism are explored in Arnold (1998).

These publications will also prepare you for mastering the materials contained in Chapter 2.

Part I

Mechanistic approaches to management accounting

Chapter 2

Towards mass production and bureaucracy

A STARTING POINT: THE CHALLENGE OF A POTTER

Josiah Wedgwood, the famous potter of Staffordshire, whose statue still stands in front of Stoke-on-Trent train station to commemorate his leading role in modernizing the pottery industry, was among the pioneers of developing English factory organization of production during the industrial revolution. His success story was, on the one hand, a series of innovations in superior product designs. What was most remarkable, on the other hand, was his success in transforming a traditional 'pot-bank' to a 'factory' where discipline of workers, the minute division of labour, the systematization of production and a system of recording and monitoring at a distance the actual performance of individuals were achieved to ensure mass production of high-quality ceramics, which brought him a massive volume of profit. However, it was not an easy task. He had centuries of local tradition to oppose him. The potters had enjoyed their independence too long to take kindly to the rules which Wedgwood attempted to enforce – the punctuality, the constant attendance, the fixed hours, the scrupulous standards of care and cleanliness, the avoidance of waste, the ban on drinking. They did not surrender easily. The stoppages for a wake or a fair or a three-day drinking spree were an accepted part of the potter's life – and they proved the most difficult to uproot. When they did work, they worked by rule of thumb. Their methods of production were careless and uneconomical. Their working arrangements were arbitrary, slipshod and unscientific, for they regarded the dirt, the inefficiency and the waste, which their methods involved, as the natural companions to pot-making. (Based on McKendrick, 1961.)

SETTING THE SCENE

You should already have read in the introductory chapter that this book concentrates on two major approaches to management accounting change, namely mechanistic and post-mechanistic. Chapters 2 to 6 will deal with the mechanistic approach, and this chapter introduces you to the historical context within which the mechanistic approach evolved. By reading this chapter you will understand that the mechanistic approach to organization and management of economic enterprises evolved against craft production, and it constitutes mass production and its associated structural properties. Hence, in this chapter, two aspects are highlighted:

- evolution of production systems from craft to mass production;
- evolution of organizational forms from aristocracy (feudal) to bureaucracy (capitalist).

The chapter is historical and contextual. That is because it concentrates mostly on the organizational and social context within which cost and management accounting began to emerge and supported the creation of what we call mechanistic organizations. Relevant materials are drawn from longitudinal cases studies and seminal papers on accounting, business and social history. The central argument is that mechanistic approaches to management emerged as an instrument of managing new contradictions and complexities within production systems and organizational forms of early capitalism (so-called monopoly capitalism).

In this chapter you will first read a brief note on the methods of historical dialectics. By reading this section, you will understand the importance of locating management accounting within its totality and contradictions in order to understand the historical change in management accounting. This section will be followed by a brief note on the broader meaning of production and its associated social relations. After reading this section you will appreciate that production has a broader meaning beyond the technical process of converting input into output and it encompasses a wider set of social relations, which Marxist theories often label as relations in and relations of production.

- Understand and appreciate the method of dialectical analysis
- Understand and appreciate that the term 'production' has a broader meaning beyond the technical process of converting input into output

Second, you will come to know different types of accounting practices that prevailed in Europe before the beginning of industrial capitalism. In this section you will understand that different methods of accounting were present in different modes of production associated with (a) large agricultural estates, (b) overseas merchants and bankers and (c) manufacturers operating what is now called a putting-out system. You will appreciate that the accounting methods in all these three spheres of economic activity were rather rudimentary record-keeping and did not assist in ascertaining cost and managing production.

- Identify three distinct economic spheres that prevailed before the industrial revolution
- Appreciate the rudimentary nature of accounting practices before the industrial revolution

Third, you will move to grasp salient features of craft production. After reading these sections you will be able to describe craft production in line with six major attributes: skilled craftsmen, infusion of planning and execution, subcontracting as the control structure, infusion of economy and society, collective employment and governance by rituals. This will immediately be followed by a brief section that deals with how craft production systems evolved into a crisis and how transition to mass production began to evolve.

■ Describe defining characteristics of craft production
■ Discuss the crisis of craft production

Fourth, you will reach the major section of the chapter – the transition to mass production. In this section you will understand what changes took place in the production system during that transition. Hence, after reading this section you will be in a position to contrast mass production with craft production. It will also expose you to four major institutional forces that underline the transition from craft to mass production, namely Taylorism, Fordism, bureaucracy and the emergence of cost and management accounting during the late and early decades of the nineteenth and twentieth centuries, respectively. After reading relevant subsections, you will be able to appreciate the contribution made by each of these institutional forces to the construction of mechanistic organizations.

■ Contrast craft production with mass production systems
■ Discuss the transition process from craft to mass production
■ Discuss major institutional forces behind the transition

Finally, you will read three alternative theoretical explanations on the emergence and development of cost and management accounting, namely transaction cost theory (TCT)-based explanations, labour process theory (LPT)-based explanations and Foucauldian explanations. After reading this section you will be able to discuss the basic arguments of these three theoretical camps which attempt to provide alternative explanations for the development of cost and management accounting techniques in the late nineteenth and early twentieth centuries.

■ Identify three major competing theoretical approaches to explain management accounting change in the early phase of capitalism
■ Discuss their main arguments

A BRIEF NOTE ON METHOD OF HISTORICAL DIALECTICS

This book adopts a dialectical approach to understand and explain the management accounting change and, hence, demands an elaboration of the method of historical dialectics. As Cooper *et al.* (2005: 957) point out, dialectical analysis involves three principles – totality, change and contradictions – each of which, on its own, would not constitute a dialectical approach. They become dialectical when they are taken together (see Figure 2.1).

> Dialectical analysis involves three principles – totality, change and contradictions – each of which, on its own, would not constitute a dialectical approach.

Totality

The principle of totality states that the social world we live in is made up of interrelated elements: various social, political and economic institutions, including organizations and their control systems. However, it should be noted that the principle of totality places its focal attention not on the elements themselves but on the relations between them. The key point is relations. It is those relations which define the nature not only of the total but also of its elements. Moreover, this means, that those constituent elements of the total cannot be understood on their own but only through an understanding of their relations to each other and to the totality. 'It is only when we grasp the relationship between the parts in the totality that we begin to understand them' (Cooper *et al.*, 2005: 957). For example, let us take the case of management accounting. Management accounting is an integral element of the total organizational system and interacts with other organizational functions such as production, marketing, human resources management, corporate strategy and so on. Not only that, through its professional alignments and systems of knowledge creation and dispersion, management accounting relates to the wider structural properties of global capitalism. One can indeed provide a 'description' of management accounting on its own by focusing on the set of tools and processes it typically encompasses (see practitioners' definitions in Chapter 1). This is internal-looking and provides only a very narrow 'description' of what it contains and ignores its ever-evolving role within wider society. A better 'explanation' of the management accounting change demands attention on a much wider spectrum: on the set of relations that management accounting holds with other elements of the organizational systems and the dynamics of global capitalism.

> Principle of totality requires us to place our emphasis on the relationships among elements that make the total. It is only when we grasp the relationship between the parts in the totality that we begin to understand them.

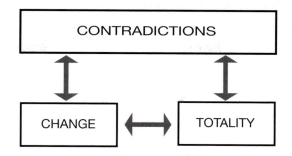

Figure 2.1 *Elements of dialectical analysis*

Contradictions

The principle of contradiction in dialectical analysis holds that deep contradictions and conflicts are inherent in relations of production. The most typical example is the contradiction between workers' interests and those of the business (shareholders). Workers struggle to maximize wages while the business struggles to minimize cost (of which wages are a part). Similarly, one can very well infer such contradictions and conflicts among all stakeholders. Not only that, there are some obvious conflicts of interest even among different functional departments and professional groups within organizations. For example, Armstrong (1985) has shown how inter-professional competition, especially between accounting, engineering and personnel, had been instrumental in new strategies for labour control.

Deep contradictions and conflicts are inherent in relations of production. Understanding those contradictions is the key to understanding production and control systems.

Change

The principle of change in dialectical analysis relates system changes to system contradictions. As we have already noted, contradictions and conflicts are inherent properties of social systems. An important consequence of such contradictions and conflicts is that they lead to system changes through interrelated cycles of crisis–solutions–crisis. This is important in understanding management accounting change. Throughout this book, we attempt to relate various technical developments in management accounting to crises in the production systems and organizational forms. Hence, it adopts a dialectical approach to management accounting change.

System contradictions lead to system changes through interrelated cycles of crisis–solutions–crisis.

MARXIST UNDERSTANDING OF PRODUCTION

So far in this chapter we have discussed the basic principles of dialectical analysis of the evolution of control systems. In the next section, we will discuss basic features of pre-modern systems of production: that is, craft production. Then we will move to discuss how this craft production transformed into mass production. However, before dealing with all this, we need to make certain clarifications as to the meaning of the term 'production'. For us, production is not simply the technical process of converting input into output. Instead, as Marx pointed out, it entails relations in production and relations of production. This distinction is important to understand how and why craft production transformed into mass production. The set of relations within which surplus labour is expropriated from the direct labour or immediate producers is termed 'relations of production' (Burawoy, 1979). Obviously, these are 'relations of economic ownership or property relations', and they are defined as 'the basis of general relations of dominance and subordination, both within and beyond the sphere of production' (Littler, 1982: 20). Relations in production or production relations, on the other hand, are the relational aspects of the *labour process* itself. They are the 'set of relations into which men and women enter as they confront nature, as they transform raw materials into objects of their imagination' (Burawoy, 1979: 15). The combination of these two types of relations entails the basic control structure pertaining to production: not only how surplus is created, but also how it is appropriated.

Production should be understood beyond the technicalities of converting input into output. It constitutes relations in production and relations of production – social relations that dictate creation of and appropriation of surplus value.

KEY TERMS

Labour process consists of (a) the actual work men and women do when they are employed, (b) the conditions under which they work and (c) social relations that they enter into while they are at work.

PRE-MODERN MODES OF PRODUCTION

We begin our exploration of the evolution of mechanistic approaches to management accounting by looking at types of accounting control before the industrial revolution. On its eve in Great Britain, according to Pollard (1965), there were three distinct economic spheres within which different systems of accounting emerged.

Large agricultural estates

The fundamental nature of relations of production in large landed estates was the notion of stewardship or agency of the servant towards the proprietor (master). The lands belonged to aristocratic lords, and were entrusted to his stewards for the purpose of management and control. These agricultural lands were laboured by peasant families and the income to the landlord was in terms of legally compulsory rent payments, dues or services. Pollard (1965: 210) describes a particular kind of a double-entry bookkeeping system used in these large landed estates. All receipts, both in money and in kind, on behalf of the master were recorded as 'charge' (debit) while all payments, including the contributions to upkeep the master's household and cash payments to him, were recorded as 'discharge' (credit). Thus, the balance usually was cash in hand with the agent.

> Large agricultural estates consist of (a) stewardship relations between aristocratic masters and servants and (b) a rudimentary system of bookkeeping consisting of 'charge' and 'discharge'.

Overseas merchants and bankers

Banking and overseas merchants were another sphere of economic activity within which distinct accounting practices emerged. Their 'counting houses' were claimed to be the oldest root of accounting practices where double-entry bookkeeping emerged (Pollard, 1965: 212). Though there were no sophisticated systems of accounting for capital and return on capital, there were systems of bookkeeping that revealed the profits of individual journeys and individual commodities. Similarly, it is claimed that some of these merchants did have rudimentary cost accounts which dealt with direct cost.

> Overseas merchant bankers had a system of bookkeeping revealing profits of individual journeys and commodities.

Manufacturers operating the putting-out system

Putting-out system refers to a kind of co-ordinating mechanism of 'domestic manufacturing' to meet a wider market. Manufacturing was fundamentally domestic and craft-based. That said, production processes such as textile, clothing, metal goods, articles of wood and leather and many more were performed in hundreds of household units by employing mainly domestic labour. The skills and knowledge of manufacturing were transferred from one generation to another on an ancestry basis and often were a speciality of a given kinship group. These domestic production units were often organized along family relations and family control, or on a gang basis with a gang-leader, often called master craftsman. These diverse units of production were co-ordinated by wealthy entrepreneurs and their agents through a kind of quasi-market mechanism where the entrepreneurs provided the fixed capital, raw materials and much of the working capital, and controlled the sale of the finished products (Littler, 1982). The recruitment and control of labour and the supervision of work processes were totally in the hands of the master craftsman. Hence, he was a kind of contractor of production from the entrepreneurs and received a lump sum for the completed work. His net income consisted of the difference between this lump sum and the wages he paid to his employees/gang plus other working capital he might have accrued. Pollard (1965: 214) argues that, unlike the agricultural estates or merchants, this system of production, by the end of the eighteenth century, did not have any accounting doctrine *per se*. Instead, entrepreneurs kept their own books as the need arose.

> Kinship relations as the basis of production relations, quasi-market mechanism of co-ordinating production by master craftsman and no clear accounting doctrine *per se* were salient features of the putting-out system.

CHARACTERISTICS OF CRAFT PRODUCTION

Of these three spheres of economic activity, the manufacturing (craft) sector is centrally important to us because it was the platform where cost and management accounting practices began to emerge. Therefore, we will go on to discuss specific characteristics of craft production and its social organization. This is important, as it will provide the basis of understanding the nature of the transition from craft to mass production. For the purpose of this chapter, and in contrast to modern capitalist societies, we identify the following characteristics of pre-capitalist systems of craft production.

Skilled workmanship

The term 'skill' has several meanings. As Littler (1982) illustrates, this term has been conceptualized in three different ways:

- Skill as job learning time. In this sense, a skilled worker is one who received a specialized 'professional' or a technical training for a given period of time (e.g., apprenticeship for a given period to qualify as a skilled worker or a professional).
- Skill as social status. This is the social legitimation of certain jobs and professions as skilled.
- Skill as job autonomy. This refers to the worker's (craftsman's) capacity to do a job from start to finish without interference or intervention from the employer.

> The term 'skill' has three different meanings:
>
> - Skill as job learning time.
> - Skill as social status.
> - Skill as job autonomy.

It is this third conception of skill – as job autonomy – we employ here. In this sense, when workers are 'skilled' (i.e., are granted a degree of job autonomy to make decisions pertaining to the design and carrying out of the job), they themselves control the production process. Craftsmen enjoyed such job autonomy and hence were deemed to be skilled. For example, Blackburn and Mann concluded that:

> A relatively skilled person was one of trust, where the worker was granted a sphere of competence within which decisions, whether routine or complex, could be taken by the worker himself. This guaranteed autonomy (skill) is the essence of traditional craft production within which the workers themselves control the production process.
>
> (Quoted in Littler, 1982: 8)

Infusion of planning and execution

A corollary to the concentration of skills in the hands of craftsmen (discussed above), both planning and the execution of jobs were done by the craftsmen themselves. This is quite contrary to the typical work scenarios we find today, where planning and design of jobs are in the hands of management and workers are simply executors of work as designed by management.

Control structures in craft production

A control structure is a set of social relations that dictates the manner in which production and appropriation of surplus value are to be carried out. In its simple terms, it is the structure that relates and co-ordinates capital and labour (which do hold conflicting interests, as we noted above). In advanced capitalist societies, this co-ordination between labour and capital is ensured by a 'chain of command' and other bureaucratic propositions within organizational hierarchies. In contrast, during the periods of craft production, this co-ordination is ensured by what has now come to be known as 'internal contracting'.

A control structure is a set of social relations that dictates the manner in which production and appropriation of surplus value are to be carried out. It relates and co-ordinates conflicting interests of labour and capital.

Littler (1982: 64–65) describes this system:

> As Hobsbawm points out, 'capitalism in its early stages expands, and to some extent operates, not so much by directly subordinating large bodies of workers to employers, but by sub-contracting exploitation and management' (Hobsbawm, 1964, p. 297). Thus, the immediate employer of many workers was not the large capitalist, but an intermediate, internal contractor who had a contractual relationship with the overarching employer, and in turn was an employer of labour himself. The employer provided the fixed capital, supplied the raw materials and much of the working capital and controlled the sale of the finished product. The contractor hired and fired, supervised the work process and received a

35

lump sum from the employer for completed work. The contractor's income consisted of the difference between the wages he paid to his employees or gang (plus the cost of any working capital he might provide) and the payments from the employer . . . In addition, the contractor was sometimes responsible for his own financial control and much of his own purchasing.

> Internal contracting was the controlling and co-ordinating mechanism of craft production.

There was not much role for accounting within this system of production and control. Effectively, the internal contract system acted as a substitute for accounting. That is because internal contracting helped the capitalists spread the capital risk among subcontractors and effectively avoided the necessity for cumbersome accounting calculations of return on capital (Littler, 1982). In fact, it was a type of quasi-market mechanism which co-ordinated units of 'domestic manufacturing' to meet the demands of a wider market without a coherent and systematic management structure.

> Accounting played no significant role in co-ordinating and controlling craft production. Instead, internal contracting acted as a substitute for accounting.

Infusion of economy and the society

Another feature of pre-capitalist societies is the relative infusion of 'economy' and the 'society'. That means organization of work by and large coincided with communal and family relations. They worked mostly in their 'domestic environments' with their communal members within a network of relations associated with the systems of internal contracts. Even within factory settings (where the work cannot be 'contracted out' due to their physical nature) in early capitalism, these 'domestic conditions' were reproduced, as people were employed as 'work gangs' owned by subcontractors. In other words, there did not exist a separate 'institution' called 'work' where people left their communal routines to work (as we do today). Instead, work was part and parcel of communal life. The accounting and managerial implications of this non-separation of economy from the society is that there did not exist distinct 'firms' or 'organizations' *per se* to account for and manage. Hence it was not organizational hierarchies and policies but kinship and communal relations coupled with aristocratic (feudal) structures of property ownership that made people accountable.

> It was not organizational hierarchies and policies but kinship and communal relations coupled with aristocratic (feudal) structures of property ownership that made people accountable.

Communal occupation in economic activities

Our discussion so far brings us to another salient feature of feudal modes of production, which is that the occupation in production activities was communal and collective rather than individualistic. Most of the subcontractors employed workers through their kinship and communal relations and formed labour gangs owned by them. A good example is provided by nineteenth-century ironworks. 'The ironmaster (master-craftsman) paid and recruited his own men, determined hours of work and discipline, and even the organization of production. Moreover, whenever an ironmaster moved to another iron-works, he took all his workers with him' (Pollard, 1965: 201).

Occupation in production activities was communal and collective rather than individualistic.

Governance by rituals and social norms

Within this pervasive structure of subcontracting, the mode of control was rather ritualistic and constituted a strong belief in traditions. There were clear skill hierarchies within work groups. For example, in the flint-glass industry, the basic work-team was called a 'chair'. It consisted of a 'gaffer', a 'servitor', a 'footworker' and a boy or 'taker-in'. Early in the nineteenth century, the 'chair' was a subcontracted work-group, and the gaffer enjoyed virtually unlimited power over the underhands (Littler, 1982: 67–68). Promotion in the skill hierarchy was a matter of length of attachment to the master craftsman. The length and the nature of the service in these attachments were generally established social norms represented as rituals and traditions.

Craft mode of control was rather ritualistic and constituted a strong belief in traditions.

In total, in a system of craft production, relations in production entail the 'skill' component of the production. That means the labour process constituted simple techniques and tools, together with a simple technical division of labour. A group of workers, which was often organized under a master craftsman, carried out a whole job and produced a marketable output. There was a set of clear hierarchical relations within such a worker-group in terms of skill hierarchies at least between the master craftsman and others. The overall system of internal contracting and the overarching relationships between subcontractors and capitalists provided the framework for relations of production – the relationship within which capitalists and intermediary internal contractors appropriated the surplus value from production.

CRISIS OF CRAFT PRODUCTION

As we noted earlier, any social system inherently contains contradictions and instabilities, and those contradictions provide the impetus for change. So did the craft production and its associated social relations structured by internal contracting. By 1900, in Britain and the USA, craft production and

37

internal contract systems were largely in demise due to the development of such internal contradictions into a crisis in the production system itself. As we noted above, craft production was dominated by the intermediate subcontractors who had a discretionary power over the control of production techniques and the labour. It was this power itself that provided the impetus for its demise, as the exercise of that power contradicted the interests of both the underhand labourers and the overarching capitalists. At the bottom end, the underhand workers reacted against the petty tyrannies of their master craftsmen. At the top end, power of internal contractors undermined and threatened the capitalist control over production and made the production system relatively inflexible to growing needs of the capitalists to meet expanding market demands. As a result, the internal contractor was squeezed from both ends and the system of internal contracting began to deform. However, an old system of production and its associated social relations would not disappear unless a superior mode of production was available to replace it. By the beginning of the twentieth century, capitalists had begun to discover a superior system of production – the technology of mass production and its associated organizational and social apparatus. The next section discusses this phenomenon.

It was the power of the internal contractor that provided the impetus for its demise, as the exercise of that power contradicted the interests of both the underhand labourers at the bottom and the overarching capitalists at the top.

TRANSFORMATION TO MASS PRODUCTION

Having discussed the salient characteristics of craft production, our problem now is to understand the transition from craft to mass production. In this respect, we have two major tasks at hand. First, we will 'describe' the changes that took place. This means we will elaborate on the 'what' of the change. Second, we will go to the 'why' aspects of the change: that is, we will 'explain' the change. This involves elaborating the reasons behind the change and providing possible theoretical explanations.

Transformation to mass production is identified in line with the six characteristics that were discussed above. Figure 2.2 summarizes and illustrates the fundamental change which occurred. It depicts the transformation as consisting of six sub-processes: de-skilling, technocratization, bureaucratization, de-domestification, individualization and the construction of governable people. They are, to a certain degree, self-explained by Figure 2.2 itself as a movement from one state of affairs to another. However, as you proceed through the next sub-sections, you will come to grasp more specific meanings and attributes of those processes.

Transition from craft to mass production consisted of six historical trends:

1. de-skilling;
2. technocratization;

3. bureaucratization;
4. de-domestification;
5. individualization;
6. construction of governable person.

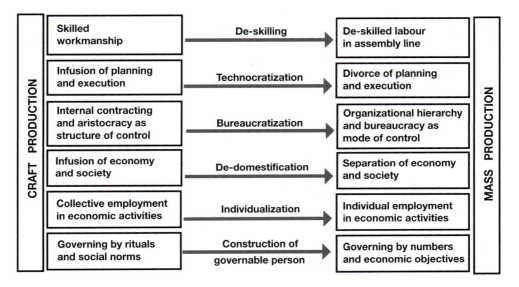

Figure 2.2 *Transformation of craft to mass production*

There are many factors which contributed to the transformation of craft to mass production. At a distance, there were global forces like the Enlightenment (which emancipated the Western world from certain religious dogmas and created the potential for scientific discovery), the French Revolution (which provided a certain impetus for a new form of government and states) and colonization (which opened up new global output and factor markets, including the supply of semi-slave labour from colonies). However, our attention will be on four interrelated managerial movements that account for most of these transitions. They are Taylorism; production control systems, especially assembly-line factory designs associated with Fordism; bureaucracy; and cost accounting. Indeed, these four factors were at the very forefront of the industry modernization agenda in the early days of monopoly capitalism. Now let us elaborate further on these movements and how they contributed to the above transition.

Taylorism, Fordism, bureaucracy and cost accounting as forces in transition from craft to mass production.

39

Rationalization of labour: Taylorism

As noted earlier, the problem of craft production for capitalists was their powerlessness over the actual techniques of production and management of labour. Real subordination of labour to capital required a system of control where managers can dictate to the workers the precise manner in which work is to be performed. This was achieved during the early decades of the twentieth century by 'labour rationalization', which includes systematization, job fragmentation and standardization. The Scientific Management Movement initiated by F. W. Taylor in the last decade of the nineteenth century provided a crucial methodological base for this labour rationalization.

Systematization refers to the process of 'gathering together all of the traditional knowledge which in the past has been possessed by the workmen and then . . . classifying, tabulating and reducing this knowledge to rules, laws, and formulae'[1] (Taylor, 1967: 36). This 'gathering of all traditional knowledge' was done by what later came to be known as 'work study', which included time and motion study. That means it became the manager's responsibility to study the work systematically, and specify the motions to be followed and time to be taken to do a given task or a job. This innovative approach to gather traditional knowledge helped not only the transfer of such knowledge to management but also the discovery of new methods, which hitherto had been unknown. As Braverman (1998: 78) argues, this process 'disassociated the labour process from the skills of the workers (hence it is de-skilled). The labour process is to be rendered independent of craft, tradition, and the workers' knowledge. Henceforth, it is to depend not at all upon the abilities of the workers, but entirely upon the practice of management.'

> Systematization refers to the process of 'gathering together all of the traditional knowledge which in the past has been possessed by the workmen and then . . . classifying, tabulating and reducing this knowledge to rules, laws, and formulae' (Taylor, 1967: 36). Systematization helped render the labour process independent of craft, tradition and the workers' knowledge.

Job fragmentation refers to breaking apart labour processes into a sequentially linked set of small 'jobs' so that an unskilled worker can perform that task to the set standards with little training. The job fragmentation not only helped de-skill the labour but also eliminated the 'collective labour' by replacing it with 'collective work' (see Figure 2.3). Workers were rendered relatively independent from each other and less interactive. They were attached individually to the tools and the work they performed rather than to each other. It was each segmented element of the job which was interdependent and collective rather than the workers performing that segment. Standardization refers to the process of prescribing, for each job, the 'standard method' and performance levels in terms of time and quantities. Indeed, standardization facilitated the linking of remuneration to the actual performance of the individual workers and effectively removed the labour management activities (hiring, firing and payments) from the master craftsmen. Taken together, Taylorist ideas on labour rationalization led to a de-skilled workforce and the divorce of planning and doing.[2]

Job fragmentation refers to breaking apart labour processes into a sequentially linked set of small 'jobs' so that an unskilled worker can perform that task to the set standards with little training.

Standardization refers to the process of prescribing, for each job, the 'standard method' and performance levels in terms of time and quantities.

Taylorist ideas on labour rationalization led to a de-skilled workforce and the divorce of planning and doing.

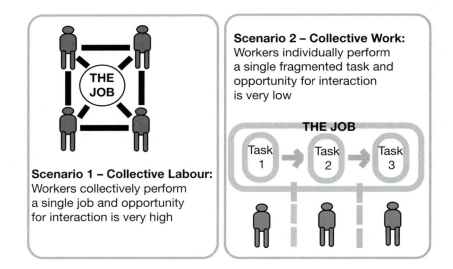

Scenario 2 – Collective Work: Workers individually perform a single fragmented task and opportunity for interaction is very low

THE JOB

Task 1 → Task 2 → Task 3

Scenario 1 – Collective Labour: Workers collectively perform a single job and opportunity for interaction is very high

THE JOB

Figure 2.3 *Collective labour versus collective work*

Rationalization of production systems: Fordism

It was the Ford Motor Company which provided the best experimental grounds for the principles of Scientific Management and began to complete the project of transition to mass production. Henry Ford was one of the few businessmen who strongly felt the limits and burden of traditional craft production in meeting the ever-increasing demand for his products, especially for his famous Model T. He also understood the value of the principles of Scientific Management and readily applied them in his factory settings. However, he carried the Scientific Management a further step forward by introducing flow-line (assembly-line) technology and a new labour control regime which revolved around the 'five dollar day'. Ford's transition from craft to assembly-line production systems was a slow but steady movement. By 1903, automobile manufacturing at Ford's still relied upon 'jack-of-all-trades' workmen who physically had to move around the factory from one car in-the-making to another, while the car in-the-making was wholly stationary in the same workstation throughout its transformation from a bare frame to a finished product. By 1908, conditions had been changed dramatically. Assemblers were stationary in their work-stations doing a limited set of unskilled jobs, while the car in-the-making was moving from one workstation to another on an assembly line to be finished at the end. Stock runners were set aside to perform various jobs that required their physical movement around the factory (cf. Sward, 1948: 32). By 1914, this system culminated in the endless-chain conveyor which could reduce the assembly time to one-tenth of what was formerly needed. By 1925, Ford could produce almost as many cars in a single day as had been produced in an entire year (cf. Braverman, 1998: 101).

> Assembly-line production in Ford's factory was a progressive innovation from jack-of-all-trades to unskilled workers which, nevertheless, resulted in a massive productivity gain.

Despite all these remarkable achievements in the speeding up of the production process, Ford faced the 'crisis of labour'. The new technology proved to be increasingly unpopular among workers and the result was remarkably high labour turnover.[3] The 'five dollar day' – the payment of five dollars a day for an eight-hour day – was the solution Ford came up with. This was so much above the prevailing rate that it halted the labour out-movement. However, it was a bargain, and to be qualified for the 'five dollar day' certain conditions had to be met: six months' continuous employment; aged over twenty-one; satisfactory personal habits both at work and home (clean-liness and prudence); and no consumption of alcohol or tobacco. Furthermore, Ford set up a new department – the Sociological Department – to check these conditions with the workers. This was indeed a further extension of the project of rationalization of labour.

> Resistance and contradictions were inevitable and, hence, new solutions were needed.

In addition to the rationalization of labour and production, mass production has another side. That is the assumption of mass markets for products, or, in other words, the assumption that the supply will find its own demand. Thus, the only challenge for capitalists is to find means and ways of speeding up the production while reducing the average cost. Hence, mass production is obvi-ously a managerial philosophy which drives the organization ever to enhance production efficiency, for which, it is assumed, there is no demand constraint.

Rationalization of organizational apparatus: bureaucracy

As we noted earlier, craft production was organized by a set of feudal relations dominated by aristocratic and kinship relations within which access to production factors and social mobility were by and large confined. It was the bureaucracy that replaced these feudal social relations of production with a set of 'rational' relationships.

One important property that defines and redefines social relations of production is the type of authority upon which those relationships are based. For Weber (1978: 215), there are three distinct types of authority: charismatic, traditional and rational. Charismatic authority derives from extraordinary grace and the magnetism of the ruler's personality, as in the case of religious leadership. It was traditional authority which was more associated with the craft and other feudal modes of production, where lineage, primogeniture and kinship were the governing principles of access to command and authority. In contrast, rational, legal precepts became the defining character of bureaucracy (at least in its ideal type).

Type of authority is central to the nature of production relations. Weber identifies three types of authority:

■ charismatic;
■ traditional;
■ rational.

Rational legitimacy to command (or authority) derives from the general obedience of organizational members to an 'objective set of rules and structures', which dictates an 'impersonal' order of things and people. Thus, on one hand, there is a set of rules that organizational members collectively believe to be necessary to achieve social objectives attached to economic enterprises. On the other hand, there is a hierarchy in which people can mobilize themselves if they follow the set rules and guidelines and if they strive to achieve the necessary credentials (merits and seniority, etc.) prescribed for the higher positions in the hierarchy. As Clegg (1990a: 38) points out, 'At the base of bureaucracy are its members' beliefs in the legitimacy of its existence, its protocols, its personnel and its policies.' Hence, bureaucracy is a technically superior form of organization that, to a certain degree, can manufacture consent of the workers to the interests of capital through the 'rational' chances of upward mobility within the hierarchy. As Weber expresses it: 'Each man becomes a little cog in the machine and aware of this, his one preoccupation is whether he can become a bigger cog' (quoted in Clegg, 1990a: 30).

In total, bureaucracy provided a technically superior form of organizational structure within which expectations of scientific management and Fordist dreams of mass production could be realized. It was finally accounting, especially cost accounting, that complemented this social movement towards mass production by providing a rational and unified mode of ascertaining the 'costs' and effectively monitoring worker behaviour at a distance.

Bureaucracy is a technically superior form of organization as it replaces aristocracy with a set of democratic rules, procedures and structures that provide 'fair' chance and hope of upward social mobility across the organizational hierarchy.

Embedding calculative practices: cost accounting

There is a dialectical relationship between cost accounting and the emergence of large bureaucratic organizations. On the one hand, emergence of large organizations necessitated cost accounting. On the other hand, cost accounting facilitated the very processes of evolution of large organizations by providing tools to monitor worker behaviour effectively 'at a distance'.

> Dialectical relationship between cost accounting and the emergence of large bureaucratic organizations.

If we are to follow the line of thinking suggested by Williamson (1975, 1988) as well as Johnson and Kaplan (1987) (transaction cost theory, which we will further discuss in Chapter 12), then the markets and hierarchical organizations (hierarchies) are competing social arrangements to co-ordinate production and exchange. In that sense, the emergence of large corporations with bureaucratic hierarchies means that the Western world moved away (at least partially) from market co-ordination of production and exchange to a system of co-ordination by hierarchies. This means that various manufacturing processes hitherto carried out by subcontractors and craftsmen outside the organizations were absorbed into the processes internal to the organizations and were now to be co-ordinated by a hierarchy of managers who were assumed to be the agents of capital. With this process of absorption, a very important element of market co-ordination was lost (i.e., market signals): demand, supply and price information (which were assumed to be autonomously pro-duced by the 'invisible hand' – the market). That means, with the absence of market mechanisms, the capitalists were left with no objective indicators about the 'value' (such as market prices) of the production they integrated into the hierarchy. The emergent solution is the subjective estimation of 'cost' of production. Cost accounting was the mechanism by which this was done.

> Markets and hierarchical organizations are competing forms of co-ordinating production and exchange.

> Integration of markets into organizational hierarchy resulted in loss of market information.

Started with rudimentary estimations of prime costs associated with the direct labour and direct materials, cost accounting systems soon evolved into those with specific techniques and procedures to allocate company-wide expenses (so-called overheads) to cost centres and cost units. These overhead absorption techniques, indeed, allowed large corporations to set competitive and more prudent prices and helped overcome financial difficulties during recessionary periods (see, for example, the Wedgwood case in Hopwood (1987)). Contribution of cost accounting to the rationalisation of economic enterprises was, however, much more than assisting the estimation of costs and setting prudent prices. Given below are some noteworthy contributions of cost accounting to the project of creating modern organizations within which individuals are governed by numbers and economic objectives.

Contribution of cost accounting to the rationalization of economic enterprises was much more than assisting the estimation of costs and setting prudent prices.

1. Cost accounting helps reconfigure organizations along manageable domains by rhetorically dividing the organization into profit centres, service centres, cost centres and costs units, etc., according to which costs and revenues estimations are carried out to ascertain relative performance. This complemented properties of bureaucracy by inserting economic objectives into the administrative apparatuses and provided economic tangibles to realize the functional division of labour within organizations further.

Cost accounting provided an alternative rhetoric to reconfigure organizations in terms of profit and costs.

2. Cost accounting provided capitalists with a powerful instrument to observe labour in economic terms. It provided a set of new lenses through which labour processes (which were hitherto 'black boxes' for capitalists and their agents) could be observed at a distance and replaced many supervisory and personal observations (Hopwood, 1987; Hopper and Armstrong, 1991). Reflecting upon the installation of cost accounting systems in Wedgwood, for example, Hopwood (1987: 218) wrote:

> observations could now be conducted indirectly. No longer did he [Josiah Wedgwood] have to rely solely on the lookout for 'unhandiness', scolding those individuals who did not follow his instructions . . . Such personal observation and supervision could start to be complemented by the exercising of control at a distance, both in time and space.

Cost accounting facilitated controlling at a distance and minimized the need for direct supervision.

3. Especially through budgeting and standard costing, cost and management accounting helped create a new regime of control where every individual within the organization was made calculable and governable by economic numbers. For example, Miller and O'Leary (1987: 242) point out:

45

possibility of a knowledge of every individual within the enterprise was established. A visibility and an allocation or responsibility could be attached to the individual. The person's activities were at last rendered knowable according to prescribed standards and deviations from the norm. Standard costing and budgeting made possible a pinpointing of responsibilities for preventing inefficiencies at the level of every individual from whom they derived. The human element of production, and most importantly the individual person, could now be known according to their contribution to the efficiency of the enterprise.

4.   Also related to the point discussed in 3 above, cost and management accounting helped create a doctrine of control which has now come to be known as 'management by exception'. That is, managers would regularly be informed of the actual performance of individuals and departments against the standards, so that managerial actions would be directed only to 'exceptional' deviations from standards, thereby saving time, effort and resources. This further helped the reduction of direct supervisory efforts and enhanced 'control at a distance'.

Cost and management accounting helped create a doctrine of control, now known as 'management by exception'.

In this way, coupled with Taylorism, Fordism and bureaucracy, emergence of conventional cost and management accounting techniques was behind the creation of specific types of organizational form which we would call 'mechanistic'. The context of this organizational form was monopoly capitalism, where large monopolistic corporations enjoyed an ever-expanding consumer market and, hence, were not constrained by limited demand but struggled against labour constraints over supply. The underlying purpose of this organizational form is to provide a stable and superordinate mechanism for the purpose of rationalization of labour to pursue the interests of capital, to contribute efficiently to the goals of capital accumulation. The main content of a mechanistic organization consists of a functionally distributed hierarchy in which planning and execution of production activities are separated and distributed, a set of impersonal rules and norms for which every member of the organization should be subordinated, highly fragmented and de-skilled jobs for which there exist specific performance expectations in terms of standards and targets, and systems of accounting for every transaction and event taking place within and across the boundary of the organization.

The main content of a mechanistic organization consists of:

■   a functionally distributed hierarchy;
■   a set of impersonal rules and norms;
■   highly fragmented and de-skilled jobs;
■   specific performance expectations in terms of standards and targets;
■   systems of accounting for every transaction and event.

ALTERNATIVE THEORETICAL EXPLANATIONS FOR EMERGENCE OF COST ACCOUNTING

So far we have discussed the nature of the transition from craft to mass production, placing much emphasis on the descriptive nature of the transition. In this section, we will provide a summary of alternative theoretical explanations of this historical transition.

In a broader sense there are three alternative theoretical explanations for accounting changes during the nineteenth century and early decades of the twentieth century. They are:

- transaction cost theory-based explanations (Johnson and Kaplan, 1987)
- labour process theory-based explanations (Hopper and Armstrong, 1991)
- Foucauldian explanations.

It should be noted, before dealing with these explanations individually, that these alternative theoretical camps are not in disagreement regarding the historical facts (events and incidents took place in chronological order at different organizational sites such as Lyman Mills Corporation or Wedgwood), but they do differ in their theoretical explanations and interpretations.

Johnson and Kaplan's approach

Core literature

Johnson and Kaplan (1987)

Underlying theory

Transaction cost theory (neoclassical economics)

Arguments

1. Organizational hierarchies and market systems are competing ways of co-ordinating production and exchange. Organizations emerge and exist as they are more efficient modes of co-ordination than market systems. They are more efficient because the cost of co-ordinating production and exchange within the organizational hierarchy (i.e., transaction cost of the organizational arrangements of production and exchange) is lower than transaction costs associated with the market system.
2. However, as organizational hierarchy replaced the hitherto prevailing market systems (subcontracting systems), there was a loss of price information to ascertain the relative efficiency of internal co-ordination of production and exchange. Hence, a new demand for cost accounting information was created and as a result, 'owners devised measures to summarise the efficiency by which labour and material were converted to finished products, measures that also served to motivate and evaluate the managers who supervised the conversion process' (Johnson and Kaplan, 1987: 7). The goal of the cost management systems was 'to identify the different costs for the intermediate and final products of the firm and to provide a benchmark to measure the efficiency of the conversion process' (ibid.: 8).
3. Promoting efficiency in the key operating activity of the organization was the basic purpose of

early cost management systems, though they helped financial reporting and pricing decisions as well.

4. Further advances in the technology of management accounting were made in conjunction with the scientific management movement by converting physical standards (that scientific management movement had already developed) into labour and material cost standards.

5. The final developments in management accounting systems occurred in the early decades of the twentieth century to support the growth of multi-divisional corporations. That is the discovery of the return on investment (ROI) measure and its decomposition into two other efficiency measures – the return on sales and sales to assets ratios.

6. By 1925, the pace of management accounting innovations seemed to stop. The period after 1925 was marked by a lack of advances. Johnson and Kaplan suggest two reasons for this failure. First is that the manufacturing firms shifted from 'cost management' to 'cost accounting'. The difference between the two is that cost management focuses upon the measurement of efficiency with which conversion processes are carried out, while cost accounting concentrates on valuing inventory for the purpose of external financial reporting. Second, they highlight the 'irrelevant contributions' by academia and the dominance of staff functions such as accounting, finance and legal (rather than engineers and owners, who understood the technology of their products and processes) in the senior positions of the hierarchy.

Labour process approach

Core literature

Hopper and Armstrong (1991)

Underlying theory

Labour process theory (Marxist structuralism)

Arguments

1. Rejects the notion that changes in the organizational forms and control systems are universally driven by searches for efficiency. As transaction cost theory is based upon this notion, it is also rejected. Instead, it is argued that organizational control systems are not neutral mechanisms for making production more efficient but are practical means through which capital extends, intensifies and exploits labour on a day-to-day basis. Hence, the labour process approach to industrial and economic history is argued to be a better theoretical framework to explain the rise and fall of management accounting.

2. Provides a theoretical critique of TCT as an insufficient explanatory tool of accounting history. The critique is, *inter alia*, based on:

   - Undue significance that TCT places upon the quest for efficiency.
   - Misleading visualization of all relationships of organizational co-ordination as contracts.
   - Vagueness of the concept of transaction cost.
   - Its assumption of competitive market.
   - Its confusion of gains from increased effort with those from increased efficiency.

3. New forms of organization and control systems emerge as strategies to eliminate or accommodate resistance and to solve associated problems of capital accumulation (i.e., profitability). These new forms of organizations and control systems, in turn, decay because they give rise to new contradictions and new forms of resistance. Their decay can also be due to disappearance of their competitive advantages as a consequence of their generalization.

4. Mid-nineteenth-century deployment of cost accounting systems was to intensify labour in response to increased competition, as well as to stimulate searches for efficiency. The most dominant rationale was the labour intensification. 'Much of the gain in profitability from the early factory organisation of production came, not from increases in the technical efficiency of the conversion process, but from the ability of the owners/entrepreneurs to intensify labour through close disciplinary control and to extend the working day' (Hopper and Armstrong, 1991: 413).

5. Management accounting techniques such as budgeting and ROI are created and deployed to intensify corporate control over managerial labour processes.

Foucauldian approach

Core literature

Hopwood and Miller (1994); Miller and O'Leary (1987); Hoskin and Macve (1994)

Underlying theory

Foucauldianism (post-structuralism)

Arguments

1. Emergence and growth of management accounting techniques are related to the growth of 'disciplinary institutions' and 'disciplinary techniques'.

2. From the late eighteenth century onwards, various society-wide disciplinary institutions started to emerge and grow. Examples are prisons, hospitals, schools, mental institutions; factories constitute just one more. Such disciplinary institutions establish set norms and rules as well as mechanisms to monitor whether their members follow them. Within the institutions, people are grouped into different categories and so arranged that their every activity is made visible to judge their behaviour against the set norms. The wide variety of methods of watching, recording, judging and so on within such disciplinary institutions are called 'disciplinary techniques', and management accounting is one of these.

3. Hence, the history of management accounting must be seen as the history of one of the central disciplinary techniques in industrial society (Loft, 1995: 35).

4. Miller and O'Leary (1987) conceptualize growth of management accounting, especially budgeting and standard costing, as an addition to a much wider set of modern apparatuses of power whose aim is to construct a governable person – that is, to construct individuals as more efficient and manageable entities. They also relate the emergence of management accounting techniques to a wider, societal-level agenda of creating efficient individuals for efficient nations. In this way, Miller and O'Leary locate the growth of management accounting techniques within a wider societal project for the social and organizational management of individual lives.

49

5. Hoskin and Macve (1994) relate the rise of management accounting to the development of giving 'marks' in educational institutions. The project of quantification of human qualities in educational institutions created a set of disciplinary techniques for constant examination and marking of individual performance. These practices of marking fed back into accounting practice through a very specific event: the creation of a sophisticated system of marking, surveillance and discipline at the United States Military Academy at West Point. Hoskin and Macve argue that it was the pupils at this disciplinary institution who facilitated the introduction of techniques of management and accounting to US industrial organizations.

HAVE YOU UNDERSTOOD THE CHAPTER?

1. What are the basic principles of the method of historical dialectics? Can you briefly discuss them and elaborate on their interrelationship?
2. How can the method of historical dialectics be related to the understanding of management accounting change?
3. What are the social relations associated with production? Why is it important to define production encompassing these relations?
4. What were the major spheres of economic activities before the industrial revolution? What role did accounting play in the organization of these economic activities?
5. What were the salient features of craft production? How do you compare and contrast craft production with mass production?
6. What were the transitional processes involved in the transformation of craft production to mass production?
7. How did Taylorism, Fordism, bureaucracy and cost accounting contribute to the transformation of craft production to mass production?
8. Can you discuss Johnson and Kaplan's 'relevance lost' thesis?
9. Can you elaborate on the labour process critique of the 'relevance lost' thesis?
10. Can you discuss major Foucauldian arguments on the evolution of cost accounting techniques?

BEYOND THE CHAPTER

1. 'Cost accounting techniques evolved to facilitate the emergence of large corporate hierarchies by enhancing their efficiency over markets.' Discuss.
2. 'Behind the evolution of management accounting during the early phase of capitalism lies the fundamental need of capital for real subordination of labour, rather than a search for technical efficiencies.' Discuss.
3. 'The history of management accounting should be seen as the history of one of the central disciplinary techniques in industrial society which helped construct governable persons within and outside economic enterprises.' Discuss.

FURTHER READING

1. For a good review of literature on management accounting history, see Loft (1995).
2. For explanations of management accounting history from transaction cost economics, labour process and Foucauldian perspectives, see the literature cited in the text as core literature of each approach.

Chapter 3

Towards product costing

A STARTING POINT: COSTING FOR ECONOMIC DEPRESSION

In 1894, Henry Rushton, an American manufacturer of canoes and small pleasure boats, faced a difficult time following the then economic depression. A small business entrepreneur, as his business matured, Rushton faced competition from mass producers, despite having a reputation for quality workmanship, character and honour in the early 1880s. Historical records indicated that he had received over 75,000 letters from customers who were satisfied with his quality work. With a view to reviving his business, from the early 1890s, he thought of processing and using detailed production costs which did not exist earlier. His prime question was whether there was a chance to make profit at the mass producers' lower price. The system Rushton had did not answer this question. He began to set some cost-finding rules, specific instructions and ideas which gave rise to an identification of cost of labour, materials and overheads. For example, on a special order for 30 boats, he had a charge for his own imputed labour for 3 working days, 37 hours' work by his brother, labour cost for other workers, and a portion to cover power and use of machinery. (Adapted from Tyson, 1988.)

This was common with many business enterprises at this time. Most aspects of the economy became worse following the Great Depression (1873–1896). Prices, profits and interest rates fell to lower levels; improved production technology enhanced the volume of production, but there was no strategy to increase profit margin. As the problem mostly lay in low prices and deteriorating profits, the only avenue available for industrial firms was to look at ways in which the cost of products could be reduced. It was in this context that industrialists such as Henry Rushton began to look for costing methods. This chapter discusses how these events unfolded into the calculative practice of 'product costing', and what techniques and meanings developed into mainstream management accounting in the late twentieth century.

SETTING THE SCENE

In previous years, you have studied costing in technical terms, where you concentrated on calculation of costs of products and services. This gave you only a technical understanding as to how costing techniques could be applied to practices. But there is an issue of adequacy of these techniques, because the historical context in which costing developed is different from the contemporary context in which those techniques are currently being applied. Now the context is highly competitive and global rather than emerging and local. Thus, the purpose of costing in the present day context must be different from that of early costing. We need to clarify this, first by a proper understanding of the development of costing techniques and their uses in an emerging and local context, and, second, by an evaluation of emerging approaches to costing. This chapter is devoted to the first objective, while Chapter 9 deals with the second. Around this broader objective, the chapter discusses two main aspects of costing:

- *ad hoc* developments in pre- and post-industrial revolution costing techniques;
- establishment of 'product costing' within mass production.

While keeping its historical tone, the chapter is mainly oriented to a technical discussion. In the previous chapter, you followed a discussion on how mass production came into shape through particular production systems and organizational forms which we called a mechanistic form. This chapter tries to explain how costing practices which developed pre- and post-industrial revolution came to be an essential technical and social device of shaping and reshaping mass production towards the construction of this mechanistic form.

First, we will address the question of what costing is. This is not only a technical definition but also highlights the organizational and social processes in which the costing function operates. This leads to achieving two learning objectives. One is about a definition of costing. The other is about an understanding of the contextual relations of costing.

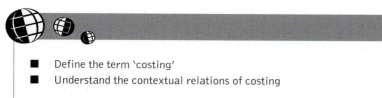

- Define the term 'costing'
- Understand the contextual relations of costing

Second, we will set two learning objectives around the issue of the development of pre- and post-industrial revolution costing techniques. Here, you will learn how different practices in the pre-industrial revolution era have transformed into 'best practices' within mass production.

- Look at historical development of costing
- Understand its transformation into 'best practices'

Third, we will undertake a presentation of cost categories which came into being. One learning objective in this presentation is to categorize costs into different themes under different 'meanings'. Another objective is to show how these cost categories link to organizational and social settings.

- ■ Define cost categories
- ■ Look at the meanings of each of these categories

Fourth, we will undertake some calculative exercises to illustrate how product costing operates as a particular technology. This leads to achieving two learning objectives. One is to understand how to calculate product costing, with a special emphasis on 'overhead allocation'. The second is to reflect on the use of overhead absorption rates under different circumstances.

- ■ Illustrate calculation of product costing
- ■ Apply overhead absorption rates

Finally, we will present an overall picture of the chapter in relation to the 'mechanistic approach' to management accounting. Here, you will learn how costing creates a particular organizational language, a control system and a pricing mechanism.

- ■ View an overall picture of the chapter
- ■ Learn how costing interlinks with the mechanistic form

WHAT IS COSTING?

Management Accounting Official Terminology (CIMA, 2000) defines costing as 'the process of determining the costs of products, services or activities'. You should have already studied this 'process' to calculate product costs. In relation to the calculation of costs, the CIMA terminology has listed a number of methods and techniques of costing: absorption costing, batch costing, continuous/process costing, contract costing, job costing, marginal costing, service/function costing, specific order costing and standard costing. While you recognize that these costing techniques have distinctive roles in the determination of costs of products and services, you tend to believe that these are scientific and unbiased, and can be practised universally.

Costing is the process of determining the costs of products, services or activities.

We believe that techniques are scientific, unbiased and can be practised universally.

Costing as a technical process

As a technical process, product costing transforms cost data into cost information. As is shown in Figure 3.1, this is reflected in a systemic approach where we identify inputs (cost data), processes (classification and calculation of costs) and outputs (information for financial reporting and decision-making purposes). The system's feedback loops generate data for standard cost, while the system includes an organizational and production environment which affects the system configuration.

In general, this system would entail four main functions:

1. Collection and recording of cost data pertinent to a particular period (through normal book-keeping procedures).
2. Classification of costs into logical categories (e.g., direct and indirect or fixed and variable).
3. Calculation of product (or service/activity) costs by using an 'appropriate' method (e.g., process costing or batch costing).
4. Use of cost information for decision-making, control or financial reporting purposes.

Technically, costing operates as a system of input/output relationship. Organizational setting and production technology comprise its immediate environment.

To a certain extent, techniques generated by this system can determine costs and influence our day-to-day life. Through their logic of calculations and rational assumptions, these techniques of costing can construct a 'truth' of value of products and services. This 'truth' of value then becomes a basis for operational decisions, including the decisions about product types, volumes, prices and customers. Despite their problems in the practices of costing, the 'truth' of costs directs the economy and society to engage in exchange relationships between employees and employers, between customers and traders, between traders and manufacturers and so on. To this extent, costing techniques underpin economic and social relationships.

Costing provided 'truth', and people's day-to-day lives are influenced by this 'truth'. This relationship creates a technical rationality.

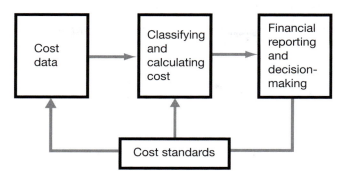

Organizational and production environment

Figure 3.1 *Costing as technical process*

The logic of calculation and rational assumptions behind these techniques would include:

1. Costs can be clearly categorized into certain elements.
2. Information for cost-calculation is readily available.
3. Available methods and techniques are generic and unbiased.
4. They can be used in any economic and organizational context.
5. Decisions taken and controls achieved through the use of these techniques and methods are conclusive.

Costing as a social process

However, costing is not only a technical process of determining costs, but also involves a social process. As a social process, costing reflects people's involvement in relation to the choice of costing techniques and use of costing information in decision-making and controls. In the choice of costing techniques, people may be biased in favour of certain 'popular' techniques rather than appropriate ones. Company managers may be inspired by certain consultants or management fads and fashions. Also, they may be in favour of certain relations with particular individuals or organizations through which 'better' costing techniques are diffused. In relation to the use of costing information, again managers may be biased towards certain decisions and controls. For example, if the manager is keen on introducing a particular product line, then he/she would manifest some justifications for the new project by providing 'helpful' cost information. Other managers on the board would argue against such justifications by providing another set of 'helpful' cost calculations. Here, what is 'correct' depends on the ways in which data are manipulated and manifested. Overall, the ways in which manipulations and manifestations operate have been captured in a number of studies of accounting which may be useful to you. Ansari and Bell (1991) highlight that accounting data would not be the means to achieve organizational controls, because accounting can play 'rationalising and hegemonic roles'. In such roles, accounting (including costing) may establish and perpetuate power for privileged groups in organizations, rather than providing data for decision-making and controls. Theoretical stances on these views will be discussed in Part III. For the time being, you may benefit from the distinction between the technical and social views of costing, summarized in Table 3.1.

Costing links with the social by shaping control systems, employing as a means of exerting power, legitimating actions and rationalizing the ways in which costs are calculated.

Table 3.1 *Technical and social views compared*

Key Questions	Technical view	Social view
What is costing?	A technical process that determines product/service costs	A social process in which people shape control systems and the ways in which the concept of rationality and efficiency is employed
What is the purpose of costing?	To provide information for decision-making, controls and financial reporting	To employ as a means of exerting power and influence
What constitutes costing techniques?	Set of rational devices that derive correct costs	Set of chosen devices that legitimize controls and manipulations
Why do new techniques come into being?	To calculate costs in a much better and rational way	To show that costs are calculated in much better and rational ways

As students of management accounting, you should not rely on only one view. Instead, you should learn from both views to complete your understanding of the subject matter of costing. You cannot see any social views if there are no technical practices in costing. Also, you cannot see the use of costing beyond 'costing itself' unless you have an understanding of social views. It is thus wise to use one view to complement the other to complete your understanding of what costing is. If one ignores this pedagogical approach, then one would come to believe that costing is a 'black box' providing just 'tools' for unproblematic calculations. The world of costing is much more complicated than this 'black box' perspective. An understanding of the history of costing will lead you to deal with such complexities in respect of social views of costing. The section below will take you there.

We must not rely on a single view. Different views give us the complete picture. Everything is problematic. Complexities must be looked at.

HISTORICAL DEVELOPMENTS IN COSTING

We need to consult history to understand the present. In particular, we can discern purposes of costing by looking at different meanings attached to costing practices in different historical epochs. In relation to historical epochs, some argue that history is evolutionary, so there are pre-industrial revolution and post-industrial revolution eras in which costing techniques were developed differently. Others argue that history is fragmented, so different costing techniques were developed under different circumstances. The former draw much on the Marxist tradition of accounting (e.g., Hopper and Armstrong, 1991), while the latter draw on Foucauldian writings (e.g., Loft, 1995). However, our aim here is not to confront the historical debate on the genesis of cost accounting. Instead, we shall understand present purposes of costing through the lens of history. When we look at historical writings on the genesis of costing, as we mentioned at the outset of this chapter, we can categorize the genesis of costing (or cost accounting) into two broader historical themes:

- *ad hoc* developments in costing techniques pre- and post-industrial revolution;
- establishment of 'product costing' within mass production.

> We need to study history to understand the present. Otherwise we are not debating history to understand how costing has come into being.

A brief discussion of these two themes is presented below. By reading it, you must remember that these arguments can be used to understand costing practice being developed in contemporary organizations.

Ad hoc developments: pre- and post-industrial revolution

How costing developed is a big historical question. One easy answer to this is to illustrate the nature of '*ad hoc*' developments. We think that such developments would have ultimately contributed to a 'uniform' system of costing. Hence, an interesting question is: What are the sources of these *ad hoc* developments? There are three inevitable sources:

- double-entry bookkeeping;
- replacing domestic system by capitalist process of production;
- entrepreneurial and engineering efforts in British industries.

Double-entry bookkeeping (DB), as we know, is one of the beautiful logics in accounting. This gave rise to a number of other accounting technologies, including costing. The technical relationship between DB and costing has been described by Solomons (1952), who undertook an examination of the historical development of costing. According to Solomons, early costing developments from the fourteenth to the nineteenth century were related to technical matters around the framework of DB. This means costing records were kept in DB accounts to illustrate how goods were internally transferred from one division to another. In such records, cost of raw materials used in production can be transferred from the raw materials account to the production cost account by crediting the former and debiting the latter. This relationship between costs and DB is also linked to inventory valuation, where the values of inventory are ascertained by costing the materials and other inputs, including labour and overheads, and by keeping records of these values through DB. Linking DB to values in this way was (and continues to be) an important economic and social phenomenon also. Max Weber (1961) emphasized this. According to him, rational calculation which was central to the development of capitalism operated through DB. In particular, he emphasized the use of 'capital accounting', which he defined as a mechanism for comparing start-of-the-year assets with the year-end assets. Costing is an important component of valuing these assets. Sombart (1953) also reasoned a direct relationship between DB and the development of capitalism. He showed that the economic world became dissolved into figures through calculations, including costing ones. DB acted as the spirit of this process. However, Yamey (1964) disagreed with this broad-brush conclusion. He contended that all economic calculations were not accounting ones, and all accounting calculations did not contribute to business decision-making. Nevertheless, when we look at the 'relevance lost' argument of Johnson and Kaplan (1987), we see that cost accounting was useful only for financial reporting through inventory valuation, which is a key area of costing.

> Double-entry bookkeeping went hand-in-hand with costing, and with the development of capitalism. But there is a debate: other than costing (and accounting) there are other aspects to be considered.

Even though historical evidence for the relationship between costing and DB is debatable, costing did influence replacing the domestic system with the capitalist mode of production. Here, we need to clarify two aspects: the distinction between capitalist mode of production and domestic system, and the role played by costing in replacing the former with the latter. As we have shown in Chapter 2, the domestic system in the late eighteenth century encompassed production within families and communities rather than within large-scale factories. Family members, through subcontracts, produced materials and parts for the principal contractors – wealthier people – and received a lump sum for the work done. This value was determined by a quasi-market mechanism. Other than the lump sum value created by this market mechanism, there was no definite costing system to value the domestic production. The capitalist production system which came to replace the domestic production system, in contrast, needed definite values for the production as the subcontracting system was absorbed into large-scale factories within mass production. As we showed in Chapter 2, these factories then looked for values of the jobs and products which had hitherto been determined by the subcontracting system. In this context, costing became an organizational and managerial need.

> The domestic system did not require costing because labour cost was determined by a semi-market mechanism. When this system ceased, industrial firms looked for costing as a mechanism of pricing labour and other resources.

The other set of historical arguments for the emergence of costing is related to entrepreneurial and engineering efforts, especially in British industries. This said, while the emergence of mass production had much to do with US industries, *ad hoc* developments of entrepreneurial and engineering enterprises had been common in British industries. Historians such as Solomons (1952) argued that sophisticated cost and management accounting developed from the mid-1880s:

the costing renaissance. In contrast, other historians, such as Fleischman and Parker (1991), argued that advanced practice of costing prevailed even before the 1850s, especially in iron and textile industries. For example, Fleischman and Parker cited Roll's (1968) study of Boulton & Watt's Saho foundry (1775–1805), which had overhead costing, scientific pricing, departmental profit analysis and process efficiency testing. The Carron Company (1760–1778), a Scottish mining and manufacturing firm, did an organizational restructuring which involved an overhead allocation practice (Fleischman and Parker, 1990). Similarly, the Wedgwood Company invented a system for employing costing data for pricing policy and production decisions (McKendrick, 1961). These developments were much more fragmented but sophisticated. The main thrust was the fact that costing was an analytical tool in industrial inventions, entrepreneurship efforts and engineering advancements.

Costing became much more useful when entrepreneurs wanted to look for alternative avenues for competing with mass producers. Cost control became one of the key strategies in the late nineteenth century.

Establishment of 'product costing' within mass production

The above *ad hoc* developments in costing came together into a 'generally accepted' costing system from the mid-1880s. An overall evaluation of this development can be found in Johnson and Kaplan's *Relevance Lost* (1987). They illustrated that with the development of transportation (e.g., railroads) and communication (e.g., telegraphs), large-scale capitalist enterprises began to use a number of costing and performance measurements as aids to management. In railroads, for example, a number of measures such as cost per ton-mile and ratios of revenues to operating costs were utilized. Similar methods were also used in large distribution enterprises, such as Marshall Field and Woolworth. Johnson and Kaplan argued that these costing-based performance measurements were used to improve internal performance, especially the process, which rationally linked to the overall profitability. This development became widespread with the popularity of the Scientific Management movement of Taylor, especially through the development of standard costing. Together with this, there was another important development: the growth of the multi-activity diverse corporation. Based on these three factors, Johnson and Kaplan went on to argue that 'by 1925 virtually all management accounting practices used today had been developed: cost accounts for labour, material and overhead; budgets for cash, income and capital; flexible budgets, sales forecasts, standard costs, variance analysis, transfer price, and divisional performance measures' (1987: 12). As a specific technology of calculation, costing became dominant in this development, and apart from 'new' developments from the 1990s onwards, these costing technologies, according to Johnson and Kaplan, have remained unchanged. However, we should not forget the historical fact that not only mass producers but also business entrepreneurs used costing techniques. Setting aside criticisms of conventional costing and the historical debates about the genesis of costing, we will now look at the details of these costing technologies.

Costing links with scientific management. Organizational performance was subject to cost-related measures, leading to measuring profitability. Mass producers have used these performance measures for over 100 years.

CATEGORIES OF COST AND THEIR MEANINGS

The costing practices used in the USA, Britain and some other European countries became widespread around the world. A number of factors such as business relations, political colonization and professional and educational practices gave impetus to this development. One of the conventions established for costing practice is about how to categorize cost. Naturally, this links to the meanings of categorization. Most textbooks present two broader 'meanings' of the categories of costs:

■   financial reporting purposes;
■   decision-making purposes.

Financial reporting

As we know, the prime aim of financial reporting is to report periodic profits. For this, we need to know costs and revenues. Costs of products cannot be ascertained if we do not know what constitutes the ultimate product cost. The constitution of ultimate costs is traditionally presented in terms of the 'resources' used in production. Three main such resources are used:

■   direct materials;
■   direct labour;
■   manufacturing overhead.

Direct materials and direct labour are called 'direct costs' because they are directly incurred, and can be directly traced from the volume of production. Hence, direct costs vary with the change in the number of units of production. In contrast, manufacturing overhead costs, such as depreciation and supervisors' salaries, are 'indirect costs', as they cannot be 'easily' traced as a cost of a unit of production. Instead, as we will show later in the chapter, certain techniques are used to calculate the 'fair share' of overheads that is to be added to the direct cost of a product or a service. However, the direct/indirect divide is an unsettled accounting issue, and debates and research on the topic, and technical solutions to the problem, are all controversial. The new cost management topic we address in Chapter 9 is an important contestable terrain in which to discuss these issues.

Whatever the product or service we produce, we cannot avoid any of the above costs. Thus, the types of resources used in production provide an inevitable guide for us to categorize costs. If we categorize costs in this way, we can collect costing data under these categories for ascertaining product cost. It is this cost which can be compared with revenue earned by selling products and/or services. Thus, costs we can ascertain are the costs of goods sold, which include the cost of inventory. This means categorization of cost and subsequent collection of cost data are important accounting inputs for inventory valuation and for subsequent financial reporting.

When Johnson and Kaplan (1987) developed their thesis of 'relevance lost', they criticized the fact that costing data contributed only to this inventory valuation purpose. However, it does not mean that the inventory valuation role of costing can be abandoned. This cost categorization and underlying inventory valuation role are key to financial reporting and auditing. This is a subject for most regulatory forms of accounting.

> Direct/indirect divide is mainly used for providing information for inventory valuation/ financial reporting. According to the 'relevance lost' thesis, costing has been bombarded with this role, rather than with the decision-making role.

Decision-making

This is about using costing data for decision-making purposes, such as pricing, make-or-buy, taking additional orders, etc. As we will illustrate in Chapter 6, the underlying theoretical guide for this categorization mostly came from economic theory rather than pragmatic practices of costing. Economists gained this understanding from their theorization of cost behaviour, so cost behaviour is an important guiding principle for managerial decision-making about the purposes mentioned above. In most textbooks, several dichotomies have been developed for explaining cost behaviour:

- fixed cost versus variable cost;
- relevant cost versus irrelevant cost;
- avoidable cost versus non-avoidable cost;
- sunk cost versus future cost;
- actual cost versus opportunity cost;
- existing cost versus incremental cost.

An analysis of cost data around these dichotomies provides managers with an economic wisdom for making choices among possible projects, products and product volumes. Fixed costs which do not vary with the change of production volume within a given capacity can be distributed to a maximum number of units, resulting in increases in variable costs. Hence, managers tend to look at cost behaviour through the fixed/variable dichotomy to see how production capacity, that is machines and facilities, is used at maximum level. However, in practice, this is much more idealistic, as the given production capacity would be a waste when there are issues in selling the products in the competitive market place. Also, managers are not clearly aware of how much production capacity is unused because of the problems of traditional costing techniques. Moreover, there are some practical issues in defining the notions of 'fixed' and variable. All fixed costs are not always fixed: some of them can be 'semi-fixed' or 'step-fixed'. Sometimes, both costs can be mixed together, where we call them 'semi-variable' or 'mixed'. We will come back to this issue later in the chapter.

> An analysis of cost data around multiple dichotomies provides managers with an economic wisdom for making choices among possible projects, products and product volumes.

Costs which do not vary with the change of production volume within a given capacity are fixed costs. Costs which vary with the change of production volume are variable costs.

The relevant/irrelevant divide is not formally categorized in accounting records, but managers deal with this divide when they are confronted with a particular decision. Relevant costs are future costs that can be changed or avoided as a result of managerial decisions. For example, when we print our work on a printer, we may consider whether we print in 'high-quality' or 'draft' mode. This consideration has implications for the cost of ink or toner and time of printing (electricity, etc.), so that these costs are relevant costs for making that choice. But in this case, cost of paper is irrelevant. This does not mean that, for the final calculation of cost of printing, we consider only ink or toner cost and cost of time. We consider these relevant costs for making the choice between 'high-quality' and 'draft' modes. Managers do not worry about irrelevant cost because their decision does not have any implication for the change in such costs, unless they consider a choice between different types of paper. However, these are rational considerations that would happen in a given situation. We need to be cautious that situations are not always rational. Some people may argue: 'Cost doesn't matter. We want quality!' But, if the managers want to avoid some unnecessary costs, they can start to identify relevant costs. We may not want always to print 'high quality'. Thus, some amount of extra costs can be 'avoidable', but still cost of paper is 'unavoidable' until we think of alternatives. For example, when the managers go for 'electronic copies', paper cost can be avoidable.

The sunk cost/future cost divide is also related to this phenomenon. Sunk costs are unavoidable and irrelevant for decision-making purposes because they have already been incurred, and whatever the decision being made, this cost cannot be reversed. If we take the printing example forward, depreciation of the printer is a sunk cost. Type of paper, quality or number of copies we make cannot change the written-down value of the printer for the period. But when you make a decision to buy a new printer in the future, you can change this depreciation cost by choosing a more durable printer. What you see here is that the above cost divides are linked to managerial decisions, corporate policies and rationalization process.

Relevant costs are future costs that can be changed or avoided as a result of managerial decisions.

Costs can be relevant or irrelevant, depending on the nature of decisions we may make. Most past costs, including sunk costs, are usually irrelevant as we make decisions for the future.

'Opportunity cost' is another economic phenomenon which is to be considered within a decision-making context. Opportunity cost is a sacrificing of income from an alternative source because of the project in question. If the above printing company accepts a particular order and decides to reduce the existing volume of the normal production, then there are two issues to be dealt with. How is the reduction of profit on the existing production covered? And on what grounds can the new order be accepted? The idea of opportunity cost permits the managers to answer these questions. Reduction of profits can be covered by regarding it as a cost of the new order – that is, the opportunity cost. The new order can be accepted if its earnings can cover at least the opportunity costs and incremental costs – that is, the additional costs to be incurred to produce the order. Thus, opportunity cost is an imputed cost into the 'actual cost'. But we must remember the point again that this imputation is only for decision-making purposes rather than for inventory valuation purposes. The idea of opportunity cost provides the managers with a perspective on the construction of value that can guide a rational-economic choice. Nevertheless, we must remember that this rationality would be subject to various other managerial perspectives, including the interest of managers and 'various influences' that they may face.

KEY TERMS

Opportunity cost is a sacrificing of income from an alternative source because of the project in question.

The idea of opportunity cost guides managers to compare between available opportunities and to calculate profits in relation to the opportunities being lost.

Finally, the existing ongoing costs of a product would routinely guide managers in their decision-making as they progress in a particular pattern of production. However, if these costs come to be increased as a result of an additional order for the same product, then there will be additional fixed costs and/or variable costs. These additional costs are called 'incremental' or 'differential' costs. Accountants tend to think that if these incremental costs include much fixed cost, there is no point in accepting the extra order. The reason is that there will be a problem recovering the fixed cost in the future if there is no substantial number of new orders. Rather, managers would be comfortable in accepting extra orders if they require only variable costs.

Incremental costs are additional costs incurred when an extra order is executed. The cost would include both fixed and variable costs.

Overall, categories of costs give shape to a managerial knowledge by which managers make decisions, legitimize their arguments and construct a particular world view. The meanings attached to these cost categories are more or less rational and calculable. But a number of accounting studies have questioned the practice of this rationality (e.g., Mouritsen, 1999) as they are subject to the individual logics of appropriateness, historical habits and institutionalized practices. However, that does not mean that the above dichotomies and economic and managerial meanings have to be avoided. Sometimes, these are complemented with other factors, or other factors may dominate these economic and managerial wisdoms.

> Practices of cost categories vary from one firm to another. Some firms prefer combining different categories.

COST CATEGORIZATION PRACTICES

Historical developments of product costing have now ended up with costing models being adopted by large and medium-sized manufacturing firms around the world. Tables 3.2 and 3.3 are two costing models adopted by two Swedish companies, ABB Motors and Denver Sala AB (Alnestig and Segerstedt, 1996). Both models represent standard costs by which firms develop their budgetary control systems, as we will show in Chapter 4. Standard costs are predetermined values of each cost category of a unit of production. Let us first look at the model adopted by ABB Motors.

ABB Motors produces electrical motors. The firm's cost categories are shown in Table 3.2. Direct materials include copper wires, aluminium and grill bearings. They keep records of these materials based on average purchase price. Material overhead includes the cost of material checking and handling costs, and material purchasing costs. Direct labour comes from multiplying the estimated standard hours by average man-hour in production centres. Production overhead 1 includes both variable and fixed cost of production. Repair and maintenance and supplies from indirect cost centres (such as tools) are regarded as variable, and all other factory overheads, including rent and depreciation, as fixed. Direct materials, semi-manufacturers include the cost of components

Table 3.2 *Example of product costing: ABB Motors model*

Direct material

Material overhead

Direct labour

Production overhead 1

Direct materials, semi-manufacturers

Production cost 1

Production overhead 2

Production standard full cost

Sales and administrative costs

Standard full cost

Source: Alnestig and Segerstedt (1996: 443)

produced by themselves, which are to be used for producing motors. This does not include production overhead 1. The total of all the above five cost categories is production cost 1. Production overhead 2 includes process design and development as well as administration and finance costs. Then ABB Motors finds production standard full cost. When sales and administration cost is added to this, they get standard full cost. You must remember that we are dealing here with cost categories rather than the mechanism of standard costing, which we present in Chapter 4. In ABB Motors, we see that costs fall into three main categories: material, labour and overhead. Following our earlier discussion on meanings of cost categories, you can see that ABB Motors follows the logic of financial reporting rather than a decision-making purpose. Here, each cost category acts as a component of full cost which leads to a calculation of value of stocks being sold.

However, we should not believe that all firms follow the same logic. Nature of business, the ways in which costing systems are developed and purposes being emphasized would lead to diverse practices. Denver Sala's somewhat complex model is shown in Table 3.3.

Table 3.3 *Example of product costing: Denver Sala AB model*

Direct material (DM)	
Direct labour (DL)	
Payroll fringe costs	VC
Variable manufacturing cost (VMC)	
Purchasing costs	FC
Carrying costs	VC
Handling charges, storage costs	FC
Rental DM – inventory	FC
Material overhead (MAO)	
Production administration – management	FC
Planning, preparing	
Rental – production unit	FC
Depreciation – equipment	Depreciation
Repairs and maintenance	FC
Heat, light and power – plant/equipment	FC/VC
Lubricants, supplies	VC
Manufacturing overhead 1 (MO1)	(depending on production)
Cost of guarantee	VC
Inventory variances/ending inventories	VC
Rental – office	FC
Heat and light – office	FC
Depreciation – office equipment	Depreciation
Depreciation – machine tools	Depreciation
Manufacturing overhead 2 (MO2)	(not depending on production)
Total manufacturing costs (TMC)	
Freight (to customers)	VC
Packaging	VC
Cars	VC
Laboratory and service cars	VC
Engineering	VC
Travel costs	VC
Purchasing – mills, etc.	VC
Non-manufacturing overhead (NMO)	
Total cost (TC)	

Source: Alnestig and Segerstedt (1996: 446)

Denver Sala AB is part of the Svedala Industries AB which caters to the mineral processing, mining and construction industries. Sala produces equipment to be used in unit operation in the mineral industry. Their manufacturing cost model shown in Table 3.3 is linked to their pricing system, so it highlights fixed cost (FC) and variable cost (VC) along with their cost categorization (We will describe the role of costing in pricing in Chapter 6.) Direct material in this model is used as a standard cost for pricing and actual cost for stock valuation purpose. Direct labour is calculated as an average cost per hour per work centre and payroll fringe cost is 83 per cent of direct labour. Variable manufacturing cost (VMC) is calculated by adding these three direct cost categories. On the question of indirect cost, two types of indirect costs are identified: material overhead and manufacturing overhead. Material overhead (MAO) is calculated to be 10 per cent of direct material. Two types of manufacturing overhead are identified: overhead for ongoing production (MO1) and others (MO2). MO1 is calculated to be 403 per cent of direct material and MO2 to be 9 per cent of VMC. Total manufacturing cost is then derived by adding all four: VMC, MAO, MO1 and MO2. Finally, non-manufacturing overhead is considered to be a variable cost, being varied with the number of units of production. As we mentioned before, it is interesting to see that Denver Sala AB has adopted this model for both inventory valuation and pricing decision purposes.

You can now make two important observations about the practices of categorization of costs in the two firms. One is that there are no drastic differences in the broader categories. Most firms adopt three-way categorization of cost (direct material, direct labour and overhead) for inventory valuation purposes, and two-way categorization of cost (fixed and variable) for decision-making. The other observation is that inventory valuation and decision-making purposes are not always treated as separate costing models. In pragmatic terms, inventory valuation and decision-making are interrelated phenomena so that, rather than keeping two separate books of costing data, firms tend to take advantage of integrating both and to provide information for both purposes.

CALCULATIVE PRACTICES OF PRODUCT COSTING

We have now considered a broad base — categories of cost — for an understanding of the calculative practice of costing. By a calculative practice, we mean the use of techniques for deriving product cost from actual and forecasted cost data. Here actual data can be accumulated only for direct costs, namely direct materials and direct labour. Forecasted data are related to overhead because actual data for individual items cannot be traced easily until the end of the accounting period. Thus, calculative practices of product costing involve two main technical steps:

- cost tracing;
- cost allocation.

Cost tracing

Cost tracing involves accumulating direct cost for individual products or jobs. We now know that direct costs include direct labour and direct materials. As long as these costs are traceable as production progresses, firms record the details of these costs on a continuous basis. For recording labour costs, firms use time sheets or job cards where they record the job number or customer number, number of hours worked and hourly pay-rate. So, time sheets/job cards allow the accounting system to assign employees' pay to individual cost objects: that is, product or service. Similarly, for recording material costs, firms use material acquisition, where they record various types and amounts of materials issued and their prices paid at the time of acquisition. Again, these costs can be recognized in terms of individual products or services through the details of the product, such as job number or customer number that is entered in the material acquisition. In examination questions on product costing problems, you are given these details as they are extracted from the time sheets and material acquisitions. Thus, these details are known and unproblematic to be included in individual product costs. Today, with the advance of information technology, these details are easily kept in computer systems, and are more easily traceable for product costing purposes.

KEY TERMS

Time sheets/job cards are data input devices (primary documents) for recording labour cost data. They record number of hours worked and pay rates, in respect of a particular product/job/customer.

KEY TERMS

Material requisitions are data input devices (primary documents) for recording material cost data. They record physical quantities used and price per unit of such quantities, in respect of a particular product/job/customer.

Instead of maintaining the actual cost records for tracing direct material and direct labour costs, some firms use a standard costing system. Rather than waiting for actual data about direct materials and labour, firms adopting a standard costing system rely on predetermined standards. These standards include the amount of materials to be consumed and expected price per unit of such materials, and the number of labour hours to be spent and rate per hour to be paid. Firms adopt such a standard costing system if they have a large number of repetitive products or services for which the managers can easily set necessary standard material and labour. In doing so, managers consider a number of factors, including engineering aspects of the product as well as dynamics in market prices. You must remember that these standards, however, are not budgets. The main difference between standards and budgets is that standards are set for individual products or services, whereas budgets are planned activities and costs/revenues for a forecasted volume of production.

Instead of actual cost data, some firms use standard costs as a proxy. This has been acceptable since the Scientific Management movement.

What you have seen here is that cost tracing is a calculative practice of product costing that has been developed in industries, and this would happen either through actual or standard cost data. In the history of cost accounting development, the accumulation of actual cost data has been common in many industries, especially during the mid-nineteenth and early twentieth centuries (see Solomons, 1952; Fleischman and Parker, 1991; Boyns and Edwards, 1997; McLean, 2006). For example, within the British steel industry, a uniform costing system (a common system for a particular industry) was adopted where the firms used to trace actual cost for each of the main products, including pig iron, soft basic billets, black sheets, railway rails, sheet bars, steel plates and steel joists. However, with the development of Taylor's ideas, firms began to use standard costing systems, especially in mass production manufacturing enterprises (see Loft, 1995). As Taylor advocated having standards for all jobs and activities, and controlling them accordingly, cost accountants must have embraced this idea to develop a standard costing system. However, whether firms adopt actual costs or standard cost for cost tracing is still a practical question that we need to explore. For example, during the Second World War, there was a debate about whether it was possible to continue with a standard costing system, given that the industrial environment in the war was unstable (see Fleischman and Parker, 1991). Nevertheless, in your exam questions, you are told what method the firm in question adopts.

Whatever the method being adopted, there is no sophisticated technique for cost tracing. You may be given straightforward data for direct calculations by multiplying physical amounts (actual or standard) by prices/rates (physical or standard). Look at Example 3.1.

EXAMPLE 3.1 THE PROBLEM

You are told that a furniture manufacturing firm adopts a system of cost tracing on an actual basis, and actual details for producing item X are as follows:

> 4 metres of timber @ £4.50 per metre
> 1 litre of polish @ £12.00 per litre
> 1.5 litres of paint @ £15.00 per litre
> 6 iron joints @ £1.50 per joint
> 4 hours of skilled labour @ £12.00 per hour
> 2 hours of unskilled labour @ £6.00 per hour

The problem is to ascertain the total cost of item X.

The calculation of direct materials and direct labour is shown in Exhibit 3.1.

Now, we have the question of assigning indirect costs to these direct costs.

Cost allocation

You saw that cost tracing was a quick calculative practice. Indirect costs cannot be traced as quickly because they are incurred periodically, irrespective of number of products being produced. For example, depreciation of machines are period costs that are allocated over a number years during the economic life of the machine. Depreciation cost per unit of production must come from a rational calculative practice which can be acceptable for stock valuation purposes. The underlying

Exhibit 3.1 *Calculation of direct material and labour costs for item X*

Cost item	£
Timber: 4 × 4.50	18.00
Polish: 1 × 12.00	12.00
Paint: 1.5 × 15.00	22.50
Iron joints: 6 × 1.50	9.00
Direct materials per unit	61.50
Skilled labour: 4 × 12.00	48.00
Unskilled labour: 2 × 6.00	12.00
Direct labour per unit	60.00

rational practice is known as cost allocation, which follows certain technical steps to assign indirect costs (overheads) to individual products. Whether or not these steps are rational is still debatable, and in response to the impediments of the traditional method of cost allocation, activity-based costing (ABC) has now emerged as an alternative. In this chapter, we will consider only the traditional method of cost allocation; a discussion of the use of ABC is presented in Chapter 9.

KEY TERMS

Cost allocation involves certain technical steps to assign indirect costs (overheads) to individual products.

You should understand that there was a growing concern about allocating overheads to individual products from the late nineteenth century. For example, concerning the shipbuilding industry, McLean (1995) revealed that there was a tendency towards using the methods of charging out overheads to final products. The rates used for this were based on price, cost and labour and machine hours (see McLean, 2006). Also, these firms tended to use a long-term ratio rather than changing it annually. Now we have a question of how this ratio can be calculated.

Cost allocation did not exist in the early nineteenth century. Later in the century, firms began to be concerned about this. Today, we have that practice as a result of these *ad hoc* developments.

The steps associated with the traditional calculative practice of cost allocation are twofold:

- calculation of overhead absorption rate;
- absorption of overhead into products.

Calculation of overhead absorption rate

Overhead absorption rate (OAR) expresses an amount of overhead costs to be added to direct costs. For example, if it is expressed as £10 per direct labour hour, it means that for each direct labour hour being spent, there is a £10 of overhead costs. The question here is how we could calculate this £10. The straightforward answer is that this rate can be calculated by adopting the following formula:

$$Overhead\ absorption\ rate\ (OAR) = \frac{forecasted\ overheads}{forecasted\ activity\ level}$$

KEY TERMS

Overhead absorption rate (OAR) is a ratio derived by dividing forecasted overheads of a particular department or of the whole plant by respective activity level, such as direct labour hours, machine hours or direct costs.

Before going on to the application of this formula, we must first understand these terms: forecasted overheads and forecasted activity level. As overhead costs are incurred periodically, until the end of the financial year, actual amount cannot be known. But the costs of products must be known on a continuous basis, especially for taking customer orders. Thus, firms use a ready-made overhead rate that could be used for absorption into direct costs. To calculate such ready-made rates, overhead for the forthcoming period must be forecasted. Activity level, the denominator of the above formula, could be a desired base, such as direct labour hours, machine hours or direct labour costs. Regarding this base, there is a debate as to what base is the most appropriate. We will come back to this later.

Overhead cost rates do not represent actual figures being derived from the same accounting period. As managers cannot wait until actual figures are produced at the end of the accounting period, ready-made rates are calculated based on past experiences. Thus rates are forecasted.

The calculative practices of an OAR vary (see Edwards, 1989). Some firms tend to use one single plant-wide OAR (a blanket OAR) so the same rate is used by all production departments. Other firms tend to use multiple rates for different production departments, so that each department uses its own OAR. The calculation of the former is simpler, and the latter is complex. To understand how to calculate these two types of OAR, we can consider an example.

EXAMPLE 3.2 OVERHEAD ABSORPTION

ABC Company produces garments in three production departments – designing and cutting (DC), sewing and finishing (SF) and packing and storage (PS) – and two service departments – material procurement (MP) and general services (GS). Its forecasted annual overhead costs are as follows:

Costs of tools and equipment

DC	£800 000
SF	£800 000
PS	£200 000
MP	£100 000
GS	£100 000

Wages for supervision

DC	£900 000
SF	£700 000
PS	£400 000
MP	£300 000
GS	£200 000

General overhead

Machine depreciation	£180 000
Machine insurance	£24 000
Maintenance and repairs	£15 000
Building rent	£220 000
Heating and lighting	£80 000
Salaries	£140 000

The company owns three machines for DC, SF and PS. Their book values are £750,000, £500,000 and £250,000, respectively. The factory occupies a single building, and all respective production and service departments share the floor area as follows: 30,000 (DC), 30,000 (SF), 20,000 (PS), 10,000 (MP) and 10,000 (GS). The company employs 1,750 people in the five departments as follows: 500 (DC), 750 (SF), 250 (PS), 125 (MP) and 125 (GS). During the year, direct labour hours in DC, SF and PS were 750,000, 1,000,000 and 50,000 hours, respectively. Machine hours required for DC and SF were 50,000 and 150,000, respectively. The company has a policy of equally weighting maintenance and repairs among all production departments. Materials issued from MP to departments were 40,000 (DC), 40,000 (SF), 20,000 (PS) and 10,000 (GS), while, as estimated by the manager-in-charge, services from GS to production departments were given in the ratio of 2:2:1.

The above details are estimates, being developed following past financial accounting data. In exams, you are given these details and asked to calculate OAR. To do this, three steps have to be followed:

1. Allocation of costs to all relevant departments.
2. Reallocation (sometimes called apportionment) of service departmental costs to production departments.
3. Calculation of OAR.

If you now look at the example, you will see costs of tools and equipment and wages for supervision are given in respect of all production and service departments. Thus, these costs can be easily allocated to these departments, as we show in Exhibit 3.2.

Exhibit 3.2 *Direct allocation of overheads*

Cost item	Production departments			Service departments	
	DC £	SF £	PS £	MP £	GS £
Tools and equipment	800 000	800 000	200 000	100 000	100 000
Wages for supervision	900 000	700 000	400 000	300 000	200 000
Total	1 700 000	1 500 000	600 000	400 000	300 000

The other overheads, namely machine depreciation, machine insurance, quality controls, building rent, heating and lighting and salaries, have not yet been allocated to any of the departments. We need to allocate them to all necessary departments based on acceptable bases. Three bases can be found from the description underneath the figures in the example: book value of machines, areas of occupation and number of employees. It is logical to accept that machine depreciation, machine insurance and maintenance and repairs can be allocated to all production departments on the basis of the book values of machines. The ratio is: 750,000:500,000:250,000 = 3:2:1. Building rent and heating and lighting can be allocated in the ratio of areas of occupation: 30,000:30,000:20,000:10,000:10,000 = 3:3:2:1:1. Salaries can be allocated in the ratio of employees in each department: 500:750:250:125:125 = 4:6:2:1:1. You must bear in mind that these ratios are rounded numbers, as it is a hypothetical case. In the real world, these numbers are not always rounded, so you need to approximate them as necessary. You can now see in Exhibit 3.3 how those costs have been allocated to respective departments. In order to differentiate this from previous direct allocation, we term it 'rational' allocation (or apportionment), to mean that those costs have been allocated on the basis of selected rational criteria.

There is another issue. Service departments are not ultimate entities producing garments. Their existence is only for serving production departments. Thus, these costs have to be reallocated to

Exhibit 3.3 *'Rational' allocation*

Cost item	Rationale of allocation	Production departments			Service departments	
		DC £	SF £	PS £	MP £	GS £
Machine depreciation	Book value of machine	90 000	60 000	30 000	–	–
Machine insurance	Book value of machine	12 000	8 000	4 000	–	–
Maintenance and repairs	Company policy of equal weighting	5 000	5 000	5 000	–	–
Building rent	Area occupied	66 000	66 000	44 000	22 000	22 000
Heating and lighting	Area occupied	24 000	24 000	16 000	8 000	8 000
Salaries	No. of employees	40 000	60 000	20 000	10 000	10 000
Total		237 000	223 000	119 000	40 000	40 000

production departments, considering them as production costs. Although most textbooks deal with complexities about this reallocation (or secondary apportionment),[1] we do not intend to go into these because our aim is to show how a broader product costing approach has developed in the history of accounting. So, totals of service department costs will have to be reallocated to other departments which received services from respective service departments. It is logical for MP's cost of £440,000 (£400,000 + £40,000) to be reallocated on the basis of the ratio of material issues: 40,000 (DC):40,000 (SF):20,000 (PS):10,000 (GS) = 4:4:2:1. As a result of this reallocation, the cost of GS has now gone from £340,000 (£300,000 + £40,000) to £380,000 (£340,000 + £40,000). This has to be reallocated to all production departments based on the ratio 2:2:1, as given in the example. All these reallocations are shown in Exhibit 3.4.

We are now in a position to add up all production costs (i.e., direct allocations, 'rational' allocations and reallocations), as shown in Exhibit 3.5. Here, you must recognize that there are no costs left in service departments as they have already been reallocated to respective production departments.

We have so far done necessary allocations. The totals in Exhibit 3.5 are the ultimate result of this process. Based on these totals, we can now calculate OARs. This is very straightforward. You need to divide each of the above totals by direct labour hours or machine hours, depending on what basis the company wants to adopt. So, the rates are shown in Exhibit 3.6.

Exhibit 3.4 *Reallocations*

Cost item	Production departments			Service departments	
	DC £	SF £	PS £	MP £	GS £
Totals of service departments				440 000	340 000
Allocation of cost of MP	160 000	160 000	80 000	(440 000)	40 000
Allocation of cost of GS	152 000	152 000	76 000	–	(380 000)
Total reallocations	312 000	312 000	156 000	–	–

Exhibit 3.5 *Total allocations*

Cost item	DC £	SF £	PS £
Direct allocations (Ex. 3.2)	1 700 000	1 500 000	600 000
'Rational' allocations (Ex. 3.3)	237 000	223 000	119 000
Reallocations (Ex. 3.4)	312 000	312 000	156 000
Total allocations	2 249 000	2 035 000	875 000

Exhibit 3.6 *Overhead absorption rates*

	DC £	SF £	PS £
A Total allocations (from Ex. 3.5)	2 249 000	2 035 000	875 000
B Direct labour hours	750 000	1 000 000	50 000
C Direct labour rates = A/B	2.99	2.03	17.50
D Machine hours	50 000	150 000	–
E Machine hour rates = A/D	44.98	13.56	–

The absorption of overhead into products

The above calculation exercise gave us an understanding of how OARs are calculated. We have ended up with three direct labour hour (DLH) rates and two machine hour (MH) rates. Based on past experience or arbitrary bases, the company may choose one or both types of rate for costing individual products. We shall consider a simple example.

EXAMPLE 3.3 ABSORPTION OF OVERHEAD INTO COST OBJECTS

Consider the same data in the previous example. Suppose that the company's policy is to absorb DC and SF costs on machine hour basis, while FS cost is absorbed on direct labour hour basis. The company had an order for 1,000 garments. The managers envisaged that the following are needed for the production of one unit:

Direct materials

3 metres of fabric @ £3.00 per metre
Sewing material cost £5.00

Direct labour

3 hours of skilled labour @ £6.50 per hour
2 hours of unskilled labour @ £4.00 per hour

Machine hours

DC   0.1
SF   2.0

You are required to calculate the cost of the order.

Here direct costs are to be taken as they are, and overheads are to be absorbed by these direct costs. OARs are to be used for the absorption, as shown in Exhibit 3.7.

OAR is used to calculate product costs when a customer order is performed. This is an exercise adding overheads to actual or standard direct costs.

Thus, in this manner, based on forecasted overhead and activity levels, companies determine the amount of overhead that should be absorbed to individual jobs, processes, activities, products, etc. (cost objects). Total absorption of overhead in this manner during the financial year should be equal to the actual overhead costs, which can be known only at the end of the accounting period. Often,

---

Exhibit 3.7 *Application of OARs*

	£	£
Direct costs		
Fabric: 3 × £3.00	9.00	
Sewing material	5.00	
Skilled labour: 3 × £6.50	19.50	
Unskilled labour: 2 × £4.00	8.00	41.50
Overheads		
DC: 0.1 × £44.98	4.50	
SF: 2.0 × £13.56	27.12	
PS: 5 × £17.50	87.50	119.12
Total cost per unit		160.62

Total costs of order: 1 000 × £160.62 = £160 620

---

there would be a difference between the two. This can be either under-absorption or over-absorption. These amounts are normally treated in the profit and loss account. This is a practice which is debatable as well.

There has been a debate in management accounting whether a firm should adopt several departmental OARs or one single plant-wide ratio. The ratios used in the above example are departmental ones. The advantage of the use of such departmental ratios is that, on the one hand, such ratios would provide more accurate overhead costs being absorbed in products and services and, on the other hand, they would give more opportunity for the senior managers to control departments, especially about/through cost controls. Church (1916) identified the need of assigning overheads to production centres, which allowed firms to develop some form of accountability and management control (see Ahmed and Scapens, 1991).

However, there are certain firms which do not have much differentiation between production departments. They tend to use a plant-wide ratio rather than several departmental ratios. Technically, it is easy for the managers: all departments use one single ratio based on direct labour hours, machine hours or direct costs. For example, suppose that the above firm's policy is to use one single ratio based on direct labour hours, then we need to divide the total overhead costs of all three production departments by total direct labour hours (DLH). You can see this calculation in Exhibit 3.8.

The plant-wide ratio can be used to calculate the total cost of production. To do this, the number of DLH spent on a particular product should be multiplied by 2.87 and the resultant overhead should be added to direct cost of that product. A recalculation of the previous customer order (Example 3.3) is provided in Exhibit 3.9.

Using a single plant-wide OAR or multiple departmental OARs is another debate. Practices vary. Both are still arbitrary, however.

Exhibit 3.8 Blanket OAR

	£	£
Overheads		
DC	2 249 000	
SF	2 035 000	
PS	875 000	5 159 000
Direct labour hours		
DC	750 000	
SF	1 000 000	
PS	50 000	1 800 000

OAR (overhead/DLH): £5 159 000/£1 800 000 = £2.87

Exhibit 3.9 Recalculation of cost using the blanket OAR

	£	£
Direct costs		
Fabric: 3 × £3.00	9.00	
Sewing material	5.00	
Skilled labour: 3 × £6.50	19.50	
Unskilled labour: 2 × £4.00	8.00	41.50
Overheads		
5 (skilled and unskilled DLH) × £2.87 =		14.35
Total cost per unit		55.85

Total costs of order: 1 000 × £55.85 = £55 850

We have calculated two costs per unit under two methods: £160.62 under 'departmental ratios' and £55.85 under 'plant-wide ratio'. Now we have to ask which ratio is correct. There is no 'right' answer to this question, other than the debate we see in the literature (see Rayburn, 1989). However, there is an interesting historical development: before cost allocation practices, overheads were written-off against profit and loss account; later on, firms used to adopt a single plant-wide ratio, while any unabsorbed overheads were written-off; then the firms tended to adopt multiple department ratios. This does not mean that there are no companies adopting single plant-wide ratios. Lamminmaki and Drury (2001) reported that they found 48 per cent of New Zealand companies (out of 85) and 26 per cent of UK companies (out of 303) adopting a plant-wide ratio. Thus, the question of what is 'correct' has to be discussed in relation to context-specific factors, including the type of industry, technology and the ways in which accounting information is used.

You should now understand the general picture of the calculative practice of product costing. A particular language has been used to describe this. In short, it is about absorption of overheads by the given direct costs. Absorption can be easily executed by using predetermined OARs. Any under-absorption or over-absorption can be adjusted in the profit and loss account at the end of the accounting year. Until such adjustments, OARs are used for inventory valuation and pricing purposes throughout the year. We do not want to take you forward regarding complex calculations. Instead, we want you to understand the essence of product costing practice which has developed over the last century. The issues about this particular practice are addressed in Chapter 9.

CONTRIBUTIONS TO MECHANISTIC APPROACH

The foregoing discussions, illustrations and arguments show you how costing as technical and social practice has emerged, and which calculative practices of costing have remained predominant. The calculative practice of costing has had a constitutive role in the construction of a mechanistic form of management accounting which we highlighted in Chapter 2. We would like to draw your attention to the ways in which the calculative practice of costing has constructed this mechanistic form. We have some observations about this construction:

■ Creation of a language of costing.
■ Linking of costing to organizational control system.
■ Transforming the firm into a pricing mechanism.

We will consider each of these points separately, despite their interrelatedness.

We have seen that categories of costs and making sense of these categories provide a particular language for the organizational members to talk with, act upon, and with which to achieve controls. As an organizational language, costing has been able to create an organizational order by translating each economic activity, be it a production of physical good or providing a service, into sensible values, together with meanings and interpretations. Drawing on the experiences of the potter Josiah Wedgwood, Miller and Napier (1993) argued that, as a particular business vocabulary, costing terms and concepts were constructed, in addition to the technology of costing. This vocabulary was required 'for making it operable'. So, costing is not only a technology but also a language that can legitimate and sustain the technology as a powerful managerial device. The creation of the calculative practice of costing is an outcome of these two aspects: language and technology.

Costing became an integral part of overall organizational control mechanism, which we will discuss further in the next chapter. Towards the end of the nineteenth century, most firms used costing as a control device by creating departments, departmental relationships and performance evaluation methods. Across the board, firms used costing as a set of tools that could generate refined controls. Worksheets, time sheets and job cards became not only the records of labour hours but also a system of surveillance for revealing how workers were engaged in production. Material requisitions and stock ledgers became not only the records of material issues and uses but also a system of preventing fraud and corruption that might occur as a result of large-scale operations. Overhead absorption ratios became not only the basis for calculating product costs, but also measures for tracking departmental efficiencies in the use of general resources and facilities. Having realized similar advantages of an established costing system, the Carron Company, a Scottish metal manufacturing firm, began to establish a proper costing system, following its financial crisis of 1760–1778 (see Fleischman and Parker, 1990). In doing so, Carron actually established a better management control system by creating costing procedures, including a system of cost allocation. Today, there is vast evidence to show that costing information is used to monitor financial aspects of performance (financial control), and as a surrogate measure to control operations (operational controls) (see Otley and Berry, 1994).

> As costing generates an organizational language, a control system and a pricing mechanism, it goes hand-in-hand with the construction of the mechanistic form of management accounting. Costs, revenues and profits then come to be an ideological structure.

Adding more to the mechanistic form of management accounting, costing became a pricing mechanism within firms. After the genesis of large-scale manufacturing firms, we showed early in this chapter that the domestic system of production remained discontinued, and the payments paid to domestic workers were replaced by the costing system. For this, costing began to act as an internal mechanism of pricing the labour. It contributed to pricing the ultimate products and service by providing direct and indirect cost information. In the early twentieth century, UK government factories relied on cost information rather than market prices to determine prices (Mitchell and Walker, 1997). Late nineteenth- and early twentieth-century firms operating in competitive environments attempted to develop uniform costing within certain industries. Mitchell and Walker (1997) reported on a case of the UK printing industry to argue that employers attempted to introduce a uniform costing system, responding to the pressures generated from both emerging market competition and trade union agitation. Within all such attempts towards determining prices, cost allocation played a vital role from the late nineteenth century (Metcalf, 1989), and internal structures of the organization were subject to formal informational processes in which costing and pricing went hand-in-hand.

HAVE YOU UNDERSTOOD THE CHAPTER?

1. Why did Henry Rushton decide to look for costing methods?
2. Why do we define costing as a process?
3. How do we differentiate the technical process of costing from its social process?
4. What assumption do you think costing techniques underlie?
5. What is meant by a 'black-box' view of costing?
6. What are the *ad hoc* contributions to the development of costing?
7. What is the rationale behind the establishment of product costing within mass production?
8. Illustrate the meanings of cost categories for financial reporting and decision-making.
9. Distinguish between cost tracing and cost allocation.
10. Why is cost allocation more difficult than cost tracing?
11. Describe the calculative process of deriving 'total allocation'.
12. What is the purpose of an 'overhead allocation sheet'?
13. What happens if overheads are not fully absorbed by products or jobs?
14. In what ways do costing practices contribute to the 'mechanistic form' of management accounting?

BEYOND THE CHAPTER

1. 'History of costing presents us with the present of costing.' Discuss.
2. 'Cost allocation is a solution.' What is the problem?
3. Is costing a job of the accountant?
4. Does costing exist without an organization?
5. 'Costing doesn't reveal but constructs costs.' How?

FURTHER READING

1. On history of costing, see Scorgie (1997), Boyns and Edwards (1997) and Mitchell and Walker (1997).
2. On costing methods, see Drury (2004) or Horngren *et al.* (2005).
3. On technical practices of costing, see Alnestig and Segerstedt (1996) and McKendrick (1961).

Chapter 4

Towards profit planning through budgeting

A STARTING POINT: CORPORATE BUDGETING IS A JOKE!

Corporate budgeting is a joke, and everyone knows it. It consumes a huge amount of executives' time, forcing them into endless rounds of dull meetings and tense negotiations. It encourages managers to lie and cheat, lowballing targets and inflating results, and it penalizes them for telling the truth. It turns business decisions into elaborate exercises in gaming. It sets colleague against colleague, creating distrust and ill will. And it distorts incentives, motivating people to act in ways that run counter to the best interests of their companies.

(Jensen, 2001: 96)

Budgeting, as most corporations practice it, should be abolished. That may sound like a radical proposition, but it would be merely the culmination of long-running efforts to transform organizations from centralized hierarchies into devolved networks that allow for nimble adjustments to market conditions. Most of the other building blocks are in place. Companies have invested huge sums in IT networks, process reengineering, and a range of management tools including EVA (Economic Value Added), balanced scorecards, and activity accounting. But they have been unable to establish a new order because the budget and the command and control culture that it supports remain predominant.

(Hope and Fraser, 2003: 108)

How has such a 'joke' become the predominant mode of corporate planning and control?

SETTING THE SCENE

In Chapter 2, we discussed the historical context within which the mechanistic form of organizations and management control techniques evolved. We highlighted two major roles of cost and management accounting within mechanistic organizational forms: product costing (i.e., product cost calculation and reporting); and cost controls and profit planning. Chapter 3 dealt with product costing. This chapter deals with profit planning through budgeting.

This chapter is historical and technical, and it lays the foundation for Chapter 5, where we will discuss controlling aspects of budgeting. It is historical because it traces how standard costing and budgeting together became the most pervasive planning and control mechanism in mechanistic organizations. It is technical because it elaborates on technical calculations and procedures involved in budgeting.

This chapter begins with a brief history of budgeting and standard costing. This section will trace the origin of budgeting and standard costing. After reading this section, you will understand that budgeting and standard costing emerged independently from two different roots, and later merged together to form a comprehensive system of operational planning and control. You will appreciate that budgeting dates back to the administrative controls in government institutions, while the roots of standard costing can be found in industrial engineers' attempts to standardize labour time, efforts and remunerations.

- Understand the historical roots of budgeting and standard costing
- Appreciate the contributions of industrial engineering and cost accounting in developing standard costing practices

Second, you will read a section that will deal with 'modernity' as the historical context within which budgeting and standard costing evolved. The objective of this section is to make you understand that it was the 'modernity', as a specific historical phase, that provided the necessary social impetus for the development of budgeting and standard costing within economic organizations. After reading this section, you will appreciate certain characteristics of modernity that facilitate the spread of budgeting and standard costing.

- Understand and appreciate how the historical phase of modernity provided the contextual background for the evolution of budgeting and standard costing techniques

Third, we will take you to a section which deals with the link between budgeting and standard costing. After reading this rather technical description, you should be able to: discuss common characteristics of budgeting and standard costing; contrast budgeting with standard costing; show how standards provide the basis for budgetary calculations; draw an outline of how various operational budgets and master budgets are derived from assumptions on market conditions; and discuss the control role that flexible budget and variances play within the overall budgetary system.

- Identify common characteristics of budgeting and standard costing
- Contrast budgeting and standard costing
- Relate budgeting with standard costing

Fourth, you will go through a fairly complex worked example of budgetary planning. The aim of this section is to make you acquainted with the calculative procedures involved in the preparation of operational and master budgets. After working through the case example in this section, you will understand how: standard costing information is recorded in a 'standard cost card'; operational budgets are prepared, in a sequential order, with the use of standard cost card and other marketing and accounting information; master budgets are derived from the operational budgets.

- Understand the calculative sequence and the logic involved in the preparation of operational and master budgets

Fifth, you will read a section that deals with different approaches to budgetary planning. The aim of this section is to introduce you to a set of approaches that organizations practically adopt to prepare budgets, such as incremental budgeting, zero-based budgeting, activity-based budgeting, programme budgeting and flexible budgeting. After reading this section, you will understand how practical approaches to budgeting deviate from the ideal-type model of budgeting for various institutional reasons.

- Understand the logic and calculative formulae of variance analysis

Finally, the chapter ends with a section that deals with the technical rationales of budgetary planning and control within mechanistic organizations. After reading this section, you will appreciate that budgeting performs the traditional managerial activities of planning, co-ordinating, communicating and controlling. You will also appreciate that budgeting has the capacity to integrate operational and administrative rationales of managing organizations. This section will conclude the chapter with a brief note on how budgetary control configures organizations as a series of budget-based performance contracts across the organizational hierarchy. The aim of this section is primarily to lay the foundation for the forthcoming theoretical and behavioural discussion in the next chapters.

■ Appreciate technical rationales that budgetary control plays within mechanistic organizations

ORIGIN OF BUDGETING AND STANDARD COSTING

As we noted in Chapter 2, most cost and management accounting techniques we use today originated in the early decades of the twentieth century. It was during this period that standard costing and budgeting evolved to constitute the most pervasive mechanism of cost control and profit planning. However, budgeting and standard costing evolved from two different sources as two distinct techniques of cost control, but later merged into a unified system of planning and control, which we may call profit planning and control.

Origin of budgeting: control of public expenditure

Budgeting is a much older technique than standard costing. The roots of formal and institutional budgeting date back at least to eighteenth-century English government when the Chancellor of the Exchequer presented his annual budget to Parliament. That budget, according to Theiss (1932: 11), was in fact an accounting report, which consisted of:

■ a statement of expenditure for the past year;
■ an estimate of expenditure for the coming year;
■ a recommendation as to the amount of taxes to be levied and methods of taxation.

Government financial controls are the historical root of budgeting.

A similar view is expressed by Dohr (1932: 31) when he asserts that the budgetary idea in industrial accounting was borrowed from the municipal field, where expenditures were controlled under the doctrine that no moneys were to be spent except as a statutory authorization or appropriation was made in advance. Budgeting in the realm of public finance, at that time, was adopted obviously to provide some means of control over the spending of public funds by public officers.[1] Those in public offices were thus held 'strictly accountable' and their future expenditures were limited by the approved budgetary appropriations which were made after a study of possible revenues for the coming year and the amounts spent over the past fiscal year (Dohr, 1932; Theiss, 1932). Hence, budgets limited the discretion of officers over public expenditure and facilitated centralized control over expenses. The notion of budgeting as it was practised in government and larger municipal councils was extensively adopted both in public and private institutions, such as educational, religious, scientific and charitable, and in business organizations. At their first appearance, these institutional budgets, including those of business organizations, by and large conformed to the procedures and purposes of government budgeting – to confine 'expenditures' to approved appropriations – and, hence, did not have a noteworthy impact upon the planning and control of core operations: production and delivery of goods and services. Budgeting began to evolve as a company-wide system of planning and controlling 'core operations' only when it started to merge with principles of Scientific Management. These principles were instrumental in the development of standard costing. Budgeting, when coupled with standard costing techniques, formed the most dominant and comprehensive system of planning and control in industrial organizations.

> The purpose of early budgets in public institutions was to control public spending by public officers.

> The purpose of early business budgeting was also to confine expenditures to approved appropriations, and had no direct role in operational planning.

Industrial engineering, labour control and concept of standards

Sowell (1973) argues that standard costing is the result of the combined efforts of American industrial engineers (who indeed led the Scientific Management movement) and American cost accountants, while English cost accounting authorities provided a certain logical background. In the early decades of the twentieth century, according to Sowell, management of industrial organization was divided mainly along the lines of 'shop management' (i.e., industrial engineering) and 'shop accounting' (i.e., cost accounting). Shop accounting was mainly in the hands of cost and work accountants, and was concerned with the systematic recording of factory input and output, distribution of expenses and determination of product costs (see Chapter 3). Shop management, on the other hand, was the line function and mainly dealt with work methods and processes: organization and supervision of machinery, materials and labour. This function was in the hands of industrial engineers, and it was evident that intensifying and enhancing labour productivity were their main objectives. Hence, most of their 'scientific inquiries' were directed to the problem of devising better incentive payment schemes to intensify and enhance labour productivity. The problem of 'work standards', against which worker efficiency had to be measured, was always at the centre of their efforts (see Table 4.1 for the progressive attempts at devising incentive payment schemes, and how the problem of 'work standards' was tackled over time by industrial engineers). Standardization of labour and concepts of standard costs were, thus, direct results of their endeavours to devise better systems of wage and incentive payments to enhance labour control and efficiency.

Two major functional areas in early business enterprises:

■ shop management;
■ shop accounting.

Work standardization was an industrial engineering task related to intensification of labour.

Integrating standards with cost accounting: formulation of standard costing

While industrial engineers had undertaken to handle labour by devising work methods, work standards and wage payment schemes, cost accountants were charged with the responsibility of factual calculation of product costs and profits. In this realm, they were faced with four major issues:

■ The problem of allocating overheads to cost centres and cost units.
■ The problem of separating manufacturing profit from trading profit: that is, separating manufacturing efficiency from trading efficiency.
■ Accounting for wastages and inefficiencies: that is, bringing wastages and inefficiencies to the attention of management.
■ Ascertainment of product cost before work is undertaken.

Table 4.1 *Evolution of notion of standards with incentive payment schemes*

Year	The incentive wage system	Basic characteristics	Nature of standard used
1888	Towne's scheme of 'Gain Sharing'	Aimed at computing additional compensation for workers due to enhanced efficiency and cost reductions. Total cost of production was compared with volume of production measured by predetermined scale of values, and difference was shared with employees on basis of wages earned during year.	Volume of production measured by predetermined scale of values, but not a standard *per se*.
1890	Halsey's Premium Wage Plan	Workers were offered a guaranteed day's wage plus an incentive to stimulate additional production. Incentive was based on arbitrary percentage of time saved, so that gain from time saved was shared between worker and employer. Time savings result from completing an operation in	Merely average of past performance.

less than standard time. For each operation, standard time was established on basis of past experiences.

1894	Taylor's Piece Rate System	Early version of Taylor's concepts, later developed into 'Taylor System' (see below). Composed of: ■ elementary rate-finding department; ■ differential rate system; ■ scheme characterized as the best method of payment.	Careful study made of time required to perform each elementary operation into which manufacturing processes might be divided.
1902	Gantt's 'A Bonus System of Rewarding Labour'	Skilled employee prepared card indicating best method of performing each elementary operation, tools to be used and standard time required to complete each operation. Standard determined by experiments. Employees who followed these instructions and exceeded standard level of output were paid bonus in addition to day rate. Bonus was fixed percentage of day's wages.	Standard determined by experiments and expressed in terms of standard number of units of production per day.
1902	Taylor's 'Shop Management' and 'Taylor System'	Offered full system of management, including incentive payment scheme based on 'Scientific Procedure'. Basic elements of scientific procedure included: ■ Experimentations: measurement, classification and systematic filing of results. ■ Standards: formulation of laws regarding use of materials, labour and machinery. ■ Planning: systematic scheduling, designing and directing work. ■ Maintenance of standards: development of systematic procedures covering performance and conditions.	Standards as laws decided by continuous experiments and record keeping. Time and motion studies as basis for setting standards.

Source: Sowell (1973)

All these problems, one way or the other, were related to the lack of acceptable standards upon which necessary calculations were to be made. It was industrial engineers' discovery of work standards that provided an acceptable solution. Accountants readily adopted them to reformulate cost accounting to become a major force in the overall administration of productive processes. Sowell (1973: 194), for example, reports a cost system developed by a certain Wildman in 1911. This case well explains the way accountants co-operated with engineers, and adopted the engineering standards to reformulate cost accounting:

He [Wildman] gave the efficiency engineer, who supervised the 'Efficiency Department' [which Wildman described as 'one of the most striking innovations in recent times'], the task of fixing standards of quantity and quality with respect to machinery, men, materials and methods; the cost accountant the task of maintaining adequate records; and both the efficiency engineer and the cost accountant the task of tying the standards and the records into cost accounting procedure.

Sowell (1973: 194) also quoted Wildman to show that:

'Standards serve to develop a predetermined cost. Taking into consideration the cost of material as determined by the standards of quantity and quality, the cost of labour as determined by the standard time of operation, the cost of overhead as determined by the standard of various elements composing it, it is possible to predetermine or obtain an estimated cost which may be used as a standard or basic cost and which provides for 100% efficiency.'

In this way, the application of work standards to cost accounting instituted the predetermination of costs, that no work shall be undertaken without its costs having been calculated in advance, and changed the whole viewpoint of cost accounting from retrospection to prospection (Harrison, 1921). In simple terms, incorporation of the notion of standards changed cost accounting from historical record keeping and reporting to a central force in operational planning and controlling. Cost accounting soon developed to incorporate techniques of variance analysis, which helped management to pinpoint and reason out potential inefficiencies, and also to operate on the basis of 'exception principle'. This planning and controlling function of cost accounting was further extended by incorporating concepts and procedures of budgeting, which were at that time widely popular in governmental institutions, to form the control technique now commonly known as flexible budgeting. The result was an organization-wide and comprehensive system of profit planning and control (see Figure 4.1). We will discuss modern systems of profit planning and control in forthcoming sections. Before that, however, it is important to discuss some extra organizational forces relating to the legitimation of standard costing and budgeting as institutional practices.

KEY TERMS

Exception principle or management by exception means that the managerial attention would be paid to those performances which are significantly deviant from the plans or standards in order to save managerial time and cost.

Standard costing, budgeting and modernity

Our discussion so far clearly illustrates the centrality of work and cost standards in the process of discovering better management systems, including incentive payments and cost accounting. Perhaps you may have thought that standard setting is rather a technical process, which was based on industrial engineering expertise. If so, you are only partly correct. Because it was not only technical but also highly political, as such standards often resulted in worker resistance and strikes. For example, Scientific Management was received rather critically at that time. Not only employees but

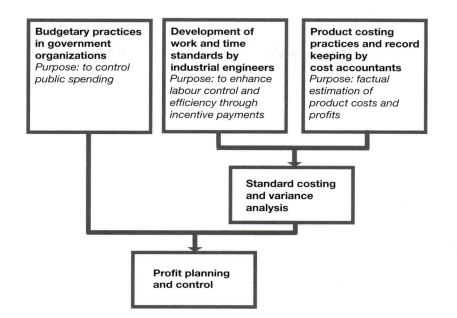

Figure 4.1 *Evolution of profit planning and control*

also some employers were sceptical about its possible effects. There were widespread social criticisms about the resulting factory organizations, especially in the media (see, for example, Charlie Chaplin's classic *Modern Times*). Initial attempts to institutionalize Scientific Management were failures in the face of such resistance and, as a result, even a 'Special Committee of the House of Representatives to Investigate the Taylor and Other Systems of Shop Management' was appointed.

Despite all this initial resistance and contradiction, principles of Scientific Management and standard cost systems were, as we now know, legitimated later as essential elements in managing industrial organizations. This legitimation was not only a process internal to the organizations but also linked to the wider socio-political changes taking place at that time. Internally, standard costing and budgeting were legitimated and institutionalized because they were supplementary to the emerging bureaucratic organizational structures. That is because they could be operationalized in line with the emerging functional division of labour and multidivisional structuring of firms. In addition, they provided a rational methodology to set, distribute and monitor performance targets in financial terms, so that their achievement could be verified and compared across the organization on a periodic basis. In that way, functional and hierarchical budgeting provided an explicit system by which the bureaucratic structures of authority and responsibility were aligned to the capitalist purpose of economic organizations – the accumulation of capital.[2]

Internally, standard costing and budgeting were legitimated and institutionalized because they were supplementary to the emerging bureaucratic organizational structures.

Externally, the emergence of 'modernity' provided the societal basis to help standard costing and budgeting penetrate almost all types of industrial organization. Modernity represents a specific stage of the history which runs from the industrial revolution to the end of the twentieth century. During this period, for example, the Western societies started to free themselves from religious dogmas, and instead came to rely upon 'science' as the basis of reality and truth. They also moved away from feudal aristocracy to democracy as the mode of political organization of society. Such social movements freed individuals from traditional systems of beliefs and social relations, and resulted in a new set of 'modern' ideas.

> Externally, the emergence of 'modernity' provided the societal basis to help standard costing and budgeting penetrate almost all types of industrial organization.

Among many others, these 'modern' ideas included:

- Idea of progress and confidence in the future. As traditional feudal social structures collapsed and the idea of free capital and labour was established, the mass public was given new hopes of progress through the social hierarchies by accumulating wealth. The future was no longer tied up to feudal kinship relations within which social mobility was confined rather than facilitated. Instead, a new mode of democracy opened up 'fair' opportunities for 'hardworking and ambitious' individuals to progress. Industrial organizations were the most immediately available institutions where individuals could realize their ambitions of progress through hard work. However, such institutions needed to be more democratic in order to open up such opportunities to the mass. Bureaucracy provided the structural apparatus for this democratization by ensuring that a rational and objective set of rules and procedures was in operation. Standard costing and budgeting, on the other hand, provided a superior technical base to assess and promote individuals objectively through the organizational hierarchy. Their legitimation as technically superior stemmed from the fact that they were predetermined on a 'scientific' basis, they were seen as impersonal, and they were transparent and open to audit and verification.
- Belief in rationalization of social life. Rationalization of social life refers to the historical tendency that economic-rational motives started to regulate the day-to-day behaviour of individuals. Individuals started to accept economic achievements (i.e., accumulation of wealth) as a core ethic, and began to self-impose short- and long-term economic goals for their lives. Given the fact that industrial organizations were the main institutions within which people could pursue their economic-rationale objectives, this tendency, on the other hand, meant that individuals began to harmonize their social behaviour with the economic objectives of industrial organizations. Budgeting and standard costing provided a technical/managerial mechanism to ensure this harmonization.
- Faith in expert systems. The industrial revolution, through a series of new innovations and miracles of 'science', built a strong faith in expert systems. Scientists were legitimated in the society as the centrepiece in social progress. Standard costing and budgeting were introduced to the people as another 'scientific' invention to make the industrial organizations better places for people to work and progress.

Certain characteristics of modernity facilitated the social acceptance of budgeting and standard costing practices:

- idea of progress and confidence in the future;
- belief in rationalization of social life;
- faith in expert systems.

In short, standard costing and budgeting emerged in a period when such a system would be mostly welcome. That period was the most dynamic historical phase in Western societies, and societies at large were undergoing massive restructuring, which embraced ideas of modernity. Concepts, techniques and purposes of standard costing and budgeting fitted nicely with this overall change which took place in the Western world and, hence, soon penetrated almost all types of industrial organization to become the dominant mode of organizational planning and control.

LINK BETWEEN STANDARD COSTING AND BUDGETING

It is important to understand the link between standard costing and budgeting because it is their integration that forms comprehensive and organization-wide profit planning and control systems. The link between the two is formed by the fact that they share five common principles (Boyns, 1998: 265):

1. The establishment of predetermined standards or targets of performance.
2. The measurement of actual performance.
3. The comparison of actual performance with the predetermined standards.
4. The disclosure of variances between the actual and the standard performance and the reasons for such variances.
5. The suggestion of corrective actions if necessary.

However, it should be noted that, though interrelated, they are not absolutely interdependent. In any given organization, there can be standard costing systems in operation without budgeting. Similarly, there can be budgeting systems without standard costing. Nevertheless, in either of these isolated applications, their usefulness could be limited. On the other hand, one can be supplementary and value-adding to the other and, therefore, integration of the two can result in a better system of profit planning and control. Their integration is sought because their best applications are in different areas, and their approaches are different. Listed below are such differences.

1. Standard costing is generally applied in manufacturing activities: that is, to 'standard cost centres', where output can be measured and input required to produce each unit of output can be specified. Typically, non-manufacturing activities are often not incorporated within standard costing. Budgeting, on the other hand, can be applied to non-manufacturing activities as well. Though budgeting can also be singularly applied to manufacturing activities, it would benefit greatly if coupled with standard costing.

2. Budgets relate to an entire activity or operation. A standard, on the other hand, presents the same information on a unit basis. Hence, standard costing often provides the basis upon which budgeted figures can be calculated.

3. Budgeting represents a top-down approach. That means calculation of budgets starts with estimates and forecasts on aggregated figures, such as sales, profits and production targets, and then goes down to elementary budgets, such as material purchase budgets and labour usage budgets, etc. Standard costing, on the other hand, employs a bottom-up approach: it starts with predetermined standards pertaining to individual units and goes on to calculate aggregates on the basis of actual volumes.

4. Budgeting provides figures on future targets: that is, expectations of the management for the budget period. Standard costing, on the other hand, provides 'figures that should have been', pertaining to the realized level of performance for that period.

5. Budgeting is more on the planning and delegation functions of management, while standard costing is more on the controlling function.

Certain differences between budgeting and standard costing:

■   relevance of quantifiability of output and input;
■   unit versus aggregate concerns;
■   top-down (i.e., from totals to units) versus bottom-up (i.e., from units to totals);
■   what should be versus what should have been;
■   planning versus controlling emphasis.

These differences and common principles imply that there are both unique and shared domains of operations for budgeting and standard costing. Figure 4.2 illustrates these domains and also the link between them. It also outlines an integrative ideal system of profit planning and control.

We can now read through Figure 4.2 to elaborate on the link between standard costing and budgeting in an integrative system. First, within the domain of standard costing, there are set standards regarding output and input of materials, labour and production overheads. They normally cover standard prices/rates of input and output; standard mixes of output and input (i.e., the standard ratios of different elements to combine to make the total, as seen in the illustrative example later in this chapter); and standard usage of input (e.g., labour hours per unit of output, material consumption per unit of output). These standards are typically set at the design stage of products and manufacturing processes, and often revised with subsequent experiences of manufacturing and selling. Hence, non-accounting functions such as operations management (OM), research and development (R&D) and marketing provide lots of basic information to arrive at these standards.

Standards are usually regarding unit level concerns such as:

■   prices and rates per unit or hour;
■   resource (material, labour, etc.) requirements per unit or standard hour.

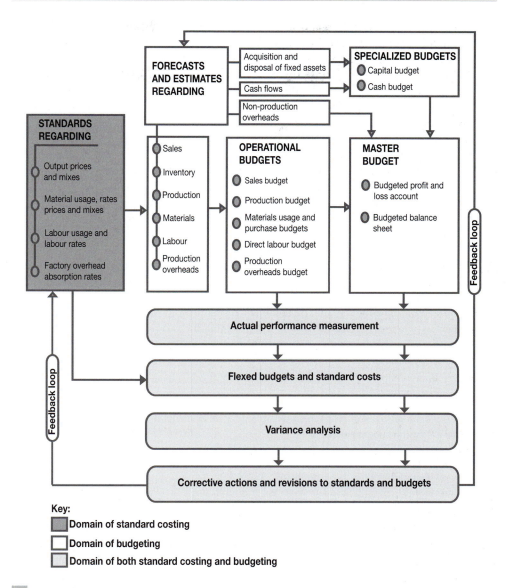

Figure 4.2 *Budgetary planning and control procedures*

Second, within the domain of budgeting, there are periodic forecasts and estimates regarding aggregate levels of operations for the company and its major subdivisions. These mainly include forecasts and targets about sales volumes, production volumes, inventory levels, etc. They are often derived from corporate planning or strategic planning exercises for the entire company, and operational programmes for its major subdivisions. After scanning the competitive environment within which the company operates, the market potentials for its products and the company's strengths and weaknesses, such long-term planning exercises decide long-term goals pertaining to market share and sales (so-called strategic goals). Then such long-term sales goals are translated into annual (and even quarterly and monthly) sales targets which provide the basis for other estimates, such as levels of production and purchases, etc.

> Budgets contain estimates and forecasts on organizational activities such as sales, production and purchasing.

> Market-related forecasts, estimates and goals are ideal starting points for the budgeting process.

Third, within the domain of budgeting, there are various operational budgets which represent budgetary targets for the major aspects of operations: sales, production, material usage, material purchase, direct labour usage and production overheads. Such budgets are indeed operational plans expressed in quantitative and/or monetary terms for a given period of time called the budget period. These are in fact arrived at by combining the various standards with budgetary estimates (we will discuss, with examples, how these operational budgets are prepared later in this chapter).

> Operational budgets are plans expressed in quantitative or monetary terms for a given period of time called the budget period.

Fourth, again in the domain of budgeting, there are forecasts and estimates regarding 'non-operational'[3] aspects of the business. These are mainly estimates on acquisitions and disposal of fixed assets, cash flows and non-production overheads. These estimates are sourced from various functional departments of the company. For example, estimates on acquisition and disposal of fixed assets can be derived from current status of the fixed assets used by various departments and their depreciation policies. Similarly, extension plans for existing facilities and new development plans can also be sources for such estimates. Cash flow estimates, for example, directly relate to estimates on sales and purchases, as well as debt collection and credit settlement policies. Estimates on non-production overheads, on the other hand, directly relate to the future plans to extend, contain or maintain the level of activities in all non-manufacturing departments. These forecasts and estimates, in turn, provide the information for two specialized budgets, namely capital budget (which contains approved capital expenditure plans) and cash budget (which shows the budgeted cash position of the firm on a suitably divided time line, say monthly). These specialized budgets, together with operational budgets and estimates on non-production overheads, on the other hand, are summarized in the master budget, which consists of the budgeted profit and loss account and the balance sheet.

Non-operational aspects of the business should also be covered by budgets, mainly non-production overhead budgets and specialized budgets, such as for capital investment.

Budgets so prepared provide a managerial framework to guide day-to-day managerial actions and decisions, as they contain specific objectives for managers in various divisions, departments and levels. Thus, managers are delegated the authority and responsibility to make sure that those budgetary objectives are met. However, at the end of the budget period, the actual performance may or may not be that which was expected. There could be deviations for various reasons. Therefore, it is necessary to ascertain whether there are any deviations from the budgeted performance (i.e., variances) and, if so, to analyse specific reasons for them. Variance analysis is a domain where standard costing and budgeting are integrated.

Budgeting is a principal mode of delegation and controlling.

In order to carry out a meaningful variance analysis, it is necessary to flex the budgeted figures. Flexing means adjusting the budgeted figures to reflect the actual levels of performance. In other words, it involves updating the 'static budget' to comply with the realized levels of production. For flexing the budgets, we reuse the elementary standards – standard prices/rates, labour and material usage standards, and so on – but with the actual volumes this time. In this context, variances mean the differences between flexed budget figures and the actual figures.

Flexing the static budgets is necessary to calculate meaningful variances.

Variance analysis provides a hierarchical structure to understand the reasons for the difference between the budgeted profit and the actual profit. Profit variance, at the outset, is explained by sales and cost variances which, in turn, are analysed in their elementary categories: material cost, labour cost and overhead. Total cost variances for each cost element would further be analysed in their causes, such as price and quantity variances.

PROFIT PLANNING THROUGH BUDGETS: PROCEDURES AND CALCULATIONS

In this section we will take you through a worked example of budgetary planning in order to understand the basic concepts, procedures and calculations involved. Required information is given in the Illustrative Case Example below.

Illustrative Case Example: Softdrink Private Limited – basic information

Softdrink Private Limited manufactures two varieties of a soft drink: Mega and Buddy; 900 ml and 450 ml in size, respectively. How the company has organized its production of these two products is depicted in Case Extract 4.1. Note that RM1, RM2 and RM3 denote raw materials.

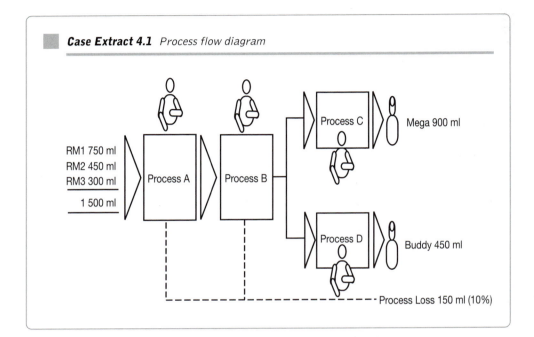

Case Extract 4.1 *Process flow diagram*

As shown in the diagram, the two products are initially processed through two common processes (Processes A and B) and then distributed to two distinctive processes for each product (Process C for Mega; Process D for Buddy). For the purpose of product cost calculations, these processes are considered as cost centres to which variable costs, including variable factory overheads, are to be allocated, according to predetermined rates. Those rates and other standards are documented in a 'standard cost card' prepared by the management accountant (see Case Extract 4.2). He periodically revises this cost card to reflect the most updated situations as informed by other functional managers. Please note that values in the standard cost card are given in pence, except for labour rate per hour and its adjoining cost per unit column.

The company's strategic objectives include achieving a market share of 20 per cent within the next five years and hence demand an annual sales growth more than the average market growth rate. Considering these strategic objectives and other relevant factors, the company has set budgeted sales for the year to be 4,000,000 bottles from Mega, and 6,000,000 bottles from Buddy. All variable factory overheads, as shown in the standard cost card, are budgeted to each process of production on the basis of direct labour hours. Estimates of fixed factory overheads and sales and marketing overheads for the budget period are given below. Note that all non-production expenses are assumed to be fixed.

Fixed factory overhead:

- Depreciation: £50,000
- Factory management salaries: £75,000
- Power (fixed element): £20,000
- Maintenance and services (fixed element): £10,000
- Factory insurance: £15,000
- Total: £170,000

Sales and marketing budget:

- Salaries: £125,000
- Commissions: £35,000
- Transport and delivery: £37,000
- Travelling: £13,000
- Advertising: £35,000
- Total: £245,000

Estimates related to general administration, accounting and personnel management overheads:

- Personnel and administration: £75,000
- CEO's office: £100,000
- Accounting and finance: £75,000
- Total: £250,000

Estimated closing stocks:

- Finished products (bottles):

  - Mega: 200,000
  - Buddy: 300,000

- Raw materials (litres):

  - RM1: 173,250
  - RM2: 103,950
  - RM3: 69,300

- Containers (bottles):

  - Mega: 197,000
  - Buddy: 299,000

- Containers at standard purchasing price (£):

  - Mega: 9,850
  - Buddy: 11,960

Case Extract 4.2 Standard cost card

Raw materials	Mega					Buddy				
	Quantity (mls)	Standard mix (%)	Standard price per 1000 ml (pence)	Cost per bottle (pence)	Total per bottle (pence)	Quantity (mls)	Standard mix (%)	Standard price per 1000 ml (pence)	Cost per bottle (pence)	Total per bottle (pence)
RM 1	500	50	20	10		250	50	20	5	
RM 2	300	30	10	3		150	30	10	1.5	
RM 3	200	20	10	2		100	20	10	1	
	1000	100				500	100			
Normal process loss	100	10				50	10			
Per bottle	900	90		15	15.00	450	45		7.5	7.50

Direct labour	Mega				Buddy			
	Standard hours	Standard rate per hour (£)	Cost per bottle (£)	Total per bottle (pence)	Standard hours	Standard rate per hour (£)	Cost per bottle (£)	Total per bottle (pence)
Process A	0.003	10	0.03	3	0.0015	10	0.015	1.5
Process B	0.002	10	0.02	2	0.001	10	0.01	1
Process C	0.003	10	0.03	3				
Process D					0.004	10	0.04	4
Total	0.008		0.08	8.00	0.0065		0.065	6.50

Table 1

Standard variable overhead rates (pence per hr)	Process A	Process B	Process C	Process D	Total per bottle (pence)
Indirect materials	200	160	160	N/A	
Indirect labour	175	175	175	N/A	
Power	180	125	160	N/A	
Maintenance	120	75	140	N/A	
Total	675	535	635	N/A	
Standard hours	0.003	0.002	0.003	N/A	
	2.025	1.07	1.905	N/A	5.00
Total variable factory cost					28.00
Standard purchasing price per bottle (container)					5.00
Provision for normal loss in bottles in processing (5%)				0.25	
Standard cost of container per bottle				5.25	5.25
Total variable cost					33.25
Standard selling price					50.00
Standard contribution margin					16.75

Table 2

	Process A	Process B	Process C	Process D	Total per bottle (pence)
Indirect materials	200	160	N/A	127	
Indirect labour	175	175	N/A	140	
Power	180	125	N/A	156	
Maintenance	120	75	N/A	140	
Total	675	535	N/A	563	
Standard hours	0.0015	0.001	N/A	0.004	
	1.0125	0.535	N/A	2.252	3.80
Total variable factory cost					17.80
Standard purchasing price per bottle (container)					4.00
Provision for normal loss in bottles in processing (5%)				0.20	
Standard cost of container per bottle				4.20	4.20
Total variable cost					22.00
Standard selling price					30.00
Standard contribution margin					8.00

The sales pattern of both products is consistent throughout the year except for the months of December and January. December sales are forecast to be 20 per cent of the total sales, while in January they would be 10 per cent. Sales in the rest of the months are forecasted to be equally distributed. All sales are on credit terms, and it is the company policy to collect all debts after one month of sales. Purchases of raw materials and containers are on credit, and all credits are settled one month after purchase. Purchases and production are equally distributed throughout the year, irrespective of the seasonal fluctuations in sales. Occurrences of all other expenses are also equally distributed throughout the year, and the settlement of them is in the same month they occur.

You are also given the opening balance sheet at the beginning of the period (see Case Extract 4.3).

Case Extract 4.3 *Balance sheet at beginning of period*

	£	£	£
Fixed assets (net book value)			500 000
Current assets			
Stocks – raw materials			
(at standard price, see notes below)			
RM1	30 000		
RM2	9 000		
RM3	5 000	44 000	
Finished products			
Mega	86 450		
Buddy	67 840	154 290	
Containers (at standard price)			
For Mega	7 500		
For Buddy	10 000	17 500	
Debtors		200 000	
Cash		220 000	
Total current assets		635 790	
Less: Current liabilities			
Creditors		75 000	
Net current assets			560 790
Total net assets			1 060 790
Capital and reserves			
Ordinary share capital			600 000
Long-term loan			150 000
Reserves			310 790
			1 060 790

Notes to the balance sheet
Quantities of stocks are as follows:
Raw materials (litres)

RM1	150 000
RM2	90 000
RM3	50 000
Containers (bottles)	
For Mega	150 000
For Buddy	250 000
Finished products (bottles)	
Mega	260 000
Buddy	320 000

You are required to prepare:

- operational budgets;
- monthly cash budget; and
- master budget (budgeted profit and loss account and balance sheet).

Planning operations: operational budgets

Operational budgets are a principal mode of planning, communicating and delegating organizational objectives. They set specific quantitative objectives (mostly expressed in monetary terms) for different operational activities in the organization. They help link dispersed activities across the organization to market-related short- and long-term objectives of the organization as a whole. In other words, operational budgeting provides a hierarchical planning and communication structure within which overall market objectives of the organization can be branched out and delegated to individual departments as budgetary targets. In that way, operational budgets spell out activity levels that each functional department and its sub-units should pursue in order to achieve the organization's sales and profit objectives.

> Operational budgeting provides a hierarchical planning and communication structure within which overall market objectives of the organization can be branched out and delegated to individual departments as budgetary targets.

Sales planning: sales budget

The most rational starting point of profit planning is the sales budget. This budget specifies the sales targets for the forthcoming budgetary period in unit terms as well as in monetary terms. Indeed, the sales budget is the most important operational budget, as it sets the basis upon which all other operational budgets are prepared, and upon which the company's overall profitability will be determined. Hence, due care and diligence is demanded in estimating the budgeted sales figures. The sales budget can appropriately be described as the linking pin between the market potential and the organizational possibilities.

> The most rational starting point of profit planning is the sales budget.

Technically, a sales budget involves two interrelated marketing decisions: deciding selling prices and sales quantities of each product that the company offers to the market. These decisions are interrelated because, in imperfectly competitive markets (the most realistic market scenario), price and demand of a given product are inversely related. This means price is the most dominant factor that determines the demand for a company's product and its sales potential. This demands careful research and analysis of market conditions. Taking this complexity into account, some companies conduct extensive market research, either by their own staff or by independent, third-party research organizations, to forecast and decide budgeted sales figures. Some others use sophisticated statistical techniques that often include analysis of market trends and external factors affecting the market demand. Yet others simply add a growth percentage to the previous year's sales to arrive at the next year's sales. This implies that, especially in companies where there is a well-organized marketing function, pricing and demand estimation are often beyond the decision scope of management accountants, though they provide necessary cost data to determine the minimum threshold above which price should be set.

> Technically, a sales budget involves two interrelated marketing decisions: deciding selling prices and sales quantities of each product that the company offers to the market.

Once the target prices and quantities are decided, it is a matter of presentation to meet information requirements of the management. For example, the sales budget of Softdrink Private Limited should spell out sales targets for each product, in line with the budgeted sales mix. Case Extract 4.4 is the sales budget prepared to reveal that information.

Case Extract 4.4 *Annual sales budget for year ending 31 December 200X*

Product	Quantity (bottles)	Price (£)	Sales (£)	Sales mix (%)
Mega	4 000 000	0.50	2 000 000	40
Buddy	6 000 000	0.30	1 800 000	60
Total	10 000 000		3 800 000	100

This sales budget shows only annual sales targets, which would not be as helpful for short-term decision forums as for monthly performance review meetings. When functional managers meet to review their progress, say monthly, they need more frequent benchmarks against which the actual can be compared, and corrective actions be taken before it is too late. Therefore, for detailed planning and control purposes, these annual budgets should be further detailed into much shorter time periods – monthly is the most common. Case Extract 4.5 is the monthly sales budget.

Please note that monthly sales figures in the Case Extract 4.5 have been calculated as follows:

- December = annual sales figures × 20 per cent
- January = annual sales figures × 10 per cent
- All other months = annual sales figures × 7 per cent (arrived at as follows: $\{100 - (20 + 10)\}/10 = 7$)

A monthly sales budget would help management to check whether the company and its departments progress towards the annual sales targets on a monthly basis, rather than waiting for the end of the year, in which case it might be too late to take corrective action.

Case Extract 4.5 *Monthly sales budget for year ending 31 December 200X*

	Mega		Buddy		Total	
	Quantity	Value (£)	Quantity	Value (£)	Quantity	Value (£)
January	400 000	200 000	600 000	180 000	1 000 000	380 000
February	280 000	140 000	420 000	126 000	700 000	266 000
March	280 000	140 000	420 000	126 000	700 000	266 000
April	280 000	140 000	420 000	126 000	700 000	266 000
May	280 000	140 000	420 000	126 000	700 000	266 000
June	280 000	140 000	420 000	126 000	700 000	266 000
July	280 000	140 000	420 000	126 000	700 000	266 000
August	280 000	140 000	420 000	126 000	700 000	266 000
September	280 000	140 000	420 000	126 000	700 000	266 000
October	280 000	140 000	420 000	126 000	700 000	266 000
November	280 000	140 000	420 000	126 000	700 000	266 000
December	800 000	400 000	1 200 000	360 000	2 000 000	760 000
Total	4 000 000	2 000 000	6 000 000	1 800 000	10 000 000	3 800 000

Production planning: production budget

Once the sales budget is prepared, all other operational budgets flow downward from it. The production budget specifies the volume of production that should be achieved in order to meet budgeted sales. Computation of the production budget is simple, in that it involves only adjustment of budgeted opening and closing stocks to the sales budget figures. The logic is that budgeted closing stock has to be added to budgeted sales, as we need to produce more than sales to retain that closing stock at the end of the period. Opening stocks, on the other hand, have to be deducted from the production requirements as they have been already produced, and can be sold during the forthcoming budgetary period. The annual production budget so prepared is given in Case Extract 4.6.

> Production budget is derived by adjusting inventory forecasts to the sales budget, such that: sales + closing stock − opening stock = production

Note that production requirements are given on both a unit and a standard hour basis. Standard hours of production spell out the number of production hours that the company should operate to meet the budgeted production. That means it is budgeted that the company should run the operations, in total, for 70,390 standard hours (31,520 for Mega and 38,870 for Buddy), if the production targets are to be met. Also note that, as in the case of the sales budget, the production budget should be detailed to monthly and weekly budgets to assist ongoing production controls. However, for simplicity, we have assumed that all activities other than sales are equally distributed throughout the year, and hence require only equal division of budgeted figures between all months. Hence, we do not reproduce those detailed monthly production budgets in this text.

Case Extract 4.6 *Annual production budget for year ending 31 December 200X*

	Mega	Buddy	Total
Budgeted sales (bottles)	4 000 000	6 000 000	10 000 000
Add closing stocks (bottles)	200 000	300 000	500 000
Less opening stocks (bottles)	260 000	320 000	580 000
Budgeted production (bottles)	3 940 000	5 980 000	9 920 000
Standard hours per bottle	0.008	0.0065	
Production budget in standard hours of production	31 520	38 870	70 390

Units of measurement in the production budget can be both physical units (such as mere units, kilos or litres, etc.) and 'standard hours of production', which indicates the number of hours that the firm should run its manufacturing process to meet the production budget.

Estimating material usage: material usage budget

The material usage budget is derived from the production budget, and it shows raw material requirements to meet the budgeted production. To calculate production requirements of materials, we need consumption rates of each raw material per unit of output, which can then be multiplied with the budgeted production to arrive at the budgeted consumption of raw materials. These consumption rates are given in the standard cost card (see Case Extract 4.2, above). Material usage budget (see Case Extract 4.7) shows material usage of RM1, RM2 and RM3, both in physical quantities (litres) and in monetary values (£). The physical quantities are translated into monetary values by multiplying them by the standard price per litre of each raw material (see standard cost card – Case Extract 4.2). Note that these usages also include 10 per cent normal loss. Also note that both physical quantities and monetary values are shown, and it is these monetary values that we will take to the master budget.

Material usage budget is derived from production budget, and it shows raw material consumption to meet the budgeted production.

Estimating spending on materials: material purchase budget

The material purchase budget should show the amount of money that the company has to spend on each raw material during the forthcoming budget period. It is arrived at by adjusting the opening and closing stocks of raw materials to the material usage budget. Case Extract 4.8 illustrates the purchase budget.

Case Extract 4.7 *Material usage budget*

	RM1	RM2	RM3	Total
Mega				
Usage per bottle including normal loss (litres)	0.5	0.3	0.2	
Production budget (bottles)	3 940 000	3 940 000	3 940 000	
Total usage (litres)	1 970 000	1 182 000	788 000	
Standard price per litre (£)	0.2	0.1	0.1	
Total usage (£)	394 000	118 200	78 800	591 000
Buddy				
Usage per bottle (litres)	0.25	0.15	0.1	
Production budget (bottles)	5 980 000	5 980 000	5 980 000	
Total usage (litres)	1 495 000	897 000	598 000	
Standard price per litre (£)	0.2	0.1	0.1	
Total usage (£)	299 000	89 700	59 800	448 500
For both (in litres):	3 465 000	2 079 000	1 386 000	
Standard price per litre (£)	0.2	0.1	0.1	
Material usage (£)	693 000	207 900	138 600	1 039 500

Case Extract 4.8 *Material purchase budget*

	RM1	RM2	RM3	Total
Material requirements to meet production – from material usage budget (litres)	3 465 000	2 079 000	1 386 000	
Add: budgeted closing stock (litres)	173 250	103 950	69 300	
Less: budgeted opening stock (litres)	150 000	90 000	50 000	
Total units to be purchased (litres)	3 488 250	2 092 950	1 405 300	
Standard price per litre (£)	0.2	0.1	0.1	
Total budgeted purchase (£)	697 650	209 295	140 530	1 047 475

It should be noted that Softdrink Private Limited has to purchase another special material – the containers. It is stated that there are two sizes of containers (bottles) for Mega and Buddy. Hence, it is necessary to prepare a usage and purchase budget for this special material as well. The procedure is similar to the above usage and purchase budgets. The only difference is that we have to adjust for the 5 per cent process loss of containers. However, to keep the number of tables to a minimum, we may join two budgets together and call it the usage and purchase budget (see Case Extract 4.9).

105

Material purchase budget shows the quantity of material to be purchased, and amount of money to be spent on such purchases, after adjusting for opening and closing inventories to the production requirements of raw materials.

Case Extract 4.9 *Usage and purchase budget for containers*

	Mega	Buddy	Total
Requirement as per production budget	3 940 000	5 980 000	
Add: 5% process loss	197 000	299 000	
Total usage (bottles)	4 137 000	6 279 000	
Price per bottle (£)	0.05	0.04	
Cost of total usage (£)	206 850	251 160	458 010
Total usage including 5% loss (from usage budget)	4 137 000	6 279 000	
Add: budgeted closing stocks	197 000	299 000	
Less: opening stocks	150 000	250 000	
Number of bottles to be purchased	4 184 000	6 328 000	
Price per bottle (£)	0.05	0.04	
Total purchase (£)	209 200	253 120	462 320

All these usage and purchases budgets are usually detailed in monthly budgets to assist the progressive and interim comparison of actual performance with that which has been budgeted.

Estimating usage and expenditure on labour: direct labour budget

The direct labour budget specifies two things. First, it shows standard labour hours required to meet the production budget. Second, it shows the total cost to employ that number of standard hours. To calculate these values, we need standard rates of labour usage per unit of production under different categories of labour, if any, and the standard wage rates for each category of labour. The standard cost card (Case Extract 4.2) contains this information: standard labour hours per unit of production, and standard wage rate per hour. The production budget provides the other relevant information. Case Extract 4.10 shows the direct labour usage budget. Please note that there is only one type of direct labour in this example (hence only one wage rate per hour), but labour is consumed by production at different rates in different processes.

Direct labour budget specifies two things. First, it shows standard labour hours required to meet the production budget. Second, it shows the total cost to employ that number of standard hours.

Case Extract 4.10 *Direct labour usage budget*

	Process A	Process B	Process C	Process D	Total
Mega					
Standard hours per bottle	0.003	0.002	0.003		
Number of bottles to be produced	3 940 000	3 940 000	3 940 000		
Total budgeted hours	11 820	7 880	11 820		
Standard wage rate (£)	10	10	10		
Total direct labour cost (£)	118 200	78 800	118 200		315 200
Buddy					
Standard hours per bottle	0.0015	0.001		0.004	
Number of bottles to be produced	5 980 000	5 980 000		5 980 000	
Total budgeted hours	8 970	5 980		23 920	
Standard wage rate (£)	10	10		10	
Total direct labour cost (£)	89 700	59 800		239 200	388 700
Total labour cost for both (£)	207 900	138 600	118 200	239 200	703 900

Estimating factory expenses: variable factory overhead budget

Factory overhead budgets show variable and fixed overheads related to factory operations. In the case of variable overhead items, it is typical to have predetermined standard overhead rates to forecast total overheads corresponding to a given level of budgeted operations. In our example, those rates are given in the standard cost card (Case Extract 4.2, above), and they are on unit basis. Please note that they are also directly related to the labour hours in each process regarding each product. For example, in Process A, the rate applicable for indirect materials is £2.00 (i.e., 200p) per hour for Mega, and £1.00 (i.e., 100p) for Buddy. Case Extract 4.11 shows the variable production overhead budget.

> In the case of variable overhead items, it is typical to have predetermined standard overhead absorption rates to forecast total overheads corresponding to a given level of budgeted operations.

Please note that figures for hours columns in Case Extract 4.11 are taken from labour usage budget (see total budgeted labour hours for each product under each process).

Case Extract 4.11 *Variable factory overhead budget*

	Process A			Process B			Process C			Process D			Total (£)
	Rate	Hours	Total (£)	Rate	Hours	Total (£)	Rate	Hours	Total (£)	Rate	Hours	Total (£)	
Mega													
Indirect materials	2.00	11 820	23 640	1.60	7 880	12 608	1.60	11 820	18 912				55 160
Indirect labour	1.75	11 820	20 685	1.75	7 880	13 790	1.75	11 820	20 685				55 160
Power	1.80	11 820	21 276	1.25	7 880	9 850	1.60	11 820	18 912				50 038
Maintenance	1.20	11 820	14 184	0.75	7 880	5 910	1.40	11 820	16 548				36 642
Total	6.75	11 820	79 785	5.35	7 880	42 158	6.35	11 820	75 057				197 000
Buddy													
Indirect materials	2.00	8 970	17 940	1.60	5 980	9 568				1.27	23 920	30 378	57 886
Indirect labour	1.75	8 970	15 698	1.75	5 980	10 465				1.40	23 920	33 488	59 651
Power	1.80	8 970	16 146	1.25	5 980	7 475				1.56	23 920	37 315	60 936
Maintenance	1.20	8 970	10 764	0.75	5 980	4 485				1.40	23 920	33 488	48 737
Total	6.75	8 970	60 548	5.35	5 980	31 993				5.63	23 920	134 670	227 210
Total for both			140 333			74 151			75 057			134 670	424 210

Estimating factory indirect expenses: fixed factory overhead budget

Fixed factory overhead items are those which do not vary with the level of production or sales. They are normally considered uncontrollable for the operations managers and are to be estimated independent of level of production mostly on the basis of various supply contracts which the company has entered into. Such estimates are reproduced in Case Extract 4.12.

Case Extract 4.12 *Fixed factory overhead budget (£)*

Depreciation	50 000
Factory managers' salaries	75 000
Power (fixed element)	20 000
Maintenance and services (fixed element)	10 000
Factory insurance	15 000
Total	170 000

Estimating other expenses: non-production overhead budgets

This budget represents estimates on various expenses that non-production departments regularly incur. They can range from stationery to telephone bills to CEO's salaries and bonuses, and many more. Each department has to estimate these individual items on the basis of past experiences, future plans to expand and specific supply contracts that they have entered into with outside parties. Thus, each department keeps detailed budgets on such expenses, and attempts to keep actual expenses within those budgetary allowances. In our example, however, we are provided with the aggregates of these estimates which, in practice, may be distributed to a large number of estimated cost sheets kept in different departments across the organization, so that managers responsible for each expense item can take actions whenever necessary. For example, as monthly or quarterly statements from suppliers (such as telephone, electricity and gas bills, etc.) reach the relevant managers' desks, they should be able to record them against those estimates and take necessary actions. The aggregate budgets are useful for compiling the master budget. Case Extract 4.13 shows the aggregate non-production expense budget.

Case Extract 4.13 *Non-production overhead budget (£)*

Sales and marketing		
Salaries	125 000	
Commissions	35 000	
Transport and delivery	37 000	
Travelling	13 000	
Advertising	35 000	245 000
Personnel and administration	———	75 000
CEO's office		100 000
Accounting and finance		75 000
Total		495 000

Forecasting cash flows: cash budget

Cash budget records estimated cash inflows and outflows for the forthcoming budget period. It is compiled by recognizing cash movements attached to budgeted operational and non-operational activities. For example, sales and debtors' collection policies would determine the budgeted cash inflows related to sales. Similarly, frequency of purchases and suppliers' settlement policies would determine cash outflows related to main purchases. A set of such policies and assumptions is given in the Illustrative Case Example regarding payments for and collections of various expenses and revenues. Most typical is to prepare the cash budget to show monthly cash position. Cash budget prepared in line with these policies and assumptions is given in Case Extract 4.14.

Putting them together: master budget

The master budget summarizes all operational budgets into budgeted profit and loss statements and balance sheet. Accordingly, the master budget is the one showing the organization-wide impact of all operational budgets. In simple terms, it shows the consequent profitability and the financial position of budgeted operations for the period. Case Extracts 4.15 and 4.16 constitute the master budget which summarizes all the operational budgets we have gone through so far. Please note that, in this case, budgeted profit and loss account has been prepared under marginal costing principles demarcating variable and fixed costs and showing the contribution (i.e., sales – variable cost). Also note that when we adopt marginal costing principles, we do not have to allocate and unitize fixed costs.

> Master budget summarizes all operational budgets into budgeted profit and loss statements and balance sheet, and shows the overall financial impact of the operational and other specialized budgets.

Understanding the link

Preparation of budgets encompasses a logical flow. It begins with the market-related assumptions, forecasts and objectives, which are translated into the sales budget. Then it logically moves to production budget, with stock adjustments. The production budget provides the level of operation upon which all other activities depend. Thus, production budget provides the basic information for material usage and purchase budgets, labour usage budgets and variable overhead budgets. However, it should also be noted that there are various expenditure items which are quite independent of production and sales, and, hence, demand different modes of forecasting and budgeting. Operational budgets, together, form the cash budget and master budget, which include the budgeted profit and loss account and balance sheet. Nevertheless, there are no universally applicable budget formats that suit the information needs of all circumstances. Instead, the formatting of each budget should be tailor-made to suit the information requirements of the management. However, we can have certain generalizations regarding the link between operational budgets and master budget. Figure 4.3 illustrates this link, in line with our Illustrative Case Example.

Case Extract 4.14 Monthly cash budget (£)

	Jan	Feb	Mar	Apr	May	Jun	Jul	Aug	Sep	Oct	Nov	Dec	Annual
Receipts													
Collections from debtors	200 000	380 000	266 000	266 000	266 000	266 000	266 000	266 000	266 000	266 000	266 000	266 000	3 240 000
Total inflows	200 000	380 000	266 000	266 000	266 000	266 000	266 000	266 000	266 000	266 000	266 000	266 000	3 240 000
Less: payments													
Payments to creditors	75 000	125 816	125 816	125 816	125 816	125 816	125 816	125 816	125 816	125 816	125 816	125 816	1 458 979
Direct labour wages	58 658	58 658	58 658	58 658	58 658	58 658	58 658	58 658	58 658	58 658	58 658	58 658	703 900
Variable factory OH	35 351	35 351	35 351	35 351	35 351	35 351	35 351	35 351	35 351	35 351	35 351	35 351	424 210
Fixed factory OH (excluding depreciation)	10 000	10 000	10 000	10 000	10 000	10 000	10 000	10 000	10 000	10 000	10 000	10 000	120 000
Sales and marketing expenses	20 417	20 417	20 417	20 417	20 417	20 417	20 417	20 417	20 417	20 417	20 417	20 417	245 000
Other overheads	20 833	20 833	20 833	20 833	20 833	20 833	20 833	20 833	20 833	20 833	20 833	20 833	250 000
Total outflows	220 259	271 075	271 075	271 075	271 075	271 075	271 075	271 075	271 075	271 075	271 075	271 075	3 202 089
Net cash flow (= inflow − outflow)	−20 259	108 925	−5 075	−5 075	−5 075	−5 075	−5 075	−5 075	−5 075	−5 075	−5 075	−5 075	37 911
Add: opening balance	220 000	199 741	308 665	303 590	298 515	293 439	288 364	283 288	278 213	273 137	268 062	262 987	220 000
Closing balance	199 741	308 665	303 590	298 515	293 439	288 364	283 288	278 213	273 137	268 062	262 987	257 911	257 911

Case Extract 4.15 *Budgeted profit and loss statement for year ending xx xx xx (£)*

		Mega	Buddy	Total
A	Direct materials (from material usage budget)			
	RM1	394 000	299 000	693 000
	RM2	118 200	89 700	207 900
	RM3	78 800	59 800	138 600
		591 000	448 500	1 039 500
B	Containers (from usage budget)	206 850	251 160	458 010
C = A + B	Total material cost	797 850	699 660	1 497 510
D	Direct labour (from labour usage budget)			
	Process A	118 200	89 700	207 900
	Process B	78 800	59 800	138 600
	Process C	118 200		118 200
	Process D		239 200	239 200
	Total direct labour cost	315 200	388 700	703 900
E	Variable factory overheads (from VFOH budget)			
	Process A	79 785	60 548	140 333
	Process B	42 158	31 993	74 151
	Process C	75 057		75 057
	Process D		134 670	134 670
	Total variable factory overheads	197 000	227 210	424 210
F = C + D + E	Total variable cost of production	1 310 050	1 315 570	2 625 620
	Add opening stock (at standard variable cost)	86 450	67 840	154 290
	Less closing stocks (at standard variable cost)	66 500	66 000	132 500
G	Variable cost of goods sold	1 330 000	1 317 410	2 647 410
H	Sales	2 000 000	1 800 000	3 800 000
J = H − G	Contribution (= sales − variable cost)	670 000	480 030	1 152 590
	Less fixed costs			
	Fixed production overheads (from FFOH budget)			170 000
	General administration overheads			250 000
	Sales and marketing overheads			245 000
	Total fixed cost			665 000
	Net profit (= contribution − total fixed cost)			487 590

Case Extract 4.16 *Budgeted balance sheet as at xx xx xxxx (£)*

Fixed assets (year beginning balance)			500 000
Less depreciation for year			50 000
Fixed assets (net book value)			450 000
Current assets			
Stocks – raw materials (at standard price):			
RM1	34 650		
RM2	10 395		
RM3	6 930	51 975	
Finished products:			
Mega	66 500		
Buddy	66 000	132 500	
Containers (at standard price):			
For Mega	9 850		
For Buddy	11 960	21 810	
Debtors		760 000	
Cash		257 911	
		1 224 196	
Less current liabilities:			
Creditors		125 816	
Net current assets			1 098 380
Total net assets			1 548 380
Capital and reserves:			
Ordinary share capital			600 000
Long-term loan			150 000
Reserves (year beginning balance)		310 790	
Add net profit for year		487 590	798 380
			1 548 380

> There are no universally applicable budget formats that suit the information needs of all circumstances. Instead, the formatting of each budget should be tailor-made to suit the information requirements of the management.

BUDGETARY CONFIGURATION OF MECHANISTIC ORGANIZATIONS

The way we presented the calculative procedures of budgetary planning and control in previous sections may have given you the misconception that budgeting is simply a technical process of assigning numerical targets/objectives for various functional sub-units in economic enterprises, which could rationally proceed from assumptions of market demands to basic production and non-production activities. Indeed, the process discussed in previous sections is an 'ideal-type model' that traditional cost and management accounting textbooks employ to 'teach' the concepts and calculative procedures of budgetary control. The actual business practices of budgeting and standard

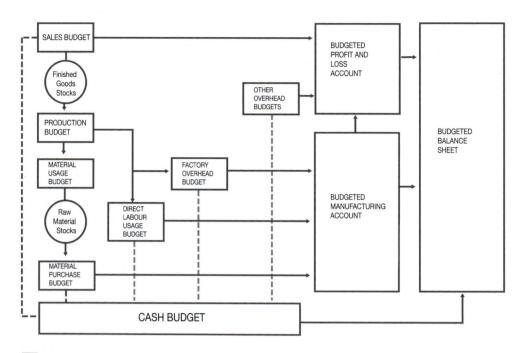

Figure 4.3 *Link between various budgets*

costing deviate from this ideal-type model due to various political, social and psychological factors that complicate the real processes of budgetary planning and control. Therefore, it should be emphasized that budgetary planning and control should be understood beyond their technical rationalities to encompass their political and sociological realities. However, it should also be noted that, by paying due attention to the contextual political and social realities within which budgetary planning and control operate, on the other hand, we never underestimate their technical rationalities. They do have a set of strong technical rationales for which they are operationalized within economic enterprises. We need to understand these technical rationalities of budgetary control within those political and social realities.

The actual business practices of budgeting and standard costing deviate from the ideal-type model due to various political, social and psychological factors that complicate the real processes of budgetary planning and control.

By paying due attention to the contextual political and social realities within which budgetary planning and control operate, we never underestimate the technical rationalities of them.

Having understood basic calculative procedures of budgeting and standard costing as integral elements of profit planning and controlling in the previous section, we will now discuss how budgeting and standard costing help develop mechanistic forms of organizations. The primary objective of this section and the next two chapters is to extend your understanding of budgetary planning and control beyond their technical and calculative procedures so that you comprehend their rational role in the management and control of economic enterprises, and appreciate their sociological and political implications for the construction of capitalistic organizations. With that purpose in our mind, in this section we will discuss:

- How budgeting and standard costing constitute a technical-rational mode of managing economic enterprises through managerial functions of planning, co-ordinating, communicating and controlling.
- How budgetary control facilitates the integration of distinct but interrelated organizational rationales: industrial engineering rationales pertaining to the management of 'relations in production', and administrative or bureaucratic rationales pertaining to systematization of 'relations of production'.
- How budgeting configures the intra-organizational relations as a series of performance contracts.

Budgeting as a rational mode of managing

Technically, as already illustrated by the example in the previous section, budgeting has been viewed as a means for a more complete, objective and rational mode of planning and control, by which organizational functions, processes, activities and people are directed towards the achievement of profit and cost objectives. It is expected that budgeting would provide a rational link between the assumed market realities and production capacities of the organization, and thereby make sure that the organization is achieving its profit potentials subject to resource and factor market constraints. In this rational sense, budgeting is a mode of planning, co-ordination, communication, motivation and control (see Drury 2004: 593). Budgeting is illustrated as a technical and rational process which refines organizations' long- and short-term planning and programming exercises by translating them into measurable terms of cost, revenues and profits. It is often described as a co-ordinating mechanism because the 'budget serves as a vehicle through which the actions of the different parts of an organization can be brought together and reconciled into a common plan' (Drury, 1994: 594). Budgeting is seen as communicating because it is through budgets that top management communicates what it expects from various sub-units in the organization, and through which organizational incumbents understand what the organization expects from them. Budgets are often quoted as a tool of motivation (or de-motivation, when they are abused), because, for example, they enhance 'expectancy', 'instrumentality' and 'valence'.[4] As budgeting provides the standards, targets and benchmarks against which performance is measured and compared for the purpose of identifying non-compliance and non-contributions to predetermined goals, it is often cited as a control mechanism. In this sense, budgeting is seen as a rational mode of managing organizations.[5]

Budgeting runs supplementary to other bureaucratic and operational apparatus of control. It supplements formal rules, regulations, procedures, policies and operational programmes that are aimed at formalizing and routinizing day-to-day organizational activities and behaviours. It runs along with the bureaucratic apparatus of functional division of labour, hierarchy of authority and

Budgeting provides a rational link between the assumed market realities and production capacities of the organization, and thereby ensures that the organization is achieving its profit potentials subject to resource and factor market constraints.

Budgeting is a mode of planning, co-ordination, communication, motivation and control.

specification of exact work duties and responsibilities. While such bureaucratic and operational measures provide a framework to regulate and stabilize day-to-day organizational activities, processes and functions, budgeting provides an objective rationale for them by specifying end results expected in terms of costs and benefits.

Budgeting runs supplementary to other bureaucratic and operational apparatus of control. It supplements formal rules, regulations, procedures, policies and operational programmes that are aimed at formalizing and routinizing day-to-day organizational activities and behaviour.

Integration of operational rationales and administrative rationales

As we noted in the first part of this chapter, budgeting and standard costing emerged from two distinct sources. Standard costing was from the Scientific Management movement, while budgeting was from fiscal controlling in state institutions. They merged later to form a comprehensive system of management planning and control. This amalgamation, on the other hand, denotes an integration of two distinctive but interrelated approaches to managing economic enterprises: the Scientific Management or industrial engineering approach, and the bureaucratic and administrative management approach. The attention of industrial engineering was rather on the rationalization of the labour process itself, which is 'relations in production'. That means it took rather a micro-perspective on work organization – on the rationalization of tasks by standardizing the work methods, tools and time. Administrative and bureaucratic approaches to management, on the other hand, took a rather macro-perspective on the organization, and attempted to rationalize relations of production – relations that determine the distribution of authority, power, access to resources across the organizational hierarchy, and, therefore, appropriation of surplus value. The technical rationality of budgeting also stems from its potential to integrate these two dimensions of managing economic enterprises. Budgeting provided a framework within which industrial engineering and administrative rationales, at least partially, could be integrated.

Budgeting provided a framework within which industrial engineering and administrative rationales, at least partially, could be integrated.

Budget-based contracts

In essence, production is the interaction between labour (human efforts, skills, knowledge and time) and capital (accumulated and natural wealth). Hence, any economic enterprise dealing with production of goods and services should entail some sort of structure to relate capital with the labour. As we noted in Chapter 2, the market is such a structure that organizes the relationship between labour and capital. In a pure market system of production, labourers would produce goods and services 'domestically', and capitalists would buy them in the open (wholesale) market and resell them in the output (retail) market, where they would appropriate a profit. In a quasi-market system of 'internal contracting' (which we discussed in Chapter 2), internal contractors organized the domestic production as a petite bourgeoisie and sold to the contracted capitalists, who would realize their final value in the output markets. In a simple organizational setting, the capitalist would buy labour and directly supervise it, to make sure that the expected surplus value was created by the labour and appropriated by the capitalist.

Today, complex organizational hierarchies have replaced these simple structures. There is a vast distance between the capitalists (shareholders, as we call them today) and the men and women who perform the activities of production. Shareholders, the ultimate owners of the economic enterprise, are not present in the day-to-day activities of production or market exchange. This absence is met by a hierarchy of managers and supervisors who perform those day-to-day activities on behalf of their principals – the higher managers and shareholders. It is easy to conceptualize that there is a series of principal–agent relationships across modern corporate hierarchies, and these relationships are explicitly and implicitly contracted through various contractual arrangements, such as job contracts, job descriptions, job specifications and so on. Budgets can also be viewed as a mode of explicitly establishing contractual arrangements between principals and agents such that they would agree on (or the principals would impose upon the agents) a set of performance outcomes. Such budget-based contracts may also specify rewards for achievement, and punishment for non-achievement, of budgetary performance targets. They can be individual-based contracts or group contracts, where collective performance targets and rewards are set. However, the challenge for the principal is to set the appropriate level of difficulty and reward structure in the budget-based contract in order to stimulate the maximum motivation and efforts from the agent. We will discuss this motivational aspect of budget-based performance contracts in the next chapter. For the time being, what we have to understand is the way that budgeting configures the organizations as a series of contractual arrangements between capital and labour through the organizational hierarchy.

> Budgets can be viewed as a mode of explicitly establishing contractual arrangements between principals and agents such that principals and agents would agree on (or the principals would impose upon the agents) a set of performance outcomes.

In brief, this section has dealt with the technical rationales that budgeting meets within a mechanistic organization. On the one hand, budgeting and standard costing constitute a rational mode of managing economic enterprises through managerial functions of planning, co-ordinating, communicating and controlling. On the other hand, budgetary control facilitates the integration of distinct but interrelated organizational rationales: industrial engineering rationales pertaining to the management of 'relations in production', and administrative or bureaucratic rationales pertaining to systematization of 'relations of production'. Finally, budgeting is a technical-rational medium for bridging the gap, together with other bureaucratic measures, between capital and labour in modern organizations where capitalists are remote from the day-to-day operations of the enterprises of which they claim ownership. This gap is filled by a series of budget-based performance contracts running from top to bottom of modern organizational hierarchies.

DIFFERENT APPROACHES TO BUDGETING

It is obvious that real-world organizations are not characterized by a similar set of attributes and features so that they can effectively adopt a universal model of budgetary planning and control. Instead, the ideal model of budgetary planning we discussed in previous sections is modified in various ways to suit various real-world contingencies. Systems of budgetary planning would be different from organization to organization, depending on the size of the organization, complexity of the organizational structure, information-processing capabilities, long- and short-term strategies, leadership style, organizational culture and many more factors. Historically, depending on various factors and historical incidents and trends, an organization would develop and institutionalize its own system of planning, which may have certain unique features, as well as other features common to many other organizations. Acknowledging such common features as well as deviations from the standard ideal-type budgetary planning models, management accounting literature has identified a few different approaches to budgetary planning. In this section, we will provide brief descriptions of the most common.

> Real-world scenarios of budgeting differ from the ideal model.

Incremental budgeting

As you have already noted, the system of budgeting we discussed throughout this chapter (the ideal-type model) would ideally start with so-called long-term strategic planning exercises, and then would logically flow downward to set sales, production and other operational budgets. Such strategic planning exercises, especially in popular management discourses, are often described as essentially characterized by futuristic thinking, such as envisioning the future, mission setting and so on. An ideal model like that, therefore, little resembles the past but has strong connections to the future as envisioned by the organizational leaders. Incremental budgeting, on the other hand, deviates from this ideal model in that it totally depends upon the past performance of the organization and its sub-units. Incremental budgeting implies a simple budgeting exercise where the future activity levels and budget targets are set by adding an agreed upon 'percentage of progress' to the previous year's figures (either the actual figures or the previous budgeted figures). This percentage of progress can be estimated by taking into account certain factors (such as inflation rates, assumed market growth rates, known price changes, specific operational changes expected and so on). Therefore, incremental budgeting exemplifies a system where the future is seen as the mere projection of the past. It also exemplifies an internal-looking paradigm, which ignores the competitive forces and conditions outside the organization. The most notable weakness with incremental budgeting is that it tends to repeat inefficiencies and wastages incurred during the previous year of operations, because it does not ask whether activities and operations financed during the last year are still necessary or are being provided in the most effective way. Incremental budgeting is mostly applied in public sector organizations where the organizational outputs cannot be readily quantified and programmed, and where the market demand, sales and profits are not explicit considerations of operational planning. Sources of income for most public sector organizations are not their market-related activities but provisions and allocations from the central government or regional governmental institutions, such as city councils. Therefore, budgeting in public sector organizations is mostly exercised as a mode of justifying resource allocation from such central funding institutions, and previous-year figures are often used (although this seems inefficient) as readily available criteria to justify current-year allocations. Thus, progress and development are often represented by mere increments in previous-year figures. Many business organizations also choose to adopt the seemingly inferior mode of incremental budgeting, especially due to resource and information constraints to engage in sophisticated planning exercises. Incremental budgeting is also adopted by business organizations in estimating budgeted figures for discretionary expenditures (such as R&D), which bear little resemblance to the budgeted operational activities (i.e., sales and production).

> Incremental budgeting implies a simple budgeting exercise where the future activity levels and budget targets are set by adding an agreed upon 'percentage of progress' to the previous year's figures.

> Many business organizations also choose to adopt the seemingly inferior mode of incremental budgeting, especially due to resource and information constraints to engage in sophisticated planning exercises.

Zero-based budgeting

Zero-based budgeting evolved, especially in the public sector, as a solution to the problem of incremental budgeting. When a zero-based budgeting system is in place, managers are required to justify all budgeted expenditure in terms of programmed service levels, activities and operations, etc. Therefore, the baseline is zero rather than the last year's budgets. This paradigm of budgeting compels managers to assess periodically whether services and activities that are being financed are still necessary, and whether they are carried out in the most efficient and effective manner.

> When a zero-based budgeting system is in place, managers are required to justify all budgeted expenditure in terms of programmed service levels, activities and operations, etc.

119

Programme budgeting

Some organizations, especially those which deal with project-based activities, use programme budgeting techniques. Rather than budgeting for recurring budgeting periods (such as annual and monthly budgets), programme budgeting considers a given programme (e.g., a construction project) as the planning frame for budgeting. Then, using various project planning techniques such as network and critical path analysis, programme activities are identified, sequentially arranged according to the precedence of activities, and resource and time consumptions are estimated. The result is a programme budget which details the timing and resource requirements for the successful completion of the programme or project.

> Programme budgeting takes a given programme as the unit of budgeting, rather than a budget period and functional activities such as sales, production and purchasing, etc.

Activity-based budgeting

Activity-based budgeting is indeed a further refinement of the ideal-type model by integrating with the activity-based costing paradigm evolved in the recent past. We will discuss the activity-based costing and budgeting practices in more detail in Part II of this book. For the time being, we would emphasize the following aspects of activity-based budgeting.

■ The activity-based paradigm of costing and budgeting understands that costs occur due to various 'activities' that the organization carries out, and to the 'capacities' that organization provides to carry out those activities. That means the costs are incurred because activities consume resources (note that costs are the value of economic resources consumed). In rather technical terms, the 'incidence of costs' comprises the activities, and therefore they can be seen as 'cost drivers' (fundamental reasons behind the occurrence of costs).
■ Since activities are the cost drivers, costs should be more meaningful and controllable if they are categorized and understood in terms of activities to which they are related. Thus, activity-based costing pools and traces the costs to cost objects (products, services, customers, etc.) on the basis of activities involved in manufacturing or serving those cost objects. The cost pooling and tracing are done through resource cost drivers and activity-cost drivers (see Chapter 9).
■ Activity-based budgeting, therefore, relies upon the activity classifications of costs. It first forecasts and estimates the level of 'activities' needed to be carried out during the forthcoming budget period. Then, on the basis of activity-cost drivers and resource cost drivers, it estimates the amount of resources that those activities would consume, and thereby the costs of activities. In this sense, budgets are prepared for each activity category.

> Activity-based budgeting estimates the costs and revenues on the basis of volume of activities, resource cost drivers and activity-cost drivers.

HAVE YOU UNDERSTOOD THE CHAPTER?

1. What was the primary purpose of early budgeting practices in government institutions such as municipal councils?
2. How did industrial engineering contribute to the development of standard costing practices in the early phases of industrial development?
3. Can you trace the evolution of the concept of standards?
4. What were the major issues that cost accountants in the early phases of industrial development had to face, and how did the concept of standards help overcome those issues?
5. How can you describe 'modernity' as a distinct phase of social evolution?
6. How did 'modernity', as a distinct phase of social evolution, help the evolution of budgeting and standard costing?
7. What is the link between standard costing and budgeting?
8. What should be the ideal starting point for the process of budgeting?
9. Why is sales budget considered to be the basis upon which all other operational budgets are prepared?
10. What adjustments should you make to derive the production budget from the sales budget? Use your own hypothetical example.
11. What additional information should you have to derive material and labour usage and purchase budgets from the production budget? What is the typical cost accounting document in which this additional information is recorded? What are the typical sources from which a cost accountant would gather this information?
12. How should a cost and management accountant go about collecting information for various non-production overhead budgets?
13. What are the sources of information needed to compile a cash budget? What purpose does a cash budget serve?
14. How are the master budget and the cash budget derived from various operational budgets? Draw a diagram to show this and also illustrate the sequential link and computational logic of various operational budgets.
15. How do budgeting and standard costing constitute a technical-rational mode of managing organizations?
16. How do budgeting and standard costing integrate technical rationales of engineering with administrative rationales of bureaucracy?
17. What does the term 'budget-based performance contracts' mean? How does budgeting help configure the organization as a series of such contracts?
18. What are some alternative approaches to budgeting? Write short notes.

BEYOND THE CHAPTER

1. 'Budgeting is not simply a technical process of forecasting and setting performance goals for managers, but a socio-political mode of configuring the whole organization.' Discuss.
2. 'Budgeting is incomplete without a complementary system of comparing budgets with the actual performance and a logical way of analysing any differences between the two.' Discuss.
3. 'Budgets do not simply limit the discretion of managers but locate them in an array of power distribution.' Discuss.

4. 'Budgeting is an organizational reality that compromises between the notions such as freedom, innovation, creativity and empowerment, etc., on the one hand, and control and stability on the other.' Discuss.

FURTHER READING

1. For technical aspects of budgetary procedures, see Drury (2004).
2. For a history of standard costing and budgeting, see Sowell (1973).

Chapter 5

Towards management control through budgeting

A STARTING POINT: MANAGEMENT CONTROL IN A STUDENTS' SURGERY

Mid-November 2006: a conversation between two final-year undergraduates

John: Hi, how're you doing? You weren't at the MA lecture were you?

Alex: No, I wasn't. I had a job interview to go to. Anyway, what did you think of that question for next week's workshop: 'How do you reconcile management accounting with management control?' Did he say something at the lecture?

John: No, he didn't. I'm still confused about those two terms. He always uses them here and there. Sometimes, I feel we are on a management course, not management accounting!

Alex: You know, I had a similar question at the job interview. I was asked to describe how I would use a budget rather than supervising people to control. Basically, I said that budgets are linked to people, not only accounting numbers, so budgets can control people. I can remember our lecturer said that once. But I'm not clear about it. I'm not sure I'll get the job.

Late November: at the workshop to discuss the question above

Tutor: I hope you have had some thoughts about this question. I think it's better to start with some ideas from you. Shall we first look at the general meaning of management control? Can you tell me what you think of management control?

Martin: It's controlling others.

Julie: Controlling subordinates.

Alex: Controlling people and activities.

John: Controlling by numbers.

Elizabeth: Controlling to achieve preset objectives.

Tutor: All that is correct. Well done! Yes. It's about controlling people by certain techniques such as numbers. I'm controlled to have this workshop, for example, by timetable and course outline. But what are they to do with management accounting?

Martin: It's not management accounting at all!

John: No. As long as numbers are involved, it's management accounting.

Alex: I don't think so. Numbers have to be financial ones to become accounting.

Tutor: Good start. I agree that accounting is defined in financial terms. But accounting can't be understood without referring to a broader control system. Also, we should not underestimate the value of non-financial information.

SETTING THE SCENE

In the previous chapter we studied how organizations historically evolved to be planned by budgets, and how they are budgeted through various operational budgets. Through an illustrative example, we discussed how operational and master budgets are prepared, and their interrelationship. The example also illustrated the fact that budgeting is a major planning device which specifies profit and costs objectives for the organization as a whole and its sub-units. A logically prepared set of budgets provides a hierarchy of objectives to cover the financial aspects of all programmable activities. In simple terms, a budget is a type of plan that managers strive to implement and achieve. However, the story of budgeting is incomplete unless we discuss the control function of budgeting. This chapter will do that.

First, the chapter discusses some of the general issues in control. This sets two learning objectives. The first is to provide a discussion on the notion of control. The second is briefly to elaborate on the development of the concept of control. Once you have accomplished these two learning objectives, you will be equipped with a better background for linking management control issues to budgeting.

- Discuss the notion of control
- Elaborate on the development of control concepts

The chapter then links the discussion to the domain of management control, a term used interchangeably with management accounting, but with a different focus. This discussion aims to achieve two learning objectives. The first is to define the term 'management control systems' under different schools of thought. The second is to highlight different interpretations of management control systems in action.

- Define the term 'management control systems' under different schools of thought
- Highlight different interpretations of management control systems in action

The discussion proceeds to an overall evaluation of management control literature. One of its objectives is to raise some practical questions that would lead the managers to design management control systems. Another is to make a link between general management control and budgetary control. This will give you a 'control background' for locating the techniques of budgetary controls.

- ■ Raise some practical questions for designing management control systems
- ■ Make a link between management control and budgetary control systems

Finally, the chapter extends the Illustrative Case Example introduced in Chapter 4 to controlling aspects of budgeting and standard costing. The extension of the Illustrative Case Example will provide some ex-post information on actual performance of the company. Then, using that information, we will go through worked examples of how various calculations relating to budgetary control are carried out, and how those calculations would be used for controlling business operations.

- ■ Use ex-post information on actual performance of the company for pertinent calculations around budgets
- ■ Illustrate how these calculations are used for controlling business operations

ON THE NOTION OF CONTROL

It is hard to limit 'control' to management accounting, but it is easy to understand management accounting from control perspectives. 'Unlimited' scope of control encompasses multiple levels of analysis, ranging from individual through organizational to social arenas, and these arenas are governed by psychology, organizational sociology and broad social theories, respectively. One fundamental question common to all these would be: who controls who, and on what grounds? When we start asking this question, there will be an array of issues for further scholarship, including mechanisms of control, consequences of control and remedial measures for control problems. When addressing these issues, some tend to highlight the root causes of control issues, while others may provide solutions. For sociologists, controls are problems; for managers, controls are solutions.

Despite its unlimited scope, control is about who controls who on what grounds. In control, mechanisms, consequences and remedies have to be learned.

Both sociological and managerial aspects of control are important for us to understand management accounting in practice, and design better control systems in which management accounting plays a constitutive role. The sociological aspect is more to highlight problems and relate them to broader socio-political factors, rather than to provide solutions. For example, if workers in an organization are inherently underperformers, then sociological analysis would suggest that this is because of the culture of those workers or political pressures from trade unions. Sociologists try to use control issues to understand organizations and society, rather than change them (Roslender, 1992).

In contrast, managerial aspects suggest that managers seek solutions, such as introducing an incentive scheme. For managers, control is used to detect differences between 'what is' and 'what ought to be' (Rathe, 1960). Having detected them, managers begin to correct these differences by taking actions which might result in positive or negative effects (Vickers, 1972). As we will see later, budgetary control systems can be used as such corrective actions and may bring either negative or positive consequences, depending on the ways in which such devices are used.

> Management accounting is integral to control systems. Sociologists highlight problems. Managers seek solutions. Both aspects are needed for a better understanding.

MANAGEMENT CONTROL

Management control stems from ideas of control. The term is defined as 'those organizational arrangements and actions designed to facilitate its members to achieve higher performance with least unintended consequences' (Ansari, 1977: 102). Management control usually refers to formal controls in an organizational setting rather than informal controls in a broader social setting. In the history of management control innovations, formal control systems were linked to the creation of a 'professional manager' and 'formal structures of control', complemented by the attempts of early management gurus such as F. W. Taylor and Henri Fayol. For Taylor (1967), control processes should be based on standardization of work, while for Fayol, formal controls should be maintained through direct supervision.

KEY TERMS

Management controls are those organizational arrangements and actions designed to facilitate higher performance with fewest unintended consequences.

These formal control systems operated through accounting. Even early writers such as Emerson (1912), Church (1918) and Diemer (1914) located management control in an accounting context. They signified that these systems should be based on: the recognition of what facts are truly significant; accurate records and conventional presentation of these facts; and judicious actions concerning these facts. Accounting orientation of management control further developed by the influence of early links between accounting and social psychology (e.g., Argyris, 1952) and accounting and organizational analyses (e.g., March and Simons, 1958; Simon, 1964). These early developments gave rise to the Harvard Model of Management Control (HMMC) and its supplementary developments into cybernetics, general systems theory and contingency theory. Having seen basic problems in this development, socio-political views of management control challenged its underlying assumptions. We will briefly consider this development and its socio-political views.

> The terms 'accounting controls' and 'management controls' are used interchangeably. However, the latter is a broader concept than the former.

Harvard Model of Management Control

HMMC was advocated by Robert Anthony and his colleagues at Harvard Business School. For them, any control system should have at least the following four components: a detector or an observer who can detect or observe what is happening; an evaluator or an assessor who can evaluate or assess performance of the activity; a director or a modifier who can change or alter performance, if needed; and a communication network that can transmit information among detector, evaluator and director (see Anthony *et al.*, 1965). A management control system should have these features, so that it may be a process of communication in which all those components act together. Anthony defined management control as 'the process by which managers assure that resources are obtained and used effectively and efficiently in the accomplishment of the organization's objectives' (Anthony, 1965: 2). According to Anthony, management control is an organizational sub-system located between strategic planning and operational controls. Thus, to understand a management control system in a firm, reference must be made to the overall organizational control system that consists of those three sub-systems: strategic planning, management control and operational controls. Strategic planning systems set strategies; operational control systems look after day-to-day checks and balances; and management control systems check the planned strategies to see that they are being pursued appropriately. HMMC views management control as a programmed activity processed through: programming; budgeting; operating and measurement; and reporting and analysis. These activities are akin to accounting: one of the fundamental tasks that accountants are entrusted with relates to controlling input costs through these programmed activities. As we will see later, budget is one such prominent control device (see Machin, 1983).

> Any control system should have a detector, an evaluator, a director and a communication network.

KEY TERMS

Management control is 'the process by which managers assure that resources are obtained and used effectively and efficiently in the accomplishment of the organization's objectives'.

Management control is a mid-range activity between strategic planning and operational controls. 'Budgeting' is the best example.

HMMC appreciates the human element in management control. Drawing on the ideas of social psychology, it regards the 'domain of interest' as 'people' rather than 'physical sub-systems'. Management control systems (MCSs) then assist those who take actions – a human interaction with other humans. The success or failure depends on the personal characteristics of the manager – his/her knowledge, judgement and ability to influence others. However, as MCSs are located in organizations' responsibility centres, some argue that the HMMC model does not emphasize the importance of human factors. Moreover, the model is criticized for its negligence of processual aspects of management control, which involves human judgement, power struggles and conflicts (see Cooper *et al.*, 1981).

Whether HMMC focuses on human aspects or sub-units is unclear and debatable.

Cybernetics and general systems theory

Cybernetics, which developed in the science of control and communication, is a conglomeration of circuits which could correct its own deviation from a planned course (Wiener, 1948). Building on this idea, the proponents of management control characterized controls in organizations with the features of co-ordination, monitoring and regulation. Through such organizational control systems, the operations and activities of the organization must be co-ordinated, monitored and checked and balanced through certain technologies on a day-to-day basis. General systems theory (GST) also developed along similar lines to establish concepts, laws and models for delineating the nature of control systems in organizations (Ashby, 1956). This latter approach models organizational control procedures to be in a system where there are inputs, processes and outputs with a feedback loop. A general system is a mechanism built with these interrelated components.

KEY TERMS

Cybernetics is a conglomeration of circuits which could correct its own deviation from a planned course.

KEY TERMS

A general system is a mechanism built with four interrelated components, namely input, process, output and feedback loop.

Both cybernetics and GST attempt to describe a management control system through the metaphor of science and communication, as well as biological systems. Assuming that human and organizational behaviour is common with natural and biological systems, the followers of this paradigm advocate that control issues can be handled through feedback loops, be they negative or positive (Otley, 1983). In such a control system, there should be four necessary conditions: the existence of an objective; measurement criteria; predictable effects of potential control actions; and reduction of deviations from the objectives (Otley and Berry, 1980). These conditions inform organizations to develop either a 'feedback' or 'feed-forward' system, where the former considers 'regulation by error', and the latter aims to 'control the future by planning' (see Wilson and Chua, 1993). Either way produces an information system that links to the organization's decision-making procedures so that control systems are reliable 'black boxes'.

Control systems can be feedback or feed-forward systems: the former is based on past data and the latter on planned data.

Despite cybernetics and GST having provided a language for conceiving of a control system, some argued that scientific analogy would be too simple to capture the complexities of management control systems in action (Vickers, 1967). Otley (1983) showed that organizational goals would not be equated to the sum of individual goals: people have self-desires which would not be appreciated by organizational management. Vickers (1967) criticized that feedback loops would often be absent or ambiguous, and uninformative. Also, due to enormous uncertainties, feed-forward systems would not be the best way of describing control systems (see Otley and Berry, 1980). Control systems cannot be 'black boxes' such as a biological nerve system, because there can be a number of unintended consequences due to continuous interplay between the organization and its uncertain environment (Otley, 1980).

Control systems in action cannot be as straightforward as 'general systems' or cybernetics. There are uncertainties and unintended consequences.

Contingency theory

Contingency theory of management (accounting) developed from cybernetics and GST (Woodward, 1965; Burns and Stalker, 1961). It argues that there cannot be a universal method of designing a management control system which can be applicable to any organization. Instead, the organization must compare its specific structure with its relevant contingencies (Otley, 1980). These contingencies include the organization's environment and technology. As we will elaborate in Chapter 13, accounting control systems must be developed by matching them with the nature of the environment and technology. For example, as Mintzberg (1979) argued, an organization operating in a stable business environment can survive with a rather mechanistic control structure, whereas an organization in a dynamic business environment would have to rely on an organic control

129

structure. Similarly, an organization would choose the best control systems that would be appropriate to the type of technology (e.g., unit production, mass production or process production) the firm has.

> There cannot be a universal management control system: the organization must compare its specific structure with its relevant contingencies, including environment and technology.

The contingency theory of management control system design has produced a small flood of studies showing relationships between a number of contingencies and the organization's control system. These include the studies by Khandwalla (1974), Earl and Hopwood (1979), Rahman and McCosh (1976), Young (1979) and Gordon and Narayanan (1984). These early studies led to another string of contemporary studies, which have continued to explore those relationships (e.g., Langfield-Smith, 1997; Chong and Chong, 1997).

> Contingency theory of management accounting was a research fashion in the 1970s and 1980s.

However, contingency theory of management accounting suffers from a number of methodological deficiencies, especially its 'scientific' orientation (for a detailed review, see Otley, 1980; Fisher, 1995; Chapman, 1997). Despite its technical limitations (Langfield-Smith, 1997), a pervasive criticism is that cross-sectional analyses based on survey methods did not produce a deeper understanding of how organizations and their accounting systems react to environmental uncertainty. The studies also enjoyed a greater functional orientation, whereby they tended to generalize the findings for managerial implementation. This is not without risk, as all organizations and their accounting systems are contingent upon circumstances, the fundamental premise of contingency theory itself. Most of these studies did not define contextually what environment is; for most researchers, environment is about competition and market stability. Researchers inadvertently neglected an important environmental aspect of how the broader socio-economic and institutional context shape accounting systems in organizations (for a critical evaluation, see Hopper and Powell, 1985).

> Contingency theory approach was criticized for its limitations: limited undefined variables, statistical relationships, negligence of social complexities.

Socio-political perspectives

The identified limitations of contingency theory of management control led a camp of management accounting researchers to study the control systems in their wider organizational and socio-political context. Rather than designing control systems based on their association with contingencies, socio-political perspectives assume complex interactions between accounting systems and the context in which they operate. Thus, the proponents of this view highlight problems and issues of control systems, rather than offering prescriptions for designing better systems. It is argued that the identification of problems is more important than blindly developing new systems (for a review, see Hopper et al., 1987).

> Socio-political perspectives emphasize the problematic nature of controls, and explore their complex socio-political ramifications.

The researchers taking this perspective apply a variety of organization and social theories, with a view to providing meaningful explanations for the problems identified. For example, researchers adopt labour process theory, which argues that control systems help accumulate capital rather than maintaining a perfect match between the control system and its environment. Workers are regarded as commodities sold in the market, and accounting systems help control the workers for the accumulation of capital. Thus, the existence of management control systems in the capitalist world is not a possibility for smoothing economic affairs; rather, it generates struggles and conflicts between capital and labour. Consequently, management controls do not represent logics of efficiency, but maintain surveillance of the labour process (see Hopper et al., 1987; Hopper and Armstrong, 1991).

> Socio-political perspectives use a social or organization theory for understanding/explaining control issues.

The socio-political perspectives on management control studies did not provide prescriptions for improvement. Based on this observation, some observe that management accounting students must contribute much to practice, as opposed to their engagement in the critical project (Scapens, 2006). They assert that while we need to understand what is happening in organizations, we need to translate our findings into applicable knowledge. Going in this direction, CIMA (UK) tends to sponsor academic conferences where researchers and practitioners sit together to share academic knowledge and practice issues. However, this does not mean that socio-political effects on management control systems are immaterial, and practical-oriented delineations are of paramount importance. Broader social and political articulations such as globalization, privatization or even customer orientation are important aspects that we need to consider when understanding the design of better management control systems.

131

Some argue that the understanding of problems must lead to creating applicable and pragmatic knowledge.

WHAT DO WE DO WITH THESE FRAMEWORKS?

The above frameworks do not provide us with techniques for management controls. Instead, they describe how control systems work, and explain why such systems operate in a particular manner. This knowledge is needed for us to accommodate certain control techniques in a meaningful framework of practices. As Ansari (1977) observed, the frameworks in practice consist of two elements:

- information networks;
- social relationships.

All control frameworks encompass information networks and social relationships.

As a network of information, a management control system measures, collects, processes and transmits information. These activities in such a network facilitate organizational communication concerning goals, outputs/outcomes and variances between them. In other words, this network is a structure that determines managerial understanding of deviations between 'what is' and 'what ought to be'. If you are to design a better control system as an information network, as Ansari (1977) pointed out, you need to begin with the following questions:

- What are the controlled variables, and how are they to be broken down and measured at different levels?
- What disturbances should be recognized and measured?
- When and how often should you communicate information on deviations to management?
- Which and how many transformations are to be performed on the information as it moves through a network?
- What feedback reports should be provided to subordinates, and how often?

Certain questions can be raised when designing a control system. These questions link to possible differences between 'what is' and 'what ought to be'.

As a web of social relationships, a management control system attempts to design a process by which the senior managers can affect the behaviour of subordinates. The frameworks we summarized earlier provide us with different ways of articulating this relationship. For HMMC, rational, economic rewards can maintain better relationships between the controllers and the controlled. Cybernetics and GST confirm this. However, contingency theory assumes that there is no one best way. Instead, relationships can be developed by considering situational circumstances. Socio-political views, in contrast, highlight the problems of sustaining such relationships, as capitalism's aim is to exploit labour by capital through the use of control systems.

Both elements – the network of information and the web of social relations – are invariably linked. The former is much more tangible and mechanistic in that it is well known and universally practised. However, the consequences of these practices are different from one firm to another, because the nature of the web of social relationships would be different across firms. Budgeting, for example, is a well-known control system, but the practices of budgeting will be different across different companies and contexts. The next section illustrates how budgeting acts as a control system by enabling firms to involve themselves in the procedures of standard costing.

> In a control system, we need to understand both the network of communications and the social relationships.

BUDGETARY CONTROL: TECHNIQUES AND PROCEDURES

In Chapter 4, through an illustrative example, we discussed how operational and master budgets are prepared and their interrelationship. The example also illustrated that budgeting is a major planning device which specifies profit and costs objectives for the organization as a whole and its sub-units. A logically prepared set of budgets provides a hierarchy of objectives to cover the financial aspects of all programmable activities. In simple terms, a budget is a type of plan that managers strive to implement and achieve.

Budgeting also has a control function. Budgetary control is one of the main controlling techniques widely used in business organizations. Technically, budgetary control refers to the process of ensuring that actual performance complies with the plans. In this sense, basic elements of a controlling system involve:

1. Plans and/or standards against which actual performances are to be compared.
2. A system of monitoring and recording actual performance – so that it can be compared with the planned.
3. A system of comparing actual performance with the planned to recognize, analyse and report deviations from the planned (variance).
4. A system of regulating the actual performance: that is, taking corrective actions to eliminate or minimize variance.

> A budgetary control system can take corrective actions when the plans deviate from the actual.

The first is derived from managerial planning exercises, including budgeting. The second is generally the accounting information system, which records and reports day-to-day transactions and events. The third and fourth basically form the central part of organizational control, and budgetary controls and standard costing play a major role therein. Figure 5.1 illustrates the phases of management control, and how budgeting can be placed within the overall system.

From Figure 5.1, it is clear that budgeting operates at both the planning and controlling phases. As we have already noted, at the planning phase, budgeting sets specific financial targets to be achieved by the organization and its sub-units. At the controlling phase, on the other hand, budgetary control compares the actual with the plans in order to identify any deviations and to analyse reasons for them. Broadly speaking, there are two major tools that management accountants use for this purpose:

- flexible budgeting;
- standard costing – analysis of variance.

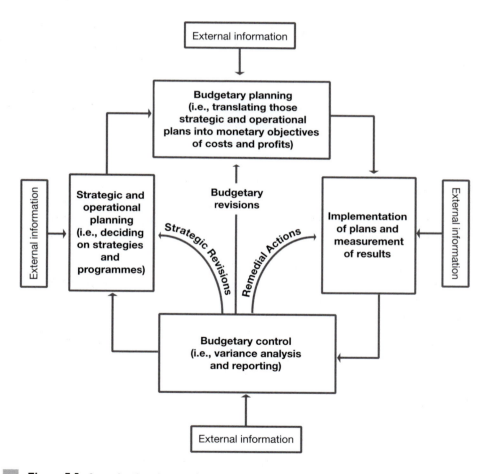

Figure 5.1 *Organizational control process and budgeting*
Source: Adapted from Anthony and Dearden (1980: 19)

It should be noted that most of the traditional textbooks discuss these two techniques in isolation, without properly addressing the relationship between the two. It is true that these two techniques can indeed be applied independently, as they are not necessarily interdependent. However, a proper amalgamation of the two would always enhance the potential of the other to recognize and analyse cost and profit variances. For our understanding, flexible budgeting provides the major tool for recognizing significant variances at the aggregate level, while standard costing provides a structured way of analysing reasons for total variances of profit, revenue and costs. In other words, standard costing technique can provide a hierarchical breakdown of profit and costs variances shown in the flexible budget.

Flexible budget

The flexible budget is an 'update' of the static budget. What we presented in the previous chapter for the Softdrink Private Limited case was a static budget. This budget is indeed a representation of future expectations, prepared before that future takes place. A flexible budget, on the other hand, is prepared to reflect what has already happened. Hence, it is more a feedback control device than a planning device, though it can provide significant inputs for future planning exercises. A flexible budget is prepared by revising the static budget to represent actual level of operations accomplished during the budget period. That means flexible budgeting makes the budgeted figures comparable with the actual by bringing them to the same (comparable) level of activity. A clear meaning of flexible budgeting can be gained by understanding the procedures and calculations involved in preparation, and the general format it takes. We will do this by extending the illustrative case example we used previously. Relevant information to prepare the flexible budget is given in Illustrative Case Example: ex-post information.

Illustrative Case Example: Softdrink Private Limited – ex-post information

The accountant of Softdrink Private Limited has recorded the following information on actual performance after the budget period:

1. Production: 4,790,000 bottles of Mega; 6,640,000 bottles of Buddy.
2. Sales: 4,800,000 bottles of Mega; 6,600,000 bottles of Buddy, at average prices of £0.48 and £0.30, respectively.
3. Material usages and actual prices were as follows:

    ■ RM1: 2,442,900 litres for Mega and 1,593,600 litres for Buddy at £0.21 per litre
    ■ RM2: 1,437,000 litres for Mega and 1,195,200 litres for Buddy at £0.09 per litre
    ■ RM3: 1,077,750 litres for Mega and 664,000 litres for Buddy at £0.10 per litre
    ■ Containers: 5,053,450 bottles at £0.05 per bottle for Mega and 6,985,280 bottles at £0.04 per bottle for Buddy

4. Closing stocks were taken to be:

    ■ Raw materials (litres): RM1 160,000, RM2 110,000 and RM3 70,000
    ■ Containers: 199,450 for Mega and 298,880 for Buddy
    ■ Finished products: 250,000 bottles of Mega and 360,000 bottles of Buddy

135

5. Labour usage and variable overheads:

	Labour hours			Variable overheads (£)		
	Mega	Buddy	Total	Mega	Buddy	Total
In Process A	11 975	6 640	18 615	89 813	26 560	116 373
In Process B	9 580	6 640	16 220	48 379	15 936	64 315
In Process C	14 370	–	14 370	86 220	–	86 220
In Process D	–	26 560	26 560	–	146 080	146 080
Total	35 925	39 840	75 765	224 412	188 576	412 988

The labour rate per hour was £12 for all processes.

6. Fixed overheads:

- Fixed production overheads: £188,000
- General administration overheads: £272,000
- Sales and marketing overheads: £416,000
- Total fixed cost: £876,000

Basically, a flexible budget report, which is often called a performance report, shows three major types of information:

- Revisions to the static budget so that it represents what the costs and revenues should have been for the actual level of activity realized during the budget period.
- Actual costs and revenues.
- Variances between the budgeted and actual costs and revenues.

Now let us turn to the Illustrative Case Example and try to understand the procedures and calculations involved in the preparation of a flexible budget. Typically, the level of activity is measured by the level of production, as it is the most immediate indicator of the production capacity. Thus Softdrink Private Limited's actual level of activities is represented by 4,790,000 bottles of Mega and 6,640,000 bottles of Buddy. On this basis we should recalculate our budgeted cost figures to comply with the realized level of activity. These production figures should be used with the standard cost data (given in the standard cost card – see Case Extract 4.2 in Chapter 4). So calculated figures will be the flexible budget figures. For example, let us take the material cost elements to flex with actual level of activity. As per the standard cost card, the total material cost per bottle of Mega and Buddy should be 15p and 7.5p, respectively. Therefore, the standard costs to produce 4,790,000 bottles of Mega and 6,640,000 bottles of Buddy should be £718,500 (= £0.15 × 4,790,000) and £498,000 (= £0.075 × 6,640,000), respectively.

These total figures can be broken down into individual raw material items by repeating the same calculation, but taking the individual raw material costs per unit of output at a time. The spreadsheet for this calculation (which shows individual raw material costs and the total for each product) is shown in Case Extract 5.1.

In this way, using the unit cost information in the standard cost card, we can recalculate budgeted figures for other cost elements as well to represent the production level of 4,790,000

Case Extract 5.1 *Calculation of standard material costs*

	Mega			Buddy			Total (£)
	Standard cost per bottle (£)	Total production (bottles)	Total cost (£)	Standard cost per bottle (£)	Total production (bottles)	Total cost (£)	
RM1	0.10	4 790 000	479 000	0.050	6 640 000	332 000	811 000
RM2	0.03	4 790 000	143 700	0.015	6 640 000	99 600	243 300
RM3	0.02	4 790 000	95 800	0.010	6 640 000	66 400	162 200
Total material cost	0.15	4 790 000	718 500	0.075	6 640 000	498 000	1 216 500

and 6,640,000 bottles of Mega and Buddy, respectively. These are the flexible budget figures that can be compared with the actual. In other words, they are the costs that should have been at the realized level of activity.

It should be noted that flexing the figures in this way applies only to variable cost elements. As fixed costs do not depend upon the level of production, they should remain constant in the flexible budget. That means static budget figures for fixed cost elements remain as they are in the flexible budget[1] as well. So do the sales figures.

Flexible budget figures can be summarized in a profit and loss statement together with actual figures, so that variances are readily available for management attention. See Case Extract 5.2 for the flexible budget statement regarding the Softdrink Private Limited case, which was prepared using the ex-post information given above, together with other information in Chapter 4.

In summary, a flexible budget contains what should have been the costs and revenues at the realized level of production, and compares them with the actual performance to identify variances. This is important to eliminate the misleading comparison that can be arrived at if we compare a static budget with a flexible budget, where a 'positive' change in costs due to an increase in level of operation could be recorded as an adverse variance. Or, on the other hand, a 'negative' change in costs due to decrease in operation could be seen as a favourable variance.

A flexible budget contains expected costs and revenues at the actual level of production. These figures are ready to compare with actual costs and revenues.

See Figure 5.2, later in this chapter, for the structured analysis of variances shown in the flexible budget.

Having identified cost, revenue and profit variances, the next task is to analyse possible reasons for them. As already mentioned, standard costing techniques of variance analysis provide a structured way of doing this. We will discuss that in the next section.

137

Case Extract 5.2 *Performance report*

	Actual (£)			Flexed budget (£)			Variances = flexed budget – actual					
	Mega	Buddy	Total	Mega	Buddy	Total	Mega		Buddy		Total	
Direct materials (from material usage budget)												
RM1	513 009	334 656	847 665	479 000	332 000	811 000	34 009	A	2 656	A	36 665	A
RM2	129 330	107 568	236 898	143 700	99 600	243 300	14 370	F	7 968	A	6 402	F
RM3	107 775	66 400	174 175	95 800	66 400	162 200	11 975	A	0		11 975	A
	750 114	508 624	1 258 738	718 500	498 000	1 216 500	31 614	A	10 624	A	42 238	A
Containers (from usage budget)	252 673	279 411	532 084	251 475	278 880	530 355	1 198	A	531	A	1 729	A
Total material cost	1 002 787	788 035	1 790 822	969 975	776 880	1 746 855	32 812	A	11 155	A	43 967	A
Direct labour (from labour usage budget)												
Process A	143 700	79 680	223 380	143 700	99 600	243 300	0		19 920	F	19 920	F
Process B	114 960	79 680	194 640	95 800	66 400	162 200	19 160	A	13 280	A	32 440	A
Process C	172 440		172 440	143 700		143 700	28 740	A	0		28 740	A
Process D		318 720	318 720		265 600	265 600	0		53 120	A	53 120	A
Total direct labour cost	431 100	478 080	909 180	383 200	431 600	814 800	47 900	A	46 480	A	94 380	A
Variable factory overheads (from VFOH budget)												
Process A	89 813	26 560	116 373	96 998	67 230	164 228	7 185	F	40 670	F	47 855	F
Process B	48 379	15 936	64 315	51 253	35 524	86 777	2 874	F	19 588	F	22 462	F
Process C	86 220		86 220	91 250		91 250	5 030	F	0		5 030	F
Process D		146 080	146 080		149 533	149 533	0		3 453	F	3 453	F
Total variable factory overheads	224 412	188 576	412 988	239 500	252 287	491 787	15 089	F	63 711	F	78 799	F

Total variable cost of production	1 658 298	1 454 691	3 112 989	1 592 675	1 460 767	3 053 442	65 623 A	6 076 A	59 547 A
Add: opening stock (at standard variable cost)	86 450	70 398	156 848	86 450	70 398	156 848	0	0	0
Less: closing stock (at standard variable cost)	86 550	78 869	165 419	83 125	79 198	162 323	3 425 A	329 A	3 096 A
Variable cost of goods sold	1 658 198	1 446 221	3 104 419	1 596 000	1 451 967	3 047 967	62 198 A	5 746 A	56 452 A
Sales	2 304 000	1 980 000	4 284 000	2 000 000	1 800 000	3 800 000	304 000 F	180 000 F	484 000 F
Contribution	645 802	533 779	1 179 581	404 000	348 033	752 033	241 802 F	185 746 F	427 548 F
Less fixed costs									
Fixed production overheads (from FFOH budget)			188 000			170 000	18 000 A		
General administration overheads			272 000			250 000	22 000 A		
Sales and marketing overheads			416 000			245 000	171 000 A		
Total fixed cost			876 000			665 000	211 000 A		
Net profit			303 581			87 033	216 548 F		

Note: flexible sales and fixed cost figures are static budget figures.

STANDARD COSTING – ANALYSIS OF VARIANCES

The variance analysis framework in standard costing goes to the basic building blocks of cost and revenues in order to analyse the variances. In basic economic terms, cost is the value of economic resources consumed in production of goods and services. This value is arrived at by multiplying the quantities consumed by the prices paid in the factor market. That means, in generic terms:

$Cost = PiQi,$
where Pi is price of input and Qi is quantity of input.

Similarly, revenue is the value of goods and services sold in product markets. As in the case of cost, this value is also arrived at by multiplying market prices by the quantities sold. Hence, in generic terms:

$Revenue = PoQo,$
where Po is price of output and Qo is quantity of output sold.

Hence, there are two basic factors that determine the costs and revenues, namely prices and quantities. Changes in either or both of these cause changes in cost or revenue. This basic logic is employed in standard costing techniques of analysing variances. At the basic level, any cost and sales variance can therefore be broken down to price and quantity variances, though they are labelled with different names. For example, in the cases of labour, 'price' variance is known as 'rate' variance, simply because in generic terms, 'prices' paid for labour are commonly known as 'rates'. Similarly, variances due to changes in quantities are known as 'usage', 'efficiency' and 'volume' variances with respect to materials, labour and overheads, and sales. Table 5.1 summarizes the different terms we use to identify price and quantity variances with respect to each cost element and sales.

> There are two basic factors that determine costs and revenues: prices and quantities. Changes in either or both of these cause changes in cost or revenue. This is the basic logic in standard costing.

It should also be noted that price or rate variances often take place due to changes in market conditions and hence can often be beyond the control of management. However, it should also be noted that they can be due to mere managerial (in)efficiencies of (not) identifying the best source of resources or uninformed pricing decisions. Hence, further analysis of price or rate variances needs qualitative explanations.

Quantity variances (i.e., usage, efficiency or volume variances), on the other hand, mostly take place due to managerial (in)efficiencies related to internal processes of production and marketing. In special cases, however, they can also be due to various external factors beyond the control of management. For example, a shortage in production can be due to an industry-wide industrial action. Hence, further analysis of quantity variances requires qualitative explanations.

Table 5.1 *Terminology of price and quantity variances*

Cost element/sales	Term for price variance	Term for quantity variance
Direct material	Price variance	Usage variance
Direct labour	Rate variance	Efficiency variance
Variable overhead	Expenditure variance	Efficiency variance
Sales	Price variance	Volume variance

> When analysing the reasons for variances, we may link them to internal management (in)efficiency, external environmental dynamics or both.

There is another point that we have to note about usage, efficiency or volume variances. When the company has more than one raw material which has to be 'mixed' in standard proportions (as in the case of Softdrink Private Limited, where three raw materials are mixed to form the final product), cost variances can occur due to changes in the proportions of each raw material. In that case, the quantity variance should be analysed further into two other variances: mix variance and yield variance. This can be true for labour as well, if different categories of labour (with different pay rates) can be substituted for one another. Note that the same logic is applicable for sales. Where there is more than one product sold at different selling prices, then sales variance can occur due to changes in the sales mix. Therefore, sales volume variance should be analysed further into its components: sales mix variance and sales quantity variance. In this way, standard costing practices have constructed a hierarchical structure to explain the net profit variances through various cost and sales variances. Figure 5.2 later illustrates this analytical structure of variances for our Illustrative Case Example. Definitions, formulae used and the detailed calculations of individual variances follow in the next sections.

> Variance analysis can be applied to the mixtures of resources, as well as sales.

Direct material cost variance

The material cost variance is the difference between the standard material cost (SCm) and the actual material cost (ACm) of production.

Material cost variance = SCm − ACm

KEY TERMS

The material cost variance is the difference between the standard material cost (SCm) and the actual material cost (ACm) of production.

Standard cost is what the cost should have been to manufacture actual quantities produced: 4,790,000 bottles of Mega and 6,640,000 bottles of Buddy. This can be calculated by multiplying actual quantity of production by the standard material cost per unit of each product. This is what the flexible budget shows. It also shows the actual cost incurred and the total variance. Thus, reading the flexible budget, we identify that there is a £42,238 adverse material cost variance. Regarding the special material, containers, the cost variance is £1,729 adverse.

The analysis of cost variances includes identifying reasons for the variance. At the outset, as we noted above, cost variance can occur because the actual material prices are different from the standard prices, because the actual quantities are different from standard quantities or both. Hence,

Material cost variance = material price variance + material usage variance

Direct material price variance

Material price variance is the difference between actual cost of material consumed (or purchased) and the cost of the same quantity of material at standard price. In other words, it is the deviation from the standard cost of manufacturing the actual quantity due to a difference in actual price from the standard price. That means the price variance attempts to isolate the deviation of actual cost from the standard, which is due to the fact that actual prices at which materials are purchased are different from those of standard. As a formula, it is:

Price variance = (sp − ap) × aq
where: sp is standard price;
         ap is actual price;
         aq is actual quantity.

KEY TERMS

Material price variance is the difference between actual cost of material consumed (or purchased) and the cost of the same quantity of material at standard price.

Calculations for the Illustrative Case Example are shown in Case Extract 5.3.

Accordingly, of £42,238 total material cost variance, £14,043 is due to price changes of raw materials. Further reasoning why the company had to buy RM1 and RM2 at a higher price (please note that price variance for RM3 is nil, as its actual price is equal to the standard price) needs qualitative explanations from the managers responsible for purchasing. If such qualitative explanations point to permanent changes in the market conditions, which are uncontrollable by the management of the firm, then they may lead to a revision of standard prices and the standard cost structure. Note that the price variance for containers is nil, as the actual prices do not differ from the standard prices.

Case Extract 5.3 *Direct material price variances*

	(sp – ap)	×	aq	=	price variance	
RM1	(0.2 – 0.21)	×	4 036 500	=	£40 365	(A)
RM2	(0.1 – 0.09)	×	2 632 200	=	£26 322	(F)
RM3	(0.1 – 0.10)	×	1 741 750	=	0	
Total					£14 043	(A)

Direct material usage variance

As we noted earlier, actual material cost can be different from the standard cost also due to a difference between the actual material consumption and the standard consumption. Material usage variance isolates this reason by calculating the difference between actual and standard consumption at standard price. In other words, material usage variance is the difference between quantity that should have been used and the actual quantity, valued at standard price:

Usage variance = (standard quantity – actual quantity) × standard price

KEY TERMS

Material usage variance is the difference between quantity that should have been used and the actual quantity, valued at standard price.

Calculations for the Illustrative Case Example are shown in Case Extract 5.4.

Accordingly, £28,195 of the total material cost variance is due to the usage variance: that is, due to the excess usage of material (rather than their price changes).

Similarly we can calculate the usage variance for containers as well (see Case Extract 5.5).

As the price variance for containers is nil, the container cost variance is solely due to the inefficiencies in usage: that is, above-standard process losses. This may require qualitative explanations from relevant process supervisors as to why this has taken place.

Material mix variance and yield variance

Material mix variance and yield variance further explain the reasons for usage variance when more than one raw material is 'mixed' for production. It should be noted that all cases where more than one raw material is used may not include 'mixing'. Mixing takes place only when raw materials can substitute one another to form the finished product. For example, production of a furniture item like a computer desk essentially requires more than one raw material, but they are not 'mixed' with one another. On the other hand, the Softdrink example we are dealing with comprises a mixing problem, as RM1, RM2 and RM3 (all liquids measured in litres) have to be mixed in standard proportions. Material mix variance arises when the actual mix of the material is different from the

Case Extract 5.4 *Direct material usage variances*

	(sq – aq)		×	sp	=	usage variance	
RM1	(4055000	– 4036500)	×	0.20	=	£3 700	(F)
RM2	(2433000	– 2632200)	×	0.10	=	£19 920	(A)
RM3	(1622000	– 1741750)	×	0.10	=	£11 975	(A)
Total						£28 195	(A)

Note that standard quantity column (sq) is calculated as follows:

	Mega			Buddy			Standard quantity for both (litres)
	Standard litres per bottle	× actual production (bottles)	= standard quantity (litres)	Standard litres per bottle	× actual production (bottles)	= standard quantity (litres)	
RM1	0.50	× 4790000	= 2395000	0.25	× 6640000	= 1660000	4055000
RM2	0.30	× 4790000	= 1437000	0.15	× 6640000	= 996000	2433000
RM3	0.20	× 4790000	= 958000	0.10	× 6640000	= 664000	1622000
Total	1.00	× 4790000	= 4790000	0.50	× 6640000	= 3320000	8110000

Case Extract 5.5 *Direct material usage variance for containers*

	Actual production (bottles)	× adjustment for standard loss	= standard quantity (containers)	– actual quantity (containers)	× standard price	= usage variance
Mega	4790000	× 1.05	= 5029500	– 5053450	× 0.05	= £1 198(A)
Buddy	6640000	× 1.05	= 6972000	– 6985280	× 0.04	= £531(A)
Total						£1 729(A)

standard mix. If a relatively cheap raw material has taken a larger proportion than the standard proportion in place of relatively expensive materials, then there would be a favourable cost variance. Similarly, if an expensive material is taken in a higher proportion than the standard, there would be an adverse variance.

KEY TERMS

Material mix variance occurs due to the difference between the actual mix and the standard mix of materials.

In this sense, material mix variance is the variance in the material cost due to the difference between the actual mix and the standard mix of materials. It is calculated as follows:

Mix variance = [aq − (taq × sm)] × (μ − sp),
where: aq is actual quantity of each raw material;
taq is total of actual quantities consumed from all raw materials in mix;
sm is standard mix proportion (per cent) for each raw material;
μ is weighted average standard price of all raw materials in mix;
sp is standard price of raw material.

Calculations regarding our Illustrative Case Example are shown in Case Extract 5.6.

Case Extract 5.6 *Direct material mix variances*

	[aq − (taq × sm)]	× (μ − sp)	= mix variance
RM1	[4036500 − (8410450 × 50%)]	× (0.15 − 0.2) =	£8 436 (F)
RM2	[2632200 − (8410450 × 30%)]	× (0.15 − 0.1) =	£5 453 (F)
RM3	[1741750 − (8410450 × 20%)]	× (0.15 − 0.1) =	£2 983 (F)
Total	8410450	100%	£16 873 (F)

Note that the weighted average standard price (μ) is calculated using the standard mix proportions (per cent) of materials as the weights. Calculation is as follows:

μ = (0.2 × 50%) + (0.1 × 30%) + (0.1 × 20%) = 0.15

Thus, there is a favourable variance of £16,873, in total, due to the actual mix being different from the standard. The variances are favourable because a more expensive material (RM1) has been substituted by less expensive materials (RM2 and RM3). Note that this favourable price variance could have resulted in an unfavourable effect on the product quality, and hence on the demand. However, the analysis of quality impact of material mix variance is often beyond the scope of management accounting.

Material yield variance, on the other hand, shows the effect on cost of the difference between the actual quantity used and the quantity that should have been used for the actual output. Calculation could be done as follows:

(sq − aq) × μ = yield variance,
where: sq is standard quantity;
aq is actual quantity;
μ is weighted average standard price of raw materials in mix.

KEY TERMS

Material yield variance shows the effect on cost of the difference between the actual quantity used and the quantity that should have been used for the actual output.

For our Illustrative Case Example, calculation is as follows:

$(sq - aq) \times \mu = yield\ variance$
$(8,110,000 - 8,410,450) \times 0.15 = £45,068\ (A)$

See the calculations for material usage variance above (Case Extract 5.3) to check how we arrive at the standard quantity (total of all raw materials). We used the same weighted average standard price as calculated for mix variance shown above.

The summary of material cost variances is shown in Case Extract 5.7.

Case Extract 5.7 *Summary of material cost variances*

The variance	For RMs		For containers	
Mix variance	£16 873	(F)	n/a	
Yield variance	£45 068	(A)	n/a	
Usage variance (mix + yield)	£28 195	(A)	£1 729	(A)
Price variance	£14 043	(A)	0	
Total cost variance (usage + price)	£42 238	(A)	£1 729	(A)

Labour variances

Direct labour cost variance is the difference between standard labour cost of the actual output and the actual direct labour cost. It is computed as follows:

$Direct\ labour\ cost\ variance = (shp \times sr) - (ahp \times ar),$
where: shp is standard hours of actual production;
      sr is standard wage rate per hour;
      ahp is actual hours of production spent;
      ar is actual wage rate paid per hour.

KEY TERMS

Direct labour cost variance is the difference between standard labour cost of the actual output and the actual direct labour cost.

See Case Extract 5.8 for Illustrative Case Example calculations.

Case Extract 5.8 *Calculation of direct labour variance*

	(shp × sr)	– (ahp × ar)	= labour cost variance	
Mega	(38320 × 10) –	(35925 × 12)	= £47 900	(A)
Buddy	(43160 × 10) –	(39840 × 12)	= £46 480	(A)
Total	(81480 × 10) –	(75765 × 12)	= £94 380	(A)

Note that standard hours of production are calculated as follows:

	Actual production (bottles)	×	standard labour hours per bottle	=	standard hours of production
Mega	4790000	×	0.008	=	38320
Buddy	6640000	×	0.0065	=	43160
Total					81480

This total direct labour cost variance can be explained by its components: the rate variance and the efficiency variance.

Labour rate variance

Labour rate variance is the price variance for labour. It is the effect of the difference between standard wage rate and the actual wage rate on total direct labour cost. It is calculated as follows:

$$Labour\ rate\ variance = (standard\ wage\ rate - actual\ wage\ rate) \times actual\ hours\ spent$$
$$= (10 - 12) \times 75,765 = £151,530\ (A)$$

KEY TERMS

Labour rate variance is the difference between standard wage rate and the actual wage rate on total direct labour cost.

Labour efficiency variance

This is the quantity variance for labour and shows the effect of the difference between standard production hours and actual hours spent on the total direct labour cost. It is calculated as follows:

Labour efficiency variance = (shp − ahp) × sr,

where: shp is standard hours of actual production;

ahp is actual hours spent;

sr is standard wage rate.

Calculation for our example is as follows:

KEY TERMS

Labour efficiency variance is the difference between standard production hours and actual hours valued at standard wage rate.

Labour efficiency variance = (81,480 − 75,765) × 10 = £57,150 (F)

Thus, the total direct labour cost variance is explained by an adverse rate variance of £151,530 and a favourable efficiency variance of £57,150.

It should be noted that we have calculated only the total variances for all production processes. Computation of labour efficiency variances for each process of production would be very helpful for managerial control, as they provide additional information regarding each labour cost centre, which should be the focus of control. The calculative procedures and the formulae will be the same.

Variable overhead variances

The total variable overhead variance is the difference between the standard variable overheads and the actual variable overheads (VOH) incurred. That means:

Total VOH variance = standard VOH − actual VOH

Generally, standard variable overheads are calculated on the basis of machine or labour hours. In the

KEY TERMS

Total variable overhead variance is the difference between the standard variable overheads and the actual variable overheads incurred.

Illustrative Case Example, the direct labour hours provide the basis for variable overhead calculations. Therefore,

Standard VOH = standard hours of production × standard rate

Now we can rewrite the total variable overheads variance as follows:

VOH variance = (shp × sr) − actual VOH

Note that, in the case of our example, variable overhead rates are different for each process and calculated on the basis of direct labour hours in each process. The standard cost card provides the standard rates for each process (note, they are in pence). We can calculate the variable overhead variance using the information in the standard cost card and actual production information. Calculations are shown in Case Extract 5.9.

Case Extract 5.9 *Calculation of variable overhead variance*

	(shp × sr)			– actual overhead	=	variable OH variance	
Process A	(24330	×	6.75)	– 116373	=	£47 855	(F)
Process B	(16220	×	5.35)	– 64315	=	£22 462	(F)
Process C	(14370	×	6.35)	– 86220	=	£5 030	(F)
Process D	(26560	×	5.63)	– 146080	=	£3 453	(F)
Total						£78 799	(F)

Note that shp column is calculated as follows:

	Mega			Buddy			Total standard hours
	Standard hours per unit	× actual unit of production	= standard hours of production	Standard hours per unit	× actual unit of production	= standard hours of production	
Process A	0.003	× 4790000	= 14370	0.0015	× 6640000	= 9960	24330
Process B	0.002	× 4790000	= 9580	0.001	× 6640000	= 6640	16220
Process C	0.003	× 4790000	= 14370			0	14370
Process D				0.004	× 6640000	= 26560	26560
Total			38320			43160	81480

This total favourable variance of £78,799 can be broken down into its components: variable overhead expenditure variance and the efficiency variance.

Variable overhead expenditure variance

This is the price variance of variable overheads and measures the difference between the actual expenditure on various overhead items and the budgeted expenditure. We can calculate this as follows:

VOH expenditure variance = (sr − ar) × actual direct labour hours spent

Regarding our Illustrative Case Example, we already know the standard rates and the actual hours (see calculations in Case Extract 5.9 above and ex-post information above). The Illustrative Case Example also provides us with the actual overheads for each process. Thus, we can easily calculate the actual rate as follows:

KEY TERMS

Variable overhead expenditure variance is the difference between the actual expenditure on various overhead items and the budgeted expenditure.

	Actual expenditure/actual hours	=	actual rate
Process A	116373 / 18615	=	6.25
Process B	64315 / 16220	=	3.97
Process C	86220 / 14370	=	6.00
Process D	146080 / 26560	=	5.50

Then, we can proceed to calculate the variable overhead expenditure variance as shown in Case Extract 5.10.

Case Extract 5.10 *Calculation of VOH expenditure variance*

	(sr – ar)	× actual hours	=	expenditure variance	
Process A	(6.75 – 6.25) ×	18615	=	£9 279	(F)
Process B	(5.35 – 3.97) ×	16220	=	£22 462	(F)
Process C	(6.35 – 6.00) ×	14370	=	£5 029	(F)
Process D	(5.63 – 5.50) ×	26560	=	£3 453	(F)
Total				£40 223	(F)

Variable overhead efficiency variance

This is the quantity variance for variable overheads which arises from the differences between actual labour hours and standard labour hours. It is calculated as follows:

Variable overhead efficiency variance = (sh – ah) × sr,
where: sh is standard hours;
ah is actual hours;
sr is standard rate of variable overhead per hour.

KEY TERMS

Variable overhead efficiency variance is the difference between actual labour hours and standard labour hours.

Calculation for the Illustrative Case Example is shown in Case Extract 5.11.

Case Extract 5.11 *VOH efficiency variance*

	(sh – ah)	×	sr	=	efficiency variance	
Process A	(24330 –18615) ×		6.75	=	£38 576	(F)
Process B	(16220 –16220) ×		5.35	=	0	
Process C	(14370 –14370) ×		6.35	=	0	
Process D	(26560 –26560) ×		5.63	=	0	
Total					£38 576	(F)

Hence, the total variable overhead favourable variance of £78,799 is due to a favourable expenditure variance of £40,223 and a favourable efficiency variance of £38,576.

Fixed overhead variances

With a marginal costing system, fixed variable overheads are assumed to remain unchanged with the level of production. Hence, they do not have quantity variations, as we show in other cost variances. However, they can change due to various factors other than production, which can generally be categorized as an expenditure variance. In other words, the amount spent on fixed overheads can change with no relation to the level of production, and changes in production have no bearing on the changes in fixed overheads. Therefore, we have only one type of fixed expenditure variance: the fixed overhead expenditure variance.

Despite the assumption that fixed overhead does not change, due to various factors this could change and, in turn, affect overall profit variance.

The fixed overhead (FOH) expenditure variance is the difference between budgeted fixed overheads (static budget) and the actual fixed overhead incurred.

FOH expenditure variance = budgeted fixed cost – actual fixed cost

KEY TERMS

Fixed overhead expenditure variance is the difference between budgeted fixed overheads (static budget) and the actual fixed overhead incurred.

For our Illustrative Case Example, it is as follows:

$$FOH \text{ } expenditure \text{ } variance = budgeted \text{ } fixed \text{ } cost - actual \text{ } fixed \text{ } cost$$
$$= 665,000 - 876,000 = £211,000 \text{ } (A)$$

SALES VARIANCES

In terms of calculative procedures, sales variances are the same as cost variances, except in the way adversity and favourableness are identified. It is simple to understand that a case where actual is higher than standard is adverse for cost but favourable for sales.

However, you should be careful enough to differentiate between sales margin variances and sales variances. In simple terms, 'sales variance' is the difference between budgeted and actual sales values. 'Sales margin variance', on the other hand, measures the effect of sales variances on the contribution or profit. Formulae used for calculation are the same except that the sales variances use price rather than contribution margin, which is the case in sales margin variances. We are dealing here with sales variances rather than sales margin variances. This is not because sales variances are superior to sales margin variances in any sense, but because we can thereby explain the sales variance shown in our flexible budget. Note that the flexible budget shows sales variance rather than sales margin variance.

> There is a difference between sales variance and sales margin variance. Sales variance measures the difference between budgeted and actual sales values, whereas sales margin variance measures the effect of sales variances on the contribution or profit.

The total sales variance shown in the flexible budget (£484,000, favourable) can be explained by sales price variance and sales volume variance. Sales volume variance can, in turn, be explained by sales mix and sales quantity variance.

Sales price variance

This is the difference in sales value due to a change in the sales price. Calculation can be done as follows:

$$Sales \text{ } price \text{ } variance = (ap - sp) \times aq$$

KEY TERMS

Sales price variance is the difference in sales value due to a change in the sales price.

For our Illustrative Case Example, calculations are as follows:

	(ap – sp)	× aq	=	price variance
Mega	(0.48 – 0.50) × 4 800 000		=	£96 000 (A)
Buddy	(0.30 – 0.30) × 6 600 000		=	0
Total				£96 000 (A)

Sales volume variance

This is the difference between budgeted sales quantities and actual sales quantities valued at standard price. The formula is as follows:

$$Volume\ variance = (aq - bq) \times sp$$

KEY TERMS

Sales volume variance is the difference between budgeted sales quantities and actual sales quantities valued at standard price.

The calculations for our Illustrative Case Example are as follows:

	(aq – bq)	× sp	=	price variance
Mega	(4 800 000 – 4 000 000) × 0.50		=	£400 000 (F)
Buddy	(6 600 000 – 6 000 000) × 0.30		=	£180 000 (F)
Total				£580 000 (F)

Thus, the total favourable sales variance of £484,000 can be explained by an adverse price variance of £96,000 and a favourable volume variance of £580,000. However, it should be noted that this separation between price and quantity variances in sales could be misleading, as they are interdependent variables. Often a price cut, which leads to an adverse price variance, could lead to a favourable volume variance.

Sales mix variance

As in the case of material mix variance, sales mix variance measures the effect of changes in standard sales mix on the total sales revenue (or sales margin). It is calculated as follows:

$$Sales\ mix\ variance = (actual\ quantity - actual\ quantity\ in\ standard\ mix) \times standard\ price$$

> **KEY TERMS**
>
> Sales mix variance measures the effect of changes in standard sales mix on the total sales revenue (or sales margin).

Calculations for our example are as follows:

	[aq – (taq × sm)]	× sp	=	mix variance
Mega	[4 800 000 – (11 400 000 × 40%)] × 0.50	=		£120 000 (F)
Buddy	[6 600 000 – (11 400 000 × 60%)] × 0.30	=		£72 000 (A)
Total				£48 000 (F)

Sales quantity variance

This is the effect of quantity changes on the sales revenue after allowing for the changes in the sales mix. The formula is as follows:

Quantity variance = (actual in standard mix – budgeted sales) × sp

> **KEY TERMS**
>
> Sales quantity variance is the effect of quantity changes on the sales revenue after allowing for changes in the sales mix.

For our example, calculations are as follows:

	[(taq × sm) – bq]	× sp	= quantity variance
Mega	[(11 400 000 × 40%) – 4 000 000] × 0.50	=	£280 000 (F)
Buddy	[(11 400 000 × 60%) – 6 000 000] × 0.30	=	£252 000 (F)
Total			£532 000 (F)

Thus, the sales volume variance of £580,000 (F) is explained by a favourable mix variance of £48,000 and a favourable quantity variance of £532,000.

A summary of all sales variances is given in Case Extract 5.12.

Note that the sum total of all variances we have so far calculated should explain the net profit variance, which is shown in the flexible budget as an adverse variance of £216,548. This summation is illustrated in Figure 5.2.

Case Extract 5.12 *Summary of sales variances*

Variance	Mega	Buddy	Total
Mix variance	120 000 (F)	72 000 (A)	£48 000 (F)
Quantity variance	280 000 (F)	252 000 (F)	£532 000 (F)
Volume variance	400 000 (F)	180 000 (F)	£580 000 (F)
Price variance	96 000 (A)	0	£96 000 (A)
Total sales variance	304 000 (F)	180 000 (F)	£484 000 (F)

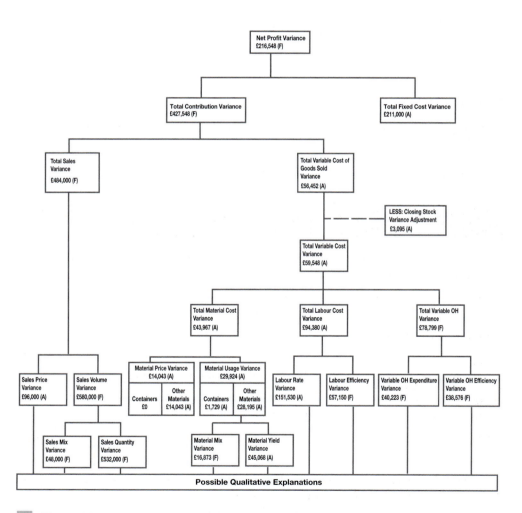

Figure 5.2 *Summary of variances: how profit variance is explained*

LEGITIMATED BUDGETS IN THE MECHANISTIC FORM

You should now be clear that budgets extend to flexible budgeting and standard costing and form a mechanism for analysing everyday operations for control purposes. This mechanism entails both a network of communication and a web of social relationship. In their network of communication, budgets enable people in organizations to talk about budgets, communicate the actual against plans, discuss the issues of variances, report through justifications and act on consequences. These communicative actions take place in social relations where people exude their consent or coercion. These social relations can be seen sometimes in negotiations, and at other times in confrontations. Thus, variance analyses and subsequent communications do not result in a 'summarized profit variance summary sheet'. Instead, these variances reflect on the ways in which people produce these variances through their contribution to 'efficiency' and 'profitability'.

> Budgets represent both communication networks and social relations, which are interrelated.

Many contemporary commercial and service organizations use budgets as their prominent, and perhaps only, management control system. Those firms accommodate budgets in their traditional organizational structure while ever-present bureaucracy reflects on the budgetary process by providing and maintaining rules and procedures. For example, taking advantage of the existence of the organization structure, top managers impose budget targets on the lower managers who, in turn, cascade them down to operational people at the grass roots. Moreover, the firm's bureaucracy helps the budgeters to command the budgetees to 'get the things done' by deploying further rules and regulations. Hence, budgeting represents structures, mechanisms, rules, regulations, procedures, etc., and most textbooks are confident that budgetary control systems play a prominent role in organizations (Wilson and Chua, 1993).

> As one of the prominent control systems, budgeting contributes to maintain the functions of organizational structures and bureaucracy.

One set of arguments lies in the belief that budgets are functional, so organizations use them to gain efficiency and enhance effectiveness. Managers in such organizations are well prepared to follow budgetary rules and get things done by people with budgets. It is assumed that budget targets can be set and imposed unproblematically, and people and sub-divisions are prepared to accommodate conditions attached to budgets passively. If this is correct, budgets constitute the total control system in an organization, as long as they carry not only targets and goals but also the 'facts of costs and revenues' which are fundamental to the functioning of capitalist work organizations. This total system then produces responsibility centres, co-ordinating mechanisms, reward systems, managerial language, etc. This is the mechanistic form of accounting.

In contrast, another set of arguments is advanced to provide a critique on this conventional wisdom of budgeting. Taking a critical–political perspective, these critiques argue that budgets are

> Budgeting produces mechanistic tools such as responsibility centres, co-ordinating mechanisms, reward systems and a managerial language.

essentially political, and operate between conflicts, disagreements and power relations. For example, Covaleski and Dirsmith (1983, 1986) presented a case study to illustrate that budgets played a role to maintain control, as well as to create loose coupling due to political bargaining. They argued that budgets are inevitably reflexive practices associated with organizational politics, so that budgets and organizational activities are involved in manoeuvring, with uneasy tensions between the two. More recently, Wickramasinghe and Hopper (2005) illustrated that budgets are shaped by local cultural political economies, so that rational use of budgets ends up with complexities which produce enormous unintended consequences. These counter-arguments about budgetary controls remind us of problems of budgets as opposed to their functional imperatives.

> Critiques argue that budgets are essentially political, and operate between conflicts, disagreements and power relations.

Even though budgets are problematic, organizations still continue using them as their prominent control systems. One explanation for this is that organizations tend to legitimize their systems as being rational, acceptable and formal, so they use formal systems such as budgets. This legitimization can occur because of regulative pressures, influences of textbooks and professional bodies, or widespread beliefs that budgets can control organizational activities and people. For example, Hoque and Hopper (1994) provided a detailed account of political turbulence in management control which challenged the advantage of budgets. Despite this, the budgeting system operated as an organizational ceremony. Thus, the mechanistic form of management accounting has been much influenced by budgetary control systems, be they functional or ceremonial. It is hard for many organizations to avoid the use of budgets in one form or another.

> Organizations tend to legitimize their systems as being rational, acceptable and formal, so they use formal systems such as budgets.

HAVE YOU UNDERSTOOD THE CHAPTER?

1. Why do we study controls in management accounting?
2. How do you reconcile the terms 'control', 'management control' and 'management accounting'?
3. How are cybernetics and general systems theory linked to the Harvard model?
4. What are main properties of the Harvard model?

157

5. What have we learned from contingency theory of management accounting, and what problems did its proponents face?
6. In relation to the understanding of management control systems, what claims did the advocators of socio-political views make?
7. How do we argue that variance analysis can constitute a prominent management control system?
8. What is the purpose of preparing a flexible budget?
9. Prepare a sheet of formulae of variances, together with a remark on their rationality and managerial purpose.
10. How do you explain that budgetary control systems have contributed to the existence of the mechanistic form of management accounting?

BEYOND THE CHAPTER

1. 'Controls are solutions for managers, problems for sociologists.' What is this difference?
2. 'Budgets have answers.' What are the questions?
3. 'Frameworks of controls cannot be applied.' Do you agree? Why?
4. 'Organizations are mechanistic. Budgets are part of them.' Is that correct? What are your views?
5. Can organizations live with budgets for ever?

FURTHER READING

1. One of the best texts is Emmanuel *et al.* (1996). This will give you further insights into systems and cybernetics-based management control systems, including the contingency theory approach.
2. Ansari's (1977) paper is a straightforward analysis of elements of a management control system. A similar source is Marginson (1999).
3. Budgetary control systems in an organizational context can be read in Flamholtz (1983). A more recent source is Otley (1994, 2003).
4. The use of budgeting in management and performance valuation can be read in Briers and Hirst (1990). A more recent source is Otley (1999).
5. More critical views on management control systems can be found in Neimark and Tinker (1986). A more recent source is Cooper and Hopper (2006).

Chapter 6

Towards economic models of decision-making

A STARTING POINT: ECONOMIC MEN IN AN ECONOMIC WORLD

Once upon a time, not long ago and not far away, there was a 'world' where the inhabitants were known as 'economic men'. They were said to be 'economic' because their behaviour was driven by their economic objectives of profit and utility maximization, by being producers of outputs and consumers of them. Their world was made of 'sectors', mainly producers, households, government. They were not only economic but also rational. They were said to be rational because their production, consumption and governing decisions were made after logical and information-based analysis and comparison of all possible alternatives so that the alternative that maximizes profit and utility could be selected.

Three categories of these economic-rational men, producers, consumers and their governors, interacted with each other in free markets and politics. In markets, it is said, they exercised their freedom of choice in consumption and production. In politics, they exercised their freedom of selecting their governors through collective voting. Thus, their system of production, consumption, exchange and governance was collectively known as 'liberal economic democracy', which they literally translated as 'economic and political freedom'.

'Equilibrium' was their 'nirvana', or their state of perfection; the path to achieve that nirvana was competition. Though they understood that producers and consumers were all in a mutually inclusive competition between one another, at the state of 'market equilibrium' they could all simultaneously maximize their individual objectives of utility and profit, and without free competition the market could never reach equilibrium. Being away from the heavenly status of market equilibrium was a shame because it meant a 'deadweight loss of social welfare'. Thus everybody, in their respective roles of production and consumption, should behave rationally to help the markets reach equilibrium. Producers especially should take as their ultimate social responsibility the maximization of profit, preached one of their prophets – Milton Friedman.

It is also mentioned that they invented management accounting as a set of rational decision-making tools that would help producers to maximize profit.

SETTING THE SCENE

In the previous three chapters we dealt a with set of management accounting techniques which primarily served the purposes of cost ascertainment and cost control. Chapter 3 dealt with the traditional methods of allocation and absorption of overhead costs to 'ascertain the product costs'.

We learned that these cost ascertainment techniques were the historical outcomes of various 'scientific' and accounting experiments to deal with the problem of knowing the 'true' costs of products and services that the economic enterprises produced and sold. Indeed, these cost accounting techniques were invented as a result of the joint efforts of practising accountants (known as work accountants in the early decades of the twentieth century), industrial engineers and entrepreneurs. It was the ever-intensifying market competition during the early decades of the twentieth century that urged the practising accountants and industrialists to search for a system to find the 'true' costs of their products.

> Cost ascertainment techniques were the historical outcomes of various 'scientific' and accounting experiments to deal with the problem of knowing the 'true' costs of products and services.

In Chapters 4 and 5 we dealt with budgeting and standard costing. We understood that the primary purpose of budgeting and standard costing was profit planning and control. Indeed, budgeting and standard costing, together, form the most widely adopted system of management control. We also learned that, similar to product costing techniques we discussed in Chapter 3, budgeting and standard costing techniques had their roots in the Scientific Management movement and evolved as solutions to the 'problem of labour control' (see also Chapter 2).

> Similar to product costing techniques, budgeting and standard costing techniques had their roots in the Scientific Management movement and evolved as solutions to the 'problem of labour control'.

In brief, the techniques of product costing, standard costing and budgeting comprised a set of techniques which evolved with practice (rather than being a product of any academic intellectual discourse), and mainly served the purposes of:

- ascertainment of 'true' cost of the product or services, with special reference to the problem of distributing overhead costs to the cost objects; and
- control of labour through standardization, budgeting and monitoring of work by comparing the actual with the standards and budgets.

It is not difficult to see that these techniques do not employ any sophisticated mathematical or economic models *per se* but a set of accounting procedures and calculative practices that evolved over time to deal with cost ascertainment and cost control problems.[1] Indeed, they are not 'theory-led' or 'theory-based' techniques but a set of calculative practices invented by practice for practice. However, on the other hand, when you go through any basic management accounting text you see that there are large numbers of techniques which are based on certain economic and mathematical models. For example, cost–volume–profit analysis, marginal costing and limiting factor analysis,

160

linear programming, capital budgeting and economic order quantity all employ certain mathematical and economic frameworks. In contrast to product costing, budgeting and standard costing techniques, these economic models of management accounting were not invented by industrial practitioners but by academics, in the hope of making managerial decision-making more effective and efficient.

> In contrast to product costing, budgeting and standard costing techniques, economic models of management accounting were not invented by industrial practitioners but by academics, in the hope of making managerial decision-making more effective and efficient.

Accordingly, we can see that there were two interdependent and interrelated sources for the development of management accounting techniques: the evolution of industrial practices as firms attempted to find solutions to crises in various phases of industrial and organizational development; and intellectual discourses in academia which attempted to help develop and understand industrial practices. For the purpose of this chapter, we would like to classify and label the academia-invented techniques as 'management accounting tools for managerial decision-making', while product costing, budgeting and standard costing will be labelled as 'techniques of cost determination and control'.

> In a broader sense, we can identify two types of management accounting tools:
>
> ■ tools for cost determination and control;
> ■ tools for managerial decision-making.

The purpose of this chapter is to elaborate on the 'tools for managerial decision-making', and to understand that these tools are certain derivations of neoclassical economics and its related branches. Thus, this chapter appreciates economics' contribution to the development of a distinct domain of knowledge which we now call management accounting. However, it should also be noted that the contribution of neoclassical economics to management accounting literature is wider than will be discussed in this chapter. Its contribution can broadly be understood in two distinct arenas of management accounting literature. The first is its contribution to the development of management accounting's *decision-making tools*, while the second is its contribution to *management accounting research*. The former is the focus of this chapter, while major economic theories that underlie management accounting research will be the focus of Chapter 10. Accordingly, this chapter is confined only to understanding neoclassical economic models that provide the theoretical foundation for short- and long-run decision-making tools in management accounting.

Two major branches of neoclassical economics, the *microeconomic theory of the firm's behaviour* and *Keynesian economic theory of investment decisions*, are discussed in this chapter in order to highlight two distinct sets of decision-making tools applicable to short- and long-run decision-making scenarios. Overall, after reading this chapter, you will appreciate the microeconomic theory of the firm as the underlying theoretical foundation behind many management accounting techniques that deal with various short-term production decisions. You will also appreciate the relevance of Keynesian economic theory of investment decisions as the foundation of management accounting techniques pertaining to capital budgeting.

The first section of the chapter provides an outline of the neoclassical microeconomic theory of the firm and its adaptation to management accounting. This section starts with an outline of the major properties of the neoclassical economic model of the firm. Thus, you will come to know the basic elements of the microeconomic theory of the firm.

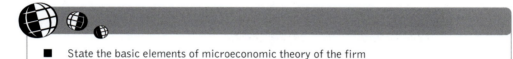

■ State the basic elements of microeconomic theory of the firm

In the second section, we move on to discuss the economic and accounting conception of profit as the primary objective of business enterprises. After reading this part of the chapter, you will be able to: appreciate the centrality of profit in economic and management models of decision-making; differentiate between accounting and economic definitions of the term 'profit'; and differentiate ways that management accounting mobilizes the economic conception of profit.

■ Appreciate the centrality of profit in managerial decision-making
■ Differentiate between economic and accounting conception of profit
■ Identify management accounting instances of using economic conception of profit

Third, the chapter addresses the economic concept of revenue as one of the two elements of profit. It will show how perfectly competitive and non-perfectly competitive market conditions give rise to different types of revenue curve. By reading this section of the chapter, you will understand how the shape of revenue curves is related to the economic assumptions about output market conditions.

■ Relate different economic assumptions about market to the different shapes of revenue curves

Fourth, the chapter deals with the relationship between production and cost functions. It will discuss economic assumptions of production and cost functions, and how they are adapted to management accounting. After reading this section you will be able to describe how production functions give rise to cost functions, and how and why accounting cost concepts and curves are different from those of economics.

- Describe how production functions give rise to cost functions
- Describe how and why accounting cost concepts and curves are different from those of economics

Having discussed revenue and cost concepts, the chapter moves on to deal with profit maximization behaviour in firms. In this section, we first discuss the basic microeconomic model of firms' profit-maximizing behaviour, and then deal with how management accounting adopts and adapts those economic concepts of profit-maximization behaviour mainly through C–V–P analysis and limiting factor analysis. Starting with a simple numerical example to explain the related concepts, we move on to a somewhat more complex example of using linear programming to solve short-run production decisions. After reading this section, you will be able to: describe the neoclassical economic rule of profit maximization; and discuss how the neoclassical economic model of the firm is adapted in management accounting as a set of short-run decision-making tools.

- Describe the neoclassical economic rule of profit maximization
- Discuss how the neoclassical economic model of the firm is adapted in management accounting

The last few sections of the chapter move on to long-run decision-making scenarios, and mobilize the Keynesian theory of investment to explain capital budgeting techniques in management accounting. We will show how Keynesian economic concepts of marginal efficiency of capital and cost of capital underlie management accounting techniques of capital budgeting. You should then be able to: appreciate the economic and management accounting criteria of long-run investment decisions; and calculate and assess net present value (NPV), internal rate of return (IRR) and the cost of capital for a given investment project.

- Appreciate the economic and management accounting criteria of long-run investment decisions
- Calculate and assess NPV, IRR and the cost of capital for a given investment project

NEOCLASSICAL ECONOMIC MODEL OF THE FIRM AND MANAGEMENT ACCOUNTING

The neoclassical economic model of the firm provides the basis for many of management accounting's decision-making techniques. It is composed of the following properties:

1. The assumption that the firm's primary objective is to maximize profit. Hence the conception and calculation of profit are the defining principles of the neoclassical economic model of the firm, because it is assumed that all decisions of the firm are directed to achieve the maximum profits possible. Profit is often represented as the 'objective function' of many decision-making models.
2. Revenue function, which is one constituent element of the profit function, as profit is the difference between total revenue (TR) and total costs (TC). It is assumed that the firm's revenue function is dependent upon the market conditions that the firm faces for its products.
3. Cost function, which is the other constituent element of the profit function. Cost is the economic value of resources consumed in production of goods and services. It is shown that cost is by and large an outcome of production technology employed and factor market conditions.
4. The mathematical tool of marginal analysis to locate optimum point of production: that is, the profit maximizing point of production, which is commonly known as the firm's equilibrium point of production.
5. A definite set of rules and propositions to locate the equilibrium of the firm.

The neoclassical economic model of the firm is based on a set of principles relating to the firm's primary objective (profit) and its components (revenue and cost), and a set of analytical rules (marginal analysis) to determine the firm's optimum behaviour.

The profit function: economic and accounting conception of profit

As we have already noted, the basic assumption of the neoclassical economic model is that firms are striving to maximize (rather than 'satisfy') their profit. Hence, the primary focus of the decision-making models of economics is to find out the level of production at which profit is maximized. This is done by analysing mathematically the profit function, which is often called the objective function of the model.

The primary focus of the analytical models of decision-making in economics is to find out the level of production at which profit is maximized.

In its simplistic form, in a single product case, the profit function is written as:

$\pi = TR - TC$,
where: $\pi = profit$;
$\quad\quad TR = total\ revenue$;
$\quad\quad TC = total\ cost$.

This is seemingly a simple conception of profit as the difference between total revenue and total cost. However, complexities arise due to the differences between the economic and accounting conception of costs and profits.

The cost is the market value of economic resources consumed in a given economic activity: that is, production of a good or service. According to neoclassical economic theories, economic resources are broadly classified into four major types, which are commonly known as 'factors of production':

1. Land – physical resources such as raw materials, land, etc., the market value of which is 'rent'. (Note that the term 'rent' captures all payments for physical resources and facilities which can, in practice, be represented by thousands of expenditure items, such as electricity, telephone bills, etc.).
2. Labour – mental and physical efforts of people directly or indirectly involved in the production process, the market value of which is wages and/or salaries.
3. Capital – accumulated wealth reinvested in the production processes, the market value of which is interest.
4. Entrepreneurship – the risk-taking element of the producer who takes the risks and responsibilities of co-ordinating all other factors of production, the market value of which is profit (or loss). In accounting practice, this is often called 'ownership capital', in contrast to 'debt capital', mentioned above.

Neoclassical economic theories classify resources into four major types, which are commonly known as 'factors of production': land, labour, capital and entrepreneurship.

Thus, for neoclassical economic theories, cost is the market value of all these resources, including entrepreneurship, consumed in production of goods and services. That is the sum total of not only rent, wages/salaries and interests, but also 'normal profits'. Any excess of revenue over these costs is the 'economic profit'. Note that there is a clear difference between the accounting and economic conception of costs and profits. In economics, there are two distinct conceptions of profits: 'normal profits' and 'economic profits' (or 'abnormal' or 'supernormal' profits, as some textbooks call them). We will show the difference between economic profit and accounting profit by way of an example (see Box 6.1).

BOX 6.1 ECONOMIC VERSUS ACCOUNTING PROFIT

Mr A is a small-scale entrepreneur engaging in the production of the product X. He has invested £30,000 of his own savings, and also borrowed a sum of £20,000, for which he pays 10 per cent interest per annum. His assessment is that he would have earned 8 per cent annual return for his savings if he had invested them in the best possible alternative available (rather than investing in the present business). In addition, he also believes that he could have earned an annual salary of £18,000 from the job he left for the full-time engagement in this business.

Given below are the operational results for the last year:

- Sales income: £120,000
- Wages and salaries: £26,000
- Raw materials and other supplies: £36,000
- Other bills and expenses (excluding bank interest): £18,000

An accountant would have calculated Mr A's profit as follows:

	£	£
Sales		120 000
Less costs:		
Raw materials and supplies	36 000	
Wages and salaries	26 000	
Other bills and expenses	18 000	
Bank interest	2 000	(82 000)
Accounting profit		38 000

An economist would have calculated his profit as follows:

	£	£
Sales		120 000
Less costs:		
Explicit costs (i.e., accounting costs):		
Raw materials and supplies	36 000	
Wages and salaries	26 000	
Other bills and expenses	18 000	
Bank interest	2 000	
	82 000	
Implicit costs (i.e., normal profit which is the earnings from the best alternative foregone):		
Entrepreneur's salary that could have been earned from the job given up	18 000	
Income possible from the best alternative investment opportunity	2 400	
Total economic cost (i.e., accounting cost + implicit costs)		(102 400)
Economic profit		17 600

For neoclassical economic theories, cost is the market value of production factors, including entrepreneurship, consumed in production of goods and services. That is the sum total of not only rent, wages/salaries and interests, but also 'normal profits'. Any excess of revenue over these costs is the 'economic profit'.

Accounting calculation of profit considers only the 'explicit costs', but not the 'implict costs' or 'opportunity costs', which are considered in economics in arriving at profit.

The economist's calculation of profits is much lower than that of the accountant. That is because the economic conception of cost involves the 'normal profit', or the 'opportunity cost' (or 'shadow price'), of the entrepreneurial resources, which is the net income possible from the best alternatives foregone for the investment in the present business (£18,000 salary and £2,400 investment income in this example). This means 'economic profit' is the net return to the entrepreneurial resources over and above the returns possible from the best alternatives foregone. Thus, Mr A's economic profit of £17,600 means that the current business has earned him that much more than he could have earned (£18,000 + £2,400) if he had invested his money and time in the best alternatives available. Accordingly, we can break the accounting profit into the two notions of economic profits:

Accounting profit = normal profit + economic profit
£38,000 = £20,400 + £17,600

Accounting profit can be split into two notions as 'normal profit' and 'economic profit'. Normal profit is the net income that could have been earned from the best alternative foregone. Economic profit is the net income earned over and above the normal profit.

This economic conception of profit has been used by management accounting, especially in the area of divisional performance measurements. The concept of 'residual income' is the management accounting derivation of economic profit – the profit earned over and above the opportunity cost of capital. The opportunity cost of capital is charged against the divisional income in the name of capital charge, which is a certain percentage of the capital employed. See Box 6.2 for the calculation of residual income and other profit-related divisional performance measures.

Note that in Box 6.2, each column shows different notions of profit: contribution, controllable income, direct income and net income. These different notions of profit have been calculated by taking the variable versus fixed, controllable versus non-controllable and direct versus indirect natures of costs. All these profit indicators are converted into economic profit (i.e., residual income) by deducting an appropriate 'capital charge' (10 per cent in this case), which is indeed the opportunity cost of capital. The notion of residual income, which was largely debated in

BOX 6.2 DIFFERENT PROFIT MEASURES IN MANAGEMENT ACCOUNTING

Summary of profit centre activities	£ million
Revenue	2 000
Direct profit centre expenses:	
Variable	1 200
Non-variable controllable	200
Non-variable non-controllable	75
Indirect profit centre expenses:	
Allocated overheads	90
Required return of capital (capital charge)	10%
Investment value appropriate to centre	2 500

	Division contribution margin (£ million)	Division controllable income/profit (£ million)	Division direct income (£ million)	Division net income (£ million)	Division net residual income (£ million)
Revenue	2 000	2 000	2 000	2 000	2 000
Less: profit centre variable expenses	1 200	1 200	1 200	1 200	1 200
Contribution	800				
Less: non-variable controllable expenses		200	200	200	200
Controllable net income of the centre		600			
Non-variable non-controllable expenses			75	75	75
Direct net income of the centre			525		
Indirect expenses of the centre				90	90
Net income				435	
Capital charge 10% on £2 500 investment	250	250	250		250
Residual income	550	350	275		185

management accounting literature in the 1970s (see, for example, Emmanuel and Otley, 1976), received renewed attention with the introduction of the performance management tool called 'Economic Value Added' (EVA™). EVA™, introduced by the Stern Stewart Corporation and still a copyright intellectual asset of that corporation, is very similar to the concept of residual income, in that it is also defined as 'accounting profit less a charge for capital employed' (Otley, 1999: 372). However, the difference between the residual income and EVA™ comes from the detailed accounting adjustments to the accounting profit that the Stern Stewart Corporation proposed before the accounting profit can be transferred to a useful economic measure of profit.

> Residual income and Economic Value Added (EVA™) are two instances of management accounting adaptation of the notion of economic profit. Residual income is arrived at by deducting a 'capital charge' from the accounting profit. EVA™ does the same, but with a set of detailed accounting adjustments as well.

Total revenue function

According to economic theory, total revenue function is derived from the demand function (the demand curve or the price curve) of the product, and the nature of demand function is a matter of the type of 'market condition' that the firm is in. For the purpose of this chapter, we consider two market conditions that the firm might face: perfectly competitive and non-perfectly competitive market conditions (which are typically classified as monopolistic competition/imperfect competition, oligopoly and monopoly in economics).

> Total revenue of a firm is dependent upon the market or demand conditions that its products face.

If the firm is in a perfectly competitive market, the following conditions apply:

■ Every firm in the market produces identical or homogeneous products. That means no firm has the power to ask for a premium price, claiming that its product is superior to the products that other firms offer to the market.
■ There are so many firms in the market that an individual firm cannot influence the market price. An individual firm is so small relative to the total market supply that any increase or decrease in the supply by an individual firm is insignificant and will not affect the market conditions. Therefore, the firm is a 'price taker', rather than a 'price setter'. That means the firm can sell any quantity, but only at the ongoing market price (so-called 'equilibrium price').
■ As a result, the firm faces a horizontal demand curve, which denotes that there is a constant price that does not vary with the quantity sold. The derivation of this firm's demand curve is shown in Figure 6.1.

Figure 6.1 contains two panels: the market and the firm. The first shows how market price (market equilibrium) is determined by the interaction of market demand and supply. Accordingly, a market price of £c has been determined by the market (we use the letter 'c' to imply that the price is 'constant' over any quantity). The second shows the firm's demand curve (i.e., demand for the

A perfectly competitive market condition is characterized, *inter alia*, by homogeneity of products and the large number of firms, such that no individual firm can enjoy any monopoly powers. Thus, every firm is a 'price taker', meaning that its products have a constant market price.

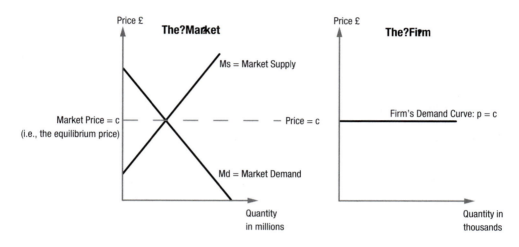

Figure 6.1 *Firm in perfectly competitive market 'takes' market price*

firm's product), which simply indicates that the firm can sell any amount it wishes, but only at the ongoing market price of £c; thus, the equation for the demand curve (which is the price curve) is $p = c$.

If the firm, on the other hand, operates in a non-perfectly competitive market (i.e., in imperfect competition, oligopoly or monopoly market), its product is not identical to the products of other firms, and the firm's supply strategies can affect the market conditions. Therefore, the firm is not a price taker but a price setter. That means it can set its own price, but subject to the demand constraint. The lower the price it sets, the higher the demand for its product; the higher the price it sets, the lower the demand. This means the demand or the price curve for the firm's product is downward sloping, denoting a negative relationship between the price and the quantity sold, which is called the 'law of demand' in economics. Figure 6.2 illustrates a demand curve for a product facing non-perfectly competitive market conditions.

In a non-perfectly competitive market, a firm's products are not identical to other products in the market and it can enjoy a certain degree of monopoly power – the power to set its own price. However, price and quantity sold are negatively related on a downward-sloping demand curve. If the firm wants to sell more, it should drop its price.

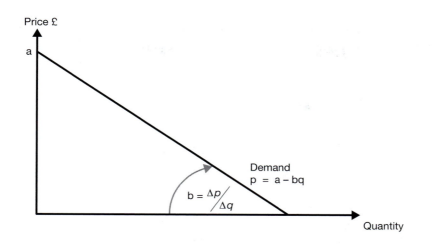

Figure 6.2 *Demand curve of product in non-perfectly competitive market*

Note that the demand curve in Figure 6.2 is mathematically expressed as a function:

$p = a - bq$,
where: a is the y-axis intercept of the curve (i.e., the value of p when $q = 0$);
b is the slope of the curve (i.e., $\Delta p / \Delta q$).

What is more important for us is the nature of the TR curve that these demand curves would produce. Total revenue is simply the total income generated from selling a certain quantity at a certain price. If the price is denoted by the variable p and the quantity sold by the variable q, then TR can be expressed as follows:

$TR = pq$

However, the p in the above equation (i.e., the demand function) is different for the two market scenarios we discussed above, resulting in two different TR functions. In the case of a perfectly competitive market scenario, it is constant at any level of quantity, whereas in non-perfectly competitive markets, price has to decrease for a higher quantity of sales. Therefore, the TR function should also get different shapes and mathematical expressions for the two different market scenarios. Box 6.3 summarizes these differences.

If perfectly competitive market assumptions are held, then the total revenue can be represented by a linear curve. If non-perfectly competitive market conditions are assumed valid, then the total revenue is represented by a non-linear curve. Thus, there is an implied assumption of perfect competition behind the linear revenue curves used in management accounting.

171

BOX 6.3 DIFFERENCES IN REVENUE CONCEPTS BETWEEN PERFECTLY AND NON-PERFECTLY COMPETITIVE MARKETS

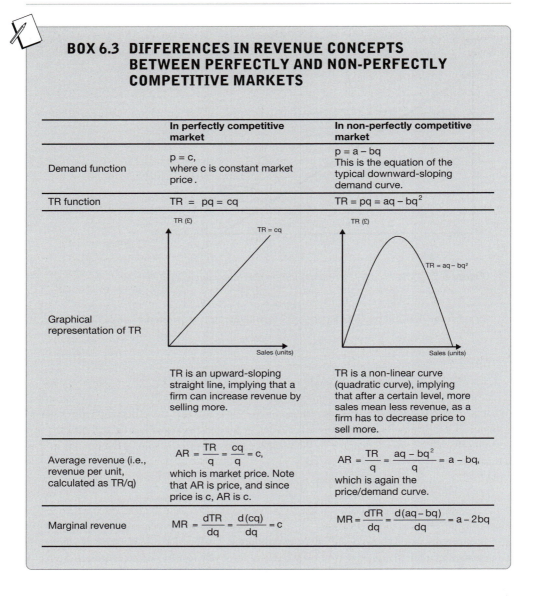

	In perfectly competitive market	In non-perfectly competitive market
Demand function	$p = c$, where c is constant market price.	$p = a - bq$ This is the equation of the typical downward-sloping demand curve.
TR function	$TR = pq = cq$	$TR = pq = aq - bq^2$
Graphical representation of TR	TR is an upward-sloping straight line, implying that a firm can increase revenue by selling more.	TR is a non-linear curve (quadratic curve), implying that after a certain level, more sales mean less revenue, as a firm has to decrease price to sell more.
Average revenue (i.e., revenue per unit, calculated as TR/q)	$AR = \dfrac{TR}{q} = \dfrac{cq}{q} = c$, which is market price. Note that AR is price, and since price is c, AR is c.	$AR = \dfrac{TR}{q} = \dfrac{aq - bq^2}{q} = a - bq$, which is again the price/demand curve.
Marginal revenue	$MR = \dfrac{dTR}{dq} = \dfrac{d(cq)}{dq} = c$	$MR = \dfrac{dTR}{dq} = \dfrac{d(aq - bq)}{dq} = a - 2bq$

The last two rows of the table in Box 6.3 reveal two important economic concepts of revenue: average revenue and marginal revenue. Average revenue is the revenue per unit of production, which is simply the unit price at any given level of sales. Marginal revenue is the addition to the total revenue of an extra unit of production or sales. Mathematically, using differential calculus, marginal revenue is the slope or the gradient of the total revenue function, derived by the first order differentiation of the total revenue function. Note that if the market conditions are assumed to be perfectly competitive, then marginal revenue and average revenue are equal to the market price. However, if the market conditions are assumed to be less than perfectly competitive, marginal revenue cannot be equal to the price of the product.

> **KEY TERMS**
>
> Marginal revenue is the addition to the total revenue of an extra unit of production or sales. Mathematically, using differential calculus, marginal revenue is the slope or the gradient of the total revenue function, derived by the first order differentiation of the total revenue function.

In summary, the point is that the total revenue of a firm depends on the nature of the market where its products are sold. Broadly speaking, the TR curve of a product operating in a perfectly competitive market condition should be different from that of a product operating in less perfectly competitive markets. In the case of a perfectly competitive market, it is a straight line, while in a less perfectly competitive market, it is a non-linear curve with a maximum point implying that a higher sales quantity beyond this point would result in a decrease of total revenue (i.e., sales income). You may recall that most management accounting textbooks adopt a straight line TR curve and, therefore, assume that the firm can sell any amount it wishes without an essential price drop (at least within a given range of production and sales), as it is in a perfectly competitive market.

Production and cost functions

While the total revenue is a matter of the output market conditions of the firm, cost is a matter of factor market conditions that determine the prices of production factors, and the production technology that determines the productivity of those factors. That is because, in very simple terms, cost is the value of economic resources used in production. For example, if 10 hours of labour are used to produce one unit of output and if the price paid for labour is £5 per hour, then the labour cost per unit of output is £50 (10 hours $\times$ £5 ph). The same applies for many other resources, such as direct materials, and if the market prices and amount of resources consumed per unit of output are not clearly apparent, as in the case of overhead expenditures, various estimations or approximations are used to ascertain overhead absorption rates (see Chapter 3). It is the technology that ultimately determines the nature and amount of resources needed to produce a given amount of output. That said, it is the technology that determines the relationship between input and output.

> Cost is a matter of factor market conditions that determine the prices of production factors, and the production technology that determines the productivity of those factors.

Neoclassical economics holds certain important assumptions about the technological relationship between input and output. First, it is important to understand that there is an analytical and behavioural classification of production factors as fixed and variable. Fixed factors are defined as those which are held constant in the short run, while variable factors are those which might change in the short run. Factory capacity includes the number of machines, factory space, maximum power constraints, etc., which are typically taken as fixed factors, while labour, materials, etc., are taken as variable factors. It is only the variable factors that are at the discretion of managers in the short run. Thus, different levels of production are achieved in the short run by changing the level of variable factor consumption.

> There is an analytical and behavioural classification of production factors as fixed and variable. Fixed factors are defined as those which are held to be constant in the short run, while variable factors are those which might change in the short run.

There are two different technological assumptions that one can hold on the relationship between input and output in the short run:

■ Constant returns to variable factors: this means if you keep on increasing the variable factor consumption while holding the fixed factor constant, the marginal production of each additional unit of variable factor should remain constant.
■ Diminishing returns to variable factors: this means if you keep on increasing the variable factor consumption while holding the fixed factor constant, the marginal production of each additional unit of variable factor should eventually diminish. The term 'eventually diminish' means here that there should be an increase of marginal productivity up to a certain level, which then starts to diminish.

> There are two different technological assumptions that one can hold on the relationship between input and output in the short run: constant returns to variable factors and diminishing returns to variable factors.

Box 6.4 illustrates these two technological assumptions.

It is the assumption of diminishing returns that neoclassical economics generally holds. The result is that economic textbooks typically deal with non-linear production and cost curves. On the other hand, management accounting textbooks adopt straight line cost curves, behind which always lies the assumption of constant returns to variable factors.

> Behind the linear cost curves that management accounting often adopts there lies the assumption of constant returns to variable factors.

Cost curves are a direct result of production curves, and show the relationship between level of production and resource cost. For example, in Box 6.5, when 5 labour units are employed, the total production is 500 units under constant returns assumption, while it is 370 under diminishing

BOX 6.4 CONSTANT AND DIMINISHING RETURNS TO VARIABLE FACTOR

Constant returns to variable factor	Variable factor (labour)	0	1	2	3	4	5	6	7	8	9	10	11	12	13	14	15	16
	Total production	0	100	200	300	400	500	600	700	800	900	1000	1100	1200	1300	1400	1500	1600
	Marginal production	100	100	100	100	100	100	100	100	100	100	100	100	100	100	100	100	100
Diminishing returns to variable factor	Variable factor (labour)	0	1	2	3	4	5	6	7	8	9	10	11	12	13	14	15	16
	Total production	0	30	86	164	260	370	490	616	744	870	990	1100	1196	1274	1330	1360	1360
	Marginal production	0	30	56	78	96	110	120	126	128	126	120	110	96	78	56	30	0

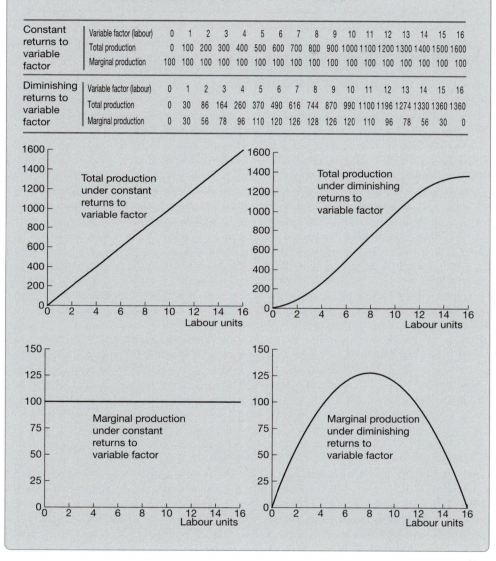

returns assumption. If we now assume that the cost per labour unit is £500, then the total cost of producing 500 units is £2,500 (5 labour units × £500 per labour unit). This labour cost will be for only 370 units of output if we take the economists' assumption of diminishing returns. Box 6.5 shows the derivation of cost curves from the production data given in Box 6.4, assuming that the cost per labour unit is £500 constant at any level of labour usage.

Cost curves are the direct result of production curves and show the relationship between level of production and resource cost.

BOX 6.5 DERIVATION OF COST CURVES FROM PRODUCTION CURVES

Constant returns to variable factor
The accounting's view

Variable factor (labour)	Total production	Total labour cost	Average labour cost	Marginal labour cost
0	0	0	–	–
1	100	500	5	5
2	200	1000	5	5
3	300	1500	5	5
4	400	2000	5	5
5	500	2500	5	5
6	600	3000	5	5
7	700	3500	5	5
8	800	4000	5	5
9	900	4500	5	5
10	1000	5000	5	5
11	1100	5500	5	5
12	1200	6000	5	5
13	1300	6500	5	5
14	1400	7000	5	5
15	1500	7500	5	5
16	1600	8000	5	5

Diminishing returns to variable factor
The economics' view

Variable factor (labour)	Total production	Total labour cost	Average labour cost	Marginal labour cost
0	0	0	–	–
1	30	500	16.67	16.67
2	86	1000	11.63	8.93
3	164	1500	9.15	6.41
4	260	2000	7.69	5.21
5	370	2500	6.76	4.55
6	490	3000	6.12	4.17
7	616	3500	5.68	3.97
8	744	4000	5.38	3.91
9	870	4500	5.17	3.97
10	990	5000	5.05	4.17
11	1100	5500	5.00	4.55
12	1196	6000	5.02	5.21
13	1274	6500	5.10	6.41
14	1330	7000	5.26	8.93
15	1360	7500	5.51	16.67
16	1360	8000	5.88	–

Total labour cost under constant returns to variable factor

Total labour cost under diminishing returns to variable factor

Marginal & average cost under constant returns to variable factor

MC = AC

Marginal & average cost under diminishing returns to variable factor

MC

AC

Equilibrium of firm and cost–volume–profit analysis

So far we have discussed the economic concepts of profit, revenue and costs, and how accountants use them. Now we will focus on the equilibrium analysis of the firm. Economists use the concept of 'equilibrium of the firm' to identify the level of production at which the firm can maximize its profits and, therefore, the level of production at which the firm should aim to operate. They use a specific economic theorem to locate this equilibrium level of production. That said, at the profit-maximizing level of production, marginal revenue (MR) should be equal to the marginal cost (MC). As we have already noted, the term 'marginal cost' means the addition to the total cost of an extra unit of production. Similarly, the term 'marginal revenue' means the addition to the total revenue of an extra unit of production. At a certain level of production, if MR > MC, then an additional unit of production will result in a greater increase in revenue than cost, and therefore the firm can further increase its profit by increasing its production. Similarly, if MR < MC, the firm is operating at a point beyond its optimum level of production. Then a reduction in production can decrease the total cost more than the total revenue and the firm can increase its profits simply by reducing its level of operation. The point is that in either case the firm is not at the optimum or profit-maximizing level of production, which can happen only if MR = MC . This neoclassical economic theory relating to the profit-maximizing behaviour of the firm is illustrated in Figure 6.3.

Economists use the concept of 'equilibrium of the firm' to identify level of production at which the firm can maximize its profits and, therefore, the level of production at which the firm should aim to operate.

KEY TERMS

Marginal cost (MC) is the addition to the total cost of an extra unit of production. Similarly, marginal revenue (MR) is the addition to the total revenue of an extra unit of production.

Profit is maximized only if MC = MR. Thus, graphically, a firm's equilibrium is at the point where the MR curve intersects the MC curve.

Figure 6.3 contains two panels. The first shows the most popular graphical presentation of the behaviour of the firm in economics. In this graph, the profit-maximizing point of the firm is arrived at through marginal and average cost and revenue curves. Thus, it shows the price, average cost and profit (the shaded area in the graph) at the profit-maximizing quantity of production. The second graph presents more or less the same, but by using the total values rather than the marginal and average values. Nevertheless, the second graph is more important to management accounting

177

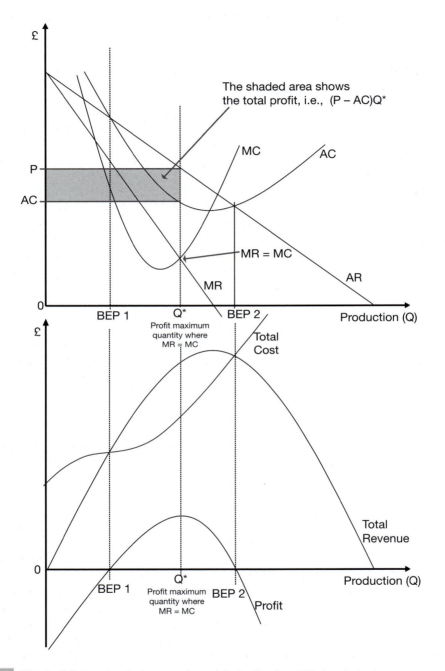

Figure 6.3 *Neoclassical economic model of a firm's equilibrium behaviour*

students, because we use that model in cost–volume–profit analysis, though with slight modifications of curves to be straight lines.

C–V–P analysis: management accounting application of the neoclassical economic model

Management accounting adaptation of the neoclassical economic model shown above is the cost–volume–profit analysis. The fundamental difference between accounting and economic application of this model is that in management accounting we adopt linear cost and revenue curves, implicating that we hold the assumptions of: perfectly competitive market scenarios which result in linear TR curves; and constant returns to variable factors which result in linear cost curves. Consequently, in the management accounting model, the problem of profit-maximization never arises, because a constant price independent of quantity offered to the market and constant returns to variable factors imply that the firm's profit potential has no limit, except for its own capacity to produce (i.e., the limits imposed by fixed factors). This is apparent in the ever-increasing gap between the TR and TC curves in the C–V–P diagram (see Figure 6.4). Hence, management accounting adaptation of the economic model ends up with identifying the break-even point (BEP), margin of safety and target profits for a budgeted level of output, etc.

> C–V–P analysis is the management accounting adaptation of the economic model of the firm. Since management accounting relies on linear cost and revenue curves, profit-maximization point of production is not applicable but concepts like BEP, margin of safety and budgeted level of output are in place.

However, this does not necessarily mean that the management accounting model is inferior to the economic model. Though it is not 'theoretically' sound, it is simple and pragmatic for managerial use, and readily applicable with the available information in organizational settings.

Fixed and variable classification of costs

The fundamental principle of C–V–P analysis is the classification of cost elements as 'fixed' and 'variable', which by and large resembles the economic classification of resources as fixed and variable factors. 'Fixed costs' relates to the fixed factors which cannot be changed in the short run. Changes in fixed costs denote long-run decisions leading to changes in the production capacity. Once committed, fixed factors bear costs which behave independently of the level of production. That is why they are called fixed costs: fixed at all levels of production within the current level of factory capacity. They could change only if there were changes in the capacity of production (i.e., fixed factors), not as a result of changes in the level of production. Figure 6.5 illustrates this property of fixed costs, which is often called 'stepping fixed costs' in popular management accounting texts. However, the C–V–P model is often adopted as a short-run decision-making model which helps to understand the profit impact of production decisions within a given level of capacity, so that fixed costs are held constant at 'possible' levels of production.

179

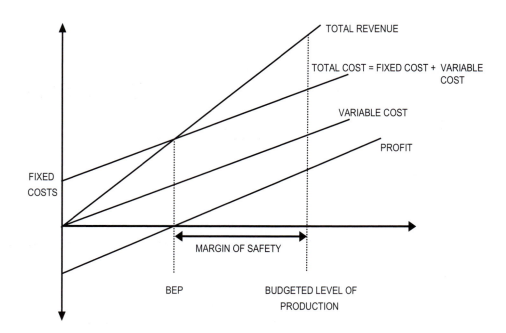

Figure 6.4 *C–V–P framework graphical presentation*

The fundamental principle of C–V–P analysis is the classification of cost elements as 'fixed' and 'variable', which by and large resembles the economic classification of resources as fixed and variable factors.

The C–V–P model is often adopted as a short-run decision-making model which helps us to understand the profit impact of production decisions within a given level of capacity, so that fixed costs are held constant at 'possible' levels of production.

It should also be noted that 'capacity' does not necessarily mean only physical facilities, such as machinery and buildings. Many other 'auxiliary facilities' to maintain them contribute to the capacity. They include, for example, managerial labour. Expenditure on such numerous resources adds up to fixed costs, for which the firm should commit, despite the level of production it aims to achieve.

'Variable costs', on the other hand, relates to the variable factors, which should vary with the level of production: to achieve a higher level of production, even within the current capacity, the firm should consume more variable factors, such as direct material and direct labour. Variable costs are easily understandable and calculable at unit level, because they often constitute the individual products (the cost objects), such as, for example, a given amount of raw material and a given

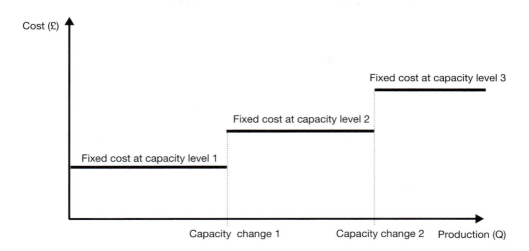

Figure 6.5 *Fixed cost and production capacity*

number of labour or machine hours per unit of output. Therefore, the fundamental element of variable cost is the variable cost per unit of output, and the total variable cost is a matter of the production level to be achieved. Thus, total variable cost is modelled as shown in the Figure 6.6.

Variable cost relates to the variable factors, which should vary with the level of production.

Changes in the variable cost per unit of output can occur for two reasons:

- Changes in market prices of resources, such as raw material prices, wage rates, etc.
- Improvements in the efficiency of resource usage in production. Under the assumption of constant returns to variable factor, efficiency improvements can be achieved only in the long

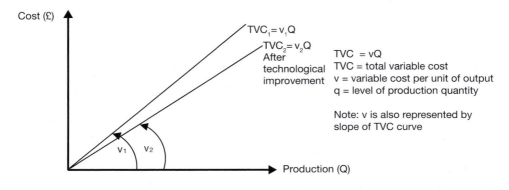

Figure 6.6 *Modelling variable cost*

run, as it demands changes in the scale or capacity of production and/or technology. Such capacity and technological changes should result in a downward pivot of the total variable cost curve, denoting a lower variable cost per unit of output.[2]

Changes in variable cost per unit of output can occur for two reasons:

■ changes in factor prices;
■ changes in efficiency of factor usage.

Again, changes in the variable cost per unit of output (the slope of the variable cost curve: v_1 and v_2, as shown in the Figure 6.6) can 'technologically' be achieved only in the long run, as they demand changes in the scale or capacity of production and/or technology. Such capacity and technological changes should result in a downward pivot of the total variable cost curve, denoting a lower variable cost per unit of output. Nevertheless, short-run changes in variable cost per unit can take place due to non-technological reasons, such as short-run fluctuations in factor prices like labour rates and material prices. This simply recalls the proposition that cost of production is a matter of: technology of production; and factor market conditions, which are subject to short-run fluctuations, while technological advancements always take place in the long run.

Putting them together: contribution, break-even and margin of safety

C–V–P analyses are based on accounting's specific profit concept, which we call the 'contribution'. As you should know from basic management accounting texts, contribution is the difference between sales and variable cost. At unit level, it is the difference between price and variable cost per unit of output. Thus,

$c = p - v$,
where: c is contribution per unit of output;
p is price per unit of output;
v is variable cost per unit of output.

KEY TERMS

Contribution is the difference between sales and variable cost. At unit level, it is the difference between price and variable cost per unit of output. Thus, $c = p - v$.

Management accounting applications of the C–V–P analysis are numerous. At the outset it is used to:

■ Determine break-even point – the level of production/sales at which the firm earns no profit and makes no losses, and beyond which the company can cover its fixed costs and earn a profit. In other words, BEP is the minimum level of production/sales needed to avoid making losses.

- Estimate profit at a target or budgeted level of production/sales.
- Estimate margin of safety (MoS). MoS is the difference between the current level of production/sales and the break-even level of sales, and indicates how far sales can be allowed to drop, in the worst-case scenario, before making any losses.
- Estimate level of sales/production required to achieve a target level of profit.

In addition, the C–V–P analysis framework can be used as a template of simulation to predict profit consequences of various possible events such as price changes, sales increases or decreases, effect of advertising, capacity developments, tax changes and so on. The Illustrative Case Example 6.1 demonstrates some ways in which the C–V–P framework can be used.

> A C–V–P analysis can be used to calculate: break-even point, margin of safety, profit at given level of output, production required for target profit and effects of changes in price, variable cost, etc.

Illustrative Case Example 6.1: C–V–P analysis

The following cost information is extracted from the standard cost card for product EXE:

- Direct material A: 10 units @ £5 per unit
- Direct material B: 2 units @ £15 per unit
- Direct labour: 3 hours @ £10 per hour
- Variable overheads: incidental on direct labour hours @ £5 per hour

It is also estimated that total fixed cost for next budget period is £18,000. Target price of product: £200 per unit.

What follows is an illustration of how these accounting data can be used in a C–V–P analysis.

Break-even point

We have the fundamental information required to carry out a C–V–P analysis: information relating to variable cost per unit of output, price and fixed costs. We begin our analysis by calculating the contribution per unit of output:

Direct materials:	
A – 10 units @ £5 per unit	£50
B – 2 units @ £15 per unit	£30
Direct labour – 3 hours @ £10 per hour	£30
Variable OH – 3 hours @ £5 per hour	£15
Total variable cost per unit (v)	£125
Price (p)	£200
Contribution (c = p – v)	£75

Note that contribution means the unit price less unit variable cost. A contribution of £75 per unit of output means that every unit of sales can 'contribute' £75 to recover the fixed costs, and thereafter, to the net profit. When this contribution is expressed as a percentage of price, it is called the contribution/sales ratio, or c/s ratio.

$$Contribution\ sales\ ratio = contribution\ per\ unit\ /\ unit\ sales\ price$$
$$= £75\ /\ £200 = 0.375$$

This means that every '£ of sales' (rather than a unit) can contribute 37.5 pence to recover fixed costs, and thereafter, to the net profit.

🔑 **KEY TERMS**

Contribution sales ratio = contribution per unit/unit sales price

---

Now, break-even point means the amount of sales required to recover the fixed costs. As fixed cost is £18,000 and as every 'unit of sales' can contribute £75 to recover that, the number of units required to recover fixed costs (i.e., BEP) is £18,000/£75 = 240 units. This commonsense logic is often represented in management accounting textbooks by the following formula:

$$BEP\ (in\ units) = \frac{fixed\ costs}{contribution\ per\ unit} = \frac{FC}{c} = \frac{FC}{(p-v)}$$

This formula can be derived mathematically as follows:

$Profit = total\ revenue - total\ cost,\ i.e.,\ \pi = TR - TC$
$Since\ \pi = 0\ at\ BEP,\ TR - TC = 0$
$As\ TR = pQ,\ and\ TC = FC + vQ$
$At\ BEP,\ \pi = pQ - (FC + vQ) = 0$
$\qquad = pQ - vQ - FC = 0$
$\qquad = (p - v)Q - FC = 0$
$\qquad = (p - v)Q = FC,\ therefore$
$\qquad Q = FC/(p - v)$
$As\ (p - v) = c,\ i.e.,\ contribution\ per\ unit,\ Q\ at\ BEP = FC/c$

Similarly, the BEP can be calculated and expressed in sales volume (i.e., in monetary value of sales rather than in physical units). The c/s ratio we calculated above indicates that every pound of sales will contribute 37.5 pence to recover the fixed costs. Therefore, the sales volume required to recover the fixed cost is £18,000/£0.375 = £48,000. Thus, a sales volume of £48,000 would provide neither profit nor loss for the company. Any sales above this point will contribute to net profit at a rate of 37.5 pence for every pound of sales (or £75 for every unit of sales). This is often stated by the following formula in management accounting textbooks.

$$BEP \ (in \ sales \ volume) = \frac{fixed \ costs}{contribution \ / \ sales \ ratio} = \frac{FC}{c \ / \ s}$$

Budgeted profit and margin of safety

The budgeted production for the period is 300 units. As contribution per unit is £75, this would result in a total contribution of £22,500 (i.e., £75 × 300). Since the fixed cost is £18,000, the net profit is £22,500 − £18,000 = £4,500. This is indeed the contribution of the units produced over and above the BEP, which are 60 units @ £75 per unit.

Margin of safety is the difference between the budgeted level of production and the BEP. As the BEP is 240 units, the margin of safety is 60 units. In sales volume, it is 60 × £200 = £12,000. This means the firm can tolerate a maximum of 60 units of £12,000 sales drop from the budgeted level of sales, as such a sales drop would not result in a loss.

Target profit

Net profit is the contribution of any units sold more than the BEP. To achieve a target profit of £6,000, number of units to be sold more than the BEP is 80 (i.e., target profit/contribution per unit = £6000/£75). As we have already calculated, the BEP is 240 units. Hence, 320 units in total (240 + 80) should be sold to achieve a target profit of £6,000. It is easy to understand that, out of 320 units, 240 units are just enough to break even while the rest contribute to the profit. This simple calculative logic can also be presented in a formula:

$$Quantity \ to \ be \ sold \ for \ target \ profit = \frac{fixed \ cost + target \ profit}{contribution \ per \ unit} = \frac{FC + \pi}{c}$$

If sales volume, rather than sales quantity, is to be estimated, then the formula takes the form:

$$Sales \ volume \ for \ target \ profit = \frac{FC + \pi}{c \ / \ s \ ratio}$$

For our example:

> *Sales volume for target profit of £6,000 = (18,000 + 6,000)/0.375 = 64,000, which is simply 320 units @ £200 per unit*

Illustrative Case Example 6.1 is graphically represented in Figure 6.7.

In summary, management accounting adaptation of the neoclassical economic model of the firm is the C–V–P analysis. In the process of translating from economics to management accounting, the model took rather a simplified version of linear functions of revenue, cost and profit, putting it in line with the cost information available through existing cost accounting systems. The theoretical implication of these linear functions is that the management accounting model of the firm assumes constant returns to variable factors and perfect market conditions. Despite these theoretical implications, the C–V–P framework remains pragmatic. Its use is extensive in managerial decision-making, because it provides a basic decision template for 'what-if analysis', where profit impact of changes in various decision variables, such as output prices, input prices, government regulations (such as tax rates) and so on, can be readily predicted and understood. This kind of analysis has been well facilitated and simplified by spreadsheet-based computer packages.

The contribution of the neoclassical economic model of the firm, and its management accounting derivatives of C–V–P analysis, to the construction of mechanistic organizational forms is deep rooted. One of the important properties of mechanistic organizational forms is the centrality of

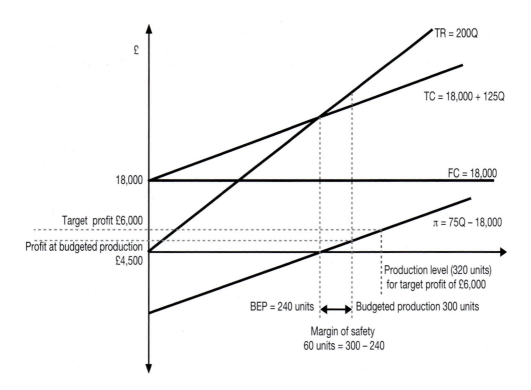

Figure 6.7 *Illustrative Case Example 6.1: C–V–P analysis – graphical representation*

186

> The C–V–P framework is simple and pragmatic. Its use is extensive in managerial decision-making, because it provides a basic decision template for 'what-if analysis', where profit impact of changes in various decision variables such as output prices, input prices, government regulations and so on can be readily predicted and understood.

profit as the main objective of the firm; in a mechanistic organization, managers are made to take it for granted that their utmost objective is to achieve greater profits. Thus, their primary decision criterion is the impact that a given decisional alternative would make upon the corporate profit. That means, in a typical decision-making scenario, managers have to make the selection that would most contribute to the organizational profit. Neoclassical economic theory of the firm, and its management accounting derivative of C–V–P analysis, provided a fundamental framework to operationalize this profit motive of the mechanistic organizations. They help capitalism to institutionalize the profit motive within organizational structures, processes and procedures, as well as in managerial ideologies, as to what constitutes better management. Thus, concepts such as contribution, opportunity cost and so on are mobilized to analyse and understand various operational decision scenarios. The next section of the chapter addresses some of these decision scenarios.

> Neoclassical economic theory of the firm, and C–V–P analysis, provided a fundamental framework to operationalize the profit motive of mechanistic organizations. They help capitalism to institutionalize the profit motive within organizational structures, processes and procedures, as well as in managerial ideologies, as to what constitutes better management.

Limiting factor analysis

Scarcity of resources is a universal truth: we do not have enough resources to do everything we need to do. This is equally applicable for managerial decision-making. Production decisions have to be made within certain resource constraints – limited availability of machine hours, man hours, raw materials, space and so on. In management accounting, these resource constraints are known as 'limiting factors'. Thus, limiting factor analysis entails the making of production decisions subject to limiting factor constraints.

The basic proposition of such analysis is the calculation of contribution per unit of limiting factor. This is an estimate of the opportunity costs of the limiting factor. In simple terms, contribution per limiting factor means the contribution that a unit allocation of the limiting factor to a given product can earn. Illustrative Case Example 6.2 will help you to understand this.

> Limiting factor analysis entails the making of production decisions subject to limiting factor constraints. The basic proposition of such analysis is the calculation of contribution per unit of limiting factor, such as contribution per labour hour, etc.

Illustrative Case Example 6.2: contribution per limiting factor

The following cost information has been extracted from the standard cost card for products X and Y.

	X	Y
Direct material cost per unit	£100.00	£120.00
Direct labour hours per unit	1.50	2.50
Direct labour cost per hour	£20.00	£20.00
Direct machine hours per unit	0.50	0.25
Machining cost per hour	£30.00	£48.00
Variable OH per unit	£20.00	£30.00
Selling price	£300.00	£400.00

Calculate the contribution of each product per direct labour hour and machine hour.

The starting point of our calculations is the contribution per unit of output, for which we have to estimate unit variable cost. We do this as follows:

	X	Y
Direct materials	£100.00	£120.00
Direct labour	£30.00	£50.00
Machining	£15.00	£12.00
Variable OH	£20.00	£30.00
Total variable cost per unit	£165.00	£212.00
Selling price	£300.00	£400.00
Contribution per unit	£135.00	£188.00

It seems that product Y has a higher unit contribution, and hence should take priority in normal production decisions if it is not subject to resource constraints. However, when we calculate the contribution per unit of man hours and machine hours (limiting factors or constrained resources), the situation may be different. Contribution per limiting factor is as follows:

		X	Y
A	Contribution per unit	£135.00	£188.00
B	Labour hours per unit	1.50	2.50
C = A/B	Contribution per labour hour	£90.00	£75.20

		X	Y
A	Contribution per unit	£135.00	£188.00
B	Machine hours per unit	0.50	0.25
C = A/B	Contribution per machine hour	£270.00	£752.00

188

Now it is clear that, in terms of labour hours, X is more profitable than Y. This means that in the case where labour hours are the scarce resource, thereby limiting the production possibility of both products, it is more profitable to produce X than Y. In the case of machine hours, Y is more profitable, and hence, it should receive priority rather than X in a case where machine hours are the limiting factor.

Let us assume that labour hours and machine hours are limited to 400 and 60 hours, respectively. And also assume that there are no demand constraints on these products – both products have market potential of selling what the firm can produce. Our problem now is to decide the most profitable product mix. Is it X only or Y only, or a specific mix of both?

Management accounting has borrowed from mathematical modelling techniques, especially linear programming, to solve this type of management problem. Thus, our problem can be modelled as follows.

The objective function is to maximize contribution. We take contribution rather than profit to be maximized because our production mix decision will not have an impact upon the fixed costs, and hence, whether we take net profit or contribution will not have an impact upon our decision. The objective function can be written as follows:

Maximize: $C_{tot} = C_x Q_x + C_y Q_y$,
  where: C_{tot} *is total contribution from both products;*
    C_x *and* C_y *are contribution per unit of X and Y, respectively;*
    Q_x *and* Q_y *are quantity to be manufactured from X and Y, respectively.*
Subject to:
    $0.5Q_x + 0.25Q_y \leq 60$ *(machine hour constraint)*
    $1.5Q_x + 2.50Q_y \leq 400$ *(labour hour constraint).*

> Linear programming is a mathematical modelling technique used to solve decision scenarios with more than one limiting factor and more than one product.

Thus, we have to find Q_x and Q_y that maximize the contribution. Using any spreadsheet application, we can easily find the solution for this model. (We used Microsoft Excel with its solver add-in.) The answer is that when we produce 57.14 units of X and 125.71 units of Y, we can achieve a maximum contribution of £31,348.57, and we will fully employ all available resources (i.e., 400 man hours and 60 machine hours). We can represent this model graphically (as far as there are only two variables to determine: i.e., two products in this case). The graphical presentation of the model is given in Figure 6.8.

This section provides us with two distinct messages. First, it shows how economic modelling is mobilized to solve management accounting problems. Second, it again exemplifies the message we highlighted above: economic concepts of the firm and associated mathematical modelling techniques help conceptualize and configure organizations in a rather mechanistic way – as an economic entity that can be modelled and programmed in the light of a unitary objective: maximization of profit.

189

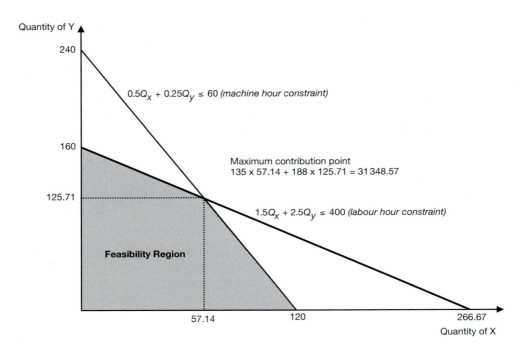

Figure 6.8 *Decision-making subject to limiting factors – graphical presentation of model*

Economic concepts of the firm and associated mathematical modelling techniques help conceptualize and configure organizations in a rather mechanistic way – as an economic entity that can be modelled and programmed in the light of a unitary objective: maximization of profit.

PROFIT MAXIMIZATION IN THE LONG RUN: ECONOMICS OF CAPITAL BUDGETING

So far, our discussion has concentrated on the economic model of short-run decision-making. It is short run because only the variable factors such as labour and machine hours are to be changed at a given level of production capacity. In that case, we understood that the decision is to determine the level of production that maximizes profits at a given production capacity. The production capacity, which is often expressed as the maximum number of machine or labour hours that can be accommodated by the available capacity, becomes the principal constraint for short-run production decisions.

Long-run decision-making, on the other hand, relates to capacity expansion in terms of acquiring new fixed assets and technologies. They are the investment decisions to shift the production possibility of the firm; once the firm commits to a capacity expansion, its production constraints shift upwards, enabling the firm to produce more, and to earn more profits in consecutive cycles of short-run production. In management accounting literature, such investment decisions to expand the production capacity of the firm are commonly known as 'capital budgeting decisions'.

Long-run decision-making relates to capacity expansions in terms of acquiring new fixed assets and technologies. They are the investment decisions which are commonly known as 'capital budgeting decisions' in management accounting.

It was John Maynard Keynes, back in 1936, who first proposed a general economic theory as to how firms should decide upon capital expenditures. From this theory popular capital budgeting techniques in management accounting have been derived. According to Keynes (1936: 135):

> When a man buys an investment or capital-asset, he purchases the right to the series of prospective returns, which he expects to obtain from selling its output, after deducting the running expenses of obtaining that output, during the life of the asset. This series of annuities Q1, Q2, . . . Qn it is convenient to call the prospective yield of the investment.

John Maynard Keynes in 1936 first proposed a general economic theory as to how firms should decide upon capital expenditures. From this theory popular capital budgeting techniques in management accounting have been derived.

In accounting terms, this series of annuities or prospective yield of the investment is known as 'future net cash flows', and calculated by adjusting non-cash flow items (such as depreciations, accruals, etc.) to the net accounting profit.

The Keynesian economic theory on capital investments is based on three interrelated concepts:

- present value of prospective yield (i.e., future net cash flows);
- marginal efficiency of capital;
- cost of capital.

The Keynesian economic theory on capital investments is based on:

- present value of prospective yield;
- marginal efficiency of capital;
- cost of capital.

Present value of future cash flows

As pointed out in the above quotation from Keynes, an expenditure of a capital nature would generate a series of annuities over the lifespan of the investment. In a very general manner, one would
think that if the sum of these future cash flows is greater than the investment made, then the given
investment is profitable. For example, suppose that we make an investment of £100,000 today and
expect a series of net profits (or net cash flows) during the lifespan of the investment (say 5 years)
as £20,000, £30,000, £30,000, £40,000 and £10,000. Thus, one would conclude at the outset
that this investment is profitable, because the sum of future cash flows (i.e., £130,000) is greater
than the initial investment (i.e., £100,000). This is the basic logic in certain capital budgeting techniques such as payback period, which does not employ the concept of 'present value of money'.

The present value concept, on the other hand, takes the opportunity cost of money into
account, and understands that a pound today is worth more than a pound next year. This means
simply a pound today can be invested somewhere and be turned into a greater sum. For example,
if the bank interest rate is 5 per cent per annum, £1 today would be £1.05 one year later, if it
is simply saved in an interest-earning bank account. This means, on the other hand, £1.05 to be
received next year is no more than just £1.00 in terms of today's money. This is what we call the
'time value' of money. The bank interest in this example is the 'opportunity cost' of money, or
'cost of capital' or 'discounting factor', as it is often called in management accounting.

> The present value concept takes the opportunity cost of money into account and understands
> that a pound today is worth more than a pound next year because of the opportunity of
> investing money today and earning a return for it next year. This possible return is the oppor-
> tunity cost of capital or simply the cost of capital.

Thus, if we take this time value of money into consideration, it is clear that simple comparison
between the sum of future cash flows and initial investment is flawed as a criterion for investment
decisions. Instead, we should consider the *sum of present value of future cash flows* discounted by an
appropriate cost of capital (k).

The present value of a future amount of money (FV) to be received in n years from now, where
the cost of capital is k per annum, is mathematically expressed as follows:

$$PV = \frac{FV}{(1 + k)^n}$$

KEY TERMS

Present value (PV) of a future sum of money (FV) is calculated as:

$$PV = \frac{FV}{(1 + k)^n}$$

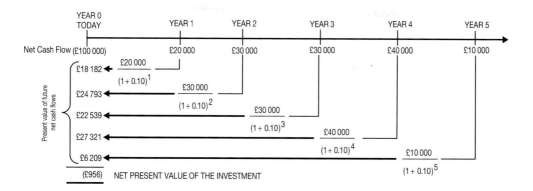

Figure 6.9 *Net present value criterion of investment*

Now we can reconsider the simple example we discussed above. Accordingly, we should convert all future cash flows into their present values so that their sum is comparable with the initial investment. Figure 6.9 illustrates this calculative logic, assuming a cost of capital of 10 per cent per annum (i.e., $k = 0.10$).

As illustrated in Figure 6.9, the 'net present value' is the decision criterion and an investment is selected as profitable in the long run only if the net present value is positive. That said, the sum of present values of all future net cash flows is greater than the initial investment at the selected rate of cost of capital. In our example, the cost of capital is taken as 10 per cent, and the investment should not be selected, as its net present value (NPV) is negative. This means the investment concerned would not earn a higher return than the return possible from the best alternative investment option, which, for example, could be saving in a bank account with an interest rate of 10 per cent per annum.

An investment is selected as profitable in the long run only if the net present value is positive. That said, the sum of present values of all future net cash flows is greater than the initial investment at the selected rate of cost of capital.

Marginal efficiency of capital (MEC) and internal rate of return (IRR)

Marginal efficiency of capital (MEC), which translates into management accounting as internal rate of return (IRR), is the Keynesian economics criterion for investment decisions. Keynes wrote (1936: 135): 'I define the marginal efficiency of capital as being equal to that rate of discount which would make the present value of the series of annuities given by the returns expected from the capital-asset during its life just equal to its supply price.'

If we use our general notation, this is the specific discounting rate at which the NPV of an investment becomes zero. For our example discussed above, this would be 9.6216 per cent. (You can easily calculate IRR for a series of values using spreadsheet formula.) If we use 9.6216 per cent

193

($= 0.096216$) as the discounting factor, the NPV of the project should be zero, and any discounting factor smaller than IRR should result in a positive NPV, which implies that the investment is profitable. Hence, the decision criterion related to MEC or IRR is that the cost of capital (k) should be smaller than the IRR for an investment to be profitable. According to Keynesian economic theory, when the cost of capital (which is called the marginal cost of capital, as it is the cost to be incurred for an additional unit of capital) is equal to the MEC, the firm is in long-run equilibrium, implying that it has reached its optimum level of capital investment. Any investment above or below this level would cause the firm to deviate from its long-run profit maximization point. However, it should be noted that, in management accounting, we never try to assess whether the firm is at its long-run profit maximization point. Instead, we assess individual investment projects or capital budgets for their long-run profitability in line with time value of money, using IRR and NPV criteria. Thus, marginal efficiency of capital (or IRR) becomes a benchmark against which we compare the cost of capital of a given investment project to assess that project independently, or to compare it with other alternatives available.

MEC, which translates into management accounting as IRR, is the Keynesian economics criterion for investment decisions. This is the specific discounting rate at which the net present value of an investment becomes zero.

The decision criterion related to marginal efficiency of capital or IRR is that the cost of capital (k) should be smaller than the IRR for an investment to be profitable.

According to Keynesian economic theory, when the marginal cost of capital is equal to the marginal efficiency of capital, the firm is in long-run equilibrium, implying that it has reached its optimum level of capital investment.

Cost of capital

The cost of capital is the opportunity cost of capital, which is the return that a similar amount of capital can earn from the best alternatives available. Thus, it represents required rate of return, as any return below that means an opportunity loss. As we already noted, the cost of capital is also the rate at which we should discount the future net cash flows to arrive at NPV of investment.

The cost of capital is the opportunity cost of capital, which is the return that a similar amount of capital can earn from the best alternatives available. Thus, it represents required rate of return, as any return below that means an opportunity loss.

However, when this theoretical meaning is borrowed for pragmatics of management accounting and finance, some complexities arise. One of these is that capital comprises different sources bearing different capital cost structures. For example, an investment project may be financed partly by equity capital (share capital) and partly by debt capital. In that case, the cost of capital that we use to assess the long-term profitability of the investment should consist of costs of both debt and equity capital elements, which would have different cost structures. The general practice is to calculate what is called weighted average cost of capital (WACC).

> In a case where an investment is financed by more than one source of capital with different capital costs, the management accounting convention is to use weighted average cost of capital (WACC).

Another complexity is the capital structure or gearing that any corporate entity should maintain. Gearing means the proportion or percentage of debt capital that the company maintains vis-à-vis equity capital. Economic theory assumes that there is an optimum gearing structure at which the firm can minimize its cost of capital. Once the firm reaches this gearing structure, any additional financing from one source of capital should accompany a proportionate amount of capital from the other sources that represent the existing capital structure in order to maintain the optimum capital structure.

Given the need to maintain the optimum capital structure (assuming that the firm is currently at its optimum structure composed of both equity and debt capital), any new investment should consist of both debt capital and equity capital, for which the firm may bear different rates of cost of capital. Thus, estimating cost of capital involves first estimating cost of individual capital elements, then estimating the WACC. We will show this by using a simple example of a hypothetical investment project (see Illustrative Case Example 6.3).

> Economic theory assumes that there is an optimum gearing structure at which the firm can minimize its cost of capital. Once the firm reaches this, any additional financing from one source of capital should accompany a proportionate amount of capital from the other sources that represent the existing capital structure.

Illustrative Case Example 6.3: cost of capital and capital structure

XYZ Limited is considering a proposal to increase its production machinery by investing £50 million, of which £10 million can be financed internally by retained earnings. Its external financing options include a debenture issue at par at an interest rate of 11 per cent per annum. Preference shares will have an 11.5 per cent gross dividend payment and will sell at their nominal value. Company ordinary shares, which have a nominal value of £1 per share, will sell at £5 per share and can be sold at net £4.50, that is, after flotation cost of 10 per cent on issue price. It is assumed that a starting dividend of 30 pence per share with an annual growth rate of 8 per cent would be

195

applicable for ordinary shares. The corporate tax rate is 40 per cent. In order to maintain the current capital structure, which is considered to be optimum, the management has decided to finance the investment project as follows:

- Retained earnings: £10 million
- New ordinary shares: £15 million
- Preference shares: £5 million
- Debentures: £20 million

What follows is an exemplified calculation of WACC.

A careful reading of the case information above reveals that the proposed capital investment should be financed by four different types of capital component: retained earnings, new ordinary share issues, preference shares and debentures, all of which would have different cost structures.

Cost of debenture capital

Calculation of cost of debenture capital is straightforward, as debentures are debt capital for which the firm should pay a definite annual interest. Thus, the annual interest rate, which is 11 per cent, represents a fair estimate of cost of capital sourced by debentures. However, it should be noted that interest is a tax-deductible expense, and hence encompasses a tax saving which should be taken into account when calculating the cost of debt capital. Therefore, economic theories express the cost of debt capital as:

After-tax cost of debt, $k_{b-t} = k_b(1-t),$
where: k_b *is interest rate;*
 t is the corporate tax rate.

As interest rate is 11 per cent and tax rate is 40 per cent in our example, the after tax cost of debt is:

$$k_{b-t} = 0.11 \times (1 - 0.40) = 0.066 = 6.6\%$$

Cost of debt is the agreed rate of interest adjusted to any tax savings: $k_{b-t} = k_b(1-t)$

Cost of preference share capital

Calculation of cost of preference share capital is also straightforward, as it carries a fixed rate of dividends. Thus, similar to debt capital, the specified preference dividend rate would be the expected cost of preference share capital. However, unlike debt capital, preference dividends are not a tax deductible expense, and thus are not affected by the corporate tax rate. For our example, therefore, 11.5 per cent can be taken directly as the cost of preference share capital element of the investment project.

Cost of preference shares is the specified rate of preference dividends.

Cost of ordinary share capital

Economics theory prescribes at least four different ways of estimating cost of ordinary share capital:

- capital asset pricing model (CAPM);
- debt yield plus equity risk premium;
- realized investor yield;
- dividend growth model.

The first three methods are fundamentally related to financial market information, while the last can largely be operationalized from internal management accounting information. Therefore, in this very brief discussion on the notion of cost of capital, we will concentrate on the last one only. This is also because our purpose here is not to engage in a detailed discussion on the methods of estimating cost of capital, but rather to clarify the notion of cost of capital in understanding how Keynesian economic theory contributed to conceptualize modern mechanistic organizations. If you are curious to gain a further knowledge of the other models, refer to any standard managerial finance textbook.

There are a number of theoretical models to calculate the cost of ordinary share capital. Some of them are related to financial market information, while others can be operationalized from internal management accounting information.

According to the dividend growth model, the cost of equity capital is generally expressed as:

$$Cost\ of\ equity\ capital = k_s = \frac{d_1}{P_o(1-f)} + g,$$

where: d_1 is expected dividend at end of first year;
P_o is issue price of ordinary share;
g is dividend growth rate;
f is flotation cost as % of the issue price.

When we apply this general formula to our case example, where d_1 is £0.30, P_o is £5, f is £0.50 and g is 8 per cent, we have:

$$k_s = \frac{0.30}{5(1-0.10)} + 0.08 = 0.1467 = 14.67\%$$

197

The dividend growth model calculates the cost of equity capital as:

$$k_s = \frac{d_1}{P_o\,(1-f)} + g$$

Cost of retained earnings

Retained earnings are the undistributed profits of a company. Simply because they are internally available, one should not consider that retained earnings have no cost. Though they do not involve any explicit payments to outside parties, they do have an opportunity cost because they, like any other source of funds, can be invested elsewhere and earn a return. Thus, they do have an expected return, which is the cost of capital. However, the problem is estimating this implied cost. The most common assumption is that cost of ordinary share capital can be readily applicable to the retained earnings as well. Thus, economic theory suggests adopting the same dividend growth model we discussed above, but with the adjustment of flotation cost. Since the retained earnings are internally available, they do not bear any issuing or flotation cost. Thus the, value of f in the above formula becomes zero and the formula itself simply becomes:

$$Cost\ of\ retained\ earnings = k_r = \frac{d_1}{P_o} + g$$

Calculations for our example, therefore, are as follows:

$$k_r = \frac{0.30}{5} + 0.08 = 0.14 = 14.00\%$$

Cost of ordinary share capital can be readily substituted for the cost of retained earnings, but with the necessary adjustments to the flotation costs, as retained earnings do not bear such costs.

Weighted average cost of capital (WACC)

According to our Illustrative Case Example information, four sources of capital have to be combined to form the total capital applicable to the investment project concerned. So far, we have calculated the individual cost of capital for each of these sources.

Now, WACC means simply the average of these component costs weighted by their relative significance in the total capital structure. Thus,

$$WACC = 14.00 \times 20\% + 14.67 \times 30\% + 11.50 \times 10\% + 46.60 \times 40\% = 10.99\%$$

Element of capital required	Component cost (%)	Proportion of total capital
Retained earnings (k_r)	14.00	10 (20%)
New ordinary shares (k_s)	14.67	15 (30%)
Preference shares (k_{ps})	11.50	5 (10%)
Debentures (k_b)	6.60	20 (40%)
		50 (100%)

WACC means simply the average of component costs of capital weighted by their relative significance in the total capital structure.

This is the rate that the firm should use to discount its future net cash flows to arrive at NPV of the project. Or, if IRR is used, this rate should be compared with the IRR, and if the IRR is greater than WACC (i.e., 10.99 per cent), then the capital investment is profitable in the long run.

Now, let us assume that this investment has a five-year lifespan and the estimated net cash flows are £10, £15, £20, £25 and £5 million, respectively, for the next five years. Together with the initial cash outflow of £50 million, these future net cash flows would result in an IRR (or MEC, if we use Keynesian terms) of 14.9737 per cent, which is greater than the WACC of 10.99 per cent, indicating that the investment is worth pursuing. The same conclusion can be arrived at through the net present value as well (see Table 6.1).

In summary, this section dealt with the contribution of Keynesian economics for the management accounting techniques of capital budgeting. Here, we understood that the most popular capital budgeting techniques of NPV and IRR are derivations of the Keynesian economic concepts of time value of money, marginal efficiency of capital and the cost of capital. As a result, we showed that Keynesian economics provided the basic theoretical foundations upon which management accounting, in practice, modelled the firm as an economic entity which attempts to maximize shareholders' wealth, which is defined as the NPV of all future net cash flows of the firm. This, of course, is long-run expansion of the short-run profit-maximization objective which we discussed in the previous section.

Table 6.1 Net present value calculation

Year	(A) Net cash flow (£ million)	(B) Discounting factor at $k = 0.1099$	(C) = (A) × (B) Present value (£ million)
0	−50	$1/(1 + 0.1099)^0 = 1.0000$	−50.0000
1	10	$1/(1 + 0.1099)^1 = 0.9010$	9.0098
2	15	$1/(1 + 0.1099)^2 = 0.8118$	12.1765
3	20	$1/(1 + 0.1099)^3 = 0.7314$	14.6278
4	25	$1/(1 + 0.1099)^4 = 0.6590$	16.4742
5	5	$1/(1 + 0.1099)^5 = 0.5937$	2.9686
Net present value			5.2569

199

ECONOMIC MODELLING OF THE FIRM

Neoclassical economics made a remarkable contribution towards the construction of mechanistic organizational forms. Neoclassical economic frameworks not only provided theoretical lenses through which we conceive organizations, but also help develop a pragmatic set of management accounting tools used in day-to-day managerial decision-making. Their combined effect was that organizations were conceptualized as mathematical 'models' with definite objective functions, decision variables and decision constraints. That means organizations are conceptualized as types of 'machines', with specific functional objectives and parameters that govern their behaviour. Attempts were made to reduce everything in those organizations to programmable objectives, constraints and variables, so that managers, with the use of appropriate mathematical or managerial tools and techniques, can effectively programme them. Thus, neoclassical economics complemented the historical project of constructing mechanistic forms of organizations started by the Scientific Management movement in the nineteenth century.

> Neoclassical economic frameworks help develop a pragmatic set of management accounting tools used in day-to-day managerial decision-making. Their effect was that organizations were conceptualized as mathematical 'models' with definite objective functions, decision variables and decision constraints.

Neoclassical economics and its derivatives of management accounting modelling of the firm encompass a set of parameters. These parameters are illustrated in Figure 6.10, and are discussed in the list below.

1. The demarcation between long- and short-run decision-making scenarios. Long-run decision-making is related to the acquisition and/or disposal of 'fixed factors' which determine the 'production capacities' of the firm, and hence release the capacity constraints on the short-run decision-making. Short-run decision-making, on the other hand, is associated with the determination of the level of production and sales within a fixed capacity of production. Thus, short-run decision-making manifests decisions on the optimum use of 'variable factors' within a fixed production capacity.

2. Specific short- and long-run objectives assigned to business enterprises. In line with the long-run and short-run demarcation of decision scenarios, neoclassical economic theories and their derivative management accounting techniques first assign shareholders' wealth maximization as the long-run objective of the firm. Having defined wealth as the NPV of all future net cash flows of the firm, profit-maximization is taken as the short-run objective of the firm.

3. Set of decision criteria to guide long-run investment decisions. Long-run decision scenarios, often termed 'capital budgeting decisions' in management accounting, are to be understood through the theoretical lenses of Keynesian economics. As we noted earlier, Keynes' theorization of how firms should make investment decisions rests on two major economic notions: marginal efficiency of capital; and marginal cost of capital. The decision criterion is that the marginal efficiency of capital, which manifests the potential of the investment to generate future cash flows, termed IRR in management accounting, should be greater than the cost of

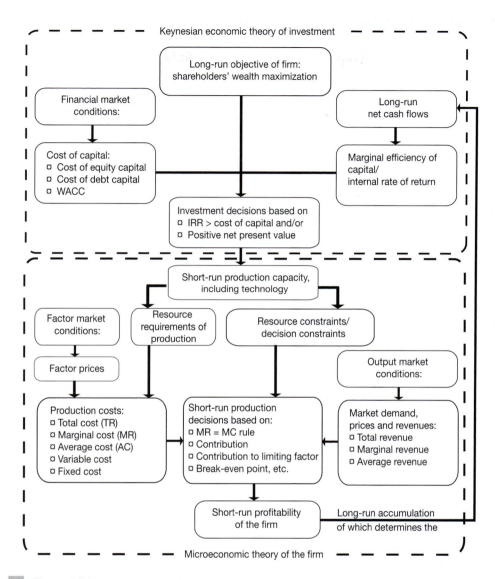

Figure 6.10 *Neoclassical economic configuration of mechanistic organizations*

capital applicable to that investment project. The same decision criterion can also be expressed slightly differently in terms of NPV of the project, such that the NPV of an investment project should be positive if it is to be selected.

4. The link between long- and short-run decision scenarios. The former are linked to the latter through production capacity. On the one hand, production capacity, including technology, is the fundamental organizational variable to be determined by capital budgeting techniques. On the other hand, once decided by capital budgeting decisions, the production capacity becomes the decision parameter which gives rise to resource constraints within which

201

short-run production decisions have to be made. Not only that, capital budgeting decisions, by way of determining appropriate production technologies, determine the fundamental technical parameters of the production and cost functions of the firm.

5. Set of decision criteria to guide short-run investment decisions. These decision scenarios are to be understood through the neoclassical microeconomic theory. Microeconomic theory postulates the relationships between production and cost, on the one hand, and market structures and the firm's sales revenue, on the other. The technical relationship within the production function between input and output is manifested by the assumptions of 'marginal returns to variable factor'. For example, as we noted earlier, assumption of constant return to variable factor in the production function results in straight line cost curves. Similarly, the perfectly competitive conditions in the output market give rise to straight line revenue curves, as often depicted in management accounting textbooks. In this way, microeconomic theory specifies that marginal revenue should be equal to marginal cost (the MR = MC rule) at the level of production that maximizes short-run profits. With adaptation of straight line cost and revenue curves, management accounting derives various decision rules and techniques, such as C–V–P analysis, limiting factor analysis, linear programming, etc., to guide various short-run decision-making scenarios.

Neoclassical economics and its derivatives of management accounting modelling of the firm encompass a set of parameters:

■ The demarcation between long- and short-run decision-making scenarios.
■ Specific short- and long-run objectives assigned to business enterprises.
■ Set of decision criteria to guide long-run investment decisions.
■ The link between long- and short-run decision scenarios.
■ Set of decision criteria to guide short-run investment decisions.

In this way, neoclassical economic theory conceptualizes economic enterprises as an economic machine with the ultimate functional objective of maximizing its shareholders' wealth, or, in other words, capital accumulation in the long run. Specific configuration of this machine is depicted in Figure 6.10. Note that the figure also summarizes all we discussed in this chapter. Accordingly, it should be clear that the primary contribution of neoclassical economic theory to management accounting is that it provided the fundamental theoretical foundation upon which we built a set of short- and long-run decision tools to ensure that the firm would achieve its assumed objectives of wealth and profit maximization.

Neoclassical economic theory conceptualizes economic enterprises as economic machines with the ultimate functional objective of maximizing their shareholders' wealth, or, in other words, capital accumulation in the long run.

THE OTHER PERSPECTIVE: ACCOUNTING AS THE META-THEORY OF ECONOMICS?

The relationship between accounting and economics was depicted in this chapter as one in which economics is the meta-theory of certain management accounting concepts and tools. That means we presented certain management accounting techniques as mere derivatives of neoclassical economics. However, this conception has its critics. Some argue the reverse, positing that the relationship between accounting and economics is one in which accounting is the 'master-metaphor' for economics (Thompson, 1998). For example, Klamer and McCloskey (1992), after analysing a series of seminal works in neoclassical economics, traced how they were based upon 'prior' accounting conventions and analytical devices, such as stock and flow concepts. Nevertheless, the conventional wisdom remains that economics is the meta-theory of accounting. It should, however, be remembered that this conventional wisdom has been reasonably challenged.

> There are alternative perspectives which argue that accounting provided the 'master-metaphor' for neoclassical economics, rather than economics being the 'meta-theory' of accounting.

HAVE YOU UNDERSTOOD THE CHAPTER?

1. In terms of their evolutionary roots, how do you differentiate between product costing and C–V–P analysis?
2. What are the defining properties of the neoclassical economic model of the firm?
3. What is the difference between economic and conventional accounting conceptions of profits? How has management accounting incorporated the economic conception of profit?
4. How should the assumptions of perfectly and non-perfectly competitive market conditions be reflected in the shape of the total, marginal and average revenue curves?
5. What are the different technological assumptions that we can hold on the relationship between output and variable factor input?
6. How should different technological assumptions on production be reflected in cost curves? What technological assumption of production is implied in linear cost curves?
7. Explain the economic rule that a firm should meet in order to maximize its short-run profits.
8. Illustrate the neoclassical microeconomic model of the firm's equilibrium behaviour. How far does C–V–P analysis in management accounting resemble this neoclassical economic model of the firm?
9. Differentiate between fixed and variable cost in relation to fixed and variable factors of production.
10. What is the difference between long- and short-run decision scenarios? Which branches of neoclassical economics are more relevant for each of these decision scenarios?
11. Prove mathematically that BEP = FC/contribution per unit.
12. Explain, in general terms and notions, how a linear programming model can be used to solve multi-product, multi-constraint short-run decision scenarios. Specify the objective function and the constraints.

13. Define the term 'shareholders' wealth maximization'.
14. List and briefly describe the main concepts of Keynesian theory of investment.
15. Explain how cost of capital is calculated when an investment project is financed by multiple sources of capital.
16. Discuss the contribution of neoclassical economics in the construction of mechanistic forms of organizations. How does it programme the short- and long-run decision scenarios in terms of economic variables and objectives?

BEYOND THE CHAPTER

1. 'The theoretical foundation of management accounting is neoclassical economics.' Discuss.
2. Discuss the link between short-run and long-run decision-making.
3. Discuss how the assumption of 'economic-rational man' is replicated in management accounting practices.
4. Discuss how Milton Friedman's doctrine that the 'social responsibility of business is to increase its profits' is replicated in management accounting.

FURTHER READING

1. For economic treatment of cost, revenue, profit and firm's equilibrium analysis, see Chrystal and Lipsey (1997).
2. For management accounting treatment of C–V–P analysis, including linear programming-based limiting factor analysis, see Drury (2004).
3. For cost of capital and investment decisions, see Gitman (2006).

Part II

Post-mechanistic approaches to management accounting

Chapter 7

Towards customer orientation and flexible manufacturing

A STARTING POINT: ENCOUNTERING JAPANESE

In the 1980s, most American firms faced a business crisis under pressure from Japanese competition. Caterpillar Inc., which has a plant in Decatur, Illinois, that produces earth-moving equipment such as motor graders, wheel tractors and scrapers and off-highway trucks, was one of them. The crisis faced by Caterpillar was marked by losses totalling almost $1 billion, which led to a closure of six plants, laying-off 44 per cent of casual and 26 per cent of salaried workers.

In response to the crisis, Caterpillar rethought its way of doing things. A new programme called 'Plant with a future' (PWAF) was introduced in the mid-1980s. In May 1989, Caterpillar opened a new plant called 'Assembly Highway'. This was a complete transformation of the production process that reordered the plant, previously located in two separate buildings, into a single building. To do this, products were identified as core and non-core, and all non-core products were outsourced. Production process of all core products was subject to enormous simplification, automation and integration. The new plant became the Assembly Highway as a value-adding entity through the concepts of lean manufacturing, where work was handled by spurs along with multi-task sub-assembly. When the redesign of the plant took place, four critical steps were considered – consolidation, simplification, automation and integration. These changes linked with the plant's control system by redefining accountability within the context of computerized plant. In doing so, the plant was to be constructed as a set of independent manufacturing cells integrated through a computer network. The accountability of individuals was redefined along with the functioning of these manufacturing cells rather than with distinct bureaucratic procedures. The cells became 'small businesses', and a group of workers collectively contributed to them as their 'proprietors'. The workers were entrusted to produce a complete part on their own, and all the cells did the same in respect of different parts. Within the Assembly Highway, all the cells became integrated through the computer network towards delivering what Caterpillar promised to the customer. Moreover, the accounting system in the plant embraced the ideal of competitor cost analysis, and this accounting system began to emphasize the need of customer focus. (Adapted from Miller and O'Leary, 1994.)

SETTING THE SCENE

The evolution of mechanistic forms of organizations and their management accounting and control apparatuses were the concerns in Part I. We noted that, with the industrial revolution in the West, the mechanistic forms of organizations began to emerge and then became the most pervasive, dominant and idealistic forms of business enterprise. However, during the last two decades or so, it is evident, as in the Caterpillar case above, that the mechanistic form has begun to transform into another configuration which we call 'post-mechanistic'. American management guru Peter Drucker (2000: 3) calls this new form of organization 'postmodern', and argues that its essence will not be mechanical but a conceptual combination of a set of emerging principles and practices such as total quality management (TQM), new manufacturing accounting, modular organization of manufacturing processes and a system approach embedding physical processes of making things in the economic processes of creating value. Indeed, Drucker focuses on certain 'managerial' implications of a period of global transition from what we have inherited since the eighteenth-century industrial revolution. Sociologists have employed a series of terms to characterize this transitional time: post-industrial, post-Fordist, postmodern, post-bureaucracy, globalization and McDonaldization are among the more popular. They are, of course, not alternative terms for the same thing but alternative theoretical phenomena addressing different aspects and levels of wider socio-economic and technological changes that have been taking place for a quarter of a century or so. Thus, one thing is clear: 'something dramatic has been happening to the international economy over the past two decades' (Hirst and Zeitlin, 1991: 1); and, as a result, new forms are emerging as alternatives to mechanistic forms of organizations and production systems.

> Something dramatic has been happening to the international economy, and mechanistic forms of organizations and production systems are in transition.

The aim of this chapter is to outline the major attributes of this transformation, and thereby set the background for the forthcoming chapters, where we will elaborate on management accounting implications of this transition. In this chapter, three particular dimensions of change are highlighted: customer orientation, flexible manufacturing and post-bureaucracy. The argument here is that customers came to be dominant over other stakeholders, and so became influential in the determination of production systems and organizational forms. These, hitherto configured to maximize shareholders' returns through standardization and economies of scale, were to be reconfigured to meet the highly dynamic, fragmented and differentiated needs of the customers. Thus, our main concern here is how and why mechanistic organizations, during the last two decades or so, had to reorient towards the customer and reconfigure themselves as market-driven, flexible organizations.

First, we will discuss the totality of the change. The aim of this section is to help you grasp the major arenas in which the post-mechanistic changes are occurring. Here, you will also be provided with a framework to understand categorically the overall change. By reading this section you will gain an overview of the multifaceted, multi-layered and paradoxical nature of the change.

■ To gain an overview of the post-mechanistic change taking place

The second section will cover changes in the global context. Along with the concept of globalization, this section will introduce you to global forces behind globalization of markets, products and brands. After reading this section you will understand two things: politico-economic forces behind globalization and business implications of globalization.

- ■ To understand politico-economic forces behind globalization
- ■ To understand business implications of globalization

The third section takes you from global context to business intents to show how changes in global context are implicated in corporate goals and objectives. After reading this section, you will understand that globalized, fragmented and volatile market contexts have forced business organizations to move beyond traditional financial to strategic emphasis in their corporate intents. You will also understand the pluralistic nature of post-mechanistic corporate stakes.

- ■ To understand how changes in global context implicate corporate goals and objectives

The fourth section deals with how and why mass production began to transform into flexible manufacturing regimes. We will begin the discussion on this transition process by concentrating on the crisis of mass production. After reading this section, you will understand this crisis in terms of specific macroeconomic, microregulatory and global political reasons, as argued in celebrated industrial sociology literature.

- ■ To understand why and how mass production entered a crisis

After dealing with the crisis of mass production, we shall introduce the notion of flexible manufacturing as an evolutionary solution to that crisis. In this section, before launching into sociological theories of flexible manufacturing, you will first learn the generic meaning of 'flexible manufacturing' as often dealt with in accounting literature. Then comes 'flexible manufacturing' in its sociological contexts, where we will deal with certain sociological theories, namely post-Fordism, flexible specialization, postmodernity and post-bureaucracy. The aim of this section is to offer you a broader sociological understanding of the flexible manufacturing regimes through the lenses of popular sociological theories.

209

- ■ To understand flexible manufacturing as it is comprehended in accounting literature
- ■ To understand flexible manufacturing in a wider spectrum of sociological theories

Finally, the chapter culminates in a discussion of how post-mechanistic changes in organizational contexts, intents and contents have implications for management accounting concepts, tools and practices.

- ■ To understand how post-mechanistic changes in business contexts, intents and contents have implications for management accounting

POST-MECHANISTIC CHANGE – UNDERSTANDING THE COMPLEXITY AND TOTALITY

Before anything else, we have to recall one important aspect of the historical transformation of production systems and organizational forms: they never take place in a socio-political vacuum. They are the products of transitions taking place in wider socio-political and economic contexts, and the challenges they raise to the prevailing production systems and organizational forms. For example, as we noted in Chapter 2, the transition from craft to mass production was the result of a set of wider politico-economic events and movements such as the industrial revolution, colonialism and the growth of 'modern' social ideologies and political apparatuses like democracy. Now, in the late modern age, which some indeed call 'postmodern' or 'post-industrial', there is another set of 'historical'[1] conditions that transforms the contexts, intents and contents of economic organizations.

Historical transformations of production systems and organizational forms are the results of wider socio-political transformations.

These historical conditions are multilayered, multifaceted and paradoxical. They are multilayered because the changes are taking place both 'out there', changing conditions of the global society, and 'in here', working on us (Hall, 1988). 'Out there' in the global arena, there is a convergence of nation states into global markets; whether they are small, big or mega, firms all converge into global markets. Managers, politicians, journalists and academics all talk about 'globalization', 'global markets', 'global competition', 'global strategies', 'global corporations' and so on. Customers from all corners of the world literally have the opportunity of buying from anyone anywhere else in the world through various modes of co-ordinating global transactions, including internet-based 'market spaces'. 'In here', at individual levels, whether we like it or not, we have been absorbed into 'global' ways of doing things: our day-to-day activities of work, consumption, communication, social interaction and so on are overwhelmed by a vast variety of 'global' products and technologies. At the organizational level, in contrast to what they believed thirty or so years ago, organizational leaders have begun to embrace flexibility and change rather than stability; empowerment rather than control; teamwork rather than individualization; multi-skilling rather than de-skilling; trust rather than power and command; and so on. This is a holistic change: changes are simultaneously taking place at all possible levels from global economy to organizational apparatus to individual psychology, making it rather difficult to trace cause and effect. We are being changed by what happens 'out there', but it is we who make that change happen, at least as consumers who are finally ready to absorb costs and benefits of what is happening 'out there'.

> Post-mechanistic historical conditions are multilayered, multifaceted and paradoxical.

> Changes are simultaneously taking place at all possible levels, from global economy to organizational apparatus to individual psychology, making it rather difficult to trace cause and effect.

The current change is multifaceted. It is technological, because it constitutes a dramatic change in the technologies we use and the technologies that are used to govern us: a shift from Fordism to post-Fordism; from mechanical to digital; from cogwheels to electronic chips; from manual assembly lines to fully automated robotic manufacturing; from close manual supervision to CCTV cameras; from telephone to web-based video conferences; and so on. It is organizational and managerial because it constitutes a fundamental change in the way we conceptualize and manage our organizations: from bureaucracy to post-bureaucracy; from mass production to lean production; from 'just-in-case' to 'just-in-time'; from shareholders to stakeholders. It is political because it is fascinated by a new global political order: from economic conservatism to liberal economics embracing a 'free' global economy; from export and imports of goods to foreign direct investments; from Cold War to global capitalism; from nation states to regional economic unions (such as the European Union); and from private capital to transnational corporations. The change is also cultural, manifested not only in art and architecture but also in corporate communication and everyday lives of people. As a whole, in cultural terms, as Hall (1988: 25–26) argues, this change 'celebrates the penetration of aesthetics into everyday life and the ascendancy of popular culture over the high arts . . . remark(s) on the dominance of image, appearance, surface-effect over depth . . . the blurring of image and reality . . . the preference for the popular and the decorative over the brutalist or functional in architectural designs'.

As Firat and Venkatesh (1993: 237) point out, there is a wide-ranging consensus among post-modernist theoreticians that one of the major characteristics of the postmodern is its paradoxical

211

Current change is multifaceted: it is technological, organizational, political and cultural. It is also paradoxical.

nature which permits the juxtaposition of anything with anything else, however contradictory they may be. Things which were hitherto seen as contradictory and conflicting are now seen as things that should and can be integrated and de-differentiated to create new wholes. Thus, simultaneous loose tight controls, specialization and flexibility, control and empowerment and so on are at the centre of agendas creating post-mechanistic organizations.

Though there is widespread agreement that something dramatic has been happening to the international economy and polity, international and national cultures, managerial ideologies, production technologies, forms of industrial organizations and control systems, there is also a great deal of confusion about how to characterize these changes. Hirst and Zeitlin (1991), for example, identify three superficially similar but theoretically divergent sociological approaches to explain the changes: flexible specialization, regulation theory and a diverse body of post-Fordist analyses, which one could easily make more complicated by adding a diverse body of postmodern analyses as well. However, the purpose of this chapter is not to engage in such a sociological debate about the characterization of these changes but to devise a simplified framework in which we can identify and appreciate the changes that management accounting has sought in the midst of such turbulence. Thus, entirely for simplicity, we will reduce these changes to three hierarchical levels: context, intent and content of post-mechanistic organizations (see Figure 7.1).

Something dramatic has been happening to the international economy and polity, inter-national and national cultures, managerial ideologies, production technologies, forms of industrial organizations and control systems, but there is a great deal of confusion about how to characterize these changes.

Though Figure 7.1 presents a hierarchical framework from global to organizational, we do not propose that the influence is one-directional. It is true that we identify wider global and society-level factors and forces to be the constituent elements of the 'context', and such forces and factors do shape and reshape 'intents' and 'contents' of industrial organizations. However, it is equally true that those global forces and factors are the cumulative results of changes in the contents and intents of organizations, at least of those organizations which define the future of markets and industries. For example, product and process innovations in industry's leading firms like Microsoft, Toyota, Sony and Panasonic (Matsushita Corporation) determine the context for many other firms. Similarly, intents of firms, which are often manifested by corporate vision, mission, philosophies and objectives, are the two-directional interface between firms' contents (technologies, processes, structures, cultures, resources and competencies, etc.) and demands imposed by the changing context. Thus, the relationship is dialectical, meaning that context, intents and contents all shape and reshape the others while simultaneously being reshaped by the others (hence, the two-directional arrows in Figure 7.1). In the next few sections, we will discuss the themes illustrated in Figure 7.1.

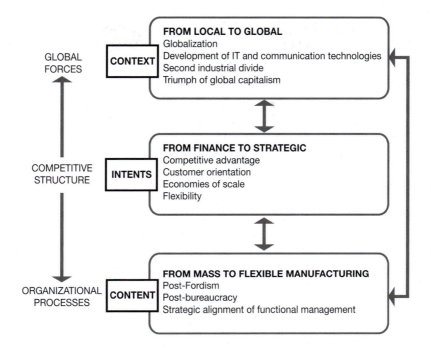

Figure 7.1 *Hierarchy of post-mechanistic changes*

The relationship between organizational context, intents and contents are dialectical; each shapes the others.

CHANGING CONTEXT: FROM LOCAL TO GLOBAL

'Globalization' is the generic term used to characterize the transition taking place in the international context. In its very generic meaning, globalization refers to the trend of global integration of economic, political and cultural activities across national boundaries. At the heart of globalization lies the convergence thesis, which asserts that societies become increasingly alike in their social, political and cultural characteristics, as well as their work organizations (Watson, 2003: 70). This integration takes place due to the emergence and growth of global markets, global firms and global brands – three defining characteristics of globalization. Global markets are the networks of exchanging relationships through which selling and consumption of global brands across national boundaries take place. Global markets signify a convergence of consumption patterns. Thus, Ohmae (1985), for example, has discussed the 'Californianization of society', with teenagers in São Paolo, Bombay, Milan and Los Angeles listening to the same music, using the same Walkman and wearing the same pair of blue jeans. This convergence of consumption is facilitated by the growth of global brands – such as Sony, Panasonic, Toyota, Kodak, Fujitsu, etc. – that have successfully established their names as symbols of global quality and prestige. Global firms, which dominate global markets through global brands, are transnational or are becoming transnational. That means their national identity is disappearing or becoming less important as their finance, production and distribution operations are diversified across national boundaries. Thus, Toyota is not necessarily 'made in Japan'. Such transnational companies' stocks and bonds are traded in major stock exchanges across the globe; their managerial expertise is recruited from everywhere; their factories are located in a number of countries; their labour force is multinational; and their products are appreciated and demanded in all corners of the world. Thus, for example, American capital can operate in China, employing Chinese labour and Korean management, to produce a Japanese design of an electronic product to be sold in the European market, which is more or less differentiated from its American or Asian counterpart by regulatory restrictions on regional differentiations. In that way, globalization is characterized by three defining trends: emergence of global markets, firms and brands.

> In its very generic meaning, globalization refers to the trend of global integration of economic, political and cultural activities across national boundaries through the emergence and growth of global markets, global firms and global brands.

Globalization is made possible by a set of underlying technological and political changes which have taken place over the last few decades. Given below is a very brief introduction to them.

1. Developments in technologies of information, telecommunication and physical transport and travel. These have made the 'distance' insignificant in terms of accessibility and costs of accessibility. Markets mean the networks of exchanging relationships, the global market being that relationship taking place across national boundaries. The basis of such a market relationship is the flow of information, which is made easy and less costly by new IT and telecommunication devices and networks so that production, consumption and distribution can be co-ordinated across the globe. Co-ordination and control of a geographically dispersed set of factories, distribution centres and service centres around the world by a central head office is no longer so challenging as to prohibit the global presence of a company. Even the physical movement of goods and people is becoming easier and less costly. Thus, Theodore Levitt (1983: 92), a Harvard-based marketing guru, noted,

    > A powerful force drives the world toward a converging commonality, and that force is technology. It has proletarianized communication, transport and travel . . . The result is a new commercial reality – the emergence of global markets for standardized consumer products on a previously unimagined scale of magnitude.

2. Triumph of global capitalism and liberal economics. Global political circumstances during the last two decades or so were very conducive to globalization. On the one hand, the collapse of the Soviet Bloc ending the Cold War marked a triumph of global capitalism, which significantly wrote off any alternative ideological policy frameworks for economic development. On the other hand, developed as well as developing countries embarked on a policy agenda of free trade among nations by gradually dismantling various international trade and investment

barriers, and also engaged in the integration of nation states into regional economic syndicates such as the European Union, which provided the necessary legal and political infrastructures for unified systems of trade, investment and businesses.

3. Second industrial divide refers simultaneously to a new global division of labour and a new paradigm of industrial organizations in the industrial West – flexible specialization. Theorists like Piore and Sabel (1984) have argued that there is a new international division of labour in which certain manufacturing industries, which heavily depend on unskilled labour working on semi-automated assembly lines, are shifted to low-wage areas of the Third World, while knowledge-intensive activities such as R&D and design are retained in the West. As a result, de-skilling and mass production have become the order of the day in the Third World, while post-Fordist variants have started to gain ground in the West. (We will discuss the concepts of post-Fordism and flexible specialization later in this chapter.)

4. The rise of Japan as a competitive threat to the Western business monopoly, especially in the automobile and electronic industries, two industrial sectors that lead industrial development, is often quoted as a competitive imperative to redefine Western models of managing industrial organizations. Indeed, the Japanese models, for the first time in history, started to question the currency of hitherto well-accepted business models of mass production. American failure vis-à-vis Japanese success is explained in two ways. First, there is the macro-economic issue of undervaluing the Japanese yen against the US dollar. It is argued that, in the case of Caterpillar and Komatsu, the latter enjoyed a 14 per cent unearned price advantage, simply due to the undervalued yen. Thus, in this sense, America's competitiveness against Japan was taken as a macroeconomic policy matter to be addressed by government policy-makers (Miller and O'Leary, 1994: 23). Second, there is an issue relating to the conduct of manufacture in American factories that leads to a relatively higher cost structure in comparison with their Japanese counterparts.

Forces behind globalization include:

- Developments in technologies of information, telecommunication and physical transport and travel.
- Triumph of global capitalism and liberal economics.
- Second industrial divide.
- Rise of Japan.

The business implications of globalization of markets were multiple and strategically critical. Markets became volatile, fragmented and risky for individual companies. No organization, big or small, is immune to the risk of failure and collapse, unless it is creative and flexible enough to deal with changing market conditions, namely competition and customer demand. Firms need to be sensitive and adaptive to changing output market conditions, more than capital market conditions. Hence, customers and competitors should receive focal attention in strategic and operational analyses and decision-making. Thus, competitive market positioning and customer satisfaction become defining parameters of 'new' decision-making models vis-à-vis hitherto

215

prevailing profit-maximization models. Profit has become a necessary condition, rather than an objective, to support achievement of other long-term purposes spelled out in company vision and mission statements.

> Competitive market positioning and customer satisfaction become defining parameters of 'new' decision-making models vis-à-vis hitherto prevailing profit-maximization models.

Globalized markets mean greater rivalry among firms in the market, and greater threat of new entrants and substitutes. Thus, firms are compelled to seek ways and means of differentiating their products from those of competitors. The result is that consumers are given a greater market choice than before, and markets are apparently fragmented and segmented. The marketing implication of this is that 'mass marketing' is replaced by S–T–P marketing, so-called strategic marketing: segmentation, targeting and positioning. Identifying strategically appropriate target market segments and effectively positioning the firm's brands in those segments using effective and efficient 'marketing mix' strategies have become the essence of marketing success (see Kotler, 2003).

> Globalized markets mean greater rivalry among firms in the market, and greater threat of new entrants and substitutes. Firms are compelled to seek ways and means of differentiating their products from those of competitors.

These market implications of globalization are clearly reflected in a remarkable transition of business ideologies and intents from financial to what we call strategic. The next section will provide a brief introduction to this strategic turn, and it will be dealt with in more detail in the next chapter.

CHANGING ORGANIZATIONAL INTENTS: FROM FINANCIAL TO STRATEGIC

Globalization and its market implications, discussed above, have definite implications on corporate intents and philosophies. By the term 'intents' we mean long-term goals for which the company as a socio-economic entity should strive. These are often communicated by companies through their vision, mission and corporate objective statements. Such communications on corporate intents manifest commonly held top-management ideologies on strategic priorities of the organizations towards which they are ready to commit their resources and opportunities. A quick reading of various company communications, such as annual reports and corporate websites, can help you easily understand the current pattern of change. The following points are noteworthy.

1. In contrast to the tendency of emphasizing financial information (i.e., accounting reports) in the past, there is now a greater emphasis on strategic intents, such as vision, mission, corporate philosophies and corporate objectives, even though companies are not legally compelled

to do this. It seems that setting a clear vision for the future and letting the world know what it is have been deemed essential tasks in postmodern corporate ideologies.

2. Pluralism is evident in the way companies communicate their intents. Moving away from neoclassical economic models of shareholders' wealth-maximization, companies now emphasize the strategic significance of balancing the conflicting needs of different stakeholders, including environmental sustainability. Everybody related to the organization, ranging from shareholders to employees to society at large, is viewed as a party whose well-being the firms must consider.

3. Operational emphasis has shifted from comparative advantage to competitive advantage. The difference is that comparative advantage holds that the firm's capacity to outperform its competitors arises from its manufacturing excellence, mainly economies of scale which ensure that a firm's opportunity costs of producing what it sells are lower than that of competitors. Competitive advantage, on the other hand, shifts attention to the market from the factory. It implies that the firm's capacity to outperform competitors rests on the market positioning strategy it selects, and the relative attractiveness of the market segments in which the firm decides to position its products (see next chapter for details).

4. As a corollary to the competitive advantage theory mentioned above, the notion of economies of scale is replaced by 'economies of scope'. It is often argued that scope, which is the domain of related or unrelated businesses included in a corporation's business portfolio, is strategically more crucial than the scale of individual businesses.

5. Organizational learning, change and flexibility have come to the very forefront of organizational philosophies, so that they are no more considered to be 'means' but 'ends' in themselves. Especially the notion of 'flexibility' has become the guiding philosophy of organizational designs; various processes and systems are designed primarily to accommodate flexibility.

6. Integration of financial and non-financial measures as the indicators of organizational, divisional and individual performance.

An overall reorientation of organizational intents has taken place from unitary objectives of profitability towards multiple, market and change-oriented strategic intents.

Popular marketing texts (e.g., Kotler, 2003) often label this transition in business philosophy as one from 'production concept' to 'marketing concept'. The production concept is a business philosophy which holds that consumers prefer products that are widely available and inexpensive. Its concentration is on high production efficiency, low costs and mass distribution. Companies tend to follow this philosophy when they do not encounter severe market competition, especially in growing markets where selling is not yet a problem. In such a case, firms enjoy monopoly power over customers, as the market choice for customers is limited. As the production value can be readily realized in output markets, efficient capacity utilization is the primary focus of management. Marketing concepts, on the other hand, become highly relevant when the markets are saturated, fragmented and highly competitive. In such a scenario, buyers enjoy relatively greater bargaining power. Firms learn that profits can be realized only through customer satisfaction. Thus, the logical starting point for all organizational activities is identifying and understanding

217

customer needs. Production systems and processes should be geared to meet the conditions these needs impose.

> A transition from production concept to marketing concept is taking place.

FROM MASS TO FLEXIBLE MANUFACTURING

Changes in the global context and their ramifications in corporate intents demand a dramatic transition from mass production to more flexible manufacturing regimes. By the term 'flexibility in production systems' what we mean is the capacity to carry out small-batch operations without compromising the quality and the costs of production. In other words, it is the capacity to carry out 'craft production', but with a cost structure equivalent to or better than that of mass production. Thus, flexible manufacturing is in a way revisiting 'craft production' with superior technologies and systems of controls. Then, we have a fundamental question: 'What made the capitalist firms revisit craft production with a new technological change?' This would lead us to understand the 'crisis of mass production' before moving into detailed discussion of the salient characteristics of flexible manufacturing.

> Flexibility in production systems means the firm's capacity to carry out small-batch operations without compromising the quality and the costs of production.

The crisis of mass production

By reading Chapter 2, you should have learned that the emergence of mass production can be explained through Taylorism and Fordism, which came into being at the start of the twentieth century. Consequently, large-scale manufacturing industries became major players on the economic front. As Murray (1988) showed, certain economic conditions should be met for mass production to be a successful economic strategy:

- There should exist a mass market. That said, the mass public should have the required purchasing power and willingness to buy standardized products.
- Mass advertising must play a central role in establishing mass consumption norms. That said, the products coming through a mass production assembly line should be made to appeal to the ego needs of the mass public, thus making consumption of them fashionable. As a result, the marginal propensity to consume, to use Keynsian economic jargon, should be at its maximum, to ensure the circular flow of funds back to the firms from households as consumption expenses (which are the firms' sales income).
- Necessary infrastructure such as housing, education and roads must be in place; the circular flow of income between firms and households should be regulated by the government through proper fiscal, monetary and international trade policies, so that economic issues such as unemployment, inflation, income disparity and poverty are kept to a minimum.

218

■ As you already know, mass production systems entail a high fixed cost, which demand a high volume of sales to recover that fixed cost and earn profits. Thus, protected national markets must be established to recoup fixed costs at home, while competing on the basis of marginal costs at the global level.

Essential conditions for mass production:

- mass markets;
- mass consumption norms;
- social infrastructure;
- protected national markets.

Overall, what the above four points spell out is the balance between demand and supply, or production and consumption. In simple terms, mass production cannot persist without a system of mass consumption. Thus, the government and other regulatory institutions should make sure that the balance between production and consumption is maintained. However, the Great Depression in the 1930s witnessed a problem of ensuring this balance across national economies around the world. In turn, large industrial firms became vulnerable to sudden falls in demand. Keynes then prescribed that actions should be taken to increase demand, which led to the development of the welfare state. Responding to such prescriptions, mass producers such as Ford began to raise workers' wages. Governments interfered to establish more effective wage and welfare systems to increase mass consumption. In this way, with the necessary infrastructure and governing systems in place, as Piore and Sabel (1984: 165) argue, for the first two decades after the Second World War, mass production systems produced great prosperity and social stability. Economic growth was rapid and steady, inflation was moderate, unemployment was generally low, and there was a general feeling of well-being, especially in industrial countries. However, this golden period was short lived.

> Starting in the late 1960s, the industrial world entered a time of troubles. One economic disruption succeeded another. As the conviction spread that events could not be explained – much less reversed – by the theories and policies of the preceding epoch, the economic disruptions merged in the public mind into a general crisis of the industrial system . . . The crisis began with widespread expressions of discontent and social unrest; then came raw-material shortages (especially oil crisis), followed by rapid inflation, rising unemployment, and finally economic stagnation. In the United States and elsewhere, these signs of crisis raised questions about the fundamental social and economic institutions. There were halting attempts to reconstruct corporations, unions, and the state.
>
> (Piore and Sabel, 1984: 165)

The balance between production and consumption is essential for the persistence of mass production regimes. The crisis stemmed from the breakdown of this balance.

219

Piore and Sabel (1984) propose two interrelated reasons for this crisis in the mass production epoch. First were external shocks to the industrial system stemming from events and trends such as labour shortage produced by the revolt of marginal labour force, especially black and immigrant labour in the USA; food shortage occasioned by poor Soviet harvests; and the oil shortages of 1973 and 1979. The results of such external shocks were slow economic growth, low productivity gains and rising unemployment, which led to a deficiency of demand for mass production, and consequently a breakdown of mass markets.

The second reason that Piore and Sabel provide was the incapacity of late 1960s institutional structure to accommodate the spread of mass production technology. That means macroeconomic policy and corporate governance frameworks which prevailed at that time were not supportive enough for further development of mass production across national boundaries. The post-war regulatory system, argue Piore and Sabel (1984: 184), had been designed to promote economic expansion within the borders of discrete nations, not outside them. However, by the late 1960s, domestic consumption of the goods that had led the post-war expansion had reached its limits, especially in the USA. On a global scale, there was no mechanism to ensure that the world economy would be accessible and grow at the rate required to justify new investments in mass production facilities. What occurred was therefore a shortfall of demand which accompanied a greater competition for larger share of a limited market.

In short, by the early 1970s, the mass production system, as a total system of production, consumption and regulation, was in crisis mainly due to its own incapacity to maintain the balance between demand and supply.

The crisis was addressed in two ways. First there were global economic and political policy reformations: economic policy-makers addressed the world-wide unemployment and stagnation with instruments of domestic economic control and global economic integration of nations (Piore and Sabel, 1984: 194). The result was the embracing of open economic policies and globalization of markets, which we discussed in earlier sections of this chapter. The second attempt to tackle the crisis was at the level of individual firms. As was shown in the case of Caterpillar, leading manufacturing firms in the USA and elsewhere, following the Japanese initiative, embarked on their own programmes of flexible manufacturing as a solution to problems of mass production. The focus of the next few sections in this chapter is to give an overview of flexible manufacturing. Specific management accounting techniques associated with it will be discussed in Chapters 9 and 10.

The crisis of mass production was addressed in two ways:

- through macroeconomic political and policy reformations;
- through the introduction of flexible manufacturing at the organizational level.

Flexible manufacturing: genesis, meaning and context

The predecessor of flexible manufacturing was mass production, which formed a context for the conventional wisdom of management accounting. As you read in Chapter 2, the fundamental proposition of mass production was that economies of scale derived from the production of similar products in high volume can sustain the profitability of business firms. However, the validity of economies of scale was questioned when competition became acute from the 1970s onward. The competitive environment did not guarantee continuous improvements in turnover, even though economies of scale guaranteed low-cost production. As you read in previous sections, the importance of customer-orientation came to outweigh the advantages of economies of scale that were embedded in production-orientation. Rather than producing similar products with similar functionalities for all customers, a need arose to produce different products with different functionalities for different customers. The question now is how a firm can deal with this new demand. Flexible manufacturing has become part of the answer to that question. Consequently, the conventional wisdom of management accounting which developed in the context of mass production no longer fitted, and alternative forms of management accounting practice have emerged around the world. The Caterpillar case is an exemplar of this. Before considering this development further, we shall clarify the notion of flexible manufacturing.

What is flexible manufacturing?

The terms 'flexible manufacturing', 'advanced manufacturing' and 'manufacturing flexibility' are used interchangeably to mean the shift from production-oriented mass production to customer-oriented flexible manufacturing. Broadly, flexible manufacturing crosscuts two main disciplines: engineering and management. In engineering terms, it is a change from a mechanical to an electronic/digital orientation of plants, machines, tools and processes. Given that the ideals of mechanical engineering are still fundamental to production technologies, the above shift marks an emergence of 'mechatronic engineering', which combines mechanical principles with computer-aided manufacturing technologies (Grimshaw *et al.*, 2002). Engineering faculties in many universities have started to offer new degree programmes in this emerging technology with a view to producing 'right personnel' for new manufacturing realities. Our aim is not, however, to explore this unfamiliar territory.

> The terms 'flexible manufacturing', 'advanced manufacturing' are 'manufacturing flexibility' are used interchangeably to mean the shift from production-oriented mass production to customer-oriented flexible manufacturing.

We need to define the term considering the implication of flexible manufacturing for management (and accounting) practices. A good starting point is the observation by Abernethy and Lillis (1995: 242): 'Manufacturing flexibility is reflected in a firm's ability to respond to market demands by switching from one product to another through co-ordinated policies and actions and a willingness or capacity to offer product variations.' According to Abernethy and Lillis, flexible manufacturing entails two main interrelated managerial tasks: flexibility and integration.

Flexibility is the firm's ability to switch from one product to another when different customers demand different production with multiple functionalities. The old mechanical engineering environment did not permit this flexibility. Within the new 'mechatronic' technological environment, plants became characterized by various electronic-oriented technologies, including computer-aided manufacturing (CAM), computer-aided design (CAD), computer-integrated manufacturing (CIM), flexible manufacturing and assembly cells (FMC and FAC), etc. These technologies allowed

> Flexible manufacturing entails two main interrelated managerial tasks:
>
> ■ flexibility;
> ■ integration.

the production engineers to reprogramme production tasks to produce different products. Dugdale and Jones (1995: 192) described this: 'Flexibility refers to the reprogramming of AMT (Advanced Manufacturing Technology) so that it can be used for several different products, with the facility to switch rapidly between them.'

Large firms such as Caterpillar realized that this technological transformation was needed to create a customer-oriented production system. With no such technological transformations, many firms suffered from the problem of continuity. As a result, a huge number of Western manufacturing firms collapsed or at least became unprofitable and untenable (Ashton *et al.*, 1995). In contrast, the firms, especially those in the Japanese automobile industry, equipped with flexibility triumphed in the market (McMann and Nanni, 1995).

The second principle is integration: linking the divisions/departments which were separated under the regime of mass production. As you saw in Chapter 2, mass production rested on the ideals of bureaucracy which created divisions and departments through a cluster of responsibilities. This separation did not allow the firms to respond quickly to market demands. For example, production departments had to wait for product design departments, and marketing departments had to wait for production departments. With the emergence of CAD/CAM-like technologies, firms began to integrate the functions of these divisions and departments with a view to responding to customers' changing needs. Mouritsen (1999: 32) observed this transformation as follows:

> firms reorganise their production spaces to support throughput and flows of goods and introduce information technology to underscore a lateral ordering of the firm. The plant with a future and new commercial agenda empowers supervisors and workers and makes them accountable to each other and to the customers. The hierarchical ordering of the firm is transformed into a lateral one, or at least the 'governable person' is supplemented with the 'governable process' across the plant's spaces of flows . . . which emphasises throughput – a set of material and information flows organised in and across organisations – and heralds flexibility, productivity and innovation.

Integration here means transformation of bureaucracy into a governable organizational process where everybody works together to satisfy the customers. It is a new accountability system where ultimate accounts are given to the customers. It is a new manufacturing space where never-ending innovations take place as the customers demand variations. It is an exciting context for management accountants in which they need to seek alternative methods of calculation, analysis and reporting. We shall elaborate on this orientation later in the chapter.

> Integration means transformation of bureaucracy into a governable organizational process where everybody works together to satisfy the customers.

One point must be noted here. The definition given above of 'flexible manufacturing' has largely drawn on accounting. However, accounting is still in its infancy in the exploitation of this concept as a broader social and organizational concept. At the moment, the concept has been taken for granted, and it is assumed that 'flexible manufacturing' is technologically superior to mass manufacturing, and could force the surrender of conventional management accounting. When we look at broader social science literature the case is debated, especially where empirical conditions are concerned. Flexible manufacturing is an ideal type requiring empirical explanations as to what extent this new production system is universal and how it is actually practised in different industries and regions. Not only that, much accounting and managerial literature on 'flexible manufacturing' considers it in isolation, detaching it from its socio-political and regulatory context, as a mere technological phenomenon that managers should strive to install within their industrial settings. Therefore, it is important to understand the sociological connotations of the concept. The next section will lead to that.

Accounting and managerial literature on 'flexible manufacturing' considers it in isolation, detaching it from its socio-political and regulatory context, as a mere technological phenomenon that managers should strive to install within their industrial settings.

Flexible manufacturing in its sociological context

Although we concentrate on organizational changes in respect of flexible manufacturing, there is a historical and social origin which would broaden our understanding of management accounting practices in modern organizations. Since the 1980s, social scientists have begun to develop concerns about the fact that 'something dramatic has been happening' to production technologies and industrial organizations (e.g., Hirst and Zeitlin, 1991). This is an observation about the emergence of a post-mechanistic form of production. Writers have used several terms to describe this form. We shall concentrate on four complementary terms: 'post-Fordism', 'flexible specialization', 'postmodernity' and 'post-bureaucracy', which provide different descriptions of the different aspects of the post-mechanistic change.

The post-mechanistic change has been associated with broader intellectual terms, along with different conceptual connotations such as post-Fordism, flexible specialization, postmodernity and post-bureaucracy.

Post-Fordism

As the wording implies, post-Fordism is something after Fordism. The notion of post-Fordism is proposed in social sciences as the end of the Fordist era and, therefore, must be understood in stark comparison to it. As we explained in Chapter 2, mass production or Fordism is the assembly-line model where special-purpose machines and unskilled labour are used to produce standard products on a large scale, with a view to selling them in mass markets. Economies of scale, efficiency of large-scale plants, separation of conception and execution, logic of comparative advantage, etc., were some of the dominant features of Fordism. These features are contextualized by a Fordist society characterized by a working class, with full-time unskilled or semi-skilled blue-collar male workers employed by large plants in large industrial cities. Their life pattern is constructed as 'proletarianized city life', in sharp contrast to the 'country life', where life is relatively self-subsistent.

> Post-Fordism is proposed in social sciences as the end of the Fordist era and, therefore, must be understood in stark comparison to it.

Drawing from Murray (1988: 8), we can identify the following technical principles upon which the Fordist industrial system is based, and from which its limitations stem (see also Chapter 2):

1. Standardization. Products and their components are standardized and, hence, their manufacture can also be standardized, which means, as we noted in Chapter 2, minute division of labour and task specialization, or, in other words, application of Taylorism.
2. Flowline production. This is the organization of divided work in a logical sequence on assembly lines. In contrast to 'nodal assembly', where workers move to and from a standstill work or product (node), flowline production keeps the workers stationary and moves the product on a conveyer belt, so that each worker or a special-purpose machine performs that work repeatedly at a standard speed determined by the speed of the flowline itself.
3. Special-purpose machines which cannot be utilized for any other purpose. Thus, Fordist manufacturing systems not only involve a huge investment and a fixed cost in special-purpose machinery but are also inflexible in their commitments to standard products. The special-purpose machineries can neither be used for manufacturing of any other products nor be discarded before their large initial investments are fully recovered.

> Defining characteristics of Fordism (from which its limitations also stem):
>
> ■ standardization;
> ■ flowline production;
> ■ special-purpose machines.

During the golden period of Fordism, inflexibility was not a problem but a necessary condition for efficient manufacturing. Inflexibility was very well twinned with the notions of standardization and bureaucratic control, where changes or deviations from standard are considered as problems (see Chapter 4 on budgeting and standard costing). In such a context, flexibility was not encouraged, as it did not possess any market relevance; there was ample demand for standardized products coming through mass-production assembly lines. As we noted in a previous section, when flexibility was made a necessary condition of manufacturing by external market conditions, and when inflexibility became a problem, post-Fordism originated as the solution. It rests on the principles of flexible manufacturing which presume that a better competitive advantage can be gained by offering different product varieties for different segments of the market through a lean production system which can manufacture differences at a competitive cost. In this sense, post-Fordism is what comes after Fordism as a solution for the evolutionary crisis of Fordism, and consists of the following characteristics:

1. Differentiation of output. In contrast to the classic case of the Model-T Ford, the symbol of mass production and mass marketing, manufacturers in the automobile industry, for example, now offer varieties. Customers are provided with choice of colours, number of doors, engine capacity and many more options, including financial options. The ultimate end of this product differentiation process is identified as 'mass customization', where a product is designed and manufactured to meet the needs of individual customers. While variety provides the choice for customers, customization provides the ability to specify the product. In a DELL web store, for example, you can specify from a given set of choices the configuration of the computer that you want to buy. In many automobile manufacturers' websites also, similar customization options are provided.

2. Modular production. While flowline or assembly-line technology resembles the technological core of Fordism, post-Fordism's flexible manufacturing systems provide for lower-cost customization and varieties through the use of modular design principles, which involves designing standardized sub-components of a product or service which can be put together in different ways to create a wide choice of varieties (Slack et al., 2004). As the product is designed as a set of modular components, each component can be manufactured independently of the others. Thus, each modularity is organized as an autonomous production centre, or can be outsourced to another company with superior technological capabilities to produce it at a lower cost. Either way, standardization and its associated economies of scale are gained at the level not of total product but of its modular components.

3. Computer-aided integration of production. Modular design of product and processes demands a sophisticated co-ordination between, and control of, autonomous production centres, both inside and outside the organization. When customization (customer given ability to choose between modular preferences) is in place, there should also be an appropriate customer interface through which the customer can communicate preferences with the relevant modular production centres and/or other organizational units. Three interrelated technological developments have facilitated this co-ordination, communication and control: computer-aided design (CAD), computer-aided manufacturing (CAM) and networking technologies. In Fordist systems, the assembly line itself provided the 'physical' means by which de-skilled labour was co-ordinated and controlled; labour and machines were physically located along the assembly line, and were made to work according to the speed enforced by the assembly line itself. As much as possible, customers were detached from the manufacturing core in order to minimize 'interference', which at that time was considered as a bottleneck for manufacturing efficiency. In post-Fordist manufacturing, on the other hand, co-ordination and control are 'virtual'; autonomous modular production centres are linked to each other through computer programs which provide online interfaces to communicate between themselves, as well as with the customers.

225

4. Multi-skilled labour. The new manufacturing realities have considerably altered the condition of factory labour. While many manufacturing tasks are robotized, factory labour is increasingly engaged in electronic control of processes. Though this may not necessarily mean a reversal of de-skilling in the sense that labour is engaged in a full cycle of production, including both conception and execution, it implies that the labour is provided with a 'new' set of skills and tasks which can effectively be perceived by the labour as 'empowerment'.

Defining characteristics of post-Fordism:

■ differentiation;
■ modular production;
■ computer-aided integration of production;
■ multi-skilled labour.

In this way, post-Fordism refers to a wider transition in industrial set-up towards more flexible markets and manufacturing systems where customers enjoy greater choice and the ability to dictate their preferences. Under this emerging system, employees have to be multi-skilled. For example, engineers must possess managerial skills, and accountants must be aware of production systems. Everybody should be able to work with teams, while having a good working knowledge of computing. Even if you are a technician in a small garage, you should be able to work on certain computer programs by which you are controlled, guided and facilitated. While this is so, the conventional unskilled worker who contributed to the assembly line is losing his job. Consequently, workers under post-Fordism are forced to be computer-literate and multi-skilled. These are, indeed, social issues, and some writers have defined them in various ways. For example, Urry (1988) sees this change as the dismantling of 'organized capitalism' towards the development of 'disorganized capitalism'. By understanding the fact that some Fordism-based industries are moving to under-developed countries, Piore and Sabel (1984) articulate this change as the 'second industrial divide'. Moreover, this change has implications for industrial relations within organizations. For example, as Clegg (1990b) has reported, in the USA there is an anti-trade-union posture reducing the union-ization of the workforce to 17 per cent.

Post-Fordism refers to a wider transition in industrial set-up towards more flexible markets and manufacturing systems where customers enjoy greater choice and the ability to dictate their preferences.

Flexible specialization

To enlighten the idea of the above change, a parallel term being used in the social sciences is 'flex-ible specialization', again in stark contrast to 'mass-production regime'. While flexible production and post-Fordism stand as its technical apparatuses, 'flexible specialization' is coined to be the broadest concept that can bracket all similar or alternative terms. Hirst and Zeitlin (1991: 2) show a difference between post-Fordism and flexible specialization. For them:

> Where post-Fordism sees productive systems as integrated and coherent totalities, flexible specialisation identifies complex and variable connections between technology, institutions and politics; where post-Fordism sees industrial change as a mechanical outcome of impersonal processes, flexible specialisation emphasises contingency and the scope for strategic choice.

Hirst and Zeitlin (1991: 10) also argue that the post-Fordist conception of industrial change 'involves, by and large, borrowing and radically simplifying the flexible specialisation approach to manufacturing. However, this borrowing is accompanied by very little attention to the wide range of forms and hybrids of flexibly-specialised production and their social and institutional conditions.' Another important difference between post-Fordist explanations and the flexible specialization thesis is that while the former relies upon firm-initiated reactions to the collapse of mass markets, the latter argues that the strategic turn towards flexible manufacturing is 'not merely the firm but inter-firm and collective regional and national patterns are crucial in the balancing of competition and co-operation necessary for their more progressive institutionalisation' (ibid.). For Piore and Sabel, also, flexible specialization is not a phenomenon confined within the boundaries of individual organizations, but a result of proper microregulation of innovative activities across industries. It is a matter of 'finding a compatible institutional answer to the problems of instigating and coordinating innovation, [because] competition of a wrong kind undermines the necessary coordination; misdirected coordination undermines competition' (Piore and Sabel, 1984: 264–265). A transition from mass production to flexible manufacturing thus requires an extra-organizational reconciliation of these apparently antagonistic principles of competition and co-ordination to facilitate financially viable innovations. According to Piore and Sabel (ibid.: 265–268), this reconciliation took place in three different settings:

- Regional conglomerations. These are the specialized industrial districts composed of a core of more-or-less equal enterprises bound in a complex web of competition and co-ordination. Michael Porter's concept of 'industrial clusters' is akin to these regional conglomerations. For him:

> Clusters are geographic concentration of interconnected companies and institutions in a particular field. Clusters encompass an array of linked industries and other entities important to competition . . . The California wine industry is a good example. It includes 680 commercial wineries as well as several thousand independent wine grape growers. An extensive complement of industries supporting both wine making and grape growing exists, including suppliers of grape stock, irrigation and harvesting equipment, barrels and labels, specialized public relations and advertising firms, and numerous wine publications aimed at consumers and trade audiences. A host of local institutions is involved with wine, such as the world-renowned viticulture and enology program at the University of California at Davis, the Wine Institute, and special committees of California senate and assembly.
>
> (Porter, 1998: 78)

227

■ Federated enterprises. This refers to the pre-war Japanese zaibatsu and the looser post-war federations of Japanese enterprises which led the industrial development in Japan towards flexible specialization. According to Miyajima (1994: 294):

> there are six corporate groups of this type in Japan. Three of them – Mitsu, Mitsubishi and Sumitomo – originated as pre-war zaibatsu and were organised as corporate groups in the early 1950s. The other three – Fuyo, Sanwa and Dai-ichi – originated as pre-war big banks and organised as corporate groups in the late 1960s.

The salient characteristics of these federated enterprises or corporate groups were cross-shareholding, a main bank system, an intermediary role for trading companies, presidents' clubs and co-operative investments of member companies, as well as sharing of financial, marketing and technological expertise between member corporations. However, according to Piore and Sabel (1984: 267), the group is not as integrated as the mass-production corporation, and member firms are not hierarchically arranged, but their sense of common identity is much sharper than that of firms in regional conglomerates or industrial clusters.

■ 'Solar' firms and workshop factories. This type of co-ordination of innovative activities consists of 'firms with a solar-system model of orbiting suppliers and its close cousin the workshop factory' (Piore and Sabel, 1984: 267). The link between the suppliers and the factory is not subordinate (as in the case of divisions of a multi-divisional mass producer) but collaborative, and the solar firm depends on the subcontractors for advice in solving design and production problems. The example Piore and Sabel provide is the Boeing Company, which produces neither the engines nor much of the avionic equipment for its aeroplanes.

Flexible specialization is not a phenomenon confined within the boundaries of individual organizations but a result of proper microregulation of innovative activities across industries.

A transition from mass production to flexible manufacturing requires an extra-organizational reconciliation of apparently antagonistic principles of competition and co-ordination to facilitate financially viable innovations. This took place in three settings:

■ regional conglomerations;
■ federated enterprises;
■ solar and workshop factories.

In essence, the flexible specialization thesis extends the post-Fordist analysis of industrial change beyond organizational boundaries to the sphere of inter-firm co-ordination and competition. It emphasizes the significance of microregulatory institutional arrangements between firms and industries to reconcile competition and co-ordination – a necessary structural condition for the development of flexible manufacturing regimes.

> The flexible specialization thesis extends post-Fordist analysis of industrial change beyond organizational boundaries to the sphere of inter-firm co-ordination and competition.

Postmodernity

Postmodernity is another parallel concept often used to characterize the change that we are dealing with here. It is quite difficult to differentiate the use of this term from those discussed above, as it is often used to capture the whole sweep of changes taking place in all the economic, social and political dimensions of society. Thus, many postmodern writers describe what we discussed above under 'Post-Fordism' and 'Flexible specialization' as 'postmodern' changes.

> The term 'postmodern' is often used to capture the whole sweep of changes taking place in all the economic, social and political dimensions of society.

For example, Clegg (1990: 181) compares modernist and postmodern organizations as follows:

> Where the modernist organization was rigid, postmodern organization is flexible. Where modernist consumption was premised on mass forms, postmodernist consumption is premised on niches. Where modernist organization was premised on technological determinism, postmodernist organization is premised on technological choices made possible through 'de-dedicated' micro-electronic equipment. Where modernist organization and jobs were highly differentiated, demarcated and de-skilled, postmodernist organization and jobs are highly de-differentiated, de-demarcated and multiskilled. Employment relations as a fundamental relation of organization upon which has been constructed a whole discourse of the determinism of size as a contingency variable increasingly give way to more complex and fragmentary relational forms, such as subcontracting and networking.

In a similar fashion, Montagna (1997: 125), for example, defines 'postmodern' as:

> Much has been ascribed to this [postmodern], from new forms of organisation to new modes of production. In its simplest form, postmodernism is defined as events that are transitory, selves that are fragmented, ideas that are constantly changing, all without any underlying universal laws or guidelines.

However, for the purpose of this text, we would rather like to confine the use of 'postmodern' to the cultural realm of changes, as we have deployed 'flexible manufacturing', 'post-Fordism', 'flexible specialization' and 'post-bureaucracy' to characterize technological, economic and organizational aspects of the change, which are of course interrelated and interdependent.

Like post-Fordism, postmodernism also implies a movement beyond something, beyond modernism this time, and, hence, understanding of postmodernism heavily depends on our understanding of modernism. As a cultural phenomenon, thus, 'postmodern' exemplifies a shift of

229

modernist values and beliefs in all realms of social life, such as work, pleasure, truth, universality, uniformity, relationships, sexuality and so on. These 'new' systems of values and beliefs provide the cultural logic for flexible manufacturing (see Jameson, 1984). At the level of market or consumer behaviour, for example, these 'new' values manifest fragmented markets, logic of product differentiation, power of subjective perception of consumers as a driving force of organizational strategies, and consumerism. Figure 7.2 illustrates salient features of the postmodern cultural shift, and how they are manifested, and implicated in, market and organizational domains.

> As a cultural phenomenon, 'postmodern' exemplifies a shift of modernist values and beliefs in all realms of social life, such as work, pleasure, truth, universality, uniformity, relationships, sexuality and so on. These 'new' systems of values and beliefs provide the cultural logic for flexible manufacturing.

Postmodern cultural change

1. The celebration of differences of interpretations, of values and of styles. Being different is more desirable than being similar, not only for organizations but also for individuals.

2. A delight in the superficial, in appearance, in image and diversity, rather than in modernistic aspirations of deep meanings, functionalities and common accord.

3. The rejection of claims to identify 'truth', on grounds that there are only versions of 'truth'. The rejection of the search for authenticity or the 'real', since everything is inauthentic. Objective judgements are superseded by subjective interpretations: things are in the eye of the beholder.

4. A superior self, and an emphasis on pleasure, explicit sexuality and shifting identities and relations rather than (as in modernity) long-term commitment to something believed to be superior to self (e.g., God, work, love, family, nation, organizations, professions, socialism and so on, to which self is to be committed).

Cultural manifestation of market and consumer behaviour

1. Market fragmentation and logic of product differentiation.

2. Customer emphasis more on aesthetic attributes (rather than functionality) of the product. Product differentiations are mainly achieved through offering varieties in aesthetic attributes (such as colour, size, appearance and optional features) but holding core functionality as standard.

3. Power of subjective perception of customer in dictating market positioning strategies of firms.

4. Power of persuasive media (advertising and public relations) in constructing customer subjectivity.

5. Consumerism. Fashion-driven buyer behaviour and speeding up of the buy-use-throw-repeat purchase cycle. (You may buy a new mobile phone not because it is out of order but because it is out of fashion.)

6. Forced obsolescence. Products are made obsolete, before their functional lifespan, by the introduction of new models (e.g., personal computers).

Changes sought in organizational systems

1. From mass marketing to strategic marketing (i.e., market segmentation, targeting and positioning).

2. Design emphasis on product modularity and customization.

3. Modular production systems integrated by CAD, CAM and networking technologies.

4. Multi-skilled workforce.

5. Post-bureaucratic organizational forms and industry networking and clustering.

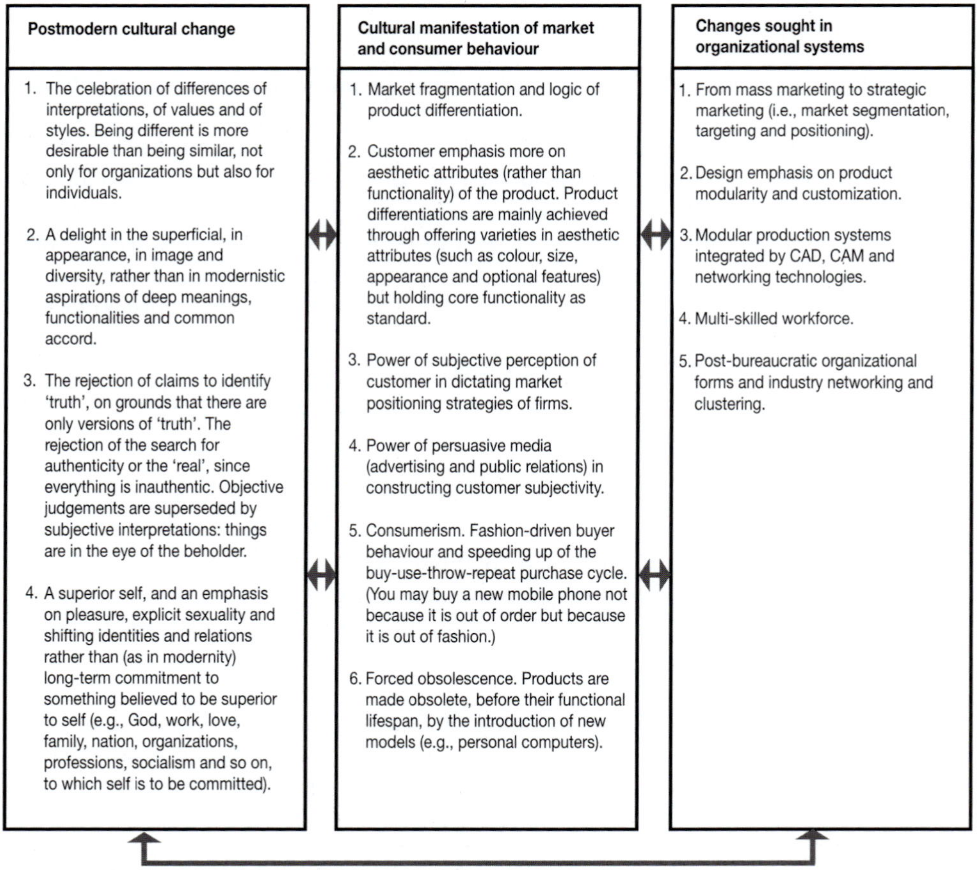

Figure 7.2 Postmodern cultural logic of flexible manufacturing

Post-bureaucracy

The issue of flexibility has also made bureaucratic organizational forms outdated and inappropriate, forcing organizations to search for new forms of organization and control that suit a flexibility regime. The result is post-bureaucracy – the emergence of alternative organizational arrangements to bureaucracy.

For Thompson and McHugh (2002), post-bureaucratization has taken the forms of decentralization, disaggregation, delayering and disorganization, resulting in less hierarchical, network-based, dispersed and informal organizational forms. According to them, within such organizational forms, spontaneity has come to replace planning; empowerment has superseded control; participation rather than command is valued; and charisma and values have taken the place of rationality (see Table 7.1).

> Post-bureaucratization has taken the forms of decentralization, disaggregation, delayering and disorganization, resulting in less hierarchical, network-based, dispersed and informal organizational forms.

For Mabey *et al.* (2000), recent developments in organizational forms beyond bureaucracy mirror a breaking of organizational boundaries and a move towards network and virtual organizations. They characterize different forms of post-bureaucratic organizations formed across

Table 7.1 *Post-bureaucratic characteristics of organizations*

Bureaucratic (Old)	Post-bureaucratic (New)
Content:	
Stability	Disorganization/chaos
Rationality	Charisma, values
Planning	Spontaneity
Control	Empowerment
Command	Participation
Centralization	Decentralization/disaggregation
Hierarchy	Network
Formal	Informal/flexible
Large	Downsized/delayered
Economies of scale	Economies of scope
Context:	
Fordism	Post-Fordism
Modern	Postmodern
Production emphasis	Consumption emphasis
Mass market	Market segmentation
Nationalism	Globalization

Source: based on Thompson and McHugh (2002: 155) and 'A guide to new times', *Marxism Today* (October 1988)

231

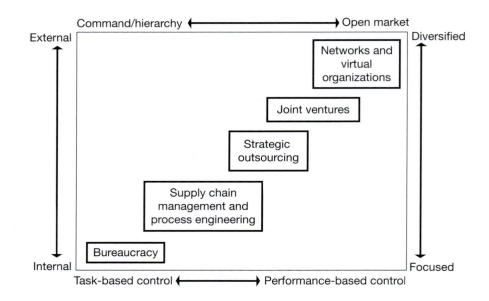

Figure 7.3 *Post-bureaucratic organizational forms*
Source: Mabey *et al.* (2000: 172)

organizations in four key dimensions: externalization of relations; diversification of activities; performance-based controls; and open-market mode of regulation. Figure 7.3 summarizes their classification of post-bureaucratic organizational forms which, along with other relevant forms, we will discuss further in Chapter 10.

SUMMING UP: POST-MECHANISTIC ORGANIZATIONS AND MANAGEMENT ACCOUNTING

In the previous sections, we discussed different aspects of the change that has been taking place since the 1970s in industrial contexts, intents and contents. In line with popular usage in the literature, notions such as globalization, flexible manufacturing, post-Fordism, flexible special-ization, postmodernity and post-bureaucracy were used to explain various dimensions of the change. Table 7.2 illustrates the overall change, of which the culmination is post-mechanistic forms of organizations and management accounting. As we mentioned previously, it should be noted that we use the terms 'mechanistic' and 'post-mechanistic' to mean the cumulative effects of various changes often labelled in interchangeable and confusingly similar terms, mainly 'modern'/ 'postmodern' and 'Fordist'/'post-Fordist'. As far as possible, for ease of comprehension, we attempted to differentiate and confine those popularly but interchangeably used terms to mean specific dimensions of a holistic change. A cautionary note, however, is needed here. Simplicity entails the loss of richness of complexity. We should always keep in mind that such sociological terms as 'modern', 'postmodern', 'Fordism' and 'post-Fordism' have been, and can be, used to mean the totality rather than a specific segment or aspect. It is our very arbitrary choice to use the terms 'mechanistic' and 'post-mechanistic' instead.

Table 7.2 *From mechanistic to post-mechanistic*

Mechanistic	Post-mechanistic
Modernity as the cultural context	Postmodernity as the cultural context
Protected, stable, mass markets	Globalized, fragmented, volatile markets
Mass production and mass marketing	Flexible manufacturing and target marketing
Emphasis on short-term operational objectives	Emphasis on long-term strategic goals
Manufacturing-driven in search for economies of scale	Market/customer-driven in search for economies of scope
Standardization as production norm	Differentiation as production norm
Assembly line and de-skilled labour	Modular systems and multi-skilled labour
Bureaucracy as mode of control	Post-bureaucratic organizational forms as mode of control
Mechanistic forms of management control that emphasize standardization and control	Post-mechanistic forms of management control that emphasize flexibility and autonomy

Now, in this section, our aim is to elaborate on the last row of Table 7.2 to explain the implications of the post-mechanistic change for management accounting.

The role of management accounting in mechanistic and post-mechanistic organizations has been fundamentally different. In mechanistic form, it was standardization and control. Driven by the quest for economies of scale and flowline-based mass production, mechanistic organizations were configured as giant unitary production and sales machines. Divisions and departments were tightly connected as sub-systems of one single, large corporate entity. Unification of different sub-systems into a single corporate entity was a primary task of top management. Return on investment (ROI) was the guiding principle: all divisions, departments and functions were designated as investment, profit or cost centres, and their operations were planned, executed and controlled through a system of responsibility accounting to make sure that they contributed to the overall profitability of the corporate entity; decision-making was primarily guided by contribution or profit criteria. Primary managerial focus was on control – making sure that plans and budgets were met by comparing budgets/standards with actual performance results, and taking necessary corrective actions. Customer and market conditions were, by and large, left in the background, mostly as a decision constraint, and marketing was a 'push system', where mass-produced goods were pushed through sales promotions. All these took place smoothly, but only until the mass markets were no longer protected, and became globalized and fragmented.

In mechanistic form, the role of management accounting was standardization and control.

In post-mechanistic organizational forms, on the other hand, the primary role of management accounting is to contribute to flexibility and autonomy, rather than standardization and control.

Driven by the quest for economies of scope and modularity-based production designs, post-mechanistic organizations are configured as a set or a cluster of autonomous, relatively small, loosely coupled entities. Big is no longer strength: 'it is seen as positively dangerous and anachronistic' (Thompson and McHugh, 2002: 154). The primary managerial concern is to enhance the long-term capacity of the company to meet the demands of segmented and ever-changing markets competitively. Thus, post-mechanistic organizations embrace a 'pull system' where organizational activities begin from the market/customers and proceed backwards to the factory to manufacture what those customers demand.

> In post-mechanistic organizational forms, the primary role of management accounting is to contribute to flexibility and autonomy.

In adapting to this postmodernist transition, management accounting has so far made some progress by making a two-way integration with two other business functions: operations management and strategic management/marketing. This two-way integration is parallel with two emerging sub-disciplines of management accounting: management accounting for flexible manufacturing and strategic management accounting.

> Post-mechanistic progress in management accounting has been made by integrating with operations management, on the one hand, and strategic management and marketing, on the other.

Integration with operations management has enabled management accounting to enhance its boundaries beyond mere 'cost accounting' to strategic 'cost management'. Arguably, the most important breakthrough that management accounting has achieved in this respect is activity-based costing/management (ABC/M). Other emerging management accounting concepts and tools that are related to manufacturing flexibility include accounting for just-in-time (JIT), enterprise resource planning (ERP), backflush costing, target costing and accounting for quality.

Inflexibilities of traditional management accounting methods generally rest on two major issues. The first is associated with the determination of economic order quantity (EOQ) and economic production batch quantity. These quantities are traditionally determined by offsetting stock-holding costs and stock-out costs. Stock-out costs are the costs incurred due to possible shortages of inventories (both raw materials and finished goods), and are the main reason for unnecessarily incurring stock-holding costs. That said, stock-holding costs are incurred due to the fact that production and purchase are carried out in quantities more than 'demanded', as a precaution to avoid possible stock-out costs. However, if each production unit can reach such a level of integration between its suppliers and buyers that avoids or minimizes informational uncertainties regarding its demand and supply, possibilities of stock-out costs are minimized to merely bearable. All management accounting concepts and tools associated with JIT, especially ERP and backflush costing, which are mostly borrowed from Japanese quality management regimes, contribute to this end.

The second inflexibility is associated with the treatment of fixed costs. Traditionally, management accounting followed a resource-based classification of costs in the lines of direct/indirect and variable/fixed. The problem with this classification is that it theoretically demands high-volume production to recover high fixed costs, especially when prices are set so competitively that contribution per unit is very low. This is the basic logic of economies of scale: the larger the scale of production, the lower the average cost of manufacturing as fixed or indirect costs are absorbed by a larger volume of units. This, of course, is a theoretical barrier to moving into economies of scope where small-volume production should be profitable enough. Activity-based costing and management offered a viable alternative to this. Costs are reclassified according to activities and traced to products, market segments and customers on the basis of activity-cost drivers, thus providing an altogether new insight to the profitability of small production volumes. Costs and revenues are budgeted and planned on the basis of activity levels rather than resource capacities. See Chapter 9 for a detailed discussion of those management accounting topics that are geared to manufacturing flexibility.

Inflexibility of traditional management accounting techniques rests on two major issues: one is associated with the determination of economic order/batch quantities, and the other with the treatment of fixed costs. New developments in management accounting mainly address these two issues.

Management accounting's integration with strategic management/marketing, on the other hand, is geared to: align operational-level activities and measures with corporate strategic intents, such as vision, mission and corporate strategies; and externally focus management accounting analysis towards competitor and customer analysis. Major innovations in management accounting in these regards are the balanced scorecard (BSC), competitor cost analysis, customer profitability analysis and product life-cycle analysis. You will read more about this strategic turn in management accounting in Chapter 8.

Management accounting's integration with strategic management/marketing is geared to: aligning operational-level activities and measures with corporate strategic intents, such as vision, mission and corporate strategies; and externally focusing management accounting analysis towards competitor and customer analysis.

In essence, management accounting's transition towards post-mechanistic has taken two streams. The first has broken away from some traditional management accounting techniques and concepts, especially those associated with determination of economic order quantities and traditional treatment of fixed costs, which theoretically prohibit the concept of economies of scope. The second has aligned with strategic management and marketing themes that link operations with corporate strategic intents and external market dynamics.

HAVE YOU UNDERSTOOD THE CHAPTER?

1. Why do we consider post-mechanistic conditions as multi-layered, multifaceted and para-doxical?
2. What is meant by globalization?
3. What are the underlying forces that promoted globalization?
4. How does globalization impact upon product market conditions?
5. How do globalization and its ramifications in product markets impact upon business intents?
6. What are the wider macroeconomic conditions essential for the persistence of mass pro-duction?
7. What were the wider social and economic forces that contributed to the collapse of mass-production systems?
8. How did the industrial world respond to the crisis of mass production? Explain in line with Piore and Sabel's (1984) thesis of 'flexible specialization'.
9. What is flexible manufacturing?
10. How would you describe the transition from Fordism to post-Fordism?
11. What are the salient features of post-Fordist manufacturing compared to the Fordist assembly line?
12. How would you compare the post-Fordist explanation of industrial change with the 'flexible specialization' thesis?
13. What are the three different settings in which, according to Piore and Sabel (1984), flexible specialization began to take place?
14. What cultural changes were brought about by the postmodern cultural turn? How would they be replicated in market and consumer behaviour?
15. What are the changes sought in organizational systems in response to the postmodern cultural turn?
16. What are the changes brought about by post-bureaucratic movements in organizations?
17. How does management accounting respond to post-mechanistic transition in organizational contexts, intents and contents?
18. What are the main sources for inflexibilities associated with traditional management account-ing tools and concepts? How do you relate emerging management accounting techniques such as ABC and ERP to those inflexibilities?
19. What purpose does the strategic turn in management accounting serve?

BEYOND THE CHAPTER

1. We cannot build it yet. But already we can specify the 'postmodern' factory . . . Its essence will not be mechanical, though there will be plenty of machines. Its essence will be conceptual – the product of . . . principles and practices that together constitute a new approach to manufacturing.

    (Drucker, 2000: 3)

    Discuss.

2. There is a widespread agreement that something dramatic has been happening to the international economy over the last two decades: rapid changes in production technology

236

and industrial organization, a major restructuring of world markets, and consequent large-scale changes in the policies of economic management at the international, national and regional levels. At the same time there is a great deal of confusion about how to characterise these changes, the mechanisation at work, and the policy implications for different groups of economic and political actors.

(Hirst and Zeitlin, 1991: 1)

Discuss, with special reference to changing management accounting practices.

FURTHER READING

1. For an interesting and 'critical' synopsis of post-Fordist/postmodern conditions, see Murray (1988) and Hall (1988).
2. For a detailed discussion of the Caterpillar case: a postmodern story of how reordering of manufacturing spaces relates to construction of 'new economic citizenship', see Miller and O'Leary (1994).
3. For a comparative and detailed discussion of the differences between post-Fordism, flexible specialization and regulation theory, see Hirst and Zeitlin (1991).

Chapter 8

Towards strategic management accounting

A STARTING POINT: ACCOUNTING'S CHALLENGE IN THE NEW WORLD

Let us look at what management gurus have said about Western business beyond the 1990s.

The Japanese challenge

> While some Western companies have had global brand positions for 30 or 40 years or more (Heinz, Siemens, IBM, Ford, and Kodak, for example), it is hard to identify any American or European company that has created a new global brand franchise in the last 10 to 15 years. Yet Japanese companies have created a score or more – NEC, Fujitsu, Panasonic (Matsushita), Toshiba, Sony, Seiko, Epson, Canon, Minolta, and Honda, among them . . . General Electric's situation is typical. In many of its businesses, this American giant has been almost unknown in Europe and Asia. GE made no coordinated effort to build a global corporate franchise . . . In contrast, smaller Korean companies like Samsung, Daewoo, and Lucky Gold Star are busy building global-brand umbrellas that will ease market entry for a whole range of businesses. The underlying principle is simple: economies of scope may be as important as economies of scale in entering global markets. But capturing economies of scope demands interbusiness coordination that only top management can provide.
>
> (Hamel and Prahalad, 1989: 12)

Significance of competitive advantage

> Competitive advantage is at the heart of a firm's performance in competitive markets . . . Today the importance of competitive advantage could hardly be greater. Firms throughout the world face slower growth as well as domestic and global competitors that are no longer acting as if the expanding pie were big enough for all.
>
> (Porter, 1985: xv)

New role of accounting

> In a globally competitive organization, everyone understands that long-term profitability is achieved by improving customer satisfaction, not by trying to sell the largest possible

quantities of what the accounting system says are the highest margin products. They under-stand both the quality imperatives of TQM and the operational imperatives of JIT. Information about customer satisfaction and about variation in processes can move companies continuously closer to achieving the imperatives of competitive excellence. Defining that information and those imperatives is the task that awaits us.

(Johnson, 1992: xi)

How far has management accounting changed to face these challenges?

SETTING THE SCENE

Especially during the last few decades, the term 'strategic' has become a very popular and attrac-tive adjective among business practitioners and academics. It has become so fashionable to qualify their respective functional disciplines by this adjective that we have a series of 'new' subjects to teach and learn: strategic marketing, strategic human resource management, strategic finance, strategic operations management and strategic management accounting. They all have begun to rewrite their respective disciplines with a 'strategic emphasis'. As a result, we have many kinds of 'strategic' courses and topics, especially at the higher stages of business school and professional accounting programmes (and in other functional disciplines, such as marketing, human resource management, finance and banking and so on). A textbook like this, which focuses on management accounting change, cannot ignore this popular trend.

Despite its long history of use in military sciences, the term 'strategy' began to enter into busi-ness management discourses strongly only in the 1980s. As we discussed in the previous chapter, this 'strategic turn' in managing various aspects of business enterprises can be linked to the growth of global competition, which made business competition analogous to warfare: markets being the territories to capture, customers being the subjects to surrender, competitors being the enemies to defeat, the four Ps[1] being the competitive weapons to use tactically, and strategy being the way in which 'business warfare' is thought out, led and executed. Much of the credit for introducing the 'warfare' analogy to business competition and bringing the notion of strategy to the forefront of business analysis should go to Anglo-American business school academics and consultants. During the 1980s, business school courses under the label of 'business policy' provided the initial peda-gogical framework to capture the notion of strategy. While functional disciplines such as accounting and finance, marketing, production and personnel management (which later became human resource management) dealt with their respective functional areas with clear-cut definitions and conceptual tools to partition them from each other, it was business policy that taught its students how to draw 'organizational' (rather than 'functional' or 'departmental') policies to project the business enterprise as a single, unified entity to its stakeholders. By definition, 'business policy' was an area of 'general managers' and 'directors' (rather than functional specialists) who led the whole business. Thus, it was this 'business policy' arena which provided the initial pedagogical framework to institutionalize militaristic notions of strategy within business discourse, and which later turned itself into the subject of 'strategic management'.

> The 'strategic turn' in managing various aspects of business enterprises can be linked to the growth of global competition, which made business competition analogous to warfare.

The last decade or so has been a golden period for strategic management discourse. Within the context of ever-increasing global competition and risk of business failure, it established itself as the central function of managing business enterprises: the higher-order 'strategic' function to oversee and co-ordinate other functional management concerns. Executing a good strategy well was understood to be the fundamental reason for business success. Business failures were readily attributed to lack of good strategies and/or bad implementation. Developing and implementing effective and efficient strategies at organizational, divisional and departmental or functional levels were presented as the primary objectives across all functional disciplines. All other business functions were thus required to align with and contribute to the 'strategic management' of the business. The result was that the functional disciplines, including management accounting, began to learn from strategic management and to provide a 'strategic flavour' to their contents. Strategic management accounting (SMA) is management accounting's response to this strategic turn of businesses.

> Strategic management accounting (SMA) is management accounting's response to the strategic turn of businesses.

The purpose of this chapter is to introduce you to this trend of integrating management accounting with theories, concepts, tools and ideologies of strategic management to form what we now call SMA. First, we try to answer the basic question: 'What is SMA?' In this section, however, our aim is not to provide a specific definition of SMA, but to help you understand the evolving character of SMA. We will do that by introducing you to three distinct ways in which SMA can be understood: SMA as a solution to a set of problems associated with the conventional management accounting paradigm; SMA as a fundamentally different management accounting paradigm from the conventional one; and SMA as the interface between management accounting and other organizational functions, especially corporate strategy, marketing and operations.

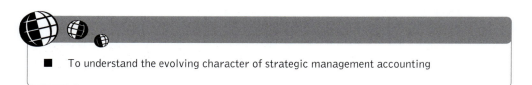

■ To understand the evolving character of strategic management accounting

In the second section of the chapter, we will construct a conceptual framework to identify different approaches to SMA. In this section, you will learn how the notion of strategy is deployed in three different arenas – corporate, competitive and manufacturing. Then the directions of SMA are conceptualized in these three arenas. After reading this section, you will understand that complexity and diversity in SMA concepts and tools are due to its three-way amalgamation with these three arenas of strategy.

■ To understand how the notion of strategy is deployed in three different arenas — corporate, competitive and manufacturing

The third section deals mainly with a set of strategic management themes, especially that of corporate strategy formulation. Concepts such as vision, mission, and corporate planning tools such as portfolio planning models are introduced, together with the strategic demands they may impose upon SMA. After reading this section you will understand the generic trend that corporate strategy follows, and appreciate the types of changes that management accounting methodology should undergo if it wants to integrate with corporate planning exercises.

■ To understand the generic trend that corporate strategy follows
■ To appreciate the types of changes that management accounting methodology should undergo to integrate with corporate planning exercises

The fourth section introduces you to the notion of competitive strategy, as formulated by Michael Porter. In this section, you will understand the centrality of Porter's concepts of competitive advantage, competitive structure, generic strategies, competitive positioning and value chain in SMA discourse. After reading this section, you will be able to describe types of strategic analysis that management accounting may perform to facilitate competitive strategy formulation, and discuss how Porter's conception of organization as a value chain helped reformulate management accounting tasks around the notion of activities.

■ To describe types of strategic analysis that management accounting may perform to facilitate competitive strategy formulation
■ To discuss how Porter's conception of the organization as a value chain helped reformulate management accounting tasks around the notion of activities

Finally, the chapter discusses the balanced scorecard (BSC) as a strategic management accounting system. In this section, the basic conceptual framework and managerial ideology of BSC will be introduced, then there will be a brief critique of the BSC framework.

- ■ To describe conceptual framework and managerial ideology of BSC
- ■ To appreciate some conceptual weaknesses of BSC

WHAT IS SMA?

Defining SMA is difficult and dangerous. That is because, as Coad (1996: 392) puts it, 'SMA is an emerging field whose boundaries are loose and, as yet, there is no unified view of what it is or how it might develop. The existing literature in the field is both disparate and disjointed.' Therefore, rather than attempting to provide a definition *per se*, in this section we will try to explain the evolving character of SMA.

SMA is an alleged solution for problems of conventional management accounting

SMA is the response to the critique that conventional management accounting systems are inadequate for today's environment (Johnson and Kaplan, 1987). During the late 1980s and 1990s, together with Johnson and Kaplan's 'relevance lost' thesis (see Chapter 2), a series of critiques on conventional management accounting emerged, arguing that its outdated characteristics were behind the competitive loss of Western business, especially to the Japanese. Johnson and Kaplan (1987: xi), for example, argue that:

> Corporate management accounting systems are inadequate for today's environment. In this time of rapid technological change, vigorous global and domestic competition, and enormously expanding information processing capabilities, management accounting systems are not providing useful, timely information for the process control, product costing, and performance evaluation activities of managers.

Similarly, Johnson (1992: 14) states that:

> American businesses in the 1970s and 1980s experienced a sharp discontinuity in the terms of competition. Comfortably ensconced before the 1970s in an enormously wealthy domestic marketplace of familiar competitors and captive customers, they were buffeted in the 1980s by new and unprecedented global competitive forces. Unfortunately, the management information in most American companies today still triggers actions that are not relevant to this new competitive environment.

This view is further exemplified by the following: 'Cost-accounting is wrecking American Business. If we're going to remain competitive, we've got to change [our costing systems]' (*Business Week*, 1988, quoted in Shank and Govindarajan, 1989: x); and 'Most large companies seem to recognise that their cost systems are not responsive to today's competitive environment . . . the methods they use to allocate costs among their many products are hopelessly obsolete' (*Fortune*, 1987, quoted in Shank and Govindarajan, 1989: x).

242

> Outdated characteristics of management accounting are behind the competitive loss of Western business.

The incapacity of conventional management accounting to deal effectively with the decision scenarios of 'today's new competitive environment' stems from a set of inherent weaknesses:

1. It is argued that conventional management accounting is excessively inward-looking and does not provide external market information, which is critical for strategic decision-making. As Bromwich (1992: 136) points out:

    > the focus of conventional management accounting reports is on a detailed understanding of the enterprise's internal costs, each categorised according to the input to which they relate, and attributed to a product or products and to a responsibility centre or centres . . . The focus is almost exclusively on activities within the enterprise rather than market results of such endeavours.

> Conventional management accounting is excessively inward-looking and does not provide external market information.

2. Another weakness commonly attributed to conventional management accounting is its detachment from the enterprise's strategies and strategic planning exercises. Cost and decision analysis tools of conventional management accounting (such as limiting factor analysis and break-even analysis) almost exclusively concentrate on short-run operational decisions rather than long-run strategic decisions. Even conventional capital budgeting techniques are nothing more than extensions of basic 'marginal analysis' (which considers marginal efficiency against the marginal cost of capital, see Chapter 6) to multi-period scenarios. They totally ignore rather critical 'strategic dimensions' of business decisions, such as impact on market share, corporate and brand image, core competencies of the firm and its competitors, competitive cost structures and possible competitive reactions to firms' investment decisions, etc. Most importantly, conventional management accounting does not account for 'benefits to customer' stemming from business decisions, which is more determinant in the long-term competitive success of the firm than the financial benefits accruing to its shareholders (i.e., net cash flows).

> Conventional management accounting is detached from an enterprise's strategies.

3. Performance measurement and control are critical for both operational and strategic success of the firm. However, conventional performance measurement and control systems, which

are largely responsibility accounting systems based on budgeting and variance analysis, including standard costing, exclusively concentrate on operational results, and do not measure the relative success of a firm's strategic moves, and, hence, do not provide feedback on the firm's strategic planning exercises. Instead, it seems that their primary objective is to assess budgetary compliance as a basis for the reward (and punishment) structure of the company.

Conventional management accounting does not measure the relative success of a firm's strategic moves, and, hence, does not provide feedback on the firm's strategic planning exercises.

4. Conventional performance measurement and control systems are financial-biased. They do not account for critical non-financial measures. Performance measures that conventional management accounting produces are directly related neither to manufacturing and marketing nor to overall corporate strategies. Not only that, they largely produce outcome measures and inherently lack the potential of producing driver measures. In general, a performance measurement system provides two kinds of measure: outcome and driver measures. Outcome measures are lagging indicators: they tell managers what has happened. In contrast, driver measures are leading indicators, showing the progress of key areas of concern (Anthony and Govindarajan, 1998: 463).

Conventional performance measurement and control systems are financial-biased.

Thus, a new management accounting regime (i.e., SMA) is sought, one which:

■ Generates external market information critical for strategic decisions.
■ Carries out 'strategic cost analysis' (Shank, 1996; Shank and Govindarajan, 1989), which:

- ■ Attributes costs to value-creating activities across extra-organizational linkages and networks.
- ■ Identifies cost drivers which relate to the firm's explicit strategic choices regarding its economic structure (such as scale, product-line complexity and vertical integration), and those which relate to determinants of the firm's cost position, and hinge on its ability to execute successfully within the economic structure it chooses (Shank 1996: 194).
- ■ Assesses the implications of cost structures on the firm's strategic positioning options of cost leadership, differentiation and focus (Porter, 1980; Shank, 1996).

■ Releases management accounting from factory floor (Bromwich and Bhimani, 1989) and 'product costing', so that management accounting can cost 'product or quality attributes' provided by the company to satisfy its customers, the basis upon which customers are attracted to and retained by the company in the long run (Bromwich and Bhimani, 1994).

■ Informs top managers about the potential and actual environmental and market consequences of their strategic decisions.

■ Links performance measurement systems with corporate vision, mission and strategies, and also strikes a balance between financial and non-financial measures, such as product quality, customer satisfaction and innovation capabilities, etc., that are indeed critical determinants of the long-term success of the organization (Kaplan and Norton, 1992, 1993, 1996a, 1996b; Norton, 2000).

SMA is understood in comparison to conventional management accounting

Another common method employed to understand the nature of SMA is to compare it with conventional management accounting. Although such comparison would normally not provide us with a detailed insight into the computational practices involved in SMA, it is helpful in understanding the overall character of SMA, and the direction in which conventional management accounting has to evolve in order to become strategic. Table 8.1 provides such a comparative picture of SMA vis-à-vis conventional management accounting.

> The nature of SMA can be understood by comparing it with characteristics of conventional management accounting.

However, a point of caution is needed here. When we attempt to understand the nature of SMA in comparison with conventional management accounting, inevitably we end up with a kind of extreme duality. We tend to understand conventional and strategic management accounting as bipolar opposites of a continuum, which is not necessarily the case. Furthermore, since SMA is still an unfinished project, many of the characteristics we attribute to it are rather idealistic

Table 8.1 *Conventional versus strategic management accounting*

Conventional	Strategic
Historical	Prospective
Single entity	Relative position
Single period	Multiple period
Single decision	Sequences, patterns
Introspective	Outward looking
Manufacturing focus	Competitive focus
Existing activities	Possibilities
Reactive	Proactive
Programmed	Unprogrammed
Overlooks linkages	Embraces linkages
Data orientation	Information orientation
Based on existing systems	Unconstrained by existing system
Builds on conventions	Ignores conventions

Source: Wilson and Chua (1993: 530)

projections constructed in opposition to conventional management accounting systems. However, SMA is not going to be a wholesale revision of conventional management accounting but a gradual evolution of it (see Bromwich and Bhimani, 1989). In such an evolutionary context, SMA will retain many of the characteristics of conventional management accounting. It is too early to predict the extent of that retention.

> SMA is not going to be a wholesale revision of conventional management accounting but a gradual evolution of it.

SMA is the intersection of management accounting with other functional disciplines

SMA is assigned with an integrative role. One salient characteristic of mechanistic organizations that have developed over the last century or so is their compartmentalization and specialization of enterprise management activities across functional lines: marketing, production, human resource management, finance and accounting, etc. This was bureaucratic rationality: where production and administrative efficiencies are the primary objectives of enterprise management, where 'special-ization' is the *modus operandi* of achieving that objective, this compartmentalization has its own rationality. Managing parts of the enterprise is deemed to be the best approach to manage the whole. Thus, organizations are conceptualized, structured and managed as bureaucratic hierarchies divided along functional departments. On the contrary, in today's competitive context, where a firm's capacity to 'deliver a superior value' to customers has become the ground rule of business success, organizations are conceptualized and managed differently, as a 'value chain' (Porter 1980, 1985). Once organizations are seen as 'value chains', integration and co-ordination across different functional domains become crucial. Managing the sum instead of the parts has become the accepted logic. Organization decisions relating to the firm's capacity of creating and delivering value are no longer made in respective functional arenas but in an integrative manner. Thus, each functional area needs an extension through which it can ideologically and procedurally link to other functional areas. SMA represents this extension to management accounting; it provides not only the ideology but also some techniques of doing so. As Nanni *et al.* (1992: 2) point out, strategic cost management brings management accounting into strategic management and operations management. It calls for a perspective which goes well beyond accounting itself. Following this logic, one might expect management accounting to become integrated with 'user' functions in the organization as it changes to meet the needs of a changing business environment. Bromwich and Bhimani (1994: 130) argue that 'strategic management accounting requires that accountants embrace new skills extending beyond their usual areas and cooperate much more with general management, corporate strategists, marketing and product development, who may not have a good image of accountants'.

> Compartmentalization and specialization of enterprise management activities across functional lines was the rationale of modern organizations; their integration is the rationale for today's postmodern organizations.

Strategic management accounting requires that accountants embrace new skills extending beyond their usual areas and co-operate much more with general management, corporate strategists, marketing and product development.

The extension and integration of management accounting with other management disciplines has mainly taken three paths. First is the integration with strategic management themes of vision, mission and business strategy, etc., so that SMA would gain a capacity to link short-term actions and performance measures with the future 'dreams' of corporate leaders or strategists. Second is its move towards market analysis by integrating with marketing that deals with segmentation and positioning the company's products/brands in final markets. Third is the move towards manufacturing by integrating with operations management. Figure 8.1 illustrates this three-way integration of management accounting with business strategy, marketing and operations management.

SMA and strategy themes

Since the 1980s, accounting scholars have drawn from strategic management literature to extend the domain of management accounting. As early as 1987, Simons attempted to draw the linkage between management control systems and business strategy. Relying upon a contingency theory framework, and drawing from Miles and Snow's (1978) typology of generic business strategies, and also their hypothesis that successful firms must ensure that their control systems are properly

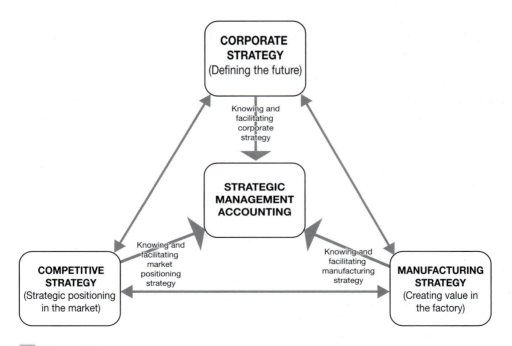

Figure 8.1 *Three-way strategic extension of management accounting*

and differentially designed to take account of their strategy, Simons demonstrated that firms embracing a prospector strategy, in comparison with firms embracing a defender strategy, use their accounting control systems more intensively. Based on a two-year field study of two competing companies and an extended view of business strategy, embracing the strategy themes of Mintzberg (1973), Utterback and Abernathy (1975) and Porter (1980), in addition to Miles and Snow (1978), the same author in 1990 demonstrated the power of management control systems in the strategy formulation process. He illustrated how interactive management control systems focus organizational attention on strategic uncertainties.

> Since the 1980s accounting scholars have drawn from strategic management literature to extend the domain of management accounting. Simons (1987, 1990) attempted to relate management control systems to business strategy.

A clearer link between business strategy and management accounting is pursued in the writings of Kaplan and Norton (1992, 1996a, 1996b) who proposed the balanced scorecard (BSC) as a strategic performance measurement system. They not only emphasized the strategic importance of linking a company's short-term actions with long-term strategy, but also proposed BSC as an 'enabling mechanism that translates strategy into action' (see Roslender and Hart, 2002: 260). It is argued that BSC lets organizations introduce four new management processes that, separately and in combination, contribute to linking long-term strategic objectives with short-term actions: translating the vision; communicating and linking; business planning; and feedback and learning. It is said that use of scorecards, by providing the means of accomplishing these strategic management processes, 'enables a company to align its management processes and focuses the entire organisation on implementing long-term strategy' (Kaplan and Norton, 1996a: 85). Later in this chapter we will deal with BSC in detail.

> In the early 1990s, BSC was proposed as a strategic performance measurement system to link business strategies with operational measures of performance.

The construction of SMA is, in this way, linked to strategic management concepts and ideologies. Thus, an SMA student would study various strategy themes such as vision, mission, corporate philosophy, competitive strategies, strategic leadership, corporate culture and so on, which, one way or the other, are linked to the notion of 'seeing the future first' (Hamel and Prahalad, 1994).

SMA and marketing

Roslender and Hart (2002: 256) argue:

> strategic management accounting's defining characteristic is the management accounting interface with marketing management rather than strategy. When conceived in this way,

strategic management accounting is a fundamentally interdisciplinary development, a potent mix of marketing and management accounting concepts and themes to be deployed in the pursuit of sustainable competitive advantage.

In the context of the interface between management accounting and marketing, SMA is understood as a generic approach to account for 'strategic positioning' – effectively locating a firm's products against its competitors' in the market to pursue sustainable competitive advantages. When seen in this way, techniques associated with SMA include competitor position analysis, target costing and life-cycle costing. In addition, it is informed by product attribute analysis, buyer value chain analysis and contestable market theory (Roslender and Hart, 2002: 258). Figure 8.2 illustrates SMA as the interface between marketing and management accounting to pursue competitive advantage through market positioning strategies.

> In the context of the interface between management accounting and marketing, SMA is understood as a generic approach to account for 'strategic positioning' – effectively locating a firm's products against its competitors' in the market to pursue sustainable competitive advantages.

SMA and operations management

Although its external market orientation is emphasized everywhere, SMA has a new internal focus as well. It revisits the factory floor to integrate management accounting with new manufacturing technologies. In addition to its market positioning strategy, manufacturing strategy constitutes an

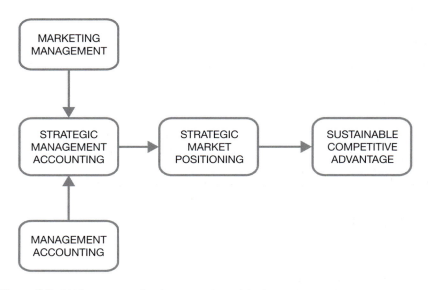

Figure 8.2 *SMA as accounting for strategic positioning*

important element of overall business strategy, which determines the firm's status on a set of 'critical success factors in manufacturing': quality, cost, speed of delivery, dependability and flexibility. The 'Japanese miracle' (Bromwich and Bhimani, 1994) is by and large attributed to that country's manufacturing environment, which embraces participative management, quality concern, low cost through waste minimization, including inventories, continuous improvement, etc. A whole new set of manufacturing technologies and ideologies, commonly bracketed under the umbrella term 'lean production' (see Chapter 9 and Chapter 7), have emerged during the last two decades or so. These posed new challenges for management accounting. Thus, strategic extension of management accounting has also taken the path of 'revisiting the factory floor' to integrate with a new set of manufacturing techniques, such as enterprise resource planning (ERP), activity-based management, computer-aided manufacturing, just-in-time (JIT), value-chain analysis, quality costing, continuous improvement and so on. We will deal with the role of management accounting in this new manufacturing environment in the next chapter.

> Strategic extension of management accounting has also taken the path of 'revisiting the factory floor' to integrate with a new set of manufacturing techniques.

DIRECTIONS IN SMA

Learning from, and integrating with, other disciplines, SMA is still evolving. Obviously, this process of evolution is rather messy and cloudy. On the one hand, at a conceptual level, some accounting academics are busy making 'accounting readings' of what is happening in other disciplines; while, on the other hand, some are attempting to fine-tune the definition of SMA by clarifying which interface (whether strategic management or marketing) with management accounting is more defining for SMA (see Roslender and Hart, 2002, 2003). For convenience, we are proposing a classification of emerging SMA contents on the basis of which elements of strategy those are directly related to. For this classification and in line with the three-way extension of SMA we depicted in Figure 8.1, we identify three major arenas of 'strategy': corporate, marketing and manufacturing/operations. Thus, we have three directions of SMA for each of these. Table 8.2 summarizes our classification, and the rest of this chapter will deal with the first two directions. Accounting for new manufacturing will be dealt with in the next two chapters.

> Three directions of SMA: accounting for corporate strategy, marketing strategy and manufacturing strategy.

ACCOUNTING FOR CORPORATE STRATEGY

Accounting for corporate strategy takes place at three different levels: ideological, conceptual and technical. At the ideological level, the accounting profession has begun to learn and internalize late modern or post-industrialist corporate ideologies (see also Chapters 7, 9 and 10) of flexibility,

Table 8.2 *Directions of/approaches to SMA*

SMA approach/ direction	Strategic questions/concerns	Underlying strategic concepts/popular techniques deployed
Accounting for corporate strategy	How do we envision our future? What should our mission be? What should our guiding principles (business philosophy) be?	Visionary leadership Strategic thinking Industry foresight
	What are our strategic business units (SBU)? What overall strategies should we adopt for them?	BCG growth share matrix, GE nine-cell matrix
	What are the external opportunities and threats for our businesses? What are the internal strengths and weaknesses of our businesses?	SWOT analysis
	How do we communicate our mission and strategies? What financial and non-financial objectives should cover our mission and strategy? How do we align short-term actions with long-term strategy? How do we measure the degree of success in implementing our strategy and achieving our mission?	Balanced scorecard (BSC)
Accounting for market/ competitive strategy	How do we understand the competitive environment within which our businesses/products compete?	Porter's five forces model
	What are the identifiable segments of our product markets? Which segments are attractive for us?	Market segment analysis/segment profitability analysis
	What competitive advantages should we aim at?	Resource and capability analysis Value-chain analysis
	What generic strategies or product market strategies should we choose for our businesses/products?	Porter's generic strategies Ansoff's product-market expansion grid
	What stages in their life cycles are our products at? What strategies should we adopt for each product in different life-cycle stages?	Product life-cycle analysis and costing
	How should we position our products in selected segments? What attributes/benefits of the product appeal for each segment? How should we position and promote our brands?	Marketing mix strategies Product attribute analysis and costing Brand management
	Do we have competitive capacity to deliver preferred product attributes at a target cost? How do we position our product attributes and cost in relation to competitive product attributes and costs?	Value-chain analysis Product attribute analysis and costing Activity-based management Strategic cost analysis
	How profitable are our customers?	Customer profitability analysis

251

Table 8.2 *continued*

SMA approach/ direction	Strategic questions/concerns	Underlying strategic concepts/popular techniques deployed
Accounting for operations strategy	Do we have operating or manufacturing capabilities to meet demands imposed by corporate and marketing strategies?	Value-chain analysis Core-competency analysis
	What should our target operating costs be?	Target costing
	Do we meet our target operating costs imposed by marketing strategies? If not, how can we improve our cost conditions?	Value-chain analysis Continuous improvement programmes
	How can we make sure our operating activities are efficient enough to meet cost and productivity targets?	Activity-based management/ budgeting and costing, value-chain analysis, standard costing
	How do we make sure that our products and processes meet quality standards set by business and marketing strategies?	Total quality management (TQM)
	How do we make sure that our day-to-day operations are carried out smoothly and efficiently without any bottlenecks due to reasons such as disturbances in resource supply? How do we keep our inventory costs to a minimum while making sure that no inventory shortages would disturb production runs? How do we make sure that our suppliers continuously meet our operational demands for supplies?	Production scheduling and resource planning techniques such as ERP, MRP and line balancing Inventory management techniques such as JIT and kanban Supply network design and supply chain planning and control
	How do we make sure that our manufacturing/ operations systems and technologies are better than those of our competitors?	Continuous improvement Business process re-engineering (BPR) Research and development activities

change, pluralism, futurism and 'imaginization' (Morgan, 1997), etc. It is at this level that they first understand the deficiency of their existing paradigm, and the necessity and inevitability for change. At the conceptual level, accountants come to know various strategic themes and to appreciate their relevance for management accounting. They embrace those strategic themes as guiding principles or theories to frame the change that they strive to bring in their profession. At the technical level, they engage in developing various managerial techniques through which those ideological apparatuses of post-industrial or late modern capitalism would be realized.[2] In the next few sub-sections we will discuss some of these strategic themes and techniques.

Accounting for business strategy takes place at three different levels: ideological, conceptual and technical.

Organizational vision

The central theme of strategic management is the organization's future. In the popular discourses of strategic management, the 'future' is portrayed as the driving force of the present, not simply as the outcome of what we do today. For management gurus like Peter Drucker (1989), Hamel and Prahalad (1994), Gareth Morgan (1997) and Theodore Levitt (1960), the future takes place before the present, in the minds of visionary leaders. Thus, Hamel and Prahalad (1994: 64) do not believe that:

> any company can get along without a well-articulated point of view about tomorrow's opportunities and challenges . . . To get to the future first, top management must either see opportunities not seen by other top teams or be able to exploit opportunities by virtue of preemptive and consistent capability-building that other companies can't.

Furthermore, the capacity for 'seeing the future first' comes from 'industry foresight' (or 'vision' for many others), which is 'based on deep insights into the trends in technology, demographics, regulation, and lifestyles that can be harnessed to rewrite industry rules and create new competitive space' (Hamel and Prahalad, 1994: 66).

Vision is not simply a projection of the present to the future or a forecast, but the ideologies of visionary corporate leaders formed with deep insights into the envisioned future. It is the future that corporate leaders believe they should and can achieve and, therefore, commit themselves to achieve.

It is stated that vision is not simply a projection of the present to the future or a forecast, but the ideologies of visionary corporate leaders formed with deep insights into the envisioned future. It is the future that corporate leaders believe they should and can achieve and, therefore, commit themeslves to achieve. Thus, the notion of 'vision', at least in the popular management press, has been given a normative social value as the definition of societal progress, to which, it is argued, every organizational member and resource should be committed. In this way, creating a 'corporate vision' (often communicated through a vision statement) has been made the starting point of the strategy formulation process. Management gurus have provided us with certain conceptual frameworks to create corporate vision. For example, Collins and Porras (1996) suggest that corporate vision should consist of two major components: 'core ideology' and 'envisioned future'. For them, 'core ideology' defines what we stand for (core values) and why we exist (core purpose, which is a *raison d'être*, not a goal or a business strategy). 'Envisioned future', according to Collins and Porras, consists of 'big, hairy, audacious goals' (BHAG as they put it, as an aide-mémoire for strategic managers) and 'vivid description' – that is, a vibrant, engaging and specific description of what it will be like to achieve the BHAG. Corporate vision, they believe, will provide the context for marching towards the 'future'.

Creating a 'corporate vision' has been made the starting point of the strategy formulation process.

What is important is not what a corporate vision should contain, or how corporate managers should go about creating one, but the type of transformation that the notion of vision exemplifies. One thing is apparent: it has made significant inroads into corporate communication. At least as a tool of public relations and advertising, many companies include vision and mission statements in their annual reports and other internal and external communication materials. By doing that, they explicitly communicate that their *raison d'être* extends far beyond shareholders' wealth, and their planning horizon extends far beyond the conventional financial planning range. More importantly, corporations are projected as having 'sacred' societal purposes, so that commitment of people and resources for corporate growth is socially justified (see Table 8.3). Finally, simply as one of many objectives, profitability is communicated to the society as a 'necessary condition' without which those 'sacred' purposes of capitalist enterprises cannot be achieved. Thus, through discourses of vision and mission, capitalist enterprises, in a way, have begun a project of representing themselves as kinds of 'not-for-profit organizations' in the long run.

Through vision statements, corporations are projected as having 'sacred' societal purposes beyond shareholders' wealth, so that commitment of people and resources for corporate growth is socially justified

Mission

The difference between 'vision' and 'mission' is not always clear when we look at the way these terms are used in company reports. However, if we follow the prescriptive discourse of management gurus, we can discern certain differences between the two concepts. While vision defines the future in terms of 'industry foresight', 'core ideology' and 'envisioned future', mission defines the current business in terms of 'company strategic goals', 'guiding principles or policies' and 'major competitive scope'. Thus, according to Kotler (2003: 91), 'to define its mission a company should address Peter Drucker's classic questions: What is our business? Who is our customer? What is of value to the customer? What will our business be? What should our business be?' In general, what Kotler and Drucker mean is that mission defines the scope of the business in terms of a set of critical dimensions such as industry, products and applications, competencies, market segments, vertical integration and geographical domain.

Even after reading popular literature on vision and mission, the difference remains unclear, we guess, not only for us but also for many practising corporate managers. Much corporate reporting, for example, does not deploy both of these concepts, but uses one or other of them in a similar

Table 8.3 *Corporate reasons for being 'not for profit' – some examples*

3M	To solve unsolved problems innovatively
Cargill	To improve the standard of living around the world
Fannie Mae	To strengthen the social fabric by continually democratizing home ownership
Hewlett-Packard	To make technical contributions for the advancement and welfare of humanity
Lost Arrow Corporation	To be a role model and a tool for social change
Pacific Theatres	To provide a place for people to flourish and to enhance the community
Mary Kay Cosmetics	To give unlimited opportunity to women
McKinsey & Company	To help leading corporations and governments be more successful
Merck	To preserve and improve human life
Sony	To experience the joy of advancing and applying technology for the benefit of the public
Telecare Corporation	To help people with mental impairments realize their full potential
Wal-Mart	To give ordinary folk the chance to buy the same things as rich people
Walt Disney	To make people happy

Source: Collins and Porras (1996: 69)

While vision defines the future in terms of 'industry foresight', 'core ideology' and 'envisioned future', mission defines the current business in terms of 'company strategic goals', 'guiding principles or policies' and 'major competitive scope'.

fashion. Even in the cases where both are used, the difference is not easy to discern, as both mission and vision statements contain similar vivid descriptions, goals and philosophies or policies. Nevertheless, one thing is clear: they are popular among corporate managers and are often deployed to convey the message that their corporations are striving for a set of 'sacred' societal purposes, far beyond shareholders' wealth. Thus, when accountants embrace strategic notions such as vision and mission, they are inevitably forced to rethink their conceptual frameworks, which were hitherto built upon the unitary notion of shareholders' wealth-maximization, in the light of these futuristic and pluralistic notions of corporate objectives and rationales.

Despite the conceptual ambiguity of vision and mission, one thing is clear: they are both deployed to convey the message that corporations are striving for a set of 'sacred' societal purposes, far beyond shareholders' wealth.

Corporate strategies and portfolio planning models

Again, like many other strategic themes, the concept of 'strategy' has multiple meanings and is deployed at multiple levels. Hence, rather than listing a set of different definitions of 'strategy', let us discuss different levels and different ways that strategies are devised in organizations. Accordingly, we will be able to understand the generic meaning that corporate managers attach to the term, and different analytical devices (or conceptual frameworks) that they use to define strategies.

> The concept of 'strategy' has multiple meanings and is deployed at multiple levels.

Strategic management literature commonly understands that organizational strategies are devised at three different levels:

- corporate strategies;
- business, product or market strategies;
- functional strategies (operations, HRM, finance, etc.).

Here the corporate level refers to a collection of different businesses, which corporate managers often call strategic business units (SBU). A corporate entity such as Sony would consist of a portfolio of SBUs competing in different markets, serving different customer groups, and deploying different technologies (see Figure 8.3). It is uniformity and diversity of the business portfolio that define the vertical and horizontal scope of the corporate entity. The fundamental question at corporate planning level is to decide upon the overall cohesiveness of the business portfolio, and future viability of each SBU in the portfolio, in the light of their internal and external contexts.

> The fundamental question at corporate planning level is to decide upon the overall cohesiveness of the business portfolio, and future viability of each SBU in the portfolio.

Corporate planning consultants have developed a few conceptual tools to evaluate a business portfolio, and to prescribe appropriate strategies for each SBU. These models are commonly known as 'portfolio planning models'. Two are especially well known: the Boston Consultancy Group's (BCG) growth share matrix and General Electric's (GE) nine-cell matrix.

The BCG matrix

The BCG matrix is a two-dimensional typology of the SBU, and its methodology is to classify and map SBUs on the basis of two related variables (see Figure 8.4):

- Market growth rate as an indicator of market attractiveness.
- Relative market share as an indicator of the company's strength in the market. It measures the market share of the business relative to the market share of the largest competitor. For

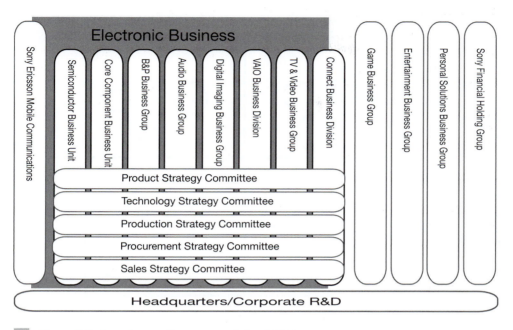

Figure 8.3 *Sony Corporation as a portfolio of SBUs*

Source: <http://www.sony.net/SonyInfo/CorporateInfo/Data/organization.html>

example, if the market share of the business is 20 per cent while the largest competitor's is 40 per cent, the relative market share of the business is 0.5. Hence, a relative market share more than 1 means the business is the market leader.

> The BCG matrix is a two-dimensional typology of the SBU and its methodology is to classify and map SBUs on the basis of two related variables: market growth rate and relative market share.

As is shown in Figure 8.4, the BCG matrix is a conceptual map divided into four distinct arenas, each equating to different 'strategic positions'. Company SBUs are located across this map according to their relative market share and market growth rate. Each SBU is represented by a circle, the size of which is proportional to the sales volume. The result is that corporate managers are provided with a graphical overview of the profit potentials of their SBUs, based upon which they can recommend 'strategies' for each SBU in the portfolio. For example, if an SBU is located in the quadrant of high market growth and high relative market share, then that SBU is identified as a 'star'. The 'strategic prescription' for a star is 'invest for growth' (see Table 8.4 for a full description of classification and strategic prescriptions). This means that corporate leaders should love the business with a bright future, and should invest in it to grow and expand. Thus, it should receive more funds from corporate head office for capacity expansion, new recruitment, research and development, market promotion and so on.

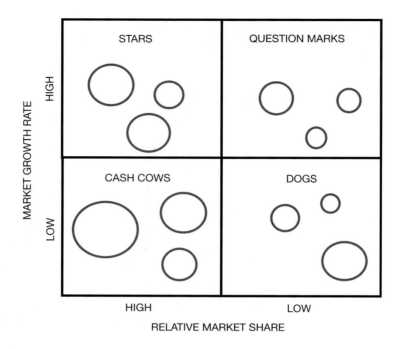

Figure 8.4 *BCG growth share matrix*

The GE nine-cell matrix

The GE nine-cell matrix, the second portfolio planning model, is an extension of the BCG methodology. The proponents of this model understand that market growth rate and relative market share alone cannot diagnose the strategic positions of SBUs. Thus, they use multiple criteria to measure 'market attractiveness' (which is measured only by market growth rate in the BCG matrix) and 'business strength' (which is measured only by relative market share in the BCG matrix). Furthermore, the strategic map is divided into nine areas, so that the marginal cases can be better analysed and a wider set of strategies can be recommended. Figure 8.5 illustrates the GE nine-cell matrix.

Similar to the BCG matrix, the GE nine-cell matrix also maps SBUs in a business portfolio using two dimensions: market attractiveness and business strength, which are, however, measured as composite indices of the number of indicators.

So, what is corporate strategy in the context of the strategic planning exercise manifested in portfolio planning models? It is a resource allocation decision among different businesses: deciding which businesses should receive more funds for growth, and which businesses those funds should be extracted from through 'milking' and 'divestments'. It is aimed at maximizing future cash flow

Table 8.4 *Strategic labelling and prescriptions in BCG growth share matrix*

Market growth rate	Relative market share	Labels	Strategic position	Strategic prescription
High	High	Stars	Strong business in high growing market High future positive net cash flows, if developed to keep up with evolving market	Invest and grow: ■ Capacity expansion ■ New recruitments in business leadership ■ Market promotion ■ Product development and improvement ■ Distribution channel development, etc.
High	Low	Question marks	An infant/weak business in high growth market Future cash flows uncertain	Selective invest/divest: ■ Need for further analysis into future potential of cash flows ■ If future potentials seem to be good, invest and grow, otherwise divest
Low	High	Cash cows	Strong business in mature market Though business is strong, future market opportunities are limited High stable positive net cash flows	Hold and milk: ■ No need of expansionary investment, market promotion or product development ■ Maintain current level of operations ■ Improve profitability through cost reduction
Low	Low	Dogs	Weak business in non-growing market Negative cash flows and no future potential of positive cash flows	Divest: ■ Operational cost-cutting programmes ■ Downsizing, redundancies and facility closures ■ Moving into niche markets, etc.

Source: based on Grant (1995)

possibilities of the corporate entity. The process of deciding strategies is rather analytical and rational: use the tool, diagnose the position, then prescribe. The methodology of portfolio planning models is simple. They diagnose the 'strategic position' of each SBU using an analytical tool, a 'strategic map', where each SBU is located using two variables: market attractiveness and business strength. Then, depending on its position on that map, each SBU is given a label (question mark, star, cash cow or dog, in the case of the BCG matrix). For each label, there are ready-made 'strategic prescriptions'. The role of corporate managers is made simple: use the tool, diagnose the position, then prescribe. In that sense, though popular until the late 1980s, portfolio models have never been up to the 'post-industrial' notion of strategy manifested in corporate vision and mission statements. Ignoring all those 'sacred' purposes of corporations expressed in vision and mission (see Table 8.3, above), portfolio models simply concentrate on profit potentials of businesses and market – a rather 'modernistic' notion of business purposes.

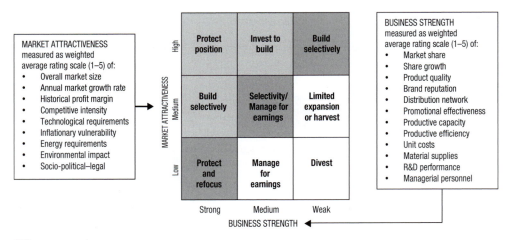

MARKET ATTRACTIVENESS
measured as weighted
average rating scale (1–5) of:
- Overall market size
- Annual market growth rate
- Historical profit margin
- Competitive intensity
- Technological requirements
- Inflationary vulnerability
- Energy requirements
- Environmental impact
- Socio-political–legal

BUSINESS STRENGTH
measured as weighted
average rating scale (1–5) of:
- Market share
- Share growth
- Product quality
- Brand reputation
- Distribution network
- Promotional effectiveness
- Productive capacity
- Productive efficiency
- Unit costs
- Material supplies
- R&D performance
- Managerial personnel

	Strong	Medium	Weak
High	Protect position	Invest to build	Build selectively
Medium	Build selectively	Selectivity/ Manage for earnings	Limited expansion or harvest
Low	Protect and refocus	Manage for earnings	Divest

MARKET ATTRACTIVENESS

BUSINESS STRENGTH

Figure 8.5 *General Electric portfolio planning model*
Source: based on Grant (1995) and Kotler (2003)

> Strategy, at the level of corporate porfolio planning, is a resource allocation decision among different businesses: deciding which businesses should receive more funds for growth, and which businesses those funds should be extracted from through 'milking' and 'divestments'.

Information requirements of portfolio models, however, extend beyond organizations to industry aggregates and trends. Computations of relative market share, market growth rate and other indicators used in the GE matrix demand such industry data, which are often beyond the domain of conventional management accounting. To attune with these strategic management tools, management accounting should acquire external orientation with a survey-type methodology of collecting market information. An alternative approach is to use industry databases run by third-party, independent organizations. A typical example is the PIMS (Profit Impact on Market Strategy) database run by the Strategic Planning Institute, which describes PIMS as:

> A large scale study designed to measure the relationship between business actions and business results. The project was initiated and developed at the General Electric Co. from the mid-1960s and expanded upon at the Management Science Institute at Harvard in the early 1970s; since 1975 The Strategic Planning Institute has continued the development and application of the PIMS research . . .
>
> The PIMS database forms the core of all services delivered by The Strategic Planning Institute. The database is a collection of statistically documented experiences drawn from thousands of businesses, designed to help understand what kinds of strategies (e.g. quality, pricing, vertical integration, innovation, advertising) work best in what kinds of business environments. The data constitute a key resource for such critical management tasks as evaluating business performance, analysing new business opportunities, evaluating and reality testing new strategies, and screening business portfolios.
>
> (<http://www.pimsonline.com/about_pims_db.htm>)

> Information requirements of portfolio models extend beyond the organization to industry aggregates and trends, which are often beyond the domain of conventional management accounting.

BUSINESS-LEVEL STRATEGIES: ACCOUNTING FOR COMPETITIVE MARKET POSITIONING

The second level at which the notion of 'strategy' is deployed is at the business, product or market level. At this level, strategies possess a rather different meaning than they have at the corporate level: they become competitive 'game plans' to achieve 'competitive advantages' by 'strategically positioning' the firm's products in a 'competitive structure', which is the industry. In essence, at business level, strategy becomes a 'competitive strategy' which is, according to Porter (1985: 1), 'the search for a favourable competitive position in an industry, the fundamental arena in which competition occurs'.

> At business level, strategy becomes a 'competitive strategy' which is, according to Porter (1985: 1), 'the search for a favourable competitive position in an industry, the fundamental arena in which competition occurs'.

The most popular conceptual frameworks employed to understand and devise market strategies are Michael Porter's competitive strategy (1980) and competitive advantage (1985). At the epi-centre of these, as the result of successful competitive strategies, lies the notion of competitive advantage – a firm's capacity to create and sustain superior performance. Porter argues that doing so depends on two major factors:

■ attractiveness of the industry in which the firm competes; and
■ the firm's relative competitive position.

Neither of these factors by itself, however, determines competitive advantage, but their combination does. That is because neither competitive leadership in an unattractive industry nor poor positioning in an attractive industry would result in superior performance.

> A firm's capacity to gain and sustain a competitive advantage depends on two factors: industry attractiveness and the firm's relative competitive position.

The way that a firm chooses to position its products/brands in the industry is the competitive strategy. Porter's framework suggests that there are three generic ways that a firm can position

261

itself: cost leadership, differentiation and focus. The firm's choice of competitive strategy is a matter of both 'competitive structure' and the firm's internal structure (the value chain). Thus, there are two strategic analyses pertaining to Porter's framework: structural analysis of the industry and value-chain analysis of the firm's operations. An overview of Porter's framework is illustrated in Figure 8.6.

> Porter's framework suggests that there are three generic ways that a firm can position itself in the industry: cost leadership, differentiation and focus.

Generic strategies

Relative positioning of a firm in the industry is a critical determinant of its performance. Figure 8.6 shows Porter's three positioning strategies from which a firm can choose: cost leadership, differentiation and focus. Cost leadership generally means that the firm attempts to gain the position of 'lowest-cost producer', so that it can offer a standard product at a lower price than its competitors. Differentiation, on the other hand, means offering a superior quality product at a premium price such that the premium price difference is more than justified by the superior-quality. Focus positioning means choosing either cost leadership or differentiation, not in a broader cross-section of the market, but in a narrower market niche. Table 8.5 summarizes the differences between these three modes of market positioning. Please pay special attention to the last row, where the management control implications are highlighted.

Industry analysis

Porter's framework of competitive strategy demands two types of strategic analysis: industry and value chain. The rationale for industry analysis comes from the assertion that 'competitive strategy

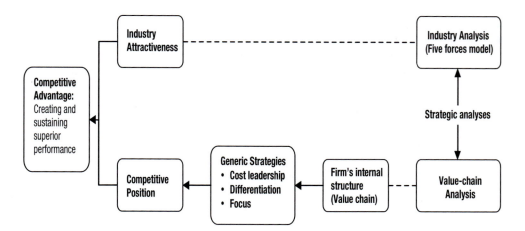

Figure 8.6 *Overview of Porter's framework*

Table 8.5 *Generic strategies of market positioning*

	Cost leadership	Differentiation	Focus
Strategic target	Broad cross-section of market	Broad cross-section of market	Narrow market niche where buyer needs and preferences are distinctly different from the rest of the market
Basis of competitive advantage	Lower cost than competitors	Ability to offer buyers something different from competitors	Either of cost leadership or differentiation: i.e., cost focus or differentiation focus
Product line	Good basic product with few lines (acceptable quality and limited selection)	Many product variations, wide selection, strong emphasis on chosen differentiation features	Customized to fit specialized needs of target segment
Production emphasis	Continuous search for cost reduction without sacrificing acceptable quality and essential features	Invent ways to create value for buyers	Tailor-made for niche
Marketing emphasis	Try to make virtue out of product features that lead to low cost	Build in whatever features buyers are willing to pay for Charge premium price to cover extra costs of differentiating features	Communicate focuser's unique ability to satisfy buyer's specialized requirements
Management control and accounting paradigm	Tight cost controls and intense supervision of labour Tendency to de-skill and automate activities Tighter integrated production scheduling and inventory controls to minimize waste and idle time Dedicated line of suppliers and integrated systems to co-ordinate with suppliers and distributors Frequent, detailed control reports emphasizing cost deviations Structured organization and responsibilities Incentives based on meeting strict quantitative/cost targets More emphasis on production-driven or factory-floor performance indicators	Strong co-ordination among functions in R&D, product development and marketing Tendency to organize work as autonomous teamwork or projects Subjective measurements and incentives instead of quantitative measures Amenities to attract high-skilled labour, scientists or creative people More emphasis on market-based performance indicators	Combination of above policies directed at particular strategic target

Source: based on Porter (1980, 1985)

263

must grow out of a sophisticated understanding of the rules of competition that determine an industry's attractiveness' (Porter, 1985: 4). However, this is no different from the conventional old school of strategic thinking of market analysis, except that Porter provides a refined conceptual framework for such analyses. For example, traditional portfolio planning models, which we discussed in the previous section, also concentrate on the same analytical dimensions, such as market attractiveness, which is of course the same as industry attractiveness, but uses different criteria to measure it (see GE nine-cell matrix's weighted average rating scale indicators for market attractiveness). The conceptual or analytical advancement that Porter brings to market analysis is that he organizes various factors that determine the competitive attractiveness under five competitive forces (so the framework is popularly known as the 'five forces model'). Figure 8.7 summarizes this analytical framework.

> The rationale for industry analysis comes from the assertion that competitive strategy must grow out of a sophisticated understanding of the rules of competition that determine an industry's attractiveness.

The management accounting implications of Porter's industry analysis are not so different from those of the portfolio planning models we discussed earlier. Like those models, Porter's five forces model also draws managers' attention to a large number of 'industry factors', and the necessity for 'external information' is created. As opposed to conventional management accounting systems,

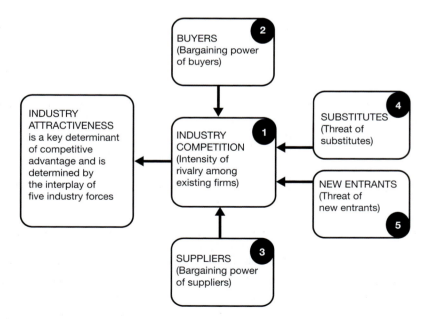

Figure 8.7 *Competitive structure – five forces model*

Source: based on Porter (1985)

which collect and organize data in an automated or semi-automated manner through 'transaction processing systems', collection, organization, interpretation and reporting of such external data require a rather non-transactional methodology that monitors and captures external environmental events and trends. Indeed, many organizations have set up separate departments, such as marketing research or economic analysis, for this information function, leaving little room for management accountants. Nevertheless, the management accounting role is more explicit and prominent in internal strategic analyses, especially in strategic cost analysis, along with value-chain analysis (see Shank and Govindarajan, 1989).

> Like portfolio planning models, Porter's five forces model also draws managers' attention to a large number of 'industry factors', and a necessity for 'external information' is created.

Value-chain analysis

This is the internal analysis of the firm to determine its potential for pursuing cost leadership or differentiation as the selected positioning strategy. Porter conceptualizes firms as 'value chains' where organizational activities can be represented as a set of:

■ Primary activities organized in a sequence of input–output relationships.
■ Supporting activities organized around primary activities to provide the necessary infrastructural conditions needed to perform those primary activities (see Figure 8.8).

> Organization as a value chain consists of primary and support activities.

According to Porter (1985), value-chain analysis consists of three interrelated phases, which are the steps in 'strategic cost analysis' for Shank and Govindarajan (1989: 40–41):

1. Define the firm's value chain and assign costs and assets to activities.
2. Investigate cost drivers regulating each value activity.
3. Examine possibilities to build sustainable competitive advantages either through controlling cost drivers or by reconfiguring the value chain.

The management accounting significance of the value-chain concept is that it draws managers' attention to activities. Activities are taken as the building blocks of a firm's value creation process, and it is understood that costs and quality are more related to activities than conventionally adopted capacity concepts, such as production volumes, labour hours and machine hours. Thus, classification of costs, especially overhead costs, which form a greater proportion of overall cost of delivering value to the customer, on the basis of activities is understood to be more managerially meaningful than the conventional costs classifications around resource categories (i.e., material, labour and expenses). Similarly, understanding cost behaviour on the basis of activity-cost drivers

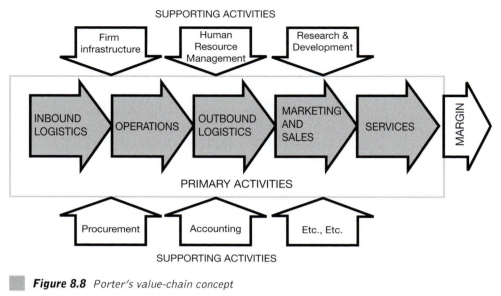

Figure 8.8 *Porter's value-chain concept*
Source: based on Porter (1985)

is more meaningful, because activities represent 'incidence of cost' closer than production volume. In other words, what are to be managed are activities not costs, because costs are the results of activities. The management accounting manifestation of this activity orientation emphasized by value-chain analysis is activity-based costing and management (ABC and ABM), which we will discuss in the next chapter.

> Activities are taken as the building blocks of a firm's value creation process, and it is understood that costs and quality are more related to activities than conventionally adopted capacity concepts, such as production volumes, labour hours and machine hours.

PERFORMANCE MEASUREMENT SYSTEMS: FROM CONVENTIONAL TO STRATEGIC

It is not an exaggeration to say that the most widely discussed and attempted (both successfully and unsuccessfully) recent innovations in management accounting are activity-based costing and the balanced scorecard. While ABC is proposed as a more accurate system of tracing product costs and a more effective way of managing costs, the BSC is proposed, initially, as a performance measurement system (PMS) that integrates financial with non-financial and operational with strategic dimensions of managing business performance.

As its name suggests, there is a specific focus for PMS – to provide information about the performance of the company or any sub-system therein. What we mean by the term 'performance' is the degree to which the company (or any sub-system therein) achieves its set targets in relation to key success factors. Hence, its focus is basically internal and measurement-oriented. Rather than merely reporting on various occurrences and activities, a PMS computes and communicates indicators or measures on the critical aspects of organizational activities. Practitioners and management accounting writers often equate a PMS with a car dashboard (e.g., Anthony and Govindarajan, 1998: 462). This analogy is a good way to understand the relationship between a PMS and a management control system (MCS). For example, a car's control system includes:

■ Mechanisms or tools of control: steering wheel, clutch, accelerator, brake, gear system, etc., that the driver handles to regulate the performance of the vehicle.
■ Performance measurement system: indicators and meters on the dashboard that inform the driver about what has happened or what is happening with respect to some selected critical factors (such as speed, RPM, etc.). By reading these meters and indicators, the driver makes decisions and carries them out by manoeuvring the control tools.

By the same token, an organizational PMS constitutes a specific sub-system of the overall control system. Its primary objective is to measure and communicate a set of indicators or measures which should accurately reflect critical factors – the factors which will determine the success of the company. Figure 8.9 shows this conception of a PMS in relation to an organizational control system.

> An organizational PMS constitutes a specific sub-system of the overall control system. Its primary objective is to measure and communicate a set of indicators or measures which should accurately reflect critical factors – the factors which will determine the success of the company.

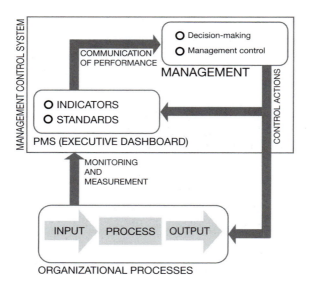

Figure 8.9 *PMS and organizational control systems*

Conventional measures of performance

During the last decade or so, PMS has become a hot topic in management accounting as well as in strategic management literature. For management accounting practitioners and academics, it has become one of the main opportunities to regain the (lost) relevance of their subject in the context of strategy formulation and implementation. Especially with the emergence of ABC and BSC, management accounting has embarked on a project of redesigning its conventional PMS to give it a strategic intent and content. However, before moving on to the issue of strategic PMS, we should explain the salient features and weaknesses of a conventional PMS. For the purpose of comparison with strategic PMS later in this chapter, we will discuss the nature of a conventional PMS in line with four dimensions: tools of measurement, dimensions of measurement, mode of operation and focus.

Tools of measurement: responsibility accounting

A conventional PMS is a collection of management accounting techniques and tools that provides segmented and detailed reports on various aspects of the company's financial performance. These techniques are mainly hinged upon the notion of responsibility accounting. Budgeting and variance analysis, divisional performance reporting and transfer pricing, and financial statement analysis (which mainly includes comparative financial statements, ratio analysis and trend analysis) are the most popular.

> Conventional PMS is mainly hinged upon the notion of responsibility accounting, and encompasses techniques such as budgeting and variance analysis, divisional performance reporting and financial statement analysis.

Dimensions of measurement: financial emphasis

A conventional PMS concentrates only on the financial aspects of the company. It attempts to measure the 'financial health' of the business. Thus, the factors it conceives as critical to the survival and growth of the company are basically financial, and often classified as profitability, efficiency, liquidity, gearing and investment attractiveness (see Table 8.6 for some measures of each of these financial dimensions). As a result, a conventional PMS is often criticized for its lack of concern for non-financial dimensions of company performance.

> Conventional PMS concentrates only on the financial aspects of the company, and, hence, is often criticized for its lack of concern for non-financial dimensions.

Even at individual and departmental levels, performance measurements are confined to budgetary targets which, within conventional budgeting and standard costing frameworks, emphasize cost and revenue targets.

Table 8.6 *Conventional PMS – critical indicators at organization level*

Dimension	What it measures	Common measures
Profitability	Firm's ability to generate profit out of sales or investment	Gross profit margin Net profit margin Return on investment (ROI) Return on capital employed (ROCE) Return on shareholders' fund (ROSF)
Liquidity	Firm's ability to meet its maturing short-term financial obligations	Current ratio Quick asset ratio
Efficiency	How efficiently firm is using its current and fixed assets	Stock turnover and/or stock-holding period Debtors' collection period Fixed asset turnover
Gearing	Extent to which firm has been financed by debt	Total debt to total assets Times interest earned
Investment attractiveness/market valuation	How attractive firm is to potential investors	Earning per share Dividend yield

Mode of operation: dis-integration

The basic principle of organizing a conventional PMS is the conceptual breakdown of overall business into a set of interrelated operations, processes and/or factors. For example, conventional budgeting compartmentalizes the overall business (represented by the master budget: i.e., the budgeted profit and loss account and balance sheet) into a set of related activities, such as sales, production, purchasing, labour usage and overhead expenses, etc. Then, on the basis of limiting factors and previous-year performances, budgetary targets are set (static budgets). After the elapse of the budget period, these budgeted figures are flexed to reflect actual level of operations, and variances are calculated and reported for the attention of management. See Chapter 4 for an illustration of this dis-integration associated with budgeting and variance analysis. Another example of this dis-integrative mode of analysis is the DuPont ratio analysis framework.

> The basic principle of organizing a conventional PMS is the conceptual breakdown of overall business into a set of interrelated operations, processes and/or factors.

Focus: emphasis on ROI and budgetary compliance

The focus of a conventional PMS is on the contribution to return on investment (ROI). It provides cost, revenue and profitability indicators on how well resources are utilized within different divisions or departments, often called 'responsibility centres', which might be cost centres, profit centres or investment centres. Thus, the main focus of a conventional PMS is to set budgetary targets in terms of revenue, costs or profits for each responsibility centre, and then to measure how well each responsibility centre contributes to the overall organizational ROI by achieving those budgetary targets.

> The focus of a conventional PMS is on the divisional contribution to return on investment.

Weaknesses of a conventional PMS

A conventional PMS is often subject to many criticisms. Drawing from a number of sources, Tangen (2004: 726–727) lists the following weaknesses of a conventional PMS that should be addressed in order to develop better ones:

- They try to quantify performance solely in financial terms. And hence they neglect non-financial aspects such as product quality, customer satisfaction and innovation capabilities, etc., which are indeed critical determinants of the long-term success of the organization.
- They largely produce outcome measures and inherently lack the potential of producing driver measures. In general, PMSs provide two kinds of measures: outcome and driver measures. Outcome measures are lagging indicators, they tell managers what has happened. By contrast, driver measures are leading indicators showing the progress of key areas of concern (Anthony and Govindarajan, 1998: 463).
- They do not have the required flexibility to suit changing circumstances over time and across different departments, which have unique characteristics and priorities.
- Financial measures that conventional PMSs produce are not directly related to manufacturing, marketing or overall corporate strategies.
- They are short-term-oriented and, for that reason, discourage long-term vision and improvements.
- They are focused on controlling processes and activities in isolation rather than as a whole system, and hence promote sub-optimization.

> Conventional PMSs are criticized for:
>
> - being biased towards financial indicators;
> - providing lagging indicators;
> - being less flexible;
> - being non-related to strategies;
> - being short-term-oriented;
> - promoting sub-optimization.

THE BSC AS AN INTEGRATIVE/STRATEGIC PMS

With the increasing emphasis on market competition, innovations, change and strategic aspects of managing business, limitations of conventional PMSs are felt more. The result is the emergence of various models that attempt to integrate PMSs with corporate strategies and non-financial aspects of businesses.

The balanced scorecard (BSC), first proposed by Kaplan and Norton (1992), is probably the most well-known strategic PMS today. It attempts to overcome weaknesses of conventional PMSs by:

- integrating financial measures with non-financial measures;
- linking performance measures to corporate strategy.

Kaplan and Norton (1993: 134) provide the following introduction to the BSC:

> The balanced scorecard . . . provides executives with a comprehensive framework that translates a company's strategic objectives into a coherent set of performance measures. Much more than a measurement exercise, the balanced scorecard is a management system that can motivate breakthrough improvements in such critical areas as product, process, customer, and market development.

Elsewhere, they also provide a description as to what a BSC contains (1992: 71):

> 'Balanced scorecard' [is a] set of measures that gives top managers a fast but comprehensive view of the business. The balanced scorecard includes financial measures that tell the results of actions already taken. And it complements the financial measures with operational measures on customer satisfaction, internal processes, and the organization's innovation and improvement activities – operational measures that are the drivers of future financial performance.

The BSC is proposed as a strategic PMS to overcome the weaknesses of a conventional PMS by:

- integrating financial measures with non-financial measures;
- linking performance measures to corporate strategy.

Perhaps a better way to have a comparative understanding of the BSC is to compare it with a conventional PMS. A summary of the comparison is given in Table 8.7 and is followed by discussions in the next sections.

Critical dimensions of measurement

In contrast to the financial over-emphasis of a conventional PMS, the BSC attempts to balance financial and non-financial dimensions of performance. These critical dimensions are presented as answers to the following questions (Kaplan and Norton, 1992: 72; see Figure 8.10).

Table 8.7 *Comparison between conventional PMS and BSC*

	Conventional PMS	BSC
Framework of measurements	Responsibility accounting	Scorecards
Critical dimensions of measurement	Financial aspects only	Financial and non-financial
Modes of operation	Dis-integration and compartmentalization	Integration of different functional perspectives
Focus	Budgetary compliance	Strategic alignment

1. How do customers see us? (Customer perspective.)
2. What must we excel at? (Internal perspective.)
3. Can we continue to improve and create value? (Innovation and learning perspective.)
4. How do we look to shareholders? (Financial perspective.)

Four perspectives of the BSC are:

- customer;
- internal;
- innovation and learning;
- financial.

By answering these four questions, it is argued, the BSC endeavours to create a blend of strategic measures: the outcome and driver measures, financial and non-financial measures and internal and external measures (Anthony and Govindarajan, 1998: 463).

- Customer perspective. Kaplan and Norton (1992: 73) state that managers should translate the company's general mission statement into specific measures that reflect the factors that really matter to customers. They also argue that customers' concerns tend to fall into four categories: time, quality, performance and service, and cost. Hence, they prescribe that companies should articulate goals for time, quality, performance and service, and then translate these goals into specific measures. In addition to these three areas, they also argue that companies must remain sensitive to the cost of their products, which encompasses not only the price of the products but also a range of other customer-driven costs.
- Internal perspective. According to Kaplan and Norton (1992: 75), this attempts to capture those critical internal operations that enable the company to meet customer expectations. Managers should identify business processes that have the greatest impact upon customer satisfaction, especially those which have a determinant impact upon cycle time, quality, employee skills and productivity. It is also necessary to identify core competencies, the critical technologies needed to ensure continued market leadership. Then they should decide what processes and competencies they must excel at and specify measures for each.

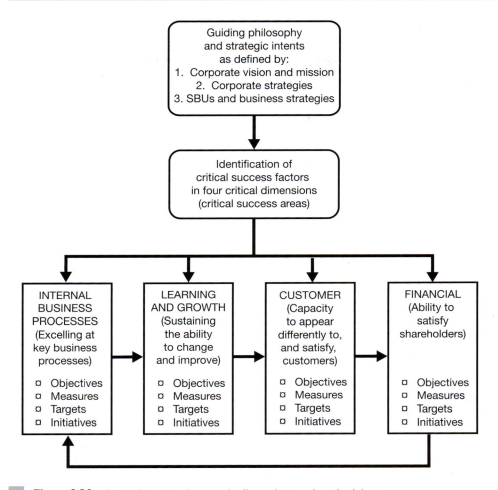

Figure 8.10 *The BSC's critical strategic dimensions and methodology*

Source: based on Kaplan and Norton (1993, 1996a, 1996b)

- Innovation and learning perspective. This relates to the capacity of the business to change continually and adapt to changing market and technological conditions. It is this potential for change and adaptation which provides the company with the capacity to grow and offer better value to its stakeholders. Continuous improvement, product, service and process innovations, and workforce empowerment are some of the crucial aspects that fall under the innovation and learning perspective.

- Financial perspective. Performance measures classified into the financial perspective indicate whether the company's strategy contributes to its bottom-line improvement: that is, profitability, growth and shareholder value. Kaplan and Norton (1992: 77) argue that it is necessary to re-examine the basic assumptions of corporate strategies if improved performance fails to be reflected in profitability and shareholder value. Hence, conventional PMS indicators, especially cash flow measures, sales growth, operating income, ROI and EPS, do have a significant role, even in the modern strategic PMS.

> The BSC is proposed to be used to translate a company's mission into specific performance indicators that reflect how customers perceive the company's products, the capacity of internal processes to satisfy customer needs, the potential of the firm to learn and grow, and to meet financial demands placed on the firm by shareholders.

Modes of operation and focus

The focus of a BSC is strategic alignment, and the mode of operation is the integration of disparate business functions into a single framework of measurement. Kaplan and Norton (1992: 73) argue that a BSC brings together, in a single management report, many of the seemingly disparate elements of a company's competitive agenda: becoming customer-oriented, shortening response time, improving quality, emphasizing teamwork, reducing new product launch times and managing for the long term, while making sure that corporate profitability and shareholders' value are increased. They also argue that scorecards guard against sub-optimization by helping managers to see whether improvement in one area may have been achieved at the expense of another.

> The focus of a BSC is the strategic alignment and the mode of operation is the integration of disparate business functions into a single framework of measurement.

The starting points for the development of a BSC are the corporate mission and vision statements (see Figure 8.10). The development of BSC begins with a definition of the company's vision for the future in terms of mission statement, vision statement and the definition of strategic business units (SBUs). Then that strategic intent is translated to financial, customer, internal and innovation perspectives in order to specify critical success factors (CSFs) in each of them. Finally, critical measurements are developed to reflect those critical factors. In this sense, Norton (2000: 3) argues that

> The Balanced scorecards . . . were designed to . . . communicate. [Their] underlying premise is that the act of measurement conveys what is important and, consequently, influence behavior. What gets measured, gets done. The BSC builds on this premise, asserting that measurement of the strategy provides a means of communicating the critical success factors to the organization, thus focusing everyone's efforts on the strategy.

CRITICAL VIEWS OF THE BSC

Despite its popularity among practitioners, the BSC has attracted some conceptual critiques. First, some have questioned its novelty, especially when it is compared with the good old French management practice of 'tableau de bord' (e.g., Bessire and Baker, 2005; Bourguignon et al., 2004; Epstein and Manzoni, 1998).

> The BSC is criticized for its novelty in the context of French *tableau de bord*.

The second criticism relates to the way in which it gained its popularity. Norreklit (2003: 611) levels a criticism that the BSC gained its popularity not due to its substance as an innovative and practical theory, but simply because of its promotional rhetoric, arguing that it

> is not unreasonable to claim that The Balanced Scorecard belongs to the genre of the management guru text: a genre in which sound argumentation is not a prevalent feature, which, by using certain stylistic devices and a composition that appeals to the emotions of the audience, persuades its audience to buy a new management theory, for instance. In the case under consideration, the authors may succeed in persuading – although without convincing – because the audience associates them with prestigious academia, but the text has little to do with scholarly work. The authors draw on the prestige and not the expertise of academia. It should be noted, however, that the prestige of academia is enhanced by the authors' claim that the BSC has been developed in interaction with practical business situations and that it has proved applicable in many companies. Kaplan and Norton [1996a, 1996b], however, offer no convincing documentation that, by using the BSC model, companies may attain the results claimed to follow from the application of the model . . . It should also be noted that the book does not document any comprehensive case study of the application of the BSC technique but only fragments of such studies.

> It is argued that the BSC lacks convincing conceptual substance but became popular through persuasive rhetoric.

Norreklit's argument that the BSC lacks substance is linked to her other critique (2000), where she argues that:

■ The assumed causality between four critical dimensions in the BSC is flawed. The BSC is projected not simply as an *ad hoc* collection of financial and non-financial measures but as a system of measurement that 'contains outcome measures and performance drivers of those outcomes, linked together in cause-and-effect relationships' (Kaplan and Norton, 1996b: 4). They assume that there is such a relationship between the critical dimensions of BSC that organizational learning and growth lead to efficient internal business processes which lead to high level of customer satisfaction which leads to good financial results. It is this central premise that Norreklit (2000) argues against. The first part of her argument is that, as a cause-and-effect relationship requires a time lag between cause and effect, and as such a time dimension is not part of the BSC, the causal relation presumed in BSC is flawed. The second part of her argument refers to the empirical validity of the claim that Kaplan and Norton make on the causal relationship between customer satisfaction and financial results.

> The assumed causality between critical dimensions in the BSC is problematic because the model does not constitute the necessary time lag between cause and effect and the empirical validity of the causal relationship is not sufficiently established.

■ The BSC as a strategic control model does not serve its intended purpose. Norreklit (2000) argues that the BSC lacks the potential of balancing company activities with its stakeholders because not all stakeholders are being included, especially suppliers and public authorities. This is made even more problematic, according to Norreklit (2000: 78), because 'the score-card does not monitor the competition or technological development', the 'focus of the model is static rather than dynamic', and it 'risks being too rigid because it measures what is required to set a strategy without asking what may block or shock the strategy'.

> The BSC as a strategic control model does not serve its intended purpose because of the number of its intrinsic limitations.

Problem of notion of strategy in the BSC

As we have already mentioned, vision and strategy have been given a central place in the BSC. It is argued that the BSC links strategy to performance measures: corporate vision and strategy can be communicated and institutionalized within the day-to-day activities of the employees by cascading strategic objectives in those four critical dimensions (see Figure 8.10, above). However, what is not explicit is the meaning that Kaplan and Norton attached to the term 'strategy'. They have never attempted to provide explicit definitions for 'strategy', 'mission' or 'vision', although they use all three terms extensively in their literature.

> Kaplan and Norton have never attempted to provide explicit definitions for 'strategy', 'mission' or 'vision', although they use all three terms extensively in their literature.

Nevertheless, through a careful reading of their texts, we can make certain inferences about the notion of strategy as it is conceived by Kaplan and Norton:

■ Company mission and vision statements necessarily contain an accurate expression of business strategy. Hence, vision and mission statements provide the most logical starting points for the BSC.
■ Visionary leadership is the source of strategy, and external change agents such as consultants are important elements in the strategy 'discovery' process.
■ Strategy formulation and implementation are essentially top-down processes: imagined and

invented at the top, communicated down, and implemented across the organization. (See Box 8.1 for an ideal-type BSC development process envisioned by Kaplan and Norton (1996a). This process exemplifies the top-down approach and the dominance of 'top management'.)

However, the point is that, at least in the field of strategic management, the notion of strategy has a much wider set of meanings than this. For Mintzberg (1987: 12), for example, defining 'strategy' as a 'plan' is not sufficient; it can also be a 'pattern that encompasses resulting behaviour – a pattern in a stream of actions . . . a consistency in behaviour whether intended or not'. Thus, strategies can stem from the bottom, rather than the top. As in Japanese practices such as quality circles and continuous improvement, top management may just be endorsing, rather than creating, strategies which emerged from below.

Strategy formulation is a bottom-up approach rather than a top-down enforcement.

BOX 8.1 BSC DESIGN AND IMPLEMENTATION – KAPLAN AND NORTON'S IDEAL-TYPE MODEL

Through a case example of successful implementation of BSC, Kaplan and Norton (1992: 42–43) present an ideal-type process of designing and implementing the BSC. Their model consists of ten basic steps that fundamentally rely upon a top-down approach to strategy formulation and implementation.

The process begins (**Step 1**) with a newly formed executive team working together for three months. A balanced scorecard is developed to translate a generic vision into a strategy that is understood and can be communicated.

Step 2 is to communicate the strategy to middle managers. The top three layers of management (100 people) are brought together to learn about and discuss the new strategy. This is done through the BSC. That means the BSC is used as a communication vehicle of strategy from top to middle management. The end result of this step is to develop business unit scorecards. Using the corporate scorecards as a template, each business unit translates its strategy into its own scorecard.

Step 3 is mainly to streamline the investment portfolio and to initiate the necessary cross-business change programmes. It is stated that the corporate scorecard, by clarifying strategic priorities, can identify many active programmes that are not contributing to the strategy and initiate cross-business change programmes. They are launched while the business units prepare their scorecards.

Step 4 is to review business unit scorecards. The CEO and the executive team review the individual business units' scorecards. The review permits the CEO to participate knowledgeably in shaping business unit strategy.

In **Step 5** top management (the executive team formed to design and implement the BSC)

continued

refine the vision: the review of business unit scorecards identifies several cross-business issues not included in the corporate strategy. The corporate scorecard is updated. Now the top management has an updated version of corporate strategy and the BSC, which is ready to communicate beyond the middle management to the whole company.

In **Step 6** the BSC is disseminated to the whole organization, and individual performance objectives are established: the top three layers of management link their individual objectives and incentive compensation to their scorecards.

Step 7 is to link long-range plans and budgets to the BSC. Five-year goals are established for each measure. The investments required to meet those goals are identified and funded. The first year of the five-year plan becomes the annual budget.

Steps 8 and 9 are for periodic reviews. In **Step 8** monthly and quarterly reviews begin. In **Step 9** annual strategy review is conducted. The executive committee lists ten strategic issues. Each business unit is asked to develop a position on each issue as a prelude to updating its strategy and scorecard.

Finally, in **Step 10**, everyone's performance is linked to the balanced scorecard: all employees are asked to link their individual objectives to the balanced scorecard. In this way, it is stated, the entire organization's incentive compensation is linked to the scorecard.

Source: based on Kaplan and Norton (1996a: 42–43)

Another problem with the BSC's notion of strategy is that it assumes an ahistorical and apolitical organization. The organizations that Kaplan and Norton assume are free from historical and structural contingencies; free from collective and individual resistances, contradictions and conflicts. People at the bottom are readily available to 'absorb' management ideologies, whatever the repercussions on their individual and collective lives as 'workers' might be.

The BSC assumes an ahistorical and apolitical organization.

The significance of political and institutional factors in the popularization, adoption and implementation of the BSC is well illustrated in a case study that Wickramasinghe *et al.* (forthcoming) conducted in a less developed country. There they noted the role that professional accounting bodies, especially CIMA (through a set of seminars and workshops) and other professional consultants, played in popularizing the BSC as a 'new' strategic management technique. Malmi (2001) has made a similar observation, based on interview data from seventeen Finnish companies, regarding the popularization of the BSC in Finland. The Wickramasinghe *et al.* case study also reports on how a BSC implementation project was jeopardized by inter-professional rivalry. While Malmi's Finnish case study notes that BSCs are used in two different ways: first as a programme of management by objectives, and second simply as an information system. Their findings suggest that the idea of linking measures together based on assumed cause-and-effect relationships was not well understood by early adopters of the BSCs.

HAVE YOU UNDERSTOOD THE CHAPTER?

1. What are the reasons behind the strategic turn in management?
2. What are the different ways in which we can understand the evolving character of SMA?
3. What are the major weaknesses in conventional management accounting in relation to strategic management accounting?
4. What roles should SMA play if it is to overcome weaknesses in conventional management accounting?
5. How do you compare salient features of conventional management accounting with SMA?
6. How do you understand SMA in relation to other functional management areas, especially marketing, operations and strategic management?
6. What directions could SMA take to expand its strategic interface?
7. What are the major strategic concerns and tools/concepts in accounting for corporate strategies?
8. What are the major strategic concerns and tools/concepts in accounting for market or competitive strategies?
9. What are the major strategic concerns and tools/concepts in accounting for manufacturing strategies?
10. How do you differentiate between corporate vision and mission?
11. What implications do the notions of vision and mission, as they are stated in corporate communications, have upon the traditional understanding of corporate objectives?
12. What do you understand by the term 'strategy' at corporate planning level and in the context of portfolio planning models?
13. What are the major dimensions that portfolio planning models consider in evaluating the relative strategic position of a corporate business portfolio? How are they measured in the BCG growth share matrix and GE nine-cell matrix? What strategic options are available in portfolio planning models?
14. What informational demands are placed upon management accounting by portfolio planning models?
15. How do you define the term 'strategy' in relation to competitive strategies?
16. What are the major factors that determine a firm's capacity to gain and sustain a competitive advantage?
17. What generic strategies are available for a firm at the competitive level? Can you differentiate between them and discuss the management control implications of following each of them?
18. What strategic analyses are demanded by Porter's framework of competitive strategy?
19. What forces would determine the relative attractiveness of an industry?
20. What are the salient features of Porter's value-chain model of the firm?
21. What are the major weaknesses of a conventional PMS?
22. What role does a PMS play within a management control system?
23. How does the BSC attempt to overcome the weaknesses of a conventional PMS?
24. How would you compare a conventional PMS with a BSC?
25. What are the major criticisms levelled against the BSC?
26. How would you describe the notion of strategy as it occurs in the BSC?

BEYOND THE CHAPTER

1. In a globally competitive organization, everyone understands that long-term profitability is achieved by improving customer satisfaction, not by trying to sell the largest possible quantities of what the accounting system says are the highest-margin products. They understand both the quality imperatives of TQM and the operational imperatives of JIT. Information about customer satisfaction and about variation in processes can move companies continuously closer to achieving the imperatives of competitive excellence. Defining that information and those imperatives is the task that awaits us.

    (Johnson, 1992: xi)

    How far has management accounting changed to face these challenges?

2. Corporate management accounting systems are inadequate for today's environment. In this time of rapid technological change, vigorous global and domestic competition, and enormously expanding information processing capabilities, management accounting systems are not providing useful, timely information for the process control, product costing, and performance evaluation activities of managers.

    (Johnson and Kaplan, 1987: xi)

    Discuss.

3. Strategic management accounting's defining characteristic is the management accounting interface with marketing management rather than strategy. When conceived in this way, strategic management accounting is a fundamentally interdisciplinary development, a potent mix of marketing and management accounting concepts and themes to be deployed in the pursuit of sustainable competitive advantage.

    (Roslender and Hart, 2002: 258)

    Discuss.

4. 'What is important is not what a corporate vision should contain, or how corporate managers should go about creating one, but the type of transformation that the notion of vision exemplifies.' Discuss.
5. 'Though popular until the late 1980s, portfolio models never captured the "post-industrial" notion of strategy manifested in corporate vision and mission statements.' Discuss.
6. 'The BSC is neither a novel nor a conceptually convincing model. Its popularity is gained not by its conceptual substance but by persuasive rhetoric in its promotion. The causality it assumes is flawed, and as a strategic control model, it does not serve its purpose.' Discuss.

FURTHER READING

1. On management accounting innovations during the last two decades, see Bromwich and Bhimani (1989, 1994).
2. On technical aspects of the BSC, see Atkinson *et al.* (2004: ch. 9).
3. On competitive strategy, see Porter (1980, 1985).
4. For alternative conceptions of strategy, see Mintzberg (1987).
5. For critiques of the BSC, see Norreklit (2000, 2003).

Chapter 9

Towards cost management

A STARTING POINT: THE COST OF COST CUTTING

Established in 1925, Marconi, a Portuguese Telecommunications company, continued its businesses under a monopolistic regime on an engineering-driven, production-oriented basis until the 1980s. Following economic liberalization in the 1980s, Marconi moved into expanded business areas. This marked a stark contrast to its costing system. Earlier, Marconi enjoyed its production orientation through glorious engineering expertise. During this time, as prices were regulated by government agencies, costing for management decisions was not so important. Rather, engineering rationalities were pre-eminent. New liberalization policies pressured Marconi to change this regime. As old historical costs which persisted over the previous regime became irrelevant to a competitive environment, telecommunications regulators forced Marconi to adopt activity-based costing (ABC).

A consulting arm of a big international accounting firm emerged between telecommunications regulators and Marconi to help in implementing ABC. Impressed by this scenario, some managers believed that ABC could enhance firm flexibility and responsiveness to the business environment through better decision-making on cost-cutting programmes, including staff reduction and out-sourcing. Other managers held the view that, as other firms were also using it, Marconi could not avoid the adoption of ABC. Consequently, Marconi initiated the ABC project through internal reorganization and restructuring, coupled with the identification of activities and processes. By doing this, the company was looking for cost information (accurate costs which can be logically linked to cost objects) for better decisions as a means to improve efficiency. However, from engineering sources, it was heard that the motive to do this arose from external pressures more than internal informational needs.

When implementing this project, certain organizational issues arose. As much as the economic liberalization programme questioned the extent of the production orientation of Marconi, ABC neglected production department needs. Some 'powerful' engineers resigned, while remaining production personnel did not support ABC implementation. For them, it was a complete organizational restructuring programme which questioned both the orientation of the business and the mode of costing. In contrast, a commercial orientation developed. Senior commercial managers were appointed and ABC information was highly appreciated by them. Despite costing data's late arrival, they highlighted that they were useful. Notwithstanding that common costs were as high as 25 per cent, commercial managers said that before ABC, these costs were even higher. In this way, both consultants (who were supported by regulators) and commercial managers (who supported the project) maintained a positive mentality towards continuing with the ABC project under the new regime of liberalization which led to a commercial orientation. (Adapted from Hopper and Major, forthcoming.)

SETTING THE SCENE

The previous chapter showed an intersection between the organization and its immediate business environment. On the one hand, the strategic turn has implications for the analysis of business performance; on the other, it creates opportunities for changing the internal mechanisms of calculations. The analysis of business performance now largely hinges upon the project of SMA and its immediate congenial technique of the BSC. Researchers tend to define a 'new' subject matter by coining these terms for different connotations and by evaluating their practices in different organizational contexts. While the external orientation of management accounting leans to strategic management accounting, the change in internal calculations is now seen in the areas of costing where practitioners and academics come out with new terms, such as 'cost management', 'strategic cost analysis', 'activity-based costing', 'activity-based management', 'target costing', 'functional cost analysis', etc. The focus of this chapter is on this development.

The case of Marconi is a starting point to place this development in a real-life context. Marconi's rise and fall of production orientation, and fall and rise of market orientation, mark a transformation through which the changes in management accounting take place. This transformation signifies the practical problems of the domain of management accounting which served the requirements of production-oriented firms and the urgent needs of new management accounting which could facilitate commercial (customer)-oriented firms. Also, Marconi's case shows us how difficult it is to establish new management accounting, such as ABC, even under the blessings of some of the parties that are involved. This story shows not only a departure of costing from its old version, but also the issues of implementation of the new form in different and distant contexts.

As you now know, costing or cost accounting is the ancestor of modern management accounting. As costing became connected with broader managerial functions, and the managerial perspectives on controls became essential subject matters in business unit performance, cost accounting became management accounting with a broader managerial emphasis. However, this shift had problems, as the techniques and usage of original cost accounting remained more or less the same. A number of commentaries highlight that the persistence of conventional costing has not been sufficient to keep pace with the demand for more and different information. Consequently, a number of approaches have been introduced, discussed and critiqued for developing a new domain of costing.

We term this new domain 'cost management'. As this encompasses several techniques, ranging from activity-based costing (ABC) to Japanese practices of costing, it is difficult for us to provide a specific definition for this development. However, due to the power of Western diffusion programmes which propagate certain practices around the globe, ABC is now increasingly seen as the 'best' alternative to conventional cost accounting. Just as the BSC gained similar popularity for similar reasons (see Chapter 8), ABC is now a technique being embraced by consultants, educators, senior managers and academics. As students of management accounting, we must not ignore this 'historical' incident. We should read the literature, pinpoint the definitions of respective terms and usages, contrast them with the conventional approaches to cost management and alternatives, explore the nature of underlying practices and so on. The learning objectives of this chapter are set around this educational and academic need.

First, we address the question of defining the notion of cost management. As there is no specific definition, we have looked at how some prominent writers viewed cost management in their own programmes. This allows us to see how early costing practices operated, and to learn which issues have been identified from later developments. Moreover, we will look at the other cost management techniques, especially Japanese management techniques, to broaden the scope of our definition of cost management. Another strand of cost management we will focus on is the academic contribution by the strategic management accounting school. This focus gives an opportunity to see the interface between strategic management accounting and cost management. We will try to show the various possible definitions of the notion of cost management, rather than providing one standard definition; and we will present a comparison of cost accounting and cost management.

- To see how early costing practices operated
- To pinpoint the issues of later developments
- To consider Japanese management techniques as part of cost management
- To look at the interface between strategic management accounting and cost management
- To compare cost accounting with cost management

Second, we will look at the rise of ABC. In this, we will see that Harvard Business School addressed the concerns of a crisis in American manufacturing and launched a programme of cost management. There were several waves of this: the development of a critique of traditional costing; the development of ABC technique; and the expansion of ABC into activity-based management (ABM). After this, we will see that Japanese cost management practices as well as some American management initiatives became part of a broader ABC programme. In relation to this development, we will point out that the ABC programme is not merely a technical practice but also a social and economic practice that responded to the requirements of the new global economy.

- To examine the three waves of ABC development: critiquing traditional costing; developing ABC; and expanding ABC to ABM
- To show that Japanese management techniques and some American management initiatives became parts of the cost management programme
- To point out that the ABC/M programme is a response to the new global economy

Third, the chapter goes on to elaborate on the technical apparatus of ABC. This will achieve several learning objectives. The first is to define the technical dimension of ABC, where we show that it entails a final calculation of a cost driver rate. The second is to present the theoretical under-pinnings of ABC, in which we include the taxonomy of cost hierarchy, and the distinction between cost of resources supplied and cost of resources used. Third, we will elaborate on the technical procedures of ABC calculations. We will raise several technical questions here. What are the activities? How are the activities identified? How do we cost the activities? How do we use activity costs in costing products/customers? In answering these questions, we will illustrate how these costs are calculated, using hypothetical figures. When doing these calculations, you may compare them with the traditional cost allocation procedure we presented in Chapter 3.

- To define the technical dimension of ABC
- To present the theoretical underpinnings of ABC
- To elaborate on technical steps towards the calculation of cost of products/customers

Fourth, we look specifically at ABM, the expanded version of ABC. In this section, we will broadly define the notion of ABM. This will lead to understanding a dichotomy of ABM: opera-tional and strategic. This has some practical implications, in that it allows managers to use ABC data for different purposes. Moreover, this section shows you how ABC links with a firm's performance, especially in terms of its market value.

- To define the notion of ABM
- To understand the dichotomy of operational and strategic ABM
- To gauge the linkage between ABC/M and the market value of firms

Fifth, the chapter proceeds to a section on academic views on the implementation of ABC projects in different organizations. One learning objective here is to summarize research findings on the implementation of ABC projects. We see that most findings highlight some positive effects, and there is a rationality as to why most researchers evaluate ABC projects positively.

- To summarize the research findings on ABC
- To point out why researchers are mostly positive

Finally, we will present an argument that ABC was a bandwagon effect rather than a unique paradigm shift. Our aim is to deal with a critical evaluation of the entire ABC project. One learning objective is to show that there is a fundamental mistake in the conception of ABC: one cannot completely eliminate indirect costs, yet this is a main plank of ABC. Moreover, this section highlights that ABC is not a superior management technology but a fabrication of a particular practice by certain actors through the development of certain networks. The section concludes that, within some projects, ABC has created managerial problems, such as resistance and mistrust.

■ To pinpoint some fundamental mistakes in the conception of ABC
■ To argue that ABC is a practice fabricated by certain actors through their networking
■ To show that some ABC projects had managerial and organizational problems

COST MANAGEMENT REVISITED

As we have explained in the preceding chapters, changes occurring in the market place and at the manufacturing site led to changing costing systems, too. Many writers now tend to bracket such new and emerging costing techniques within 'cost management' (e.g., Johnson and Kaplan, 1987; Monden, 1989; Yahikawa *et al.*, 1994). This does not mean, however, that new costing techniques are 'cost management', and old techniques are 'cost accounting'. Writers use this terminology interchangeably, as well as separately. Some of these usages are presented below.

Johnson and Kaplan (1987) used the term 'cost accounting' to present certain historical events in cost accounting. They used 'cost management' in the contexts of 'early New England textile mills' (p. 21), 'late nineteenth-century steel works' (p. 32), 'railroads' (p. 34) and 'distributing and urban retailing' (p. 38). By referring to these early cost accounting practices in the USA context, Johnson and Kaplan argued that the aim of these practices was to use cost information for management purposes, such as cost control and pricing within single-activity firms. As costing was used for such purposes, Johnson and Kaplan were inclined to term the practices 'cost management'. Advancing the argument of 'relevance lost', they illustrated that, when cost accounting began to provide information for inventory valuation and, in turn, financial reporting, costing was no longer a service for management decision-making and (cost) control. Thus, cost management persisted only in the nineteenth century, while new 'cost management techniques' were introduced only in the 1980s.

Cost management persisted only in the nineteenth century. New 'cost management techniques' were introduced only in the 1980s.

Reconstituting cost accounting, which was confined to the accountant's office, Cooper and Kaplan (1988) once again began to use the term 'cost management' or 'cost management systems' by referring to a 'new' cost allocation system called activity-based costing (ABC). As we will explain later in this chapter, the proponents argue that this costing system was meant to provide information for management decisions in a competitive environment where customer satisfaction became vital. Rather than being subservient to financial reporting, this system, Cooper and Kaplan (1988: 103) illustrate, 'helps managers make better decisions about product design, pricing, marketing, and mix, and encourages continual operating improvements'. When Cooper and Kaplan compiled a textbook to illustrate the technique of ABC, they entitled it *The Design of Cost Management Systems* (originally published 1991; 2nd edn, 1999). Textbook writers then began to use this term in place of 'cost accounting' (e.g., *Activity-based Management: Emerging Practices in Cost Management* and *Handbook of Cost Management* (Brinker, 1994, 1992)). The term now connotes a trend in cost accounting practice being developed for management and control purposes.

KEY TERMS

New cost management is an emerging accounting paradigm that helps managers make better decisions about product design, pricing, marketing and mix, and encourages continual operating improvements.

While the contribution of Kaplan and his colleagues became momentous in the 1990s, another stream of 'cost management' had already emerged in the 1980s within the programme of Japanese management accounting. One of the key figures in this programme is Monden, who reported on emerging Japanese management accounting practices (Monden and Sakurai, 1989). One of the key features of these practices was the incorporation of Japanese methods of management in management and cost accounting. These include: quality costing stemming from total quality management (TQM), target costing developed from broader strategic management, costing in a just-in-time (JIT) environment developed especially in Toyota and functional cost analysis developed from value analysis or value engineering. All this was a collective response to combat the Western monopoly and towards enhancing competitiveness for Japanese products, especially cars. The underlying management accounting practice within this broader programme has been termed 'cost management' (McMann and Nanni, 1995). McMann and Nanni suggest the Japanese cost management programme is characterized by several features: eyes of the market – 'everything originates from the customer'; focus on quality – 'no trade-off between cost and quality'; fixation with waste as excess cost – 'money spent that does not promote customer value is simply waste'; continual improvement – 'reducing errors, matching customers' functionality requirements better and eliminating waste'; and integration through communication – 'formal, but open two-way channel of communication . . . between upper and lower levels'. These features constitute a stark contrast to traditional management accounting in the mass production regimes of organizations.

Another influence has been the voice of alternative academic research. With no intention to launch a particular programme, a theme emerged in the late 1980s and early 1990s under the title 'strategic management accounting' (see Chapter 8). This has some links to the development of cost management. Shank (1989: 50) developed the idea of 'strategic cost management' (SCM), which he described as a 'paradigm shift', and defined as 'managerial use of cost information explicitly directed at one or more of the four stages of the strategic management cycle'. As a new paradigm,

Key features of Japanese methods of cost management:

- eyes of the market;
- focus on quality;
- fixation with waste as excess cost;
- continual improvement;
- integration through communication.

Shank articulated SCM around three strategic management themes: value-chain analysis, strategic positioning analysis and cost driver analysis. Next, Bromwich (1990) made a theoretical analysis of costing practices in the context of strategy. He reviewed two economic theories: product attributes and costs in competitive markets. The first suggested that accountants must understand the cost structure of not only their own products but also the products of competitors and potential entrants. The second suggested that the existing cost structure must be considered to determine whether it can sustain a market strategy when there is a challenge from potential entrants. These two complementary economic theories have been used to highlight the significance of the strategic orientation of cost management. Both Shank and Bromwich represent a school of academics which promotes an alternative to traditional cost accounting, and its underlying views have informed us how cost management can be constituted.

KEY TERMS

'Strategic cost management' (SCM) is defined as 'managerial use of cost information explicitly directed at one or more of the four stages of the strategic management cycle'.

SCM entails three strategic management themes: value-chain analysis, strategic positioning analysis and cost driver analysis.

The above academic and pragmatic enterprises lead us to differentiate the 'cost management' domain from its predecessor, 'cost accounting'. Table 9.1 highlights the differences.

We do not intend to provide a standard definition for cost management. Instead, you could formulate your own by taking the distinct characteristics highlighted in Table 9.1 into consideration. In general, we must know that there was a shift from early cost management to modern cost accounting, where cost accounting became subservient to financial reporting rather than a service for decision-making and control. Recent trends developed by Kaplan and his colleagues and Japanese management once again witness an emergence of cost management, by which cost information is coming to be a useful guide for decision-making and control. While this is so, academics tend to endorse the significance of cost management in a strategic context.

287

Table 9.1 *Cost accounting and cost management compared*

Aspects of comparison	Contemporary cost accounting	Emerging cost management
Purpose as in actual practice	To provide information for inventory valuation and financial reporting	To provide information for management decisions and control
Operational context	Mass-production manufacturing firms – mostly monopolistic	Mass-production and flexible specialization – both manufacturing and service firms in a stiff competitive environment
Technical focus	Unit cost ascertainment	Ascertainment of hierarchy of costs of activities – unit, batch and product sustaining
Dominant techniques	Calculation of a single factory/plant-wide overhead rate	Calculation of multiple activity rates and analysis of multiple perspectives on costs
Role of accountants	Provision of information to internal and external parties	Collaborating with other managers to search for better information
Mode of operation	Disintegrated from manufacturing/operations	Integrated with computer-aided manufacturing techniques

ABC AS A POWERFUL PROGRAMME OF COST MANAGEMENT

As we have already seen, the proponents of the ABC programme include Robert Kaplan and his colleagues from Harvard Business School. They presented their ideas in two journals: the *Harvard Business Review* and the *Journal of Cost Management*. Subsequently, Kaplan and Robin Cooper compiled two accessible textbooks: *Cost & Effect* (Kaplan and Cooper, 1998) and *The Design of Cost Management Systems* (Cooper and Kaplan, 1999). Towards the end of the 1990s, big accounting firms also developed consulting arms to 'do business' in ABC at a global level. Numerous organizations, including large multinational manufacturing firms, public sector organizations and banks have now implemented ABC as a new cost management technique.

> The proponents of the ABC programme include Robert Kaplan and his colleagues from Harvard Business School. They presented their ideas in two journals: the *Harvard Business Review* and the *Journal of Cost Management*.

In the development of ABC, Kaplan and his colleagues had a common challenge in relation to a broader economic programme in the USA. It was in the 1980s that American business became less competitive in the global market (Miller and O'Leary, 1993). Stiff competition against US products came from Japanese manufacturers, especially in the car industry. It has been shown that the success of Japanese manufacturing lies in several unique management techniques, such as total quality management (TQM), just-in-time (JIT), target costing, etc. These techniques were not management accounting techniques *per se*. However, they provided a useful conceptual context for cost management practices. Rather than manipulation of costing data for financial reporting purposes through traditional cost accounting techniques, Japanese firms were successful in cost reduction and quality improvement programmes through adopting those new management techniques, and their products became very competitive in the global market. This was a challenge for Western management practices, and Kaplan and his colleagues aimed to do something about it.

> Japanese firms were successful in cost reduction and quality improvement programmes through adopting new management techniques, and their products became very competitive in the global market.

They did not reject Japanese management techniques, but found a common label for all of this – ABC. They rode several waves while developing this. In the first wave, they criticized traditional costing by providing historical evidence from company cases. In the second, they developed ABC by determining how some companies do costing differently. In this case, as we will elaborate later in the chapter, ABC was not Kaplan and his colleagues' own discovery but a collaborative consulting effort, together with Robin Cooper and Computer-Aided Manufacturing International (CAM-I), a company propagating advanced manufacturing technologies. In the third wave, they expanded the scope of ABC's costing calculations to management use – activity-based management (ABM). In this development, they combined all emerging management techniques in cost reduction programmes. They accommodated not only Japanese management techniques, such as JIT and TQM, but also American initiatives such as business process re-engineering (BPR), downsizing and outsourcing. Consequently, as Jones and Dugdale (2002) argued, ABC became one of the 'global expert systems'.

> The proponents of ABM accommodated not only Japanese management techniques, such as JIT and TQM, but also American initiatives, such as business process re-engineering (BPR), downsizing and outsourcing. Consequently, ABC became one of the 'global expert systems'.

Broadly, ABC represents a response to the social and economic transformation we discussed in Chapter 7. It purported to create flexibility in the sphere of costing by looking for an avenue for transforming most indirect costs into direct costs which can be directly attributed to cost objects, such as products and customers. ABC also aimed to link costing to strategic management requirements, especially by making products and production processes more customer-oriented. Thus, we should not see the study of cost management purely as a technical exercise which concentrates on 'how to do it'. Instead, it is a social and organizational study which can explore its development in a broader sense. Our aim in this chapter is to take this second option.

ABC purported to create flexibility in the sphere of costing by looking for an avenue for transforming most indirect costs into direct costs which can be directly attributed to cost objects, such as products and customers.

DEFICIENCIES AND MISCONCEPTIONS OF TRADITIONAL COSTING

The 'glorious' development of cost management had a small seed: the identification of problems in traditional costing. First, as the cost allocation system was based on direct labour (or cost), cost centre managers tended to believe that direct labour cost should be reduced in order to reduce overheads and, in turn, to improve profitability. However, in the face of a competitive environment since the 1980s, firms have been inclined to spend more on overheads than on direct labour. Without understanding the significance of this increase in overheads, managers continued to look for means of reducing direct labour cost with a view to eliminating its impact on the calculation of overheads. As the root of the problem lies in escalating overheads, attempts to reduce direct labour cost had little impact on enhancing competitive advantage (see Johnson and Kaplan, 1987).

As the cost allocation system was based on direct labour (or cost), cost centre managers tended to believe that direct labour cost should be reduced in order to reduce overheads and, in turn, to improve profitability.

Second, the traditional cost allocation system could prompt managers to make unwise decisions. For instance, when managers realized that labour-intensive processes were expensive, because the overhead was allocated based on direct labour hours, they tended to subcontract such processes to outside suppliers. In the USA, as Johnson and Kaplan (1987) highlighted, such subcontracting orders went to Latin America or East Asia, where labour is cheap. However, this was a mistake. Despite some increases in labour cost at home, managers did not understand that the basis of calculation of cost was inaccurate: cost accountants were concerned about the accuracy of the last digit, not the inaccuracy of the first digit, as Johnson and Kaplan noted. Consequently, in the 1980s, in response to competition, a huge outsourcing programme was launched, rather than paying attention to the recalculation of overhead costs and taking action accordingly. Later, the firms that took the above misguided outsourcing action incurred more overhead costs, as subcontracting involves numerous additional costs, such as investing in qualified vendors, visiting the plants to check quality, scheduling orders, keeping sufficient stocks in storage, making payments, etc.

Managers tended to subcontract processes to outside suppliers because they did not understand that the basis of calculation of cost was inaccurate: cost accountants were concerned about the accuracy of the last digit, not the inaccuracy of the first digit.

Third, as a result of the above interrelated issues, the traditional costing system was not suffi-ciently flexible to accommodate different production situations. In a competitive environment where production systems are becoming customer-oriented, rigid calculative practices, such as direct labour-based cost allocation, cannot be compatible with the changing needs of customers. Rather than demanding similar products with similar functionalities, customers tend to shift their interests from one product to another, as competitors continuously create a host of different models and convince customers to buy them. Firms operating in such environments then have to shift their production system from mass production to flexible manufacturing, or to a hybrid system featuring both. Under such circumstances, direct labour would not be the only basis for understanding the behaviour of overhead costs. The traditional cost allocation system was not designed to see any others, as it developed only through, and for, the regimen of mass production. It survived under mass production and served the customers who relied on production-oriented firms.

> The traditional costing system was not flexible enough to accommodate different production situations.

Fourth, it was observed that the traditional costing system was associated with the problem of timeliness, a basic accounting principle. Based on this traditional cost allocation system, firms tended to prepare monthly performance reports, together with variance analysis. As different predicaments arise in different months, last month's experience does not help to solve the current month's problems. Monthly performance reports from the accounting department were found to be 'too late' and 'too aggregated' for operational decisions at hand. Instead, some firms regarded the incoming of official reports as a ceremonial practice, and developed a local system to pinpoint operational issues. Sometimes, some divisions employed accountants to help the production man-agers by providing information on a daily or even hourly basis. To this extent, they used computer spreadsheets, etc., to make this local system more efficient. While this was so, the fundamental problem of the traditional cost allocation system went unnoticed.

> Monthly performance reports from the accounting department found to be 'too late' and 'too aggregated' for operational decisions at hand.

Last, when the traditional system was not of help in providing accurate and timely information for product costing and operational decisions, profit centre managers in large hierarchical organizations looked for other avenues to make bigger profits, avenues other than increasing sales, enhancing market share, innovating new products, etc. As Johnson and Kaplan (1987) reported, profit centre managers wanting to get the credit for better return on investment tended to adopt 'non-productive' strategies, including financial accounting conventions. For example, as the aim was to show better period profits, managers tended to switch from accelerated to straight-line depreciation, or extended depreciable life of fixed assets. These managers used cost accounting

291

for these financial accounting needs, rather than making actual profits under the guidance of cost information. In respect of this tendency, Johnson and Kaplan (1987: 198) came out with a tough statement: 'management accounting therefore followed, and became subservient to, financial reporting practices'.

> Profit centre managers wanting to get the credit for better return on investment tended to adopt 'non-productive' strategies, including financial accounting conventions.

Overall, the above deficiencies led to the new programme of cost management initiated by Harvard Business School academics and allied professional journals. The arguments levelled against traditional management accounting were largely supported by these deficiencies, and developed a market for new cost management techniques. The 1987 historical analysis of the 'relevance lost' thesis became a turning point in the history of management accounting, and the genesis of subsequent cost management techniques, as we will show later in this chapter, eventually became the 'juggernauts' and 'bandwagon' (Jones and Dugdale, 2002) of postmodern management accounting. The new techniques which emerged from this programme are detailed below.

WHAT IS ABC?

In a technical sense, ABC is a system of overhead cost allocation which is said to eliminate the problems of a traditional cost allocation system. In contrast to the traditional system, ABC allows us to calculate a number of ratios based on 'activity-cost drivers'. As we will show later, 'activity-cost drivers' are the most relevant determinants of overhead costs of a product/service. Rather than beginning from determining the resources supplied to a product/product line, ABC begins with an analysis of activities involved in production and selling. The analysis can determine 'activity-cost pools' – the total cost of respective activities, and relevant cost drivers. For example, suppose that there is an activity of material movement/handling between one place and another. The most relevant determinant of cost activity would be the number of material movements over a particular batch of production. In this case, the 'number of material movements' is the cost driver. When we divide total cost of material movements/handling by the number of movements, we can derive 'cost driver rate'. When we have calculated such cost driver rates for each activity-cost category, by considering the volume of activities of respective categories of activities we can determine overhead cost by totalling the activity costs of each product/product line.

KEY TERMS

ABC is a system of overhead cost allocation which allows us to calculate a number of ratios based on 'activity-cost drivers'.

ABC is essentially simple, in that it involves only the calculation of activity-cost rates, which can be applied to assign overhead cost to each product. However, it has been suggested that this simple practice has a profound impact, in that it guides better management of resources, enhances competitiveness and market share and, finally, gains competitive advantage by satisfying customers. Thus, ABC has become not only an accounting technique but also an advancement of management and control. Subsequently, the proponents of ABC have extended it to ABM, implying that it relates not only to accounting but also to a broader management initiative.

> Despite the apparent simplicity of ABC, it has been suggested that it has a profound impact, in that it guides better management of resources, enhances competitiveness and market share and gains competitive advantage by satisfying customers.

A salient feature of ABC is that there is an attempt to eliminate common/indirect costs by allocating almost all indirect costs to cost objects, usually to products and customers. In a sense, this is a process of making all indirect and fixed costs direct and variable. In a way, this coincides with broader attempts to make everything flexible under the emerging regime of flexible specialization, as we discussed in Chapter 7. If flexibility is imputed to costing through ABC, then one can argue that there are virtually no indirect costs, as such. Thus, ABC appears to be a technical practice which has an impact on the ways people think about costing. In other words, ABC points out to managers that costing is a powerful managerial device that can do wonders, including turning the entire business in new directions.

> ABC's technical logic coincides with broader attempts to make everything flexible under the emerging regime of flexible specialization.

Theoretical underpinnings of ABC

Before proceeding to discuss how ABC is meant to work as a cost management technique, we must first look at how this technique has been theoretically articulated. Two theoretical discoveries underpinned the development of ABC, as Kaplan (1994) observed:

- taxonomy of cost hierarchy;
- cost of resources supplied versus cost of resources used.

The taxonomy of cost hierarchy is an understanding of different levels of activity in respect to a product or service. Understanding such activities is important for identifying suitable cost drivers which can be used to calculate cost driver rates. Cooper (1990) reported three levels of activity:

- Unit-level activities. These are directly related to product/service units so that they increase (or decrease) in proportion to production and sales volume. Cost drivers stemming from these activities are used directly for a volume of production. Traditional direct labour hours/costs and machine hours are such unit-level cost drivers. All organizational overhead costs which lead to increased (or decreased) production volume are to be allocated to units of production based on such unit-level cost drivers. This was not a new discovery by the proponents of ABC, but it provided a starting point from which to arrange overhead costs into a hierarchy.

KEY TERMS

Unit-level activities are directly related to product/service units so that they increase (or decrease) in proportion to production and sales volume.

■ Batch-level activities. These include the activities related to each batch of production. A batch could be a production run (e.g., a round of machine operation) or a bulk of services (e.g., processing of a set of customer orders). The activities involved in a batch are independent of number of units. For example, the number of items included in a customer order is not related to the order-processing cost. Identification of batch-level activities can then lead to identifying batch-level cost drivers. For example, the number of customer orders processed is a cost driver for the allocation of order-processing cost to a particular order. Kaplan (1994) observed that the traditional costing system assumed that these costs are fixed, so that, irrespective of the complexities of having different types of batches of production, such batch-level costs were allocated based on unit-level cost drivers. ABC has revealed that this was a miscalculation.

KEY TERMS

Batch-level activities include the activities related to each batch of production, which are independent of number of units.

■ Product-sustaining activities. The activities related to retaining customers fall into this category. Other than producing and delivering a particular product, in a competitive environment firms tend to retain customers by providing additional services, such as updating product specification (e.g., updating software packages which have already been sold), and providing supplementary products and services (e.g., providing home insurance services to customers of a bank). Related activities involved at this level are independent of the number of the other two levels of activity. The traditional costing system regarded the costs of these activities as fixed, because it did not have a mechanism to assign such costs to individual products and services.

> ## KEY TERMS
>
> Product-sustaining activities are related to retaining customers through additional services and supplementary products.

Identification of the above levels of activity and, in turn, respective cost drivers has been regarded as a powerful contribution to the development of cost management. Kaplan (1994) claimed this was significant for the following reasons:

■ It provides 'visibility' for managers (who had been blinded by traditional costing, as it did not reveal the true cost of production) thinking of cutting a particular cost. If the managers want to reduce a particular cost, they need to cut related activities rather than adopt cost-controlling mechanisms. By thinking of activities, the managers need to understand which level of activities they need to eliminate. In this way, they can establish clear-cut cause-and-effect relationships between activities and costs.

■ It provides knowledge for separating the selling of high-volume products with few complexities in production (as in traditional mass production) from low-volume products with more complexities in production (as in flexible specialization). Kaplan (1994) comments that the importance of this separation was also noted by early contributors, such as Skinner (1974) and Hayes and Wheelwright (1979).

■ It allows engineers to link the costing system to flexible manufacturing technologies, such as computer-aided design (CAD), computer-aided manufacturing (CAM) and computer-aided software engineering (CASE). This change in manufacturing helped to reduce batch-level and customer-sustaining costs. Thus, the development of flexible manufacturing and ABC have gone hand-in-hand (Jones and Dugdale, 2002).

■ It extends the service of management accounting from its traditional 'accounting' mode to a new management programme. As we will explain later in this chapter, this happened as emerging Japanese management techniques became useful in the reduction of identified cost categories. Following these techniques, Western engineers began to focus on potential avenues for reducing cost driver volumes: for example, reducing set-up times.

The second theoretical contribution in cost of resources supplied versus cost of resources used assumed a fundamental change in the ways in which cost could be assigned to individual products and customers. Traditionally, it was assumed that the assignment of all organizational expenses to products and customers is essential. The underlying problem of this assumption is that all such expenses were not actually incurred for adding value to products and customers. As long as different customers demand different product attributes, some products will be more expensive than others. However, traditional costing seemed unaware of this, given that overhead absorption rates were blindly determined, based on the arbitrary ratios we presented in Chapter 3. The theoretical discovery by the proponents of ABC is then a calculation of costs of 'using resources' rather than costs of 'supplying resources'.

> ABC aims to calculate costs of 'using resources' rather than costs of 'supplying resources'.

295

As traditional costing provided information for financial reporting, it was sufficient to know the cost of resources supplied: that is, the resources available for productive purposes for a particular financial period. Thus, managers were aware of the amount of the overhead resources supplied to production departments, and assumed that they must have been actually used. As relevant cost drivers were not analysed for deciding whether or not those resources were used, Cooper and Kaplan (1991, 1992) demonstrated that managers were unaware of any 'unused capacity'. Having analysed the cost drivers, they noticed how capacity is used. This led them to recognize how economists' 'long-term variable costs' could be made visible to managers: all fixed costs would become variable when the demand for such resources changes. Demand changes for two reasons: because of increased volume or because of increased activities due to increased 'variety and complexity'. This fact offers two guides to cost management: an understanding to provide more resources when there are more demands; and an understanding to reduce activities and enhance continuous improvement when there are costly activities. This theoretical explanation, however, offers little challenge to neoclassical economics, which claims that cost can be fixed and variable, and that most fixed costs can be variable in the long run. The proponents therefore built upon this economic theory and demonstrated how cost can be ascertained in a changing business environment where flexibility and customer orientation are inevitable.

> ABC recognizes how economists' 'long-term variable costs' can be made visible to managers: all fixed costs would become variable when the demand for such resources changes.

Technical procedures of ABC

The technical procedures involved in the calculation of 'activity-based costing' are straightforward: calculation of overheard costs based on activities rather than direct labour hours or direct labour costs. Figure 9.1 provides a broader sketch of this calculative practice.

In relation to the above costing procedure, some fundamental technical questions need to be explored:

- What are these activities?
- How are the activities identified?
- How do we cost the activities?
- How do we use 'activity costs' in costing a product/customer?

We will address each of these questions to explore how the technical procedures have been laid down by the proponents of ABC.

> ABC calculates overheard costs based on activities rather than direct labour hours or direct labour costs.

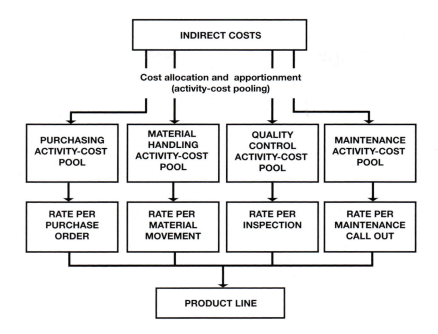

Figure 9.1 *The ABC cost allocation model*

What are the activities?

Traditionally, economists consider production as a process that transforms inputs into outputs – that is, products. Cooper and Kaplan redefined the production process by breaking down its steps into 'activities', so that costs of activities can determine the cost of a product or a customer. Brimson (Brimson, 1991: 46), a follower of Cooper and Kaplan, defined an activity as 'a combination of people, technology, raw materials, methods and environment that produces a given product or service', and claimed that 'activities transcend all steps within the chain of value – product design, manufacturing engineering, production, distribution, marketing, and after sales service'. Looked at closely, we can see that an activity contains diverse resources: for example, billing a customer would involve all of them.

> An activity is a combination of people, technology, raw materials, methods and environment that produces a given product or service.

Moreover, Brimson distinguished activity from function, business process, task and operation: function is the broader responsibility assigned to a functional area (e.g., marketing and sales); activity is the action to be executed to accomplish the function (e.g., travelling to the customer); business process is the main job of that functional area (e.g., selling the product by the activity of travelling to the customer); task is a specific action (e.g., driving a car to travel to the customer);

operation is the ultimate action involved in the task (e.g., talking to the customer to introduce him/herself). This hierarchical arrangement tells us that activity, rather than anything else, is the central base for costing. Costing for a function is too global or broad, so such costings cannot guide us to better cost management in a competitive environment. Costing for an operation is too local or insignificant for making decisions and taking action. The hierarchical arrangement helps us to distinguish the 'central activity' from 'other activities', such as function, business process, task and operation, and it is this central activity that has been labelled 'activity' in ABC. It has been argued that this activity is neither too global nor too local for costing purposes.

KEY TERMS

Function is the broader responsibility assigned to a functional area; activity is the action to be executed to accomplish the function; business process is the main job of that functional area; task is a specific action; operation is the ultimate action involved in the task.

Impressed by the importance of activities, Brimson emphasized the rationality of 'activity accounting' with the following slogans: 'activities are action', 'activities improve product cost accuracy', 'activities drive costs', 'activities facilitate evaluation of alternatives', 'activities focus corporate strategy', 'activities complement continuous improvement', 'activities are compatible with Total Quality Management', 'activity accounting is cost effective', 'activities are easily understood by the users', 'activities link planning and control', 'activities integrate financial and non-financial measures', 'activities facilitate life-cycle management' and 'activities improve decision support'. These slogans embrace every aspect of modern business management.

How are the activities identified?

An activity is identified by making a reasonable aggregation of operations into tasks and tasks into an activity. When this is done, one important accounting principle has to be considered: an activity must be linked to a product, service or any other reporting objective for which the management seeks information for decision-making and control. In other words, a series of activities should constitute overhead costs of a product or service. When such a focus is maintained on a product or service, an activity should not be 'too global or too local' for information purposes. Rather, relevant activities should be identified by focusing on the product or service.

An activity is identified by making a reasonable aggregation of operations into tasks and tasks into an activity.

Taking the notion of activity further into an accounting context, Brimson (1991) showed that an activity can be reduced to the processing of a transaction. A transaction process involves an event and resources, and ends with documentary evidence. For example, if a customer made a complaint about a fault in the product he/she bought, then the receipt of the complaint is the event. In this case, a salesperson would attend to this and correct the fault, either by getting the product repaired or by exchanging it. This is an important customer-related event which would generate a number of activities, including recording the complaint, sending the product for repair, informing the customer when the product is repaired, or sending the new product back to the customer, etc. All these activities involve resources which lead to customer-related costs, and produce documents which can provide evidence for those activities. This evidence can form a basis for accounting records which link to costing procedures. As long as paying attention to a customer complaint is part of the cost of after-sales service, the activities involved in this particular event are neither too global nor too local, but relevant.

> An activity can be reduced to the processing of a transaction which involves an event and resources and ends with documentary evidence.

As Kaplan and Cooper (1998) reported, companies used to develop 'activity dictionaries' which defined every major activity related to production facilities. The definitions could then be used as a template for labelling activities. According to this template, every activity is described by a particular verb, together with a relevant object: for example, receive a customer order, schedule production, receive materials, move materials, set up machines, respond to customers, etc. One primary task of consulting companies has been to develop such dictionaries. The technical literature on ABC has been based on verbs and objects contained in those dictionaries. A sample of a collection of these is reported by Kaplan and Cooper in their appendix (1998: 108–110). Broadly, they have categorized these 'activities' under two main service types which involve overhead costs: operation processes and management and support processes. The main activities under each are shown in Table 9.2.

> Companies used to develop 'activity dictionaries' which defined every major activity related to production facilities.

However, there are no hard and fast rules for identifying activities. As Innes and Mitchell (1995) showed, the final choice of activities is subjective. Twenty activities identified in the production of a particular product could be increased to thirty in another firm producing the same product with the same technology. No one can argue that the costing system in the former is better than the latter, or vice versa. What is real is the existence of such a subjective element which would lead to some arbitrary costing practices. No organization can be fully rational or fully attentive to choose the 'right' number of activities. Consequently, no one knows what the right number of activities is. While this is so, proponents of ABC have pinpointed the centrality of activities before doing anything else in product costing.

299

Table 9.2 *Activities in a business enterprise*

Activities within operation process:

Understand market and customers
Develop vision and strategy
Design products and services
Market and sell
Produce and deliver products and services
Produce and deliver for service organizations
Invoice and service customers

Activities within management and support process:

Develop and manage human resources
Manage information resources
Manage financial and physical resources
Execute environment management programmes
Manage external relationships
Manage improvement and change

Source: adapted from Kaplan and Cooper (1998)

How do we cost the activities?

The simplest answer to this question is that costs can be determined by tracing the resources involved in performing respective activities. Expenses categories coming from financial accounting systems are not activity-based. Instead, they represent broader categories – for example, salaries, office expenses, depreciation, maintenance, etc. When we look at the item 'salaries', we understand that it could be payments to various people engaged in different support activities, ranging from market research to final delivery of products and services. According to ABC procedures, 'salaries' can be broken down into these 'activities'. Similarly, all overhead costs coming from financial accounting classifications can be reclassified in line with identified activities. To go further, we shall consider an example, shown in Exhibit 9.1.

Costs can be determined by tracing the respective resources involved in performing activities.

Exhibit 9.1 *Overhead expenses of Company X*

Suppose that Company X has extracted the following overhead expenses from the financial accounting records for a particular accounting period:

Salaries	£250 000
Office expenses	£50 000
Depreciation	£350 000
Materials for common use	£75 000
Maintenance	£125 000
Total	*£850 000*

As we saw, these expenses do not tell us anything about the activities on which they are actually spent. An identification of activities and an understanding of the volume of resources these activities require would guide us to reclassify the above expenses categories into activity-based expenses categories. Suppose that this reclassification resulted in the figures shown in Exhibit 9.2 (adapted from Kaplan and Cooper, 1998).

Now, you should question how we have arrived at the figures in Exhibit 9.2. To answer this, we need to understand the emergence of activity-cost pools. In traditional cost allocation, as you saw in Chapter 3, we used to narrow down all departmental costs to production departments. In ABC, all costs need to be reallocated to activity-cost pools, which are contributed to by different resource expenses, such as salaries, office expenses, etc. The rows in Exhibit 9.2 add up to these activity-cost pools. Consequently, customer-order processing, materials purchasing, etc., con-

Exhibit 9.2 *Reclassification of overheads of Company X (£)*

Activity	Salaries	Office expenses	Depreciation	Materials for common use	Maintenance	Total
Customer-order processing	25 000	5 000	50 000	3 000	25 000	108 000
Materials purchasing	35 000	4 000	30 000	2 000	15 000	86 000
Production scheduling	40 000	6 000	80 000	4 000	10 000	140 000
Materials movements	50 000	7 000	30 000	6 000	25 000	118 000
Machine setting up	30 000	4 000	10 000	10 000	5 000	59 000
Inspecting for quality control	15 000	4 000	40 000	12 000	10 000	81 000
Production information processing	5 000	3 000	20 000	13 000	8 000	49 000
Performing engineering changes	25 000	8 000	30 000	18 000	12 000	93 000
Responding to customers	15 000	4 000	40 000	2 000	10 000	71 000
Attending to quality matters	10 000	5 000	20 000	5 000	5 000	45 000
Total	250 000	50 000	350 000	75 000	125 000	850 000

stitute activity-cost pools. In their initial stage, firms wanting to develop an ABC system tend to establish these activity-cost pools through careful monitoring of how resources are spent on different activities, rather than on 'departments'.

> All costs need to be reallocated to activity-cost pools, which are contributed to by different resource expenses, such as salaries, office expenses, etc.

How do we use 'activity costs' in costing a product/customer

When activity-cost pools are ready, costing can proceed to calculate the costs of products or services. At this stage, ABC advocates focusing on activity-cost drivers, which are regarded as the main determinants of costs of each activity. Traditional costing viewed overarching cost drivers as direct labour hours, etc. However, as long as activities are central to ABC, the volume of activity should be the cost driver. Kaplan and Cooper (1998: 95) stated that 'an activity cost driver is a quantitative measure of the output of an activity'. It has been emphasized that by closely observing production and support activities, these activity-cost drivers can be determined. Initially, there are several possible cost drivers. Through discussion and further observation, the most determinative cost drivers can be identified.

KEY TERMS

An activity-cost driver is a quantitative measure of the output of an activity.

Suppose that Company X has identified the cost drivers shown in Exhibit 9.3.

Exhibit 9.3 *Activity-cost drivers*

Activity	Activity-cost driver	Activity volume
Customer-order processing	Number of customer orders	1 080 orders
Materials purchasing	Number of invoices	430 invoices
Production scheduling	Number of production runs	280 runs
Materials movements	Number of movements	1 180 movements
Machine setting up	Number of set ups	590 set ups
Inspecting for quality control	Number of inspections	810 inspections
Production information processing	Number of production runs	280 runs
Performing engineering changes	Number of changes	93 changes
Responding to customers	Number of contacts	3 550 contacts
Attending to quality matters	Number of cases	450 cases

Having seen the hypothetical figures in Exhibit 9.3, you can understand that activity-cost drivers are always quantitative measures which can be used for further calculations. With these figures, the ABC system seeks the calculation of 'activity-cost driver rates'. It is a simple procedure: you need to divide respective activity costs by respective activity-cost driver volume. Exhibit 9.4 has the calculation of these rates.

KEY TERMS

'Activity-cost driver rate' equals respective activity costs divided by respective activity-cost driver volume.

Exhibit 9.4 Activity-cost driver rates

Activity costs	Activity-cost driver volume	Activity-cost driver rate (£)
Customer-order processing £108 000	1 080	100 per order
Materials purchasing £86 000	430	200 per invoice
Production scheduling £140 000	280	500 per run
Materials movements £118 000	1 180	100 per movement
Machine setting up £59 000	590	100 per set up
Inspecting for quality £81 000	810	100 per inspection
Production information processing £49 000	280	175 per run
Performing engineering changes £93 000	93	1 000 per change
Responding to customers £71 000	3 550	20 per contact
Attending to quality £45 000	450	100 per case

The cost driver rates can now be used for costing overheads for individual products and services. Rather than using a single 'overhead absorption rate', as in a traditional overhead allocation system, ABC allows us to use a number of 'cost driver rates' to absorb overheads to individual products and services. These rates can be ready-made, and when customer orders are executed, they can be a useful guide for costing differently for different customers.

To understand this procedure, we continue with our hypothetical example. Suppose that two different customers placed orders for the same products, but with different product specifications. Having looked at these specifications, the company's ABC system processed the data as shown in Exhibit 9.5.

It is noticeable that customer B should be more expensive than customer A because A's products demand more volume of activities than B's. As long as cost driver rates are now available, we can calculate the different overhead costs for each customer, as shown in Exhibit 9.6.

Continuing this example, suppose that direct materials and direct labour per unit of these products are £3.50 and £5.50, respectively. We can now calculate unit cost for both customers, as shown in Exhibit 9.7.

Exhibit 9.5 *Customer differences on activity-cost drivers*

Activity	Customer A	Customer B
Customer-order processing	1 order for 850 units	1 order for 500 units
Materials purchasing	3 invoices	5 invoices
Production scheduling	4 runs	7 runs
Materials movements	5 movements	8 movements
Machine setting up	4 set ups	8 set ups
Inspecting for quality control	2 inspections	5 inspections
Production information processing	4 runs	7 runs
Performing engineering changes	4 changes	8 changes
Responding to customers	2 contacts	6 contacts
Attending to quality matters	3 cases	6 cases

Exhibit 9.6 *Activity-based costing of customers*

Activity	Customer A	Customer B
Customer-order processing	1 × £100 = £100	1 × £100 = £100
Materials purchasing	3 × £200 = £600	5 × £200 = £1 000
Production scheduling	4 × £500 = £2 000	7 × £500 = £3 500
Materials movements	5 × £100 = £500	8 × £100 = £800
Machine setting up	4 × £100 = £400	8 × £100 = £800
Inspecting for quality control	2 × £100 = £200	5 × £100 = £500
Production information processing	4 × £175 = £700	7 × £175 = £1 225
Performing engineering changes	4 × £1 000 = £4 000	8 × £1 000 = £8 000
Responding to customers	2 × £20 = £40	6 × £20 = £120
Attending to quality matters	3 × £100 = £300	6 × £100 = £600
Total activity cost	*£8 840*	*£16 645*
Unit cost	*£8 840/850 = £10.40*	*£16 645/500 = £33.29*

Exhibit 9.7 *Customer order costing*

Unit costs	Customer A	Customer B
Direct materials	£3.50	£3.50
Direct labour	£5.50	£5.50
Overheads	£10.40	£33.29
Total	*£19.40*	*£42.29*

The final technical outcome of ABC is the calculation of costs. By doing this, it is argued, the right costs for the right customers can be determined, which leads to a product differentiation strategy under flexible specialization. It has been suggested that a traditional costing system over-costs high-volume products and under-costs low-volume products, as all product costs are calculated on the basis of a single overhead absorption rate. Now, flexibility has been created to use different costs for products with different functionalities for different customers. Possibilities have been developed for focusing on customers and rearranging production processes and facilities. This has led ABC's advocates to argue that it is not just about costing: it is cost management – activity-based management.

ABC can calculate the right costs for the right customers, which leads to product differentiation strategy under flexible specialization.

ACTIVITY-BASED MANAGEMENT

We do not intend to review this topic in detail. However, we cannot neglect the important extension of ABC into activity-based management (ABM). According to Cooper and Kaplan (1999: 277), 'ABM refers to the entire set of actions that can be taken, on a better formed basis, with activity-based cost information'. The aim of these actions is to lower the demand for resources for an organization's output without lowering the revenue that those outputs can earn. In simple terms, it is about the management of cost in a competitive environment in which advanced manufacturing technology is widely used.

'ABM refers to the entire set of actions that can be taken, on a better formed basis, with activity-based cost information.'

Cooper and Kaplan showed that there are two types of ABM practice: operational and strategic ABM. Operational ABM aims to 'do things right' towards gaining efficiency through lower costs, and enhancing asset utilization. Even though this is hardly a magical new management system, it does appear to be a new way of doing things in the context of flexibility and customer focus. Under operational ABM, managers tend to play around within the given system that demands resources. Three operational aims are to be accomplished under such a practice. The first is to reduce costs by lowering supplying resources, which can lead to lower cost driver rates. The second is to earn higher revenues by better resource utilization, which creates opportunities to produce more than before. The third is to avoid costs which would have been incurred for additional resources if a better resource utilization policy had not been implemented.

KEY TERMS

Operational ABM aims to 'do things right' towards gaining efficiency by lowering costs, and enhancing asset utilization.

Improvement of operational ABM requires some additional techniques. In pursuit of these, Cooper and Kaplan (1999) have been attracted by continuous and discontinuous improvement programmes. The former continues with existing attempts to optimize the operational benefits of reducing costs and maximizing resource utilization. The latter is applied when the former does not guarantee the radical changes required by ABM programmes. TQM programmes, which have been popular in Japanese firms, were seen as suitable for continuous improvement programmes. In TQM, firms tend to search for every aspect of business process which needs continuous improvement. Business process re-engineering (BPR) programmes, launched by most US firms, were considered suitable techniques in discontinuous programmes. BPR seeks radical changes in business process when continuous programmes come to an optimal point. Both continuous and discontinuous programmes were used to implement the practices of operational ABM. Having come to this point, Cooper and Kaplan suggested five steps to be followed in the implementation of operational ABM:

- develop the business case by starting with activity analysis;
- establish priorities in the profile of the firm's business;
- provide cost justification for the implementation of new programmes;
- track the benefits by refreshing and updating the ABC/M model; and
- measure performance for ongoing improvement by focusing on both cost objects and other performance measures.

TQM programmes, which have been popular in Japanese car firms, were seen as suitable for continuous improvement programmes.

Five steps to be followed in the implementation of operational ABM:

- develop the business case;
- establish priorities;
- provide cost justification;
- track the benefits; and
- measure performance.

While keeping the operational ABM practices constant, strategic ABM attempts to change the activity mix by shifting activities from unprofitable products, services and customers to profitable ones. This would result in a reduction of activity volumes in non-profitable revenue sources, and in an increase of such volumes in productive sources. ABC advocates suggests that the opportunity for engaging in activity analysis, spotting unused capacity, eliminating non-value-added activities, etc., can lead to such strategic-oriented practices. In economic terms, this has been termed as a shift from 'economies of scale' to 'economies of scope', where managers are engaged in exploiting better opportunities rather than perpetually increasing production. For instance, unused capacity spotted by the analysts can be redirected to better economic actions, or such capacity can be eliminated by stopping supplying resources. On the one hand, this can reduce the costs of existing products and services; and, on the other, by redirecting idle capacity, firms can earn more revenue. In this way, strategic ABM tends to recast the existing expensive operational processes into more profitable ones, in both manufacturing and service organizations.

KEY TERMS

Strategic ABM is a set of attempts to change the activity mix by shifting activities from unprofitable products, services and customers to profitable ones.

Towards implementing strategic ABM, firms tend to deal with several areas of management action, including product mix and pricing, customer relationships, supplier selection and relationships, and product design and development. These areas are not automatically triggered by ABM. Rather, as Cooper and Kaplan (1988: 103) pointed out, more accurate cost information generated from ABC systems can lead managers to focus attention on those areas 'with the most leverage for increasing profits'. Rather than taking cost information only for one particular purpose, ABC systems create flexibility to act upon numerous strategic areas with a greater enthusiasm for innovative decisions. As shown in Figure 9.2, the ultimate goal of this broader engagement in the implementation of ABC/M is to create better market value (Kennedy and Affleck-Graves, 2001).

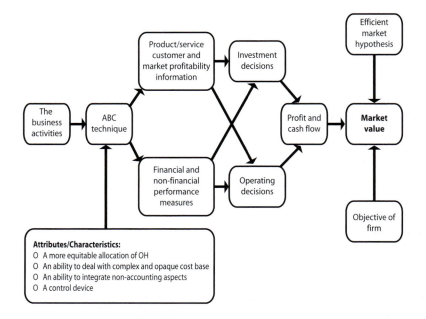

Figure 9.2 *Link between ABC and market value*

Source: adapted from Ward and Patel (1990), cited in Kennedy and Affleck-Graves (2001)

307

ABC IMPLEMENTATION: RESEARCHERS' VIEWS

We have seen that ABC seems to be a breakthrough in the field of cost management. From the perspectives of its advocates, it is the solution to the problem of 'relevance lost' in management accounting. From the 1990s onwards, mainstream academic researchers have evaluated the impact of the implementation of ABC/M projects to explore whether or not the original claims are correct. We shall look at some major contributions, summarized in Table 9.3.

Table 9.3 *Mainstream ABC academic studies: issues in implementation*

Study	Focus	Findings	Issues identified
Mitchell (1994)	Rationales and limitations of application	ABC has proved attractive not only to accountants as a costing technique but also to other managerial users as a guide to decision-making	Can lead to unrest among employees; rigid organizational forms would not match ABC requirements; behavioural issues could arise
Bjornenak (1997)	Diffusion of ABC in Norway	An understanding of diffusion of accounting innovations	Innovation takes place through influence of consultants, media, pressures for change, etc.; otherwise ABC would not be adopted
Foster and Swenson (1997)	Measuring the success of ABC/M based on alternative methods of measurement – decision-making, decision actions, dollar improvements and management evaluation	ABC/M has been successful in implementation in those areas, provided determinants of success are fulfilled	No specific issue pinpointed; however, it is implied that, if determinants are not fulfilled, problems of implementation would occur
Malmi (1997)	Failure in a decentralized organization	ABC failures are not failures: rather, they are problems of implementation and those problems are associated with broader organizational issues, such as resistance, power and politics	When implementing new techniques, such as ABC, resistance develops through non-consonance with dimensions of organizational power and organizational paradigm
Innes *et al.* (2000)	Comparison of two survey results to assess changes in firms adopting ABC	While adoption of ABC is significantly higher among large firms and those from the finance sector, few significant changes can be seen between 1994 and 1999; however, firms adopting ABC have been experimenting for more than five years	Majority of respondents have not been attracted enough to adopt ABC; whether users are loyal to ABC is not conclusive; there is a considerable rejection rate

Kennedy and Affleck-Graves (2001)	Impact of ABC on firm performance	Firms adopting ABC perform better by adding value through better cost control and asset utilization, coupled with greater use of financial leverage	Superior stock performance of ABC not immediate, taking until the second half of the three-year study period to manifest itself
Cagwin and Bouwman (2002)	Association between ABC and improvement in financial performance	Positive association between ABC and improvement in ROI when ABC is used concurrently with other strategic initiatives, even under complex business conditions	No specific issues identified despite possible methodological problems of cross-sectional data analysis, especially issue of causality
Soin *et al.* (2002)	ABC and organizational change in clearing department of UK-based multinational bank	ABC team succeeded in establishing a less radical version of ABC through developing new links between costs and products; however, they did not succeed in transforming strategic thinking of bank's senior management	Early stage of implementation, formal change preferable, but in later stage; this cannot be continued as some managers demand informal changes; evolutionary changes undesirable as ABC was new management accounting initiative; no progressive change as ABC data not properly linked with strategic dimensions
Cardinaels *et al.* (2004)	ABC in competitive pricing decisions	ABC provides benefits over volume-based costing in market segments; even in less informative market settings, ABC outperforms traditional costing	No specific issue identified; ABC evaluated positively through estimating statistical significance

The mainstream academic research findings represent another phase of ABC/M development. As Lukka and Granlund (2002) argue, once the proponents (be they consultants or researchers) – in this case Kaplan and his followers – sell their concepts (by providing convincing arguments), academic researchers come to the scene as independent evaluators to see how this concept has been implemented in actual organizational contexts. Their role is not to sell the concept but to provide some analysis and clarification. If you look at Table 9.1, you can see that some have analysed by showing the statistical relationships between ABC and organizational performance. Others levelled criticisms against organizational settings – their politics and resistance. In general, for these researchers, problems in ABC application as a costing technique or ABM implementation as a strategic initiative lay in organizational resistance rather than in the ABC/M technique/method itself. Thus, as Lukka and Granlund (2002) showed, these researchers are implicitly positive towards the concept. They do not tend to criticize it but engage in an academic exercise, assuming that ABC/M is now a well-accepted technique which does not need questioning. However, ABC/M has also been evaluated by critical researchers. We shall consider their contributions in the next section.

309

> Once the proponents (be they consultants or researchers) – in this case Kaplan and his followers – sell their concepts (by providing convincing arguments), academic researchers come to the scene as independent evaluators to see how this concept has been implemented in actual organizational contexts.

> Problems in implementation lay in organizational resistance rather than the ABC/M technique/method itself.

ABC has been a bandwagon!

The bandwagon is 'the car that carries the band in a circus procession: a fashionable movement' (Jones and Dugdale, 2002: 121). Naturally, a bandwagon attracts everybody's attention and shows how well the people in the wagon perform. Some critical researchers in accounting have come forward to illustrate how 'key actors' in the development of new management technologies, such as ABC/M, perform well in making their technologies attractive (Gosselin, 1997; Jones and Dugdale, 2002; Armstrong, 2002; Lukka and Granlund, 2002). This particular development is called the 'bandwagon effect' of new management technologies (Gosselin, 1997). If the band-wagon effect in a particular new management technology is much more significant than being a 'real' management innovation, then the underlying technology is said to be a 'fad' or 'fashion' (Innes et al., 2000). If this is the case in respect of ABC/M, then there is a question as to whether its underlying techniques represent a 'real' calculative practice.

> If the bandwagon effect in a particular new management technology is much more significant than being a 'real' management innovation, then the underlying technology is said to be a 'fad' or 'fashion'.

Starting from the definition of direct and indirect costs, regarding the question of 'real', Armstrong (2002) has made some interesting points. He admits that direct costs do not entail any issue of calculation, as they can easily be assigned to cost objects. In this sense, as he argues, direct costs are real. '[T]hey are external to cost accounting as a practice' (p. 104); only a bookkeeping methodology is sufficient to record and assign direct costs to cost objects; thus, any approach to costing cannot change the amount of direct costs. If this observation is correct, then Armstrong raises the question of whether indirect costs are real in the same sense. Quoting Wilson and Chua (1993: 107), Armstrong illustrates that indirect costs are 'both unknown and unknowable, given that there is no definitive basis for apportioning or absorbing indirect costs. However, some bases are better than others.' What we infer from this is that direct costs are always accurate and real, and indirect costs might not always be.

Direct costs are always accurate and real, but indirect costs might not be.

However, the advocates of ABC/M appear to make indirect costs accurate and, in turn, real. As you saw earlier in the chapter, Kaplan, Cooper and their followers said that traditional costing miscalculated and distorted indirect costs, while ABC has corrected this miscalculation and distortion. If they did this, the outcome should be that all indirect costs should now be direct costs in relation to the behaviour of cost objects. As all costs are now direct, the world of costing should be real. However, as Armstrong (2002: 106) argues, this cannot be a practical reality:

> In practice, most applications of ABC make arbitrary allocations of common costs. The search for the activities which connect costs to products and processes, and for the cost drivers which proxy for them, needs to compromise between representational accuracy and manageability. The result is that some indirect costs – hopefully a small portion of the total – are virtually bound to be excluded from the cost pools associated with a practical set of cost drivers.

Having done this, Armstrong terms this process of indirect costing 'the concealment of indirect costs allocations within activity-based costing'. Taking staff department costs as an example, he highlights that 'the more of the labour within a staff department which is indirect in terms of its output activities, the greater will be the proportion of arbitrary allocation within activity costs' (ibid.).

What we could conclude from these critical comments is that, despite the fact that ABC's indirect cost calculation may be better than that of traditional absorption costing, ABC still calculates indirect costs on an arbitrary basis, just as traditional costing did. To put the matter another way, ABC, albeit inadvertently, still distorts product costs by concealing indirect costs behind the curtain of cost drivers. If the product costs are still not 100 per cent accurate, then there arises a question of the utility of such costs for management and strategic purposes – a question of the validity of ABM.[1] Without questioning this 'fundamental error', some researchers tend to 'appreciate and evaluate' the effects of ABC/M on firms' performance.

The more indirect (in terms of its output activities) the labour in a staff department is, the greater will be the proportion of arbitrary allocation within activity costs.

Also, despite the above 'error', the ABC/M project stands up as a powerful global expert system. Drawing on Giddens (1990: 27), Jones and Dugdale (2002: 124) define expert systems as 'systems of technical accomplishments or professional expertise that organise large areas of the material and social environments in which we live today'. Focusing on the diffusion of ABC, Jones and Dugdale go on to show that expert systems become global and encircle us with their knowledge and authenticity. However, this does not happen automatically. This knowledge and authenticity come from certain actors and networks rather than through individual academic contributions. Jones and Dugdale have discovered this story of the network-building process which made ABC a 'global expert system', rather than a true solution to the problem of miscalculation of product costing.

> There is a story of a network-building process which made ABC a 'global expert system', rather than a true solution to the problem of miscalculation of product costing.

The story begins with comments that ABC was not a discovery by Robin Cooper, but a practice in an American company visited by Robert Kaplan. It was Kaplan who was associated with a programme of introducing advanced manufacturing systems which was regarded as a requirement of American firms struggling against Japanese competition. In this context, Kaplan initiated the building of the Harvard University network of academics and consultants, and expanded it to the manufacturing consulting firm CAM-I (Computer-Aided Manufacturing International). This network worked hard to establish ABC as a solid and valid answer to the problems of miscosting. In their development to this point, they had problems with some counter-actors, such as Goldratt, who were ultimately fought off, and also some disagreements within the Harvard network itself. Despite these struggles, the network gradually became settled, and ABC solidified as an accepted concept of product costing, especially in the context of modern computing systems and a programme of downsizing. Jones and Dugdale emphasized that this process involved a cycle of translation: from company practices to case studies, from case studies to expositions, from expositions to theoretical improvements, from improved theories to new company practices and so on.

> Robert Kaplan initiated the building of the Harvard University network of academics and consultants and expanded it to the manufacturing consulting firm called CAM-I (Computer-Aided Manufacturing International).

We now can conclude the chapter by revisiting the case of Marconi. Other than this networking effect of ABC, as Marconi suggested, it is hard to see any technical superiority of ABC/M over traditional absorption costing. Marconi provided empirical evidence that the technical problems of ABC, especially on the choice of activities and cost drivers, led to managerial resistance through the development of disagreements and distrust. This is not only an issue of the organizational setting in which the ABC project was implemented (in this case, a public utility), but also a problem of ABC itself, which allowed the managers to exercise subjective judgements on indirect costs as they were not inherently 'real'. The diffusion of ABC as a global expert system which appears to transform indirect costs into direct costs owed more to the power of global networks of consultants than to the superiority of ABC/M. As long as ABC cannot create 'real costs', when charged with resistance, some managers can manipulate the practice of ABC and create unintended control problems. In the case of Portuguese Telecommunications, 'ABC did not trace a high proportion of costs to products as predicted by instigators. Its arbitrariness was reinforced when some employees deliberately rendered slow and inaccurate time sheets, seeing them as unwarranted and threatening controls' (Hopper and Major, forthcoming).

ABC led to managerial resistance through the development of disagreements and distrust. This is not only an issue of organizational setting but also a problem of ABC itself, which allowed the managers to exercise subjective judgements on indirect costs as they were not inherently 'real'.

SUMMING UP: ALIGNMENT WITH THE POST-MECHANISTIC FORM

By reading Chapter 7, you know that the post-mechanistic form is a dramatic transformation of both production systems and organizational forms. This transformation has created a flexible manufacturing regime in the sphere of production systems, and a post-bureaucratic organization in the sphere of organizational forms. Manufacturing flexibility does not stand alone: it requires a logical synchronization with customer needs reflected in market behaviour. The strategic turn in management has established this synchronization. This sustenance of ABC/M has much to offer for the post-mechanistic approach to management accounting in these two strands: contributing to flexibility, while synchronizing with the strategic turn in management accounting (see Armstrong, 2002).

Together with the underlying economic-theory justification, traditional costing had the famous dichotomy of costs: fixed and variable (from its behavioural perspective) or indirect and direct (from its inventory-valuation perspective). The fixed/indirect group of costs generate from 'inflexible' production processes and 'invisible' common facilities. When production systems and facilities became flexible, and managers began to respond to customers' needs accordingly, instigators of new cost management sought to impute the same flexibility and responsiveness to customers in the same sense. Thus, almost all indirect costs have to be fully allocated to products and customers, and almost all unallocated costs have to be eliminated through programmes such as outsourcing, downsizing and restructuring. The ultimate aim is to make all costs flexible (direct or variable), as opposed to living with the above traditional dichotomy of costs. To put it another way, instigators wanted to synchronize flexible manufacturing and the strategic orientation of management with a potential regime of 'flexible costing'.

'Flexible costing' can go hand-in-hand with flexible manufacturing in two mutually inclusive ways. One is that manufacturing flexibility can easily eliminate many sources of fixed/indirect costs through the replacement of production plants with CAM/CAD-type facilities. Consequently, the cost of the use of plants can 'logically' be allocated to individual products/customers in terms of appropriate cost drivers, such as number of production runs. Second is that, by making all costs 'visible' to managers, cost management can promote the possible elimination of 'unnecessary' production facilities which cannot directly contribute to customers' needs. This is possible because CAM/CAD is able to perform multiple functions that had previously operated separately This has a pragmatic logic for eliminating separate functions that become idle. The Caterpillar case in Chapter 7 illustrated the accommodation of multiple functions in single plant, the Assembly Highway. In this way, Caterpillar's 'Plant with a Future' created a future for new cost management, too. As we saw earlier in this chapter, the mutuality between costing and a CAM/CAD programme was substantially exploited by ABC/M instigators by expanding their network to CAM-I. Moreover, various management programmes, such as TQM and JIT, emerged from this environ-

313

ment of manufacturing flexibility, and simultaneously those management programmes enhanced that manufacturing flexibility.

Also, 'flexible costing' became synchronized with strategic management accounting, which focused on customer requirements and, in turn, on external market dynamics. Now, making changes to product attributes is not an engineering problem. Production flexibility is now meant to respond to the needs of customers. Consequently, firms are now continuously engaged in dropping unwanted products and product attributes and adding new ones. This can be better justified when product costs are more visible to managers, and when manufacturing technology is ready for any required changes. The interface between strategic management accounting and cost management, which we mentioned earlier, has to be noted here again. ABC/M provides product costing according to the needs of customers. However, before embarking on a batch of products for a particular sector of customers, managers tend to look beyond the organization by collecting demand information and related external data to be combined with ABC/M information, as Bromwich (1990) suggested. Even though such external information is vitally important, managers cannot go ahead with producing for the above particular sector of customers unless ABC/M provides useful information for making that production decision.

To sum up, as is shown in Figure 9.3, traditional costing survived under the regime of mass production through the maintenance of standardized management control systems, along with widespread bureaucracy. This whole configuration is now being dismantled, and a new configuration is being constructed. In this new configuration, ABC/M seems to be located at the interface between flexible manufacturing and the customer-oriented strategic management regime. This

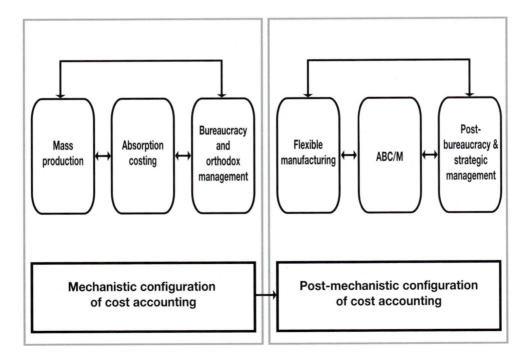

Figure 9.3 *Transformation from the mechanistic to the post-mechanistic*

wholesale transformation is now taking place, while ABC/M is becoming a justifiable postmodern technology through the development of powerful global networks. Despite its potential problems of implementation, actors in networks are continuously attempting to translate this Western-origin technology into the contexts of other parts of the world. Despite its simplicity of calculation, the underlying programme of ABC/M seems to be powerful: 'the juggernaut of modernity' (Jones and Dugdale, 2002).

HAVE YOU UNDERSTOOD THE CHAPTER?

1. What are the main differences between nineteenth-century cost management and twentieth-century cost accounting?
2. As the terms are used in contemporary management accounting textbooks, what are the differences between 'cost accounting' and 'cost management'?
3. What are the main contributions to the development of contemporary cost management?
4. Describe the main steps in the development of an ABC/M programme.
5. Distinguish between the technical procedures in traditional absorption costing and ABC.
6. Why are activities more important than functions, business processes, actions and operations?
7. Define 'ABM'. Describe its operational and strategic dimensions.
8. What did mainstream academic researchers learn about the implementation of ABC/M programmes?
9. Outline the critical comments regarding ABC/M implementation.
10. How does ABC/M promote the post-mechanistic form?

BEYOND THE CHAPTER

1. 'ABC is not only a costing technique but also a business enterprise in modern capitalism.' Discuss.
2. 'The ABC "solution" creates more problems.' Discuss.
3. 'ABC is not a problem, but the context is.' Is this true?
4. On ABC/M, some researchers are positive, others are critical. Why?
5. On the application of ABC, reflect on the lessons you learned from Marconi.

FURTHER READING

1. The best starting point is Kaplan (1994) which gives you a broader context to this topic.
2. Cooper and Kaplan (1988) is essential for an understanding of the technical foundation of ABC and ABM.
3. Broader evaluation of the application of ABC can be found in Mitchell (1994) and Foster and Swenson (1997).
4. The nature of research on ABC is in Lukka and Granlund (2002).
5. More critical commentaries on ABC application can be found in Armstrong (2002), Jones and Dugdale (2002) and Hopper and Major (forthcoming).

Chapter 10

Towards new management control and governance in new organizations

A STARTING POINT: GOVERNING BY RELATIONS

Supermarkets are proliferating, and their success is due largely to the use of communication and information technology, and subsequent changes in the form of organization. Consider sales of sandwiches at any supermarket. When you buy the sandwiches, sales occur. At the point of sale, numbers of sales are calculated automatically through a scanning system. As programmed, the scanning system speaks to the ordering system, which is facilitated by EDI (electronic data interchange). The ordering system can transmit this requirement to the supplier's production planning system. The job of the latter is to calculate and process information needed for the order: that is, labour, raw materials, etc., the number of units to be produced and details of distribution. As soon as planning and calculations are complete, sandwiches are produced, outputs are put in lorries, distributions are made straight to depots, boxes are despatched to respective stores, sandwiches are put on shelves and then into customers' trolleys. Again, sales are registered through the scanning system. To complete a round of sales – from ordering to selling again – takes forty-eight hours! One of the fundamental reasons behind this success is the supermarkets' uniqueness in organizing their activities through network relations and communication and information technology. The supermarkets have shown that they cannot function as stand-alone firms operating by their own rules and regulations. Instead, they need to adapt to the ways in which supplier relations operate through the use of new technologies. The supermarkets have then come to be super-organizations, extending and blurring the traditional boundaries of inter-firm relations and networks. (Adapted from Frances and Garnsey, 1996.)

SETTING THE SCENE

The above is an inevitable, upcoming context for management accounting. As we showed in Chapter 7, this context reflects an emerging trend in manufacturing technology and a changing orientation in marketing philosophy. The manufacturing technology was seen through three sociological concepts: post-Fordism, postmodernism and flexible specialization. The marketing philosophy was viewed in the light of the escalation of global competition in product markets, which empowered the customer rather than the firm and/or employee. In relation to this context, in Chapters 8 and 9, we reviewed two inevitable new directions in management accounting approaches: strategic management accounting and cost management. The implications of the above changing context and the resultant management accounting approaches are seen in the construction of a new management control and governance mechanism coupled with the changing forms of organizations. A study of new management accounting can thus conclude by investigating and characterizing the underlying principles of those changing forms of new organizations and their companion management controls and governance mechanisms. These mechanisms can broadly define the notion of new management accounting which this book is unveiling.

New organizations are thus the micro-context, and the resultant management control and governance are its content. This micro-context is an inevitable shift in the orthodox form of organization which stemmed from the Weberian model of bureaucracy to a post-bureaucratic form. The content marks a transformation of the conventional management control model, which reproduced the principles of bureaucracy, into a blurred form of management control in both intra-organizational and inter-organizational spheres. In Chapter 7, we showed that this micro-contextual transformation can be seen as a gradual trend of deconstructing fundamental principles of bureaucracy which promoted task-based controls under the blessing of an internal-oriented command economy and reconstructing new organizational principles which encouraged performance-based control under a context of an external-oriented open market. Learning objectives of this chapter are set to elaborate this broader transformation and its implications for the mechanisms of new management control and governance upon which we can define 'new management accounting'.

First, we will provide a conceptual framework for organizing the subsequent sections of the chapter. In this framework, we will present a typology of transformation: from bureaucracy to post-bureaucracy, and from intra-organizational changes to inter-organizational changes. This typology will provide us with four arenas of management control: intra-organizational and inter-organizational controls under bureaucracy and under post-bureaucracy.

- To categorize the principles of management control as bureaucracy and post-bureaucracy
- To divide the arenas of management control into intra-organizational and inter-organizational
- To define a typology of transformation for the study of changing organizational forms and their implications for management control and governance

Second, the chapter will elaborate on the perceived crisis in bureaucracy. Having outlined the connection between bureaucracy and orthodox management control, this section will address several issues of how an orthodox management control model would be problematic in both intra-organizational and inter-organizational arenas. It will be shown that, as bureaucracy aims to establish 'rationalized, well-ordered manufacturing settings', the changes occurring mainly in the areas of production systems, costing methods and marketing philosophies come to be incompatible with the functioning of the bureaucratic forms of management control. The section will emphasize how this problem can present itself in both intra-organizational and inter-organizational arenas.

- To introduce the concept of bureaucracy as the organizing principle of orthodox management control
- To highlight the problem of incompatibility of bureaucratic forms of management control with changing organizational environment
- To discuss the magnitude of the above problem in relation to the functioning of controls in both intra-organizational and inter-organizational arenas

Third, the chapter proceeds to outline the emerging forms of organizations within the regime of post-bureaucracy. In this, we will briefly characterize major forms being merged, together with a focus on their management control ramifications. As there cannot be exact types of organizational forms that have been established like bureaucratic forms, this section will highlight the fragmentation of this trend and the evolutionary nature of their development. We will show these ramifications in relation to the practice of management control in the two arenas we are considering: the intra- and inter-organizational.

- To outline the emerging forms of organizations within the regime of post-bureaucracy
- To review the nature of management control systems emerging from the above regime
- To focus on intra-organizational and inter-organizational relationships and their underlying management control systems and governance mechanisms

Fourth, we will illustrate from case studies the emerging practices of management control systems under which organizations are changing. Specifically, the section will draw on research findings which contribute to our knowledge of management control practices within post-bureaucracy. Despite its infancy, a reflection on this emerging body of literature will guide us to a reconfiguration of the orthodox management control model into one that could facilitate flexible specialization, strategic management initiatives and cost management practices.

- To illustrate emerging practices of management control systems stemming from new forms of organization
- To reflect on a reconfiguration of orthodox management control into one that could go hand-in-hand with new management accounting technologies

Finally, we sum up the chapter by outlining how these organizational changes contribute to the formation of the post-mechanistic approach to management accounting. In particular, we will highlight in what sense new management accounting operates under the blessing of these changes in organizational forms.

- To sum up the chapter by outlining the contributions to the overall post-mechanistic approach
- To reflect on the practice of new management accounting under these changes in organizational forms

This context and content give rise to a particular typology.

A TYPOLOGY OF ORGANIZATIONAL TRANSFORMATION

The typology of organizational transformation, as is shown in Figure 10.1, creates two dichotomies in two continuums: bureaucracy versus post-bureaucracy and intra-organizational versus inter-organizational. The dichotomy of bureaucracy versus post-bureaucracy represents a continuum rather than two distinct forms of organizations. In contemporary organizations, there would be characters of both bureaucratic and post-bureaucratic forms with some variation reflected in a continuum. The vertical axis in Figure 10.1 represents this. The other dichotomy of intra- versus inter-organizational relationships is seen in a continuum on the horizontal axis, again with variations in practice more towards appreciation of either intra-organizational or inter-organizational relationships. The two dichotomies then allow us to tease out three types of organization: the orthodox rational, the team-based horizontal and the network. In this, it is hard to see a type of organization which promotes inter-organizational relationships under bureaucracy, as this form is mostly confined to legal boundaries.

The two dichotomies allow us to tease out three types of organization: the orthodox rational, the team-based horizontal, and the network.

Based on the typology above, we can discern that a study of forms of organizations and their implications for management control and governance depend on the orientation of bureaucracy and the nature of relationships the firms wish to maintain. What we want to emphasize is that the broader contextual changes we outlined in Chapter 7 are now coming to force organizations to adopt more post-bureaucratic forms with an appreciation of more team-based horizontal organization structures and network organizations. Thus, the typology above aids an exploration of how these changes occur, what concepts of organizations we can identify and how these concepts explain emerging management control and governance. The subsequent sections of the chapter will address these issues.

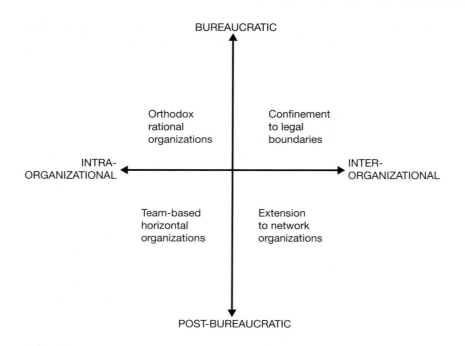

Figure 10.1 *Forms of organizations and arenas of management control*

Contextual changes are now forcing organizations to adopt more post-bureaucratic forms, with an appreciation of more team-based horizontal organization structures and network organizations.

MANAGEMENT CONTROL AND GOVERNANCE UNDER BUREAUCRACY

In Chapter 5, we defined 'management control' as 'those organizational arrangements and actions designed to facilitate members to achieve higher performance with least unintended consequences' (Ansari, 1977: 102). These arrangements and actions can constitute a broader governance mechanism that would hold the organization conceptually as an integrated institution. The question of how we should understand the functioning of such management control and governance mechanisms has been addressed by Max Weber in his writings on bureaucracy (see, for example, Weber, 1930, 1958, 1964). In this section, we shall outline such conceptual underpinnings and their implications for questioning the scope of the bureaucratic form of management control and governance.

Bureaucratic form is a mechanism of governance by which modern organizations (those which developed towards the end of the nineteenth and the start of the twentieth century) are run by rules and regulations. As is seen in Box 10.1, Max Weber described how these rules and regulations worked in the German state in the nineteenth century. Soon after the development of the German model of the state, especially after the First World War, large-scale corporations in the USA began to take the model of bureaucracy as their superstructure of management. These corporations developed into the model of 'rational-efficient' organizations, where 'rationality' refers to the 'logical nature of beliefs and actions'. In these beliefs and actions there appeared designed structures and practices built upon the processes of planning, organizing, staffing, co-ordinating, motivating, controlling and so on (see Thompson and McHugh, 2002). These aspects of organizations constituted management control and governance systems which aimed to accomplish predetermined aims and objectives, calculated and formulated mostly in financial terms.

BOX 10.1 GOVERNING PRINCIPLES OF BUREAUCRACY

1. There is the principle of fixed and official jurisdictional areas, which are generally ordered by rules: that is, by laws or administrative regulations.
2. The principles of office hierarchy and of levels of graded authority mean a firmly ordered system of super- and sub-ordination in which there is supervision of the lower offices by higher ones. Such a system offers the governed the possibility of appealing against decisions of a lower office to higher authority, in a definitely regulated manner. With the development of bureaucratic type, the office hierarchy is monocratically organized. The principle of hierarchical office authority is found in all bureaucratic structures, in state and ecclesiastical structures as well as in large party organizations and private enterprises. It does not matter for the character of bureaucracy whether its authority is called 'private' or 'public'.
3. The management of the modern office is based upon written documents ('files'), which are preserved in their original or draft form. There is, therefore, a staff of subaltern officials and scribes of all sorts. The body of officials actively engaged in a 'public' office,

continued

along with the respective apparatus of material implements and files, makes up a 'bureau'. In private enterprise 'the bureau' is often called the 'office'.

4. Office management, at least all specialized office management – and such management is distinctly modern – usually presupposes thorough and expert training. This holds increasingly for the modern executive and employee of private enterprises, in the same way as it holds for the state official.

5. When the office is fully developed, official activity demands the full working capacity of the official, irrespective of the fact that his obligatory time in the bureau may be firmly delimited. In the normal case, this is only the product of a long development, in the public as well as in the private office. Formally, in all cases, the normal state of affairs was reversed: official business was discharged as a secondary activity.

6. The management of the office follows general rules, which are more or less stable, more or less exhaustive, and which can be learned. Knowledge of these rules represents a special technical learning which the officials possess. It involves jurisprudence, or administrative or business management.

Source: Weber (1964), Clegg *et al.* (2005)

Following the development from around 1900 of the ideas of the American mechanical engineer F. W. Taylor (1967), the above bureaucratic model became the foundation for factory management. Taylor prescribed: the development of science for each element of work; scientific selection and training of workers; co-operation between management and workers to ensure the work is done according to the science; and equal division of work and responsibility between management and workers, each side doing what suits it best. These prescriptions became widespread in the organizing of economic and social activities. Taylorism came to emphasize the fact that social organization can be made operable by introducing engineered technical arrangements into the organization with a view to 'getting the job done'. To put it another way, rational actions were regarded as essential to achieving efficiency, a combined conceptualization of Weber's bureaucracy and Taylor's scientific management. This combined concept was extended by Henry Ford in his motor company, where he adopted Taylorist principles with the introduction of technical control through the flow of the assembly line (see Littler, 1982). While Taylorist principles enhanced rigidity and inflexibility, Fordist principles allowed certain job fragmentation for a greater level of labour intensity towards speeding up of lines and increased payments to combat labour turnover (see Williams *et al.*, 1992). Moreover, Taylorist principles developed into neo-Taylorist schemes in other parts of the world through concurrent consulting efforts. For example, Charles Bedeaux, a French management consultant, promoted a cheap and quick method that did not need to have major consequences for existing management structures (Littler, 1982).

Taylorism is about: the development of science for each element of work; scientific selection and training of workers; co-operation between management and workers to ensure that work is done according to the science; and equal division of work and responsibility between management and workers, each side doing what suits it best.

How organizations are structured is also an important aspect we must look at in our attempt to understand management control and governance mechanisms. On this specific issue, Pugh (1997: 18) has presented a useful guide for understanding the dimensions of an organization structure. His categorization includes six dimensions:

- specialization – dividing activities into specialized roles;
- standardization – laying down standard rules and procedures;
- standardization of employment practices;
- formalization – producing written instructions, procedures, etc.;
- centralization – placing authority for making certain decisions at the top;
- configuration – shaping the organization's roles through: chain of command (whether it is short or long); span of control (whether superiors have a few or a large number of subordinates); and percentage of specialized/support personnel (whether there is a large or small percentage).

When we study the changing nature of organizations' management control and governance mechanisms, the above dimensions can be used as variables for testing how organizational structures would change due to the nature of, and changes in, them. Based on the above classification, Pugh concluded that there can be three forms of bureaucracy: personal bureaucracy, with a centralized structure; workflow bureaucracy, with a fully structured production system; and full bureaucracy, with a system of impersonal control. Thus, fully structured, organizational and manufacturing features can promote fully developed, bureaucratic management control and governance mechanisms (such as budgeting, which we discussed in Chapter 5) which had been better synchronized with the tendencies of mass production and production-oriented marketing philosophies. It was believed that organizations would be more effective and efficient if these structured features were developed.

Fully structured, organizational and manufacturing features can promote fully developed, bureaucratic management control and governance mechanisms. Budgeting is one example.

In this organizational context, intra-organizational controls operated through those structured mechanisms. Here, intra-organizational controls are all internal arrangements that create (power) relationships between superiors and subordinates, as well as among employees. Governing principles for the substance of these internal relationships and subsequent intra-control processes come from the above structured characteristics. For example, organizations develop budgeting processes where budget targets are set according to standards (standardization); the set targets are to be achieved by designated responsibility centres (formalization); the responsibilities are divided into expert knowledge areas (specialization and standardization of employment practices); top managers make decisions and/or take actions about the performance of budgetees (centralization); and a chain of command is developed for communication and co-ordination through budgeting (configuration).

As these practices promote rigidity rather than flexibility, there is less scope for the development of inter-organizational relationships and subsequent management control systems and

> ### KEY TERMS
>
> Intra-organizational controls are all internal arrangements that create (power) relationships between superiors and subordinates, as well as among employees.

governance beyond the legal boundaries of organizations. When it comes to inter-organizational control systems, organizations had to maintain their autonomy through legal definitions: firms are regarded as 'separate legal entities'. Thus, an inter-organizational control system hardly developed, and the firms operating within mass production regimes had little requirement for maintaining such inter-organizational control and governance mechanisms. Instead, the orthodox, bureaucratic systems celebrated the existence of such intra-oriented control systems and governance mechanisms. However, when both 'flexible manufacturing' and 'customer orientation' came to penetrate the organization structures and, in turn, management control and governance mechanisms, the bureaucratic form faced a crisis. The next section outlines this.

> An inter-organizational control system hardly developed within bureaucracy, and the firms operating within mass-production regimes had little requirement for maintaining such inter-organizational control and governance mechanisms.

CRISIS IN THE BUREAUCRATIC FORM OF MANAGEMENT CONTROL AND GOVERNANCE

By the term 'crisis' we do not mean that the bureaucratic form has to be abandoned. It cannot be completely abandoned and replaced with another form, as the impact of large-scale bureaucracy on the power structures of modern organizations and society cannot be easily neglected. However, we can discuss a 'crisis' in two main areas: first, by referring to neo-Weberian organization literature that developed some concerns about the practice of bureaucracy; and second, by summarizing some of the remedial measures suggested in managerial writings.

From neo-Weberian organization literature

Neo-Weberian organization literature which developed the debate on bureaucracy is diverse and complicated. We do not wish to review all of it, but the following highlights some major problems of the practice of bureaucracy.

- One of the issues is the notion of efficiency. Merton (1949) observed that excessive use of bureaucracy leads to the development of 'red tape' which hinders innovation and creativity. He termed this development 'trained incapacity' through which managers tend to 'work to rules' rather than responding to contingencies. When people in organizations propose 'new' ways of improving efficiency, bureaucracy tends to arrest this behaviour. Even though mass-production regimes required such repetitive practices, the changes in production technology and diversified customer needs challenged this.

> Bureaucracy leads to the development of 'red tape', which hinders innovation and creativity.

- On the notion of rationality, Blau (1955) argued that it is a form of centralization. He emphasized that rationality comes only from the top and is imposed on subordinates 'to get the job done'. This tendency reduced the opportunities for the exercise of individual autonomy and employees' participation in decision-making. Blau found that this centralized 'rationality' led to lowering of both productivity and employee morale. This also has adverse implications for innovation and discoveries at the individual level.

> Rationality comes only from the top and is imposed on subordinates 'to get the job done'.

- Even though it was thought that the development of expertise (specialization) and rigid hierarchies can be functional to overall organizational goal, Crozier (1964) found that highly specialized employees tend to exercise their power and discretion over other workers. Rather than getting things done by following rules and regulations, these 'powerful' employees create their own 'rules and regulations' to exercise their power. Classic empirical work by Selznick (1949) reported that in the Tennessee Valley Authority, specialized officials formed power cliques and frustrated the citizens who wanted to participate in decision-making.

> Highly specialized employees tend to exercise their power and discretion over other workers.

- There are problems of employment relations when bureaucratic controls are exercised. Edwards (1979) showed that, because of bureaucracy, the workforce has been subject to grading and stratification which lead to the breaking up of the homogeneity of the workforce. This is better for securing job identity and careers. But lack of homogeneity creates problems in the carrying out of collective tasks. Rigid rules and highly defined grades limit flexibility and creativity. Employees tend to focus on their career and job rather than the task and overall organizational goal. Collective actions are needed to develop these characteristics, but too much bureaucracy can hinder this.

> Because of bureaucracy, the workforce has been subject to grading and stratification which lead to the breaking up of the homogeneity of the workforce.

325

■ By dividing organization types into mechanistic and organic, Burns and Stalker (1961) argued that too much bureaucracy limits the capacity of organizations to react to changing environmental conditions. The mechanistic form of organization is rigid and rule-bound, with more bureaucratic characteristics. It has little scope to change in response to changing environmental needs, including changes in customer demands. The organic form can make these reactions to external changes. It is widespread bureaucracy which has limited organizations' capacity to be more organic.

> Too much bureaucracy will limit the capacity of organizations to react to changing environmental conditions.

Emerging managerial writing

Through the experience of different practices of bureaucracy, or the realization that different organizational forms are needed, a number of organizational formulations have emerged since the 1980s. These have implied some problems with the orthodox bureaucratic form of organization and offered some alternatives that they claim will improve practices of management and control. To indicate this trend, we chose three of them: Henry Mintzberg (1983); Gareth Morgan (1997); and Peter Senge (1990). We will briefly consider how these writers have questioned the orthodox form and offered alternatives.

Mintzberg (1983) suggested that organizations should be structured by considering a number of situational factors, including the size and age of the organization, the nature of the environment in which it operates, the technological processes it has developed and so on. Rather than adopting a universal structure copied from the orthodox bureaucratic form, Mintzberg stressed that both the design parameters and the situational factors should be clustered to create what he called 'configurations'. He introduced five configurations, together with identified dimensions: simple structure with direct supervision; machine bureaucracy with standardization of work; professional bureaucracy with standardization of skills; divisionalized form with standardization of outputs; and 'adhocracy' with mutual adjustments. Our intention here is not to elaborate on each of these configurations but show that the orthodox form cannot be appropriate to all circumstances. Instead, we need to configure organizational structure into one of the most suitable forms. However, when we try to configure structure into one of the above types, we may end up with a completely different one. The ultimate configuration might have characteristics of two or three types of configuration. But, as Mintzberg himself argued, this does not mean that the configurations have to be rejected. They can act as a guide for us to start developing an appropriate system. The nature of management accounting and control system would be a product of this appropriate system.

> Five configurations have been identified: simple structure with direct supervision; machine bureaucracy with standardization of work; professional bureaucracy with standardization of skills; divisionalized form with standardization of outputs; and 'adhocracy' with mutual adjustments.

The next piece of work is *Imaginization* (Morgan, 1997). Like Mintzberg's book, this also provides a managerial prescription which emphasizes images and ideas for portraying an art of creative management. For Morgan, it is all about:

- improving our abilities to see and understand situations in new ways;
- finding new images for new ways of organization;
- creating shared understanding;
- personnel empowerment; and
- developing capacities for continuous self-organization.

Having developed these definitions, Morgan described how changing organizational forms are useful for developing new ways of managing organizational affairs. He illustrated this with a number of case studies to show how organizational images and ideas can be used to explain and create flexible organizations, network relations, strategic thinking and so on. He took this position by understanding the broader changes taking place in a number of areas within and outside the organization. These included the change in the environment from stable to highly turbulent, strategic change from defensive to proactively entrepreneurial, structural change from bureaucratic to flexible, cultural change from static to innovative and management-style change from authoritarian to highly collaborative. Again like Mintzberg, this attempt highlights, on the one hand, the problematic nature of the old bureaucratic form, and, on the other hand, the inevitable changes taking place in response to identified problems of bureaucracy.

> Organizational images and ideas can be used to explain and create flexible organizations, network relations, strategic thinking and so on.

The last work we chose is by Peter Senge (1990). Having doubts about the conventional approach to the design of organizational systems which relied on bureaucracy, Senge introduced five 'technologies' which come together in the functioning of an effective organization: system thinking – an understanding of interconnected patterns of organizational functions; personal mastery – having a special level of proficiency over other people; mental models – exposing to better thinking and opening that thinking to the influence of others; building shared vision – binding people together around a common identity and destiny; and team learning – improving team intelligence over individual intelligence. When organizations develop these organizational technologies, Senge calls them learning organizations. When these technologies are bound together by system thinking, it is the fifth discipline that drives the organizations to learn at every level in the company. Senge illustrated from his own case studies that, from the 1990s, firms became learning organizations as they applied the above technologies alongside the complexities stemming from a turbulent environment. Again as with other prescriptions, the launch of learning organizations implies a rejection of static organizations that reproduced bureaucracy and associated control and governance mechanisms.

This review so far has revealed two recurring points. One is about theoretical problems of sustaining bureaucratic organizational form and its underlying management control and governance mechanisms which reproduced rigidity and rule-bound rationality. The other is about the

> Five 'technologies': system thinking – an understanding of interconnected patterns of organizational functions; personal mastery – having a special level of proficiency over other people; mental models – exposing to better thinking and opening that thinking to the influence of others; building shared vision – binding people together around a common identity and destiny; and team learning – improving team intelligence over individual intelligence.

inclination of consultants and popular management writers to provide solutions to the above problem. Both points contribute to a systematic critique of orthodox management control and governance mechanisms within which management accounting operated as a vital component. So we are left with the question of how we conceive new management accounting stemming from the changing organizational form. The next section will deal with this fundamental issue.

> Emerging literature contributes to a systematic critique of orthodox management control and governance mechanisms within which management accounting operated as a vital component.

Rise of post-bureaucratic management control and governance

Post-bureaucracy represents the lower quadrants in Figure 10.1 (above). While we see that there is no neat definition for the term, we generally regard 'post-bureaucracy' as all aspects of organizational arrangements which respond to the programmes of flexible manufacturing and customer-oriented marketing philosophies. These aspects of organizational arrangements represent a number of areas, ranging from structural changes to changing roles of people in organizations. One of the ways of looking at these changes could be by gaining an understanding of what Clegg (1990a: 203) has labelled a change from modernity to postmodernity. Here, bureaucracy and post-bureaucracy can be alternatives for modernity and postmodernity, respectively. To explain changing organizational arrangements, Clegg used seven dimensions: mission, goals, strategies and main functions; functional alignments; co-ordination and control; accountability and role relationships; planning and communications; relations of performance and rewards; and leadership. We do not intend to elaborate on all this, but we want to see how, in these dimensions, the form of organizations changed from bureaucratic to post-bureaucratic, and how they produced differences in intra- and inter-organizational controls. While this change can be understood by referring to Clegg, it must be emphasized that there cannot be a sudden change from one form to another. As Mabey *et al.* (2000) argued, what really happened was a gradual and/or multiple transformation of the form from bureaucracy to networks and virtual organizations. Having looked at the above dimensions and their implications for management control change, we will come back to this point later in the chapter. Below is a brief consideration of the above dimensions.

- Regarding the change in mission, goals, strategies and main functions, Clegg has shown that postmodern organizations tend to know what business they are in, rather than expanding their economic activities through mergers and acquisitions. Thus, post-bureaucratic organizational forms have come to facilitate focused specific businesses through 'deep-rooted and substantive knowledge' (Clegg, 1990a: 185) rather than facilitating multiple businesses through conventional co-ordination mechanisms and associated management accounting calculations, usually based on ROI. Under this broader mission and goal, specialization of employees' skills and the development of occupational/professional structures are inappropriate. Instead, employees tend to serve broader organizational tasks rather than their own occupations/professions. Moreover, instead of reacting to an internal labour market, employees in these organizations tend to be innovators. As we saw earlier, Senge and Morgan also explain this transformation which reflects a change in mission, goals and functions.

> Post-bureaucratic organizational forms facilitate specific businesses through 'deep-rooted and substantive knowledge' rather than facilitating multiple businesses.

- Functional alignment in post-bureaucratic form is about a movement from rigid hierarchical relationships to more horizontal ones. However, although economic theorization of organizations saw markets and hierarchies as two opposing extremes, post-bureaucratic forms tend to use markets and internal arrangements simultaneously. For instance, by adopting JIT methodology, it has been proved that transaction costs can be minimized where firms tend to develop supply chains through vertical integration and complex market and subcontracting relations. While such external relationships are developed on the basis of market principles, internal quasi-democratic workers' teams are formulated on the basis of principles of self-management, where opportunities are open for innovation. In these arrangements, work teams are collective, and information flows are multi-directional.

> Economists saw markets and hierarchies as two opposing extremes, but post-bureaucratic forms tend to use markets and internal arrangements simultaneously.

- Mechanisms of co-ordination and control are different in post-bureaucratic form in that they largely rest on the principles of worker empowerment and industrial policy. Unlike in bureaucratic form where workers were disempowered and strategies were governed by capital markets, emerging co-ordinating and control mechanisms are institutionalized through employment relations aligned around quasi-democratic teams whose ideas are highly accepted, and through strategic consideration where customer orientation is considered to be vital. Consequently, co-ordination and controls tend to be reconstructed into horizontal and flatter power relationships while responding to product market dynamics.

> Emerging mechanisms are institutionalized through employment relations, quasi-democratic teams and strategic consideration for customer orientation.

■ In bureaucratic forms, accountability and role relationships have been regarded as extra-organizational matters. With the emergence of post-bureaucratic forms, internal rather than external accountability systems and associated role relationships are becoming commonplace (Clegg, 1990a). This is because skill formation is organizationally rather than individually determined, which leads to the development of multi-skills, allowing the workers to work across disciplines (Grimshaw *et al.*, 2002). Thus, accountability systems are formed around teams for evaluating team performance, so that these systems have now come into being as an intra-organizational phenomenon rather than an issue to be dealt with outside the organization through financial reporting. Consequently, teams rather than individuals will have to deliver accountability internally, through the mechanisms of management control and governance.

> Accountability systems aim to evaluate team performance. Thus, these systems are an intra-organizational phenomenon rather than an issue to be dealt with outside the organization through financial reporting.

■ Planning imperatives in bureaucratic forms have fallen into short-term traps through excessive reliance on ROI measures. Profit centre managers wanting to be appraised by ROI criteria and capital budgeting techniques tend to increase short-term profit with little long-term investment. This did not allow technology to change in response to the changing demands of product markets. In contrast, managers in post-bureaucratic organizations are trying to use strategic investment decisions to invest in advanced manufacturing technologies. In this respect, it has been argued that traditional accounting measures can handicap the ability of investing strategically (Dugdale and Jones, 1995). However, this is only a trend rather than a complete transformation, because some organizations with an inclination to a post-bureaucratic form still use traditional accounting measures, such as ROI and capital budgeting.

> Post-bureaucratic organizations use strategic investment decisions to invest in advanced manufacturing technologies with or without traditional accounting measures.

■ In conjunction with the above changes taking place in post-bureaucratic organizations, reward and performance measurement systems tend to be made collective rather than individual. On the one hand, skill formation is taking place through the formation of worker-teams which allow the workers to be multi-skilled and innovative; and, on the other hand, teams rather than individuals perform certain tasks. Under such circumstances, there is a strong case for developing team-based performance measures and reward systems. These practices are prevalent in East Asian enterprises, and a trend is emerging to develop such measures in the West as well (Alston, 1982, cited in Clegg, 1990a: 200–201).

■ The last dimension relates to changes in leadership style. Traditionally, bureaucracy was meant to provide leadership through rigid rules and regulations. The implied assumption was that rules were needed because nobody can be trusted. So mistrust was the driving force for

With the workers' multi-skilled and innovative orientation, there is a strong case for developing team-based performance measures and reward systems.

formation of a leadership style. However, when the skill formation took place through teams, and when organizational members became innovative and loyal to the enterprise (as in Japan), the notion of mistrust came to be replaced by one of trust. This change gave rise to the regimens of employee empowerment, quasi-democratic, self-managed teams and so on. The role of leaders was to follow the system being changed rather than imposing it through charismatic or autocratic influence.

Reliance on trust has given rise to the regimens of employee empowerment, quasi-democratic, self-managed teams and so on.

We have summarized the above features and their implications for the practices of management control and governance in Table 10.1.

Looking at Table 10.1, we can discern that control and governance systems in post-bureaucratic forms tend to be more democratic, with a deep-rooted commitment to achieve strategic goals which developed from an understanding of markets and customers. Leaders in such a context are governed by social and organizational networks developed from trust relations.

However, as we mentioned earlier, transformation from bureaucratic to post-bureaucratic forms is still in a flux, and there can be variations in the continuum from supply chain relationships to virtual organizations. Drawing on Mabey *et al.* (2000), we have shown in Chapter 7 that this transformation has created five major alternatives to bureaucracy: supply chain management and process engineering; strategic outsourcing; joint ventures; networks; and virtual organizations.

Table 10.1 *Post-bureaucracy: implications for management control and governance*

Dimensions	In post-bureaucracy	Control and governance
Mission, goals, strategies and main functions	Diffused at all levels	Broader organizational tasks
Functional alignment	More horizontal relationships	Lateral relations
Mechanisms of co-ordination and control	Based on workers' influence	Empowerment and industrial policy
Accountability and role relationships	Developed to evaluate team performance	Team performance
Planning imperatives	Based on strategic measures	Strategic initiatives
Reward and performance measurement systems	Collectivized	Collective efforts
Leadership style	Based on trust	Trust

Most of these forms tend to reproduce some of the postmodern, post-bureaucratic dimensions we presented in the previous section. Following our typology shown above in Table 10.1, we can see these variations from both intra- and inter-organizational change perspectives to understand the changes in management control and governance mechanisms.

> Transformation from bureaucratic to post-bureaucratic forms is still in a state of flux, and there can be variations in the continuum from supply chain relationships to virtual organizations.

CHANGES IN INTRA-ORGANIZATIONAL CONTROL AND GOVERNANCE

Numerous changes have occurred in the sphere of intra-organizational control. We will illustrate four major aspects: horizontalization of relationships; digitalization of information systems; hybridization of knowledge and skills; and localization of accountability and governance. Even though these changes seem to be overlapping and interrelated, we suggest that there are good grounds for exploring them separately.

Horizontalization of relationships

Horizontalization is a change in internal role relationships from vertical arrangements, where commands come from the top, to horizontal arrangements, where collaboration and collective efforts are held in high regard. With the rise of flexible manufacturing and strategic turns in management philosophy, horizontal arrangement became essential, whereas vertical systems produced delays, malfunctions and customer dissatisfaction. In emerging horizontal systems, people with different knowledge backgrounds tend to come into physical proximity to maintain lateral relations (Monge and Fulk, 1995). Computer-based information technology (IT) has facilitated these relations by providing the means for information and document sharing. With an entrepreneurial mindset, workers tend to maintain such horizontal relations for innovative products and services.

> **KEY TERMS**
>
> Horizontalization is a change in internal role relationships from vertical arrangements, where commands come from the top, to horizontal arrangements, where collaboration and collective efforts are held in high regard.

As Fulk and DeSanctis (1995) have shown, these relationships are particularly evident in product design. Traditionally, product design and the subsequent production process were planned separately by a separate group of experts. In post-bureaucratic forms, this 'separated planning' function has now come to be participative with executors, hence horizontal relationships. For Fulk and DeSanctis (1995), this is 'concurrent engineering', and for Piore (1994), a replacement of 'traditional hierarchy with more egalitarian relationship'. Under the horizontal system, individuals work in teams. Rather than waiting for someone else to complete his/her task, everybody works together on designated IT.

> Rather than waiting for someone else to complete his/her task, everybody works together on designated IT.

What we learn from this new trend is that management control systems cannot be commanding and coercive when the above relationships are coming into being. Instead, top managers tend to appreciate teamwork by introducing more inter-functional performance measures. As Abernethy and Lillis (1995) illustrated, the level of worker co-operation and strength of interdependent relationships can be established by introducing suitable performance measures and rewards that will appraise them. They argue that management accounting's role is vital in this transformation rather than leaving the task to engineering personnel. Thus, control and governance mechanisms are now shaping the set of interconnected teams, in which horizontal relationships seem to be governing principles, where performance, measurement and reward systems tend to be collectivized.

> Management control systems cannot be commanding and coercive when horizontal relationships are coming into being.

Digitalization of information systems

Digitalization refers to the extensive use of computer-based technologies in information processing within and between organizations. When we look at how this trend has impacted upon management control systems and governance mechanisms in organizations, we may pose the fundamental question as to which processes have been taking place in respect of implementing information systems. Among many such processes, one popular system is enterprise resource planning (ERP). This is an integrated information system used for integrating the organizational functions which have hitherto been separated. SAP, Oracle and Baan are some of the popular software packages being used for this purpose. All they do is provide the functional managers with an information infrastructure for processing prompt decisions and taking actions quickly, rather than waiting for traditional information processors, such as accountants.

KEY TERMS

Digitalization refers to the extensive use of computer-based technologies in information processing within and between organizations.

As Scapens and Jazayeri (2003) reviewed, ERP has the ability to integrate, standardize, routinize and centralize information processing, including management accounting. The system then promotes information and knowledge sharing, horizontal relations and teamwork. As O'Connell (1995) emphasized, ERP can establish new forms of organizations where impediments such as delays and rigidities can be eliminated. This allows the managers to cope with competition by responding quickly to the demands of customers. The resultant management control system is one that can be flexible, responsive and proactive. It does not, however, mean that there is no role for management accountants at all, even though some expected this to be the case. Granlund and Malmi (2002) reported that, in the longer-run implementation of ERP projects, management accountants tend to provide more support for business decisions.

> ERP has the ability to integrate, standardize, routinize and centralize information processing, including management accounting.

It must be noted, however, that there can be limits to ERP implementation. Such limits are present not because of the technical limitations of ERP, but because of the processes in which ERP systems have to be implemented. These are the organizational processes in which organizational structures and personnel roles are changing, and they cannot be directly accomplished, as resistance from organizational members is always possible. For example, as Quattrone and Hopper (2001) reported, when ERP systems such as SAP are introduced, personnel involved in use of the system must be properly trained. However, when training them, they would not understand why changes are needed by introducing ERP. This is because organizations already have established systems, so organizational members prefer to follow the legacy system. Thus, as Quattrone and Hopper (2001) argued, training (learning) is a more complex phenomenon than giving instructions on how the software package should be used. However, the vendors of these programs assume that training is merely another step in the process of implementation. Thus, the change occurring though digitalization of information systems can be slow and evolutionary, rather than radical and revolutionary.

> ERP processes cannot be easily accomplished, as resistance from organizational members is always possible.

Hybridization of knowledge and skills

As we mentioned earlier, the mode of skill formation has implications for the design of management control systems. Following the emerging trend in the building of teams and sharing of knowledge through extensive use of information and communication technology (ICT), organizational members require multi-skills rather than being trapped in traditional career paths. As reported by Grimshaw et al. (2002), employees in changing forms of organizations develop their skills through their experience in network relations, joint ventures and subcontracting arrangements. At intra-organizational level, employees find this development challenging, but the trend is inevitable. As a result, universities and professional bodies have now come to identify this market need and modify their training programmes for creating multi-skilled personnel.

Teamwork and sharing of knowledge require multi-skills: accordingly, universities and professional bodies tend to modify their training programmes.

It may be useful if we look at how management accountants react to this intra-organizational change. Until the 1990s, accountants were accustomed to engage in routine transaction processing such as record-keeping, preparing periodical accounts reports, and reporting them to their respective managers (Granlund and Malmi, 2002). However, the change in the organization structure and IT has eliminated this need for transaction processing activities. As Granlund and Malmi reported, from the mid-1990s, most technologically advanced firms began to use accounting packages for processing those transactions, leaving little for accountants to do. As we mentioned earlier, though, this does not mean that management accountants are not needed any more. Burns and Baldvinsdottir (2005) found that, from the late 1990s onwards, a new type of 'hybrid accountant' emerged, whose role lies in the interface between finance and production functions. Being financial managers and financial analysts, these hybrid accountants process strategic and operational information needed by business managers. To do this properly, the hybrid accountants tend to be very knowledgeable about production and markets through their association with business managers. This is possible through advanced manufacturing technology linked to information processing. Unlike earlier, business managers are now happy, as they get what they need from accountants; and accountants are happy, as they provide what the business managers want (Burns and Baldvinsdottir, 2005). What we learn from this is that there is a trend towards the hybridization of accountants as organizational forms change through increased use of IT.

Hybrid accountants' role lies in the interface between finance and production functions.

However, in practice, hybridization does not take place without limitations. The transition from old accounting systems which facilitated routines and hierarchies cannot be made immediately. Sometimes, traditional accountants are opposed to change (Friedman and Lyne, 1997). At other times, business managers still think that accountants do not provide necessary information: for instance, they tend to complain that accountants are unaware of engineering aspects (Wickramasinghe *et al.*, 2004). Consequently, new systems generate new problems, as opposed to old problems in old systems. One example is a company adopting a new accounting system which was confronted with rivalry between engineering and accounting personnel (Wickramasinghe *et al.*, forthcoming). This is a problem generated by the solution. However, hybridization is a compromise rather than a rejection of traditional accounting. This has an implication for training and education of accountants: they need to be trained in inter-disciplinary areas such as accounting, IT, marketing, operations management, management of technology, etc.

335

> New systems generate new problems, as opposed to old problems in old systems.

Localization of accountability and governance

Changes have occurred in the accountability and governance mechanism. As we mentioned earlier, traditionally, accountability was regarded as a functional matter of organization-wide budgeting, accounting and auditing. However, with the change in the organizational form, there emerged small autonomous business units through decentralization. Business managers who look after these business units have become much more accountable for making the unit more profitable and viable. Under this changing regime of accountability, managers tend to be empowered to prepare and manage their own budgets.

> Business unit managers have become much more accountable for making the unit more profitable and viable. They themselves process and use accounting.

For example, as we mentioned in Chapter 7, in Caterpillar in the USA (Miller and O'Leary, 1993), following the introduction of a flexible manufacturing regime, production cells were created and were accountable for their performance. These cells became local centres of accountability and the whole governance mechanism became fortified with this localization of accountability. Managers who looked after the cells created a kind of 'citizenry', who appreciated calculating their own performance and living a better life accordingly. Burns and Baldvinsdottir (2005) reported that the localization of accountability and new management control mechanisms have become arts of management alongside the hybridization of accountants. All this tells us that changing organizational forms from bureaucratic structures to more flexible local structures has reconstructed the ways in which we should think of organizational accountability. Now, we tend to appreciate small business units rather than large multinational corporations which serve local accountability and associated governance structures rather than their external stakeholders.

Again, this change has limitations. In former bureaucratic organization forms, members of the organizations were somewhat relaxed. All they needed to do was comply with rules and regulations rather than take responsibility to innovate and satisfy customers. When this post-bureaucratic form brings the above accountability and governance systems into the organization, as in the case of hybridization, integration of those elements into the organization's overall control system is not so easy. Resistance can occur in any form. In Caterpillar, for example, there were enormous trade union agitations against the changes that were made (Froud *et al.*, 1998). Thus, the modernization being seen in the form of 'new' accountability systems demonstrates limits and contradictions as well (Arnold, 1998).

> When the post-bureaucratic form brings new accountability and governance systems into the organization, integrating them into the overall control system is not easy, hence resistance.

CHANGES IN INTER-ORGANIZATIONAL CONTROL AND GOVERNANCE

The right quadrants of Figure 10.1 (p. 320) represent inter-organizational control and governance. In bureaucracy, these controls operate within the legal boundaries of firms. In contrast, post-bureaucracy blurs the boundaries and creates 'boundary-less' organizations (Grimshaw *et al.*, 2002). This development is a useful context for us to understand the change in management accounting, controls and governance mechanisms. In this section, we will look at this development and focus on inter-organizational relationships that create different control and governance mechanisms. In this respect, for illustration, we will consider three types of development: supply chain management, strategic outsourcing and network/virtual organizations.

To illustrate the nature of inter-organizational relationships, three types of development can be considered: supply chain management, strategic outsourcing and network/virtual organizations.

Supply chain management

Most businesses in today's competitive markets are successful when they manage to sustain successful suppliers. 'Supply chain management' is a term that has been used to describe the development of relationships between such suppliers and firms. In a broader sense, these relationships become supply networks linked with the firms' sale of final products and services. Within such a network, an efficient supply chain ensures that there is a continuous flow of products and services along the production and distribution chain (Frances and Garnsey, 1996). As Slack *et al.* (2004) explained, such supply networks are made of supplier's suppliers and customer's customers. One example drawn by Frances and Garnsey (1996) is British supermarkets, which have been successful in managing and sustaining suppliers. Their investigation suggests that supply chain management aims to create 'close interdependence' with suppliers, and takes collective actions to reduce costs while enhancing 'positive feedback effects'.

An efficient supply chain ensures that there is a continuous flow of products and services along the production and distribution chain.

The development of such relationships between firms and suppliers certainly reshapes the nature of management control and accounting systems, as Frances and Garnsey (1996) reported. As the organization and management of supply chains require a massive transformation of business processes internally, internal control systems change accordingly. The resultant control system operates within inter-organizational relationships rather than within the traditional boundaries of the organization. The sustenance of such a control system is possible as information and communication technologies facilitate their processes. In most British supermarkets, such technologically

337

generated information flows run through the interrelationships between customers and stores, stores and supermarket HQ, supermarket HQ and suppliers, suppliers and warehouses and so on. IT allows the relationship to be active, quick and reliable. For instance, selling performance at the supermarket level is regularly recorded and communicated to the suppliers. Following this, orders are placed automatically to fill the gaps between sales and purchases. When this happens, throughout the network, information is transmitted to respective suppliers and their suppliers to take action to prepare the next shift. The information processing at this stage is detailed, in that it calculates all requirements, including raw materials, labour, means of production and distribution, etc.

> As the organization and management of supply chains require a massive transformation of business processes internally, internal control systems change accordingly.

However, managing supply chains has a cost. Seal *et al.* (1999) reported that this is a transaction cost, and it must be minimized by adopting an optimal governance mechanism across the supply chain. In developing and studying such a system, they argue it should be possible by reflecting on the development of trust relations, focusing on costing data and information sharing, and the formation of organizational partnerships. In respect of these areas, accounting can play a constitutional role in fixing profitable relationships and maintaining suitable governance mechanisms. However, traditional management accounting, which regarded the processing of internal information as a job only for internal managers, has limits to playing that constitutional role. Instead, there is a trend of developing 'open-book accounting' systems where partners are allowed to 'inspect' each other's costs and revenue. This would enable the partnership to make collective decisions openly and quickly (Seal *et al.*, 1999).

> Accounting can play a constitutional role in fixing profitable relationships and maintaining suitable governance mechanisms.

Strategic outsourcing

Outsourcing has come to deconstruct the ways in which businesses are run, exerting a dramatic influence on changes in the organizational form. Before going into a consideration of this organizational change, we shall first consider the meaning of the term. 'Outsourcing' refers to contracting out internal business activities to specialized third-party service suppliers. Even though this term has been manifested as a novel business strategy, outsourcing is a revitalization of conventional 'make or buy decisions' by externalizing production and services, as Mabey *et al.* (2000) and Sartorius and Kirsten (2005) have noted. In practice, several varieties of such externalization programmes are becoming popular. Labour recruitment, office cleaning, IT services and security services are some of the more common examples of outsourcing. There are various degrees of outsourcing: Nike has outsourced all manufacturing; General Motors has outsourced car-body painting; IBM has outsourced most of its human resource management function; and British Telecom has outsourced its accounting and finance function.

KEY TERMS

'Outsourcing' is the contracting out of internal business activities to specialized third-party service suppliers.

Outsourcing is part of the broad strategic initiative of a firm. The purpose of outsourcing is strategic, in that it can improve products and service quality, reduce costs and enhance the profitability of businesses. For Langfield-Smith and Smith (2003), outsourcing is a popular method of strategic alliance. In line with such strategic expectations, firms tend to identify core and non-core products: core products are strategically important, so their production will remain in-house; non-core products are outsourced. You may recall that Caterpillar launched a programme of advanced manufacturing through a large-scale outsourcing programme. The starting point for this was classification of its products as core and non-core. Caterpillar's philosophy was to outsource all costly products and components if they were not strategically important as a result of being subject to advanced manufacturing technologies (Miller and O'Leary, 1993). Focusing on transaction costs of production and services, Sartorius and Kirsten (2005) have outlined the strategic advantages of outsourcing as follows: it can avoid in-house duplication of support facilities; economies of scale gained by suppliers can reduce cost; some other firms can be more efficient at producing certain products than in-house production; it can avoid fixed costs, including training and development costs for non-core products; and the firm can focus on its core business rather than being worried about ancillary services. In a competitive market, these benefits are strategically advantageous.

The purpose of outsourcing is strategic in that it can improve products and service quality, reduce costs and enhance profitability of businesses.

Outsourcing has implications for changes in organizational forms. Basically, it is a development of strategic alliance containing a broader governance system along inter-organizational relationships. In most cases, the relationship can be formal and written. Management control systems usually stem from the conditions laid down in formal documentation. Considering outsourcing of an IT project, Langfield-Smith and Smith (2003) provided case study evidence about how such an inter-organizational structure develops. Initial relationships are built upon contracts between partners, even though a high level of uncertainty can create some difficulties. Usually partners prefer to have tightly written contracts. The firm then engages in monitoring not only the relationship *per se* but also the agreed performance of supplies in their quality and continuity. Even though performance criteria cannot be explicitly set in uncertain circumstances, they are developed for measuring performance of the quality of delivery through discussions and negotiations. In implementing close monitoring and control, regular communications and reviews are carried out.

339

Information sharing, keeping open books and building trust are cornerstones in the maintenance of such control systems. In this, outcome control (controls based on output) and social controls (controls by social interaction, reputation, social networks, etc.) play vital roles. Amid a number of experiments and developments, trust-based inter-firm control systems have gained much popularity (see Seal and Vincent-Jones, 1997).

Initial relationships are built upon contracts between partners, even though a high level of uncertainty can create some difficulties. Usually, partners prefer to have tightly written contracts.

Joint ventures

Joint ventures are separate entities owned by two or more partners which develop co-operative agreements between themselves (Groot *et al.*, 2000). With the proliferation of globalization, joint ventures have now come to be 'international joint ventures' as well, where partners come from different nations and engage in businesses globally. For example, British Telecom has developed more than seventy joint ventures and overseas distribution arrangements. Many Chinese business operations are now forming joint ventures with US firms. Many pharmaceutical companies engaged in new product development have joint ventures globally. As Mabey *et al.* (2000) pointed out, these developments imply a common objective: large firms are exploiting their 'marketing expertise and systems' to market the products developed by small firms abroad more effectively and faster than the latter could if operating alone. As we will highlight later, with the opening of China as a market economy and its qualification to be a member of the World Trade Organization (WTO), many joint ventures have mushroomed with a view to achieving such objectives (Chalos and O'Connor, 2004). Groot *et al.* (2000) reported that, since the 1980s, US joint ventures have being growing by 27 per cent per year. This creates an opportunity for us to understand how underlying inter-organizational relations operate and how new management accounting and control mechanisms emerge.

KEY TERMS

Joint ventures are separate entities owned by two or more partners which develop co-operative agreements between themselves.

Large firms exploit their 'marketing expertise and systems' to market the products developed by small firms abroad more effectively and faster than the latter could if operating alone. Hence, the joint ventures.

Like outsourcing, joint ventures begin with legal contracts in which the rights and obligations of partners are laid down. The business operation according to these rights and obligations creates a particular management control system through which information on performance of each partner is monitored. In practice, on the one hand, the control mechanisms can facilitate the implementation of legal agreement; and, on the other hand, they can act as an alternative mechanism, as everything cannot be enforced legally. Chalos and O'Connor (2004: 592) summarized the aim of such controls as follows:

> These controls serve to influence behaviour in such areas that could not be included in the JV (joint ventures) agreement that are difficult to legally enforce. The aim of such control is to align partner differences and to promote a better understanding of the intangible strengths and relationships that each partner brings to the alliance.

While control mechanisms can facilitate the implementation of legal agreements, they can also act as an alternative mechanism, as everything cannot be enforced legally.

In developing alliances, as Chalos and O'Connor (2004) show from drawing on management accounting research (Dekker, 2004; Groot and Merchant, 2000), three types of controls are possible: cultural controls, behavioural controls and output controls.

Cultural controls attempt to develop alignments over diverse cultural values and interests. As joint ventures tend to extend their relationships internationally, such cultural issues must be addressed in designing a control system. The literature suggests that through staffing by expatriates and promoting socialization practices, such cultural controls can be tenable. Behavioural controls, in contrast, aim to monitor respective managers, making them aligned with the expectations of the alliance. Both cultural and behavioural controls attempt to maintain the relationships between firms entering the joint venture contracts, which is a primary requirement. Output controls aim to get the managers to perform well in line with strategic goals and objectives. Even though controls highlight the roles of control mechanisms, the actual operations of these controls depend on certain determinants. Among these, knowledge-based and asset specificities are major. For example, in respect of joint ventures between US and Chinese firms, knowledge (or intangible assets) of US firms came to be greater than that of Chinese. Thus, the nature of management control is a result of the influence of US firms (Chalos and O'Connor, 2004).

Three types of controls are possible: cultural, behavioural and output controls.

In practice, control systems in joint ventures remain under-researched. Some exploratory studies have been made to develop working hypotheses as to how these control systems work. Some have identified factors which determined the elements of control systems (Groot and Merchant, 2000), including breadth of partners' objectives, alignment of joint venture products with the rest of partners' businesses, level of trust in partners, partners' unique knowledge and

341

capacities, partner management style and partners' need for short-term performance. This implies that control systems in joint ventures cannot come from a universal model. Rather, they are outcomes of certain practices akin to different contexts and relationships. Consequently, the above factors would tell us what control mechanisms can be developed, with what focus and tightness, as Groot and Merchant (2000) tried to model.

> Controls systems in joint ventures cannot be universal: they are outcomes of certain practices akin to different contexts and relationships.

Network/virtual organizations

The final form of organization we chose is network organizations: network relations between people who have common objectives in carrying out a business. Network organizations operate through the interaction of autonomous systems of goals and sharing of each other's resources. These organizations usually share costs and risks, while keeping a lookout for updated information (Castells, 2000). While a network operates in a collective manner, the partners in the network would carry out their own businesses independently, even though there are influences of individual activities on the affairs of the network. Although networks also present an inter-organizational relationship, the former are somewhat more complex than the latter as relations are multiple, and compromises on goals can be difficult. Consequently, the operations of networks raise a fundamental issue of what control systems they need. The answer is still inconclusive, despite a recent upsurge of research in this area.

KEY TERMS

Network organizations refer to network relations between people who have common objectives in carrying out a business.

It is worth reading Mouritsen and Thrane (2006). They suggest that there are two alternative forms of control in networks: self-regulating and orchestrating. In self-regulating mechanisms, frictionless network interaction is maintained through relationships. The primary purpose of this type of interaction is to commence projects and allow the partners to engage in them collectively while reducing conflicts, free riding and competition. If this happens, there will be an incentive for partners to continue interactions while concentrating on projects. The benefit of this system is that it enhances transparencies. By contrast, in the orchestrating mechanism, the system develops an entity with a common objective which would be effective in developing better strategies and boundaries of activities. However, this would present some issues of conflict between individual interests and collective behaviour.

Most network organizations tend to be virtual organizations in which common goals and objectives are monitored by information and communication technologies (ICT). Ahuja and Carley

> There are two alternative forms of control in networks: self-regulating and orchestrating.

(1999: 742) defined virtual organization as 'a geographically distributed organisation whose members are bound by long-term common interest or goal, and who communicate and coordinate their work through information technology'. Virtual organizations tend to operate in non-formal structures and systems. As Krackhardt (1991) found, they are controlled through personal and interactive communications, especially through emails. Through such informal communication, an emergent structure could appear which can be the backbone of the management control and governance system. Such a network structure also implies particular organizational behaviour better than formal structures (Monge and Contractor, 1998). In this, relationships are maintained through lateral means rather than through hierarchy. Thus, control issues present in hierarchical relationships cannot exist in such lateral relationships. For instance, power relations or professional rivalries which are prevalent in traditional hierarchical organizations are not an issue, as there is no physical space available for rivalries to operate (Sproull and Kiesler, 1986). However, some studies have suggested that personal characteristics can influence patterns of email communication (Zack and McKenney, 1995).

KEY TERMS

A virtual organization is a geographically distributed organization whose members are bound by long-term common interests or goals, and who communicate and co-ordinate their work through information technology.

Both network organizations and virtual organizations benefit from the roles of accounting and management control, either for enhancing trust or to operate in the absence of trust. In both situations, accounting acts as an enabling institution, making relationships and controls visible and possible. As network relations have few structures and hierarchies, we cannot expect that accounting would serve the networks as it does for a rigid hierarchy. Sometimes, accounting calculations can persist in networks as open-book arrangements, allowing the parties to be more flexible and interactive (Mouritsen and Thrane, 2006). At other times, accounting can legitimize the status quo, which leads to the development of trust (Tomkins, 2001). Even though trust seems to be a fundamental operating principle in network relations, it cannot perform independently as an abstract system. Accounting helps develop its legitimacy.

> Accounting acts as an enabling institution, making relationships and controls visible and possible.

SUMMING UP

We have seen that organizational life is changing due to a number of factors, including the changes in technology and severe economic pressures towards making everything for customer satisfaction. As we elaborated in this chapter, the resultant forms of organizations are becoming more innovative, entrepreneurial, learning-oriented and participative, as opposed to the rigid bureaucratic form. Heydebrand (1989: 327) defined these post-industrial organizations:

> A general, simplified profile of the typical post-industrial organisation would indicate the following: it would tend to be small or located in small sub-units of larger organisations; its object is typically service or information, if not automated production; its technology is computerised; its division of labour is informal and flexible; and its managerial structure is functionally decentralised, eclectic, and participative, overlapping in many ways with non-managerial functions.

The control and governance systems in these organizations are now emerging, changing, and subject to experiment and innovation. The controls are escaping from the trap of bureaucracy, formal rules and regulations and rigid control tools governed by budgeting and ROI-based measurements.

At intra-organizational levels, emerging controls are premised on the orientation towards lateral relations, flexibility, team-based skilled formation, internalization of accountability systems, trust-based leadership, etc. This orientation falls into a single theme – breaking up of formal controls which served a regime of mechanistic forms of control, together with mass production and production orientation. The resultant system is post-mechanistic, postmodern, crystallized within a programme of digitalization and customer orientation. However, we must not forget that these changes are occurring fully only in some organizations, while others embrace them only gradually and in an evolutionary fashion.

Inter-organizational relationships are much more common. They present either as supply chain, outsourcing, network or virtual organizations. The underlying controls are based on open-book arrangements, trust and legal contracts, rather than the formal procedures that dominated in large bureaucracies. How networks are built and maintained, how strategic goals are set and how each partner's objectives come to be aligned with the aims of the networks are still inconclusive, despite interesting research findings which point to some emerging practices. It seems that researchers in management accounting have not kept pace with the speed of these developments.

HAVE YOU UNDERSTOOD THE CHAPTER?

1. What is a new organization?
2. What are the main factors responsible for creating new organizations?
3. Why did bureaucratic organizations have problems?
4. How did managerial writers respond to the problems of the bureaucratic form?
5. What new imperatives did the new forms of organizations bring out?
6. What are the intra-organizational changes and their implications for new management controls and governance?
7. How did outsourcing bring new controls?
8. Why did supply chain management reject traditional control mechanisms?

9. What differences did network organizations make to inter-organizational controls?
10. Why did virtual organizations operate informally?

BEYOND THE CHAPTER

1. 'New organizations is an incomplete project.' Discuss.
2. Can old problems still persist in new organizations?
3. Has bureaucracy been abandoned?
4. Can management accountants survive now?
5. Are accounting systems really changing?

FURTHER READING

1. For a broader understanding of classical bureaucracy and its limitations, see Mouzelis (1967).
2. For the development of postmodern/post-bureaucratic organizations, see Clegg (1990a).
3. Research materials on intra-organizational controls can be found in Cuganesan and Lee (2006).
4. A good summary of the literature on inter-organizational relationships can be found in 'Editorial', *Management Accounting Research* 17 (2006), and Dekker (2004).
5. A good literature review and a further analysis on network organizations can be found in Mouritsen and Thrane (2006).

Part III

Rational perspectives on management accounting change

Chapter 11

Neoclassical economic theories of management accounting change

A STARTING POINT: MARKET VERSUS HIERARCHY

The Fisher Body–General Motors dealings in the early twentieth century constitute one of the most famous cases in economics literature concerning the 'theory of the firm' and the 'agency problem'. Established in 1908 by Fred Fisher and his five younger brothers, the Fisher Body Corporation (FBC), by 1916, had become the largest body builder in the automobile industry. It made bodies for all the leading automobile manufactures at that time: Cadillac, Buick, Hudson, Chalmers, Studebaker, Chandler, Cleveland and, of course, Ford. Its success was by and large attributed to the shift of body manufacture from 'open bodies', largely consisting of wood, to 'closed metal bodies', which was the defining transition in the automobile industry at the time.

In 1919, General Motors (GM), one of the largest automobile manufacturers at that time – ignoring its other two options of manufacturing its own closed metal bodies or buying them on the open market – entered into a ten-year contract with FBC which committed it to buy all its closed bodies from FBC at a price with a mark-up of 17.6 per cent over the production cost. However, FBC was not allowed to charge GM more than it would charge other customers for the supply of similar bodies. And, as part of the deal, GM invested additional capital of 500,000 shares at $92 per share in FBC, which gave GM a 60 per cent stake in FBC. However, shares owned by GM and Fisher Brothers were deposited in a voting trust to last for five years. The trust consisted of four trustees, two named by FBC and two by GM. Most importantly, the trust contained an exclusive clause that no action of voting trustees would be valid unless unanimous, which in effect provided a safeguard for FBC for at least another five years, as GM's majority shares could not be used to vote against them. In May 1926 FBC was dissolved. GM acquired all its assets and assumed all of its obligations and liabilities. So FBC effectively became a division of GM and four of the Fisher brothers became directors of GM.

When R. H. Coase (a proponent of the neoclassical economic theory of the firm whose seminal paper entitled 'The nature of the firm' (1937) provided an initial breakthrough for the branch of economics now known as transaction cost economics) made a visit to GM in 1932, he found that the firm had a major purchasing relationship with A. O. Smith, a producer of automobile frames. Interestingly, that firm had a high degree of 'asset specificity'; GM was its main customer, and much of the equipment in its highly automated plant was specifically designed to manufacture frames only for GM's products. As late as 1987, Coase found that harmonious relations between them had continued for many decades, in contrast to the FBC–GM dealings that ended with complete acquisition of FBC by GM. However, the contracts between GM and A. O. Smith were formulated in an open-ended way, making the relationship more like an open-market arrangement than a binding contract, with prices being renegotiated periodically in line with changing circumstances.

GM's two types of dealings – with FBC and A. O. Smith – manifest the classical scenario for the neoclassical economic debate on market and hierarchy as alternative arrangements of co-ordinating production and exchange. (Based on Coase (1937, 1988a, b and c, 2000); Casadesus-Masanell and Spulber (2000); Klein (1988).)

SETTING THE SCENE

As we have already noted, this book deals with two aspects of management accounting change: approaches and perspectives. 'Approaches' emphasizes the management accounting practice, while 'perspectives' draws our attention to management accounting research. In the first two parts of the book, we dealt with the transition from mechanistic to post-mechanistic 'approaches'. In Chapter 6, we also dealt with the contribution of economics to management accounting practices, especially for short-run and long-run decision-making models. Now, in this chapter, we again turn towards economics. However, this is not to understand how economics shaped and reshaped the approaches to management accounting practices but to appreciate key economic theories that provided conceptual frameworks for management accounting research. Here, we address economic 'perspectives' (rather than approaches) on management accounting change so that we can understand management accounting change through the theoretical lenses of economics.

Economics has long provided a theoretical perspective for management accounting research. In its early phases, management accounting research largely took a normative economic orientation with the aim of discovering better decision-making and control models for practitioners to follow (Jensen, 1983; Jensen and Meckling, 1976). Reflecting on his personal journey in management accounting research, Scapens (2006: 3), for example, comments:

> The 1970s was a time when much of the academic accounting world was thinking in terms of marginal economic analysis and quantitative models, and researchers in management accounting were adopting an economic approach to management decision making and control; with many, both simple and complex, mathematical models which were intended to prescribe what management accounting practitioners should do . . . At the time, the general feeling of academics, including myself, was that all the relevant theory had been developed and we just needed to communicate it to practitioners. We believed that once practitioners became aware of the new models they would apply them in practice. So we saw the essential role of academics as one of communicating marginal economic analysis to students and practitioners; but particularly to students, as they would become the next generation of practitioners. In this way, management accounting practitioners would eventually learn how to apply the new economic models. The problem was that they never really did.

Early research in management accounting has taken a normative economic orientation.

This, of course, is a contribution to the management accounting approaches which we discussed in Chapter 6. And it should be noted that this normative orientation of management accounting research – to contribute to the practice of management accounting by discovering better models of decision-making, planning and control – is a popular approach among many (especially among North American) academics and consultants, who promote a so-called 'action research' agenda. Perhaps the best examples for this continuing interest in contributing 'practical solutions' for management accounting are the balanced scorecard (BSC) and activity-based costing (ABC), which we discussed in Part II.

> 'Action-research agenda' is an example of a present-day normative approach to management accounting research.

Economic thinking has two facets: 'normative' and 'positive'. Normative economic thinking is rather 'prescriptive' and attempts to construct concepts, models and tools to help practitioners reach 'optimum' conditions and results. Positive economic thinking, on the other hand, aims to 'describe' and 'explain' what actually happened, is happening or will happen. While guided by optimality conditions such as 'equilibrium', positive economics attempts to construct theories and models that describe and explain how and why economic agents (such as consumers, managers and employees) and systems (such as organizations, markets and economies) reach, or deviate from, optimum conditions of equilibrium. The usefulness of such positive models and theories is judged by their ability to predict economic behaviour of agents and systems. Thus, in essence, positive economic models attempt to describe, explain and predict behaviours of economic agents and systems. Especially after the late 1970s, positive economic theories, especially those which can be categorized as branches of agency theory, have increasingly been used to explain management accounting phenomena (Baiman, 1982, 1990).

> Positive economic models attempt to describe, explain and predict the behaviour of economic agents and systems; normative models try to prescribe the best behaviour for them.

The purpose of this chapter is to explain the implications of economic theories for management accounting research. In doing so, we will pay particular attention to two major branches of neo-classical economic research: the principal–agent model and transaction cost theory.

First, we will elaborate the 'agency problem' upon which both the principal–agent model and transaction cost theory are based. This section will provide an overview of the agency relationship, neoclassical behavioural assumptions of agency relationships and the agency problem itself.

■ To gain an overview of agency relationship, its neoclassical behavioural assumptions and the agency problem

Second, we will describe a generic, normative model of principal and agent. In this section, we will describe analytical objectives and methods employed by agency theory to identify an optimal solution to the agency problem.

■ To understand analytical objectives and methods in agency theory

Third, we will introduce a basic, non-stochastic mathematical/graphical model that illustrates the principal variables and analytical rationale of the principal–agent model. After reading this section, you should be able to illustrate graphically and describe how the principal would determine the optimum relationship with agent.

■ To illustrate and describe how the principal would determine the optimum relationship with agent

Fourth, we will provide a brief introduction to management accounting research based on agency theory. After reading this section, you will identify key issues and empirical conditions for which agency theory could provide an explanatory framework in management accounting research.

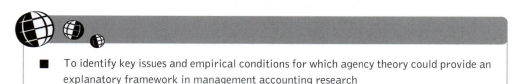

■ To identify key issues and empirical conditions for which agency theory could provide an explanatory framework in management accounting research

Fifth, we will move on to transaction cost economics (TCE). We will first explain the theoretical question which TCE tries to answer, and the basic logic that TCE employs to understand the choice between alternative mechanisms for co-ordinating economic activities.

■ To understand the basic theoretical question of TCE and its logic as to the choice between alterative co-ordinating mechanisms of economic activities

Sixth, how the agency problem is manifested in TCE is discussed next. In this sub-section, we will explain the behavioural assumptions that TCE holds on economic agents and how those assumptions affect agency contracts and organizations.

■ To understand behavioural assumptions that TCE holds on economic agents and how those assumptions affect agency contracts and organizations

There are then two sub-sections dealing with how transactions differ, how governance structures differ and how a discriminatory match between transactions and governance structures is reached. By reading these sub-sections, you will gain an understanding of: attributes according to which TCE differentiates between transactions; relative strengths and weaknesses of alternative governance mechanisms available to control economic transactions; and how agency theory differs from TCE.

■ To gain an understanding of: attributes according to which TCE differentiates between transactions; relative strengths and weaknesses of alternative governance mechanisms available to control economic transactions; and how agency theory differs from TCE

Finally, we will introduce you to management accounting research that uses, critiques and extends TCE as a theoretical framework to explain management accounting phenomena. After reading this section, you should have an understanding of management accounting issues that have been explained through TCE, and the relative strengths and weaknesses of TCE in explicating them.

■ To gain an understanding of management accounting issues explained through TCE, and the relative strengths and weaknesses of TCE in explicating them

THE AGENCY PROBLEM

Two branches of neoclassical economic theories of the firm, which we discuss in this chapter, rest on the notion of the 'agency problem'. According to Baiman (1990: 342): 'an agency relationship exists when one or more individuals (called principals) hire others (called agents) in order to delegate responsibilities to them'. Examples for such agency relationships include those between owners (principals) of a firm and the managers (agents); owners of an estate (principals) and their stewards (agents); a superior manager (principal) and his/her subordinates (agents); a client (principal) and a service provider (agent), such as a physician, a lawyer or an accountant, who makes decisions that affect the client. Thus, it is clear that such agency relationships can be intra-organizational as well as inter-organizational. Organizational hierarchies, for example, manifest intra-organizational agency relationships, while inter-firm arrangements such as franchising, licensing, subcontracting and so on are also examples of agency relationships.

> An agency relationship exists when one or more individuals (called principals) hire others (called agents) in order to delegate responsibilities to them.

Agency relationships are governed by implicit or explicit contracts between agents and principals. Such agency contracts spell out specific objectives, duties, responsibilities and authorities delegated to the agent; compensation arrangements for carrying out those delegated responsibilities; information and communication arrangements; allocation of ownership rights; and so on. Various managerial techniques and tools, such as management by objectives, budgeting and responsibility accounting, as well as human resource management practices of job descriptions, prescriptions and letters of appointment, form complementary methods of contractual arrangements between agents (employees) and the principal (the firm). Such methods of contractual arrangements not only define the agency relationships between the firm and its employees but also construct the organization as a nexus of contracts (Fama and Jensen, 1983a and b).

> Agency relationships are governed by implicit or explicit contracts between agents and principals.

An organization as a nexus of contracts demands co-operative behaviour to reach an optimality condition which, according to neoclassical economic theories, is shareholders' wealth-maximization. The 'agency problem' arises when agents' interests and behaviour are not consistent with the principal's interests, or the firm's profit-maximizing objective. According to Baiman (1990: 342), the agency problem occurs

> if the employment relations are such that, given that everyone else is acting cooperatively, one or more individuals could make themselves better off by deviating from their cooperative behaviour. Of course, if one or more individuals are expected to deviate from their

354

cooperative behaviour, others may find it is in their best interest to deviate. The end result is that when cooperative behaviour is not consistent with self-interested behaviour . . . the group suffers from a loss of efficiency and all individuals are potentially made worse off.

The 'agency problem' arises when agents' interests and behaviour are not consistent with principals' interests.

The assumption of 'self-interest' underlies the agency problem, which assumes that individuals (agents) are motivated solely by self-interest that may oppose and undermine co-operative behaviour and corporate goals. If 'self-interested' behaviour is the 'nature', then an arbitrary set of 'controls' is needed to make agents' behaviour comply with corporate goals, and such controls define the nature of agency relationships within economic enterprises. Budgeting, standard costing and similar responsibility accounting systems, for example, define the parameters within which agency relationships are to be defined and controlled, so that possible efficiency losses due to the agency problem are minimized. In that sense, especially when we are concerned with management accounting research, the analytical focus of agency theory-based research is on the implications of different governance and control systems and processes for mitigating the loss of efficiency due to the agency problem (Baiman, 1990). Being concerned with the agency problem, agency research in management accounting thus attempts to model agents' behaviour, principals' expectations underlying organizational and information contexts that give rise to the agency problem. Through such modelling, agency research attempts to understand parameters of agency problems so that they can be solved. Thus, the expected outcome of agency research is, in a normative sense, to derive optimal contractual relationships between agents and principals which maximize the principals' objective functions. In a positive sense, such models would help researchers to assess empirically and understand the optimality of existing control structures and relations.

The assumption of self-interest is the basis of the agency problem.

Drawing on Baiman (1990), we identify three major streams of agency research – the normative agency or the principal–agency model, transaction cost theory and information economics – each of which elaborates on different aspects of the agency problem, bearing different behavioural assumptions on agents, principals and the informational context within which they operate. What follows is a discussion of the first two streams of agency research on management accounting. We leave out the third branch, information economics, as it stays far from the scope of this book.

Baiman's (1990) classification of agency research: principal–agent model; TCE; and information economics.

355

THEORY OF PRINCIPAL AND AGENT

As we have already noted, the 'agency problem' is the analytical root for economic theories on the nature of the firm and relations therein. Agency theory or the theory of principal and agent attempts to handle the agency problem in a rather normative or deductive way by modelling agency relationships and solving them for optimal contractual relationships between the agent and the principal. It should be noted that 'optimality' means here a solution that would maximize the net return for the principal, which is the firm. Thus, agency theory fundamentally concerns devising contractual relationships between the agents (employees) and the principal (the firm) that produce the required level of effort and risk from the agents to maximize the firm's profits. According to neoclassical economic terminology, this profit-maximization contractual relationship is an equilibrium, as it balances the conflicting needs of agent and principal. The agency theory employs marginal analysis as its analytical device to determine this equilibrium, and it holds the assumptions that both agent and principal are rational, wealth-seeking and utility maximizers (Ezzamel and Hart, 1987: 262). Thus, in essence, agency theory is a neoclassical economic theory aimed at devising equilibrium contractual relationships between agent and principal to mitigate the loss (to the principal) caused by the agency problem.

A normative model of principal and agent

Agency theory suggests two fundamental behavioural reasons for the agency problem. First is the goal incongruence between agent and principal. It is assumed that the 'employee or agent, while economically rational, acts out of self-interest rather than necessarily in the interests of his employer or principal' (Ashton, 1991: 106). When this self-interest is coupled with the risk and work aversion of the agent, goal incongruence between agent and principal becomes the norm rather than the exception.[1] The second reason is information asymmetry, which is the agent's possession of private information about his/her level of efforts to which the principal cannot gain access without incurring additional costs. In other words, information asymmetry is the issue of how well the principal can observe the agent's behaviour. In typical situations, the principal has no information about the agent's behaviour other than some signals concerning the agent's level of effort. For example, output by the agent would constitute a signal concerning the agent's level of effort. However, that would never be a perfect piece of information on the agent's level of effort, as output is determined not only by that effort but by many other random variables beyond the control of the agent.

> Self-interest, risk and work aversion and information asymmetry are bases of the agency problem.

Given the agent's risk and work aversion and information asymmetry, the challenge of the principal is to devise a 'contract' that motivates the agent to exert a level of effort that would maximize the firm's (i.e., principal's) profit. There are two contrasting employment contracts that a principal can devise, though neither is likely to maximize the principal's payoff. A combination of these two is also possible, which is more likely to maximize the principal's payoff.

356

The principal's challenge is to devise a contract that motivates the agent to exert a level of effort that would maximize the firm's (principal's) profit.

For example, suppose that you have an estate which you think would be better managed by hiring a capable manager (an agent). It is easy to understand that you have three basic contractual options under which you could hire the manager:

- A wage contract, where you agree to pay a fixed monthly wage irrespective of effort and performance by the manager. In this case, you (the principal) bear the total risk of the business, and the agent has no incentive to exert greater effort or perform better. It is you, the principal, who ultimately has to bear the losses due to managerial inefficiency and/or any other factors.
- A rent contract, where you rent out the estate for a fixed monthly payment and the manager agrees to pay a fixed monthly rent irrespective of performance so that any extra net income (or loss) generated from the estate goes to the manager. In that case, it is the agent who bears the total business risk as your return is fixed. Although a rent contract surely motivates the manager to perform better, his performance brings no additional gains for you.
- Your third option is a combination of the above two, where you and the manager share the risk and return. So, you would pay a base salary plus an incentive payment based upon the manager's performance.

Contractual options available to a principal recruiting an agent: wage contract; rent contract; or combination of the two.

The third option is subject to agency theory analysis, as it is the most problematic as well as the most probable to maximize the principal's profit. At the outset, according to agency theory propositions, there are two major issues that the principal has to determine:

- Level of risk that the agent should be made to bear in order to maximize the principal's profit.
- Basic salary and the incentive pay that would motivate the agent to accept the profit-maximizing level of risk.

Major issues that the principal has to determine: risk to be delegated to agent and latter's wage structure.

The principal–agent model is based on two components:

- Principal's expected payoff curve (also known as principal's utility function).
- Agent's utility curve (or indifference curve).

> Two components of the agency model: principal's expected payoff curve and agent's utility curve.

The principal's expected payoff curve, which could be measured in revenue, profit, contribution or any other dimension, is said to be a positive function of the amount of risk borne by the agent. The greater the agent's risk, the greater the principal's payoff. In simple terms, the principal's payoff curve can be stated as:

$$P = a + bR$$

where: P is the principal's payoff (or profit before deducting payments for agent);
R is level of risk that the agent bears;
a is the principal's payoff when the agent bears no risk at all, i.e., payoff when the agent is employed under a fixed wage contract (risk-free contract for the agent);
b is the marginal contribution of the agent's additional risk to the principal's payoff i.e., the increment in the principal's payoff due to one unit increment of the agent's risk proportion.

> Principal's payoff curve can be expressed as a linear function of agent's risk.

Figure 11.1 illustrates this payoff curve. You should note that the equation above is a non-stochastic curve, which we adopted solely for simplicity. In advanced modelling of the agency problem, researchers often adopt stochastic models with an additional random variable whose expected mean value is zero (see Gietzmann (1995) for a worked example). Since our purpose here, however, is not to elaborate on the mathematics behind the modelling of the agency problem but to provide an overview of agency theory, a simple, non-stochastic framework serves our purpose.

The second element of the agency model is the agent's utility curve for risk and return. As we have already noted, the agent is assumed to be wealth-maximizing, but work and risk averse. Hence, s/he would trade-off between risk and money returns. In other words, s/he would be willing to accept more risk and exert more effort only if there is an additional income to compensate for that additional risk and effort. Figure 11.2 illustrates a typical preference curve (indifference curve), showing the trade-off between risk and return (wage income).

Curve U represents one of the agent's utility or indifference curves. At any point on this utility curve s/he is indifferent (that's why these curves are also known as indifference curves). For example, s/he is indifferent between points x and y, which shows the trade-off between effort/risk and money income. That means s/he would bear a higher risk (R_2) if and only if s/he is paid a higher wage (W_2).

358

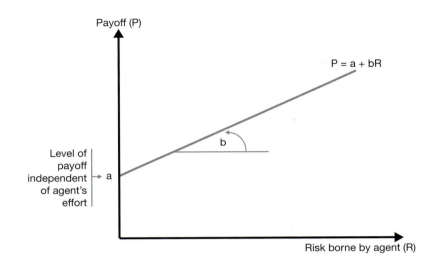

Figure 11.1 *Principal's payoff curve*

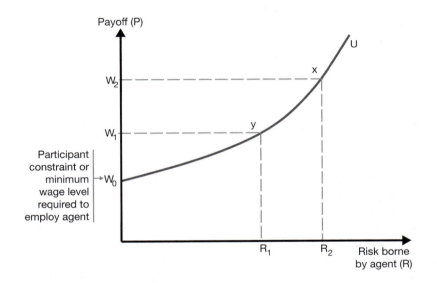

Figure 11.2 *Agent's indifference curve*

W_0 is the participation constraint, which is the money income that the agent can receive elsewhere when s/he bears no risk at all. Thus, the agent should be paid this minimum wage in order to persuade him/her to accept the job. It is the risk-free wage for the agent.

Having explained the two basic components of the agency model, now we can combine them in a single graph to show the marginal analysis of determining optimum risk/effort and wage level. Figure 11.3 illustrates the mathematical derivation of the optimum risk level that the principal should try to shift on to the agent in order to maximize his/her own payoff.

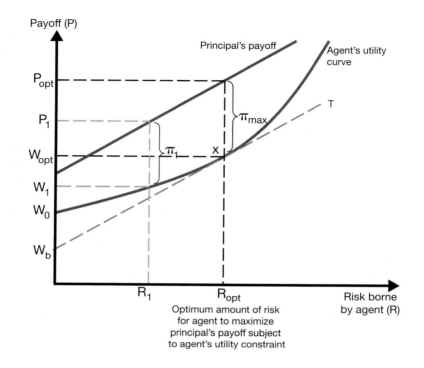

Figure 11.3 *Optimum employment contract with information symmetry*

Looking at Figure 11.3, we should first remember that the principal's objective is to determine the optimum amount of agent's risk that would maximize his/her own profit. The principal can influence and determine the agent's level of risk by determining the wage structure, simply because the agent is ready to trade-off higher risk for higher return. However, that decision needs to be on the agent's utility curve as that represents the agent's readiness to trade-off between risk and return. For example, if the principal wants the agent to exert R_{opt} level of risk, then s/he should pay the agent W_{opt} level of wage. Similarly, for an R_1 level of risk, the agent should be paid W_1 wage. In that way, the principal can expect the agent to bear a level of risk corresponding to a wage level given by the utility curve.

The principal's payoff curve, on the other hand, shows the relationship between the agent's risk and the payoff before deducting the agent's wage. Thus, the net profit for the principal at a given amount of agent's risk is the difference between the payoff curve and the utility curve (note that the utility curve is also a wage curve, as it represents the minimum wage that the agent expects at a given amount of risk s/he bears). For example, at R_1 level of risk, the principal would gain a net profit of π_1, which is the difference between P_1 and W_1. However, π_1 is not the maximum profit that the principal can achieve, and hence does not constitute an optimum for him/her. The profit maximum risk level is the one corresponding to the maximum gap between payoff curve and the utility curve. Mathematically, this is the point at which the slope of the payoff curve is equal to that of the utility curve. R_{opt} is the risk level at which that condition is met, and hence constitutes the optimum risk level for the principal where s/he can earn a π_{max} level of profit paying W_{opt} level of wage.

There is a specific level of agent's risk at which principal's profit can be maximized which is, mathematically, the point where the slope of the principal's payoff curve is equal to that of the agent's utility curve.

The principal can motivate the agent to bear an R_{opt} level of risk by devising an incentive payment structure corresponding to the line T in Figure 11.3.[2] In this case, the contractual agreement should be that the agent is paid a basic wage of W_b (the intercept of the line T) plus an incentive payment for every additional amount of risk (which the principal cannot directly observe or measure, see below). The incentive will be equal to the slope of the curve T, which is the marginal contribution of the agent's risk to the principal's payoff (note that the slope of line T is equal to that of the principal's payoff curve). When the wage structure is set in this way, it would be irrational for a utility-maximizing agent to be at a point other than R_{opt}, which is also the principal's profit-maximizing level of risk. Note that at any point other than point x (which corresponds to the risk level of R_{opt}), the agent's level of utility will be lower than that of point x.

The principal can motivate the agents to bear the level of risk at which the principal's payoff is maximized by devising an appropriate reward structure.

However, it should also be noted that, under the condition of information asymmetry, the principal cannot directly observe the effort or risk level of the agent. Thus, in devising the incentive payment structure, the principal has no choice other than to base it on some other performance indicators that only signal the effort level. For example, the principal can base incentives on productivity, profitability, cost savings and so on. However, they are all simply approximations to the agent's effort, because they are all combined results of a number of factors, including effort and chance. In some other cases, where there is no measurable output of the job, even such signalling information is lacking. This is what we call information asymmetry: the non-observability of the agent's true effort by the principal, who has access only to output measures which are dependent not purely on the agent's effort but also on many other factors (random variables, as agency theorists call them).

In devising the incentive payment structure, under the conditions of information asymmetry, the principal has no choice other than to base it on some other performance indicators that only signal effort level.

Information asymmetry, first-best and second-best solutions

Now let us assume that the information condition is symmetrical; the employment conditions are such that the principal can observe the agent's level of effort and/or the principal has access to private information about the agent's level of effort and performance. It is easy to imagine that

361

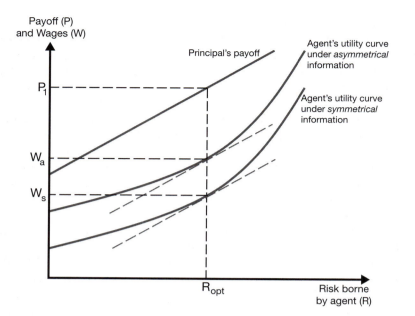

Figure 11.4 *Information symmetry and asymmetry – differences in agent's utility and principal's payoff*

such information symmetry would provide the principal with greater bargaining leverage over the agent's trade-off between wages and effort. This means that, under information symmetry, the agent is ready to be in a lower-level utility curve. Figure 11.4 illustrates this scenario.

In Figure 11.4, two utility curves are shown: one for information asymmetry and the other for information symmetry. Information symmetry renders the agent's private information open to the principal, and the agent is now ready to bear the R_{opt} level of effort for a lower wage level (W_s) than s/he could gain under information asymmetry (W_a). Thus, the principal's profit with information symmetry (i.e., $P_1 - W_s$) is greater than with information asymmetry ($P_1 - W_a$).

From the principal's point of view, the solution to the agency problem under the conditions of information symmetry is always better than any solution under information asymmetry. The former is known as a first-best solution, while the latter is known as a second-best solution. The difference between the two solutions indicates the value of information that makes the agency relationships symmetrical. It is the ability of the principal to 'know' about agents' (employees') activities and efforts that makes them controllable by the principal (the firm).

> The value of symmetrical information is the difference between first-best and second-best solutions.

Agency theory and management accounting research

Agency theory has long been a popular framework for management accounting research. One reason for this is its capacity to incorporate conflicts of interest, information imperfections and mechanisms for control into analytical models (Lambert, 2001). As a theoretical framework, the agency model provides management accounting researchers with a theoretical lens through which an organization can be seen as a network or a hierarchy of 'potentially' dysfunctional agency relationships with divergence of interests and imperfect information. The existence of incentive schemes, performance measurement systems and various responsibility accounting systems is theoretically legitimized as a means to mitigate possible losses due to the 'agency problem'. Thus, various management accounting systems and procedures can be understood as systems of 'monitoring', 'metering' (see Sharma, 1997) and incentives to mitigate the agency problem. In that sense, management accounting researchers have deployed agency theory, according to Lambert (2001: 4), to address two fundamental questions. How do features of information, accounting and compensation systems affect (reduce or worsen) the agency problem? And how does the existence of the agency problem affect the design and structure of information, accounting and compensation systems? For Walker (1989), agency theory has been given two complementary interpretations in accounting research: as a normative theory of accounting, on the one hand; and as a positive theory on the other. As a normative theory, it has been deployed to determine economically efficient accounting practices: that is, determination of accounting practices which would mitigate the agency problem and help firms achieve optimality in production and resource allocation. As a positive theory, on the other hand, it has been employed to test the optimality of empirically observed contractual arrangements (compensation, incentives, information systems, responsibility accounting systems, etc.), or to test the empirical validity of the presumptions of the agency model in the light of empirical observations. Given below are a few examples of accounting research based on agency theory frameworks.

Various management accounting systems and procedures can be understood as systems of 'monitoring' and incentive systems to mitigate the agency problem.

Agency theory has been deployed in management accounting research to address two fundamental questions. How do features of information, accounting and compensation systems affect the agency problem? And how does the existence of the agency problem affect the design and structure of information, accounting and compensation systems?

Moers (2006), for example, examined how delegation choices are affected by an (in)ability to resolve the agency problem caused by those delegations. Based on agency theory frameworks proposed by Grossman and Hart (1986) and Holmstrom and Milgrom (1987, 1994), he argues that ability to resolve the agency problem depends on the contractibility (which is measured in terms of sensitivity, precision and verifiability of performance measures) of financial and non-financial measures of performance. His study shows how quality of performance measures (i.e., contractibility) increases delegation, and how the design of decision-making processes is constrained or facilitated by the contractibility of performance measures.

Towry (2003) has employed the agency theory framework to examine control in a teamwork setting. His findings report on two financial incentive systems which rely on mutual monitoring,

> Ability to resolve the agency problem depends on contractibility of financial and non-financial measures of performance.

systems where team members monitor each other's actions. He compares the optimality of two different mutual monitoring systems: vertical (where team members report their observations on their peers' actions upwards); and horizontal (where team members themselves use their observations to control their peers) in the context of team identity (whether strong or weak). He concludes that when the team identity is high, a self-managed team structure of delegation is optimal, rather than an extractive reporting mechanism through peer observation.

> When the team identity is high, a self-managed team structure of delegation is optimal, rather than an extractive reporting mechanism through peer observation.

Arya *et al.* (1997) studied information system design in an agency model incorporating a double moral hazard scenario of a decision problem and a control problem. Their empirical conclusion was that an information system that provides less information (rather than more information to mitigate information asymmetry) will be closer to the optimal when the interaction between those two moral hazards is considered. However, if those double moral hazards are considered in isolation, an information system that provides more public information is preferred. In this way, Arya *et al.* describe conditions under which either less or more information might be optimal.

> Arya *et al.* (1997) describe conditions under which either less or more information might be optimal.

While the researchers cited above embrace the presumptions and propositions of agency theory, there are others who cast doubt on them. Seal and Vincent-Jones (1997), for example, argue that the contractual view of the world as portrayed by agency theory is an unrealistic description of business relationships, where trusting and co-operative relations are the norm rather than the exception, and where the vast majority of businesses do not engage in single-games or discrete contracting. Instead, they opt for collective agreements or standard employment contracts. Drawing from cognitive evaluation theory, Kunz and Pfaff (2002) focus on the notion of the agent's intrinsic motivation to justify scepticism towards agency theory postulations on incentives. In contradiction to agency theory, they doubt that the principal may be worse off when providing an incentive contract to the agent, as it may undermine the agent's intrinsic motivation. Ogden's (1993) study of UK government proposals relating to profit related pay (PRP) schemes shows that, contrary to the expectations of agency theory, employers were not prepared to contemplate the disclosure of the financial information required to make profit sharing effective in motivational terms, as it involves too many risks of exacerbating the very conflicts of interest that profit sharing is intended to reduce (Ogden, 1993: 201). However, in line with Armstrong (1991), he argues that the agency concept, in order to be meaningful in management–worker relations, must be theorized in ways which take account of the critical importance of the power relations that mediate agency relations (Ogden, 1993: 201).

> The contractual view of the world as portrayed by agency theory is an unrealistic description of business relationships, where trusting and co-operative relations are the norm rather than the exception, and where the vast majority of businesses do not engage in single-games or discrete contracting.

> The agency concept, in order to be meaningful in management–worker relations, must be theorized in ways which take account of the critical importance of the power relations that mediate agency relations.

TRANSACTION COST ECONOMICS

Unlike agency theory, where the focus is on the contractual relationship between self-interested principal and agent, transaction cost economics (TCE) takes transaction as the focal unit of analysis. Its focus is on comparative understanding of the alternative arrangements within which transactions take place. In his seminal paper, which marks the beginning of TCE, Coase (1937: 388) raises the fundamental question which TCE attempts to answer:

> we find islands of conscious power in this ocean of unconscious co-operation like lumps of butter coagulating in a pail of buttermilk. But in view of the fact that it is usually argued that co-ordination will be done by the price mechanism, why is such organization necessary? Why are there these 'islands of conscious power'? Outside the firm, price movements direct production, which is co-ordinated through a series of exchange transactions on the market. Within a firm, these market transactions are eliminated and in place of the complicated market structure with exchange transactions is substituted the entrepreneur-co-ordinator, who directs production. It is clear that these are alternative methods of co-ordinating production. Yet, having regard to the fact that if production is regulated by price movements, production could be carried on without any organization at all, well might we ask, why is there any organization?

> The Coasian origin of TCE is to answer the basic question: 'Why is any organization necessary when economic co-ordination is to be done by the price mechanism?'

Though he raises a fundamental question about the *raison d'être* of firms, implied in the Coase question above is the point that markets and hierarchies (organizations) are alternative institutional arrangements of co-ordinating production and exchange. The empirical and theoretical question that TCE raises is: 'Why are some transactions more likely to be executed within one form of institutional arrangements, whereas others tend to be associated with different ones?' (Spekle, 2001: 419). Going back to our opening case, transaction cost economists still debate the theoretical and empirical/historical reasons why GM entered into a long-term contract with Fisher Body, ignoring other alternative institutional arrangements that were open to them (purchasing from the open market or producing in-house), and then later decided to acquire Fisher Body while maintaining a long-term open-market relationship with A. O. Smith.

> The empirical and theoretical question that TCE generally raises is: 'Why are some trans-actions more likely to be executed within one form of institutional arrangements, whereas others tend to be associated with different ones?'

Transaction cost logic of co-ordinating economic activities

TCE identifies three alternative institutional arrangements to co-ordinate production and exchange: market, hierarchy and hybrid (Williamson, 1991).[3] The transaction cost logic of their co-existence can be summarized as follows:

1. Transactions differ. They differ in respect of their key characteristics (such as frequency, uncertainty and asset specificity, see below) and contractual and agency problems that they pose.
2. Markets, hierarchies and their hybrid forms offer different solutions because they have different problem-solving and control apparatuses, which would be suitable for certain kinds of transactions but not for others.
3. Therefore, a specific institutional arrangement is chosen to co-ordinate and govern a specific type of transaction because that combination offers the most economic means of doing so. Whether a given institutional arrangement is more economic than another to co-ordinate a specific type of transaction is explained in terms of 'transaction costs' related to each institutional arrangement. Thus, for example, it is argued that a firm has a role to play in the economic system if transactions can be organized within the firm at less cost than if the same transactions were carried out through the market (Williamson, 1988: 65).

> TCE's logic of choosing a governance structure is that a specific institutional arrangement is chosen to co-ordinate and govern a specific type of transaction because that combination offers the most economic means of doing so.

In this way, TCE adopts a 'comparative contractual approach' (Williamson, 1988: 66), as it attempts to discern and explicate the alignment of viable forms of contractual arrangements (markets, hierarchies and hybrid) and distinct characteristics of transactions, which together determine the transaction costs within such contractual arrangements. In the long run, TCE proposes, it is this comparative transaction cost that would determine the most viable contractual arrangement for a given type of transaction. As Williamson (1988: 73) argues, TCE's strategy employs the following organizational imperative: align transactions (which differ in their attributes) with governance structure (the costs and competencies of which differ) in a discriminating (mainly transaction cost economizing) way.

The agency problem in TCE

TCE employs two critical behavioural assumptions about economic agents and their behaviour. First is the assumption of 'bounded rationality', which assumes that human agents are 'intendedly rational, but only limitedly so' (Simon, 1961: xxiv, quoted in Williamson, 1988: 67). Human agents are boundedly rational due to their cognitive, computational, informational and emotional limitations. The second assumption is about opportunistic behaviour. Similar to the principal–agent model's assumption of self-interest behaviour, TCE also assumes that human agents, although constrained by bounded rationality, are 'given to opportunism, which is a deep condition of self-interest seeking that contemplates guile' (Williamson, 1988: 68). The direct contractual implication of these assumptions is that all forms of comprehensive contract are infeasible and all viable forms of contract are unavoidably incomplete. This means there exist possible but unforeseen events in the future for which the contract does not stipulate the appropriate actions at the time of contracting, and such events would provide ample opportunities for either of the parties to the contract to act opportunistically and deviate from corporative solutions. In other words, conditions for 'moral hazards' (loss of efficiency due to opportunistic behaviour by either party to the contract) are unavoidable at the point of devising contracts. In this sense, Williamson (1988: 68) argues, the organizational imperative is to 'organize economic activity so as to economize on bounded rationality while simultaneously safeguarding the transactions in questions against the hazards of opportunism'. When we couple this imperative stemming from behavioural imperfection with the transaction cost economic logic of co-ordinating economic activities (see previous sub-section), then we have the following propositions about transaction cost theory:

TCE holds two critical behavioural assumptions: bounded rationality; and opportunistic behaviour of economic agents.

The implication of bounded rationality and opportunistic behaviour is that all forms of comprehensive contract are infeasible, and all viable forms of contract are unavoidably incomplete.

367

1. As transactions differ in their attributes, and as different institutional arrangements or governance structures to co-ordinate economic activities (i.e., market, hierarchy and hybrid) bear different problem-solving and control apparatuses, transactions should be matched discriminately with governance structures. Some may be better left to market mechanisms, while others may be better off with hierarchies or hybrid forms of governance.

2. The decision as to which institutional arrangement should govern a certain transaction would be based on the potential of each governance structure to economize on transaction costs.

3. However, this discriminatory match between transactions and governance structures should allow for economic agents' behavioural limitations of bounded rationality and opportunistic behaviour. Since these two behavioural conditions make 'comprehensive contracts' infeasible, institutional arrangements to co-ordinate economic activities would be effective if they provided for adaptive and sequential decision-making. Table 11.1 summarizes these contractual implications of bounded rationality and opportunism.

> TCE embraces the logic of discriminatory match between transactions and governance structures subject to behavioural conditions of bounded rationality and opportunism.

How transactions differ

For the purpose of a discriminatory match between transactions and alternative structures available to govern them, it is important to understand critical dimensions according to which transactions differ from one another. Transaction cost theorists (see Williamson, 1988: 70) employ three critical dimensions to differentiate between transactions: frequency with which they occur; degree of complexity to which they are subjected; and condition of asset specificity. These transaction attributes are important determinants not only of the transaction costs but also of the possibilities of opportunistic behaviour.

> Transactions differ due to frequency, complexity and asset specificity.

Table 11.1 *Implications of bounded rationality and opportunism*

	Behavioural assumptions	
	Bounded rationality	Opportunism
Implications for contractual theory	Comprehensive contracting is infeasible	Contract as promise is naive
Implications for economic organization	Exchange will be facilitated by modes that support adaptive, sequential decision-making	Trading requires support of spontaneous or crafted safeguards

Source: Williamson (1988: 69)

■ Frequency. Typically, less frequent or one-off transactions[4] are more transaction-cost econo-mizing in spot markets than a company's internal production or long-term, contract-based supplies. For example, it would not be transaction-cost economizing for a manufacturing company to set up its own building construction department for its new head office building rather than spot market contracting through open bidding. On the other hand, companies often opt to enter into long-term supply contracts with reliable, high-quality suppliers for raw materials and other services, which should be frequently and steadily supplied on a day-to-day basis to facilitate smooth production schedules.

■ Complexity. *Inter alia*, this refers to the degree of private information (or information asym-metry) in the transaction. That means one party knows more than others about some aspects of the transaction. This is the case where the quality and quantity of the transaction are difficult to measure. The higher the complexity involved in a transaction, the greater the chance to act opportunistically.

■ Asset specificity. This is the degree to which an asset can be redeployed to alternative uses and by alternative users without sacrifice of productive value (Williamson, 1988: 70). In other words, if the supplier to a contract is required to make a buyer-specific investment, then there is an asset specificity to the contract. Going back to the opening case example, one of the disagreements between GM and FBC was about the latter's refusal of GM's proposal that FBC should build a dedicated plant adjacent to one of the GM assembly plants so that efficiency would improve by cutting transport time and costs, as well as the need for inventory. FBC's refusal, it is argued, was due to the high asset specificity of the investment, which would pro-vide GM with a considerable opportunity for ex-post opportunistic behaviour. The solution that GM found for this agency issue was to integrate closed-body manufacturing vertically by acquiring FBC.

Transaction cost theorists identify several types of asset specificity. The first is site or location speci-ficity, where geographical location of the asset confines its use to a specific buyer or set of buyers. The second is type specificity, where the asset can produce only a particular input for a particular firm. The third is human resource specificity, where an investment is made to train or recruit personnel with specific knowledge or skills which are not easily transferable for any other use.

> Site or location specificity, type specificity and human resource specificity are different types of asset specificity.

When a transaction involves asset specificity, the consequence is that parties to the transaction are bilaterally dependent, which complicates the inter-temporal governance of contractual rela-tions (Williamson, 1988).

How governance structures differ

According to Williamson (1991), governance structures (i.e., mainly market, hierarchies and hybrid forms) differ in three basic dimensions: the contract law that governs each type of contractual arrangement; adaptability of each governance structure to changing circumstances;

and incentive and control instruments in use under each governance structure. It would be helpful, especially in the context of management accounting, to elaborate on the second and third of these dimensions.

> Governance structures differ in three basic dimensions: the contract law; adaptability; and incentive and control instruments that are in use.

Drawing from Hayek and Barnard, Williamson (1991) describes two types of adaptation. First is type A, or autonomous, adaptation, where the price mechanism provides the necessary and sufficient signals, in response to which individual participants can take adaptive actions. This is the ideal-type neoclassical economic condition where buyers and sellers in a market transaction can respond independently to price changes so as to maximize their profit and/or utility functions (Williamson, 1991: 278). The second is type C, or co-ordinated (non-autonomous), adaptation which becomes important when possibilities of adaptation through price mechanism fail due to market and contractual imperfections. Thus, it is easy to understand that these two types of adaptation, A and C, are associated with market and hierarchy, respectively, in bipolar oppositions, while hybrid forms of governance combine them to various degrees.

> Autonomous and co-ordinated are the two types of adaptation that market and hierarchy embrace, respectively.

Governance structures also differ in their use of incentive and control instruments. It is argued that market as a governance structure of economic activities is strong in 'incentive intensity', while hierarchy is weak in that respect. In a competitive market, there is a very strong incentive for individual participants in transactions to reduce cost, increase quality and adapt efficiently in order to appropriate individual streams of net profits. In other words, when economic activities are governed by a competitive market mechanism, actions of individual participants are strongly linked to their market outcomes of profits or losses, and, therefore, markets offer strong incentives for individual actors to perform efficiently. Hierarchies as a governance structure, on the other hand, are argued to be stronger in the sense of 'administrative controls' than markets. Administrative controls of economic activities become important when market conditions are imperfect and when bilateral dependencies intrude into economic relationships, especially when transactions are conditioned by asset specificities, complexity and high frequency (see above). However, hierarchies[5] are weak in incentive intensity because the link between actions of individual parties (such as departments, divisions and levels) and the collective outcome of the hierarchy is blurred. Thus, one division may make plausible claims for its contribution to the co-ordinated outcome. Similarly, there are a number of accounting methods to distribute and redistribute arbitrarily the co-ordinated outcome of the hierarchy among its divisions and subdivisions. Examples are transfer pricing, allocation and absorption of overheads, budgeting and inventory conventions, which all arbitrarily link actions of individual parties to their collective outcome.

> Market is strong in 'incentive intensity', while hierarchy is weak in that respect.

> Hierarchies as a governance structure are argued to be stronger in the sense of 'administrative controls' than markets.

Thus, in the sense of two types of adaptability, incentive intensity and administrative controls, markets and hierarchies are bipolar opposites, while hybrid forms occupy a middle ground. Table 11.2 illustrates these differences between market, hierarchy and hybrid forms of governance structures.

Table 11.2 *How governance structures differ*

Attributes	Governance structure		
	Market	Hybrid	Hierarchy
Instruments:			
Incentive intensity	Strong	Semi-strong	Weak
Administrative controls	Weak	Semi-strong	Strong
Performance attributes:			
Autonomous adaptation	Strong	Semi-strong	Weak
Co-ordinated adaptation	Weak	Semi-strong	Strong
Contract law	Strong	Semi-strong	Weak

Source: Williamson (1991: 281)

Differences between TCE and the principal–agent model

It would be helpful at this time to explain some of the key differences between agency theory and transaction cost theory. However, one of the striking similarities is that the agency problem occupies the focal point in both theoretical perspectives. The two theories, nevertheless, approach the agency problem from two different angles. Under the assumptions of self-interest and information asymmetry, and taking a rather relationship focus, the principal–agent model sees the agency problem as the possibility of deviating from Pareto-optimal contractual relationships between an agent and principal where such deviations would result in gross loss of economic efficiency due to the agent's lack of motivation to perform. Thus, the agency problem is ultimately reduced to a motivational one. Transaction cost theory, on the other hand, under the assumptions of opportunism and bounded rationality, conceptualizes the agency problem as a possible mismatch between a transaction and alternative structures available to govern that transaction. In that sense, the economic loss related to the agency problem is manifested by higher transaction costs due to governance of transactions by incorrect governance structures.

The agency problem occupies the focal point in both the principal–agent model and TCE, though with different interpretations.

The two approaches also differ in their theoretical orientation. The principal–agent model takes a rather normative theoretical stance, while TCE takes a positive one. Based on the neoclassical economic assumption of rationality, the principal–agent model assumes that perfect contractual arrangements between principal and agent are possible. Thus, its analytical focus is on modelling the agency problem in line with its associated profit and utility variables, so that model-based solutions would provide an equilibrium solution (perfect contractual terms between principal and agent to maximize the principal's profit subject to the agent's utility constraints). Based on new institutional economics' assumption of bounded rationality, TCE, on the other hand, assumes that perfect contracts are infeasible and all viable contracts are imperfect. Thus, its analytical focus is to explain, in rather a positive manner, why particular transactions are governed by certain governance structures while others are not. Thus, for TCE, the issue is not 'how they should be governed', but rather, 'why they are governed in that way'.

The principal–agent model and TCE differ in their analytical focus.

The two also differ in their focal unit of analysis. The principal–agent model takes the micro-level relationship between the parties (principal and agent) to economic activities and transactions. As already noted, its focus is therefore to devise an optimal contractual relationship between them. It adopts a neoclassical marginal analysis to determine the optimality. In contrast, TCE studies dimensions according to which transactions differ from one another; or, in other words, it studies the salient attributes of a transaction to distinguish it from others. Then it also studies alternative structures available to govern that transaction in comparative terms, by differentiating between their relative strengths and weaknesses to govern a specific kind of transaction. In that way, transaction cost theory can perform a 'discriminatory analysis' of transactions and their governance structures to explicate why those transactions are governed by a particular structure.

The principal–agent model and TCE differ in their focal unit of analysis.

Consequential to this micro-level relational and transactional focus of the two approaches, their empirical domains also differ. The principal–agent theory largely concentrates on empirical contexts that manifest interpersonnel or superior–subordinate relationships. Thus, as we have already noted, the management accounting research-based agency theory framework by and large concentrates on motivational or incentive issues related to management accounting techniques such as budgeting, transfer pricing, standard costing and performance-related reward structures. TCE, on the other hand, concentrates more on empirical contexts that manifest governance structures which are often situated across organizational boundaries. Thus, its empirical domain is rather macro compared to that of agency theory. In the next section, we will discuss how transaction cost theory has been deployed in management accounting research.

Principal–agent model and TCE differ in their empirical domains.

TCE AND MANAGEMENT ACCOUNTING RESEARCH

TCE has long been deployed in explicating various management accounting phenomena. For the purpose of this text, we can identify three major areas in which it has provided an influential theoretical framework: management accounting history; inter-organizational relationships; and management control structures.

Explaining management accounting history through transaction cost economics

Perhaps the most famous application of transaction cost economics in management accounting is its application by Johnson and Kaplan (1987) in their 'relevance lost' thesis to explicate the evolution of management accounting practices (see also Chapter 2). In line with transaction cost theory arguments, Johnson and Kaplan consider 'managed organizations' (or hierarchies) as alternatives to the market as a co-ordinating mechanism of economic activities. Thus, the emergence of large corporations is equated to integration of producers who were hitherto co-ordinated by 'price' information in an open-market context. Once this integration took place, they argue, a new demand for management accounting information was created to supersede the 'price' information, which was lost within the transition from markets to hierarchies. In that way, Johnson and Kaplan locate management accounting within hierarchical forms of co-ordinating economic activities vis-à-vis autonomous price information in market co-ordination. For them, therefore, management accounting is an essential administrative control and information device that is needed to ensure co-ordinated adaptation of hierarchies to changing circumstances. Thus, management accounting emerged and evolved to facilitate transaction cost minimization through co-ordinated adaptation within hierarchies. They also argue that the period between the 1920s and the 1990s marks a historical epoch, where management accounting failed to perform this function due to its excessive reliance on external reporting and academic influences. This explanation for the failure of management accounting, however, is far short of a transaction cost theory-based explication (see Chapter 2).

The TCE-based explanation for the emergence of management accounting is that a new demand for management accounting information was created to supersede 'price' information once market-based transactions were integrated into hierarchies.

As we noted in Chapter 2, Hopper and Armstrong (1991) are critical about the capacity of transaction cost economics to explain the historical evolution of management accounting. One of their critiques is targeted at the lack of clarity regarding the meaning of basic concepts employed by TCE, mainly transactions and transaction costs. As they argue, it is far from clear what these are, and Johnson and Kaplan, while making no attempt to clarify these concepts, have explicitly reduced the notion of transaction cost simply to 'efficiency'. Overall, their argument is that the evolution of hierarchical organizations and their control apparatuses of management accounting cannot necessarily be equated to the entrepreneurial search for mitigating transaction cost through the invention of new organizational forms and controls. Instead, they argue that the creation of large corporations through acquisitions and mergers may be carried out with monopoly profits in view, rather than minimization of transaction costs. Most importantly, they argue that the need for progressive subordination of labour is a better explanation for the emergence of hierarchical organizations and their management accounting apparatuses.

Explaining inter-organizational relations through transaction cost economics

As we noted in Chapter 10, the last decade or so has witnessed a dramatic change in organizational forms. Organizational boundaries tend to be rather blurred and various forms of long-term inter-organizational relations have become the defining characteristics of industries. For example, outsourcing, joint ventures and networking have become increasingly common modes not only of securing a dependable, low-cost and innovation-supported supply of components and services, but also of enhancing competitive advantages through sharing resources and competencies across organizational boundaries. This turn in industrial reconfiguration has led to a proliferation of academic research in several social science disciplines, including management accounting. Some of these researches have not only deployed theoretical propositions of TCE to explicate the new changes but have started to acknowledge their limitations. In other words, these evolutions in inter-organizational forms have provided ample opportunities to revisit TCE with a new set of empirical evidence.

Defining inter-organizational relationships

One of the important issues when researching emerging inter-organizational relations is to provide a theoretical definition for them. As we have already noted, TCE identifies three discrete governance mechanisms: market, hierarchy and hybrid, where hybrid is an intermediate form of governance, encompassing all alternative contractual arrangements between the extremes of markets and hierarchy. It is also shown that hybrid forms represent a mixture of market and hierarchical attributes to form a middle-ground governance structure that sacrifices, to a certain degree, the autonomous adaptation and incentive intensity of market in favour of the co-ordinated adaptation and administrative controls of hierarchy (see Table 11.2, above). In line with this market, hierarchy and hybrid classification of governance, conventionally, TCE tends to define all forms of inter-organizational relationship as forms of hybrid governance.

TCE tends to define all forms of inter-organizational relationship as forms of hybrid governance.

Recent studies of inter-organizational relations have pointed out that this conventional TCE treatment of such relationships as generic intermediate forms between markets and hierarchies is hardly insightful. For example, Dekker (2004) argues that TCE's prediction that the form of governance structure is a function of transaction characteristics (such as frequency, complexity and asset specificity – see above) is insufficient to explain management and control of inter-organizational relationships adequately for the following reasons:

- The singular focus of TCE on the notion of transaction cost minimization as the sole determinant of governance forms lacks due recognition of variety in forms and goals of inter-organizational relationships.
- The static nature of TCE has resulted in a neglect of the organizational mechanisms used in governance of inter-organizational relationships. In particular, TCE has taken little account of the social mechanisms of governance associated with inter-organizational relationships.

> Dekker argues that TCE's prediction that the form of governance structure is a function of transaction characteristics is insufficient to explain management and control of inter-organizational relationships adequately.

Thus, in contrast to TCE's proposition that the hybrid form is a homogeneous category integrating distinct characteristics of markets and hierarchies to form a middle ground, so that they would be economizing transaction costs on certain kinds of transaction, Dekker (2004) argues that inter-organizational relationships actually comprise a rather heterogeneous phenomenon. According to him, inter-organizational relationships can cover a wide range of transaction forms, and can serve a greater variety of functions than merely economizing on transaction costs. Mouritsen and Thrane (2006: 244) extend this view by taking network organizations into consideration. They argue that 'network helps firms develop their capabilities and allows flexibility because it can be reconfigured by including and excluding members . . . it is a socio-economic rather than an economic entity'. Their point is that network collaboration between firms focuses on a wider set of implications, such as strategic, learning, competency and structural, rather than the single focus of economizing on the cost of transactions.

> Inter-organizational relationships can cover a wide range of transaction forms, and can serve a greater variety of functions than mere economizing on transaction costs.

Control issues of inter-organizational relationships

Management accounting research on inter-organizational relationships and networks, in line with TCE, identifies two major control issues (Dekker, 2004; Mouritsen and Thrane, 2006): safeguarding against opportunistic appropriations by parties to the network; and co-ordination of activities across organizational boundaries. As we have already noted, TCE asserts an agency problem created by the combination of transactional attributes (especially asset specificity and complexity, including uncertainty of future outcome of the collaborative efforts of the alliance) and behavioural conditions of economic agents (bounded rationality and opportunism). Inter-organizational networks often demand heavy network-specific investments from participating organizations, and thus create a high degree of interdependence on each other, making it possible for one participant opportunistically to appropriate the transactional values from the others. Thus, safeguarding against this kind of opportunistic appropriation (or 'generation of trust', as it is called by Tomkins, 2001) is one of the major concerns in inter-organizational relationships.

> There are two major control issues in inter-organizational relationships: safeguarding against opportunistic appropriation; and co-ordination of activities across organizational boundaries.

As Dekker (2004) points out, inter-organizational relationships involve pooling resources and competencies, planning for tasks to be carried out by the collaboration, and deciding on a division of labour between each party. This is where the second challenge, 'co-ordination of interdependent tasks' (Dekker, 2004) or 'mastery of events' (Tomkins, 2001), comes into the picture. As Mouritsen and Thrane (2006: 242) put it, 'a network is a fragile accomplishment because its form, in principle, has no strategic apex and hierarchy'. In TCE terms, it is a relational contract between opportunistically behaving and boundedly rational parties which have their own self-interests, but are ready to pool their resources and competencies with others, as that provides opportunities for economizing on transaction costs. Within such a fragile institutional arrangement, co-ordination of independent tasks (because they are not solidified through a bureaucratic hierarchy, as in the case of internal manufacturing) is a real managerial concern.

Management accounting in inter-organizational relationships

The role of management accounting in inter-organizational relationships is linked to mechanisms of governance. TCE holds a rather contractual view on governance, and argues that in hybrid form, governance consists of legal and private ordering (Dekker, 2004: 31). Legal ordering comprises the writing and third-party enforcement of legally binding contractual agreements to govern the relationship and transactions, whereas private ordering consists of 'formal self-enforcing mechanisms or hostages created intentionally to align the economic incentives of the transacting parties' (Dekker, 2004: 31). In this view, the role of management accounting within inter-organizational relationships is rather ambiguous.

> TCE holds a rather contractual view on governance, and argues that in hybrid form, governance consists of legal and private ordering.

Dekker's (2004) observation is that this contractual view of governance is incomplete, as it lacks the examination of organizational mechanisms of governance. It is his argument that firms in an inter-organizational relationship align their joint processes through organizational mechanisms such as command structures and authority systems, standard operating procedures, incentive systems, dispute-resolution procedures and non-market pricing systems (e.g., transfer pricing). Thus, it is in this context that one can place the role of management accounting within inter-organizational relationships.

Dekker observes that this contractual view of governance is incomplete, as it lacks the examination of organizational mechanisms of governance.

Mouritsen and Thrane (2006) suggest that accounting may work in network organizations through two different kinds of operation: self-regulating mechanisms and orchestration mechanisms, both of which provide safeguards against the appropriation and co-ordination concerns discussed above. They argue that:

> The relations between partner firms could hardly flow without the help of certain management technologies that (imperfectly) execute the relations between the partners. Some of these management technologies were constituted through technologies of accounting, but generally they came as self-regulating mechanisms and orchestration mechanisms.
>
> (Mouritsen and Thrane, 2006: 273)

Self-regulating mechanisms are in place to facilitate routine financial transactions and flows between partnering firms, and they are by and large constructed through preset transfer prices and fees. Orchestration mechanisms, on the other hand, are concerned with non-routine but strategically important changes in network relationships, and demand renegotiations on the network membership, contractual terms and the redesigning of self-regulating mechanisms.

Mouritsen and Thrane (2006) suggest that accounting may work in network organizations through self-regulating mechanisms or orchestration mechanisms.

Explaining management control structures

As we have already noted, TCE asserts that opportunism and bounded rationality of economic agents, on the one hand, and complexity, frequency and asset specificity of transactions that those economic agents are contracted for, on the other hand, give rise to task co-ordination, incentive, monitoring and enforcement problems. Hence, a control structure is an efficient solution to mitigate losses arising from this agency problem. This is often depicted as the problem of governance structure in root sources of TCE, and explained through the threefold generic classification of market, hierarchy and hybrid forms of governance (e.g., Williamson, 1988, 1991). From TCE's position, it is seen that a 'specific institutional arrangement is chosen to govern a specific transaction because that arrangement offers some distinctive set of control devices – a set that cannot be replicated within alternative arrangements – in a relative sense – to the control needs of that transaction' (Spekle, 2001: 420).

A few accounting researchers have made noteworthy attempts to clarify and extend this generic TCE perspective on governance by replicating it in management control literature and empirical case studies (e.g., Covaleski *et al.*, 2003; Spekle, 2001; van den Bogaard and Spekle, 2003). A brief outline of Spekle's study (2001) is sufficient, within the scope of this text, to explain how one particular piece of research situates management control within the theoretical parameters of TCE.

Spekle identifies a fundamental difference in the level of analysis between the management control literature and TCE. He shows that TCE's focus, as we noted above, is on explaining the trade-off between generic modes of governance (i.e., market, hierarchy and hybrid). The management control literature, on the other hand, is focused on the control issues within just one mode: the hierarchy. Thus, he believes that the management control literature can raise its understanding of control of economic activities to a higher level by drawing on TCE. Similarly, by integrating management control variables with TCE variables, he argues, a more detailed study of governance than is usual in TCE-based studies will ensue.

> TCE's focus is to explain the trade-off between generic modes of governance (i.e., market, hierarchy and hybrid). The management control literature, on the other hand, is focused on the control issues within just one mode: the hierarchy.

Accordingly, Spekle (2001: 427) proposes three 'variables that define the nature of activities to be controlled and the control problems to which they give rise': uncertainty; the degree of asset specificity; and the intensity of post hoc information impactedness. Relative status (high, moderate and low) of these variables and their different combinations, Spekle argues, would determine the potential 'control archetypes', which he defines (2001: 427) as 'a discrete configuration of a control device that is descriptively and theoretically representative of a significant group of observable management control structures and practices'. In this way, he extends the generic governance structures of TCE to nine different control archetypes, five of which belong to a hierarchical mode of governance, and correspond to well-known patterns of control from the management control literature. Those archetypes are: market control; arm's length hierarchical control; arm's length hybrid control; action-oriented machine control; result-oriented machine control; hierarchical exploratory control; hybrid exploratory control; hierarchical boundary control; and market-based boundary control.

> Spekle (2001) extends the generic governance structures of TCE to nine different control archetypes, five of which belong to the hierarchical mode of governance, and correspond to well-known patterns of control from the management control literature.

378

HAVE YOU UNDERSTOOD THE CHAPTER?

1. Briefly describe the theoretical orientation that management accounting research took in its early phases of development.
2. Differentiate between normative and positive stances of management accounting research.
3. What is meant by the 'agency problem'? Explain the conditions under which it arises.
4. What are the basic assumptions that agency theory holds about economic agents and their relationships?
5. What are the basic variable components of the principal–agent model?
6. Explain briefly the mathematical logic involved in the solution to the agency problem.
7. Differentiate between first-best and second-best solutions to the agency problem. How do you explain the value of symmetrical information in terms of first- and second-best solutions?
8. How do you locate various management accounting techniques and procedures, such as incentives, performance measurement and responsibility accounting systems, within the parameters of agency theory?
9. Discuss how agency theory has been deployed to explicate various management accounting issues.
10. What are the basic theoretical questions that TCE attempts to address?
11. What are the basic behavioural assumptions that TCE holds on economic agents?
12. Explain briefly the transaction cost logic of co-ordination and governance of economic transactions.
13. What are the major attributes by which different types of transaction are differentiated?
14. Briefly discuss the implications of bounded rationality and opportunism for contract theory and governance of economic organizations.
15. As governance structures, how do market and hierarchy differ ?
16. Discuss briefly the differences between agency theory and TCE.
17. How can TCE explain the historical evolution of management accounting?
18. Explain inter-organizational relationships through the theoretical parameters of TCE.
19. Explain management control structure variety through TCE parameters.

BEYOND THE CHAPTER

1. [W]e find islands of conscious power in this ocean of unconscious co-operation like lumps of butter coagulating in a pail of buttermilk. But in view of the fact that it is usually argued that co-ordination will be done by the price mechanism, why is such organisation necessary? Why are there these 'islands of conscious power'?

   (Coase, 1937: 388)

   Discuss.

2. 'Agency theory, in order to be meaningful in management–worker relations, needs to be theorized in ways which take account of the critical importance of the power relations that mediate agency relations.' Discuss.

FURTHER READING

1. For a very good synthesis of agency theory and contracting relations, see Baiman (1982, 1990) and Lambert (2001).
2. For TCE and organizational control dynamics, see Williamson (1991) and Jensen and Meckling (1976).

Chapter 12

Towards contingency theory of management accounting

A STARTING POINT: GENERALIZED CONTINGENCIES

A conversation between a professional management accountant and a research student in the former's office

Management accountant: I can't understand why you want to study our system. Ours is the same as everybody's. There isn't any difference across systems in different companies.

Student: That might be right, but I think your system must have developed under the specific circumstances you are in. Can you think of any?

Management accountant: Well, I suppose that ours is a generic system, except that we have more regular information processing. Because we are operating in a competitive market, we need to collect and analyse information about production every day. So we get email attachments on production data from the mills every day at 6.00 p.m. We start the next day with this information.

Student: That's interesting. Your system has been designed to respond to a competitive market, hasn't it?

Management accountant: Of course, we have to respond to the market. That's obvious. What do you have to study here, then?

A conversation between a supervisor and the student

Supervisor: How was your preliminary interview with the management accountant?

Student: It went OK. He doesn't agree that their system is unique. He has a view that all systems are the same. But later on, he admitted that their system was unique in that they process information on a more regular basis to respond to the market.

Supervisor: Ah. That's the view of contingency theory. So you can do more interviews with people there. You could come out with more, broader factors and their relationships.

Student: I agree. I hope that I can test the relationships between their systems and various contingent factors. So far, I've identified market environment. Do you think I can do this only with interviews?

Supervisor: Good question. Yes and no. You may do interviews. Also, collect data from other, secondary sources, such as documents, reports and so on.

Student: What do you think of that market environment?

Supervisor: That is a good finding. Can you find something different, any new factor or any new relationship? That will be a good contribution to the literature. Also, see if everything can be explained by contingency theory. Find some limitations and respond to them.

SETTING THE SCENE

Rather than emphasizing what management accounting change is, in this chapter we aim to highlight how management accounting change can be understood by means of a contingency theory framework. We chose contingency theory as it has now been revisited with a greater enthusiasm for explaining management accounting change. From the above conversation, we can see that environmental pressures have an impact on the designing of a management accounting and control system. This is a starting point for us to ask the question of how we can understand this impact systematically. Contingency theory provides us with a framework for this end. Learning objectives of this chapter are set to address this broader question.

First, the chapter elaborates on the contingency theory of management accounting as a perspective for understanding recent changes. In this, we will highlight the problem of the conventional view held to understand management accounting systems. We will then identify how, in the 1970s, researchers began to draw on the view of contingency theory to challenge the conventional one. In particular, we will look at how far these studies developed in the 1970s and 1980s, and in what sense this development has continued since the 1990s. In doing so, we will also see how this approach has identified recent changes in management accounting, especially within the post-mechanistic approach.

- Highlight the problem of the conventional view held to understand management accounting systems
- Identify the developments of the 1970s and 1980s
- Define the perspective on contingency theory of management accounting

Second, the chapter will elaborate on the key concepts that underlie contingency theory. Drawing on classical management studies, we will define how contingent factors have been identified and used in organizational studies. Also, we will look at how a particular domain of research and a debate developed in the literature in relation to the development of contingency theory perspectives within development studies.

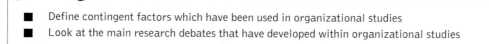

- Define contingent factors which have been used in organizational studies
- Look at the main research debates that have developed within organizational studies

Third, we will discuss the development of the contingency theory of management accounting. One important consideration here is to spot some general frameworks through which researchers undertook respective studies. Moreover, we will look at a major review in this area to understand how this perspective has been established and what limitations it has created.

- Spot two general frameworks through which researchers undertook respective studies
- Look at a major review to understand the establishment of the perspective and to highlight its limitations

Fourth, we will consider some of the major studies to highlight how researchers have engaged in research to aid both the design and the explanation of management and accounting control systems. This will enable us to understand contingency theory not only as a means of designing systems but also as a way of understanding existing systems. This review will categorize the studies by major contingent factors, namely environment, technology, structure and strategy.

- Consider some of major studies to highlight how researchers have engaged in research in this area
- Categorize the studies by major contingent factors, namely environment, technology, structure and strategy

Fifth, the chapter proceeds to evaluate the whole programme of contingency theory of management accounting critically. This evaluation will focus on two main aspects – conceptual and methodological deficiencies – and will form a systematic critique through which we can broaden our understanding of the validity of this research programme.

- Critically evaluate the whole programme of contingency theory of management accounting
- Categorize the identified deficiencies into two main aspects: conceptual and methodological

Finally, we will revisit the literature with a view to exploring new changes which have occurred in this research programme. We have spotted two strands of development: theoretical and methodological. In respect of theoretical developments, we have been attracted by the ways in which contingency theory is extended by economic and institutional theories. A noteworthy methodological development has been some researchers' inclination to conduct longitudinal case studies.

- ■ Revisit the literature to explore new changes which have occurred
- ■ Categorize the strands of development as theoretical or methodological

CONTINGENCY THEORY AS A PERSPECTIVE

When we look for perspectives to aid understanding of management practices, including recent changes from the mechanistic to the post-mechanistic, a large number of researchers tend to see contingency theory as the most appropriate. Researchers with this perspective, and others, wish to explain why and how management accounting practice exists and changes. More specifically, contingency theorists tend to explore under what circumstances management accounting systems work better or worse. This section provides a general introduction to contingency theory as a theoretical perspective on management accounting research.

Contingency theorists tend to explore under what circumstances management accounting systems work better or worse.

Until the 1970s, management accounting researchers believed that there was a universal model of management accounting systems that could be adopted by any organization. Within the programme of contingency theory of management accounting, which became active from the 1970s, the view of universality of management accounting systems was questioned. It was asked whether a particular system could operate under any circumstances for providing information for decision-making and management control. Contingency perspectives came to refute this and proposed a way of designing and studying accounting systems under different circumstances. To put it another way, contingency theory of management accounting provides us with both a view of the world of management accounting (in research philosophy, this is termed 'ontology') and a way of studying that nature of management accounting (this is termed 'epistemology').

Contingency theory of management accounting provides us with both an ontology and an epistemology.

The contingency theory of management accounting refers to the premise that there is no universally appropriate accounting system equally applicable to all organizations in all circumstances (Gordon and Miller, 1976; Otley, 1980, 1994). Instead, accounting systems are shaped by environmental (Khandwalla, 1977; Otley, 1978; Hofstede, 1984; Harrison, 1992) and organizational factors (Khandwalla, 1972; Bruns and Waterhouse, 1975; Chenhall and Morris, 1986). As we will explain later, these factors are considered to be contingent factors. Simply, as shown in

384

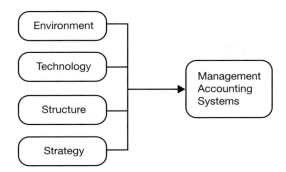

Figure 12.1 *Contingency theory perspective on management accounting*

Figure 12.1, what contingency theorists argue is that management accounting systems (MAS) are functions of certain contingent factors. Management accountants can follow this mantra and design a suitable accounting system, rather than believing in one best system which is available everywhere for everybody.

KEY TERMS

The contingency theory of management accounting refers to the premise that there is no universally appropriate accounting system equally applicable to all organizations in all circumstances.

CONTINGENCY THEORY: CLASSICAL STUDIES IN ORGANIZATION THEORY

A contingency is an unavoidable business circumstance rather than something which arises from an emergency. It has to be acknowledged and dealt with by managers rather than avoided (Clegg *et al.*, 2005). For example, as we will see below, external environment such as hostile competition and its underlying uncertainty are contingencies rather than emergencies that a firm must deal with, especially in designing organizational structures and management systems. Contingency theory focuses on contingent factors associated with such business circumstances and their relationships with organizational systems and effectiveness. The main contingent factors which have been subject to investigation are: environment, technology, size and structure. This section will look at how these factors and their relationships have been analysed by early management researchers.

KEY TERMS

A contingency is an unavoidable business circumstance rather than something which arises from an emergency.

Environment

In general, environment constitutes the market and its associated factors, such as prices, products, competition, government policies, etc. In specific terms, such an environment is a business environment which affects the functioning of business organizations. This implies that there must be a relationship between business environments and the functioning of business organizational systems. Contingency theorists aimed to explain this relationship.

One classic study is by Burns and Stalker (1961). In their study, they categorized environments into two extremes: stable and uncertain. They then developed a testable hypothesis which helps researchers and business managers to understand and design organizational systems, respectively. One extreme of the hypothesis is that firms operating in a stable business environment are much more mechanistic. Because of the stability of the environment, these firms do not tend to be innovative, either in their products or their organizational structures. Instead, they maintain their mechanistic form of organization, which is normally developed through the ideals of bureaucracy. The other extreme is that firms operating in unstable and uncertain environments tend to be much more organic and less bureaucratic. Because of the uncertainty, these organizations tend to change their products and services through innovation and differentiation. Thus, they cannot afford the problems of inflexibility generated from mechanistic forms of organizations. Burns and Stalker found that those firms operating in such changing environments developed more organic and informal structures, as opposed to mechanistic and formal ones. The implications of these two extremes for the functioning of organizational systems are summarized in Table 12.1.

> Firms operating in a stable business environment are much more mechanistic; firms operating in unstable and uncertain environments tend to be much more organic and less bureaucratic.

A number of studies carried out from the 1960s onwards confirmed the above hypothesis. For instance, Lawrence and Lorsch (1967) examined the impact of uncertainty on the differentiation (differences in functional departments) and integration (collaboration between departments) of an organization. They found that better-performing organizations under uncertainty are highly differentiated as well as integrated while similar organizations in stable conditions are less

Table 12.1 Structures in two forms of organizations

	Mechanistic	Organic
Standardization	High	Low
Formalization	High	Low
Centralization	Concentrated	Diffuse
Discretion	Small	Extensive
Authority levels	Many	Few
Administrative components	Large	Small
Specialization	Depth	Breadth
Communication	Minimal	Extensive

Source: Pennings (2002: 6)

386

differentiated and less integrated. Hage and Aiken (1970) found a strong association between environmental uncertainty and participation in decision-making. Chandler (1962) found that market diversification leads to divisionalized forms of organizations. And Child (1972) confirmed that firms operating in more hostile environments adopted more centralized and tightly controlled organizational structures.

> Better-performing organizations under uncertainty are highly differentiated as well as integrated while similar organizations in stable conditions are less differentiated and less integrated.

Technology

Technology refers to the methods of production adopted by firms. This was considered to be a contingency in a classic study by Woodward (1965). She classified technology into three major types: small-batch and unit production; large-batch and mass production; and process production. Based on this classification, she explained how different technologies can produce different organizational systems. For example, the first type is usually aimed at customized production where there are special orders from special customers. Production runs are short, and the units of production are normally small. The second type, in contrast, aims at gaining economies of scale by producing similar types of product in large numbers. This dichotomy led Woodward to identify some implications for organizational functions because the degree of production complexity had some links with the degree of controllability of production process.

Small-batch/unit-production methods required closer attention to changes, as different batches were associated with different product functionalities. Thus, the degree of controllability was not so straightforward, and it was difficult to predict the outcome of the behaviour of the production process. In contrast, in large-batch/mass-production methods, controllability and predictability were less complex, so they became standardized and formal. Consequently, organizational features such as the span of control, the nature of supervision, and the ratio of management to workforce became compatible with production methods. Woodward found that firms adopting similar production methods developed similar organizational features, and vice versa.

> In small-batch/unit-production methods, the degree of controllability is not straightforward and it is difficult to predict the outcome of the behaviour of the production process. In large-batch/mass-production methods, controllability and predictability are less complex so that they become standardized and formal.

The study by Woodward had more lessons for organizational systems. When the organizations are usually bureaucratic and formal there is little opportunity to engage in small-batch/unit production. These organizations are less innovative, so different customer requirements cannot be met. Instead, their main organizational issue is to manage administrative issues associated with the management and continuity of large-scale production. If this cannot be achieved then there is an issue of gaining advantage from economies of scale. When organizations are inclined to be less bureaucratic they can exploit the opportunity of producing small units in small batches. Rather than gaining advantage from economies of scale, they would gain economies of scope in which they serve multiple customers with multiple product functionalities. As there are not many repetitive processes, the processes are less vulnerable to standardization and formalization. One important lesson of the Woodward study for managers was that most successful firms developed their structures according to the nature of production methods. To put it another way, if the firm failed to match its technology with its structure, it could not succeed as a sustained organization.

> Bureaucratic organizations are less innovative, so different customer requirements cannot be met.

> When a firm fails to match its technology with its structure, it does not succeed as a sustained organization.

Following the work of Woodward, Perrow (1967) sought to categorize technology as routine, technical-professional, craft and non-routine. He found that these types of technologies drive firms to design appropriate organizational structures. It was suggested that, in craft and non-routine technologies, the organizational processes are organized through 'unanalysable search processes' while, in routine and technical-professional technologies, they are organized through 'analysable search processes'. The lesson here is that the more the technologies become routine and professional, the more the structures become formal and understandable, and vice versa.

> In craft and non-routine technologies, the organizational processes are organized through 'unanalysable search processes' while, in routine and technical-professional technologies, they are organized through 'analysable search processes'.

Despite the above studies being subject to substantive debate (e.g., Harvey, 1968; Child, 1972) and criticism (e.g., Pennings, 2002; Wood, 1979), contingency theorists have not underestimated the impact of technology on the design of organizational structures. Subsequently, business managers did not neglect the fact that changes in technology must follow suitable changes in organizational structures and underlying control mechanisms. In brief, complex technology requires simple and informal control mechanisms, and standardized technology (routine and professional) requires more complex control mechanisms.

> Complex technology requires simple and informal control mechanisms, and standardized technology (routine and professional) requires more complex control mechanisms.

Size

Since the 1960s, size has also been an important element in understanding the nature of organizational structures. The study by Pugh *et al.* (1969) is a notable one. They found that there is a clear association between the size of a firm (e.g., in terms of number of employees or the value of assets) and its structure. In particular, they concluded that large firms had much specialization, standardization, formalization, etc. This corroborates with the Weberian theory that bureaucracy is a feature of large organizations. In contrast, in small organizations, the above features are less important, so they are less likely to be highly structured and bureaucratic. This implies that size can create suitable management systems. In other words, if the managers do not attend to the size matter adequately, then there will emerge inappropriate systems which create more managerial and control issues.

> Large firms have much specialization, standardization, formalization, etc., but in small organizations, these features are less important.

Having found that size is an important contingency, some have come to conclude that it is more significant than other factors, such as technology. For example, Khandwalla (1974) and Hall (1977) argued that size is a key factor in the determination of the nature of control systems and organizational structures. According to their findings, we can discern that, when firms develop from small to large scale, there is a need for gradual introduction of formal procedures and standards, together with professional staff. Complex organizational and control issues emerge in such later development stages. As issues are related to size, managers tend to de-size firms by adopting a variety of strategies. A notable one is decentralization.

> When firms develop from small to large scale, there is a need for gradual introduction of formal procedures and standards, together with professional staff.

Structure

Structure refers to the establishment of certain relationships between people with specified goals and tasks. We have considered the phenomenon of structure in Chapter 10 when we discussed emerging managerial writings on the concerns of bureaucratic structures. There we focused on the change of structures from a more bureaucratic orientation to a more flexible orientation. We want to reiterate that here to emphasize structure as a contingent factor as well. In Chapter 10, we drew from Mintzberg (1987), who argued that the nature of structural devices is a determinant of certain contingencies. Structural devices here include span of control, forms of decentralization, degree of job enlargement, extent of formalization and so on. Mintzberg showed that these features developed in response to contingencies such as size, technology, environmental complexity, etc.

KEY TERMS

Structure refers to the establishment of certain relationships between people with specified goals and tasks.

What we learn from this is that management control systems cannot be designed without considering one best-fit structure. Poorly fitting structure can be nothing else but a waste of resources, and leads to the ultimate collapse of the business the organization aimed to set up. Thus, as we showed in Chapter 10, Mintzberg suggested several types of structure, of which one can be chosen as appropriate. They are: simple structure, machine bureaucracy, professional bureaucracy, divisionalized form and adhocracy. Some of these structures, such as machine bureaucracy and professional bureaucracy, are more formal and more bureaucratic, while the others are less formal and less bureaucratic. If an organization adopts one of these, we can analyse if their choice is sensible. In designing a control system, the choice of a sensible structure can bring organizational effectiveness. Contingency theory, it is argued, can test this sensibility.

Poorly fitting structure can be nothing else but a waste of resources, and leads to the ultimate collapse of the business the organization aimed to set up.

We have so far considered four main contingencies: environment, technology, size and structure. These contingencies were regarded as the main ones, but later researchers used the contingency theory approach to discover more. For example, factors such as strategy, ownership, age and power relations have also been considered as important contingencies (see Ezzamel and Hart, 1987). Also, a fruitful debate has emerged to argue which contingency is most important (see Clegg *et al.*, 2005). Both early studies and subsequent debates led accounting researchers to discover the contingency theory of management accounting, which is still in use as a popular theoretical framework for understanding management accounting change from mechanistic to post-mechanistic approaches. We will discuss this development in the next section.

IN MANAGEMENT ACCOUNTING: MODELLING AND REVIEWING OF CONTINGENCIES

We have already seen that the existence and development of management control systems are contingent upon various contingent factors. In Figure 12.1 above, we showed this relationship in relation to general organizational systems. Following this general articulation, several attempts were made to propose a contingency theory of management accounting. Two seminal models are by Gordon and Miller (1976) and Otley (1980, 1994). In this section, we will elaborate on and discuss the properties of these models as a contingency theory perspective on understanding management accounting system design.

Normative modelling: Gordon and Miller (1976)

Gordon and Miller's (1976) modelling of contingency theory from an accounting perspective was influenced by early organizational and accounting studies. Among others, these include Burns and Stalker (1961), Woodward (1965), Perrow (1970), Khandwalla (1972), Bruns and Waterhouse (1975) and Waterhouse and Tiessen (1978). Gordon and Miller's framework encompasses four variables: environment, organization, decision-making style and accounting information system (AIS). They articulated that while AIS and organization interact with each other, environment affects organization, accounting information system and decision-making style, and organization affects decision-making style. Even though there can be effects of decision-making style on organization and AIS, Gordon and Miller did not make an attempt to elaborate. In brief, their perspective is that the designing of AIS is contingent upon three variables: environment, organization and decision-making style. In order to substantiate the contingent effects of these variables, several characteristics of AIS have been pinpointed: information load, centralization reporting, cost allocation methods, frequency of reporting, method of reporting, time element of information, performance evaluation, measurements of events and valuation methods. Also, they defined environment in terms of three key dimensions: dynamism, heterogeneity and hostility.

> The designing of AIS is contingent upon three variables: environment, organization and decision-making style.

Following the usual characteristics of environmental dynamism, such as changing nature of consumer demands, rapidly changing technologies, etc., Gordon and Miller developed certain hypotheses. By reviewing these hypotheses, what we learn is that a contingency perspective can lead us to develop certain practical guides for managerial purposes and for theoretical guides for further studies. Drawing on Gordon and Miller, some of these hypotheses are summarized below:

> Contingency perspective can lead us to develop certain practical guides for managerial purposes and for theoretical guides for further studies.

1. The more environmental dynamism, the more frequent and wide-ranging is the information processing that is required.
2. High environmental heterogeneity, characterized by environmental diversity in terms of

391

consumer characteristics, production technologies, etc., would enhance the effectiveness of AIS if such systems could respond to those environmental diversities.

3. In respect of environmental hostility, managers may tend to engage in frequent information processing to combat dangers, and employ somewhat sophisticated cost accounting and control systems.

4. With environmental dynamism, heterogeneity and hostility, organizations would develop decentralized and divisionalized structures and adopt sophisticated and frequent information processing.

5. When the organizations have different sub-units, AIS would provide information suitable for their specific needs.

6. When sub-unit differentiation is present, there is a need for integration, and AIS would provide information for an integrative mechanism: for example, better co-ordination through a proper budgetary control system.

7. When the organizations are highly bureaucratic, AIS would provide information for the needs of hierarchical authorities.

8. When some resources have been abandoned or are not fully utilized, AIS would provide information for creating avenues for using them effectively.

9. Concerning decision-time horizon, AIS would provide information for multiple periods, including long-term ones.

Having developed such hypotheses, Gordon and Miller argue that contingency theory of management accounting can widen the scope of AIS design by taking an inflexible rather than a narrow view of information processing.

Constructive comments and a linear model: Otley (1980)

Otley's (1980) contribution is an encouragement for management accounting researchers. While appreciating the importance of this perspective, he expresses some concerns about the insufficient articulation of theoretical models. Despite our previous presentation of classical management and organization studies on basic contingent factors and their interrelationships, Otley has added some explicit accounting studies on technology, structure and environment. He has then undertaken a critical evaluation of some theoretical modelling of contingency theories of management accounting. This overall review has led him to present his own model. We shall briefly consider these accounts.

Regarding the effect of technology, Otley argues that production method must have an effect on the manner in which accounting information is provided. Drawing on the work of Piper (1978), he shows that the complexity of existing tasks is an essential determinant of the financial control system of an organization. Moreover, he draws from Daft and Macintosh (1978) and points out that 'task variety and task knowledge' in a particular production technology are unavoidable factors affecting the design of accounting information systems. Regarding the effect of organizational structure, Otley reveals a classic debate between himself (Otley, 1978) and Hopwood (1972). According to Hopwood, organizational structures affect how budgets are used. For example, when they are more profit conscious, budgets are used to maximize profits rather than merely adhering to budgetary controls. What was inferred here was that more flexible use of budgets can lead to better performance. However, according to Otley (1978), rigid use of budgets can also lead to better performance. Despite the argument, Otley emphasizes that the existence of accounting information systems such as budgeting depends on the nature of organizational structures.

Finally, regarding the effect of environment, he draws on several accounting studies. One is Khandwalla's (1972) work which concluded that, in a more competitive environment, AIS became more sophisticated. The other is his own 1978 study which concluded that budgetary information (for evaluation of unit manager's performance) can be used by senior managers differently within different (tough or liberal) operating environments.

This overall review thus shows us that contingent factors identified by classical theorists have been similarly considered by accounting researchers to form a basis for contingency theory of management accounting, as Otley shows. We will show further findings in subsequent sections where we catalogue the studies within this framework.

> Contingent factors identified by classical theorists have been considered by accounting researchers to form a basis for contingency theory of management accounting.

Having introduced the accounting perspectives on contingent variables, Otley presented his own framework. As is shown in Figure 12.2, this is a linear model incorporating four variables. Contingent variables such as environment and technology lead to the design of organizations which are characterized by a number of features, such as shape, centralization and interdependencies. Such a design then affects the type of AIS in terms of both its technical and its behavioural characteristics. Finally, the model ends up with organizational effectiveness, which can be measured in relation to organizational objectives. Having placed this model in a literature review of contingency theory studies in management accounting, Otley found that most studies inadvertently neglected the 'organizational effectiveness' variable. The exception to this is the study by Hayes (1977), which considered departmental effectiveness. Moreover, he elaborated on the model by providing explicit definitions for its variables. In particular, he emphasized that the organizational control system cannot be equated with accounting controls. Rather, it contains the total control package, which may include AIS designs, management information systems (MIS), organizational design and other organizational arrangements. Also, he argued that there can be intervening variables between the organizational control package and organizational effectiveness. Thus, the framework he proposed is a minimum one: it is a matter of continuing the empirical studies which would make the framework more meaningful.

> This is a linear model incorporating four variables: environment and technology lead to the design of organizations which affects the type of AIS. The model ends up with organizational effectiveness, which can be measured in relation to organizational objectives.

Figure 12.2 *Linear framework for AIS design*

A SMALL FLOOD OF ACCOUNTING RESEARCH

As we have already mentioned, accounting researchers followed the early propositions to explain how external environment could produce different structures and, in turn, management accounting systems. In the previous section, we showed some major studies that have been reviewed by Otley (1980) and Chenhall (2003). We show some of these studies in Table 12.2 to highlight a continuous flow of accounting research. It must be emphasized, however, that it is impossible

Table 12.2 *Accounting studies on contingency theory*

Researchers	Dominant contingencies	Conclusions
Khandwalla (1972)	Competition	Needs more sophisticated accounting information systems
Gordon and Narayanan (1984), Mia (1993), Chong and Chong (1997)	Environmental uncertainty	Needs broader scope of accounting information
Mia and Goyal (1991), Gul (1991), Gul and Chia (1994)	Environmental uncertainty	More sophisticated accounting information
Simons (1987)	Competition for product development	Needs elaborated budgets
Khandwalla (1977), Otley (1978), Merchant (1990), Chapman (1997)	Environmental hostility	Needs more sophisticated accounting information
Anderson and Lanen (1999)	Economic liberalization	Changes occurred in management control systems
Gupta and Govindarajan (1984), Gordon and Narayanan (1984), Mia (1993), Chong and Chong (1997)	Environmental uncertainty	More subjective forms of performance evaluation
Piper (1978), Daft and Macintosh (1978), Hopwood (1976), Otley (1978), Innes and Mitchell (1995)	Organizational structure	Formal structures require traditional and routine accounting information systems, as where decentralized organic structures require more broad-scope accounting systems
Porter (1985), Miles and Snow (1978)	Strategy	Strategies to cope with competition require more informal and broad-based information, and strategies to maintain cost leadership require tight controls and formal systems

to cover all pieces of research because of its breadth of coverage and continuity of effort. It is a small flood!

Environmental matters

Environmental matters were high on the agenda of accounting researchers from the early 1970s. One of the early studies is by Khandwalla (1972) who examined the relationship between management control systems and competition. This led to a number of subsequent management accounting studies. Gordon and Narayanan (1984), Mia (1993) and Chong and Chong (1997) reported on firms confronting more uncertain environments' use of broad-scope accounting information, including external-oriented qualitative. In contrast, firms operating in more stable environments use more formula-based accounting approaches, such as budget and ROI. The message here is that formula-based accounting is less useful in highly uncertain environments.

> Formula-based accounting is less useful in highly uncertain environments.

This line of research continued with Gul (1991), Mia and Goyal (1991) and Gul and Chia (1994), who found a strong association between accounting sophistication and perceived environmental uncertainty (for a review of this literature, see Tillema, 2005). Simons (1987) studied how firms competing in product development use elaborate budgeting techniques. Focusing on budgeting and performance evaluation systems, some others found how a hostile and uncertain external environment shaped accounting systems in organizations into a particular sophistication (e.g., Khandwalla, 1977; Otley, 1978; Merchant, 1990; Chapman, 1997). Concerning the liberalization of the Indian economy, Anderson and Lanen (1999) reported on the changes in management accounting practices in fourteen Indian firms. In relation to performance evaluation and environmental uncertainty, Gupta and Govindarajan (1984) found that high-performing firms operating in a high-uncertainty environment relied more on subjective forms of performance evaluation. This is comparable with the findings of Gordon and Narayanan (1984), Mia (1993) and Chong and Chong (1997), who reported that firms adopted a broad scope of accounting measurements.

> High-uncertainty environments rely more on subjective forms of performance evaluation.

Technological matters

Apart from early studies on the relationships between technology and management accounting systems (e.g., Piper, 1978; Daft and Macintosh, 1978), recently Chenhall (2003) reiterated the finding when focusing on budgeting practices. One aspect is that, when firms possess standardized and automated technology, they tend to use traditional budgeting processes and produce less slack. Moreover, their financial control systems are rather formal and traditional. These firms are usually not confronted with task uncertainties, thus budgets normally operate as a top-down system. However, the firms facing task uncertainty cannot be satisfied with such traditional procedures.

395

Instead, they rely less on standard procedures and emphasize more informal and organic practices, including participative budgeting, more personal and clan controls, and broad-scope management accounting systems. When the firms are confronted with a high level of technological interdependency, again traditional management control procedures have little support. Instead, these firms develop control practices with frequent statistical planning reports and informal co-ordination, less emphasis on budgets, more frequent interaction between subordinates and superiors, and greater use of aggregated and integrated management control systems.

> Firms possessing standardized and automated technology use traditional budgeting processes, with less slack, and formal and traditional financial control systems. Firms facing task uncertainty cannot be satisfied with such traditional procedures.

Moreover, Chenhall (2003) reviewed and developed propositions concerning the relationships between contemporary technologies and management accounting systems. In respect of the use of TQM technologies, firms tend to use broad-scope management accounting systems, including time, flexible and externally focused information. Also, these firms maintain a close relationship between advanced technologies and companion strategies, and they rely largely on non-financial performance measurement systems. When these firms use such performance measures, they perform well, as they relate them to reward and compensation schemes. Similarly, firms adopting JIT and FMS technologies follow similar control systems characterised by informal control and non-financial performance measures. Also, firms developing supply chains greatly rely on non-financial performance measures, informal meetings and interactions.

> Firms tend to use broad-scope management accounting systems, including time, flexible and externally focused information.

Structural matters

Through the Otley (1980) review, structure was considered in the context of the debate between Hopwood (1972) and Otley (1978). Chenhall (2003) extended this review by including more accounting studies on structure. With the definition that structure is an organizational mechanism that specifies tasks and roles of organizational members for achieving predetermined goals and objectives, Chenhall reviewed more studies and concluded with a set of propositions. In this, two types of management control system associated with two structural types were highlighted.

KEY TERMS

> Structure is an organizational mechanism that specifies tasks and roles of organizational members for achieving predetermined goals and objectives.

One structural type comes from large organizations with sophisticated technologies. The proposition about the types of management control system in this context is that they are largely formal and traditional: for example, traditional budgeting and formal communication (see Innes and Mitchell, 1995). However, when such management control systems come to serve more decentralized structures, they become more integrated and aggregated. Indeed, conventional management accounting emerged and was sustained within these large organizational structures, and budgets and formal co-ordination mechanisms became much more prevalent.

> With formal structures in large organizations with sophisticated technologies, management control systems are largely formal and traditional: for example, traditional budgeting and formal communication.

The second type is the structure developed from new forms of organization, where flexibility and informality are held in high regard. These structures developed teams, decentralized units and organic features. Management control systems associated with these structures follow a broad-scope approach. Their orientation is informal and participative, and their performance measures are team-based and collectivized. Since these structures rely more on interdependency, they cannot be successful if they adopt formal and traditional accounting measures, such as rigid budget constraint styles (see Hopwood, 1976; Otley, 1978). The bottom-line message is that emerging, new organizational forms require more informal and team-based management accounting systems, as opposed to traditional, formal ones.

> In informal and participative structures, where performance measures are team-based and collectivized, there are broad-scope management control systems.

Strategic matters

The relationship between strategy and the design of management control systems was also studied within the vogue of contingency theory. Porter's (1985) prescriptions of two strategies, namely 'low cost' and 'product differentiation', formed a contingency theory explanation. That said, the firms adopting low-cost strategies require management control systems characterized by intense supervision, tight cost control, frequent and detailed control reports, together with a formally structured organization. In contrast, firms choosing product differentiation strategies tend to develop a control system with strong co-ordination between functional areas and subjective performance measurement and incentives. Moreover, their control systems must be developed as integrated and timely information systems for operational purposes. Thus, the firms must understand that alternative strategies require appropriate management control systems if they want to succeed in a competitive environment.

Another well-known dichotomy of strategy is found in the 'defender' and 'prospector' strategies of Miles and Snow (1978). Firms tend to adopt the former strategy when they operate in a

397

Firms adopting low-cost strategies require intense supervision, tight cost control, frequent and detailed control reports, together with a formally structured organization.

Firms choosing product differentiation strategy rely more on strong co-ordination between functional areas and subjective performance measurement and incentives, together with integrated and timely information.

more stable market with limited product lines and routine technologies. Such firms' control systems are highly structured and formalized, together with leadership in cost, quality and service. Firms adopting the prospector strategy are more innovative and explorative. Rather than relying on structured and formal control systems, these firms use more subjective, broad-based information with ingredients of both financial and non-financial data. Again we have a general message here: when the strategy is aimed at coping with more competitive pressures, the management accounting system becomes broad in terms of combining financial analyses with non-financial analyses which incorporate both external and future-oriented data.

Firms adopting a defender strategy and operating in a stable market have highly structured and formalized control systems, together with leadership in cost, quality and service.

Firms adopting the prospector strategy are more innovative and explorative, and they use more subjective, broad-based information, with ingredients of both financial and non-financial data.

IS CONTINGENCY THEORY A PANACEA FOR ACCOUNTING RESEARCH?

Despite its outbreak of research and continuous attraction, the contingency theory of management accounting, critics argue, suffers from a number of deficiencies. These criticisms are useful because they could lead to this perspective being employed more sensibly and meaningfully. We will consider the criticisms in two categories: conceptual and methodological.

Conceptual deficiencies

On the development of contingency theory of management accounting, several conceptual deficiencies have been identified (Otley, 1980; Chenhall, 2003). First, most studies were limited by few general contingencies, such as environment, structure, technology, etc. Rather than exploring new contingencies and broadening our understanding of the practices of management accounting, the studies tended to replicate what organizational theorists found in the 1960s and 1970s. While we can agree that these variables are inevitable and obvious, there should be an avenue for refining them into more focused and meaningful ones. Because of this lack of conceptual refinement, any study on environment or technology, for instance, is regarded as a contingency theory study. This has limited the scope of the contingency perspective as a broader means of learning management accounting practices.

> Most studies were limited by few general contingencies, such as environment, structure, technology, etc.

Second, and related to the above deficiency, is the lack of clarity in the definitions of variables. Loosely defined variables led researchers to replicate what seminal writers found, rather than making a real contribution to knowledge. For example, most of these studies did not contextually define what 'environment' is: for most of the researchers, environment is simply about competition and market stability. Researchers inadvertently neglected an important environmental aspect of how broader socio-economic and institutional contexts shape accounting systems in organizations (for critical evaluations, see Otley, 1980; Hopper and Powell, 1985). Given that most contingencies have different connotations, proper conceptual developments are needed to test the relationships and produce exciting results.

> Contingency variables are loosely defined, leading researchers to replicate what seminal writers found, rather than making a real contribution to knowledge.

Third, there is an issue about the definition of the term 'management control systems'. As Chenhall (2003) commented, several terms, such as management accounting (MA), management accounting systems (MAS), management control systems (MCS), accounting information systems (AIS), etc., have been used interchangeably. Despite some differences between these terms, one of the aspects the researchers have neglected is the evolution of the meaning of 'management accounting and control systems'. Within a mechanistic form, management accounting provided formal routine information through traditional techniques, such as budgeting and costing. However, with the change of these systems into a post-mechanistic form, management accounting's role has shifted into a regime of providing more informal and non-financial information, together with team-based co-ordination mechanisms. Nevertheless, contingency theory of management accounting, to a large extent, still focuses on traditional accounting tools such as budgeting, rather than on emerging techniques, such ABC and the BSC.

Fourth, as Otley (1980) showed, most studies have not properly linked contingent explanations to organizational effectiveness. As the ultimate aim of any organizational function is to achieve organizational effectiveness, the test of relationships between contingencies and management accounting systems must have implications for the degree of achievement of organizational

> Several terms, such as management accounting (MA), management accounting systems (MAS), management control systems (MCS), accounting information systems (AIS), etc., are used interchangeably.

effectiveness. As we showed earlier, Otley considered organizational effectiveness to be measured in terms of organizational objectives. Accordingly, one can explore how different accounting information systems which are affected by certain contingencies could contribute differently to achieve organizational effectiveness. However, researchers have overlooked this opportunity to explain those relationships and implications.

> Most studies have not properly linked contingent explanations to organizational effectiveness.

Finally, the overall theoretical frameworks developed by accounting researchers have suffered from serious limitations. They were non-theoretical, in the sense that the relationships have not been explained in theoretical terms. Instead, they presented frameworks as sets of mere relationships supported by statistical significances. For example, 'why' questions – such as 'Why do large organizations need formal accounting?' and 'Why do informal accounting systems operate in organic settings?' – cannot be properly answered unless they can be justified through economic or social theoretical explanations. Sometimes, the answers to these questions can be context-specific, which can be explained in a social or cultural theory. Contingency theorists have not gone that far to develop a proper framework. Instead, the models have become much more hypothetical and abstract, and have been developed through 'armchair' research (Otley, 1980).

> The frameworks were non-theoretical in the sense that the relationships have not been explained in theoretical terms.

Methodological deficiencies

This line of research also suffers from certain methodological problems. First, as several reviews have underlined (Otley, 1980; Hopper and Powell, 1985; Chenhall, 2003), a pervasive criticism is that cross-sectional analysis based on survey methods did not produce a deeper understanding of how organizations and their accounting systems react to contingencies. The fundamental assumption behind this methodological tradition is that 'objective' data collected through questionnaires can construct the organizational reality. But this cannot be the case in practice because fully structured questions in them can limit the respondent's ability to express fully what is actually the case. Researchers are usually unaware of full responses, as the questionnaires are traditionally administered by post. Thus, these surveys can create a distance between the knowledge of practices and the data being collected.

 400

The predominant survey methods did not produce a deeper understanding of how organizations and their accounting systems react to contingencies.

Second, the collected data are analysed through cross-sectional methods of analysis. These methods merely test the relationship between dependent (accounting information system) and independent (contingency) variables. Other than discovering whether the relationship is statistically significant or not, nothing can be explained. The only methodological advantage is to test predetermined hypotheses. Again, there are problems with hypothesis-testing procedures. Hypotheses come from previous studies or from further normative judgements. They cannot discover anything. Instead, they learn whether the hypotheses are true or false. This limits our opportunity to explore novel scenarios concerning the functions of management accounting systems and their underlying influential factors.

Other than discovering whether a relationship is statistically significant or not, the method of cross-sectional data analysis can explain nothing.

Third, and related to the second deficiency, contingency theorists in accounting look for linear relationships between contingencies and accounting information systems. Most models, such as Gordon and Miller's (1976) or Otley's (1980), assumed that relationships will always be linear and unidirectional. This may not be true. For example, while technology can affect the functioning of accounting, accounting can explore better technologies through calculations and analyses (Hopwood and Miller, 1994). Also, accounting can influence structures by guiding the formulation of programmes of downsizing (Otley, 1994). Hence, in most cases, relationships can be multi-directional and complex because of the interdependency of variables, and not only prescribed variables but also a variety of intervening variables that create more complexities about the ways in which accounting systems function. Contingency theorists underscored this practical reality.

Researchers look for linear and unidirectional relationships which might not be the case in practice.

Fourth, these studies directly or indirectly provide prescriptions for managerial practices, assuming that hypothesis testing and cross-sectional data analysis are functionally useful for everyday practice (Hopper and Powell, 1985). This is dangerous. On the one hand, the findings cannot be generalized to every situation, although these researchers seem to argue that they are generalizable. On the other hand, prescriptive implications of those findings cannot be applied without a proper consideration of other factors, such as contextual matters including culture,

401

politics, social values, etc. Indeed, the purpose of research is not to guide practice so directly, even though it can have long-term influence.

> Studies provided prescriptions for managerial practice, assuming that hypothesis testing and cross-sectional data analysis are functionally useful for everyday practice, which is dangerous.

Finally, despite the recent reviews (e.g., Chapman, 1997; Chenhall, 2003), the results of contingency theory are still fragmentary and contradictory. One of the general problems is that researchers have failed to link their findings to previous accounting studies. Knowledge cannot develop without systematic cataloguing of previous findings. In such a process, continuous debates and conclusions have to be conducted and reached for further research, further debates and more proper conclusions to be possible. However, this cannot be achieved unless the research programme in question is governed by a particularly rich theoretical framework. Unfortunately, contingency theory's theoretical framework is armchair-based. Chapman (1997: 189) summarized this problem as follows: 'reviews are largely negative . . . proclaiming the lack of an overall framework for analysis of the relationship between contingent factors and accounting, leaving no obvious starting point for an explanation of an interesting body of often contradictory results'. The message is that lack of proper framework leads to fruitless conclusions and contributions.

> The results of contingency theory are still fragmentary and contradictory.

CONTINGENCY THEORY REVISITED

The contingency theory of management accounting has been revisited, and two important contributions have been made as a result. One is theoretical, the other methodological. In their theoretical stance, some researchers have now begun to provide explanations of the relationships between contingencies and accounting systems. In the methodological stance, a trend is emerging to conduct case studies. In understanding management accounting change from mechanistic to post-mechanistic forms, this development in contingency theory has given us new insights. This section underlines the two stances.

> Revisiting the contingency theory of management accounting has made two important contributions.

Theoretical developments

Otley (1980) observed that contingency theory has evolved without a coherent theoretical framework. In other words, there are no explicit explanations as to why, for example, environmental uncertainties demand more advanced management accounting systems. Contingency theory research has demonstrated the relationships in statistical terms only to describe it rather than to explain it theoretically. We have chosen two theoretical developments: Tiessen and Waterhouse's (1983) application of agency theory to contingent explanations, and the Evans *et al.* (1986) economic modelling of contingency theory. In general, these represent a 'marriage' of organization theory with economic theories, and an extension of the scope of contingency theory.

Having reviewed the economic frameworks of agency theory and markets and hierarchies, Tiessen and Waterhouse (1983) developed a descriptive framework of management accounting. Their fundamental assertion was that, as both agency theory and markets and hierarchies are concerned with information, structures and control, contingency theory can be enriched by combining the three approaches. They identified that ex ante uncertainty is a common variable for all three sets of literature. There are two extreme cases of this uncertainty. One is that, when the ex ante uncertainty is very low, then, on the one hand, there should be plentiful information being symmetrically distributed and, on the other hand, contractual agreements among the organizational members are clearly written. This should give rise to a more structured organizational setting where controls through procedures such as budgets, supervision and standard cost systems can be clearly specified and implemented. Here, the control system constitutes a set of contractual arrangements. The role of accounting information in such a system is to specify the financial and non-financial compensation for managers. The existence of such a system offers cost-saving advantages. This explains why management accounting systems exist within a structured organizational setting together with routine technologies. In contrast, at the other extremity, when ex ante information is not clear, contracts cannot be so specific. Under such circumstances, contracting procedures might be complex and unpredictable. However, accounting can play a constitutional role here to establish a high degree of co-operation and control.

As both agency theory and markets and hierarchies are concerned with information, structures and control, contingency theory can be enriched by combining the three approaches.

Under low ex ante uncertainty, there can be a more structured organizational setting where controls through procedures such as budgets, supervision and standard cost systems can be clearly specified and implemented; but under high ex ante uncertainty, systems become complicated and costly.

In both cases, the role of ex post information is to assist in determining whether specified contracts have been fulfilled. When uncertainty is very low, the role of ex post information is clear, in that information can compare the outcomes with the expected results. However, when uncertainty is very high, for ex post information to play an effective role, accounting measurement procedures have to be well documented and specific. As Tiessen and Waterhouse concluded, this economic explanation for the existence of accounting systems is somewhat paradoxical when we compare it with some previous contingency theory studies (e.g., Gordon and Narayanan, 1984). Previous accounting studies had pointed out that, in situations of high uncertainty, the accounting system would provide broad-scope, unspecific information, including non-financial. However, despite this paradoxical conclusion, overall Tiessen and Waterhouse's model explains why responsibility accounting systems still exist, even though changes are occurring, and environmental uncertainties are growing and becoming increasingly complex.

> Even when uncertainty is high, for ex post information to play a constitutional role, accounting measurement procedures must be well documented and specific.

Evans *et al.* (1986) made a similar theoretical contribution. Again drawing on information economics and agency theory, they observed that there is a relationship between environmental uncertainty and the nature of control systems. To explain this relationship, they used two analytical models: a planning model and an auditing model. In the first model, the role of the accounting control system is to provide information as to whether the future environment is favourable, unfavourable or neutral. Production planning will be more accurate if the accounting control system provides more accurate information. If this happens, the firm can earn more profit by producing the right amount for the market with no waste or loss. For this to happen, there should be an effective accounting control system which can only be developed by investing more in it. Informed by such an effective system, managers and owners, for instance, can reduce unit production cost by planning to produce more under favourable environmental conditions, and vice versa. However, the owner cannot develop an information system by investing as much as he/she wants, because it is costly. Thus, the owner has the freedom to trade-off between the quality of information system and its costs. To put it another way, individual economic behaviour can be a device that explains the relationship between the nature of control systems and the environment.

> In the planning model, the role of the accounting control system is to provide information as to whether the future environment is favourable, unfavourable or neutral. Systems, managers and owners can reduce unit production cost by planning to produce more under favourable environmental conditions, and vice versa.

In the auditing model, Evans *et al.* added two assumptions to the above analysis: the manager can discover in advance the actual environmental conditions; and the owner cannot know the efforts of the manager. Under such circumstances, the owner has little chance to gain knowledge of the actual behaviour of the manager because the manager can manipulate information. Consequently, production decisions have to be made based on the manager's report rather than on reports produced by the control system. Thus, on the part of owners and top managers, the control system takes the form of an audit function concerning the manager's report on product environment. As long as the owners and top managers cannot monitor production inputs directly, the resultant control system is full of alternative means of controls, such as budgets, internal audits, incentive plans, etc. When the production/operation manager has the above opportunity, s/he behaves in such a manner as not to reveal true information, hoping to get the maximum compensation from the owners. Like Tiessen and Waterhouse's model, this model offers an economic explanation as to why control systems operate in this way in conditions of environmental uncertainty.

> In the auditing model, the manager can discover in advance the actual environmental conditions, and the owner cannot know the efforts of the manager. Systems take the form of an audit function full of alternative means of control, such as budgets, internal audits, incentive plans, etc.

A methodological breakthrough

When we looked at the methodological deficiencies of contingency theory, we saw that administration questionnaires and cross-sectional data analyses do not collect substantively rich accounts which can offer a proper understanding of underlying organizational and social realities about the functioning of management control systems. Researchers have called for more detailed and in-depth studies to eliminate this methodological problem (Hopper and Powell, 1985; Hopper *et al.*, 1995). Responding to these calls, some researchers conducted case studies and provided contingency theory explanations. They include Roberts (1990), Knights and Willmott (1993) and Tillema (2005). Below is a brief introduction to their studies.

> Researchers have called for more detailed and in-depth studies to eliminate this methodological problem.

- Roberts (1990) reported that accounting controls in a UK conglomerate created conflicts against the successful implementation of new strategy, and described how non-accounting controls such as managerial conferences can resolve such issues. This confirms that there would not be strategic responses to external uncertainty, because of the persistent accounting control systems and managerial prerogatives.
- Archer and Otley (1991) offered a detailed description of how an agricultural manufacturing company reacted to a declining industry by reproducing the persistent strategy, which was supported by formal and informal controls, as well as managers' perception. This is a detailed description of the relationship between strategy and a management control system.
- By focusing on its implementation of a new expenses control system, Knights and Willmott (1993) graphically contextualized a UK insurance company. This emphasized how external competitive pressures have undermined a particular paternalism prevailing in both the industry and the firm. More specifically, the internal change in the managerial philosophy pointed to a broader political ('a shift to the right') and economic transformation ('a restoration of market principles') of the external environment.
- Tillema (2005) undertook a comparative case study to identify several contingency factors for the sophistication of accounting instruments. Findings emphasized that several conditions determine whether a firm needs average or broad-scope accounting instruments.

405

These types of study are now generating a post-contingency theory by minimizing the method-ological deficiencies of orthodox theory. Methodologically, they offer some common procedures to follow:

■ Focus on a single firm and study the historical development of the control system alongside the external factors.

■ Rely on in-depth interviews rather than questionnaire-based survey methods so that the researcher may become more familiar with events and scenarios.

■ Use accessible documentation for validating the data collected through in-depth interviews.

■ Follow up interviews and documents to improve the reliability of the data and to increase their validity.

■ Write a 'story' combining important events and scenarios into a set of logical and meaningful relationships which can be linked to contingency theory explanations.

■ Assume that the case in question is unique, so that findings cannot be generalized to other firms.

■ Encourage further case studies to replicate the same findings or to compare and contrast with previous ones.

SUMMING UP

Despite the development of multiple theoretical frameworks of management accounting research, which we will explore in the following chapters, contingency theory persists as a popular research tradition. Unlike other frameworks, it plays a dual role: academic and managerial. Playing an academic role, researchers contribute to the literature and enhance our understanding of the relationships between various contingencies and management accounting systems. Even though this effort has not created an interesting debate, research continues to produce voluminous papers. A recent review of such studies is the paper by Chenhall (2003), which presents a list of existing references. The first issue of the first volume of *Accounting, Organizations and Society* published the paper by Gordon and Miller (1976), and publication of these papers continues.

Even explicitly, playing a managerial role, the contingency theory of management accounting teased out two broader MAS types. In the first, under certain environmental conditions and with routine technologies and organizational structures, the systems are still traditional and formal. These systems reproduce the conventional wisdom of management accounting by appreciating the roles of responsibility accounting, budgetary control systems, standard costing methods, formal top-down reporting, etc. In the second type, under uncertain environmental conditions with flexible technologies and organization structures, MAS take a broad-scope form. Unlike the first type, these systems tend to discontinue the use of traditional management accounting and incor-porate non-financial information and performance measures, including ABC/M and the BSC. Also, management accountants in such firms have become internal consultants working with other managerial teams.

HAVE YOU UNDERSTOOD THE CHAPTER?

1. Why can business organizations not avoid contingencies?
2. How would you define contingency theory as a perspective for accounting studies?
3. According to classical organization theory, what are the fundamental propositions about the relationship between an organization and (1) environment, (2) technology and (3) structure?

4. In Gordon and Miller's (1976) terms, what is the contingency theory of AIS?
5. As Otley (1980) showed, what is the missing element in most contingency theory studies of management accounting? What is Otley's proposal?
6. Under what circumstances may a firm adopt formal and traditional accounting information systems?
7. Why do firms want to incorporate more non-financial and external-oriented information in their information systems?
8. What are the conceptual problems of the contingency theory of management accounting?
9. What are the methodological limitations in this research programme?
10. How has contingency theory now been revisited?

BEYOND THE CHAPTER

1. Why did contingency theory of management accounting emerge?
2. Why did the research programme of the contingency theory of management accounting produce fragmentary results? How could this be resolved?
3. Why weren't the contingencies properly contextualized?
4. Can revisiting this programme eliminate its functionalist orientation?
5. Why is the case study approach more relevant for some contingent studies?

FURTHER READING

1. For a broader understanding of contingent factors in classical organization theory, see Ezzamel and Hart (1987: ch. 1).
2. For start-up concepts of the contingency theory of management accounting, see Gordon and Miller (1976) and Otley (1980).
3. For a recent comprehensive review of this research programme, see Langfield-Smith (1997) and Chenhall (2003).
4. For a case study in this research tradition, see Knights and Willmott (1993).

Part IV

Interpretive and critical perspectives on management accounting change

Chapter 13

Towards interpretations, institutions and networks in management accounting

A STARTING POINT: A BEGINNING OF THE END

The decade of the 1980s was a 'beginning of the end' in the domination of mainstream accounting research. One salient, historical incident was the launching of *Accounting, Organizations and Society* in 1976. In the inaugural editorial, Anthony Hopwood, the journal's editor, embarked on a new agenda of accounting research. He pointed to the importance of accounting: 'terminology and underlying calculus of "profits" and "costs" continue to exert a profound impact on human consciousness and action' (Hopwood, 1976: 1). Also, he distinguished the conventional view of accounting from the view that we should see the actual functioning of accounting: 'accounting has been seen as a rather static and purely technical phenomenon . . . The purposes, processes and techniques of accounting, its human, organizational and social roles, and the way in which . . . information is used . . . have never been static' (ibid.).

Having underlined a duality associated with the functioning of accounting, he said: 'Not only can it assist the processes and techniques of accounting to respond more rapidly to emerging economic, social and organizational circumstances, but also the resultant changes in accounting can often help to further the underlying changes' (ibid.: 2).

With regard to explaining these complex relations of accounting, Hopwood pointed out the limited current knowledge of accountants and researchers: 'The behavioural and social sciences . . . were less familiar to most accountants in terms of both the body of knowledge and the underlying values. And the integration of accounting and social perspectives was a very different endeavour from the integration of finance and accounting' (ibid.: 3). So, Hopwood called for a new research agenda: 'There is now an urgent need for research . . . for seeing accounting as both a social and organizational phenomenon . . . Even what might be the quite significant ritualistic role of many accounting systems needs to be recognized . . . [O]pportunity should be taken to move beyond static forms of analysis to study the complexities of . . . [the] dynamic process of accounting' (ibid.).

SETTING THE SCENE

The starting point for this chapter has shown you that a new agenda for accounting research emerged in the late 1970s. The 1980s was then a wonderful era which pursued this agenda by furthering novel perspectives, issues and methodologies. On the one hand, this programme developed concerns about the ways in which conventional accounting research was dominated by economic and contingency theory-based perspectives; and, on the other hand, it proposed alternatives, among which were interpretive and critical perspectives which articulated a vibrant research programme in contemporary accounting research. This chapter covers the relevant material on the interpretive perspective, and the next will deal with the critical perspective.

Both perspectives shared common criticisms of conventional research in (management) accounting. Concerning their understanding about how we conceive of the (social) world, and how we learn about that world, conventional, economic and contingency theory-based research perspectives were subject to severe criticisms. For conventional researchers, management accounting was seen as static and technical, functional to organizational effectiveness. Moreover, for them, management accounting had (universal) solutions, and the role of researchers was to look for problems waiting to be resolved. In contrast, alternative perspectives offered different viewpoints, from which accounting has to be seen as a dynamic and social institution, subject to changes under historical circumstances, and socially constructed even though it seems to be technical. The primary aim of this chapter is to unfold these two contrasting perspectives of management accounting and to illuminate one of the major alternatives: interpretive sociology and its parallel developments in institutionalism and actor–network theory. The learning objectives of this chapter are reflected in this broader aim.

> For conventional researchers, management accounting was a static and technical function, it had (universal) solutions, and the role of researchers was to look for problems waiting to be resolved.

> For alternative researchers, accounting has to be seen as a dynamic and social institution subject to change under historical circumstances, and it is socially constructed even though it seems to be technical.

First, the chapter addresses the methodological and theoretical issues of the conventional perspective. One of the prevalent labels to define these issues is 'functionalism'. Thus, we will elaborate this notion of functionalism and proceed to outline the problems in relation to five subjects: context, people and organizations, controls, accounting and research. From this section, you will reflect on how to problematize the perspectives on conventional management accounting in relation to its fundamental assumptions about its existence, knowledge and methodology.

- To elaborate on the notion of functionalism as a medium for critiquing the conventional perspective
- To outline the problems in relation to five subjects: context, people and organizations, controls, accounting and research

■ To reflect on the problems of the conventional management accounting *per se*, in relation to fundamental assumptions about its existence, knowledge and methodology

Second, in the next section, by drawing on the work of interpretive sociology, we will explain how researchers have presented solutions to the problems of functionalism. The section starts with a brief introduction to interpretive sociology. This will enable us to identify the academic roots of the development of symbolic interactionism, which became a key sociological concept used in accounting studies. We will then reflect on a number of accounting studies. To summarize some of these findings, we will again look at the subjects of context, people and organizations, controls, accounting and research.

■ To introduce interpretive sociology by identifying the academic roots of symbolic interactionism
■ To reflect on a number of interpretive accounting studies in relation to context, people and organizations, controls, accounting and research

Third, we will explore how researchers have used specific theoretical perspectives in studying interpretive cases. As we will show, one such commendable project has been institutional theory built on old institutional economics and evolutionary economics. This project emerged in response to identification of a perceived gap between management accounting theory and practice. As you will see, this gap is largely due to the problems of underlying assumptions of neoclassical economic theories of management accounting models. Despite these problems, institutional theory has been introduced to explain management accounting practice, particularly changes occurring in contemporary practices. We will show how these developments have come about.

■ To explore how researchers have used specific theoretical perspectives in studying interpretive cases
■ To sketch out a perceived gap between management accounting theory and practice
■ To highlight the problems of underlying assumptions of neoclassical economic theories of management accounting models
■ To summarize institutional theory and its recent contributions to management accounting research

413

Fourth, this chapter reveals another institutional theory perspective which developed from new institutional sociology. Having highlighted the major pillars of this perspective, we will present some studies which explain how and why organizations under similar circumstances have developed similar management accounting and control systems. Also, we will reveal that there is a framework which combines the institutional theory developed from old institutional economics and evolutionary economics with new institutional sociology.

- To reveal another institutional theory perspective developed from new institutional sociology by highlighting its major pillars
- To present some studies which show how and why organizations under similar circumstances have developed similar management accounting and control systems
- To reveal a framework that combines the old institutional theory with new institutional sociology

Finally, the chapter summarizes the work of a number of researchers inspired by actor–network theory. As we will see, they have also produced interpretive case studies to illustrate how management accounting practices have come into being. We will briefly outline the properties of this theory, and the magnitude of management accounting studies which emerged to explain new practices.

- To summarize the properties of actor–network theory, which has been used to produce more interpretive case studies
- To outline the magnitude of management accounting studies which emerged to explain new practices

FUNCTIONALISM: MEANING AND PROBLEMS

Meaning

We introduced the term 'functionalism' in the previous chapter as a means to explain that management accounting systems can operate as independent and objective machines. In these machines, there are operational functions, such as planning, co-ordinating, enforcing, controlling, evaluation, etc. It is believed that, once the system has been set up, it works independently, being detached from human consciousness and organizational imperatives. When implementing such systems, even though there are problems on the part of, for instance, people and organizations, they are not the problems of the systems themselves. Rather, they are 'implementation problems'.

So, it is implied that, when implemented properly, management accounting systems can overcome those problems. Thus, it is a duty of the organizational managers to do all that is necessary to ensure the system is correctly implemented.

It is believed that, once a management accounting system has been set up, it works independently, being detached from human consciousness and organizational imperatives.

Functionalism in this case constitutes the manner in which management controls operate like a physical entity. Such control systems are usually designed with an understanding of some linear relationship between causes and effects. Consequently, systems which developed from management accounting ideals such as rational economic models, budgetary control principles and ABC should be effective if they can overcome the problems of implementation. Drawing on Burrell and Morgan (1979), Hopper and Powell (1985: 433) summarized this characteristic of functionalism as follows:

> The work [classical management theories] espouses a scientific basis to administration, based on beliefs that the organisational world possesses the characteristics of the physical one. Thus, it is claimed, administrative principles can be derived by systematic study of cause and effect relationships. The behaviour of the employee is taken to be passive and determined by managerial manipulation of situational variables.

Hopper and Powell's concern here is the functionalists' belief about the inactive role of the human element in the function or dysfunction of management accounting systems. As you have seen in the previous chapters, both economists and contingency theorists believe in such functionalist prescriptions: when organizations operate in a highly uncertain environment, accounting systems should be developed to process frequent information for detailed and complex analyses. For this to happen, on the one hand, managers will have to provide necessary technologies and facilities, and, on the other hand, both managers and employees will be trained for predetermined purposes. If this happens, the accounting system in place should be functional; that is, it should be inherently unproblematic.

KEY TERMS

Functionalism constitutes the manner in which management controls operate like a physical entity.

Systems, which developed from management accounting ideals such as rational economic models, budgetary control principles and ABC should be effective if they can overcome the problems of implementation.

415

Thus, most conventional management accounting approaches have been developed on the basis of functionalism. The approaches you have studied within both economic theories (e.g., C–V–P analysis, marginal costing and DCF techniques) and organization and control theories (e.g., budgeting, performance measures and reward systems) are largely functional. Both conventional researchers and practitioners in management accounting believe that these approaches are highly rational, so that the employees' role is to implement them under the guidance of top managers. In this situation, those techniques work like physical objects, and employees work like passive human beings. For techniques, behaviour of human beings is taken for granted; for human beings, techniques are given and problem-free. Thus, conventional textbook writers in management accounting took the necessary care to differentiate the technical side of accounting from its behavioural ramifications. They did not want to admit that the two are connected. Instead, they view the technical and behavioural aspects as two different subjects.

> Most conventional management accounting approaches have been developed on the basis of functionalism.

Functionalism is governed by the assumption of objectivity (Burrell and Morgan, 1979; Cooper, 1983; Hopper and Powell, 1985; Chua, 1986; Hopper *et al.*, 1987). Objectivity is the notion that the world is full of objects (e.g., materials and systems) independent of human behaviour. Once these objects are available for human beings to use, any interaction between those objects and human beings cannot problematize the function of the former. Consequently, objects have their own goals and meanings, and they function unproblematically. If problems do occur, they can either be technical problems of the objects or independent behavioural problems of the humans, but not problems of the interaction between the objects and human beings. By interacting with objects, it is assumed, human beings do not question the usefulness or existence of those objects. Nor do they provide different meanings or definitions and reject the objects. Management accounting provides such objects, and employees in organizations use them without any influential consciousness.

> Functionalism is governed by the assumption of objectivity, which assumes that the world is full of objects independent of human behaviour.

Moreover, as Hopper and Powell (1985) described, the functionalism in management accounting can only maintain regulations about respective practices. If accounting should be subject to formal regulations, then there are further assumptions that organizations are run with predetermined, unitary goals (e.g., profit maximization), and human beings are taken to be calculative and rational. The role of accounting is to plan and execute the behaviour of human beings in relation to the programmed organizational processes which focus on using resources effectively in a dynamic and competitive context. In these programmed processes, organizational positions are created based on goals and sub-goals, formal feedback mechanisms are in place to evaluate the performance of these positions, and rewards are offered according to such evaluation.

Changes can only be possible either in line with top managers' desires or in response to market needs. Otherwise, whole organizational processes, together with management accounting components, operate like a real physical machine.

> Functionalism in management accounting maintains regulations. Thus, organizations are run on predetermined, unitary goals, and human beings are taken to be calculative and rational. The role of accounting is to plan and execute human behaviour.

The assumptions about objectivity formed a philosophical basis for a number of researchers in management accounting who accept the existence of functionalism. These researchers tend to assume that organizations and social systems are purely objective empirical sites for collecting value-free, quantifiable data. By adopting certain research methods, the aim of the researchers is to maximize the objectivity of data and the entire research process by eliminating subjective judgements of respondents. Assuming that everybody has the same story, researchers select a sample and collect data through questionnaires, quantify the answers by adopting statistical methods, and test the relationships between independent and dependent variables. Finally, they conclude by grouping the findings into generalizable theoretical props for executing further tests. This whole process is governed by the fundamental assumption of objectivity, which is linked to the existence of functional organizations and management accounting systems.

> For functionalists, organizations and social systems are purely objective. Empirical sites such as organizations can provide us with opportunities for collecting value-free, quantifiable data.

Problems

The problem with functionalism lies in its assumptions. A number of interpretive and critical researchers in management accounting have unveiled the unrealistic nature of some of those assumptions (e.g., Tinker *et al.*, 1982; Cooper, 1983; Hopper and Powell, 1985; Chua, 1986; Hopper *et al.*, 1987). We will categorise their concerns into five subjects: context, people and organizations, controls, accounting and research.

Context

One of the problems of functionalism relates to the unproblematic treatment of wider socio-economic and political context in which organizations operate. The researchers in this camp do not envisage that the wider context can shape the organization into a different specific regime of control. Consequently, for these researchers, organizational practices such as management accounting systems are universal: irrespective of the context in which they operate, these systems should work in a similar pattern across the globe. This is unrealistic. Subsequent, researchers have found that different socio-economic and political contexts have produced different consequences of management accounting (e.g., Harrison and McKinnon, 1998; Uddin and Hopper, 2001; Wickramasinghe and Hopper, 2005). For example, Wickramasinghe and Hopper (2005) reported that the budgeting practice in a factory they studied was shaped into a particular local, cultural practice rather than an objective, rational system, because of the influence of the employees' unique behaviour. This particular behaviour is context-specific. Thus, functionalists' belief about the universal nature of management accounting is flawed.

> Functionalists do not envisage that the wider context can shape an organization into a different specific regime of control. Thus, they believe that management accounting systems are universal, so they operate in a similar pattern across the globe.

People and organizations

Another problem is related to the manner in which functionalists treat the organization. For them, the organization is a mechanistic form charged with unitary goals, rational allocation of tasks and activities, formal positions created for people, standardized procedures and systems, etc. Of course, these characteristics can be found in any organization. However, on the one hand, such systems are created by people, and for people, and, on the other hand, those systems are continuously manipulated by people for their own individual purposes rather than for achieving organizational goals. Consequently, formal and unitary organizations can be dysfunctional. Based on the findings of Selznick (1949), Gouldner (1954) and Merton (1968), Hopper and Powell (1985) argued that formal and bureaucratic organizations are dysfunctional due to the formation of individual and local goals, as opposed to organizational goals. Thus, individual consciousness rather than unitary goals shapes the functions of organizations, including their management accounting systems. However, the functionalists fail to appreciate this reality about the nature of people in organizations and the nature of organizations themselves.

> Functionalists treat the organization as a mechanistic form with unitary goals, rational allocation of tasks, formal positions and procedures, etc. In practice, such systems are created by people, and for people, and are continuously manipulated by people for their own purposes.

Controls

For functionalists, control systems are effective mechanisms to achieve organizational goals. As we explained in Chapter 5, organizational control systems aim to use resources effectively by adopting necessary mechanisms, such as budgeting. In this, controls are solutions for organizational problems. This is unrealistic. Controls themselves also create problems. Building on pluralistic ideas of management control and accounting, Hopper and Powell (1985) argued that accounting and control can be used to maintain the interests of individuals, reflecting that accounting plays a political role rather than providing legitimate solutions for organizational problems. Within a context of university budgeting, Covaleski and Dirsmith (1986) showed that budgeting played a mediatory role between the university and its higher authorities. Concerning the production planning and control system in the UK National Coal Board, Berry *et al*. (1985) reported that accounting controls created ambiguity rather than played a functional role. Moreover, Scapens and Roberts (1993) reported that, because of the new accounting control initiatives in one division of a large multidivisional company, a considerable amount of resistance developed. All this tells us that while management accounting might resolve problems, it may also create different and/or more problems.

> Functionalists believe that controls are solutions for organizational problems. This is unrealistic: they also create problems. Controls can be used to maintain the interests of individuals.

Accounting

Functionalists maintain the proposition that accounting can provide objective information for decision-making and management control. For them, as a value-free information processing system, management accounting facilitates organizational processes like a component in a physical machine. Again, as with control, this understanding of accounting is partially fictitious. Accounting would appear to be an information system functional to the organization, but it also mediates between people and their interests. Building on the labour process theory, Hopper *et al*. (1987) argued that accounting served sectional interests in the era of the development of capitalism rather than being congruent with organizational goals and objectives. Cooper (1983) observed that accounting can be a muddle rather than a force for tidiness when interacting with organizational realities such as conflicts and interests. Berry *et al*. (1985) found that physical controls rather than accounting dominated within the production culture of the National Coal Board. Thus, functionalism provides a rather narrow and unrealistic depiction of accounting by disregarding organizational and social ramifications.

> For functionalists, accounting can provide objective information. However, while accounting would appear to be an information system functional to the organization, it also mediates between people and their interests.

Research

Management accounting within a functionalist perspective assumes a given context, goal-oriented organizations, functional control systems and objective accounting roles. Consequently, problems such as contextual ramifications, organizational imperatives, dysfunctional control systems and politics of accounting were regarded as 'irrelevant and outside' subjects in a study of management accounting. Functionalists believed that, by foregrounding those subjects, value judgements would inevitably develop which may have hindered the scientific spirit of their research. However, as will

419

be seen later in this chapter, value judgements can also provide meaningful insights for understanding the practices of accounting. Referring to Max Weber (1949), Chua (1986) showed that the distinction between value and fact is itself a value judgement. Why people make value judgements, and how accounting is shaped by them, may be an interesting issue to explore, but functionalist researchers would not see it as important.

> Problems such as contextual ramifications, organizational imperatives, dysfunctional control systems and politics of accounting were regarded as 'irrelevant and outside' subjects in a study of management accounting.

We have seen how the notion of functionalism can be used to describe the unproblematic nature of management accounting and control function. For functionalists, the mainstream management accounting techniques we discussed in Part I are problem-free if they are implemented formally and correctly. We have also seen that, despite the dominance of those techniques in the conventional wisdom of management accounting, functionalism suffered from some serious flaws. In response to these flaws, from the 1980s onwards, there emerged a group of accounting researchers using different perspectives to see how and why management accounting can exist and how changes in practice can occur. In the subsequent sections, we shall discuss how those perspectives provided new ways of understanding (the problems of) management accounting, especially its change from a mechanistic to a post-mechanistic form. The main perspectives we consider are interpretive sociology, old institutional economics (institutional theory), new institutional sociology and actor–network theory.

INTERPRETIVE SOCIOLOGY

Perspective

From the 1980s, accounting researchers identified the problems of functionalism (Tinker *et al.*, 1982; Cooper, 1983; Hopper and Powell, 1985; Chua, 1986; Hopper *et al.*, 1987; Hopper and Armstrong, 1991), and, during the same decade, they proposed a few alternatives. One of these, the interpretive approach or naturalism, appealed to a group of accounting researchers. Based on the ideas of interpretive sociologists such as Max Weber, George Mead, Charles Cooley and Herbert Blumer, who emphasized the roles of symbols, images and human interaction, the researchers created an alternative theoretical approach for researching how accounting is implicated in those symbols (Colville, 1981; Hopwood, 1983; Tomkins and Groves, 1983; Berry *et al.*, 1985). This section reports on how this research tradition helped us understand management accounting change from a mechanistic to a post-mechanistic form.

> Using the ideas of interpretive sociologists who emphasized the role of symbols, images and human interaction, accounting researchers embarked on a new strand of research.

420

As a branch of sociology, the interpretive approach developed to highlight the significance of interpretations of events and things. The governing principle of interpretive sociology is that there is a constitutional role for human consciousness in creating meanings and values by reflecting on things. Functionalists believe that such things as organizations and accounting information systems exist independently of human beings (see Hopper and Powell, 1985; Chua, 1986). In contrast, interpretive researchers believe that such things (organizations and accounting information systems) exist only because of the meanings and labels given to them by human beings through their everyday life experience of those things. As a result, without those meanings and labels, one cannot tell if those things exist: the existence is *always* associated with meanings and labels, and the meanings and labels are constructions of human beings. Thus, life experience, understanding, giving meanings, using the things to reproduce such meanings, etc., are all interpretive acts of human beings. Organizations, control systems and accounting functions are such things, all interpreted by people through interpretive acts.

> The governing principle of interpretive sociology is that there is a constitutional role for human consciousness in creating meanings and values by reflecting on things.

Interpretive sociology was first developed by Max Weber (1949), who emphasized the importance of social actions as opposed to social structures. For Weber, social actions create social reality (e.g., organizational issues), so, as researchers, we need to study those actions and their underlying 'rationalities'. In studying 'actions', Weber considered the importance of focusing on individuals. In defining 'interpretive sociology', he (quoted in Gerth and Mills, 1991: 55) said:

> Interpretive sociology considers the individual and his action as the basic unit, as its 'atom' – if the disputable comparison for once may be permitted. In this approach, the individual is also the upper limit and the sole carrier of meaningful conduct . . . In general, for sociology, such concepts as 'state', 'association', 'feudalism', and the like, designate certain categories of human interaction. Hence, it is the task of sociology to reduce these concepts to 'understandable' action, that is, without exception, to the actions of participating individual men.

Weber, however, did not go on to theorize as to how these human actions are generated. Nevertheless, this idea of 'actions' was a powerful intellectual input for the subsequent development of a coherent theoretical framework. For example, contributions by Mead (1934), Blumer (1969) and Schutz (1967) led to the development of interpretive sociology into the frameworks of symbolic interactionism on which we focus here. To put it another way, interpretive sociology was extended into the refined notion of symbolic interactionism.

> The task of sociology is to reduce certain concepts to 'understandable' action: that is, the actions of participating individuals.

421

Symbolic interactionism can be understood with reference to its historical roots: pragmatism and behaviourism. Pragmatists do not believe that reality exists 'out there'. Instead, it is actively created by people through their everyday acts (Hewitt, 1984; Shalin, 1986). Consequently, knowledge is a pragmatic phenomenon, in that people believe in something as knowledge as long as it is useful to them. Equally, pragmatists define physical objects in terms of their usefulness. Combining these ideas, Ritzer (1992) highlighted that pragmatism encompasses three principles: interaction between the actor and the world; the dynamic nature of both the actor and the world; and the actor's capacity to interpret the world. Thus, when understanding any social phenomenon, pragmatism focuses on people's understanding and their active involvement in the event, incident or situation in question.

Symbolic interactionism can be understood by referring to its historical roots: pragmatism and behaviourism.

Pragmatism encompasses three principles: interaction between the actor and the world; the dynamic nature of both the actor and the world; and the actor's capacity to interpret the world.

Behaviourism is more concerned with the socio-psychological aspects of people's behaviour. The researchers in this school mainly focus on human acts, especially people's stimulus and response: for example, eating food when we are hungry. Building on the ideas of George Mead, Meltzer (1978) developed the concept of 'act', which emphasizes people's behaviour within a specific study. Meltzer explained (1978: 23): 'the unit of study is "the act", which emphasises both overt and covert aspects of human action . . . Attention, perception, imagination, reasoning, emotion, and so forth are seen as parts of the act . . . the act, then, encompasses the total process involved in human activity.'

Behaviourism encouraged sociologists to focus on the importance of understanding human action in specific situations, namely multiple 'acts'. In 'the acts', as Mead argued, the actor creatively and actively developed dynamic images through interactions between the mind and things (including society).

Behaviourism is more concerned with the socio-psychological aspects of people's behaviour, focusing on human acts, especially people's stimulus and response.

Both pragmatism and behaviourism influenced the development of symbolic interactionism, which became the backbone of interpretive sociology. In 1937, Herbert Blumer coined the term 'symbolic interactionism'. Blumer stressed that, rather than reducing human behaviour to the notion of 'attitudes', it is important to emphasize how 'attitudes' are formed through actions and interactions. The results of such acts are implicated in symbols. For example, being a powerful symbol, 'language' can provide meanings and make communication. It does so when people interact with it (symbolically) and create meanings, emotions and so forth. But this meaning creation process is social, not merely psychological. Blumer showed that this happens when a number of socio-cultural factors affect the act. These factors include social systems, social roles, customs, institutions, collective representation, social norms and values.

> According to symbolic interactionism, rather than reducing human behaviour to the notion of 'attitudes', it is important to emphasize how 'attitudes' are formed through actions and interactions.

Interpretive accounting research

Interpretive sociology and its extension of symbolic interactionism influenced the ways in which accounting researchers developed critiques of functionalist accounting research. To distinguish this line of research from functionalism, accounting researchers have used different but existing terms to emphasize the role of human actions in accounting practices: for example, Gambling (1977) described it as the 'magic of accounting', Colville (1981) as 'behavioural accounting', Tomkins and Groves (1983) as 'everyday accounting', Chua (1986) as 'the interpretive alternative', and Hopper *et al.* (1987) as 'naturalism'. All the above analyses agree that accounting is a socially constructed function by giving specific meanings to various acts of accounting, such as measurements and controls. As a perspective for understanding management accounting change, we shall look at how these accounting researchers have extended the ideas of our previous categories: context, people and organizations, controls, accounting and research.

> Accounting researchers have used different but existing terms to emphasize the role of human actions in accounting practices, namely: 'magic of accounting', 'behavioural accounting', 'everyday accounting', 'the interpretive alternative' and 'naturalism'.

Context

Earlier in the chapter, we saw that functionalist researchers considered context as a given phenomenon. Consequently, they did not want to discern how context can be an explanatory variable for understanding management accounting change. In contrast, interpretive researchers made calls for an understanding of the interplay between the context and the function of accounting (Burchell *et al.*, 1980). Following the ideas of interpretive sociology and symbolic interactionism, accounting researchers then began to conduct case studies by locating them in respective contexts. For example, focusing on work role perspectives on accountants, Rosenberg *et al.* (1982) made their studies in the context of local government service departments. They illustrated how this particular organizational context produced contrasting occupational values, goals and identities. Concerning

423

the roles of accounting control systems, Ansari and Bell (1991) provided a graphical illustration of how social and power relationships between three owners of a Pakistani company interacted with the formal control structure to produce a particular accounting practice. They found that the accounting in this context was more symbolic than rational. In another pioneering interpretive study, Berry *et al.* (1985) claimed that their analysis was context-specific in that they produced a set of detailed ethnographic accounts of how the production culture of coalmining came to underscore the merit of financial controls. Consequently, accounting became a second-order function creating ambiguities as well as legitimacies for the existence and dynamics of accounting roles.

People and organizations

Interpretive researchers called for an understanding of the interplay between the context and the function of accounting.

Whereas functionalists consider that people and organizations play passive roles in relation to the functioning of accounting, interpretive researchers look at how people create meanings and values for those functions. As a result, management accounting's contribution to the organization depends on how people conceive its purpose because, according to interpretive researchers, there are no independent meanings of social categories such as 'management accounting', 'organization' and the like. Rather, meanings are the constructions of individuals who act upon, and interact with, those social categories. For example, referring to the budgeting study of Boland and Pondy (1983), Chua (1986) contended that budgeting can create an everyday language by which people in organizations give meanings to the budgets and their implications for organizational functions. Sometimes, according to Boland and Pondy (1983), people see budgets as 'rational devices' which guide top managers to control people and activities, while, at other times, budgets are implicated in the everyday lives of people by giving opportunities for negotiation and compromise. Providing a similar analysis, Ansari and Bell (1991) demonstrated that, based on their cultural values, people interpret and create values and meanings for controls, as opposed to their managers' expectations of controls. Thus, one cannot argue that budgeting is only a rational and objective management accounting technique operating independently of people's interactions and interpretations. Moreover, it must be emphasized that if the people in organizations create meanings and values in this way, 'organization' cannot be an independent social category. Rather, it is a collection of individuals with different interests. Thus, individuals rather than organizations have goals. The interpretive accounting researcher's focus of analysis must be these individual goals and their roles in interpreting accounting: that is, social interaction (see Hopper *et al.*, 1987).

Interpretive researchers look at how people create meanings and values for organizational functions.

An organization cannot be an independent social category: it is a collection of individuals with different interests on which interpretive accounting researchers focus their analysis.

Controls

According to the interpretive perspective, controls cannot be described merely in terms of quantitative formulas, such as incentive plans, reward systems and performance measurements. Even though such controls persist as dominant systems in those forms, they function through continuous negotiation and interpretation. Consequently, the practice of controls can either be functional or dysfunctional. There is research evidence for both. Taking an interpretive stance, Rosenberg *et al.* (1982), for instance, demonstrated how professional accountants in the UK Social Service Department increased their credibility by initiating new financial controls. In this case, the accountants' negotiations and compromises with Social Service officers became positive, so that newly appointed accountants were able to create a wider perspective on control as opposed to a narrow view which merely confined itself to financial terms. This negotiable space created a wider sphere of control. Thus, control is a practice developed from individuals' desires, expectations and negotiations.

In some other cases, though, it has been reported that the outcomes of control can be dysfunctional. For instance, Berry *et al.* (1985) reported that financial controls were not effective in controlling the workers in the National Coal Board. Instead, as we mentioned earlier, the production culture, which was interpreted and understood as dominant, stressed the importance of production control. Consequently, financial controls enhanced ambiguities, and production departments became somewhat detached from the head office. This was not the intention of the financial control system. Rather, it came about because the control system was given meanings and values by people. Thus, despite the classic claim that control systems can achieve organizational goals (Anthony, 1965), they are actually participants' social constructions and situational articulations.

Controls cannot be described merely in terms of quantitative formulas: they function through continuous negotiation and interpretation and have either functional or dysfunctional effects.

Accounting

For interpretive researchers, accounting is an everyday practice rather than merely something promulgated by regulators such as governments and professional bodies (Colville, 1981; Tomkins and Groves, 1983). For regulators, accounting should be practised in line with standards, concepts and procedures, so that practices should be universal. For instance, in a budgetary control system, budget targets should be set according to rationally identified criteria: that is, by understanding market requirements. Once these requirements have been identified, budget targets are set, budgets are prepared and, in turn, people achieve the targets unless there are adverse impacts of the market. Interpretive researchers do not expect that accounting would act like this. On the one hand, accountants manipulate accounting. For instance, quoting his own inaugural lecture, Gambling (1977: 144) said:

425

> Interpretive researchers do not expect accounting to act like a machine. Rather, they manipulate it.

I remember I once checked some of the pricing in a very large inventory and found some gross manipulation over a long period of years. When I tackled the local director about it, he said, 'Ah, so you noticed that – I was wondering when someone would! You see the way I do the accounts, I get them completed without the inventories, and then I can see what the inventory values ought to be. If I didn't do that, the profits down here would fluctuate, and the main board would get worried quite unnecessarily.' When I made a few remarks about the Companies Act, secret reserves, and the like, the chap replied, 'But that's how everybody does it, you know'.

On the other hand, when accounting is mediated through wider organizational members, interpretive researchers contend that it is subject to negotiation. For instance, concerning the budgeting practice in the University of Wisconsin, Covaleski and Dirsmith (1986) argued that budget targets are outcomes of negotiations between the university and the government, rather than a formal and value-free practice expected by the government. As Hopper *et al.* (1987: 441) showed, management accounting in this context is an 'inter-subjective meaning system competing with others for recognition and priority'.

> When accounting is mediated through wider organizational members, interpretive researchers contend that it is subject to negotiation.

Research

To understand management accounting in practice, interpretive researchers conduct case studies rather than surveys. In such case studies, the researchers explore the ways in which organizational participants interpret the 'actual' practice by relying largely on qualitative data collected from interviews, observations and documentation. Through these methods, they appreciate the respondents' interpretations, as opposed to looking for 'facts' independent of subjective judgements. Alongside the methodological belief that data are value-laden, interpretive researchers attempt to articulate how reality is constructed by organizational members through their subjective interpretations. The researcher's role is then to report what has been interpreted and presented to him/her. In reporting, the researcher follows a methodology of storytelling (as in Rosenberg *et al.*, 1982; Berry *et al.*, 1985; Covaleski and Dirsmith, 1986), an approach of grounded theory (as in Parker and Roffey, 1997; Goddard, 2005) or sociological theory (as in Scapens and Roberts, 1993; Jones and Dugdale, 2002). Our intention here is not to elaborate on how to do research but to highlight that interpretive researchers merely describe what is happening from the participants' perspective, rather than prescribing what ought to be. In short, these researchers explore subjective judgements as the social and organizational reality in which management accounting change is contemplated. However, with a flavour of interpretive sociology, some researchers extend this research paradigm by applying certain sociological theories. The sections below will consider these developments.

> Interpretive researchers conduct case studies rather than surveys and explore the ways in which organizational participants interpret the 'actual' practice.

CONCERNING A GAP: OLD INSTITUTIONALISM

While the interpretive perspective developed from a critique of functionalism, there emerged another perspective called institutional theory from a critique of the neoclassical economic perspective. Institutional theory's main aim was to provide an alternative framework with a sociological flavour. Since the 1990s, it has become one of the popular theoretical frameworks in management accounting studies. For example, most of the research papers on management accounting presented at the 2006 Annual Congress of the European Accounting Association (one of the largest accounting conferences in the world) were based on institutional theory. In this section, we will examine how this framework came about, what properties it has and which contributions it has made to the knowledge of management accounting change.

> Institutional theory emerged from a critique of the neoclassical economic perspective and provided an alternative framework with a sociological flavour.

> Most of the research papers on management accounting presented at the 2006 Annual Congress of the European Accounting Association (one of the largest accounting conferences in the world) were based on institutional theory.

Problem of neoclassical economics: the issue of 'gap'

Institutional theory is a product of Robert Scapens and his followers at the University of Manchester (Ahmed, 1992; Ahmed and Scapens, 1991; Scapens, 1994; Burns and Scapens, 2000). This research programme goes back to the 1980s, when Scapens (1984) identified a gap between management accounting 'theory' and 'practice'. By 'theory', Scapens meant textbook techniques (e.g., books by Charles Horngren and his colleagues) developed from the 1970s, which were primarily based on neoclassical economics. Their observation was that neoclassical economics can only be a theoretical tool for predicting industry and market-level scenarios, such as costs, prices, sales volume, rather than a tool for explaining the behaviour of managers who use management accounting within an organization. Thus, Scapens and his colleagues were sceptical about the application of agency theory (Baiman, 1982, 1990) and transaction cost theory (Spicer and Ballew,

427

1983; Spicer, 1988) as they did not provide adequate explanations as to how and why managers respond to management accounting techniques in a particular manner. Nevertheless, as you saw in Chapter 11, these theories turned into mainstream theoretical frameworks in management accounting research.

> Neoclassical economics can predict industry and market-level scenarios, such as costs, prices, sales volume. But it cannot explain the behaviour of managers who use management accounting within an organization.

Scapens' (1984) survey results showed that most UK and US firms did not use highly sophisticated, mathematical-oriented decision-making models which developed from neoclassical economic theories and were presented in mainstream management accounting textbooks, such as Horngren (1977), Shillinglaw (1977) and Arnold and Hope (1983). (For a discussion of the theoretical problem of these textbooks, see Hopper *et al.* (1987).) Rather than reflecting on 'actual practices', these textbooks provided normative models, expecting that they would aid decision-making and organizational control. However, this modelling effort in economic-based management accounting theories was not robust enough to explain the pragmatic and complex issues in practice, especially managers' responses to decision-making and control techniques. Critiquing the theories, Tinker *et al.* (1982) defined them as 'normative origins of positive theories'. In other words, economic assumptions underpinning these management accounting models constrained them being used in practice. Scapens and his colleagues' main concern was this 'gap' between theory and practice. (For a more recent discussion, see Scapens (2006).)

> Scapens identified a gap between theory and practice: most UK and US firms did not use highly sophisticated, mathematical-oriented decision-making models presented in mainstream management accounting textbooks.

Never mind the gap: arguments for institutional theory

Writing in the 1990s, Scapens (1994: 301) pointed out that, rather than being concerned about the 'gap', focus should turn to 'the study of management accounting practice *per se*'. He must have meant that practice should be studied to develop a theory, rather than attempting to predict a practice by use of a normative theory. However, there is an issue as to how we study practice. Addressing this broader epistemological issue (in this case, about what constitutes knowledge of practice and how we obtain that knowledge), Scapens argued that practice has to be studied with the aid of a theory. In this case, theory acts as a tool for helping the researcher to understand and theorize the practice. Unlike neoclassical economists who used theory to predict practice, Scapens aimed to introduce a theory that would help us understand why and how managers behave in relation to the use of management accounting (see Humprey and Scapens, 1994). In response to this epistemological need, Scapens argued for an institutional perspective.

428

Focus should be on 'the study of management accounting practice *per se*': 'never mind the gap, study management accounting practice'.

In developing an institutional perspective, Scapens consulted the ideas of old institutional economics and, to a certain extent, evolutionary economics. Having highlighted the critiques of mainstream neoclassical economics (e.g., Bell and Kristol, 1981; Drucker, 1981), he found that old institutional economics was an avenue for the analysis of social institutions and processes which govern economic activities within a firm. To reach this point, Scapens distinguished old institutional economics from new institutional economics: whereas the latter (as an extension of neoclassical economics) focuses on rationality and equilibrium, and regards institutions as static and tacit, the former focuses on dynamics (change) and the active roles of institutions that can help us understand accounting practices. Scapens used old institutional economics to develop an alternative framework for understanding management accounting change rather than claiming his framework was superior to neoclassical frameworks. At this point we have two important questions. What are these institutions? And how can they aid understanding of management accounting change?

New institutional economics focuses on rationality and equilibrium, and regards institutions as static and tacit. Old institutional economics focuses on dynamics and the active roles of institutions that can help us understand accounting practices.

Scapens borrowed the definition of institutions from several early original sources. Two important ones were Veblen (1994) and Hamilton (1932). The former defined institutions as 'settled habits of thought common to the generality of men' (p. 239), and the latter as 'a way of thought or action of some prevalence and permanence, which is embedded in the habits of a group or the customs of a people' (p. 84). Following Scapens, we can identify at least three intuitive properties from the above definitions. First, institutions are formed from the habitual behaviour of people which cannot necessarily be explained merely in economic terms. To put it another way, people's habits, customs, cultures, values, human interactions and the like form these institutions. Second, economic behaviour cannot be reduced just to rational-equilibrium analysis. Rather, for a fuller and more complete understanding of economic behaviour, it should be supplemented with social dimensions, that is institutions. Third, together with institutional explanations, economic behaviour should not be confined to a state of static equilibrium. Instead, one can see how equilibrium can be deconstructed and alternative possibilities can be constructed through the dynamics of institutions, which can help us understand change. Thus, in brief, by bringing social, cultural and historical dimensions into the analysis, institutions can broaden the conventional wisdom of economics.

The other question we raise is on the issue of the understanding of management accounting change. The answer to this was the emergence of the institutional theory of management accounting. Scapens sketched out three important elements in this framework: routines, rules and actions (see also Burns and Scapens, 2000). People normally develop routines from their actions. The

429

KEY TERMS

- Institutions are 'settled habits of thought common to the generality of men' (Veblen, 1994: 239).
- They are 'a way of thought or action of some prevalence and permanence, which is embedded in the habits of a group or the customs of a people' (Hamilton, 1932: 84).

actions come from institutions, and, in turn, actions develop institutions. Along the process of this duality, before actions become permanent institutions, people develop routines. How do they do this? The starting point is following rules. People are always confronted with rules. Take the example of driving. To become a driver, you need to follow rules (and regulations). By following rules over and over again, you become more familiar with them. Afterwards, subconsciously, you slow down at a bend, change gear when necessary, signal when turning and so on. This is programmatic behaviour. As Burns and Scapens (2000) showed, this programmatic behaviour produces 'routines'. People's actions are then governed by these routines; they act through habit. When this happens, according to institutional theory, routines are said to be institutionalized. However, unlike in driving, actions within organizations do not merely conform to rules and routines. Instead, people choose what action they want to execute when rules are imposed. Thus, the process of institutionalization is more social and cultural than economic and psychological. In this social and cultural process, human interaction, inter-subjective judgements, available resources for making choices, etc., determine the actions of people. As the above social and cultural dimensions are subject to historical changes, current actions lead to (different) future actions. Thus, always, current actions are the result of past actions, and future actions the result of current actions. This happens because, as Burns and Scapens (2000) articulated, the duality between 'institutional realm' and 'realm of actions' operates interactively, subject to historical change.

People normally develop routines from their actions. The actions come from institutions, and, in turn, actions develop institutions. Along the process of this duality, before actions become permanent institutions, people develop routines.

This duality has been further explained by drawing on Giddens' (1984) structuration theory (Roberts and Scapens, 1985; Macintosh and Scapens, 1990). According to structuration theory, there is an interactive relationship (a duality) between 'agency' and 'structure'. Here, as Burns and Scapens summarized, agency refers to the capacities of human actors, and structure refers to the structural properties of institutions. Through 'signification', 'domination' and 'legitimation', the interaction between agency and structure is enhanced. Consequently, structural properties are reconstituted. These reconstituted structures influence the capacities of human actions, which can, in turn, reconstitute the structure. Thus, the essence of structuration theory is grounded in this concept of duality.

Institutional theory shares the views of structuration theory, except that, as Burns and Scapens argued, the latter is less confident about explaining the process of change. While building on

430

> Through 'signification', 'domination' and 'legitimation', the interaction between agency and structure is enhanced. Consequently, structural properties are reconstituted, which can influence the capacities of human actions, which can, in turn, reconstitute the structure.

fundamental props of structuration theory, Burns and Scapens drew on Barley and Tolbert (1997) to incorporate the idea of 'scripts', which, they quoted, are 'observable recurrent activities and patterns of interaction . . . in a particular setting' (p. 9). Thus, by focusing on empirical 'scripts' in organizations, management accounting change can be studied in respect of how new management accounting initiatives bring rules, how rules become routines and how routines become institutionalized. Building on evolutionary economics (Nelson, 1995), Burns and Scapens further argued that management accounting change can be seen as an evolutionary process.

> By focusing on empirical 'scripts' in organizations, management accounting change can be studied in respect of how new management accounting initiatives bring rules, how rules become routines and how routines become institutionalized.

Following the above developments, a considerable number of management accounting studies have been conducted to explain and report on management accounting change (e.g., Brignall and Modell, 2000; Modell, 2001; Soin et al., 2002; Seal, 2006; Lukka, 2007). For instance, focusing on some recent cost accounting initiatives in a clearing department of a UK multinational, Soin et al. applied the Burns and Scapens (2000) model to analyse and explain underlying changes. They characterized the change as formal, evolutionary and regressive, as opposed to informal, revolutionary and progressive. The message here is that, despite the idealistic expectations of ABC, the change from a mechanistic type of management control and cost accounting procedures to a post-mechanistic type was rather difficult. Consequently, only a particular version of ABC was institutionalized: ABC became a routine in the areas of product costing, not in those of strategic transformation. In other words, despite the ideal expectations of consultants, the new ABC system had little impact on revolutionizing the bank's strategic thinking.

> Building on institutional theory, Soin et al. (2002) characterized the change as formal, evolutionary and regressive, as opposed to informal, revolutionary and progressive.

In a more recent study, Lukka (2007) reported how change is associated with stability. In order to make sense of his story, in addition to the Burns and Scapens (2000) model, he drew on some ideas of 'loose-coupling' (Orton and Weick, 1990). The findings are interesting. On the one hand, in the case company, there was an initiative of management accounting standardization. In terms of Burns and Scapens, this standardization represents new rules. The question is how these rules can

431

be transformed into routines. Lukka explored this relationship through the notions of loose-coupling. Instead of changing rules into routines directly, Lukka found that a series of informal arrangements were made to make them informal routines. As new initiatives are not accepted directly, resistance as well as accommodation is possible through complex relations between formal rules and informal routines. Thus, the relationships are loosely coupled. Consequently, rather than either change or stability occurring, both can be present simultaneously through the multiple informal arrangements which Lukka saw as loose-coupling. This is an important contribution to institutional theory, in that it broadens our understanding of what actual practices look like.

> Instead of changing rules into routines directly, a series of informal arrangements were made to make them informal routines. As new initiatives are not accepted directly, resistance as well as accommodation is possible through complex relations between formal rules and informal routines.

Similar significant contributions are now being made to management accounting by adopting institutional theory. Considerable critique or overall evaluation of the use of this framework has not yet been made. However, irrespective of what (old) institutional theory offers, some researchers tend to follow more sociological rather than organizational aspects of institutions. Based on new institutional sociology, these researchers try to link external factors to internal processes. In the next section, we will look at how this development has occurred.

NEW INSTITUTIONALISM

Several accounting researchers have come forward to take new institutional sociology or new institutionalism (hereafter, NIS) as a framework of analysis (Covaleski and Dirsmith, 1988a; Modell, 2003; Covaleski et al., 2003; Dillard et al., 2004; Hopper and Major, forthcoming). Concerning the studies of management accounting change, NIS begins by defining 'institutions' as socio-political and cultural practices which produce legitimacy (meanings and rules) for the conduct of organizations and the existence of management accounting therein. The institutions produce political and cultural reasons rather than technical justification for the existence of certain organizational practices. These political and cultural reasons for the existence of those practices would be hidden under a technical veneer – that is, jargon, procedures, routines, etc. (Carruthers, 1995) – and organizations would continue to adopt such practices, despite not contributing to actual functioning. Consequently, many organizations use techniques partly as artefacts and ceremonies, and partly as devices of actual operations (Hopper and Major, forthcoming). Even though they are functional, the underlying functionality tends to be institutionally legitimized.

KEY TERMS

As per NIS, 'institutions' are socio-political and cultural practices which produce legitimacy (meanings and rules) for the conduct of organizations and the existence of management accounting therein.

The institutions come from institutional environments such as the legal, the regulatory, the professional, the cultural, etc. Following Weber (1968), Berger and Luckmann (1967), Meyer and Rowan (1977) and Scott (1995, 2001) defined the basic components of institutions: the normative, the regulative and the cognitive-cultural. The normative element emphasizes certain rules that prescribe both goals and means to be followed by organizations. For example, the BSC model provides rules for performance measurements and means to implement such systems (Kaplan and Norton, 1992). Regulators, consultants and managers then tend to believe that these systems provide solutions to the issues of performance measurement. Consequently, this social belief legitimizes the existence of such systems. The regulative element stresses rules, regulations and sanctions imposed by the state and regulatory agencies. For example, governments demand that firms must adhere to certain rules of regulated industries which become implicated in performance measurements (see Major and Hopper, 2005). The cognitive-cultural element constructs common beliefs and conceptions that become hidden logics for human behaviour. For example, when an organization cannot judge how it becomes 'financially effective' in a particular competitive game, then that organization unconsciously imitates major players in that game (Covaleski and Dirsmith, 1988a). Under such circumstances, performance measurement systems become imitations, fads and fashions (Malmi, 2001) rather than the systems generated from managerial purposes.

> Scott (1995, 2001) defined the basic components of institutions: the normative, the regulative and the cognitive-cultural.

NIS in management accounting research rests on the above institutional explanations of the adaptation of management accounting techniques and the existence of subsequent management accounting practices. How institutional explanations would be used to develop theoretical frameworks is debatable, however. As we now know, there are variants of institutional theory ranging from old institutional economic (OIE) (Burns and Scapens, 2000) to NIS perspectives (Meyer and Rowan, 1977; Scott, 1995, 2001). The former adopts an organizational level of analysis, while the latter uses a social (institutional) level. An interesting integration of both approaches is the model presented by Dillard *et al.* (2004), which combines NIS with Burns and Scapens' framework.

The Dillard model argues for an 'institutionalization process' by hierarchically linking political and economic (PE) level with organizational level through the organizational field (OF). The PE level provides the most general and widely accepted norms and practices influenced by politically developed symbolic criteria (CPE), such as accounting standards, laws and regulations. These general norms and practices pass into the organizational field (e.g., industry, professional bodies). When this happens, those norms are translated into a somewhat different shape, depending on the expectations of the actors in the organizational field. These expectations provide certain organizational field criteria (COF) which are the functions of CPE. COF provide legitimacy for the actions at the OF level, while CPE provide legitimacy for the existence of COF. Within the OF level, there are certain practices (POF) which are the functions of COF. At the organization level, individual organizations can either be innovators (I) or later adopters (LA): innovators have new practices (PI) which are adopted by late adopters (PLA). For PLA, legitimacy comes from both OF and PI. In organizations adopting innovator practices, there could be actual practices which are decoupled or loosely coupled from PLA.

433

> The Dillard model argues for an 'institutionalization process' by hierarchically linking political and economic (PE) level with organizational level through the organizational field (OF).

The Dillard model has theoretical roots characterized by three axes of tension along with three structural types (Weber, 1930, 1961, 1978; Giddens, 1976, 1979, 1984). The axes of tension are 'representation', 'rationality' and 'power', social actions that explain how the institutionalization process operates. The structural types, another way of categorizing social actions, are 'signification', 'legitimation' and 'domination'. Dillard *et al.* (2004) argue that the axes of tension and structural types coincide with each other: representation with signification, rationality with legitimation and power with domination. These pairs of social actions take place at all levels: PE, OF and organizational. Consequently, institutionalization, de-institutionalization or re-institutionalization processes would be generated through choosing important norms, values, beliefs, etc. (representation of signification), through justifying the choices (rationality or legitimation), and through maintaining the same (power and domination). In a similar institutionalized fashion, management accounting systems would be institutionalized, de-institutionalized or re-institutionalized through the above processes of social actions. In other words, the emergence of management accounting systems cannot be justified merely through economic rationalities; rather, such practices become institutionalized through the social and political processes of institutionalization (or de-institutionalization and re-institutionalization). Such processes take place only if the axes of tension occur.

> The axes of tension are 'representation', 'rationality' and 'power', social actions that explain how the institutionalization process operates. The structural types are 'signification', 'legitimation' and 'domination', almost similar social actions.

Limited space here does not allow us to provide a fuller review of studies within NIS. Our aim is to show how management accounting change can be conceived from a different perspective. It must be emphasized that, while the institutionalization process can be a framework for understanding why new practices develop, Dillard *et al.* (2004) show that empirical cases can be complex and variable. Organizations produce different responses to institutional pressures even within similar institutionalized environments (Eden *et al.*, 2001): some organizations may resist (Coveleski and Dirsmith, 1988a, cited in Dillard *et al.*, 2004); others may accommodate (Carruthers, 1995, cited in Dillard *et al.*, 2004). At the PE level, CPE would develop through the presence of competing coalitions producing alternative norms, values, beliefs, assumptions, etc. This would lead to changes in the institutionalization process and organizational practices within individual organizations. However, results are complex and variable in organizations depending on the nature of organizational resistance and accommodation (Zucker, 1987, cited in Dillard *et al.*, 2004). Thus, the Dillard model can capture dynamics and complexities in the PE and organizations which can explain why new management accounting techniques develop and are adopted by firms. Given that the Dillard model provides a broader perspective when compared to old institutional theory, some researchers have now begun to apply it to explain upcoming management accounting practices informed by new management accounting techniques (e.g., Hopper and Major, forthcoming).

> Organizations produce different responses to institutional pressures, even within similar institutionalized environments: some organizations may resist while others accommodate.

ACTOR–NETWORK THEORY

Actor–network theory (ANT) is another avenue for interpretive case studies to aid understanding of management accounting change. ANT, drawn on by Bruno Latour and his followers (Latour, 1987, 1991, 1999, 1999; Latour and Woolgar, 1979; Callon et al., 1986; Law and Hassard, 1999), is a framework that has been in use within accounting research for quite some time (Pinch et al., 1989; Preston et al., 1992; Robson, 1991, 1992; Miller, 1991; Chua, 1995; Ogden, 1997; Mouristen et al., 2001; Briers and Chua, 2001; Jones and Dugdale, 2002; Quattrone and Hopper, 2005; Preston 2006). Hence, a fuller account of the features of the theory has been introduced to the accounting literature, and a number of models of analysis have been used to illuminate the theory, together with rich accounts of empirical illustrations. In this section, we will look at how ANT has been used to conduct interpretive case studies which aimed to explain management accounting change.

In ANT, a number of concepts have been developed with the aim of defining social realities in the construction of science and technology. By 'science and technology', the researchers mean not only 'pure' engineering and technical aspects but also systems developed for 'getting things done'. Management accounting is regarded as such a system (see Jones and Dugdale, 2001). Another concept associated with ANT is the actor–network. The argument here is that there are certain 'actors' who are active and innovative in developing and propagating a particular science and technology. These actors work in networks to make their efforts acceptable and popular. Moreover, these networks achieve their ultimate objectives through 'boundary objects', which create possibilities for translating a commonly known technology into local circumstances. Thus, translation of technologies such as management accounting can be activated from a 'distance'. That is why, for instance, US models of management accounting could be popular in the Far East, and vice versa. Together with this translation process, some or all aspects of such technologies can emerge as 'fabrication of images' or 'inscription and representation of technology' (Preston et al., 1992). These associated concepts have been interchangeably and complementarily used in accounting research as metaphorical devices to illuminate ANT, on the one hand, and to explain the nature of the development of accounting technologies from a broader, social and historical context, on the other.

> Management accounting is regarded as a technology of control which is subject to actors' promotional roles through networks.

'Science and technology', according to Latour (1987), is not a neutral term that can be defined as mere discoveries and innovations or pre-existing natural orders. Rather, it represents established knowledge stemming from a particular 'system-building' process which embodies 'enrolling and controlling' human and non-human allies (see Jones and Dugdale, 2002). Human allies may include academics, consultants, colleagues, readers and the like, while non-human allies can be all other inputs, such as concepts, ideas, theories, instruments and models. These allies are enrolled in, and controlled by, system-building processes until science and technology becomes 'facts and machines' or 'black boxes': taken-for-granted technology. Thus, science and technology cannot be seen as being in a 'pre-existing natural order' to be rational and legitimate (see Robson, 1991, 1992). Instead, it comprises artefacts of a system-building process representing some collective achievements of certain human efforts and non-human influences.

> Science and technology, such as management accounting, represents established knowledge through a 'system-building process': 'enrolling and controlling' human and non-human allies. Human allies may include academics, consultants, colleagues and readers; non-human allies can be all other inputs, such as concepts, theories, instruments and models.

As we mentioned earlier, management accounting is a technology of decision-making and control which is subject to the above 'enrolling and controlling' processes through the involvement of 'human and non-human allies'. In the developing of management accounting technologies, 'human allies', such as consultants, professional bodies, managers and accountants, come together with non-human allies, such as the ideas of performance measures and software packages for enterprise-wide information systems. If such management accounting systems were to become institutionalized (see Burns and Scapens, 2000), they would be 'facts and machines' creating conditions and possibilities in the functioning of organizational management. A number of studies has shown how such technologies of accounting are translated from a 'big' idea into certain practices (Miller, 1991) or fabricated through specific processes (Preston *et al.*, 1992; Briers and Chua, 2001), how such systems are maintained for diverse purposes (Ogden, 1997; Preston, 2006), and how these systems become problematic under certain social and political conditions (Preston, 2006).

> In the developing of management accounting technologies, 'human allies', such as consultants, professional bodies, managers and accountants, come together with non-human allies, such as the ideas of performance measures and software packages for enterprise-wide information systems.

In the creation of 'facts and machines' such as management accounting systems, 'actors' ('human and non-human allies') build 'networks' through relationships which Callon (1991) calls 'intermediaries'. According to Callon, actors influence each other in the network through these intermediaries, namely written texts, technical artefacts, human beings and money (see Jones and

Dugdale, 2002). The intermediaries may also operate through complex relations, creating varieties of combinations of intermediaries ('hybrids' or 'monsters': see Law, 1991). Thus, networks are the products of intermediaries, and facts and machines are the products of networks. As facts and machines, management accounting systems are then the products of networks of human and non-human allies. We therefore need to study how these networks have been built, and how management accounting systems have been created.

> 'Actors' influence each other in a 'network' through 'intermediaries', namely written texts, technical artefacts, human beings and money.

Moreover, in relation to this reality, we may be guided by the dichotomy of global and local networks. Global networks are extended to the actions of global players: that is, 'cosmopolitans' (see Briers and Chua, 2001: 241), who are rich in 'concepts, competence and connections'. The global players have 'boundary objects' which represent certain abilities and specialities (repositories of things, ideal types, coincident boundaries and standardized methods – see Star and Griesemer, 1989, cited in Briers and Chua, 2001). In the construction of management accounting systems locally, locals follow the global players through the threads of intermediaries. Latour's term 'action at a distance' (see Preston *et al.*, 1992; Robson, 1991; Miller, 2001) can be a better explanation for these actions of global players influencing locals. However, if the local networks are more powerful, perhaps global influences would be minimal.

> Global players have 'boundary objects' representing certain abilities and specialities. In the construction of management accounting systems locally, locals follow the global players through the threads of intermediaries.

The above exposition tells us that 'networks' cannot be studied without due consideration being given to the nature of 'intermediaries'. In the construction of management accounting systems in firms, actors follow documentary guides and conceptual frames, as well as technical procedures and rules of programmes. Moreover, they spend huge amounts of money to employ experts such as consultants and advisers. If we need to gain a thorough understanding of the creation of management accounting systems, we need to study how these intermediaries have to operate in a certain manner under given circumstances. This is a better way of answering the questions of how and why certain management accounting systems have come into being.

> Actors follow documentary guides and conceptual frames, as well as technical procedures and rules of programmes. They also spend huge amounts of money to employ experts such as consultants and advisers.

437

SUMMING UP: HOW DO WE UNDERSTAND THE CHANGE?

Our concern has been to understand management accounting change. This chapter focuses on one common perspective on this, which has been outlined in terms of four interrelated theoretical frameworks: interpretive sociology, old institutional theory, new institutional sociology and actor–network theory. All these frameworks share a common sociological proposition that social realities can be studied by concentrating on social aspects of human behaviour rather than mere economic rationalities and market equilibrium. Thus, management accounting change is a social phenomenon in which economic rationales are also reflected. The more we look for economic rationales of new management accounting initiatives, the more we see how social they are.

> A common sociological proposition: social realities can be studied by concentrating on social aspects of human behaviour rather than mere economic rationalities and market equilibrium.

The agenda opened on the contributions of interpretive sociologists who believe that human subjectivity implicated in interpretations, symbols and interactions is more important than non-human objectivity implicated in systems, methods, techniques and the like. Systematizing this original idea, a number of sociological frameworks were developed to conduct interpretive case studies. According to the proponents of this perspective, management accounting change can be examined by exploring how human interactions operate. The role of researchers is thus to artic-ulate these interactions by describing and explaining what happens, rather than prescribing what ought to happen. Theories are used as explanatory devices rather than as ultimate models that hold 'absolute truth'.

> Management accounting change can be examined by exploring how human interactions operate. The researcher articulates these interactions by describing and explaining what happens, rather than prescribing what ought to happen.

The four theoretical frameworks we presented in the chapter contribute to our understanding of management accounting change by focusing on different dimensions of subjectivities. Institutional theorists depart from economic rationales and appeal for studies on management accounting rules and routines. According to them, rules become routines through a social process in which human subjectivity plays a vital role. These researchers' interest largely lies in the issue of whether or not the use of management accounting techniques has become habitual behaviour. NIS researchers, on the other hand, focus on the imitation of others' management accounting methods which comes along through institutional pressures. The pillars of institutions, namely the nor-mative, the regulative and the cognitive-cultural, are capable of mobilizing new management accounting in different organizations. For these new institutional theorists, how the institutions play this mobilizing role is a vital area of interest. Some researchers inspired by these ideas of institutional theory became concerned about levels of analysis – that is, old institutional theorists' negligence of macro-level analysis, and new institutional theorists' negligence of micro-level analysis. As we saw in the chapter, to eliminate this negligence, the Dillard model articulated a framework that combines both theories.

> Institutional theorists depart from economic rationales and appeal for studies on management accounting rules and routines.

ANT shares the same essence of sociology. With an interest in studying management accounting change, the researchers in this camp attempt to follow actors who mobilize new technologies. They investigate 'boundary objects' which are capable of translating commonly known management accounting methods into specific methods for specific situations. By following actors, these researchers tend to examine how these boundary objects are created by actors and their networks, and how actions are taken from a distance in translating, fabricating and inscribing new technologies of management accounting. Again, as with institutional theories, management accounting researchers within the ANT camp tend to produce interpretive case studies in which new technologies are fabricated. However, the level of analysis of these studies also lies in 'boundaries of translation', upon which broader analyses are made, rather than merely describing intra-organizational scenarios.

> Sharing the same essence of sociology, ANT researchers attempt to follow actors who mobilize new technologies. They investigate 'boundary objects' which are capable of translating commonly known management accounting methods into specific methods for specific situations.

As a postscript, it is important to note that all the above perspectives tend to produce apolitical analyses. Researchers inadvertently neglect the significance of politics, which mobilizes class interests in a wider capitalist society. Because of this, issues such as how labour processes are organized in relation to new management accounting systems and how power relations might make new techniques effective or ineffective cannot be meaningfully addressed within those interpretive perspectives. Moreover, these researchers have failed to locate their studies in respective historical contexts in which management accounting systems' evolution occurs. Despite the studies' tendency to be longitudinal in nature, researchers have avoided situating their case studies in broader historical contexts. Consequently, the apolitical and ahistorical character of an interpretive project demanded another alternative perspective which we shall examine in the next chapter.

All the above perspectives tend to produce apolitical analyses: hence, they neglect the significance of politics. Because of this, issues such as how labour processes are organized in relation to new management accounting systems and how power relations might make new techniques effective or ineffective cannot be meaningfully addressed within those interpretive perspectives.

HAVE YOU UNDERSTOOD THE CHAPTER?

1. What do we mean by functionalism?
2. What are the theoretical problems of functionalism?
3. What do we mean by interpretive sociology?
4. How did interpretive sociology develop into symbolic interactionism?
5. What benefits did accounting research gain from symbolic interactionism/interpretive sociology?
6. How did interpretive accounting researchers treat the notion of subjectivity?
7. What is the perceived gap between theory and practice in management accounting?
8. What are the theoretical properties of institutional theory which developed from old institutional economics and evolutionary economics? How did this framework treat the notion of 'gap'?
9. What have we learned from the (old) institutional theory research in understanding management accounting change?
10. What are the pillars of NIS? Describe each of them.
11. What are the contributions of NIS research to the knowledge of management accounting change?
12. What do we mean by ANT?
13. What contributions did ANT make to the understanding of management accounting change?
14. What are the general problems of the interpretive case study project in management accounting research?

BEYOND THE CHAPTER

1. 'Interpretive sociology generates subjective judgements.' What are the implications of this for accounting change?
2. 'Never mind the gap, study the practice' (Scapens, 1994). Why did Scapens make this observation?
3. 'Institutionalism provides a variety of theoretical perspectives.' How did accounting researchers operate within this variety?
4. What are the commonalities as well as the differences between NIS and ANT?
5. 'The interpretive project is apolitical.' Discuss.

FURTHER READING

1. For the fundamentals of interpretive accounting research, see Tomkins and Groves (1983).
2. When you have time for a good reflection on empirical findings from an interpretive sociology perspective, see Rosenberg *et al.* (1982) and Berry *et al.* (1985).
3. For the basic frameworks of old institutional theory and management accounting, see Scapens (1994) and Burns and Scapens (2000).
4. If you are interested in practical stories, a good empirical work on institutional theory is Lukka (2007).
5. The best recent NIS work is Hopper and Major (forthcoming).
6. For an overall understanding of actor–network theory and its application to recent management accounting changes, see Briers and Chua (2001) and Jones and Dugdale (2001).

Chapter 14

Towards political economy of MACh

A STARTING POINT: POLITICS OF STRUGGLES

According to Karl Marx and Friedrich Engels (1985), perhaps the most radical political thinkers on the history of capitalism, the history of all hitherto existing society is the history of class struggle. They understand all earlier epochs of history almost everywhere in the world as a complicated arrangement of society into various orders, 'a manifold gradation of social rank'. For example, in ancient Rome we had patricians, knights, plebeians and slaves. In the Middle Ages, this social order was manifested by feudal lords, vassals, guild-masters, journeymen, apprentices, serfs and so on. Modern capitalism, they argue, has not done away with class antagonism; instead it has established new classes, new conditions of oppression, new forms of struggle in place of the old ones.

Michel Foucault (Foucault, 2002), the French post-Marxist philosopher, also believes that forms of oppression and struggles are the defining forces of social evolution. For him, there are three types of struggle: against forms of domination (ethnic, social and religious); against forms of exploitation that separate individuals from what they produce; and against forms of subjectivity and submission (that which ties the individual to himself and submits him to others in this way). For Foucault, the dominance of each of these forms distinguishes one historical epoch from another. For example, in feudal societies, struggles against ethnic or social domination were prevalent, even though economic exploitation could have been very important among the causes of revolt (Foucault, 2002: 331). The struggle against exploitation came into the foreground during the nineteenth century. Nowadays, Foucault believes, the struggle against subjection, against submission and subjectivity, is becoming more and more important, even though the struggles against domination and exploitation have not disappeared.

How can these political perspectives on modes of oppression and struggles illuminate our understanding of management control, management accounting and their changes?

SETTING THE SCENE

We have reached the final phase of this text, which could be your starting point for going beyond this book and researching the changing world of management accounting. Thus, at this stage, it would be useful to recollect our journey so far. As you will recall, we initially dealt with various management accounting techniques (Chapters 3–6), which stemmed from the Scientific Management movement during the early decades of the twentieth century, and which characterized mechanistic organizations. Then, in the second part of the book (Chapters 7–10), we dealt with the context and content of the transition of those mechanistic forms of organization and management accounting techniques towards post-mechanistic forms. In that way, the first and second parts of the book portrayed a historical transformation of the approaches to management control and accounting.

Chapters 11, 12 and 13 of the book took us beyond management accounting practices into the theoretical world of management accounting. There we went through a set of alternative theoretical perspectives that we can deploy to research changing management accounting practices. First, by reading about neoclassical economic perspectives (Chapter 11), mainly agency theory and transaction cost economics, we started to understand management accounting techniques and their changes as a set of evolving solutions to the 'agency problem' within and between organizations, across markets, hierarchies and their hybrid forms. Second, by exploring contingency theories on management accounting (Chapter 12), we brought in various non-economic contingency factors, such as environment, technology, organizational structure and strategy to explain management accounting practices beyond their economic face. Third, we went on to present the main propositions of 'alternatives' to the conventional economic and contingency theory-based research perspective (Chapter 13). There we learned how interpretive sociology and institutional economics and sociology influenced research into management accounting practices.

Now, in this chapter, we will turn towards 'critical theories' to explain management accounting practices and their changes within a wider political domain, with 'political' denoting how various modes of social struggle for power, domination and resistance are reproduced within organizational settings, and how management accounting can constitute an inherent element of such social struggles.

Thus, the aim of this chapter, and the next, is to introduce you to a set of critical theories popular among critical accounting researchers. This chapter will mainly concentrate on Marxist and neo-Marxist theories, while in the next chapter you will read about some postmodern and post-structuralist extensions to the critical research agenda.

We will first discuss the meaning of the term 'critical research'. We will present four basic characteristics that define and distinguish critical research from other types. Thus, after reading this section, you should be able to describe salient characteristics of critical research on management accounting.

■   Describe salient features of critical research

Second, we will introduce you to the orthodox Marxist reading of society, its fundamental antagonisms and evolution. We will first present the basic Marxist theoretical notions of mode of production, labour process and formal and real subsumption of labour, etc. Next, we will discuss a seminal work in the Marxist tradition of analysing organizational control, Braverman's *Labor and Monopoly Capital* (1974). Thus, after reading this section, you will be able to: describe a set of basic theoretical notions of orthodox Marxism; describe the major contribution of Braverman's *Labor and Monopoly Capital*; and discuss Braverman's influence on critical accounting research with a set of examples from management accounting research.

443

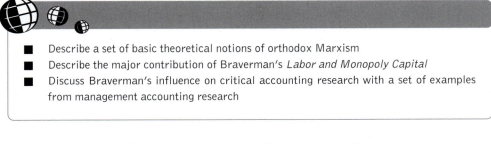

- Describe a set of basic theoretical notions of orthodox Marxism
- Describe the major contribution of Braverman's *Labor and Monopoly Capital*
- Discuss Braverman's influence on critical accounting research with a set of examples from management accounting research

Third, the chapter will introduce you to the 'problem of missing subjectivity' in the Braverman version of the labour process. By reading this section you will be able to: differentiate between alternative meanings that we can attribute to the term 'subjectivity'; and describe alternative approaches to rectify the problem of missing subjectivity.

- Differentiate between alternative meanings that we can attribute to the term 'subjectivity'
- Describe alternative approaches to rectify the problem of missing subjectivity

Fourth, the chapter will deal with how the issue of subjectivity is dealt with by neo-Marxist thinkers, mainly Friedman and Burawoy, and how their structuralist perspectives on subjectivity can illuminate the conception of management accounting and its evolution. In this section, you will learn how 'consent' is manufactured through the particular organization of labour processes. After reading the section, you will be able to: describe the notions of Friedman's 'responsible autonomy' and Burawoy's 'manufacturing consent'; and relate those concepts to the dialectical evolution of management control systems.

- Describe the notions of Friedman's 'responsible autonomy' and Burawoy's 'manufacturing consent'
- Relate those concepts to the dialectical evolution of management control systems

Then, you will go through a section that will mainly deal with Burawoy's conception of politics of production and the historical evolution of factory regimes. This section will help you understand how wider political apparatuses of state intervention in economic enterprises could shape and reshape control at the point of production. Having introduced you to Burawoy's conception of despotism and hegemony in factory regimes, this section will also direct you to a couple of pieces of research that mobilize the notion 'politics of production' to explain Third World idiosyncrasies.

After reading this section, you will be able to: describe Burawoy's typology of factory regimes; explain how Burawoy conceptualizes the interplay between factory regimes and the state apparatus; and describe how Burawoy's notion of factory regimes has been deployed to explain the politics of production in the Third World, or the 'hidden abode of underdevelopment'.

- Describe Burawoy's typology of factory regimes
- Explain how Burawoy conceptualizes the interplay between factory regimes and the state apparatus
- Describe how Burawoy's notion of factory regimes has been deployed to explain the politics of production in the Third World

Finally, the chapter moves to the Gramscian conception of hegemony and its use in critical management accounting research. In this section, you will learn the neo-Marxist perspective on how consent is manufactured beyond the immediate apparatus of labour processes by diffusing and popularizing ruling-class ideologies through civil society institutions. After reading this section, you will be able to: describe the Gramscian notion of hegemony; describe the dialectical relationship between economy, political state and civil society; and explain how institutions in civil society can be influential in shaping and reshaping control at the point of production.

- Describe the Gramscian notion of hegemony
- Describe the dialectical relationship between economy, political state and civil society
- Explain how institutions in civil society can be influential in shaping and reshaping control at the point of production

WHAT IS CRITICAL?

Defining 'critical theory' is not an easy task, especially when 'taking a critical perspective has become a catch-phrase and something of a cliché' and when 'most academics think their work is critical because the topics they study are important and because they criticise other research' (Jermier, 1998: 235). However, the term 'critical' is used in 'critical management studies' to mean something different from the mere significance or the criticism, denoting a distinctive approach to study social relations in and beyond organizational boundaries. We have identified four defining and distinguishing characteristics of 'critical theory' perspectives on management accounting change.

Critical management studies mean something more than the mere significance or the criticism. They denote a distinctive approach to study social relations in and beyond organizational boundaries.

Seeing through wider society

Critical theorists believe that organizational phenomena of management control and accounting cannot be fully appreciated unless they are linked to the wider socio-political context within which they operate. That said, organizational phenomena of management control and accounting cannot have emergence, existence or evolution independent from wider social transformations, especially from the transformative character of capitalism, whether it is early capitalism, monopoly capitalism, advanced capitalism, late capitalism, post-capitalism or any kinds of capitalism found, for example, in the Third World. Thus, critical research into management accounting demands a thoughtful examination of wider social structures and discourses to locate various management accounting phenomena within those social structures and discourses. Emphasizing the reciprocity between the macro and micro, Jones and Dugdale (2001: 58), for example, define an 'accounting regime' as 'a system of governance that operates at the *macro level* of national and international society, polity, and economy; at the *micro level of organization*; and permeates the *personal level* where accounting constitutes both rules and resources for action'. Most importantly, therefore, critical theorists situate management accounting not simply within organizational and market parameters but within the historically evolving character of capitalism. Accordingly, Cooper and Hopper (2006: 5) argue that 'accounting is not an inevitable outcome of market forces or technological change but is implicated in, and reflects, political, social and economic struggles, the outcomes of which are contingent'.

Critical research into management accounting demands a thoughtful examination of wider social structures and discourses in order to locate various management accounting phenomena within those social structures and discourses.

Seeing through conflicts and contradictions

Social relations are the focus of critical studies; and for critical theorists, social relations are political. By the term 'political' we mean that men and women, in the social reproduction of their lives, enter into contradictory and conflicting relations with not only other men and women but also with various social institutions such as economic enterprises and the state. Societies are stratified and divided along various material and ideological lines, such as class, gender, ethnicity and race, as well as professional and occupational affiliations and identities. These stratifications are not simple categorizations of men and women into different kinds, but structural bases upon which social conflicts and struggles are constructed, through which power is exercised to dominate and exploit others, and individual identities and subjectivities are constituted. Most importantly, replicating these wider social stratifications, 'the workplace becomes an arena of politics that constructs and mobilises different identities, not just worker identities but also gender and racial identities' (Burawoy, 1996: 298). For critical philosophers like Marx and Foucault, social struggles provide the social impetus for revolutionary or evolutionary changes in the social system. By the same token, critical accounting researchers also believe that their focus should be on contradictions, conflicts and struggles within and beyond economic organizations the better to explicate changes in management accounting practices, because, for them, these conflicts and struggles, in the first place, create the need for control. Thus, for example, Hopper and Armstrong (1991) emphasize the significance of capitalist struggles to subsume labour in explaining the evolution of management accounting. And Armstrong (2000) provides an example of how the fundamental conflict between capital and labour is replicated in 'flexible' work arrangements. For many Foucauldian writers (e.g., Hopwood and Miller, 1994; Miller and O'Leary, 1987; Hoskin and Macve, 1994), management accounting techniques and practices constitute disciplinary mechanisms and technologies by which men and women are constituted to be governed by numbers, but at a distance.

> The focus of critical accounting research should be on contradictions, conflicts and struggles within and beyond economic organizations in order to explicate changes in management accounting practices.

Seeing through social history

For critical management accounting researchers, historical analysis is a profound methodological element. This is because, for them, 'accounting history is likely to have a much enhanced and wider impact to the extent that it can demonstrate how the emergence and operation of accounting as a highly distinctive knowledge, body of expertise or know-how is formed and deployed with the potential of shaping and transforming the types of social relations we inhabit' (Miller et al., 1991: 399). However, one distinguishing point should be emphasized here. For critical researchers, 'historical' means much more than the chronological ordering of historical events in terms of who invented what, when and where. A good example of the latter kind of study is that of Sowell (1973), where he documented the chronology of inventions in standard costing techniques and theories from the late nineteenth century to the mid-twentieth. Critical accounting histories, or 'new' accounting histories as they are often called, on the other hand, focus on the reciprocal relationship between 'social history' and 'accounting history' (see Tinker, 1980). For them, social history is inseparable from accounting history. Any story of the evolution of management accounting techniques and practices which is told independent of, and detached from, social history would serve only a narrow informational purpose, as it does not 'explain' wider structural reasons that resulted in the social (re)production of those control practices within the micro-organizational context. For critical theories, therefore, accounting histories are the micro-analysis of macro-level social changes.

> Management accounting histories are inseparable from social histories. Accounting histories are the micro-analysis of macro-level social changes.

447

Emancipatory engagement for the mistreated

When you were reading about neoclassical economic theories and contingency theories in Chapters 11 and 12, you might have understood that their implicit and explicit aims are to serve the capitalist objective of profit-maximization, although with the assumption that an 'equilibrium' can be reached in that way, where all parties to a firm's transactions and relations can 'maximize' or 'satisfy' their respective objectives. Interpretive theories, which we discussed in Chapter 13, somewhat differently, attempt to be politically neutral by 'describing' and 'interpreting' social relations in an apolitical stance by assuming a 'neutral' (but not necessarily objective) role for the 'researchers'.[1] So they implicitly assume that their contribution is to 'knowledge', which is assumed to be neutral because it is open for any political actor, whether it is capital, labour or any other. Critical theorists, on the other hand, are different from both these political stances in that they, as Jermier (1998: 236) argues, 'maintain that in stratified and divided societies, more powerful groups and individuals reap the benefits of participating in processes through which less powerful people and the natural environment are mistreated'. Therefore, they take, often explicitly, the side of the mistreated: labour, females, marginalized groups such as ethnic, race and other minority groups, society and nature and so on. Thus, for example, taking the perspective of workers' well-being, Armstrong's (2000: 383) study on flexible budgeting and other employment relations concludes with the assertion that 'the achievement of the long-standing trade union aim of security of income and employment will depend, in part, on changing these systems of control'. For Jermier (1998: 241), as an another example, affiliation with the mistreated is needed to produce a better understanding of the circumstances of the mistreated, thereby facilitating initiatives and struggles to address and rectify the problems stemming from abusive control. In essence, therefore, critical research involves not only socially informed critiques and rejection of accounting practices and research that contribute to the reproduction of social injustices, inequality, dominance and exploitation, but also active engagement and activism in struggles to build social awareness and alternatives.

> Critical researchers, often explicitly, take the side of the mistreated: labour, females, marginalized groups such as ethnic, race and other minority groups, society and nature, and so on.

In summary, our use of the term 'critical research' in this text is confined to a spectrum of management accounting research which: attempts to understand micro-level management accounting practices in the light of macro-level social and political transformations; depicts the society and its institutions as characterized by contradictions and conflicts in unequal and exploitative social relations; attributes to socio-political history the power to explain the evolution of management accounting; and calls for self-reflexive engagement and activism for the emancipation of the mistreated (see Figure 14.1). Nevertheless, there is no general uniformity, consistency or consciousness among critical management accounting researchers. Critical theory is a loose collection of widely debated (within the critical research circle itself) and ever-evolving research, whose theoretical roots spread across a wider set of social theories holding fundamentally different ontological assumptions on the social world. Management accounting researchers' ontological assumptions are by and large derived from the social theories they embrace and the idiosyncrasies

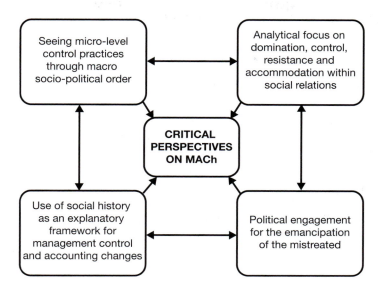

Figure 14.1 *Defining characteristics of critical perspectives*

of the empirical sites with which they are associated. Mainly on the basis of the social theories that fascinate them, we can identify three distinct schools of thought that fall under the broader heading of critical management accounting research.

■ Marxist and neo-Marxist research in management accounting, or political economy (or even cultural-political economy) of management accounting.
■ Post-modern perspectives, mainly Foucauldian and Derridian perspectives.
■ Habermasian or the Frankfurt school's 'Critical Theory'.

> Three major branches of critical research are: Marxist and neo-Marxist approaches; post-modern or post-structuralist approaches; and Habermasian approaches.

MARXIST AND NEO-MARXIST PERSPECTIVES ON MANAGEMENT ACCOUNTING

Marx's influence in social sciences is pervasive. It is hardly possible to name any social science discipline where a Marxist theory or perspective is not present. Accounting has never been exceptional but, especially in UK accounting academia, Marx is present and debated more than any other political philosopher. It is not an exaggeration to say that the whole set of projects constructing a critical thought of management and accounting is in, around and beyond the labour process theory – the epicentre of Marxist understanding of production and control.

Harry Braverman's seminal work, *Labor and Monopoly Capital* (1974), first brought the labour process theory to the forefront of the theoretical analysis of control at the organizational level. It

449

gave the initial impetus to a range of rich academic factions which entered into the famous 'labour process debate', the influence of which on accounting academia was especially remarkable. However, before getting into the labour process debate and its ramifications for management accounting research, it would be helpful to understand the conceptual framework that Marx offers us in terms of labour process and the mode of production.

Marxism's influence on critical accounting research is pervasive.

Labour process, mode of production and labour control

As we noted at the beginning of this chapter, Marxist ontology of society is the class struggle. That said, the fundamental social antagonism that shapes everything else is the division of society into labour and capital. Labour processes are the intervening social spaces in which this abstract antagonism between capital and labour (or any other categories, such as gender or castes, if applicable) is brought to the behavioural surface in terms of coercion, resistance and consent. For Marx, therefore, the labour process is at the centre of social analysis (Littler, 1982). If work organizations are viewed as emergent properties of the class struggle (Storey, 1983), then labour processes are specific social spaces in which the class struggle is materialized in the struggles for subordination of labour power to capital. They are the productive social spaces in which labour is directly entangled with capital. As control of labour aims to 'translate labour power into labour and thereby to realise surplus value' (Storey, 1983: 123), labour processes constitute the basis of control structures and relations.

Labour processes are specific social spaces in which the class struggle is materialized in the struggles for subordination of labour power to capital, and therefore constitute the basis of control structures and relations.

According to Marxist understanding, there are two sets of relations in and around the labour process: relations *of* production and relations *in* production. The set of relations within which surplus labour is expropriated from the direct labour or immediate producers is termed relations of production (Burawoy, 1979). Obviously, these are 'relations of economic ownership or property relations' and they are defined as 'the basis of general relations of dominance and subordination, both within and beyond the sphere of production' (Littler, 1982: 20). Relations in production, or production relations, on the other hand, are the relational aspects of the labour process itself. They are the 'set of relations into which men and women enter as they confront nature, as they transform raw materials into objects of their imagination' (Burawoy, 1979: 15). Thus, relations in production determine how surplus value is created, while relations of production dictate the way in which that surplus value is appropriated.

The combination of relations of production and relations in production forms the economic basis on which the superstructure of society is raised. Superstructural elements such as forms of

> There are two sets of relations in and around the labour process: relations *of* production and relations *in* production.

consciousness and culture, systems of ideology, types of politics and states correspond to the level of development of this economic base. For Marx (1976), men and women, in the social production of their lives, enter into definite relations that are indispensable and independent of their will. He calls the sum total of these relations of production the economic structure of society, the real foundation on which a legal and political superstructure as well as definite forms of social consciousness (ideology) are based.

Nevertheless, despite this profound influence, it is argued that there is a dialectical determination between the economic basis of society and its superstructural elements. This dialectic allows the superstructure and its constituent elements a history which is in part their own (Peet, 1980). Such dialectics between the economic foundation and the superstructure make the mode of production (see Figure 14.2) pertaining to a given society in a specific historical phase. Thus, according to orthodox Marxism, the mode of production is the defining character of different social formations. That means, for example, feudalism is different from capitalism, while advanced capitalism is different from early phases of capitalist development or capitalist underdevelopment, because the mode of production in each of these historical phases encompasses its own historical conditions. In essence, the notion of mode of production depicts the 'totality' of the social system, of which historical evolution is dependent upon its inherent contradictions, both those embedded in the relations of and in production, and those between structural and the superstructural elements.

> Mode of production is the defining characteristic of different social formations, and consists of an economic base and the superstructure.

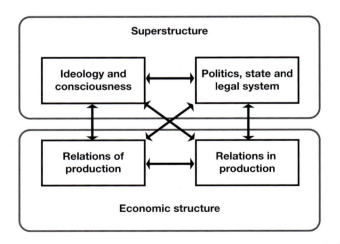

Figure 14.2 *Elements in mode of production*

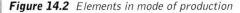

As shown in Figure 14.2, the parameters of mode of production include both economic and superstructural elements, namely relations in and of production (the economic structure), ideology and governing institutions of state, politics and legal system. Within these parameters lies the problem of labour control. At its most abstract level, this denotes subordination of labour for the interests of capital. Marxist writers identify two types of subordination (subsumption): formal subordination and real subordination. According to Marx (1976: 1019), formal subordination of labour under capital takes place when the labour process is subsumed under capital and the capitalists intervene in the process as its directors and managers. Indeed, this takes place when the independent producers of archaic modes of production turn into wage labour. Hence, the essence of formal subordination of labour is the wage relationship between labour and capital, whereby labour becomes dependent upon capital for its existence and reproduction. However, in the absence of real subordination, 'capital subsumes the labour process as it finds it, that is to say, it takes over an existing labour process, developed by different and more archaic modes of production' (Marx, 1976: 1021). Hence, the 'practical aspects of labour process' (Burawoy, 1979: 15) are, to a larger extent, under the control of the direct producer (labour). This is the subordination of labour outside the realm of production, but within labour market relations. In the transition from feudalism to capitalism, labour was freed from its archaic relationship with the land and made dependent upon capital, so labour is 'formally' subordinated to capital. In this phase, the dominant mode of extracting surplus is the absolute surplus value: that is, the surplus value produced by prolonging the working day.

> Labour control, at its most abstract level, denotes subordination of labour for the interests of capital: both formal and real subordination. Formal subordination is the subordination of labour outside the realm of production, but within labour market relations.

Real subsumption, on the other hand, occurs within the realm of production, when capital develops its capacity to take control of 'practical aspects of the labour process'. This happens through technological and managerial innovations, which shorten the labour time socially necessary for the reproduction of the value of labour. In this case, therefore, the creation of surplus value is enhanced through improving the productiveness of labour, as opposed to prolonging the working day. This is called the relative surplus value, as opposed to the absolute surplus value.

> Real subsumption occurs when capital develops its capacity to take control of 'practical aspects of the labour process'.

The development of the capitalist labour process is generally conceived in the line of transition from formal subordination to real subordination (e.g., Braverman, 1998; Edwards, 1979; Littler, 1982; Marx, 1976). Nevertheless, there are major controversies regarding the transition from formal subordination to real subordination. For example, Marx suggests that the crucial transition to real subordination occurred during the industrial revolution with the mechanization of craft production, whereas Braverman suggests that real subordination took place under monopoly capitalism in the form of the detailed labour process controls of Taylorism (see next section, and Chapter 2).

Debating the labour process: Braverman's beginning

Long after Marx's *Capital* but before Braverman's *Labor and Monopoly Capital*, there was a mythical man (rather than a woman, of course) in the minds of many industrial sociologists who were analysing human behaviour in work organizations. This man was rather atomic, in the sense that he was an individual psychic entity whose need hierarchy was the underlying force of his behaviour. He was apolitical because he himself had created a great impenetrable wall between his working life and his (personal) political life, which is often understood to be voting and electing his political masters. In the discourses of business school education, it was largely acknowledged that this man was remotely affected by political, economic, social and technological environments, which were magnificently depicted by different segments of a surrounding dot-lined circle. The conflicting and resistant character that he often exemplified in the work setting, it was understood, was due to irrational management thought and consequent irrational work arrangements and incentives (rather than expressions of his political identity and local-level reproduction of wider social antagonisms). The relationship that managers had with this man, it was assumed, was one-to-one in nature, and the central task of management was to design and implement efficient and effective behavioural devices (such as MBO, incentive schemes, grievance handling systems and many more) so that he would indeterminately be motivated by and committed to company objectives. Like a machine, he needed the right behavioural grease. So, this man was given a special name: human resource.

Neoclassical assumptions of human behaviour in work organizations were rather apolitical and ahistorical.

Braverman's *Labor and Monopoly Capital* converted this neoclassical image of human resource into the labourer within the Marxist class framework. As Spencer (2000: 225) stated: 'Braverman's key contribution was to position the issues of class and history at the centre of the analysis of work. He located workplace transformation in a broader understanding of the specificities of capitalist production, demonstrating the determining role played by class conflict in shaping organisational outcomes.' He located the then dominant managerial ideology and practice – Scientific Management – within the historical dynamics of capitalism. For Braverman, contrary to Marx, the real subordination of labour occurred not through the mechanization of the labour process but as a result of 'Taylorization'. Braverman argued that Taylorism facilitated real subordination first by dislocating the labour process from the skills of the worker, and then by rendering the labour process independent of craft, tradition and workers' knowledge. 'Henceforth it is to depend not at all upon the abilities of workers, but entirely upon the practices of management,' he declared (Braverman, 1998: 78). Second, he argued, Taylorism was instrumental in controlling and cheapening the worker by rendering conception and execution separate spheres of work. He stated (Braverman, 1998: 81):

For this purpose the study of work processes must be reserved to management and kept from the workers, to whom its results are communicated only in the form of simplified job tasks governed by simplified instructions which it is thenceforth their duty to follow unthinkingly and without comprehension of the underlying technical reasoning or data.

Third, he argued, the management's monopoly thus created over knowledge of work was used to control each step of the labour process and its mode of execution; so labour is now really subordinated to the 'work knowledge of capital': 'The more science is incorporated into the labour process, the less the worker understands of the process; the more sophisticated an intellectual product the machine becomes, the less control and comprehension of the machine the worker has' (Braverman, 1998: 295).

> For Braverman, contrary to Marx, the real subordination of labour occurred not through the mechanization of the labour process but as a result of 'Taylorization'.

The effect of the application of Taylorism in subordinating the labour process extends beyond the labour process itself to the labour market. Taylorism is substantiated by 'a general principle of maximum fragmentation' (Littler, 1982: 51), which converts workers to a 'homogeneous grouping of interchangeable parts' and 'mere appendages to machines requiring little on-the-job training' (Foster, 1998: xiv). Thus, labourers are readily interchangeable not only between different job elements in the labour process, but also for one another in the labour market. This means widening the application of Taylorism, whereby the labourer loses his dominance not only in the 'abode of production' but also in the outer space of the labour market.

> The effect of the application of Taylorism in subordinating the labour process extends beyond the labour process itself to the labour market; the labourer loses his dominance not only in the 'abode of production' but also in the outer space of the labour market.

In this manner, Braverman adds the phase of monopoly capitalism to the evolution of capitalism in advanced societies. Then, he discusses how various categorical elements such as science and mechanization, surplus value and surplus labour, the modern corporation, the universal market and the state operate within this overall mode of monopoly capitalism. Finally, he further extends his discussion into the dynamics of various working-class occupations in line with his central theme: the degradation of work in the twentieth century.

Braverman's inspiration was far reaching. A series of studies concerning the labour process in different industrial settings immediately followed (e.g., case studies in the edited collection by Zimbalist, 1976). Renewed attention was paid to the theorization of class struggle at the point of production (e.g., Boreham *et al.*, 1986; Clegg and Dunkerly, 1980; Glenn and Feldberg, 1976; Nichols and Beynon, 1977; Yates, 1999). The neoclassical economic history of management accounting was challenged and a 'new' Marxist history of management accounting was written

(Hopper and Armstrong, 1991; see also Chapter 2 of this volume). Various issues of organizational control received labour process insight (e.g., Armstrong 1986, 1989, 1991; Clegg, 1981, 1990a and b; Hakken, 2000; Hopper *et al*. 1986; Storey 1983, 1985, 1986; Teulings, 1986). Extended insights of the labour process debate have been in the forefront of analysing emerging organizational phenomena such as TQM and BPR (e.g., Knights and McCabe, 1998a and b, 2000; McCabe, 2000). And a few studies were located outside the context of advanced capitalism (e.g., Burawoy, 1985; Hoque and Hopper, 1994; Uddin and Hopper, 2001; Warhust, 1998). Most important are the diverse (and diluted) critiques in the Bravermanian debate, which brought 'other tools of analysis' (e.g., Jaros, 2001; Thompson, 1990) into the labour process debate. These extensions, say Thompson and Smith (2001: 45), 'could have branched from any body of theory, but it just happened to coincide with the labour process debate'. Most of these extensions hinge upon the notion of 'subjectivity', to which we will introduce you in the next section.

Braverman's inspiration was far reaching; the Marxist framework, especially labour process analysis, was pervasively used to understand various organizational phenomena in the light of class antagonisms.

Orthodox Marxist framework and accounting research: some examples

Orthodox Marxist understanding of relations in and of production has long been a framework for accounting research. In the early phase of critical research in accounting, mainly in the late 1970s and early 1980s, the basic orientation was to offer a radical alternative to the dominance of neo-classical economics in accounting research. Tinker's (1980) paper is a classic example of this.

In the early phase of critical research in accounting, the basic orientation was to offer a radical alternative to the dominance of neoclassical economics in accounting research.

Tinker (1980) offers a radical alternative to the marginalist theoretical base in accounting. He mobilizes Marx's labour theory of value to show that the magnitude of expenses in the income statement and their resulting profit are indicative of the social, institutional and monopolistic power of capital, rather than social efficiency and productivity, as is assumed by neoclassical economics. The significance of this paper is that it brings power relations, or social relations of production, to the forefront in interpreting and understanding accounting information. Tinker vividly exemplifies the differences between marginalist interpretations of accounting information and Marxist interpretations. According to him, neoclassical economics' marginalist explanation of profit is akin to the engineering treatment of production: a mere technological treatment of converting input into output where profit figures are the efficiency criteria of that technological conversion. Political economics' interpretations, on the other hand, rely on an analysis of the division of power between interest groups in a society, and the institutional processes through which interests may be advanced. Thus, from a political economics perspective, profit is indicative of something more than technological efficiency: namely, the distribution of power in society and the socio-political and institutional structure that mirrors that distribution of power (Tinker, 1980: 147).

> From a political economics perspective, profit is indicative of something more than techno-logical efficiency: the distribution of power in society and the socio-political and institutional structure that mirrors that distribution of power.

Tinker uses a historical case study, Delco – a UK-based multinational operated in Sierra Leone – to crystallize the differences between these theoretical alternatives. His political economics explanations of Delco's accounting profit is advanced by a theoretical regression of the Delco accounting history with the social and political conditions underlying each phase of the history. For that, he divides the Delco accounting history into three distinct historical phases: early colonial, late colonial and post-colonial. An income statement is then prepared for each period that summarizes the distribution of the firm's income for that period. The differences between the three income statements are then linked with changes in the social and political conditions underlying the figures. In that way, Tinker shows that the income data are products of the socio-economic reality that constitutes unequal distribution of power between capital and labour, and a socio-political and institutional structure that mirrors that distribution of power.

> Income data are products of the socio-economic reality that constitutes unequal distribution of power between capital and labour, and a socio-political and institutional structure that mirrors that distribution of power.

As we have already noted in Chapter 2, the Marxist notion of labour process has been a popular theoretical framework to explain management accounting history (Hopper and Armstrong, 1991). There is another set of historical research in accounting, especially Bryer (1991, 1993, 2000, 2005, 2006), which deploys orthodox Marxism as an explanatory framework. However, in contrast to Hopper and Armstrong's emphasis on the social conflicts and contradictions embedded in labour processes, Bryer's accounting histories concentrate more on Marx's labour theory of value and the historicities that helped develop capitalist calculative mentalities, especially in British trade and agriculture (in contrast to Hopper and Armstrong's concentration on American manufacture[2]). His papers provide a series of historical accounts of the evolving character of class conflicts in British agriculture and trade, and support, *inter alia*, the assertions that the 'calculative mentality of modern capitalism, the maximization of the rate of return on capital employed in production, emerged from the historical interaction of capitalistic mentalities in agriculture and trade' (Bryer, 2000: 327). There is another important point to note about Bryer's accounting histories: while he uses Marx's labour theory of value to explicate accounting history, he also uses history to validate and justify theoretical assertions in Marx's theories of value and capitalist development.

Marx's labour theory of value has been instrumental in explicating economic and accounting histories beyond manufacture, in agriculture and trade.

Cooper and Taylor's (2000) study is a classic test of Braverman's de-skilling thesis in accounting craft. By 'accounting craft' they mean the accounting jobs carried out by non-professional elements of the accounting industry, mainly bookkeeping clerks. They present a study that traces the historical tendency of de-skilling in the accounting craft from the mid-nineteenth century to 1996. By doing that, they propose that the majority work experience in the accounting industry is one of de-skilling according to Tayloristic Scientific Management principles (Cooper and Taylor, 2000: 556). While illustrating how Braverman's de-skilling thesis can illuminate our understanding of the 'progress' in the accounting industry during the 1970s, 1980s and 1990s, they also shed some light on its future when 'new management philosophies' might marginalize accounting as a 'non-core function', leading to its outsourcing in a fashion similar to cleaning and catering functions.

The historical tendencies in accounting craft, according to Cooper and Taylor, offer a classic example of Braverman's de-skilling thesis.

The problem of 'subjectivity' in the labour process

In the foreword to the original edition of Braverman's *Labor and Monopoly Capital*, Paul Sweezy (in Braverman, 1998: xxv) wrote: 'Harry Braverman, however, does not attempt to pursue the inquiry into what may be called the subjective aspects of the development of the working class under monopoly capitalism. That task remains to be tackled'. What Sweezy preferred to call the 'subjective aspects of the development of the working class' was attached to the issues of subjectivity, identity and post-structuralism. It is argued that 'a major limitation of orthodox labour process theory . . . [is] its rudimentary conception of the nature and significance of subjectivity and identity for analysing the dynamics of workplace relations' (O'Doherty and Willmott, 2001b: 112). Then, it is proposed that this deficiency 'can be addressed by reconstructing labour process theory through a careful and sustained engagement with poststructuralist thinking' (ibid.).

Braverman's *Labor and Monopoly Capital* was initially criticized for its neglect of the subjective dimensions of the labour process.

The notion of subjectivity has had different meanings, content and intentions in the labour process debate. Foucault (2002: 331) provides a good starting point to review these differences when he claims that 'there are two meanings of the word "subject": subject to someone else by control and dependence, and tied to his own identity by a conscience or self-knowledge'. The

457

implication of this dual meaning of 'subject' is expressed in his typology of struggles and modes of objectification. He notes three modes of struggle, the prevalence of which varies according to different historical epochs. His typology of modes of objectification – different modes by which human beings are transformed into subjects – identifies three such modes. The first is the mode of inquiry that tries to give itself the status of science. The second is the 'dividing practices' that either divide the subject inside him/herself or divide him/her from others (examples are, according to Foucault (2002: 326), the divisions between the mad and the sane, between the sick and the healthy and between criminals and 'good boys'). The third is the mode by which a human being turns him/herself into a subject (ibid.: 326–327). Table 14.1 synthesizes the interrelationship of different modes of subject, struggle and objectification, as proposed by Foucault.

> Foucault identifies two meanings of the term 'subject': subject to someone else by control and dependence, and subject to his/her own identity by conscience or self-knowledge.

A careful review of attempts to bring agency back into labour process theory reveals that there are two broader branches of thought in this respect, which more or less align with the above typology of the 'subject'. Depending on the domain of empirical inquiry and the phenomenological emphasis given to the empirics, studies exemplify either of the two meanings attached to 'subject': subject to someone else by control and dependence; and subject to his/her own identity by conscience or self-knowledge, or reflexive capacity of human agency.

First, subjectivity is conceptualized and empirically validated within the modes of struggle against domination and exploitation. It was soon understood that 'the workplace becomes an arena of struggle for shaping subjectivities – it becomes an arena of politics that constructs and mobilizes different identities, not just worker identities but also gender and racial identities, harnessed to managerial interests' (Burawoy, 1996: 298). These initial theorizations of subjectivity within the labour process debate began as a result of attempts to correct the 'objectivist bias' of Braverman's version of the labour process in monopoly capitalism. Classic examples of these types of theorization of subjectivity are the 'responsible autonomy' of Friedman (1977) and the 'manufacturing consent' of Burawoy (1979). An important feature of these studies is that they seek to explain subjectivities and identities within the fundamental dualism of control and resistance. They find that control strategies of capitalist organizations create social spaces for the individual subjectivities and identities that are not necessarily antagonistic to the control strategies, but adjusting and accommodating. They acknowledge the dualism between capital and labour but attempt to signify the role of agency of labour within the structures of a capitalist work arrangement. However, their orientation to address the issue of subjectivity in the labour process is more akin to Foucault's first definition of subjectivity, mentioned above. For example, for Burawoy (1979), it is the specific organization of the labour process itself that manufactures consent. Thus, for neo-Marxists, the structural conditions to which human agents are subjected provide the necessary social space within which they can exercise their subjectivities.

Second, the issue of subjectivity is addressed by moving beyond the Marxist ontology of structural antagonism between capital and labour, especially by bringing in Foucauldian and Derridian theories of post-structuralism. Here, 'subjectivity' is defined as 'a person's ability to make decisions

Table 14.1 *Subject, modes of struggles and modes of objectification*

Meaning of subject	Mode of struggles*	Mode of objectification	Empirical domains in organizational studies
Subject to someone else (and perhaps something else)	1. Against forms of domination 2. Against forms of exploitation	1. Science 2. Dividing practices (and perhaps dividing ideologies) 3. Self-objectification	Control practices and strategies, resistance, accommodation, manufacturing consent, etc.
Subject to own identity by conscience or self-knowledge	3. Against forms of subjectivity and submission		Self and identity politics (within postmodern) and modes of consciousness (in pre-LP studies: for example, Goldthorpe *et al.*, 1969; McKenzie and Silver, 1968; Newby, 1977; Nichols and Beynon, 1977)

Note:

* We should emphasize at this point that there is a conceptual ambiguity in the de-differentiation between these different modes of struggle. Other than the paragraph quoted above, Foucault does not provide a detailed clarification of the differences between the terms 'domination', 'exploitation' and 'submission'. Perhaps one implication of his description is that 'domination' refers to the social aspects of control of one social category by another (such as ethnic and religious), whereas 'exploitation' is its economic front which separates the producer from the product (a form of alienation). 'Submission' can then be interpreted as psychological dimensions which include reflexivity or (false) consciousness. Another interpretation is to project these Foucauldian terms into the traditional sociological terminology of coercion and hegemony such that domination and exploitation are different modes of coercion, whereas subjection is hegemonic. Thus, the following typology can be constructed:

	Economic	Extra-economic
Coercive	Exploitation	Domination
Hegemonic	Submission (constitution of subjectivities)	

The first stream of attempts to rectify the neglect of subjectivity in the labour process seeks to explain subjectivities and identities within the fundamental dualism of control and resistance.

in the context of social constraints' (Grugulis and Knights, 2001: 22), or as 'the degree to which workers can exercise agency to shape their experiences' (Jaros, 2001: 38). O'Doherty and Willmott (2001b: 114) acknowledge the same when they define subjectivity as 'the open, reflexive, embodied quality of human agency'. We will deal with these Foucauldian and Derridian perspectives in the next chapter.

459

> The second stream of attempts to rectify the issue of subjectivity moves beyond the Marxist ontology of structural antagonism between capital and labour, especially by bringing in Foucauldian and Derridian theories of post-structuralism.

CONTROL, RESISTANCE AND CONSENT: NEO-MARXIST EXTENSIONS OF LABOUR PROCESS AND CONTROL

In this section, we will briefly introduce you to three major neo-Marxist extensions of the Marxist theorization of labour process and organizational control:

- Friedman's and Burawoy's conceptualization of subjectivity within the labour process.
- Burawoy's theory of factory regimes.
- Gramscian theory of hegemony.

Friedman's responsible autonomy and Burawoy's manufacturing consent

Friedman (1977) was critical of the Marxists' lack of concern about the capacity of labour resistance to force accommodating changes within the capitalist mode of production. He attributed this weakness to the Marxists' concentration on 'the pressure of the industrial reserve army, which allowed capitalists to maintain harsh disciplinary procedures to enforce managerial authority over the majority in factories' (Friedman, 1977: 79). Accordingly, he argued that 'Marxists have generally treated the direct control strategy as the theory and practice of capitalist control over the labour process' (ibid.: 80). His contribution to the labour process debate arises from the understanding that the growing importance of organized worker resistance and internal labour markets gave the impetus to co-opt what he called 'responsible autonomy'. According to Friedman, 'responsible autonomy' and 'direct control' are the two strategies that top management can use to subordinate labour. In the case of responsible autonomy, top management delegates status, authority and responsibility with the aim of winning labour's loyalty. This is akin to what we now call 'empowerment', but within a limited scope. 'Direct control', on the other hand, tries to limit scope for labour power by coercive threats, close supervision and minimizing individual worker responsibility (i.e., a form of de-skilling). According to Friedman (ibid.: 78), 'the first type of strategy attempts to capture benefits particular to variable capital, the second tries to limit its particular harmful effects and treats workers as though they were machines'.

> Friedman identifies two strategies that capital deploys to subordinate labour: direct control and responsible autonomy.

The important point here is the dialectic between control and resistance. The emergence and coexistence of responsible autonomy together with direct control are the results of this dialectic.

Transformations of control practices, according to Edwards (1979), occur as a resolution of intensifying conflict and contradiction in the firm's operations. Resistance is inherent within the labour process and new forms of resistance 'occur under definite historical circumstances, or, what is the same, within specific economic and social contexts' (Edwards, 1979: 15). The existing forms of control no longer effectively contain worker resistance, and capital is forced to experiment with new strategies of control to substitute or supplement the older ones. Within this 'control–resistance' postulation, Edwards posited a secular trend in control strategies from the 'simple' to 'technical' and through to 'bureaucratic control'. This is the basic theoretical notion that Hopper and Armstrong (1991) deploy in their construction of the 'labour process history of management accounting'. According to them (p. 406), the core presupposition of the labour process perspective is that social and economic conflicts arising from the models of control pertaining to a particular phase of capitalistic development stimulate the creation of new forms of control. These new forms of control are intended to eliminate or accommodate resistance and to solve the associated problems of profitability, and they, in turn, decay, partly because their competitive advantage disappears as a consequence of their generalization and partly because they give rise to new contradictions and forms of resistance.

> New modes of control are the product of historical dialectics between existing modes of control and their accommodations, conflicts and resistance. Thus, modes of control evolve in a cycle of crises and solutions.

Burawoy's contribution to the labour process debate is important in three ways. First, he emphasizes the notion of consent in the control–resistance dichotomy of labour process analysis.[3] Second, he locates the labour process in its wider political context by entwining production politics with the state apparatus to conceptualize historically specific factory regimes. Finally, he extends labour process analysis to the 'hidden abode of underdevelopment' (Burawoy, 1985).

Burawoy's distinction arises from his focus on the manufacturing of consent within the labour process. His main thesis in this respect is that the evolution of capitalist political apparatuses, especially state politics, pushes the capitalist to supplement coercion by consent. He is sympathetic to Marx's neglect of consent, given that Marx's original theorization of the labour process was in the context of nineteenth-century capitalism, where the arena for consent was insignificant. However, he argues that 'with the passage of time, as the result of working-class struggles, the wage becomes increasingly independent of the individual expenditure of effort. Accordingly, coercion must be supplemented by the organization of consent' (Burawoy, 1979: 27). Hence, the organization of consent becomes an integral element of the conscious efforts of capital to exercise control over labour.

To Burawoy, consent is manufactured and not a 'subjective state of mind that individuals carry around with them' (ibid.). It is the specific organization of the labour process that manufactures the consent. For him, consent is expressed through, and is the result of, the particular organization of activities in the labour process. He clearly distinguishes the consent from the specific consciousness or subjective attributes of the individual who engages in those activities. When the labour process is organized in such a manner that the worker is presented with real choice, however narrow it might be, the consent is manufactured through the exercise of that choice by the worker.

461

This sense of choice (and chance) underlying manufacturing consent is produced and reproduced by three sets of historical developments within and around the capitalist organization of production: gaming behaviour, an internal labour market and an internal state.

> Consent is manufactured by making the worker exercise choice. The sense of choice and chance underlying the manufacturing of consent is produced by three developments in capitalist organizations: gaming behaviour, an internal labour market and an internal state.

Gaming in the labour process

Burawoy (1979: 51) treats the 'activities on the shop floor as a series of games in which operators attempt to achieve levels of production that earn incentive pay'. However, his ethnographic accounts of the gaming behaviour in Allied Corporation reveal that the game is not simply to achieve incentive pay but extends to the interpersonal dependencies and antagonisms among the workers on the production line. Thus, it becomes a power play between the workers who are placed in dependent elements of the production line. Hence, the game of 'making out' frames not only the productive activities of the individual employee with company interests (which are manifested in incentive targets) but also the social relations among fellow workers in which they are constituted as competing and conflicting with each other. One consequence of this gaming behaviour is that, according to Burawoy (ibid.: 81), it 'inserts the worker into the labour process as an individual rather than as a member of a class distinguished by a particular relationship to the means of production'.[4] Another is that it reconstitutes hierarchical conflicts inherent in a capitalist organization of production into lateral conflicts, in which individual labourers face one another in conflict or competition. Most important is that 'the very activity of playing the game generates consent with respect to its rules' (ibid.), which are the explicit behavioural manifestation of capitalist interests in the labour process.

> When activities on the shop floor are organized to stimulate gaming behaviour among workers, it is capable of: inserting the worker into the labour process as an individual rather than as a member of a class; and reconstituting hierarchical conflicts into lateral conflicts.

Internal labour market

This is the second organizational element that, according to Burawoy, helps manufacture consent within the labour process. The internal labour market is a structural and institutional arrangement of administrative rules and procedures internal to a firm so as to promote mobility within the firm and reduce it between firms. According to Burawoy (1979: 98), the internal labour market is characterized by six structural and institutional arrangements:

a differentiated job structure, an institutionalised means of disseminating information about submitting applications for vacancies, non-arbitrary criteria for selecting employees for vacancies, a system of training on the job, ways of generating a commitment to the firm that makes jobs in other firms unattractive, and finally, maintaining the allegiance of employees after they have been laid off.

The consequences of the internal market on the labour process, according to Burawoy, are the same as those of gaming, in that the internal labour market also promotes individual autonomy, breaks down collectivities based on skills groups, mitigates hierarchical conflicts and promotes lateral conflicts. Thus, the internal labour market reconciles the interests of capital and labour within limited structural opportunities for labour to upgrade, and thereby contributes to the manufacture of consent.[5]

> The internal labour market is a structural and institutional arrangement of administrative rules and procedures internal to a firm which promotes mobility within the firm and reduces it between firms. It promotes individual autonomy, breaks down collectivities based on skills groups, mitigates hierarchical conflicts and promotes lateral conflicts.

Internal state

This is the mechanism by which labour struggles are internalized into the managerial prerogatives by way of collective bargaining and grievance procedures. To Burawoy (1979: 110), the internal state 'refers to the set of institutions that organise, transform or repress struggles over relations in production and relations of production at the level of enterprise'. The main strategies of internalizing these worker struggles into management prerogatives include the explicit acknowledgement of the right of the trade union to be operative within the organizational rationales, and institutionalizing the rules of collective bargaining and grievance. Thus, as Burawoy argues, the internal state explicitly acknowledges the potential antagonism between the interests of workers and capital, and emphasizes the need to co-ordinate them by framing the autonomy of not only the management but also the workers. It sets explicit rules for management prerogative so that managerial discretion within such rules is legitimated and consented. The internal state also 'inserts the labourer into the political process as an industrial citizen with a set of contractually defined rights and obligations, together with a commitment to a more tedious "social contract"' (ibid.: 113). Consequently, the functional role of the internal state is similar to that of the internal labour market. Each supplements the other in co-ordinating the interests of worker and corporation in the expansion of profit. Both obscure capitalist relations of production in the labour process by constituting workers as individuals – industrial citizens with attendant rights and obligations – rather than as members of a class (ibid.: 119). Management accounting, especially through budgeting and standard costing, could facilitate this 'social contract' between capital (the firm) and labour by explicating them through 'budget-based contracts' (see Chapter 4).

Politics of production and factory regimes

In *The Politics of Production*, Burawoy (1985) expands the notion of the internal state to the politics of production by attempting to incorporate political and ideological regimes in production into the

> The internal state is the mechanism by which labour struggles are internalized into managerial prerogative by way of collective bargaining and grievance procedures. Like the internal labour market, it co-ordinates the interests of worker and corporation in the expansion of profit, and obscures capitalist relations of production in the labour process by constituting workers as individuals.

labour process analysis. In this attempt, he stands on the premise that 'the process of production contains political and ideological elements as well as a purely economic moment. That is, the process of production is not confined to the labour process . . . It also includes political apparatus which reproduces those relations of the labour process through the regulation of struggles' (Burawoy, 1985: 122). He calls these struggles the politics of production. These link the 'modes of factory controls' or 'factory regimes' to the state and global politics and explain the macro-political rationale for the historical existence of specific factory regimes (Uddin and Hopper, 2001).

> The process of production is not confined to the labour process. It also includes political apparatus which reproduces those relations of the labour process through the regulation of struggles.

Factory regimes, which refer to the 'political practices and ideological assumptions embedded in the labour process and related aspects of production' (Smith, 1990: 367), are historically shaped and reshaped by two explanatory 'variables' of the political apparatus: first, the institutional relationship between apparatus of factory and of state; and second, the intervention of the state in factory regimes. Possible combinations of these two variables in the political apparatus give impetus to different factory regimes. Under this typological scheme, Burawoy identifies three types of factory regime: hegemonic, market despotism and bureaucratic despotism.

> Burawoy identifies three types of factory regime: hegemonic, market despotism and bureaucratic despotism.

Characteristic differences between different factory regimes are mapped in terms of: the prevalence of coercion and consent; and the political apparatus underlying the rationale of coercion or consent. Accordingly, in despotism, coercion prevails over consent. In market despotism, the rationale for the prevalence of coercion is economic, and is constituted by the economic whip of the market: that is, the transactional dependency of labour on capital for maintenance of their lives. The state intervention in this case is indirect – that is to make sure free market conditions prevail to facilitate labour mobility and Pareto-efficiency in macro-economic resource allocation. Thus, 'for their economic survival, workers are presumed to be totally at the mercy of the capitalist or his

464

agent, the overseer, who can arbitrarily intensify the work, provided that his demands are compatible with the reappearance of the worker the next day (and sometimes not even then) and that they remain within certain broad and often unenforced legal limits' (Burawoy, 1979: 27). Despotism is reproduced when state protection, trade union and workers' struggles remain weak.

In contrast, bureaucratic despotism occurs where the source of rationale for the prevalence of coercion is constituted through the administrative hierarchy of the state. In this case, the factory and the state are institutionally fused together to form a kind of state-owned enterprise. Furthermore, the state intervention in the factory regime is direct: that is, the state intervenes in the internal organization of the factory regime, and the labour is subject to the mercy of the state's bureaucratic power structure. In either case of despotism, whether market or bureaucratic, coercion is the governing principle.

> Characteristic differences between different factory regimes are mapped in terms of: the prevalence of coercion and consent; and the political apparatus underlying the rationale of coercion or consent.

In hegemonic factory regimes, on the other hand, consent prevails over coercion. The institutional relationship between the apparatus of factory and state is separate. The state, however, intervenes directly in factory regimes by stipulating, for example, mechanisms for the conduct and resolution of struggles at the point of production (Burawoy, 1985: 12)

In dealing with the 'hidden abode of underdevelopment', Burawoy identifies another form of despotism specific to post-colonial economies – 'colonial despotism'. As in the case of market or bureaucratic despotism, it is despotic because coercion prevails over consent. However, the domination and exploitation is colonial because 'one racial group dominates through political, legal and economic rights denied to others' (ibid.: 226). While in market despotism the coercion stemmed from the labour market dependency of workers, in colonial despotism it came from the arbitrary power that the dictatorial colonial state and its affiliated mercantile capital could exercise outside the work organization or labour process. For Burawoy, the organizing principle of colonial despotism was explicit racism.

> For Burawoy, the organizing principle of colonial despotism was explicit racism.

The generic character of the factory regime is, according to Burawoy, independent of both the form of the labour process and the competition among the firms. Instead, there are two interrelated factors that determine the generic character of the labour process: the dependence of workers' livelihood on wage employment; and the tying of the latter to performance in the workplace (ibid.: 126). The state political apparatus then becomes a determinant factor of the form of factory regimes by intervening in these labour–capital dependencies. First, social insurance legislation not only ensures a certain minimum level of subsistence independence for the workers from wage employment but also sets a minimum threshold for the wages. Thus, in turn, the market apparatus is no longer capable of reproducing conditions for despotism: total dependency of labour at the mercy of capital and capital's managerial discretion to tie wages to performance. Second, labour legislation such as compulsory trade union recognition, grievance machinery and collective bargaining protects the workers from the capitalists' despotic powers of firing, wage reduction and fining, etc. All these culminate in the demise of despotism. Thus,

> now management can no longer rely entirely on the economic whip of the market. Nor can it impose an arbitrary despotism. Workers must be persuaded to cooperate with management. Their interests must be coordinated with those of capital. The despotic regimes of early capitalism, in which coercion prevails over consent, must be replaced with hegemonic regimes, in which consent prevails (although never to the exclusion of coercion).
>
> (ibid.)

There are two interrelated factors that determine the generic character of the labour process: the dependence of workers' livelihood on wage employment, and the tying of the latter to performance in the workplace.

In that way, Burawoy offers us an alternative theoretical framework to conceptualize how control at the point of production would historically transform from despotic to hegemonic regimes as the regulatory environment (especially the state apparatus that governs employment relations) evolves. This evolutionary framework has been especially useful in analysing Third World idiosyncrasies of control at the point of production.

Theorizing Third World politics of production

Burawoy's theory of production politics is present in the analysis of Third World politics of production in two specific case studies. The first is Burawoy's (1985) own analysis of the 'hidden abode of underdevelopment', a case of Zambian coal mines. The second is by Uddin and Hopper (2001) in a Bangladeshi soap-manufacturing company.

In his case study, Burawoy attempts to analyse the Zambian transition from colonialism to post-colonialism. He mobilizes his argument by advancing the critique that orthodox theories of underdevelopment have failed to examine the labour process or its relationship to the state as mediated by the political apparatus of production. His claim is that, in explaining the causes of underdevelopment, theories have never looked into the 'hidden abode of production', but simply remained at a surface level of analysis in the 'noisy sphere of market place' (Burawoy, 1985: 210).

Conventional theories of underdevelopment have never gone to the deeper level of production relations to explain underdevelopment, but remain at surface levels of market analysis.

He thus attempts to extend his analysis of the relationship between production politics and state politics to the hidden abode of underdevelopment. Elaborating on colonial state politics, he argues that the 'colonial state is interventionist and its function was to establish the supremacy of the capitalist mode of production' (Burawoy, 1985: 214). Its *modus operandi* was to ensure primitive accumulation in two ways. The first was to proletarianize the natives by separating them from their means of production, and the second was to extract surplus from pre-capitalist modes of production by merchant capital. In short, it was concerned with constructing the structural background for the penetration of mercantile capital into the colonial economy for a capitalist social formation. Hence, the state apparatus and the production apparatus were separate, and the intervention of the state in production regimes was indirect. The result, therefore, was colonial despotism in which the rationale for coercion was not the whip of the market but the colonial political apparatus of military supremacy and racial discrimination.

> Colonial states are interventionist, and the *modus operandi* was to ensure primitive accumulation in two ways: first, to proletarianize the natives by separating them from their means of production; and second, to extract surplus from pre-capitalist modes of production by merchant capital.

Operational doctrines of colonial despotism, as they were found in African copper mines, were manifested in what is called the 'compound system'. Burawoy reveals that paternalism was used within this system of despotism, and was institutionalized not only through the regulation of recreational activities of the workers, such as beer drinking, but also by adopting tribal kinship relations among workers. The compound population was made up of different tribes, and tribal elders were their respected representatives. Jurisdiction powers vested in them by tribal rituals were effectively used by the compound management for surveillance and regulation of workers who were the binding subjects of those tribal rituals.

But neither the compound system nor its associated paternalistic impetus was capable of sustaining the colonial despotism for ever. The very form of the compound system and the 'corporate' labour strategies of the companies themselves sowed the seeds for dissolving the 'company state' of the compound system. Hence, it consolidated the unitary structure of the mining community and encouraged the development of class consciousness and the collective struggle (Burawoy, 1985: 229). The compound itself provided a rationale for working-class solidarity and struggles across ethnic, language, skill and racial boundaries (ibid.: 230). Thus, mine workers became effectively organized in the common identity of 'Africans'. In the shadow of the changing political apparatus, the company state fragmented, lost its despotic powers and gave way to a weaker and more bureaucratic administrative apparatus. Adjustments were made in the labour process, often in the direction of greater worker control demanding prevalence of consent over coercion (ibid.: 235).

> Colonial despotism in compound systems itself provided the necessary structural impetus to organize resistance against the despotism, and dissolve it into a more hegemonic structure.

Uddin and Hopper (2001) used Burawoy's framework of factory regimes to theorize historical transformations of control in a Bangladeshi soap-manufacturing company – a prototype of manufacturing industries in South Asian economies which passed through dramatic ownership changes from colonial through public to private. Drawing on Burawoy, they benchmarked three ideal-type factory regimes – colonial despotism, hegemonic and market-based despotism – against which actual regimes of control were located to examine the historical deviation between the two. The ideal-typical expectation was that there would be a historical transformation of factory regimes from colonial despotism to hegemony, and then to a market-based despotism as ownership structure changed from colonial private ownership to post-colonial public ownership and then to post-colonial private ownership. This ideal-type construction of factory regimes indeed meets the rosy predictions of the reformation projects launched at each phase of the post-colonial history under the patronage of international development finance agencies. But Uddin and Hopper reveal that the peculiar political set-up in post-colonial Bangladesh acted as a moderating variable in manufacturing the unexpected.

Based on Burawoy's formulations, it was expected that independence struggles coupled with the nascent labour/trade union struggle should have transformed colonial despotism to a hegemonic regime where consent is manufactured through internal markets, internal states and games. Instead, a politicized and factionalized state coupled with party-patronage trade unionism mediated this ideal-typical transformation to form a 'political hegemony' in which consent is manufactured through political intervention.

This political hegemony signalled a policy failure amounting to over-politicization of production and lethargic loss-making public enterprises. The policy solution was to reform the public enterprises by transferring ownership and control to private capital. The ideal-typical expectation was a market-based hegemonic despotism in which consent is manufactured through economic transactions. But weak trade unions, divided workers and weak state regulations resulted in the formation of a new crony capitalistic despotism in which coercion was re-established under non-colonial private capital.

> Burawoy's Zambian and Uddin and Hopper's Bangldeshi cases demonstrate two episodes in the evolution of factory regimes from colonial despotism to post-colonial. Thus, different historical circumstances give rise to different evolutionary patterns of factory regimes, which emphasizes difficulties in generalization and the need for case-specific analysis of changes in control structures.

GRAMSCIAN THEORY OF HEGEMONY

The orthodox Marxist perspective of society is that it consists of an economic base upon which certain superstructural elements, such as ideologies, legal systems and the political state, are determined (see Figure 14.1, above). Thus, Marx's own conception of the relationship between the economic base and the superstructure holds rather a deterministic position that the economic base is the determinant of everything else. Gramsci's framework of cultural politics takes us beyond this orthodoxy by bringing the state, ideology and culture, especially 'intellectual leadership', to the forefront of political analysis of systems of governance and control. Its basic proposition is dialectical: economic base and superstructure can influence each other in a reciprocal manner.

> Gramsci's framework of cultural politics takes us beyond Marxist orthodoxy by bringing the state, ideology and culture, especially 'intellectual leadership', to the forefront of political analysis of systems of governance and control.

In the previous section, we discussed Burawoy's analysis of how consent was manufactured through interrelated organizational mechanisms of gaming behaviour, internal labour market and internal state. The Gramscian notion of 'hegemony' can take us to another realm of this analysis: to the cultural and ideological context of the wider society that helps diffuse the ideology of the ruling class and turn it into the popular ideology, and thereby manufactures consent of the mass to the ruling-class ideology. Thus, like Burawoy's analysis of 'factory regimes' and 'manufacturing consent', Gramscian analysis of hegemony addresses the question of how capital subordinates labour beyond the labour process, and shows us that dynamics of organizational conflicts, resistance, accommodation and consent rest on a much wider set of cultural, ideological and regulatory (state) factors.

> Gramscian analysis of hegemony addresses the question of how capital subordinates labour beyond the labour process, and shows us that dynamics of organizational conflicts, resistance, accommodation and consent rest on a much wider set of cultural, ideological and regulatory (state) factors.

The use of Gramsci in critical accounting studies hinges upon the notion of hegemony. In simple terms, the notion of hegemony tries to explicate the politico-cultural mechanisms through which consent of the mass is manufactured. As Cooper (1995: 176) argues, 'hegemony is concerned with the way in which the status quo (or the position of the ruling class) is sustained despite the existence of much larger groups with different economic and political interests'. As Richardson (1989) argues, it seeks to explain why systematically disadvantaged groups would voluntarily support hierarchical political or control structures (including corporatism) through which they are dominated and exploited. Joseph's (2002: 1) reading of Gramsci's concept of hegemony reveals that, in its simplistic form, hegemony concerns the construction of consent and the exercise of leadership by the dominant group over subordinate groups. However, when it is located within its complex structural, historical and political context, the notion of hegemony deals with issues such as the elaboration of political projects, the articulation of interests, the construction of social alliances, the development of historical blocs and state strategies and the initiating of passive revolutions.

> The use of Gramsci in critical accounting studies hinges upon the notion of hegemony, which tries to explicate the societal-level mechanisms through which consent of the mass is manufactured.

469

The 'intellectual leadership' (which is also called cultural, political or organic leadership) is the principal mechanism through which consent of the mass is constructed by diffusing and popularizing the world view of the ruling class. Thus, on certain occasions, hegemony is equated to intellectual and moral leadership (see Richardson, 1989; Cooper, 1995). However, the intellectual leadership is not simply something to do with interpersonal qualities of leading individuals in the society, but is inherent and dynamically evolving with the structural properties of the society. Indeed, intellectual leadership is an institutional arrangement within the dialectical relationships between major structural forces in society (see below). This is why hegemony is still a structural theory, though not deterministic.

> The 'intellectual leadership' is the principal mechanism through which consent of the mass is constructed by diffusing and popularizing the world view of the ruling class.

Hegemonic analysis employs a different set of sociological categories from orthodox Marxism. The latter places its primary focus on the class antagonisms between capital and labour, and therefore holds classes as the fundamental structural forces in society. The Gramscian theory of hegemony, on the other hand, considers the dialectics between economy, civil society and political state as the primary relationship within which hegemonic domination takes place (see Figure 14.3). However, this does not mean that the Gramscian notion of Marxism rejects class antagonism. Instead, it shows how class antagonisms are 'managed' within hegemonic arrangements between the ruled and the ruling classes. Such hegemonic arrangements are historically constructed through the interaction between economy, civil society and the political state.

> The Gramscian theory of hegemony considers the dialectics between economy, civil society and political state as the primary relationship within which hegemonic domination takes place.

Various elements of the superstructure form the state (see Cooper, 1995: 176), and categorically, the state consists of two major structures: political state and civil state. The dichotomy of political state and civil state rests on the recognition that there is sharing of power between the orthodox state and other forms of state, especially institutions in the civil society. The concept of the orthodox state encompasses 'a set of tightly connected governmental institutions, concerned with the administration of a geographically determined population, the authority of which is recognized by other states through international law' (Faulks, 1999: 2). This is the political state. Beyond the political state, there has been an eruption of power of governance within such voluntary associations of citizens as political parties, trade unions, businesses, media organizations, religious bodies, professional bodies, pressure groups, etc. (Gramsci, 1971). It should also be noted that the terms 'civil state' and 'civil society' are often used interchangeably. The civil society bears certain characteristics of the 'state' when it penetrates into the political state and becomes part of the 'government'. Simultaneously, the civil state is a society, in that it is subject to the government of

470

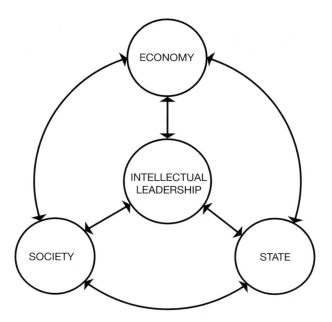

Figure 14.3 *Intellectual leadership in its structural context*

which the civil society is an integral element. Gramsci (1971: 263) reflects on this nature of civil society when he states, 'for it should be remarked that the general notion of State includes elements which need to be referred back to the notion of civil society (in the sense that one might say that State = political society + civil society, in other words hegemony protected by the armour of coercion)'.

> The dichotomy of political state and civil state rests on the recognition that there is sharing of power between the orthodox state and other forms of state, especially institutions in the civil society.

This takes us to another important point. As Richardson (1989: 419) emphasizes, there are two faces for hegemony: the hegemony of consent and the hegemony of coercion. It is true that the general attention of hegemonic analysis is on the civil state and the consensual dimension of the hegemony. However, the presence of the political state implies that the potential for coercion is always in the background. As Richardson (ibid.) argues, 'hegemonic states thus represent a balance of coercion and consent but one in which consent by the majority is clearly present'.

> There are two faces for hegemony: the hegemony of consent and the hegemony of coercion.

471

Gramscian discourses place a greater emphasis on the power of civil society, because it is through civil society institutions that the 'intellectual leadership' is mobilized for the construction of hegemony. As Cooper (1995: 205, n. 5) points out, organizations that make up the civil society are the result of a complex network of social practices and relations, and manifest different ways people are grouped and organized by class, sex, race, ethnicity, local community, professionals and other epistemic communities and so on. It is through these civil society institutions that the intellectual leadership is organized and mobilized to diffuse and popularize ruling-class ideology, and for which consent is manufactured at an ideological level. In that way, intellectual and moral leadership plays an 'agential role' in organizing ruling and proletariat classes into 'historical blocs', a political unison or an 'organic cohesion' between rulers and ruled, leaders and led, and intellectuals and the people (Gramsci, 1971). In this sense, hegemony is not a simple ideological domination of one class over the other, but a historical construction of an organic cohesion or an alliance within and between economy, political state and the civil society, to which both the ruler and the ruled are subjected. However, in the last analysis, the historical role of this organic arrangement is to reproduce the hegemonic relations within which domination and exploitation are structured.

> Gramscian discourses place a greater emphasis on the power of civil society, because it is through civil society institutions that the 'intellectual leadership' is mobilized for the construction of hegemony.

Critical accounting studies drawing on the Gramscian version of political economy, one way or the other, try to explain the hegemonic role of accounting (or the accounting profession as an intellectual leadership). For example, Cooper (1995) explores the role of accounting in the 'maintenance' of advanced capitalism. Using case empirics from the National Union of Journalists (NUJ), she demonstrates the multi-dimensionality of how capitalist state hegemony and ideology are put into action through accounting rhetoric and practices. According to her, as a spontaneous provider of explanations of the world, accounting freezes out other ways of seeing. Thus, for example, together with the economic context within which the union was operating and the coercive aspects of state hegemony, capitalist accounting rhetoric and practices were able to signify financial imperatives, rather than political ones, for the strategic decisions of the union, though the union is an overtly political organization. The specific historical and structural relations within which the union operated signified its financial strength as a critical leverage in political nego-tiations. As a result, 'the accounts of the union became mythological or metaphysical in the sense that they could be used to signify the ability of the union to negotiate on behalf of its members' (Cooper, 1995: 203). In that way, Cooper argues that: accounting is not an ideology but a par-ticular discourse; but ideology, within accounting discourse, is a particular set of effects which, within our current ideological order, arises in part because certain forms of signification are materially but silently excluded.

> Cooper (1995) demonstrates the multi-dimensionality of how capitalist state hegemony and ideology are put into action through accounting rhetoric and practices.

Goddard (2005) deploys the Gramscian notion of hegemony in a different way – to theorize changes in accounting and financial management in UK local government since the mid-1970s. The principal theoretical framework he uses is the 'regulation theory', which is a synthesis of: a regime of accumulation; a mode of regulation; and a hegemonic structure. For Goddard, a 'regime of accumulation' is a systematic organization of production, income generation, exchanges of the social product and consumption. 'Mode of regulation', on the other hand, refers to the specific local and historical collection of structural forms or institutional arrangements through which economic life is transacted and which result in a regular overall process in economic reproduction. Similar to other writers we have quoted throughout this section, he defines 'hegemony' as political leadership based on the consent of the led, a consent which is secured by diffusion and popularization of the world view of the ruling class. As a synthesis of these three elements, regulation theory explains how capitalist social relations are reproduced in the face of internal contradictions. Within these theoretical parameters, Goddard argues, a post-Fordist regime of stable capital accumulation is emerging, where private capital is extended into arenas which were hitherto provided by the state under a Fordist regime. This extension has been possible because: the new labour process relation and introduction of technology have made such activities profitable; a new mode of regulation and a hegemonic structure has brought with it a hollowing out of the state with fragmentation of government and the emergence of governance; and a new mode of competition with new heterarchic structures is emerging alongside simpler hierarchical forms and markets (Goddard, 2005: 40).

> Regulation theory is a synthesis of a regime of accumulation, a mode of regulation and a hegemonic structure.

In Alawattage and Wickramasinghe (forthcoming), we use Gramscian hegemonic analysis to explain the non-constitutive role of accounting in a Third World political hegemony. Using eleven-month ethnographic empirics on labour control practices and rituals in a Sri Lankan plantation company, we demonstrate how labour control is manifested in a complex hegemonic structure, which infuses economic enterprise, civil state and the political state to blur the formal boundaries of organizational hierarchy. Our theoretical framework, drawn on cultural-Marxist discourses on hegemony, explains the emergence and sustenance of political hegemony as the dominant mode of control in Third World enterprises. In contrast to the Western experience that accounting plays a constitutive role in labour control, we argue that the role accounting has assumed within Third World political hegemonies is rather representational and reproductive: it reproduces rather than constitutes the constitutive role of the political hegemony by representing it as a calculated 'truth' or a 'nature'.

> Gramscian hegemonic analysis is helpful in explicating the dominance of political hegemonies in the control of labour, and the non-constitutive role that accounting plays therein.

HAVE YOU UNDERSTOOD THE CHAPTER?

1. Briefly describe the defining characteristics of 'critical research' in management accounting.
2. List major theoretical camps that fall under the category of critical research.
3. Describe relations in and of production.
4. Describe the concept of mode of production.
5. How do you describe management control in the light of antagonism between capital and labour?
6. Briefly describe Braverman's key contributions to the literature of control.
7. Briefly describe a few accounting studies that deploy orthodox Marxist perspectives of labour theory of value and Braverman's de-skilling thesis.
8. Briefly describe the 'subjectivity' critique levelled against Braverman's *Labor and Monopoly Capital*.
9. How do you define the term 'subject'? How do you relate that definition to alternative approaches to address the subjectivity issue in the labour process debate?
10. Briefly describe Friedman's notion of 'responsible autonomy'.
11. Briefly describe Burawoy's concept of 'manufacturing consent'. What are the specific organizational mechanisms that would help manufacture consent at the point of production?
12. Differentiate between despotic and hegemonic forms of factory regimes.
13. How do you explain the Gramscian notion of 'hegemony'? What role does 'intellectual leadership' play in that?

BEYOND THE CHAPTER

1. 'The magnitude of expenses in the income statement and their resulting profit is indicative of the social and institutional power of capital, rather than social efficiency and productivity as assumed by neoclassical economics.' Discuss.
2. 'Social and economic conflicts arising from the models of control pertaining to a particular phase of capitalist development stimulate the creation of new forms of control.' Discuss.
3. 'It is the specific organization of the labour process that manufactures the consent of the workers.' Discuss.
4. 'Critical accounting studies drawing on the Gramscian version of political economy, one way or the other, try to understand the hegemonic role of accounting or the accounting profession as an intellectual leadership.' Discuss.

FURTHER READING

1. For a comparison of labour process theory with other accounting theories, see Neimark and Tinker (1986) and Hopper *et al.* (1987).
2. For alternative classification of accounting research, see Baxter and Chua (2003).
3. For a detailed explanation of fundamental qualities of 'critical research', see Jermier (1998) and Cooper and Hopper (2006).
4. For a basic terminology of the labour process debate, see Grugulis and Knights (2001).

Chapter 15

Beyond political economy of MACh

A STARTING POINT: THE CRITICAL DIVIDE

Recently, one of the authors attended a seminar which focused on the state of a critical accounting project. The main presenter's leading question was 'What is to be critical?' He drew much from neo-Marxist political economy to substantiate his definition of 'critical'. His concern was that, as critical researchers are now somewhat silent about broader structural (e.g., socio-economic and political) contexts in which accounting plays a significant role, a remarkable critical accounting project is becoming inactive. He provided substantive evidence to prove his argument.

The author raised the following question: 'I agree with the fact that neo-Marxists can argue for a critical project. But do you agree that post-Marxists can have the same right to provide a critique of the conventional theorization of accounting, so that they can also be "critical?"'

The presenter replied: 'Good question. You are talking about postmodernism and post-structuralism. These views are concerned with actual practices which I appreciate. But they neglect the structural reasons for the existence of such practices. Partly, they are critical in that they reveal actual circumstances largely from micro-perspectives. But where is the connection between the micro and the macro? To that extent, they are not critical.

Another question from the audience followed: 'Then, as Marxists neglect the very practices of the micro, aren't they "partly" critical? Who are "fully" critical?'

The presenter's response was: 'I don't want to divide the critical into "partly" and "fully". I want to explore the "real" critical by applying macro-level, structural reasoning. Those micro-practices cannot exist without structural influences. It is the structures that shape such practices. Why do you want to talk about "effects" without "causes"? "Causes" such as class struggle, politics, culture, etc.?'

SETTING THE SCENE

The questions addressed at the above seminar set the scene for the scope of this chapter. Here we address the problem of structural approaches to critical research in accounting and the post-structural/postmodern alternative which could resolve such problems. In the previous chapter, we used the term 'critical' to define a spectrum of management accounting research which: attempts to understand micro-level practices in the light of macro-level, social and political transformation; depicts societal institutions through the lenses of contradiction and conflict; uses social/political history to explain management accounting change; and engages in activities for emancipation from mistreatment of management accounting practices. This 'macro to micro' (top-

475

down) approach has been questioned by some alternative critical researchers, and a debate has been generated on what is to be critical. The purpose of this chapter is to unfold this debate by focusing on two main forms of critical research: the Foucauldian approach and the Habermasian approach. Despite a variety of alternative approaches having emerged from a number of philosophical schools, those two have become the major alternatives to the Marxist and neo-Marxist political economy of management accounting.

> The 'macro to micro' (top-down) approach has been questioned by some alternative critical researchers and a debate has been generated on what is to be critical.

> The purpose of this chapter is to unfold the debate between neo-Marxist and post-Marxist research by focusing on two main forms of critical research: the Foucauldian approach and the Habermasian approach.

The chapter begins with a summary of critiques levelled against the Marxist and neo-Marxist stance of critical accounting research. The question raised at the start of the chapter will be explored with reference to the main critiques that have developed recently. Why we want to go for the alternative can be substantiated by understanding these critiques, and this understanding will provide a foundation for exploring basic concepts contained in the alternative approaches.

> - To elaborate the main critiques of Marxist and neo-Marxist critical accounting
> - To establish a foundational understanding of the basic concepts contained in the alternative approaches

Second, drawing from sociological writings, the chapter will clarify the terms 'postmodernism' and 'post-structuralism'. An attempt will be made to distinguish between modernism and postmodernism. The term 'post-structuralism' will be defined alongside a comparison with the notion of structuralism. These clarifications are a prerequisite for us to understand the Foucauldian approach to management accounting studies, which we will summarize subsequently.

> - To clarify the terms 'postmodernism' and 'post-structuralism' by providing suitable definitions
> - To distinguish between modernism and postmodernism as well as structuralism and post-structuralism

Third, we will look at Foucauldian accounting research under three themes: management accounting history; management accounting as a disciplinary practice; and governance and governability. On management accounting history, we will distinguish between traditional and Foucauldian historiographies of management accounting and will highlight some of the Foucauldian management accounting historical studies. On management accounting as a disciplinary practice, we will look at Foucault's ideas of disciplinary principles and their implications for power/knowledge relations. Some relevant studies of this genre will be highlighted. On the matters of governance and governability, we will draw on some conclusions of the major studies in management accounting which act as guides for us to define those notions in a certain context.

- To look at Foucauldian accounting research under three themes: management accounting history; management accounting as a disciplinary practice; and governance and governability
- To distinguish between traditional and Foucauldian historiographies of management accounting and to highlight some of the Foucauldian management accounting historical studies
- To look at Foucault's ideas of disciplinary principles and their implications for power/knowledge relations
- To draw some conclusions from the major studies in management accounting on matters relating to the notions of governance and governability

Fourth, the chapter will present the contributions of Habermasian accounting studies. This section will begin with definitions of three fundamental concepts: 'life-world', 'systems' and 'language decentration'. These concepts have been used repeatedly in developing theoretical perspectives for doing management accounting research. Within such frameworks, the issue of internal 'colonization' of life-worlds has been addressed. We will highlight this issue. The section will then go on to discuss language processes in terms of four stages: the quasi-ignorance stage, the critical theorem stage, the enlightenment stage and the stage of selection of strategies. The section will end with a discussion of the use of 'middle-range thinking' as a particular methodological approach to conducting accounting studies.

- To define three fundamental concepts: 'life-world', 'systems' and 'language decentration'
- To highlight the issue of internal 'colonization' of life-worlds
- To discuss language processes in terms of four stages: the quasi-ignorance stage, the critical theorem stage, the enlightenment stage and the stage of selection of strategies.
- To discuss the use of 'middle-range thinking' as a particular methodological approach to conducting accounting studies

477

A CRITIQUE OF THE CRITICAL

We saw at the start of this chapter that a debate is still going on with regard to the use of the notion of 'critical theory' in accounting. If we want to see how management accounting operates and changes, we need to choose a better theory which can provide a sensible perspective for management accounting to be more visible and understandable. In the previous chapter, you saw how Marxist and neo-Marxist theories formed a perspective to see the functioning of management accounting in the light of broader socio-political and historical dynamics. However, subsequent research suggests that there is a number of alternatives which have come to challenge that grand theorization. In this section, we will briefly consider some important points that have developed alongside this challenge.

Marxist and neo-Marxists in accounting worked for the project of modernity. In its ontological dimension, modernity implies a type of society characterized by rational-economic planning through a much ordered, large-scale, hierarchical bureaucracy. Willmott *et al.* (1992: 70) specified this by commenting that 'its ideal is the expertly designed, perfectly ordered and controlled world'. Fordism is a good example for describing this modernity project, which involved mass production, mass fixed capital investment, mass consumption of product, the commodification of culture and increased control of labour (Montagna, 1997). This ontology then hinges upon the assumption of economic determinism, where broader structures in society are led by an economic base which consists of the above well-ordered rational institutions, including large-scale economic organizations. For modernists, management accounting then facilitates the sustenance of this type of society by providing a particular language of business. Moreover, this ontology has an implication for a particular epistemology, a type of knowledge. That means modernity is also about a particular way of thinking based on grand narratives derived from reason and science. These narratives argue for a coherent framework of society and social institutions which progress according to the ideals of such narratives. For instance, accounting as a social and institutional practice can be understood by reference to the totality of the social rather than merely to its underlying technical procedures (Hopper *et al.*, 1987).

KEY TERMS

Modernity implies a type of society characterized by rational-economic planning through a much ordered, large-scale, hierarchical bureaucracy.

Modernity hinges upon the ontology of economic determinism and the epistemology of gaining knowledge through reason and science.

The above ontological and epistemological dimensions have been challenged by postmodernist critiques (e.g., Arrington and Francis, 1989; Hoskin, 1994; Montagna, 1997). First, with empirical data, they illustrated that the world now is not that ordered: there are fragmentations, differences and complexities which cannot be captured by the ontology of modernism. Organizations are full of different issues, including the experiences of women, ethnic minorities and post-colonial societies (see Arnold, 1998). Consequently, management accounting practices cannot be reduced to a function of an 'ordered' organizational setting. In response to such critical observations, the researchers charged with postmodern thoughts revealed such complexities and their relationships with management accounting practices and their histories (e.g., Loft, 1986; Miller and O'Leary, 1987, 1994).

> The modernity project has been challenged. The world now is not that ordered: there are fragmentations, differences and complexities which cannot be captured by the ontology of modernism.

Second, the epistemology of modernism is incorrect in that a better understanding of management accounting cannot be achieved by looking at accounting practices merely from broader structural perspectives. Those perspectives are not close enough to analyse what happens at micro-levels. Even though there can be some relationships between the two levels (macro and micro), those relationships would present themselves rather implicitly. Local issues, which appear to be fragmented, are more explicit and influential in relation to the practices of accounting. These issues are not only about the rationalization of the world and bureaucracy, but also about the discontinuities of such systems due to various local and global circumstances. Thus, there cannot be a universal epistemology that would lead us to understand management accounting as a homogeneous practice. Instead, 'practices and discourses', on which we will elaborate later, can play a particular role in establishing dominant forms of accounting practice (see Hoskin, 1994).

> The epistemology is incorrect in that a better understanding of management accounting cannot be achieved by looking at accounting practices merely from broader structural perspectives.

However, it must be emphasized that postmodern/post-structural accounting researchers have conducted certain studies on their own, rather than critiquing the grand theorization of Marxist and neo-Marxist accounting researchers (Miller and O'Leary, 1987, 1994; Laughlin, 1987, 1995). Two notable exceptions are two debates, one involving Neimark (1990), Hoskin (1994), Armstrong (1994) and Grey (1994), and the other involving Miller and O'Leary (1994, 1998), Froud et al. (1998) and Arnold (1998). These debates pointed to an issue of ontological and epistemological validity of two approaches and their implications for the nature of accounting. At the time of writing this book, several researchers continue to maintain their positions by carrying out more studies to substantiate the validity of both ontology and epistemology in each framework. We cannot see any prospect of the abandonment of one framework in favour of the other.

Postmodern/post-structural accounting researchers have conducted certain studies on their own rather than critiquing the grand theorization of Marxist and neo-Marxist accounting researchers. We cannot see any prospect of the abandonment of one framework in favour of the other.

WHAT IS POSTMODERNISM/POST-STRUCTURALISM?

Postmodernism is a way of thinking about postmodernity, a historical era that is supposed to have succeeded the modern era. Also, it is way of critiquing the theoretical foundation of the modernity project. Postmodernism constitutes a 'different' conception, by which we can understand the contemporary world differently. The key to understanding this concept is 'difference' (Cooper and Burrell, 1988). In this, we cannot accept one singular meaning of anything. Instead, we give self-reference to the thing in question by looking at its opposites and contradictions. By rejecting grand narratives which focus on a singular meaning, postmodernism aims to construct such different meanings through language rather than fixing meanings through grand theorization (Thompson and McHugh, 2002). The notion of 'difference' is also implicated in similar terms such as 'incoherence', 'fluidity', 'fragmentation', 'discontinuity', 'contradictions' and the like. Reality is often constructed in relation to emerging and changing circumstances with a view to exploring 'differences'. Consequently, in postmodern terms, 'reality' is not a single phenomenon: by using language, for instance, media can construct a number of 'realities' which can be contradictory with each other. In a postmodernist social world, researchers aim to explore social realities through understanding changing local circumstances and their local meanings as constructed through the use of language. Hassard (1994: 9) described this: 'truth is a product of language games.' Consequently, we can construct a meaning by re-reading a text, rather than establishing an authentic explanation, by which we can reveal a difference. It is this task that the postmodern social scientist has to achieve. Eventually, the researcher would end up with limited explanations or even no explanations at all (Ritzer, 1992).

Postmodernism is about constructing different meanings (realities) through language rather than fixing meanings though grand theorization. Researchers explore social realities through understanding changing local circumstances and their local meanings.

For management accounting researchers and accountants, the world of postmodernism (postmodernity) is about the nature of contemporary social and organizational setting. As Montagna (1997: 130) summarized, postmodernity is characterized by a number of features (see also Clegg, 1990a; Harvey, 1989):

1. Flexibility in production: the concept of flexible manufacturing which replaces mass production and associated technologies that create opportunities for 'economies of scope' rather than 'economies of scale'.

480

2. Flexibility in labour market: the concept of the formation of multi-skills and exploiting the advantage of cheap labour in secondary markets.
3. Flexibility in consumption: the concept of creating opportunities to consume disposable goods, to use banking and credit facilities through IT, to buy on-line, etc.
4. Flexibility in capital market: the concept of the global stock market which allows instantaneous fund transfers.
5. Flexibility in organizations: the concept of changing the form of organization from administrative centralization and hierarchy to functional decentralization and pluralism, and from conventional structures to networked and virtual organizations.

In this book, when we turned our attention from 'mechanistic' to 'post-mechanistic' form, we emphasized the effects of the postmodernity project on management accounting. The above features are then not new to you. We have re-emphasized here the change occurring in the name of postmodernism. Indeed, postmodernism is not only a discourse that we can conceptualize but also a kind of reality that we experience in our time.

Features of the postmodern world:

■   flexibility in production;
■   flexibility in labour market;
■   flexibility in consumption;
■   flexibility in capital market;
■   flexibility in organizations.

As a social theory, postmodernism takes various forms, according to different theorists. At one extremity is Jean Baudrillard, one of the 'most radical and outrageous of this genre' (Ritzer, 1992: 616). In his seminal work *The Mirror of Production*, Baudrillard (1975: 39) criticized Marxist political economy for its 'mirror image of conservative political economy' which led to conservative ideas like 'work' and 'value' (ibid.: 83). He saw a contemporary society dominated by 'symbolic exchange' which involves an uninterrupted cycle of 'giving and receiving' and 'taking and returning'. For Baudrillard, contemporary society is no longer dominated by production. Instead, as Kellner (1989: 61) commented, it is dominated by 'media, cybernetics models and steering systems, computers, information processing, entertainment, knowledge industries, and so forth'. Baudrillard also described this as a society of 'simulations', which leads to the creation of 'simulacra', or 'reproduction of objects or events' through the use of the above materials such as media and cybernetics models (see Kellner, 1989: 78). Thus, reality cannot be seen as an ordered and perfect phenomenon. Instead, we can construct reality by using the above tools. From these perspectives, management accounting cannot be an ordered function providing a single meaning for the operation of organizations. Instead, on the one hand, it is subject to the construction of multiple realities, and, on the other hand, it can create such realities subject to the use of the above tools.

Another form of postmodernism is post-structuralism. Before defining this concept, it must be pointed out that it is hard to draw a clear line between these two terms. Ritzer (1992) commented that postmodernism is an extension and exaggeration of post-structuralism. As postmodernism has

481

> Contemporary society is full of 'symbolic exchange', an uninterrupted cycle of 'giving and receiving' and 'taking and returning', not dominated by production. Rather, it is dominated by 'media, cybernetics models and steering systems, computers, information processing, entertainment, knowledge industries, and so forth', a society of 'simulations', which leads to the creation of 'simulacra', or 'reproduction of objects or events'.

been so advanced in a number of disciplines, today we see post-structuralism as part of post-modernism. Ritzer (1992: 607) went on: 'post-structuralism has been overtaken and passed by postmodernism', despite the former having laid the groundwork for the latter. As with postmodernism, post-structuralism constructs social realities by exploring the issues of 'micro-politics of power' rather than the issues of power at the societal level. Rather than confining analyses to 'economy', post-structuralism aims to focus on a range of institutions within broader structures, such as economy, state and culture. Thus, post-structuralism rejects grand theorization based on grand narratives derived from structural explanations. Instead, researchers in this tradition are concerned with local explanations derived from complex and disordered situations within contexts such as micro-politics and power–knowledge relations. Rather than providing macro-explanations for micro-issues, post-structuralism provides micro-explanations *per se* for a fragmented web of relations within specific sites.

> There is no clear line between postmodernism and post-structuralism. Postmodernism is an extension and exaggeration of post-structuralism but 'post-structuralism has been overtaken and passed by post-modernism'. As with postmodernism, post-structuralism constructs social realities by exploring the issues of 'micro-politics of power'.

These basics of post-structuralism were developed by Michel Foucault and continued by Jacques Derrida. At the same time, Jürgen Habermas defended the position of structuralism by embarking on 'the unfinished project of modernity' through which he engaged in a programme of emancipation towards protecting the 'life-world' of people. This debate is important for us to understand more about the concepts of postmodernism and post-structuralism. Accounting researchers drew from multiple sources and developed two salient theoretical perspectives, one from Foucault's (sometimes in combination with Derrida: e.g., Arrington and Francis, 1989) ideas, and the other from Habermas'. The next two sections will consider these two programmes of accounting research.

> Accounting researchers drew from multiple sources and developed two salient theoretical perspectives, one from Foucault's (sometimes in combination with Derrida) ideas, and the other from Habermas'.

482

THE FOUCAULDIAN WAY: EMPHASIZING THE DISCIPLINARY

The postmodern version of accounting research has largely drawn on Michel Foucault and, to some extent, Jacques Derrida and Pierre Bourdieu (Loft, 1986; Knights and Collinson, 1987; Miller and O'Leary, 1987, 1993, 1994, 1998; Hopwood, 1987; Hoskin and Macve, 1988; Arrington and Francis, 1989; Hopper and Macintosh, 1993; Marsden, 1998; Arrington and Watkins, 2002; Watkins and Arrington, 2007; Roberts *et al.*, 2006; McKinlay and Wilson, 2006). All these studies focused on micro-settings, and they illustrated how management accounting has been implicated in complex local events and their underlying issues. The use of the Foucauldian model in management accounting research can be seen in two interrelated areas: management accounting history and management accounting as a disciplinary practice. We will briefly review each of these categories.

> The use of the Foucauldian model in management accounting research can be seen in two interrelated areas: management accounting history and management accounting as a disciplinary practice.

Management accounting history

We discussed some aspects of costing history in Chapter 3. Our aim there was to provide some historical evidence as to how costing came into being in the nineteenth and twentieth centuries. We did not develop a particular theoretical perspective on presenting that history. Here, we will draw on Foucauldian views to develop a theoretical framework of the history of management accounting by which we can understand why and how management accounting has come to occupy a constitutive role in our time. Studying the past from such a theoretical perspective should enable us to understand the present, as Loft (1995) remarked.

> Studying the past from a theoretical perspective based on Foucault should enable us to understand the present.

The traditional perspective on studying history was premised on the assumption that technological development and the emergence of large-scale business enterprises led to the emergence of various techniques, including costing and accounting systems (Littleton and Zimmerman, 1962; Chandler, 1962, 1977; Kaplan, 1984; Johnson and Kaplan, 1987). This is the evolutionary view of the Chandlerian approach to accounting history, which produces histories of certain situations with reference to those broader structural events seen in accounting's external environment. Underlying this view is that macro- (environmental) factors have teleological effects in the shaping of micro-practices. The theoretical problem in this approach is that it neglected local circumstances that led to the emergence of accounting systems (see Hopper and Armstrong, 1991; Hoskin and Macve, 1988). For Foucauldians, the neglect of such local circumstances would miss out very important historical events, such as the development of discourses and associated disciplinary practices. As Miller and O'Leary (1987: 236) remarked, accounting practices can always be enmeshed with a 'range of other social practices, in relation to mode of operation of power', which has been overlooked by conventional accounting historians.

> According to the traditional perspective, technological development and the emergence of large-scale business enterprises led to the emergence of various techniques, including costing and accounting systems. However, this perspective neglected local circumstances which led the development of certain discourses, such as accounting.

Foucauldian historians also reject the classical political economy approach which relies on an analysis of class struggle. This particular history assumes that accounting is no longer a neutral, technical apparatus. Instead, it serves a certain class with a particular economic and/or political interest (see Tinker, 1980; Hopper and Armstrong, 1991). Fundamental to this approach is that the function of, and changes in, management accounting in a particular historical epoch privilege class interest rather than a broader socio-economic transformation. In respect to control and accounting, Foucauldian researchers comment that this line of thinking is an attempt to 'substitute for notions of progress or evolution in standard histories' (Miller and O'Leary, 1987: 237). Again, the issue here is the neglect of 'other social practices' which gave rise to the functioning of, and changes in, accounting and control systems.

> Foucauldian historians also reject the classical political economy approach, which relies on an analysis of class struggle.

Foucault emerged with a different perspective on the subject of history. For him, there is no well-ordered history shifting clearly from one era to the next. Instead, Foucault articulated a theory of history with some interrelated concepts, on which management accounting researchers have formulated a 'different agenda for the interpretation of accounting past' (Miller and O'Leary, 1987: 236). Also, Miller and O'Leary have argued that Foucault's analysis of the formation of the modern era through the emergence of human sciences around 1800 can be a meaningful context in which we can understand how management accounting practices developed. To unfold this history, Miller and O'Leary have teased out three interrelated concepts, derived from Foucault's ideas: genealogy, archaeology and the power–knowledge relationship.

> Foucault's analysis of the formation of the modern era through the emergence of human sciences can be a meaningful perspective from which we understand how management accounting practices developed.

 484

Genealogy

This explores multiple and complex historical causes rather than a single historical event which may be deemed crucial. The approach here is that the origin of current practices can be traced by understanding fragmented and multiple historical events which can be combined for a complete explanation. For instance, as Miller and O'Leary (1987: 238) pinpointed, the origin of accounting can be traced through a variety of events such as 'the political objectives of states, historical contingency, particular national conditions, and the development of related disciplines'. According to Foucault, this examination of history is nothing else but the exploration of the 'genealogy of power'. In the case of management accounting, it is about the investigation of the power of calculation, which makes people calculable and governable. Genealogical method allows us to understand this 'reality' with reference to other multiple social practices which dominate certain historical periods, but within local circumstances which form 'mini-regimes of truth' (Foucault, 2002; Macintosh, 1994).

Genealogy is concerned with exploring the origin of current practices by tracing fragmented and multiple historical events which can be combined for a complete explanation.

Archaeology

This is the examination of social conditions that give rise to discourses: such as, law, medicine, economics, psychiatry and accounting. In other words, it is about the 'archaeology of knowledge' which aims to examine discursive events as well as the spoken and written statements which make discourses possible. In particular, archaeology of knowledge directs us to understand the rules and practices of various discourses and their roles in converting the people into the 'objects' of such heterogeneous discourses. For instance, with regard to the emergence of costing, a number of other discourses which led to the formation of standardization and formalization of work practices within organizations have to be consulted when we try to understand the archaeology of accounting knowledge. Accounting notions such as efficiency and standards are then seen among complex relations between heterogeneous discourses. Consequently, over time, 'different emphases have been incorporated into accounting practices' (Hopwood, 1987: 207). Following the archaeological method, we can investigate the changes in such different emphases and the eventual explanations for the emergence of, and changes in, management accounting.

The archaeological method aims to examine the social conditions that give rise to discourses: such as, law, medicine, economics, psychiatry and accounting.

Knowledge and power relations

Foucault engaged in a profound articulation of an inevitable relationship between power and knowledge. He did this by illustrating the transformation of the sovereign power of controllers (of

485

economic and social activities in our daily lives) into disciplinary power. The latter is very influential in that it can penetrate into our daily lives through a range of regulations and tools for administering the entire population. These disciplinary power regimens can be seen in many fields and institutions, including schools, hospitals, workshops and prisons. The overarching observation here is that the knowledge of various discourses, such as medicine, psychology, public administration and accounting, entails that disciplinary power to control, regulate and administer the people in those fields and institutions. When we attempt to study management accounting history, this line of argument can act as a guide for us to understand how organizations have imposed disciplinary power on organizational subordinates, and what roles management accounting played in such impositions. As Miller and O'Leary (1987) illustrated, this is possible by examining the roles of human sciences such as accounting which created a number of techniques for the supervision, administration and disciplining of the population. We will elaborate on this point when we describe management accounting as a disciplinary practice.

> The overarching observation is that the knowledge of various discourses, such as medicine, psychology, public administration and accounting, entails the disciplinary power to control, regulate and administer people.

Building on the above interrelated theoretical perspectives, a number of management accounting researchers produced some pioneering historical studies (Loft, 1986; Miller and O'Leary, 1987; Hopwood, 1987; Hoskin and Macve, 1988), which we will summarize below.

Loft (1986)

Based on the genealogical method, Loft argued that the emergence of cost accounting in the UK is a result of complex interrelations between knowledge, techniques, institutions and occupational claims. Focusing on the professionalization of management accounting, Loft illustrated that, through various activities, professional accounting associations played a significant role in establishing management accounting as an acceptable discourse. She highlighted that 'their publications, meetings, examination syllabi and other activities . . . play a role in defining and furthering . . . accounting, deciding who is competent to practise, and in elaborating the discourse' (p. 140). Thus, management accounting, according to its genealogy, is a result of multiple social and organizational functions occurring in specific historical epochs.

> The emergence of cost accounting in the UK is a result of complex interrelations between knowledge, techniques, institutions and occupational claims.

Miller and O'Leary (1987)

Taking all three concepts together, Miller and O'Leary (1987) reported on how the first three decades of the twentieth century gave rise to standard costing and budgeting. The argument was that the construction of 'efficiency' was linked to the development of a diverse body of knowledge, including engineering, psychology, accounting, medicine, politics, journalism, etc. These bodies of expertise have profoundly affected the lives of people, making them governable. Together with these diverse bodies of expertise, costing and budgeting emerged to be part of the 'alliance of scientific management', and accounting should be viewed as a 'more general project of socio-economic management'.

The construction of 'efficiency' was linked to the development of a diverse body of knowledge, including engineering, psychology, accounting, medicine, politics, journalism, etc.

Hopwood (1987)

In a similar vein, but referring to different empirical settings, Hopwood argued that diverse practices and processes of organizations must be considered in an exploration of the emergence of accounting. He provided detailed accounts from three different cases. Taking the first case, Hopwood illustrated that roles of costing were diverted from mere pricing and product volume decisions to broader interventional roles in economic management and governance. This work also highlighted how certain social and economic conditions provided ground rules for the emergence of certain discourses, such as, in this case, costing. With the second case, Hopwood showed how accounting became proactive rather than reactive in shaping the functions of an organization, especially in the areas of reappraisal of product lines, strategies, and subsequent implications for internal efficiency and productivity. The third case was taken to illustrate how accounting had been associated with internal control operating in conjunction with such functions as manufacturing, marketing, distribution and administration. In all cases, Hopwood's aim was to argue that accounting's history pointed to its acts of surveillance, discipline, punishment and normalization.

Diverse practices and processes of organizations must be considered in an exploration of the emergence of accounting.

Hoskin and Macve (1988)

These researchers provided an interesting case study which argued that the genesis of new managerialism in some US businesses and factories in the nineteenth century was connected with the production of engineering and military graduates in the US Military Academy at West Point. Hoskin and Macve found that the system for accountability which prevailed in US armouries and railways was a reproduction of the meticulous 'grammotocentric' and 'panoptic' one for human

487

accountability. As another detailed illustration of how Foucault's 'disciplinary power' became a pervasive social programme of which accounting was a part, this study used similar concepts to those employed in the previous studies.

> The genesis of new managerialism in some US businesses and factories was connected with the production of engineering and military graduates in the US Military Academy at West Point.

Management accounting as disciplinary practice

The notion of 'disciplinary power' has been attractive for critical management accounting researchers who produced interesting case studies. The theoretical framework in these studies was the same as the one we mentioned earlier. Fundamental to this is the proliferation of the knowledge–power relations implicated in various disciplinary practices which are linked to the modern strategies of surveillance and discipline. Power here, according to Foucault (1979), is not restricted merely to individuals but to strategies which are mobilized in a series of relations and tactics. Power also involves continuous tensions implicated in the depths of the social structure, and it is hard to separate power from knowledge. Foucault (1979: 27) remarked that 'power produces knowledge . . . power and knowledge directly imply one another; and there is no power relation without correlative constitution of a field of knowledge'. Therefore, the history of power is also the history of forms of knowledge. Management accounting studies are premised on this fundamental idea and define management accounting as a disciplinary practice. It represents a particular form of knowledge and contributes to the strategies of surveillance and discipline within organizations.

> The proliferation of knowledge–power relations is implicated in various disciplinary practices which are linked to the modern strategies of surveillance and discipline.

As a disciplinary practice, management accounting is implicated in the regulation of human behaviour through a 'panoptic' system of surveillance (see Dandeker, 1990). It is about a transformation of relationships between observer and observed. In such a system, as Foucault (1979: 202) articulated, each individual who is subject to disciplinary controls is 'seen without ever being seen'. For instance, in schools and prisons, everybody is seen as they are in classes and cells, respectively. Those observed become disciplined through certain rules and regulations derived from certain disciplinary practices contained in administrative procedures. In a similar fashion, workers in a factory become disciplined through a variety of regulations, rules and procedures, including management accounting controls. The underlying principles (of disciplinary society) of all these disciplinary practices can be categorized into three: the principle of enclosure (the use of cells, useful sites and rankings); the principle of efficient body (timetabling, manoeuvres and dressage, and the exhaustive use of time); and the principle of disciplinary power (hierarchization, panopticons, normalizing, sanctions and examination). To the extent that Weber emphasized the significance of bureaucracy, Foucault signified the importance of the operations of these disciplinary principles in modern societies. His thesis is that the modern era can be distinguished from its traditional form with reference to these principles. The development of management accounting practices is then part of the development of the practices of those disciplinary principles. To illustrate this understanding of management accounting, we will highlight three major studies: Knights and Collinson (1987), Hopper and Macintosh (1993) and McKinlay and Wilson (2006).

> Disciplinary practices can be categorised into three: the principle of enclosure, the principle of efficient body and the principle of disciplinary power.

Knights and Collinson (1987)

These researchers focused on the political power of accounting as a disciplinary practice, especially within management–worker relations. Their case study illustrated that a particular financial accounting regime in a US multinational firm came to force the workforce into a redundancy programme against which their resistance was unsuccessful. The firm was able to exercise the power of this financial discipline remotely through creating 'individualisation effects of management policy'. Financial justification was more powerful than potential collective reactions on the part of the workers. Rather than opposing collectively, workers supported the closure of the plant and the subsequent redundancy programme. This financial accounting discipline was able to leave the workers divided and indifferent, which made it difficult for them to organize collective resistance. This disciplinary power became much more rigorous, as there was a combined effect when (accounting) techniques, power, class and gender differentiations, etc., led the labour force to be enormously disadvantaged in organizing collective resistance. Knights and Collinson remarked that this negative effect on the part of the labour force could not be controlled, as the disciplinary power of accounting was 'inscribed in disciplinary mechanisms of hierarchical surveillance, normalising judgement and the examination case' (Foucault cited in Knights and Collinson, 1987: 475). Instead, academic involvement in the 'deconstruction of knowledge' would be a kind of emancipation.

> A particular financial accounting regime forced the workforce into a redundancy programme against which the workers' resistance was unsuccessful.

Hopper and Macintosh (1993)

These researchers used Foucault's general principles of the disciplinary society (detailed previously) to analyse a case study of how a company CEO maintained certain disciplinary practices. Having outlined the features of those principles and their applicability to the case company, ITT, Hopper and Macintosh showed that the management control system in ITT resembled the features of those disciplinary principles. Most of these basic principles were mastered by Harold Geneen, the CEO,

489

when he was at a boarding school during his childhood. Hopper and Macintosh presented this story alongside the case of the 'West Point connection' reported by Hoskin and Macve (1988). In ITT, Geneen clearly 'refined the principles of disciplinary power through the aggregative abstractions of management accounting controls' (p. 209) in the light of his own disciplinary training at boarding school. By doing this, Geneen 'constituted managers as subjects and amenable, docile, obedient bodies, and established ITT as a large international conglomerate' (p. 181). In other words, the underlying control practices became institutionalized in the minds of managers in terms of what managers must do to get things done effectively, by which ITT developed into a giant capitalist firm. However, while these analyses were regarded as fitting into the Foucauldian model, Hopper and Macintosh had some reservations also. On the one hand, while accounting controls can be seen from the perspective of disciplinary power, there are other features of these control systems which cannot be explained by the same framework. On the other hand, accounting was not the only control mechanism in ITT, especially in relation to its historical changes. Moreover, other factors, such as the influence of financial markets, relationships with states, technological developments and various forms of internal resistance, are not well captured by the Foucauldian model.

> Geneen 'refined the principles of disciplinary power through the aggregative abstractions of management accounting controls'.

McKinlay and Wilson (2006)

These researchers illustrated another interesting case of the development of bureaucratic careers in the mid-nineteenth century. Even though this is a historical study, its argument helps understand the power of organizational disciplines which aim to monitor the day-to-day activities of employees. It builds on the work of Savage (1998), who articulated that bureaucratic careers became the key to the development of control systems over individual performance and to the eventual formation of the self. Taking the Bank of Scotland as their case, McKinlay and Wilson focused on the clerical labour process in the late nineteenth century, which was subject to an inspection system. Their argument was that the emergence of an internal labour market within the bank was due to the opportunities available for the banking clerks to progress in their career, which was articulated as an 'economic and moral project'. The employees were then subject to rigorous scrutiny through regular appraisal and centralized records, coupled with an inspection system. This led to the formation of a 'career' to be a self-regulatory system of surveillance, as 'conformity' with the above appraisal resulted in promotions and career progression. In this process, clerks became the subjects of bureaucratic forms of banking management, where central managers exercised a kind of monarchical power. McKinlay and Wilson concluded that, with the articulation of career and the setting up of surveillance through inspections and records, the individual was rendered visible as a self-managed employee. The proliferation of similar events must have then led to the development of the modern era from the nineteenth century.

> The emergence of an internal labour market within the bank was due to the opportunities available for the banking clerks to progress in their career, which was articulated as an 'economic and moral project'.

THE HABERMASIAN WAY: UNDERSTANDING AND CHANGING ACCOUNTING SYSTEMS

Within the critical accounting research project, a group of researchers have built on Habermas' critical theory (Laughlin, 1987; Arrington and Puxty, 1991; Broadbent *et al.*, 1991; Chua and Degeling, 1993; Broadbent and Laughlin, 1997; Power and Laughlin, 1996). A Frankfurt school philosopher, Jürgen Habermas pointed to a way of engaging in a critical project that allows us both to understand and change the status quo. On 'critical', Habermas held the view that there cannot be an independent category of science and technology which can bring development and change without any influence of the social. He argued that there are movements of 'scientization of politics' through 'communicative actions' towards the 'rationalization of life-world' (see Power and Laughlin, 1996). Although Habermas did not address accounting issues explicitly, the above group of researchers built on Habermas' social theory, especially drawing from such works as *Knowledge and Human Interests* (1978), *Theory and Practice* (1974) and *The Theory of Communicative Action* (1984, 1987).[1] More importantly, Habermas argues for a general 'theory of social evolution', in which he emphasizes the role of language: for example, the communicative capacities of societal members in the development of Western societies. He termed this the 'logic of development', a discursive device which has been used by accounting researchers in their development of a general methodology for 'understanding and changing accounting systems' (Laughlin, 1987: 484). In this section, we will outline this connection between Habermas' social theory and critical accounting scholarship.

> There cannot be an independent category of science and technology. There are movements of 'scientization of politics' through 'communicative actions' towards the 'rationalization of life-world'. Accounting researchers embarked on a critical project with a view to understanding and changing accounting systems.

Three fundamental concepts

Before considering the above theoretical and methodological accounts in more detail, we shall look at three related concepts: 'life-world', 'systems' and 'language decentration'. We will first consider their meanings.

Life-world

This, according to Habermas, refers to a cultural space which articulates meanings for our societal life in which we use numerous tangible systems. For example, when we use a public service, we may characterize it as an 'efficient' or 'corrupted' system and interact with it according to this particular understanding. This characterization can come not only from the actual characteristics of that service but also from the human interpretations which are rooted in 'cultural space'[2] (Laughlin, 1987). However, life-world is not another sub-system of the wider social system. Power and Laughlin (1996: 444) read Habermas and stressed this point: 'Habermas is committed to the concept of a life-world as a symbolic space . . . which is a normative context within which culture, tradition and identity can be reproduced.' It is this symbolic space which interacts with tangible systems (such as organizations and accounting systems) for them to be characterized as particular 'actual systems'. The actuality does not simply represent the technical imperatives of such systems but a combination of both technicalities and symbolic interpretations. Thus, life-world is an epistemological device for us to understand a system such as an organization or its accounting system from a cultural perspective.

KEY TERMS

'Life-world' refers to a cultural space which articulates meanings for our societal life in which we use numerous tangible systems. It is not just another social sub-system but a normative context within which culture, tradition and identity can be reproduced.

Systems

As mentioned above, systems such as organizations and accounting systems act as self-regulatory mechanisms. Thompson (1983: 2855, cited in Laughlin, 1987: 486) defined this as 'self-regulating action contexts which co-ordinate actions around specific mechanisms or media such as money or power'. While money and the power of individuals play vital roles in maintaining systems as distinct elements in a society, they can be differentiated from the life-world. To put it another way, being differentiated from the life-world, systems have definable functional arrangements, but these arrangements operate through power relations and the influence of money (see Power and Laughlin, 1996). For instance, as a system, a hospital has specific functions that can be operationally defined; its operational mechanism can be understood with reference to its power structures and the role of money. However, the life-world of a hospital system is a cultural dimension which provides meanings to the function of the hospital in a particular manner. Eventually, the hospital is a self-regulating functional arrangement, while its functional expression is a function of the life-world. This means that the system and the life-world need each other for development as well as for separation.

KEY TERMS

Systems are defined as self-regulating action contexts which co-ordinate actions around specific mechanisms or media, such as money or power.

Language decentration

This concerns the communicative capacities of societal members who use their language skills. The fundamental assumption here is that a language is not merely a medium of communication, but also a device for constructing some social realities. On the one hand, individuals develop their language skills to differentiate the life-world from systems. In this way, the life-world is a distinct, symbolic resource which can guide individuals to keep it protected from systems. On the other hand, language skills are used to develop both the life-world and systems. On the whole, as Laughlin (1987) noted, these language skills of individuals develop society by moving from a position of a 'primitive egocentrism' towards a language capacity for coping with the external world, the social world and the world of inner subjectivity. In other words, language skills can create differences as well as integrations simultaneously between the technical (the external world), the cultural (the social world) and individuality (the world of inner subjectivity). Habermas showed that, because of these communicative actions, one can identify cultural systems separated from tangible institutions and systems.

> Language decentration concerns the language skills of individuals that develop society by moving from a position of a 'primitive egocentrism' towards a language capacity for coping with the external world, the social world and the world of inner subjectivity.

Building on the above concepts, Laughlin (1987) developed a methodology for understanding and changing accounting systems. Seen from the Habermasian perspective, such a methodology would be a sensible theoretical choice. First, because traditional theorists have been overconfident about the technical imperatives of accounting, in that there is a common belief that construction of profit and loss accounts, balance sheets, budgets, performance reports, etc., can improve efficiency. However, as Laughlin (1987) highlighted, there has been an underestimation of the connection between the technical world and the social world: conventional accounting researchers kept the technical divorced from the social (see Neimark and Tinker, 1986; Cooper and Hopper, 2006). Thus, there is a need to correct this 'unbalanced situation' by focusing on the connection between the technical and the social. Second, for Laughlin (1987), Habermas' methodology is instrumental if we need a change in the existing accounting systems. Presently, accounting systems are highly separated from the social by providing a persuasive language of business for emphasizing accounting's technical imperatives. Because of this separation, most textbook techniques are rarely practised: it is the cultural world that hinders such a synchronization between techniques and practice (see Scapens, 1994). If this is correct, then the language process *per se* can reveal this issue of disintegration and explore the interconnection between the social and the technical. The language process will then generate a change in both as Laughlin pointed out.

> The Habermasian perspective would be a sensible theoretical choice for two reasons: to bring the social dimension to analysis of accounting phenomena; and to make changes to both the social and the technical aspects of accounting systems within organizational contexts.

493

The issue of colonization

Bringing the Habermasian perspective further into the foreground, we can discern that, if the language skills of individuals are not sufficiently strong, the life-world will become subject to an 'inner colonization' by the technical world because the latter 'overpowers' the former, as Laughlin (1987) interprets Habermas. This is socially undesirable because 'unintended consequences' such as resistance and conflict would be inevitable. In this case, the life-world could either defend itself against the process of 'inner colonization' or revitalize its own significance. In either case, individuals use their language skills to protect cultural identity from the upsurge of externally generated technical systems, such as those of accounting. Rather than commenting on the nature of this colonization, Laughlin and his colleagues have been involved in a project of promoting a methodology of how interconnections between the social and the technical can be established by adopting language processes which we will explain later in this section. Thus, the Habermasian critical project in accounting is not only a theory of explanation (as to why there are discrepancies between the social and the technical), but also a programme of change which reflected on those language processes (for more details on this point, see Puxty, 1993; Alvesson and Willmott, 2003).

> If the language skills of individuals are not sufficiently strong, the life-world will become subject to 'inner colonization' by the technical world because the latter 'overpowers' the former. This is socially undesirable because 'unintended consequences' such as resistance would be inevitable.

> There has been a project promoting a methodology of how interconnections between the social and the technical can be established by adopting language processes, so the Habermasian approach is not only a theory of explanation, but also a programme of change.

Language processes

Language processes (or discursive processes) are seen to be 'actions' in case study research which have been undertaken by the above Habermasian accounting researchers. These processes contain four interconnected phases: the stage of quasi-ignorance; the formation of critical theorems; the process of enlightenment; and the selection of strategies. We will outline the nature of each process.

Quasi-ignorance stage

At this stage, both the researcher and the researched have few concerns about any issue regarding current or potential conflicts between the social and the technical elements. Instead, the researcher secures access to the organization in order to conduct an in-depth case study (Broadbent and Laughlin, 1997). However, they begin with a 'discursive process' whereby the researchers and the researched are exposed to the nature of important variables and develop some understanding about the connections between the two worlds, even though the two worlds have not been properly identified and defined. For example, they would first see that budgets are merely technical but, at the same time, they would realize that there can be some human consciousness that would enable or condition the roles of budgeting as an accounting control system. Even though such understandings have been developed, at this stage researchers collect data and keep them as descriptive as possible until they analyse them more closely and critically. As Laughlin (1987) drew on Habermas, this basic understanding of the connection between budgets and people would be an important prerequisite for the formation of critical theorems, the next stage of the language process.

Language processes are seen as 'actions' in case study research. These processes are: the stage of quasi-ignorance; the formation of critical theorems; the process of enlightenment; and the selection of strategies.

At the quasi-ignorance stage, both the researcher and the researched have few concerns about any issue, but they expose the nature of important variables and develop some understanding about the connections between the two worlds.

Critical theorems stage

At this stage, the researcher begins to explore more about the functioning of the accounting system by focusing on both its technical and social elements. With regard to the technical, the researcher exposes the actual shape of the current accounting system. For instance, s/he would recognize that there is a financial control system dominated by a tight budgetary control system, and the system of budgeting is characterized by a top-down process. In this way, the researcher identifies and synthesizes the technical imperatives of the current system before exploring underlying social reasons for the existence of such a system. Concerning the technical, the researcher now goes on to explore the hidden roots for the persistence of such a system. Laughlin (1987) pointed out that these roots can be twofold: technical and social. The technical roots relate to various technical initiatives which establish the technical dimensions of the current system. For instance, the above budgeting system would come from a government law which promulgates that all public enterprises should adopt such top-down budgetary control systems for enhancing better public financial management. The social roots relate to the development of a particular life-world and its steering mechanism, which co-exist with the technical imperatives of the current accounting systems. This life-world and its steering mechanism would guide the actual functioning of the technical dimension. For instance, the tightness of the above financial control system could be visible in the budgeting process, but these controls would not be linked to innovations which could have enhanced the scope of organizational activities. This is because the life-world would reproduce the top-down approach to budgeting as a ceremony, without a commitment to innovate. The researcher could identify this as a form of resistance developed by the life-world system. In this way, the critical theorem stage can explore more about the practice of an accounting system from both technical and social perspectives.

At the critical theorems stage, the researcher begins to explore more about the functioning of accounting systems by focusing on both their technical and social elements.

Enlightenment stage

At this stage, both the researcher and the researched develop some common understanding of the issues from both technical and social perspectives. As in the previous stage, all technical and social roots are identified. However, as Laughlin (1987) remarked, there are two unique features of the enlightenment stage. The first is related to the researcher's attempts to regard the researched as a 'discursive partner' and the associated problems of this very effort. The language process now becomes a joint endeavour where the researcher turns her/his project into a kind of 'action research'. The second is related to the resolution mechanism for associated problems which arise from disagreements and misunderstandings. As Laughlin (1987) drew from Habermas, these problems can be resolved by introducing what Habermas called prior 'therapeutic discourses'. The researched then not only understand the processes of accounting systems and their underlying technical and social roots, but also engage in producing more meaningful explanations which can be useful for further 'understanding and change'. If this happened more effectively and successfully, then both the researcher and the researched would be prepared for the last stage, the selection of strategies.

At the enlightenment stage, the researcher and the researched develop some common understanding of the issues. The researched then not only understand the processes and their roots, but also produce more explanations for further understanding and change.

Selection of strategies

This is the last stage which makes necessary strategic choices for changing the current system. Having borrowed from Habermas, Laughlin (1987) introduced three such strategies. The first relates to changes in the life-world. Even though a change in socio-cultural aspects (the life-world) seems to be difficult, an attempt is feasible as both the researcher and the researched have already developed common understanding of the issues in question. The potential changes in the life-world can then lead subsequent changes in technical aspects rather than the latter leading the former. Conventional accounting assumed that the technical would lead the cultural changes, but the outcomes were often problematic. The second strategy relates to the possible changes to be made to the technical aspects of the accounting system. The necessary guide for such changes can now be provided by the life-world. For example, if the life-world has been developed to accept the spirit of participation, then a top-down budgetary control system can be changed into a participative one. This can be a radical change, maybe against external imposition of top-down systems. The last strategy is to ensure that the life-world is congruent with the system elements where the organizational members are subject to a positive inner colonization. If this strategy is achieved, then the change can be regarded as 'cultural adaptation' rather than resistance.

> Strategic choice stage follows three separate strategies: changes in the life-world; changes in the technical aspects; and making the life-world congruent with system elements. The ultimate outcome is 'cultural adaptation' rather than resistance.

On middle-range thinking

Habermasian researchers in accounting promoted the above language processes alongside their approach to 'middle-range thinking' (Laughlin, 1995; Broadbent and Laughlin, 1997). The term 'middle-range thinking' refers to a medium position with regard to the understanding of theory, methodology and change. At one extreme, theory can be highly specific, and the methodology can be perfectly structured. Positivistic research methodology, where researchers seek to test hypotheses, usually locates in this extreme. Rather than relying on qualitative case studies, the researchers within this school rely heavily on quantitative analyses and seek statistical generalizations. For them, theory is taken to be a series of testable hypotheses rather than a guide for understanding the world, hence the specific predetermined models. While both the theory and methodology are seen to be 'high' in their specificities, change (in accounting systems) is given a low priority. Thus, by undertaking such testing of hypotheses, little can be offered to make any change to the status quo. Most economic-oriented management accounting research falls into this category: for example, Spicer and Ballew (1983), Baiman (1982, 1990), Johnson and Kaplan (1987).

The other extreme represents the 'low' position in theory, methodology and change. The researchers within this school undertake qualitative, longitudinal case studies with no prior theory in mind. Instead, they seek patterns and understand the status quo in descriptive ways. Similarly, their methodology is free of predetermined procedures and structures. Instead, the researcher explores the ways in which the status quo could be studied and reported. Also, as within the scientific extreme, the researchers within this school do not contemplate any change in the status quo. The best examples for this category of management accounting research are Colville (1981), Rosenberg et al. (1982) and Berry et al. (1985).

Laughlin and his colleagues illustrated that the execution of the two extreme cases above cannot be practically tenable, as research endeavours are not always perfect and impartial; hence, middle-range thinking.

KEY TERMS

The term 'middle-range thinking' refers to a medium position with regard to the understanding of theory, methodology and change.

> It has been illustrated that the execution of the two extreme cases cannot be practically tenable, as research endeavours are not always perfect and impartial; hence, middle-range thinking.

In middle-range thinking, the researcher relies on a theory to be a guide for understanding the status quo. However, at this level, theory is not regarded as the ultimate truth. Rather, it is a 'skeleton' theory of organizational change process which can be used as a tool for exploring analyses and informing appropriate changes. On the one hand, a theory provides a particular focus for a longitudinal case study by means of defining possible factors and their relationships. On the other hand, the theory can be flexible so that, with empirical experience, it can be modified and/or improved. The output is a theoretical construction with better analyses and explanations rather than mere descriptions. Within this school, the methodology is seen as a predetermined plan of data collection and analysis subject to modifications and changes as the project progresses: it is not highly structured as in scientific methodology, and it is not highly unplanned as in purely interpretive case studies. Moreover, in middle-range thinking, a substantive weight is given to changing the status quo. As we saw through the execution of language processes within the Habermasian way of conducting case studies, the researcher and the researched unite to contemplate culturally desirable changes.

> In 'middle-range thinking', theory is a guide for understanding the status quo; the methodology is a predetermined plan of data collection and analysis, subject to modifications and changes; substantive weight is given to culturally desirable changes.

Laughlin and his colleagues argue that the Habermasian way of conducting case studies can be an exemplar for middle-range thinking. Its theory is a 'skeleton' framework which can be modified and changed for the benefit of both the researcher and the researched (Broadbent and Laughlin, 1997). Its methodology is partially structured, subject to potential changes through an actual research process which can also be located in the study in the particular historical context of the organization in question (ibid.). Furthermore, it seeks changes in the status quo 'in a constructive way', by moving from 'quasi-ignorance' to 'selection of strategies' (ibid.).

The main thrust of this approach is that it can differentiate changes at both social and organizational levels by focusing on the three elements we presented earlier: life-world, steering media and systems. As Laughlin and others have observed, in an ideal world, these three elements should be present in equilibrium. However, when we begin to undertake a case study, we see various forms of disequilibrium, or 'disturbances'. By following the language processes, we could explore these 'disturbances' and, in turn, we would unearth ways of moving such forms of disequilibrium into equilibrium: a movement from 'first-order' to 'second-order' changes. If change occurs as a result of a change in the life-world, such a change can be a 'revolution', and if the life-world is forced to adopt certain changes occurring in the steering media, then the resultant change can be a 'colonization'. Habermasian researchers are engaged in an emancipatory project and prefer the revolutionary approach where they strive for a culturally desirable change in the life-world, as well as in the steering media and systems. However, moving from 'first-order' change to 'second-order' change is arduous and requires careful execution of the research project in question.

Broadbent and Laughlin (1997) reported on a case study of UK GP practices and schools, areas which underwent substantive 'reforms' in last two decades of the twentieth century. They demonstrated an application of the Habermasian discourse model which we described above. The 'reforms' which were implemented in these two public sector settings were mainly focused on the

In an ideal world, life-world, steering media and systems should be present in equilibrium. In practice, there are various forms of disequilibrium. The actual change can be seen as a 'revolution' or a 'colonization'.

delegation of finances, along with a tighter definition of services and enhanced accountability for actions. The aims of the research programme were to understand and evaluate these 'reforms' and to 'achieve some level of emancipation' through action strategies. The research sites comprised four schools and six GP practices. Unlike in the original model of middle-range thinking, where the discursive process starts with 'quasi-ignorance' (Laughlin, 1987), this programme was initialized with 'critical theorems'. In this first stage, Broadbent and Laughlin gathered data on an 'interpretive scheme' by focusing on the culture and values which can be understood by exploring the nature of design archetypes (steering media) and systems in the organization. Sometimes, they understood them well and developed better 'critical theorems', but, at other times, the discursive process was not necessarily productive. Continuous efforts through preliminary and follow-up interviews enabled the researchers to develop 'draft academic papers' which were subject to 'writing and rewriting' and further discussions with the researched. This initial stage led to the stage of enlightenment, where the researchers had to convince the researched of their understanding despite some difficulties. The final 'selection of strategies' involved some emancipation by means of facilitating the researched in resolving issues. This happened through mutual understanding and collaboration. For instance, in the case of schools, one of the researchers was requested to join the school's governing body.

On the whole, by applying this discursive approach, the researchers were able to produce a number of academic papers as an achievement of academic aims, and to guide the researched to refine their strategies as an achievement of emancipation. However, it must be noted that the entire discursive process overlapped, rather than starting at the first stage and finishing everything at the last stage. Also, there were more issues in the execution of the process. First, the whole process was influenced by the subjectivity of the researchers despite the influence of a critical theoretical framework. Second, the 'let it go' type of influence can give rise to conflicts between the researchers' desires and the expectations and understanding of the researched, as there emerged diverse views on strategic choices. Third, the success of emancipation largely depended on the nature of the power structure of the organization rather than the influence of the discourse partners: ultimately, the researched rather than the researchers make the final choice.

The aims of the research were to understand and evaluate the 'reforms' and to 'achieve some emancipation'. The whole process was influenced by the researchers' subjectivity; the 'let it go' type of influence can lead to conflicts between the researchers and the researched; and the success of emancipation largely depended on the nature of the power structure of the organization.

SUMMING UP

This chapter looked at some important works of management accounting which have been built on Foucauldian and Habermasian perspectives. While the former represents a particular space in postmodernism with a bent for the fundamentals of post-structuralism, the latter attempts to defend the project of modernity by reinventing the lines of societal development. Against the fundamentals of post-structuralism, some critical researchers within the domain of a broader political economy approach have levelled a series of criticisms at the Foucauldians' neglect of broader factors outside micro-settings (Neimark, 1994; Armstrong, 1994; Copper and Tinker, 1994). In response to such criticisms, Foucauldian researchers in accounting made an attempt to save Foucault (Hoskin, 1994; Grey, 1994) by providing counter-arguments and refined analyses of the problem of political economy. While we do not aim to arouse this debate in this limited space, we wish to invite you to think that there is no single perspective which aids understanding of management accounting change. 'Change' would be a 'reality', depending on the nature of theoretical assumptions and approaches by which we see it. What we can do, according to postmodernism, is construct a reality about change; or, according to a political economy perspective, we can explore realities in the light of class struggle.

> There is no single perspective which aids understanding of management accounting change. 'Change' would be a 'reality', depending on the nature of theoretical assumptions and approaches by which we see it.

The Habermasian perspective would come into the middle ground to resolve the problem of structuralism and post-structuralism. While the researchers who take this perspective developed a theoretical and methodological groundwork, they have not been confronted with a Foucauldian framework to reject or deconstruct. While the researchers have been working side by side, some have thought of making a union between Foucault and Habermas. The attempt by Arrington and Watkins (2002) is viewed in this regard. They considered both Foucault and Habermas as important intellectual resources to contribute to the debate of 'postmodern politics', in which management accounting change can be highly implicated. Arrington and Watkins' plea (2002: 139) is that this union 'may provide a useful way to think about the shape and character of critical research in accounting'.

> Some have thought of making a union between Foucault and Habermas, which may be a useful way of thinking about critical accounting.

HAVE YOU UNDERSTOOD THE CHAPTER?

1. In line with the observations of postmodern researchers, what is the fundamental problem of the political economy perspective?

2. What is the relationship, and differences, between postmodernism and post-structuralism?
3. In terms of a Foucauldian framework, what is 'critical accounting'?
4. What are the main theoretical aspects employed in Foucauldian management accounting studies? Describe each of them.
5. What have you learned from 'management accounting history' within Foucauldian studies?
6. What do we know about management accounting as a disciplinary practice?
7. In terms of Habermas' theory of societal development, what is to be 'critical'?
8. How does 'colonization' operate in our modern lives, and what roles do accounting systems play in this regard?
9. What is the ideal-type equilibrium in relation to the practice of management accounting? Why is this often not the case in practice?
10. How is 'middle-range thinking' processed through the discursive programmes of communicative actions? What can we learn from this for management accounting?

BEYOND THE CHAPTER

1. In terms of postmodern critiques, what is the problem of employing a political economy perspective in exploration of management accounting change?
2. 'Postmodernism constructs multiple realities.' Is this valid for Foucauldian accounting studies?
3. 'Management accounting cannot be understood without reference to other forms of technologies.' Discuss.
4. In terms of a Habermasian framework, what is management accounting change?
5. Is middle-range thinking a theoretical framework or a research methodology?

FURTHER READING

1. For a summary of the Foucaldian framework used in accounting, see Miller and O'Leary (1987) and Hopper and Macintosh (1993).
2. For the debate between Foucauldian and Marxist accounting, see Neimark (1994) and Hoskin (1994). For a balanced but critical review of Foucauldian research accounting, see Armstrong (1994).
3. Two excellent, empirically grounded works on management control and accounting are Hopper and Macintosh (1993) and Hoskin and Macve (1988).
4. For a good example of a Habermasian framework used in accounting, see Laughlin (1987, 1995).
5. For empirical studies in Habermasian accounting research, see Broadbent et al. (1991) and Broadbent and Laughlin (1997).

Notes

CHAPTER 1: LEARNING MANAGEMENT ACCOUNTING CHANGE

1   S–T–P marketing stands for market segmentation, targeting and positioning strategy. This marketing philosophy, which is the opposite of mass marketing, acknowledges that a market is not a homogeneous set of customers with a unitary set of wants. Instead, it recognizes that a market can be analytically broken down into a set of distinct segments, each of which demands a unique marketing mix, i.e., product, price, promotion and distribution strategies (see Kotler, 2003).

2   After Henry Ford's innovation of the assembly line and its associated managerial structure and higher wage rates, 'Fordism' refers to a form of industrial organization and employment policy in which de-skilling is organized along an assembly line to achieve economic efficiencies of mass production (i.e., mass-scale production of a standard product such as the Model-T Ford), coupled with a higher wage rate. Behind these higher wage rates there lies the assumption that not only the workplace efficiency of employees but also their earning potential and attitudes as consumers affect the success of enterprises. Though Fordism is economically efficient, it has inherent problems in lack of flexibility and incapacity to produce 'varieties' with a competitive level of efficiency.

3   This is an arena of economic theories shifted from classical economics. Classical economists such as Adam Smith and David Ricardo saw economics through a theory of production surplus. In this, they implicated political and social aspects of economic behaviour. Neoclassical economics which emerged in the second half of the nineteenth century depoliticized economic theory by deliberately neglecting politics, value judgements and social impacts of economic actions, such as income distribution (see Tinker *et al.*, 1982).

4   These costs are termed 'transaction costs'. Even though these costs are fundamental to this approach, there is no clear-cut definition of what they are. For a critique of this, see Hopper *et al.* (1987).

5   The difference between the two: postmodernists are more oriented towards cultural critique while post-structuralists emphasize method and epistemological matters. For example, post-structuralists concentrate on deconstruction, language, discourse, meanings and symbols, while postmodernists cast a broader net.

CHAPTER 2: TOWARDS MASS PRODUCTION AND BUREAUCRACY

1   This is the first principle of Taylor's Scientific Management.

2   This is Taylor's second principle, which reads 'all possible brain work should be removed from the shop and centred in the planning or laying-out department' (Taylor, 1964: 98–99).

3   Sward (1948: 48–49) states: 'So great was labour's distaste for the new machine system that toward the close of 1913 every time the company [Ford's] wanted to add 100 men to its factory personnel, it was necessary to hire 963.'

CHAPTER 3: TOWARDS PRODUCT COSTING

1   Complexities of reallocating service department costs to production department arise from the fact that service departments often simultaneously offer their services to each other. As you may recall, in such scenarios you may adopt a continuous reallocation method or 'simultaneous equation' algebra to determine the final amounts that production departments should receive from each service department.

CHAPTER 4: TOWARDS PROFIT PLANNING THROUGH BUDGETING

1   However, it should be noted, governmental budgeting today has extended its aims to encompass a broader set of objectives, such as minimizing unemployment, public welfare, economic stability, economic development and so on.
2   Note that bureaucracy as a form of organization first appeared in state institutions such as the army, where profit motive was not explicit. It was in business organizations that the bureaucracy explicitly had to assume the objective of profit: that is, capital accumulation.
3   The term 'non-operational' is used here just to mean that they fall outside the scope of operational budgets, i.e., sales, production, material and labour usage and purchases.
4   Expectancy, instrumentality and valence are the basic elements of expectancy theory of motivation, which provides an explanation for why human beings behave in certain ways. According to this theory, one would be more likely to behave in such a way if: (a) s/he is certain that his/her efforts lead to the expected performance (i.e., 'expectancy' = effort $\times$ performance); (b) s/he is certain that his/her performance leads him/her to the expected outcome, such as reward (i.e., 'instrumentality' = performance $\times$ rewarding outcome); and (c) the value s/he places upon that expected outcome (i.e., 'valence'). Thus:

motivation = f (expectancy, instrumentality and valence).

This reads as: motivation (effort) is a function of expectancy, instrumentality and valence.
5   Traditional management textbooks, especially Anglo-American ones, define management as a process of planning, organizing, co-ordinating, directing (i.e., leading, motivating and communicating) and control (cf. Koontz and Weihrich, 1990).

CHAPTER 5: TOWARDS MANAGEMENT CONTROL THROUGH BUDGETING

1   Note that we are following marginal costing principles in this example. This would be different if we adopted absorption costing principles where the demarcation between variable and fixed costs is not made at all. In that case, all overhead elements would be absorbed into unit costs according to selected absorption bases.

CHAPTER 6: TOWARDS ECONOMIC MODELS OF DECISION-MAKING

1   However, there are certain academic refinements of these practices with certain mathematical and economic models. Especially when these cost ascertainment and control techniques were reproduced through the academic discourses of textbook writing, they were given a certain

academic flavour by combining with and explaining through various conceptual frameworks (mainly mathematical). One good example is the use of simultaneous equations in the secondary apportionment of service centre overheads to production centres. This is, of course, a late textbook addition to cost ascertainment techniques by academics.

2   However, it should be noted that the variable cost per unit of output can decline even in the short run, if we assume a learning curve effect. Which means variable cost per unit of output can decrease due to 'learning effect', when we employ the same labour repeatedly in a given technological setting. The mathematical model of 'learning curves' replicates this scenario, and is a hot topic in many management accounting textbooks.

CHAPTER 7:   TOWARDS CUSTOMER ORIENTATION AND FLEXIBLE MANUFACTURING

1   Here the term 'historical' is not used necessarily to mean something which has already happened (in the past), but to mean a set of incidents, events or movements that is capable of changing the (future) history of mankind.

CHAPTER 8:   TOWARDS STRATEGIC MANAGEMENT ACCOUNTING

1   According to marketing principles, a marketer has four weapons to compete in a given market: product, place, promotion and price, which are together known as the four Ps (see Kotler, 2003).

2   Nevertheless, a set of 'others', especially some academics, who do not buy into or resist those postmodern ideologies, are critical and sceptical about the new social order and domination that they would bring forward (see Chapters 13, 14 and 15).

CHAPTER 9:   TOWARDS COST MANAGEMENT

1   However, as Armstrong (2002) discerns, ABC has changed the organizational accountability system for staff departments whose services are indirect. Traditionally, these departments were not directly accountable for cost control as their costs were regarded as common. By making these common costs 'direct' through directly linking them to cost objects, these departments were subjected to the surveillance of cost control discourses.

CHAPTER 11:   NEOCLASSICAL ECONOMIC THEORIES OF MANAGEMENT ACCOUNTING CHANGE

1   Lambert (2001: 5–6) identifies four reasons for the goal incongruence between principal and agent: differences in the perceived time horizon where the principal would normally be seeking the agent's long-term commitment to the organization, while the agent may be seeking to resign in the short term; differences in the principal's and agent's risk aversion; the possibility that the agent may opportunistically use the principal's resources for his/her own personal benefit, not covered by the agency contract (also known as moral hazard or hidden actions); and there is scope for effort aversion by the agent.

2   The line T is parallel to the principal's payoff curve, and drawn tangentially to the agent's utility curve in order to determine the maximum gap between the payoff curve and the utility curve, which is the maximum payoff after deducting the agent's wages.

3   Hybrid forms constitute a range of possibilities, such as long-term relations between buyers and suppliers, joint ventures, business groups, informal networks, franchising and so on, which have been increasingly popular in recent times, and thus subject to a stream of management accounting research. See later sections of this chapter.

4   It should be noted that, in the context of transaction cost theory, the term 'transactions' is employed to mean those between 'firms', where one party purchases materials or services from others for the purpose of production. This should not be confused with transactions in the final goods markets, where 'consumers' purchase for final consumption.

5   Note that hierarchy represents integration of individually operating production units into a single administrative structure, which otherwise would function as suppliers and buyers in open markets. For example, the acquisition of Fisher Body by General Motors is an instance of creating a larger hierarchy by integrating hitherto independently operating firms which transacted through market contracts.

CHAPTER 14: TOWARDS POLITICAL ECONOMY OF MACh

1   For critical researchers, however, projecting oneself as a politically disinterested neutral researcher is as political an act as being involved in change, as it implicitly reinforces the status quo (Cooper and Hopper, 2006: 5; see also Tinker, 1991; Willmott et al., 1993).

2   This is because Hopper and Armstrong's labour process history of management accounting was advanced as a critique to Johnson and Kaplan's transaction cost theory-based explanation of management accounting history. Both are primarily based on Chandler's (Chandler and Tedlow, 1985) accounts of American industrial history.

3   Burawoy was not the only or the first person to talk about consent in the workplace. Much earlier, Gramsci brought this concept to the theoretical arena in his political writings on the contradictions and accommodation between the political state and the civil state (hegemony). While Burawoy's contribution in bringing the concept of hegemony and consent to the forefront of labour process analysis is noteworthy, there are many others whose empirical works reflect the presence of consent in workplace politics. For example, it is reflected, more or less, in Friedman's notion of 'responsible autonomy' (discussed above). Similarly, Nichols and Beynon (1977) presented it in terms of 'resigned acquiescence'. A materialistic instrumentality as the basis of accepting managerial power in Goldthorpe et al. (1969) also resembles the idea of consent in the workplace.

4   However, it should be noted that Burawoy's study took place in North America, where the associated discourses of shop-floor collectivism were largely destroyed during the anti-union campaign of the 1930s and Cold War suspicion of anything that smacked of communism. Thus, generalization of the idea that gaming is always individualistic and always manufactures consent beyond that context is problematic. There are studies which point out that gaming is carried out at the collective level and in which it is seen through the lens of some form of collective consciousness (e.g., Brown, 1972).

5   However, it seems that Burawoy infers the effectiveness of the internal labour market as individualization from the fact of its existence. But there always exists the possibility that not all workers buy into the opportunities for individual promotions, especially when the competition among workers is so high that winning the 'game' becomes a remote chance. On the other hand, internal labour markets are often the subject of collective negotiations and agreement.

CHAPTER 15: BEYOND POLITICAL ECONOMY OF MACh

1   For a sketch of Habermas' contribution to social theory and philosophy, see Ritzer (1996).

2   Habermas used the term 'life-world' interchangeably with similar terms such as 'social' world and 'cultural' world.

Bibliography

Abernethy, M. A. and Lillis, A. M. 1995, 'The impact of manufacturing flexibility on management control system design', *Accounting, Organizations and Society*, vol. 20, no. 4, pp. 241–258.

Ahmed, M. N. 1992, 'A critical evaluation of the methodological underpinnings of management accounting research: an alternative institutional economics framework', Ph.D. thesis, University of Manchester.

Ahmed, M. N. and Scapens, R. W. 1991, 'Cost allocation theory and practice: the continuing debate', in *Issues in management accounting*, 1st edn, D. Ashton, T. Hopper and R. W. Scapens, eds, Prentice-Hall International, London, pp. 39–60.

Ahuja, M. K. and Carley, K. M. 1999, 'Network structure in virtual organizations', *Organization Science*, vol. 10, no. 6, pp. 741–757.

Alawattage, C. and Wickramasinghe, D. Forthcoming, 'Appearance of accounting in a political hegemony', *Critical Perspectives on Accounting*.

Alnestig, P. and Segerstedt, A. 1996, 'Product costing in ten Swedish manufacturing companies', *International Journal of Production Economics*, vols 46–47, pp. 441–457.

Alston, J. P. 1982, 'Awarding bonuses the Japanese way', *Business Horizons*, vol. 25, no. 5, pp. 46–50.

Alvesson, M. and Willmott, H. 1992, *Critical management studies* Sage, London.

—— 2003, *Studying management critically* Sage, London.

Anderson, S. W. and Lanen, W. N. 1999, 'Economic transition, strategy and the evolution of management accounting practices: the case of India', *Accounting, Organizations and Society*, vol. 24, nos. 5–6, pp. 379–412.

Anderson, S. W., Glenn, D. and Sedatole, K. L. 2000, 'Sourcing parts of complex products: evidence on transactions costs, high-powered incentives and ex-post opportunism', *Accounting, Organizations and Society*, vol. 25, no. 8, pp. 723–749.

Ansari, S. L. 1977, 'An integrated approach to control system design', *Accounting, Organizations and Society*, vol. 2, no. 2, pp. 101–112.

Ansari, S. L. and Bell, J. 1991, 'Symbolism, collectivism and rationality in organisational control', *Accounting, Auditing and Accountability Journal*, vol. 4, no. 2, pp. 4–27.

Anthony, R. N. 1965, *Planning and control systems: a framework for analysis* Harvard University Press, Cambridge, MA.

Anthony, R. N. and Dearden, J. 1980, *Management control systems*, 4th edn, Irwin, Homewood, IL.

Anthony, R. N. and Govindarajan, V. 1998, *Management control systems*, 9th edn, Irwin McGraw-Hill, Chicago.

Anthony, R. N., Dearden, J. and Vancil, R. F. 1965, *Management control systems: cases and readings*, Irwin, Homewood, IL.

Archer, S. and Otley, D. 1991, 'Strategy, structure, planning and control systems and performance evaluation – Rumenco Ltd.', *Management Accounting Research*, vol. 2, pp. 263–303.

Argyris, C. 1952, *The impact of budgets on people* Cornell University Press, Ithaca, NY.

Armstrong, P. 1985, 'Changing management control strategies: the role of competition between accountancy and other organisational professions', *Accounting, Organizations and Society*, vol. 10, no. 2, pp. 129–148.

—— 1986, 'Management control strategies and inter-professional competition: the cases of accountancy and personnel management', in *Managing the labour process*, D. Knights and H. Willmott, eds, Gower, Aldershot, pp. 19–43.

—— 1989, 'Management, labour process and agency', *Work, Employment and Society*, vol. 3, no. 3, pp. 307–322.

—— 1991, 'Contradiction and social dynamics in the capitalist agency relationship', *Accounting, Organizations and Society*, vol. 16, no. 1, pp. 1–25.

—— 1994, 'The influence of Michel Foucault on accounting research', *Critical Perspectives on Accounting*, vol. 5, no. 1, pp. 25–55.

—— 2000, 'Accounting for insecurity', *Critical Perspectives on Accounting*, vol. 11, no. 4, pp. 383–406.

—— 2002, 'The costs of activity-based management', *Accounting, Organizations and Society*, vol. 27, nos. 1–2, pp. 99–120.

Arnold, J. 1998, 'The limits of postmodernism in accounting history: the Decatur experience', *Accounting, Organizations and Society*, vol. 23, no. 7, pp. 665–684.

Arnold, J. and Hope, T. 1983, *Accounting for management decisions* Prentice-Hall International, Englewood Cliffs, NJ.

Arrington, C. and Francis, J. R. 1989, 'Letting the chat out of the bag: deconstruction, privilege and accounting research', *Accounting, Organizations and Society*, vol. 14, nos. 1–2, pp. 1–28.

Arrington, C. and Puxty, A. G. 1991, 'Accounting, interests, and rationality: a communicative relation', *Critical Perspectives on Accounting*, vol. 2, no. 1, pp. 31–58.

Arrington, C. and Watkins, A. L. 2002, 'Maintaining "critical intent" within a postmodern theoretical perspective on accounting research', *Critical Perspectives on Accounting*, vol. 13, no. 2, pp. 139–157.

Arya, A., Glover, J. C. and Sivaramakrishnan, K. 1997, 'The interaction between decision and control problems and the value of information', *Accounting Review*, vol. 72, no. 4, pp. 561–574.

Ashby, W. R. 1956, *An introduction to cybernetics* Chapman and Hall, London.

Ashton, D. 1991, 'Agency theory and contracts of employment', in *Issues in management accounting*, 1st edn, D. Ashton, T. Hopper and R. W. Scapens, eds, Prentice-Hall International, London, pp. 106–125.

Ashton, D., Hopper, T. and Scapens, R. W. 1995, 'The changing nature of issues in management accounting,' in *Issues in management accounting*, 2nd edn, D. Ashton, T. Hopper and R. W. Scapens, eds, Prentice-Hall Europe, Essex, pp. 1–20.

Atkinson, A. A., Kaplan, R. S. and Young, S. M. 2004, *Management accounting*, 4th edn, Pearson/Prentice-Hall, Upper Saddle River, NJ.

Baiman, S. 1982, 'Agency research in managerial accounting: a survey', *Journal of Accounting Literature*, vol. 1, no. 1, pp. 154–213.

—— 1990, 'Agency research in managerial accounting: a second look', *Accounting, Organizations and Society*, vol. 15, no. 4, pp. 341–371.

Barley, S. R. and Tolbert, P. S. 1997, 'Institutionalization and structuration: studying the links between action and institution', *Organization Studies*, vol. 18, no. 1, pp. 93–117.

Baudrillard, J. 1975, *The mirror of production*, Telos Press, St Louis, MO.

Baxter, J. and Chua, W. F. 2003, 'Alternative management accounting research – whence and whither', *Accounting, Organizations and Society*, vol. 28, nos. 2–3, pp. 97–126.

—— 2006, 'A management accountant from "down-under": the research of Professor Bill Birkett (1940–2004)', *Management Accounting Research*, vol. 17, no. 1, pp. 1–10.

Bell, D. and Kristol, I. 1981, *The crisis in economic theory* Basic Books, New York.

507

Berger, P. L. and Luckmann, T. 1967, *The social construction of reality: a treatise in the sociology of knowledge* Penguin, London.

Berry, A. J., Capps, T., Cooper, D., Ferguson, P., Hopper, T. and Lowe, E. A. 1985, 'Management control in an area of the NCB: rationales of accounting practices in a public enterprise', *Accounting, Organizations and Society*, vol. 10, no. 1, pp. 3–28.

Bessire, D. and Baker, C. R. 2005, 'The French tableau de bord and the American balanced score-card: a critical analysis', *Critical Perspectives on Accounting*, vol. 16, no. 6, pp. 645–664.

Birkett, W. P. and Poullaos, C. 2001, 'From accounting to management: a global perspective', in *A profession transforming: from accounting to management*, W. P. Birkett and C. Poullaos, eds, International Federation of Accountants, New York, pp. 1–20.

Bjornenak, T. 1997, 'Diffusion and accounting: the case of ABC in Norway', *Management Accounting Research*, vol. 8, no. 1, pp. 3–17.

Blau, P. M. 1955, *The dynamics of bureaucracy: a study of interpersonal relations in two government agencies* University of Chicago Press, Chicago.

Blumer, H. 1969, *Symbolic interaction* Prentice-Hall, Englewood Cliffs, NJ.

Boland, J. and Pondy, L. R. 1983, 'Accounting in organizations: a union of natural and rational perspectives', *Accounting, Organizations and Society*, vol. 8, nos. 2–3, pp. 223–234.

Boreham, P., Clegg, S. and Dow, G. 1986, 'The institutional management of class politics: beyond the labour processes and corporatist debates', in *Managing the labour process*, D. Knights and H. Willmott, eds, Gower, Aldershot, pp. 186–210.

Bourguignon, A., Malleret, V. and Norreklit, H. 2004, 'The American balanced scorecard versus the French tableau de bord: the ideological dimension', *Management Accounting Research*, vol. 15, no. 2, pp. 107–134.

Boyns, T. 1998, 'Budgets and budgetary control in British businesses to c.1945', *Accounting, Business and Financial History*, vol. 8, no. 3, pp. 261–301.

Boyns, T. and Edwards, J. R. 1997, 'British cost and management accounting theory and practice, c.1850–c.1950; resolved and unresolved issues', *Business and Economic History*, vol. 26, no. 2, pp. 452–462.

Braverman, H. 1974, *Labor and monopoly capital: the degradation of work in the twentieth century* Monthly Review Press, New York/London.

—— 1998, *Labor and monopoly capital: the degradation of work in the twentieth century*, 25th anniversary edn, Monthly Review Press, New York.

Briers, M. and Chua, W. F. 2001, 'The role of actor–networks and boundary objects in management accounting change: a field study of an implementation of activity-based costing', *Accounting, Organizations and Society*, vol. 26, no. 3, pp. 237–269.

Briers, M. and Hirst, M. 1990, 'The role of budgetary information in performance evaluation', *Accounting, Organizations and Society*, vol. 15, no. 4, pp. 373–398.

Brignall, S. and Modell, S. 2000, 'An institutional perspective on performance measurement and management in the "new public sector"', *Management Accounting Research*, vol. 11, no. 3, pp. 281–306.

Brimson, J. A. 1991, *Activity accounting: an activity-based costing approach* Wiley, Chichester.

Brinker, B. J. 1992, *Handbook of cost management* Warren, Gorham and Lamont, Boston, MA.

—— 1994, *Activity-based management: emerging practices in cost management* Warren, Gorham and Lamont, Boston, MA.

Broadbent, J. and Laughlin, R. 1997, 'Developing empirical research: an example informed by a Habermasian approach', *Accounting, Auditing and Accountability Journal*, vol. 10, no. 5, pp. 622–648.

Broadbent, J., Laughlin, R. and Read, S. 1991, 'Recent financial and administrative changes in the NHS: a critical theory analysis', *Critical Perspectives on Accounting*, vol. 2, no. 1, pp. 1–29.

Bromwich, M. 1990, 'The case for strategic management accounting: the role of accounting information for strategy in competitive markets', *Accounting, Organizations and Society*, vol. 15, nos. 1–2, pp. 27–46.

—— 1992, 'Strategic management accounting', in *Management accounting handbook*, C. Drury, ed., Butterworth-Heinemann, London, pp. 129–153.

Bromwich, M. and Bhimani, A. 1989, *Management accounting: evolution not revolution* Chartered Institute of Management Accountants, London.

Brown, W. A. 1972, 'A consideration of custom and practice', *British Journal of Industrial Relations*, vol. 10, no. 1, pp. 42–61.

Bruns, W. J. and Waterhouse, J. H. 1975, 'Budgetary control and organization structure', *Journal of Accounting Research*, vol. 13, no. 2, pp. 177–203.

Bryer, R. A. 1991, 'Accounting for the "railway mania" of 1845 – a great railway swindle?', *Accounting, Organizations and Society*, vol. 16, nos. 5–6, pp. 439–486.

—— 1993, 'The late nineteenth-century revolution in financial reporting: accounting for the rise of investor or managerial capitalism?', *Accounting, Organizations and Society*, vol. 18, nos. 7–8, pp. 649–690.

—— 2000, 'The history of accounting and the transition to capitalism in England. Part two: evidence', *Accounting, Organizations and Society*, vol. 25, nos. 4–5, pp. 327–381.

—— 2005, 'A Marxist accounting history of the British industrial revolution: a review of evidence and suggestions for research', *Accounting, Organizations and Society*, vol. 30, no. 1, pp. 25–65.

—— 2006, 'The genesis of the capitalist farmer: towards a Marxist accounting history of the origins of the English agricultural revolution', *Critical Perspectives on Accounting*, vol. 17, no. 4, pp. 367–397.

Burawoy, M. 1979, *Manufacturing consent: changes in the labour process under monopoly capitalism* University of Chicago Press, Chicago and London.

—— 1985, *The politics of production* Verso, London.

—— 1996, 'A classic of its time', *Contemporary Sociology*, vol. 25, pp. 296–299.

Burchell, S., Clubb, C., Hopwood, A., Hughes, J. and Nahapiet, J. 1980, 'The roles of accounting in organizations and society', *Accounting, Organizations and Society*, vol. 5, no. 1, pp. 5–27.

Burns, J. and Baldvinsdottir, G. 2005, 'An institutional perspective of accountants' new roles – the interplay of contradictions and praxis', *European Accounting Review*, vol. 14, no. 4, pp. 725–757.

Burns, J. and Scapens, R. W. 2000, 'Conceptualizing management accounting change: an institutional framework', *Management Accounting Research*, vol. 11, no. 1, pp. 3–25.

Burns, T. and Stalker, G. M. 1961, *The management of innovations* Tavistock, London.

Burrell, G. and Morgan, G. 1979, *Sociological paradigms and organisational analysis: elements of the sociology of corporate life* Heinemann Educational, London.

Cagwin, D. and Bouwman, M. J. 2002, 'The association between activity-based costing and improvement in financial performance', *Management Accounting Research*, vol. 13, no. 1, pp. 1–39.

Callon, M. 1991, 'Techno-economic networks and irreversibility', in *A sociology of monsters: essays on power, technology and domination*, J. Law, ed., Routledge, London/New York, pp. 103–131.

Callon, M., Law, J. and Rip, A. 1986, *Mapping the dynamics of science and technology: sociology of science in the real world* Macmillan, Basingstoke.

Cardinaels, E., Roodhooft, F. and Warlop, L. 2004, 'The value of activity-based costing in competitive pricing decisions', *Journal of Management Accounting Research*, vol. 16, pp. 133–148.

Carruthers, B. G. 1995, 'Accounting, ambiguity, and the new institutionalism', *Accounting, Organizations and Society*, vol. 20, no. 4, pp. 313–328.

Casadesus-Masanell, R. and Spulber, D. F. 2000, 'The fable of Fisher Body', *Journal of Law and Economics*, vol. 43, no. 1, pp. 67–104.

Castells, M. 2000, *The rise of the network society*, 2nd edn, Blackwell, Oxford.

Chalos, P. and O'Connor, N. G. 2004, 'Determinants of the use of various control mechanisms in US–Chinese joint ventures', *Accounting, Organizations and Society*, vol. 29, no. 7, pp. 591–608.

Chandler, A. 1962, *Strategy and structure: chapters in the history of the industrial enterprise* MIT Press, Cambridge, MA.

509

—— 1977, *The visible hand: the managerial revolution in American business* Belknap Press, Cambridge, MA.

Chandler, A. and Tedlow, R. S. 1985, *The coming of managerial capitalism: a casebook on the history of American economic institutions*, Irwin, Homewood, IL.

Chapman, C. S. 1997, 'Reflections on a contingent view of accounting', *Accounting, Organizations and Society*, vol. 22, no. 2, pp. 189–205.

Chartered Institute of Management Accountants (CIMA) 2000, *Management accounting official terminology*, Chartered Institute of Management Accountants, London.

Chenhall, R. H. 2003, 'Management control systems design within its organizational context: findings from contingency-based research and directions for the future', *Accounting, Organizations and Society*, vol. 28, nos. 2–3, pp. 127–168.

Chenhall, R. H. and Morris, D. 1986, 'The impact of structure, environment, and interdependence on the perceived usefulness of management accounting systems', *Accounting Review*, vol. 61, no. 1, pp. 16–35.

Child, J. 1972, 'Organizational structure, environment and performance: the role of strategic choice', *Sociology*, vol. 6, no. 1, pp. 1–22.

Chong, V. K. and Chong, K. M. 1997, 'Strategic choices, environmental uncertainty and SBU performance: a note on the intervening role of management accounting systems', *Accounting and Business Research*, vol. 27, no. 4, pp. 268–276.

Chrystal, K. A. and Lipsey, R. G. 1997, *Economics for business and management* Oxford University Press, Oxford.

Chua, W. F. 1986, 'Radical developments in accounting thought', *Accounting Review*, vol. 61, no. 4, pp. 601–632.

—— 1995, 'Experts, networks and inscriptions in the fabrication of accounting images: a story of the representation of three public hospitals', *Accounting, Organizations and Society*, vol. 20, nos. 2–3, pp. 111–145.

Chua, W. F. and Degeling, P. 1993, 'Interrogating an accounting-based intervention on three axes: instrumental, moral and aesthetic', *Accounting, Organizations and Society*, vol. 18, no. 4, pp. 291–318.

Church, A. H. 1916, *The proper distribution of expense burden* Engineering Magazine Co., New York.

—— 1918, *The science and practice of management* Engineering Magazine Co., New York.

Clegg, S. 1981, 'Organization and control', *Administrative Science Quarterly*, vol. 26, pp. 545–562.

—— 1990a, *Modern organizations: organization studies in the postmodern world* Sage, London/Newbury Park, CA.

—— 1990b, 'Sociologies of class and organisation', in *Organisation Theory and Class Analysis*, S. R. Clegg, ed., Walter de Gruyter, Berlin, pp. 1–51.

Clegg, S. and Dunkerly, D. 1980, *Organization, class and control* Routledge & Kegan Paul, London.

Clegg, S., Kornberger, M. and Pitsis, T. 2005, *Managing and organizations: an introduction to theory and practice* Sage, London.

Coad, A. 1996, 'Smart work and hard work: explicating a learning orientation in strategic management accounting', *Management Accounting Research*, vol. 7, no. 4, pp. 387–408.

Coase, R. H. 1937, 'The nature of the firm', *Economica*, vol. 4, no. 16, pp. 386–405.

—— 1988a, 'The nature of the firm: influence', *Journal of Law, Economics, and Organization*, vol. 4, no. 1, pp. 33–47.

—— 1988b, 'The nature of the firm: meaning', *Journal of Law, Economics, and Organization*, vol. 4, no. 1, pp. 19–32.

—— 1988c, 'The nature of the firm: origin', *Journal of Law, Economics, and Organization*, vol. 4, no. 1, pp. 3–17.

—— 2000, 'The acquisition of Fisher Body by General Motors', *Journal of Law and Economics*, vol. 43, no. 1, pp. 15–31.

Colbert, G. J. and Spicer, B. H. 1995, 'A multi-case investigation of a theory of the transfer pricing process', *Accounting, Organizations and Society*, vol. 20, no. 6, pp. 423–456.

Collins, J. C. and Porras, J. I. 1996, 'Building your company's vision', *Harvard Business Review*, vol. 74, no. 5, pp. 65–77.

Colville, I. 1981, 'Reconstructing "behavioural accounting"', *Accounting, Organizations and Society*, vol. 6, no. 2, pp. 119–132.

Cooper, C. 1995, 'Ideology, hegemony and accounting discourse: a case study of the National Union of Journalists', *Critical Perspectives on Accounting*, vol. 6, no. 3, pp. 175–209.

Cooper, C. and Taylor, P. 2000, 'From Taylorism to Ms Taylor: the transformation of the accounting craft', *Accounting, Organizations and Society*, vol. 25, no. 6, pp. 555–578.

Cooper, C., Taylor, P., Smith, N. and Catchpowle, L. 2005, 'A discussion of the political potential of social accounting', *Critical Perspectives on Accounting*, vol. 16, no. 7, pp. 951–974.

Cooper, D. 1980, 'Discussion of towards a political economy of accounting', *Accounting, Organizations and Society*, vol. 5, no. 1, pp. 161–166.

—— 1983, 'Tidiness, muddle and things: commonalities and divergencies in two approaches to management accounting research', *Accounting, Organizations and Society*, vol. 8, nos. 2–3, pp. 269–286.

Cooper, D. and Hopper, T. 2006, 'Critical theorizing in strategic management accounting research', paper delivered at the Interdisciplinary Perspectives on Accounting Conference, Cardiff.

Cooper, D. and Tinker, T. 1994, 'Accounting and praxis: Marx after Foucault', *Critical Perspectives on Accounting*, vol. 5, no. 1, pp. 1–3.

Cooper, D., Hayes, D., and Wolf, F. 1981, 'Accounting in organized anarchies: understanding and designing accounting systems in ambiguous situations', *Accounting, Organizations and Society*, vol. 6, no. 3, pp. 175–191.

Cooper, R. 1990, 'Cost classifications in unit-based and activity-based manufacturing cost systems', *Journal of Cost Management*, Fall, pp. 4–14.

Cooper, R. and Burrell, G. 1988, 'Modernism, postmodernism and organizational analysis: an introduction', *Organization Studies*, vol. 9, no. 1, pp. 91–112.

Cooper, R. and Kaplan, R. S. 1988, 'Measure costs right: make the right decisions', *Harvard Business Review*, vol. 66, no. 5, pp. 96–104.

—— 1991, 'Profit priorities from activity-based costing', *Harvard Business Review*, vol. 69, no. 3, pp. 130–135.

—— 1992, 'Activity-based systems: measuring the costs of resource usage', *Accounting Horizons*, vol. 6, no. 3, pp. 1–13.

—— 1999, *The design of cost management systems: text and cases*, 2nd edn, Prentice-Hall, Upper Saddle River, NJ/London.

Cooper, R. and Slagmulder, R. 2004, 'Interorganizational cost management and relational context', *Accounting, Organizations and Society*, vol. 29, no. 1, pp. 1–26.

Covaleski, M. A. and Dirsmith, M. W. 1983, 'Budgeting as a means for control and loose coupling', *Accounting, Organizations and Society*, vol. 8, no. 4, pp. 323–340.

—— 1986, 'The budgetary process of power and politics', *Accounting, Organizations and Society*, vol. 11, no. 3, pp. 193–214.

—— 1988a, 'An institutional perspective on the rise, social transformation, and fall of a university budget category', *Administrative Science Quarterly*, vol. 33, no. 4, p. 562.

—— 1988b, 'The use of budgetary symbols in the political arena: an historically informed field study', *Accounting, Organizations and Society*, vol. 13, no. 1, pp. 1–24.

Covaleski, M. A., Dirsmith, M. W. and Samuel, S. 2003, 'Changes in the institutional environment and the institutions of governance: extending the contributions of transaction cost economics within the management control literature', *Accounting, Organizations and Society*, vol. 28, no. 5, pp. 417–441.

Crozier, M. 1964, *The bureaucratic phenomenon* Tavistock, London.

Cuganesan, S. and Lee, R. 2006, 'Intra-organisational influences in procurement networks controls:

the impacts of information technology', *Management Accounting Research*, vol. 17, no. 2, pp. 141–170.

Daft, R. L. and Macintosh, N. B. 1978, 'A new approach to design and use of management information', *California Management Review*, vol. 21, no. 1, pp. 82–92.

Dandeker, C. 1990, *Surveillance, power and modernity: bureaucracy and discipline from 1700 to the present day* Polity Press, Cambridge.

Dekker, H. C. 2003, 'Value chain analysis in interfirm relationships: a field study', *Management Accounting Research*, vol. 14, no. 1, pp. 1–23.

—— 2004, 'Control of inter-organizational relationships: evidence on appropriation concerns and coordination requirements', *Accounting, Organizations and Society*, vol. 29, no. 1, pp. 27–49.

Diemer, H. 1914, *Factory organization and administration*, 2nd edn, McGraw-Hill, New York.

Dillard, J. F., Rigsby, J. T. and Goodman, C. 2004, 'The making and remaking of organization context: duality and the institutionalization process', *Accounting, Auditing and Accountability Journal*, vol. 17, no. 4, pp. 506–542.

Dohr, J. L. 1932, 'Budgetary control and standard costs in industrial accounting', *Accounting Review*, vol. 7, no. 1, pp. 31–33.

Drucker, P. F. 1981, 'Towards the next economics', in *The crisis in economic theory*, D. Bell and I. Kristol, eds, Basic Books, New York, pp. 4–18.

—— 1989, *The new realities: in government and politics – in economy and business – in society – and in world view* Heinemann Professional, Oxford.

—— 2000, 'The emerging theory of manufacturing,' in *Markets of one: creating customer-unique value through mass customization*, J. H. Gilmore and B. J. Pine, eds, Harvard Business School, Cambridge, MA, pp. 3–10.

Drury, C. 2004, *Management and cost accounting*, 6th edn, Thomson Learning, London.

Dugdale, D. and Jones, C. 1995, 'Financial justification of advanced manufacturing technology', in *Issues in management accounting*, 2nd edn, D. Ashton, T. Hopper and R. W. Scapens, eds, Prentice-Hall Europe, Essex, pp. 191–214.

Duray, R., Ward, P. T., Milligan, G. W. and Berry, W. L. 2000, 'Approaches to mass customization: configurations and empirical validation', *Journal of Operations Management*, vol. 18, no. 6, pp. 605–625.

Earl, M. J. and Hopwood, A. G. 1979, 'From management information to information management', paper delivered at the IFIP Working Conference on the Information Systems Environment, Bonn.

Eden, L., Dacin, M. T. and Wan, W. P. 2001, 'Standards across borders: crossborder diffusion of the arm's length standard in North America', *Accounting, Organizations and Society*, vol. 26, no. 1, pp. 1–23.

Edwards, R. 1979, *Contested terrain: the transformation of the workplace in the twentieth century* Heinemann, London.

Edwards, R. 1989, 'Industrial cost accounting developments in Britain to 1830: a review article', *Accounting and Business Research*, vol. 19, no. 76, pp. 305–317.

Emerson, H. 1912, *The twelve principles of efficiency* Engineering Magazine Co., New York.

Emmanuel, C. R. and Otley, D. 1976, 'The usefulness of residual income', *Journal of Business Finance and Accounting*, vol. 3, no. 4, pp. 43–51.

Emmanuel, C. R., Otley, D. and Merchant, K. A. 1996, *Accounting for management control*, 2nd edn, International Thomson Business Press, London.

Epstein, M. and Manzoni, J. F. 1998, 'Implementing corporate strategy: from tableaux de bord to balanced scorecards', *European Management Journal*, vol. 16, no. 2, pp. 190–203.

Evans, I. I. I., Lewis, B. L. and Patton, J. M. 1986, 'An economic modeling approach to contingency theory and management control', *Accounting, Organizations and Society*, vol. 11, no. 6, pp. 483–498.

Ezzamel, M. and Hart, H. 1987, *Advanced management accounting: an organisational emphasis* Cassell, London.

Fama, E. F. and Jensen, M. C. 1983a, 'Separation of ownership and control', *Journal of Law and Economics*, vol. 26, no. 2, pp. 301–325.

—— 1983b, 'Agency problems and residual claims', *Journal of Law and Economics*, vol. 26, no. 2, pp. 327–349.

Faulks, K. 1999, *Political sociology: a critical introduction* Edinburgh University Press, Edinburgh.

Fincham, R. and Roslender, R. 1995, 'Information technology and the strategy process: the UK financial services industry', *Critical Perspectives on Accounting*, vol. 6, no. 1, pp. 7–26.

Firat, A. F. and Venkatesh, A. 1993, 'Postmodernity: the age of marketing', *International Journal of Research in Marketing*, vol. 10, no. 3, pp. 227–249.

Fisher, J. 1995, 'Contingency-based research on management control systems: categorization by level of complexity', *Journal of Accounting Literature*, vol. 14, pp. 24–53.

Flamholtz, E. G. 1983, 'Accounting, budgeting and control systems in their organizational context: theoretical and empirical perspectives', *Accounting, Organizations and Society*, vol. 8, nos. 2–3, pp. 153–169.

Fleischman, R. K. and Parker, L. D. 1990, 'Managerial accounting early in the British industrial revolution: the Carron Company, a case study', *Accounting and Business Research*, vol. 20, no. 79, pp. 211–221.

—— 1991, 'British entrepreneurs and pre-industrial revolution evidence of cost management', *Accounting Review*, vol. 66, no. 2, pp. 361–375.

Foster, G. and Swenson, D. W. 1997, 'Measuring the success of activity-based cost management and its determinants', *Journal of Management Accounting Research*, vol. 9, pp. 109–141.

Foster, J. B. 1998, 'Introduction to the new edition', in H. Braverman, *Labor and monopoly capital: the degradation of work in the twentieth century* Monthly Review Press, New York.

Foucault, M. 1979, *Discipline and punish: the birth of the prison* Penguin, London.

—— 1998a, *Michel Foucault: aesthetics, method and epistemology – essential works of Foucault 1954–1984 – Volume II* Penguin, London.

—— 1998b, *Michel Foucault: ethics, subjectivity and truth – essential works of Foucault 1954–1984 – Volume I* Penguin, London.

—— 2002, *Power: essential works of Foucault 1954–1984 – Volume III* Penguin, London.

Frances, J. and Garnsey, E. 1996, 'Supermarkets and suppliers in the United Kingdom: system integration, information and control', *Accounting, Organizations and Society*, vol. 21, no. 6, pp. 591–610.

Friedman, A. L. 1977, *Industry and labour: class struggle at work and monopoly capitalism* Macmillan, London.

Friedman, A. L. and Lyne, S. R. 1997, 'Activity-based techniques and the death of the beancounter', *European Accounting Review* , vol. 6, no. 1, pp. 19–44.

Froud, J., Williams, K., Haslam, C., Johal, S. and Williams, J. 1998, 'Caterpillar: two stories and an argument', *Accounting, Organizations and Society*, vol. 23, no. 7, pp. 685–708.

Fulk, J. and DeSanctis, G. 1995, 'Electronic communication and changing organizational forms', *Organization Science*, vol. 6, no. 4, pp. 337–349.

Gambling, T. 1977, 'Magic, accounting and morale', *Accounting, Organizations and Society*, vol. 2, no. 2, pp. 141–151.

Gerth, H. H. and Mills, C. W. eds 1991, *From Max Weber: essays in sociology* Routledge, London.

Giddens, A. 1976, *New rules of sociological method: a positive critique of interpretative sociologies* Hutchinson, London.

—— 1979, *Central problems in social theory: action, structure and contradiction in social analysis* Macmillan, Basingstoke.

—— 1984, *The constitution of society: outline of the theory of structuration* Polity Press, London, in association with Blackwell, Oxford.

—— 1990, *The consequences of modernity* Stanford University Press, Stanford, CA.

Gietzmann, M. 1995, 'Introduction to agency theory in management accounting', in *Issues in*

513

management accounting, 2nd edn, D. Ashton, T. Hopper and R. W. Scapens, eds, Prentice-Hall Europe, Essex, pp. 259–268.

Giovanni, B. G. and Arthur, G. B. 1974, 'A conspectus of management control theory: 1900–1972', *Academy of Management Journal*, vol. 17, no. 2, pp. 292–305.

Gitman, L. J. 2006, *Principles of managerial finance*, 11th edn, Addison-Wesley, Boston, MA.

Glenn, E. N. and Feldberg, R. L. 1976, 'Proletarianizing clerical work: technology and organizational control in the office', in *Case studies on the labour process*, A. Zimbalist, ed., Monthly Review Press, New York, pp. 51–72.

Goddard, A. 2005, 'Reform as regulation – accounting, governance and accountability in UK local government', *Journal of Accounting and Organizational Change*, vol. 1, no. 1, pp. 27–44.

Goldthorpe, J. H., Bechhofer, F., Lockwood, D. and Platt, J. 1969, *The affluent worker in the class structure* Cambridge University Press, London.

Gordon, L. A. and Miller, D. 1976, 'A contingency framework for the design of accounting information systems', *Accounting, Organizations and Society*, vol. 1, no. 1, pp. 59–69.

Gordon, L. A. and Narayanan, V. K. 1984, 'Management accounting systems, perceived environmental uncertainty and organization structure: an empirical investigation', *Accounting, Organizations and Society*, vol. 9, no. 1, pp. 33–47.

Gosselin, M. 1997, 'The effect of strategy and organizational structure on the adoption and implementation of activity-based costing', *Accounting, Organizations and Society*, vol. 22, no. 2, pp. 105–122.

Gouldner, A. W. 1954, *Patterns of industrial bureaucracy* Free Press, Glencoe, IL.

Gramsci, A. 1971, *Selections from prison notebooks* Lawrence and Wishart, London.

Granlund, M. and Malmi, T. 2002, 'Moderate impact of ERPS on management accounting: a lag or permanent outcome?', *Management Accounting Research*, vol. 13, no. 3, pp. 299–321.

Grant, R. M. 1995, *Contemporary strategy analysis: concepts, techniques, applications*, 2nd edn, Blackwell Business, Cambridge, MA/Oxford.

Grey, C. 1994, 'Debating Foucault: a critical reply to Neimark', *Critical Perspectives on Accounting*, vol. 5, no. 1, pp. 5–24.

Grimshaw, D., Cooke, F. L., Grugulis, I. and Vincent, S. 2002, 'New technology and changing organizational forms: implications for managerial control and skills', *New Technology, Work and Employment*, vol. 17, no. 3, pp. 186–203.

Groot, T. L. C. M. and Merchant, K. A. 2000, 'Control of international joint ventures', *Accounting, Organizations and Society*, vol. 25, no. 6, pp. 579–607.

Grossman, S. J. and Hart, O. D. 1986, 'The costs and benefits of ownership: a theory of vertical and lateral integration', *Journal of Political Economy*, vol. 94, no. 4, pp. 691–719.

Grugulis, I. and Knights, D. 2001, 'Glossary', *International Studies of Management and Organization*, vol. 30, no. 4, pp. 12–24.

Gul, F. A. 1991, 'Size of audit fees and perceptions of auditors' ability to resist management pressure in audit conflict situations', *Abacus*, vol. 27, no. 2, pp. 162–172.

Gul, F. A. and Chia, Y. M. 1994, 'The effects of management accounting systems, perceived environmental uncertainty and decentralization on managerial performance: a test of three-way interaction', *Accounting, Organizations and Society*, vol. 19, nos. 4–5, pp. 413–426.

Gupta, A. K. and Govindarajan, V. 1984, 'Business unit strategy, managerial characteristics, and business unit effectiveness at strategy implementation', *Academy of Management Journal*, vol. 27, no. 1, pp. 25–41.

Habermas, J. 1978, *Knowledge and human interests*, 2nd [English] edn, Heinemann Educational, London.

—— 1984, *The theory of communicative action: reason and the rationalization of society, Vol. 1* Polity Press, Cambridge.

—— 1987, *The theory of communicative action: critique of functionalist reason, Vol. 2* Polity Press, Cambridge.

Hage, J. and Aiken, M. T. 1970, *Social change in complex organizations* Random House, New York.

Hakansson, H. and Lind, J. 2004, 'Accounting and network coordination', *Accounting, Organizations and Society*, vol. 29, no. 1, pp. 51–72.

Hakken, D. 2000, 'Resocialing work? Anticipatory anthropology of the labor process', *Futures*, vol. 32, pp. 767–775.

Hall, R. H. 1977, *Organizations: structure and process*, 2nd edn, Prentice-Hall, Englewood Cliffs, NJ.

Hall, S. 1988, 'Brave new world', *Marxism Today*, October, pp. 24–29.

Hamel, G. and Prahalad, C. K. 1989, 'Strategic intent', *Harvard Business Review*, vol. 67, no. 3, p. 63.

—— 1994, 'Seeing the future first', *Fortune*, vol. 130, no. 5, pp. 64–70.

Hamilton, W. H. 1932, 'Institution', in *Encyclopedia of social sciences*, 8th edn, E. R. A. Seligman and A. Johnson, eds, Macmillan, New York, pp. 84–89.

Harrison, G. 1992, 'The cross-cultural generalizability of the relation between participation, budget emphasis and job related attitudes', *Accounting, Organizations and Society*, vol. 17, no. 1, pp. 1–15.

Harrison, G. and McKinnon, J. 1998, 'Editorial: culture and management accounting', *Management Accounting Research*, vol. 9, no. 2, pp. 113–118.

Harrison, G. C. 1921, *Cost accounting to aid production: a practical study of scientific cost accounting* Engineering Magazine Co., New York.

Harvey, D. 1989, *The conditions of postmodernity: an inquiry into the origins of cultural change* Blackwell, Oxford.

Harvey, E. 1968, 'Technology and the structure of organizations', *American Sociological Review*, vol. 33, no. 2, pp. 247–259.

Hassard, J. 1994, 'Postmodern organizational analysis: toward a conceptual framework', *Journal of Management Studies*, vol. 31, no. 3, pp. 303–324.

Hayes, D. C. 1977, 'The contingency theory of managerial accounting', *Accounting Review*, vol. 52, no. 1, pp. 22–39.

Hayes, R. H. and Wheelwright, S. G. 1979, 'The dynamics of process–product life cycles', *Harvard Business Review*, vol. 57, no. 2, pp. 127–136.

Hewitt, J. P. 1984, *Self and society: a symbolic interactionist social psychology*, 3rd edn, Allyn and Bacon, Boston, MA.

Heydebrand, W. V. 1989, 'New organizational forms', *Work and Occupations*, vol. 16, no. 3, pp. 323–357.

Hirst, P. and Zeitlin, J. 1991, 'Flexible specialization versus post-Fordism: theory, evidence and policy implications', *Economy and Society*, vol. 20, no. 1, pp. 1–56.

Hobsbawm, E. J. 1964, *Labouring men: studies in the history of labour* Weidenfeld & Nicolson, London.

Hofstede, G. 1984, 'The cultural relativity of the quality of life concept', *Academy of Management Review*, vol. 9, no. 3, pp. 389–399.

Holmstrom, B. and Milgrom, P. 1987, 'Aggregation and linearity in the provision of intertemporal incentives', *Econometrica*, vol. 55, no. 2, pp. 303–328.

—— 1994, 'The firm as an incentive system', *American Economic Review*, vol. 84, pp. 972–991.

Hope, J. and Fraser, R. 2003, 'Who needs budgets?', *Harvard Business Review*, February, pp. 108–115.

Hopper, T. and Armstrong, P. 1991, 'Cost accounting, controlling labour and the rise of conglomerates', *Accounting, Organizations and Society*, vol. 16, nos. 5–6, pp. 405–438.

Hopper, T. and Macintosh, N. 1993, 'Management accounting as disciplinary practice: the case of ITT under Harold Geneen', *Management Accounting Research*, vol. 4, no. 3, pp. 181–216.

Hopper, T. and Major, M. Forthcoming, 'Extending new institutional theory: a case study of regulation and activity based costing in Portuguese telecommunications', *European Accounting Review*.

Hopper, T. and Powell, A. 1985, 'Making sense of research into the organizational and social

515

aspects of management accounting: a review of its underlying assumptions', *Journal of Management Studies*, vol. 22, no. 5, pp. 429–465.

Hopper, T., Otley, D. and Scapens, B. 2001, 'British management accounting research: whence and whither: opinions and recollections', *British Accounting Review*, vol. 33, no. 3, pp. 263–291.

Hopper, T., Storey, J. and Willmott, H. 1987, 'Accounting for accounting: towards the development of a dialectical view', *Accounting, Organizations and Society*, vol. 12, no. 5, pp. 437–456.

Hopper, T., Annisette, M., Dastoor, N., Uddin, S. and Wickramasinghe, D. 1995, 'Some challenges and alternatives to positive accounting research', in *Accounting theory: a contemporary review*, S. Johnes, J. Ratnatunge and C. Romano, eds, Harcourt Brace, Sydney, pp. 515–550.

Hopper, T., Cooper, D., Lowe, T., Capps, T. and Mouritsen, J. 1986, 'Management control and worker resistance in the National Coal Board: financial controls in the labour process', in *Managing the labour process*, D. Knights and H. Willmott, eds, Gower, Aldershot, pp. 109–141.

Hopwood, A. G. 1972, 'An empirical study of the role of accounting data in performance evaluation', *Journal of Accounting Research*, vol. 10, no. 3, pp. 156–182.

—— 1976, 'Editorial', *Accounting, Organizations and Society*, vol. 1, no. 1, pp. 1–4.

—— 1983, 'On trying to study accounting in the contexts in which it operates', *Accounting, Organizations and Society*, vol. 8, nos. 2–3, pp. 287–305.

—— 1987, 'The archeology of accounting systems', *Accounting, Organizations and Society*, vol. 12, no. 3, pp. 207–234.

Hopwood, A. G. and Miller, P. 1994, *Accounting as social and institutional practice* Cambridge University Press, Cambridge.

Hoque, Z. and Hopper, T. 1994, 'Rationality, accounting and politics: a case study of management control in a Bangladeshi jute mill', *Management Accounting Research*, vol. 5, no. 1, pp. 5–30.

Horngren, C. T. 1977, *Cost accounting: a managerial emphasis*, 4th edn, Prentice-Hall, London.

Horngren, C. T., Bhimani, A., Datar, S. M. and Foster, G. 2005, *Management and cost accounting*, 3rd edn, Financial Times–Prentice-Hall, Harlow.

Hoskin, K. 1994, 'Boxing clever: for, against and beyond Foucault in the battle for accounting theory', *Critical Perspectives on Accounting*, vol. 5, no. 1, pp. 57–85.

Hoskin, K. and Macve, R. 1986, 'Accounting and the examination: a genealogy of disciplinary power', *Accounting, Organizations and Society*, vol. 11, no. 2, pp. 105–136.

—— 1988, 'The genesis of accountability: the West Point connections', *Accounting, Organizations and Society*, vol. 13, no. 1, pp. 37–73.

—— 1994, 'Writing, examining, disciplining: the genesis of accounting's modern power', in *Accounting as social and institutional practice*, A. G. Hopwood and P. Miller, eds, Cambridge University Press, Cambridge, pp. 67–97.

Humprey, C. and Scapens, R. W. 1994, 'Theories and case studies: limitation or liberation', working paper, University of Manchester.

Innes, J. and Mitchell, F. 1995, 'Activity-based costing', in *Issues in management accounting*, 2nd edn, D. Ashton, T. Hopper and R. W. Scapens, eds, Prentice-Hall Europe, Essex, pp. 115–136.

Innes, J., Mitchell, F. and Sinclair, D. 2000, 'Activity-based costing in the UK's largest companies: a comparison of 1994 and 1999 survey results', *Management Accounting Research*, vol. 11, no. 3, pp. 349–362.

Jameson, F. 1984, 'Postmodernism, or the cultural logic of late capitalism', *New Left Review*, vol. I/146, July–August, pp. 53–92.

Jaros, S. J. 2001, 'Labor process theory: a commentary on the debate', *International Studies of Management and Organization*, vol. 30, no. 4, pp. 25–39.

Jensen, M. C. 1983, 'Organization theory and methodology', *Accounting Review*, vol. 58, no. 2, pp. 319–339.

—— 2001, 'Corporate budgeting is broken – let's fix it', *Harvard Business Review*, November, pp. 94–101.

Jensen, M. C. and Meckling, W. H. 1976, 'Theory of the firm: managerial behavior, agency costs and ownership structure', *Journal of Financial Economics*, vol. 3, no. 4, pp. 305–360.

516

Jermier, J. M. 1998, 'Introduction: critical perspectives on organizational control', *Administrative Science Quarterly*, vol. 43, pp. 235–256.

Johnson, H. T. 1992, *Relevance regained: from top-down control to bottom-up empowerment* Free Press, New York.

Johnson, H. T. and Kaplan, R. S. 1987, *Relevance lost: the rise and fall of management accounting* Harvard Business School Press, Cambridge, MA.

Jones, C. T. and Dugdale, D. 2001, 'The concept of an accounting regime', *Critical Perspectives on Accounting*, vol. 12, no. 1, pp. 35–63.

—— 2002, 'The ABC bandwagon and the juggernaut of modernity', *Accounting, Organizations and Society*, vol. 27, nos. 1–2, pp. 121–163.

Joseph, J. 2002, *Hegemony: a realist analysis* Routledge, London.

Kaplan, R. S. 1984, 'The evolution of management accounting', *Accounting Review*, vol. 59, no. 3, pp. 390–418.

—— 1994, 'Management accounting (1984–1994): development of new practice and theory', *Management Accounting Research*, vol. 5, nos. 3–4, pp. 247–260.

Kaplan, R. S. and Cooper, R. 1998, *Cost & effect: using integrated cost systems to drive profitability, performance* Harvard Business School Press, Cambridge, MA.

Kaplan, R. S. and Norton, D. P. 1992, 'The balanced scorecard – measures that drive performance', *Harvard Business Review*, vol. 70, no. 1, pp. 71–79.

—— 1993, 'Putting the balanced scorecard to work', *Harvard Business Review*, vol. 71, no. 5, pp. 134–147.

—— 1996a, *The balanced scorecard: translating strategy into action* Harvard Business School Press, Cambridge, MA.

—— 1996b, 'Linking the balanced scorecard to strategy', *California Management Review*, vol. 39, no. 1, pp. 53–79.

Kellner, D. 1989, *Critical theory, Marxism and modernity* Johns Hopkins University Press, Baltimore, MD.

Kennedy, T. and Affleck-Graves, J. 2001, 'The impact of activity-based costing techniques on firm performance', *Journal of Management Accounting Research*, vol. 13, pp. 19–45.

Keynes, J. M. 1936, *The general theory of employment, interest and money* Macmillan, London.

Khandwalla, P. N. 1972, 'The effect of different types of competition on the use of management controls', *Journal of Accounting Research*, vol. 10, no. 2, pp. 275–285.

—— 1974, 'Mass output orientation of operations technology and organizational structure', *Administrative Science Quarterly*, vol. 19, no. 1, pp. 74–97.

—— 1977, *The design of organizations* Harcourt Brace Jovanovich, New York.

Klamer, A. and McCloskey, D. 1992, 'Accounting as the master metaphor of economics', *European Accounting Review*, vol. 1, no. 1, pp. 145–160.

Klein, B. 1988, 'Vertical integration as organizational ownership: the Fisher Body–General Motors relationship revisited', *Journal of Law, Economics, and Organization*, vol. 4, no. 1, pp. 199–213.

—— 2000, 'Fisher–General Motors and the nature of the firm', *Journal of Law and Economics*, vol. 43, no. 1, pp. 105–141.

Knights, D. and Collinson, D. 1987, 'Disciplining the shopfloor: a comparison of the disciplinary effects of managerial psychology and financial accounting', *Accounting, Organizations and Society*, vol. 12, no. 5, pp. 457–477.

Knights, D. and McCabe, D. 1998a, 'Dreams and designs on strategy: a critical analysis of TQM and management control', *Work, Employment and Society*, vol. 12, no. 3, pp. 433–456.

—— 1998b, 'When "life is but a dream": obliterating politics through business process reengineering?', *Human Relations*, vol. 51, no. 6, pp. 761–798.

—— 2000, '"Ain't Misbehavin"? Opportunities for resistance under new forms of "Quality" management', *Sociology*, vol. 34, no. 3, pp. 421–436.

Knights, D. and Willmott, H. 1993, '"It's a very foreign discipline": the genesis of expenses control in a mutual life insurance company', *British Journal of Management*, vol. 4, no. 1, pp. 1–18.

517

Koontz, H. and Weihrich, H. 1990, *Essentials of management*, 5th edn, McGraw-Hill, New York/ London.

Kotler, P. 2003, *Marketing management* Prentice-Hall, Englewood Cliffs, NJ.

Krackhardt, D. 1991, 'The strength of strong ties: the importance of philos in organization', in *Organizations and networks: theory and practice*, N. Nohira and R. Eccles, eds, Harvard Business School Press, Cambridge, MA.

Kunz, A. H. and Pfaff, D. 2002, 'Agency theory, performance evaluation, and the hypothetical construct of intrinsic motivation', *Accounting, Organizations and Society*, vol. 27, no. 3, pp. 275–295.

Lambert, R. A. 2001, 'Contracting theory and accounting', *Journal of Accounting and Economics*, vol. 32, nos. 1–3, pp. 3–87.

Lamminmaki, D. and Drury, C. 2001, 'A comparison of New Zealand and British product-costing practices', *International Journal of Accounting*, vol. 36, no. 3, pp. 329–347.

Langfield-Smith, K. 1997, 'Management control systems and strategy: a critical review', *Accounting, Organizations and Society*, vol. 22, no. 2, pp. 207–232.

Langfield-Smith, K. and Smith, D. 2003, 'Management control systems and trust in outsourcing relationships', *Management Accounting Research*, vol. 14, no. 3, pp. 281–307.

Latour, B. 1987, *Science in action: how to follow scientists and engineers through society* Open University Press, Milton Keynes.

—— 1991, 'Technology is society made durable', in *A sociology of monsters: essays on power, technology and domination*, J. Law, ed., Routledge, London/New York, pp. 103–131.

—— 1999, *Pandora's hope: an essay on the reality of science studies* Harvard University Press, Cambridge, MA/London.

Latour, B. and Woolgar, S. 1979, *Laboratory life: the social construction of scientific facts* Sage, Beverly Hills, CA/London.

Laughlin, R. 1987, 'Accounting systems in organisational contexts: a case for critical theory', *Accounting, Organizations and Society*, vol. 12, no. 5, pp. 479–502.

—— 1995, 'Empirical research in accounting: alternative approaches and a case for "middle-range" thinking', *Accounting, Auditing and Accountability Journal*, vol. 8, no. 1, p. 63.

Law, J. 1991, 'Introduction: monsters and sociotechnical relations', in *A sociology of monsters: essays on power, technology and domination*, J. Law, ed., Routledge, London/New York, pp. 1–23.

Law, J. and Hassard, J. 1999, *Actor network theory and after* Blackwell, Oxford.

Lawrence, P. R. and Lorsch, J. W. 1967, *Organization and environment managing differentiation and integration* Division of Research, Graduate School of Business Administration, Harvard University, Cambridge, MA.

Levitt, T. 1960, 'Marketing myopia', *Harvard Business Review*, vol. 38, no. 4, pp. 45–56.

—— 1983, 'The globalization of markets', *Harvard Business Review*, vol. 61, no. 3, May–June, pp. 92–101.

Littler, C. R. 1982, *The development of the labour process in capitalist societies: a comparative study of the transformation of work organization in Britain, Japan and the USA* Heinemann Educational, London.

Littleton, A. C. and Zimmerman, V. K. 1962, *Accounting theory: continuity and change* Prentice-Hall, Englewood Cliffs, NJ.

Llewelyn, S. 2003, 'What counts as "theory" in qualitative management and accounting research? Introducing five levels of theorizing', *Accounting, Auditing and Accountability Journal*, vol. 16, no. 4, pp. 662–708.

Loft, A. 1986, 'Towards a critical understanding of accounting: the case of cost accounting in the UK, 1914–1925', *Accounting, Organizations and Society*, vol. 11, no. 2, pp. 137–169.

—— 1995, 'The history of management accounting: relevance found', in *Issues in Management Accounting*, 2nd edn, D. Ashton, T. Hopper and R. W. Scapens, eds, Prentice-Hall Europe, Essex, pp. 21–44.

Lukka, K. 2007, 'Management accounting change and stability: loosely coupled rules and routines in action', *Management Accounting Research* vol. 18, no. 1, pp. 76–101.

Lukka, K. and Granlund, M. 2002, 'The fragmented communication structure within the accounting academia: the case of activity-based costing research genres', *Accounting, Organizations and Society*, vol. 27, nos. 1–2, pp. 165–190.

Mabey, C., Salaman, G. and Storey, J. 2000, 'Beyond organizational structure: the end of classical forms?', in *Understanding business: organizations*, G. Salaman, ed., Routledge, London/New York, pp. 171–185.

McCabe, D. 2000, 'Factory innovations and management machinations: the productive and repressive relations of power', *Journal of Management Studies*, vol. 37, no. 7, pp. 932–953.

Machin, J. L. J. 1983, 'Management control systems: whence and whither?', in *New perspectives in management control*, E. A. Lowe and J. L. T. Machin, eds, Macmillan, London, pp. 22–42.

Macintosh, N. B. 1994, *Management accounting and control systems: an organizational and behavioural approach* Wiley, Chichester.

Macintosh, N. B. and Scapens, R. W. 1990, 'Structuration theory in management accounting', *Accounting, Organizations and Society*, vol. 15, no. 5, pp. 455–477.

McKendrick, N. 1961, 'Josiah Wedgwood and factory discipline', *Historical Journal*, vol. 4, no. 1, pp. 30–55.

McKenzie, R. and Silver, A. 1968, *Angels in marble: working class Conservatives in urban England* Heinemann, London.

McKinlay, A. and Starkey, K. 1998, *Foucault, management and organization theory: from panopticon to technologies of self* Sage, London.

McKinlay, A. and Wilson, R. G. 2006, '"Small acts of cunning": bureaucracy, inspection and the career, c.1890–1914', *Critical Perspectives on Accounting*, vol. 17, no. 5, pp. 657–678.

McLean, T. 1995, 'Contract accounting and costing in the Sunderland shipbuilding industry 1818–1917', *Accounting, Business and Financial History*, vol. 5, no. 1, pp. 109–145.

—— 2006, 'Continuity and change in British cost accounting development: the case of Hawthorn Ieslie, shipbuilders and engineers, 1886–1914', *British Accounting Review*, vol. 38, no. 1, pp. 95–121.

McMann, P. J. and Nanni, A. 1995, 'Means versus ends: a review of the literature on Japanese management accounting', *Management Accounting Research*, vol. 6, no. 4, pp. 313–346.

Magee, R. P. 2001, 'Discussion of "contracting theory and accounting"', *Journal of Accounting and Economics*, vol. 32, nos. 1–3, pp. 89–96.

Major, M. and Hopper, T. 2005, 'Managers divided: implementing ABC in a Portuguese telecommunications company', *Management Accounting Research*, vol. 16, no. 2, pp. 205–229.

Malmi, T. 1997, 'Towards explaining activity-based costing failure: accounting and control in a decentralized organization', *Management Accounting Research*, vol. 8, no. 4, pp. 459–480.

—— 2001, 'Balanced scorecards in Finnish companies: a research note', *Management Accounting Research*, vol. 12, no. 2, pp. 207–220.

March, J. and Simons, H. A. 1958, *Organization* Wiley, New York.

Marginson, D. E. W. 1999, 'Beyond the budgetary control system: towards a two-tiered process of management control', *Management Accounting Research*, vol. 10, no. 3, pp. 203–230.

Marsden, R. 1998, 'A political technology of the body: how labour is organized into a productive force', *Critical Perspectives on Accounting*, vol. 9, no. 1, pp. 99–136.

Marx, K. 1976, *Capital: a critique of political economy, Vol. 1* Penguin, London.

Marx, K. and Engels, F. 1985, *The communist manifesto* Penguin, London.

Mead, G. H. 1934, *Mind, self, and society from the standpoint of a social behaviorist* University of Chicago Press, Chicago.

Meltzer, B. 1978, 'Mead's social psychology', in *Symbolic interaction: a reader in social psychology*, 3rd edn, J. Mains and B. Meltzer, eds, Allyn & Bacon, Boston, MA, pp. 15–27.

Merchant, K. A. 1990, 'The effects of financial controls on data manipulation and management myopia', *Accounting, Organizations and Society*, vol. 15, no. 4, pp. 297–313.

519

Merton, R. K. 1949, *Social theory and social structure: toward a codification of theory and research* Free Press, Glencoe, IL.

—— 1968, *Social theory and social structure*, enlarged edn, Free Press/Collier-Macmillan, New York.

Metcalf, D. 1989, 'Water notes dry up: the impact of the Donovan reform proposals and Thatcherism at work on labour productivity in British manufacturing industry', *British Journal of Industrial Relations*, vol. 27, no. 1, pp. 1–31.

Meyer, J. W. and Rowan, B. 1977, 'Institutionalized organizations: formal structure as myth and ceremony', *American Journal of Sociology*, vol. 83, no. 2, pp. 340–363.

Mia, L. 1988, 'Managerial attitude, motivation and the effectiveness of budget participation', *Accounting, Organizations and Society*, vol. 13, no. 5, pp. 465–475.

—— 1993, 'The role of MAS information in organisations: an empirical study', *British Accounting Review*, vol. 25, no. 3, pp. 269–285.

Mia, M. and Goyal, M. 1991, 'Span of control, task interdependence and usefulness of MAS information in not-for-profit government organizations', *Financial Accountability and Management*, vol. 7, no. 4, p. 249.

Miles, R. E. and Snow, C. 1978, *Organizational strategy, structure, and process* McGraw-Hill, New York.

Miller, P. 1991, 'Accounting innovation beyond the enterprise: problematizing investment decisions and programming economic growth in the UK in the 1960s', *Accounting, Organizations and Society*, vol. 16, no. 8, pp. 733–762.

—— 2001, 'Government by numbers: why calculative practices matter', *Social Research*, vol. 68, no. 2, pp. 379–386.

Miller, P. and Napier, C. 1993, 'Genealogies of calculation', *Accounting, Organizations and Society*, vol. 18, nos. 7–8, pp. 631–647.

Miller, P. and O'Leary, T. 1987, 'Accounting and the construction of the governable person', *Accounting, Organizations and Society*, vol. 12, no. 3, pp. 235–265.

—— 1993, 'Accounting expertise and the politics of the product: economic citizenship and modes of corporate governance', *Accounting, Organizations and Society*, vol. 18, nos. 2–3, pp. 187–206.

—— 1994, 'Accounting, "economic citizenship" and the spatial reordering of manufacture', *Accounting, Organizations and Society*, vol. 19, no. 1, pp. 15–43.

—— 1998, 'Finding things out', *Accounting, Organizations and Society*, vol. 23, no. 7, pp. 709–714.

Miller, P., Hopper, T. and Laughlin, R. 1991, 'The new accounting history: an introduction', *Accounting, Organizations and Society*, vol. 16, nos. 5–6, pp. 395–403.

Mintzberg, H. 1973, 'Strategy-making in three modes', *California Management Review*, vol. 16, no. 2, pp. 44–54.

—— 1979, 'An emerging strategy of "direct" research', *Administrative Science Quarterly*, vol. 24, no. 4, pp. 582–589.

—— 1983, *Structure in fives: designing effective organizations* Prentice-Hall, Englewood Cliffs, NJ.

—— 1987, 'The strategy concept I: five Ps for strategy', *California Management Review*, vol. 30, no. 1, pp. 11–25.

Mitchell, F. 1994, 'A commentary on the applications of activity-based costing', *Management Accounting Research*, vol. 5, nos. 3–4, pp. 261–277.

Mitchell, F. and Walker, S. P. 1997, 'Market pressures and the development of costing practice: the emergence of uniform costing in the UK printing industry', *Management Accounting Research*, vol. 8, no. 1, pp. 75–101.

Miyajima, H. 1994, 'The transformation of zaibatsu to postwar corporate groups – from hierarchically integrated groups to horizontally integrated groups', *Journal of the Japanese and International Economies*, vol. 8, no. 3, pp. 293–328.

Modell, S. 2001, 'Performance measurement and institutional processes: a study of managerial responses to public sector reform', *Management Accounting Research*, vol. 12, no. 4, pp. 437–464.

—— 2003, 'Goals versus institutions: the development of performance measurement in the Swedish university sector', *Management Accounting Research*, vol. 14, no. 4, pp. 333–359.

Moers, F. 2006, 'Performance measure properties and delegation', *Accounting Review*, vol. 81, no. 4, pp. 897–924.

Monden, Y. 1989, 'Characteristics of performance control systems in Japanese corporations', in *Japanese management accounting: a world class approach to profit management*, Y. Monden and M. Sakurai, eds, Productivity Press, Cambridge, MA, pp. 413–423.

Monden, Y. and Hamada, K. 1991, 'Target costing and Kaizen costing in Japanese automobile companies', *Journal of Management Accounting Research*, Fall, pp. 16–34.

Monge, P. R. and Contractor, N. S. 1998, 'Emergence of communication networks', in *The new handbook of organizational communication*, F. M. Jablin and L. A. Putnam, eds, Sage, Thousand Oaks, CA.

Monge, P. R. and Fulk, J. 1995, 'Global network organizations', paper presented to the International Communication Association, Albuquerque, NM, May.

Montagna, P. 1997, 'Modernism vs. postmodernism in management accounting', *Critical Perspectives on Accounting*, vol. 8, nos. 1–2, pp. 125–145.

Morgan, G. 1997, *Imaginization: new mindsets of seeing, organizing and managing* Berrett-Koehler, San Francisco, CA.

Mouritsen, J. 1999, 'The flexible firm: strategies for a subcontractor's management control', *Accounting, Organizations and Society*, vol. 24, no. 1, pp. 31–55.

Mouritsen, J. and Thrane, S. 2006, 'Accounting, network complementarities and the development of inter-organisational relations', *Accounting, Organizations and Society*, vol. 31, no. 3, pp. 241–275.

Mouritsen, J., Larsen, H. T. and Bukh, P. N. D. 2001, 'Intellectual capital and the "capable firm": narrating, visualising and numbering for managing knowledge', *Accounting, Organizations and Society*, vol. 26, nos. 7–8, pp. 735–762.

Mouzelis, N. P. 1967, *Organisation and bureaucracy: an analysis of modern theories* Routledge & Kegan Paul, London.

Murray, R. 1988, 'Life after Henry (Ford)', *Marxism Today*, October, pp. 8–13.

Nanni, A., Dixon, J. R. and Vollmann, T. E. 1992, 'Integrated performance measurement: management accounting to support the new manufacturing realities', *Journal of Management Accounting Research*, vol. 4, pp. 1–19.

Neimark, M. 1990, 'The king is dead. Long live the king!', *Critical Perspectives on Accounting*, vol. 1, no. 1, pp. 103–114.

—— 1994, 'Regicide revisited: Marx, Foucault and accounting', *Critical Perspectives on Accounting*, vol. 5, no. 1, pp. 87–108.

Neimark, M. and Tinker, T. 1986, 'The social construction of management control systems', *Accounting, Organizations and Society*, vol. 11, nos. 4–5, pp. 369–395.

Nelson, R. R. 1995, 'Recent evolutionary theorizing about economic change', *Journal of Economic Literature*, vol. 33, no. 1, pp. 48–90.

Neu, D., Cooper, D. J. and Everett, J. 2001, 'Critical accounting interventions', *Critical Perspectives on Accounting*, vol. 12, no. 6, pp. 735–762.

Newby, H. 1977, *The differentiated worker* Penguin, London.

Nichols, T. and Beynon, H. 1977, *Living with capitalism: class relations and the modern factory* Routledge & Kegan Paul, London.

Norreklit, H. 2000, 'The balance on the balanced scorecard: a critical analysis of some of its assumptions', *Management Accounting Research*, vol. 11, no. 1, pp. 65–88.

—— 2003, 'The balanced scorecard: what is the score? A rhetorical analysis of the balanced scorecard', *Accounting, Organizations and Society*, vol. 28, no. 6, pp. 591–619.

Norton, D. P. 2000, *Should balanced scorecards be required? Balanced scorecard report* Harvard Business School and the Balanced Scorecard Collaborative, Cambridge, MA.

O'Connell, H. A. 1995, 'Microsoft's foundation for business', *Management Accounting* [USA], vol. 77, no. 3, pp. 46–47.

O'Doherty, D. and Willmott, H. 2001a, 'Debating labour process theory: the issue of subjectivity and the relevance of poststructuralism', *Sociology*, vol. 35, no. 2, pp. 457–476.

—— 2001b, 'The question of subjectivity and the labour process', *International Studies of Management and Organization*, vol. 30, no. 4, pp. 112–132.

Ogden, S. G. 1993, 'The limitations of agency theory: the case of accounting-based profit sharing schemes', *Critical Perspectives on Accounting*, vol. 4, no. 2, pp. 179–206.

—— 1997, 'Accounting for organizational performance: the construction of the customer in the privatized water industry', *Accounting, Organizations and Society*, vol. 22, no. 6, pp. 529–556.

Ohmae, K. 1985, *Triad power: the coming shape of global competition* Free Press/Collier-Macmillan, New York/London.

Orton, J. D. and Weick, K. E. 1990, 'Loosely coupled systems: a reconceptualization', *Academy of Management Review*, vol. 15, no. 2, p. 203.

Otley, D. 1978, 'Budget use and managerial performance', *Journal of Accounting Research*, vol. 16, no. 1, pp. 122–149.

—— 1980, 'The contingency theory of management accounting: achievement and prognosis', *Accounting, Organizations and Society*, vol. 5, no. 4, pp. 413–428.

—— 1983, 'Concepts of control: the contribution of cybernetics and general system theory to management control', in *New perspectives in management control*, E. A. Lowe and J. L. T. Machin, eds, Macmillan, London, pp. 59–87.

—— 1994, 'Management control in contemporary organizations: towards a wider framework', *Management Accounting Research*, vol. 5, nos. 3–4, pp. 289–299.

—— 1999, 'Performance management: a framework for management control systems research', *Management Accounting Research*, vol. 10, no. 4, pp. 363–382.

—— 2003, 'Management control and performance management: whence and whither?', *The British Accounting Review*, vol. 35, no. 4, pp. 309–326.

Otley, D. and Berry, A. J. 1980, 'Control, organization and accounting', *Accounting, Organizations and Society*, vol. 5, no. 2, pp. 231–244.

—— 1994, 'Case study research in management accounting and control', *Management Accounting Research*, vol. 5, no. 1, pp. 45–65.

Parker, L. D. and Roffey, B. H. 1997, 'Methodological themes back to the drawing board: revisiting grounded theory and the everyday accountant's and manager's reality', *Accounting, Auditing and Accountability Journal*, vol. 10, no. 2, p. 212.

Peet, R. 1980, 'Historical materialism and mode of production: a note on Marx's perspective and method', in *An introduction to Marxist theories of underdevelopment*, R. Peet, ed., Research School of Pacific Studies, The Australian National University, Canberra, pp. 9–26.

Pennings, J. M. 1975, 'The relevance of the structural-contingency model for organizational effectiveness', *Administrative Science Quarterly*, vol. 20, no. 3, pp. 393–411.

—— 2002, 'Structural contingency theory: a reappraisal', in *Central Currents in Organizational Studies I: Frameworks and Applications, Vol. 3*, S. R. Clegg, ed., Sage, London, pp. 3–41.

Perrow, C. 1967, 'A framework for the comparative analysis of organizations', *American Sociological Review*, vol. 32, no. 2, pp. 194–208.

—— 1970, *Organizational analysis: a sociological view* Tavistock, London.

Pinch, T., Mulkay, M. and Ashmore, M. 1989, 'Clinical budgeting: experimentation in the social sciences: a drama in five acts', *Accounting, Organizations and Society*, vol. 14, no. 3, pp. 271–301.

Piore, M. J. 1994, 'Corporate reform in American manufacturing and the challenge to economic theory', in *Information technology and the corporation of the 1990s: research studies*, T. J. Allen and M. S. Scott-Morton, eds, Oxford University Press, New York, pp. 46–60.

Piore, M. J. and Sabel, C. F. 1984, *The second industrial divide: possibilities for prosperity* Basic Books, New York.

Piper, J. 1978, 'Determinants of financial control systems for multiple retailers: some case study evidence', unpublished paper, University of Loughborough.

Pollard, S. 1965, *The genesis of modern management: a study of the industrial revolution in Great Britain* E. Arnold, London.

Porter, M. E. 1980, *Competitive strategy: techniques for analyzing industries and competitors* Free Press, New York.

—— 1985, *Competitive advantage: creating and sustaining superior performance* Free Press/Collier-Macmillan, New York/London.

—— 1998, 'Clusters and the new economics of competition', *Harvard Business Review*, vol. 76, no. 6, pp. 77–90.

Power, M. and Laughlin, R. 1996, 'Habermas, law and accounting', *Accounting, Organizations and Society*, vol. 21, no. 5, pp. 441–465.

Preston, A. M. 2006, 'Enabling, enacting and maintaining action at a distance: an historical case study of the role of accounts in the reduction of the Navajo herds', *Accounting, Organizations and Society*, vol. 31, no. 6, pp. 559–578.

Preston, A. M., Cooper, D. J. and Coombs, R. W. 1992, 'Fabricating budgets: a study of the production of management budgeting in the National Health Service', *Accounting, Organizations and Society*, vol. 17, no. 6, pp. 561–593.

Pugh, D. S. 1997, *Organization theory: selected readings*, 4th edn, Penguin, London.

Pugh, D. S., Hickson, D. J. and Hinings, C. R. 1969, 'An empirical taxonomy of structures of work organizations', *Administrative Science Quarterly*, vol. 14, no. 1, pp. 115–127.

Puxty, A. G. 1993, *The social & organizational context of management accounting* Academic Press in association with the Chartered Institute of Management Accountants, London.

Quattrone, P. and Hopper, T. 2001, 'What does organizational change mean? Speculations on a taken for granted category', *Management Accounting Research*, vol. 12, no. 4, pp. 403–435.

—— 2005, 'A "time-space odyssey": management control systems in two multinational organisations', *Accounting, Organizations and Society*, vol. 30, nos. 7–8, pp. 735–764.

Rahman, M. and McCosh, A. M. 1976, 'The influence of organisational and personal factors on the use of accounting information: an empirical study', *Accounting, Organizations and Society*, vol. 1, no. 4, pp. 339–355.

Rathe, A. W. 1960, 'Management controls in business', in *Management control systems*, D. G. Malcolm and A. J. Rowe, eds, Wiley, New York.

Rayburn, L. G. 1989, *Principles of cost accounting: using a cost management approach*, 4th edn, Irwin, Homewood, IL.

Richardson, A. J. 1989, 'Corporatism and intraprofessional hegemony: a study of regulation and internal social order', *Accounting, Organizations and Society*, vol. 14, nos. 5–6, pp. 415–431.

Ritzer, G. 1992, *Sociological theory*, 3rd edn, McGraw-Hill, New York.

Roberts, J. 1990, 'Strategy and accounting in a UK conglomerate', *Accounting, Organizations and Society*, vol. 15, nos. 1–2, pp. 107–126.

Roberts, J. and Scapens, R. 1985, 'Accounting systems and systems of accountability – understanding accounting practices in their organisational contexts', *Accounting, Organizations and Society*, vol. 10, no. 4, pp. 443–456.

Roberts, J. Sanderson, P., Barker, R. and Henry, J. 2006, 'In the mirror of the market: the disciplinary effects of company/fund managers meeting', *Accounting, Organizations and Society*, vol. 31, no. 3, pp. 277–294.

Robson, K. 1991, 'On the arenas of accounting change: the process of translation', *Accounting, Organizations and Society*, vol. 16, nos. 5–6, pp. 547–570.

—— 1992, 'Accounting numbers as "inscription": action at a distance and the development of accounting', *Accounting, Organizations and Society*, vol. 17, no. 7, pp. 685–708.

Roll, E. 1968, *An early experiment in industrial organisation: being a history of the firm of Boulton & Watt 1775–1805*, A. M. Kelley, New York.

Roodhooft, F. and Warlop, L. 1999, 'On the role of sunk costs and asset specificity in outsourcing decisions: a research note', *Accounting, Organizations and Society*, vol. 24, no. 4, pp. 363–369.

Rosenberg, D., Tomkins, C., and Day, P. 1982, 'A work role perspective of accountants in local government service departments', *Accounting, Organizations and Society*, vol. 7, no. 2, pp. 123–137.

Roslender, R. 1992, *Sociological perspectives on modern accountancy* Routledge, London.

—— 1996, 'Relevance lost and found: critical perspectives on the promise of management accounting', *Critical Perspectives on Accounting*, vol. 7, no. 5, pp. 533–561.

Roslender, R. and Hart, S. J. 2002, 'Integrating management accounting and marketing in the pursuit of competitive advantage: the case for strategic management accounting', *Critical Perspectives on Accounting*, vol. 13, no. 2, pp. 255–277.

—— 2003, 'In search of strategic management accounting: theoretical and field study perspectives', *Management Accounting Research*, vol. 14, no. 3, pp. 255–279.

Sartorius, K. and Kirsten, J. 2005, 'The boundaries of the firm: why do sugar producers outsource sugarcane production?', *Management Accounting Research*, vol. 16, no. 1, pp. 81–99.

Savage, M. 1998, 'Discipline, surveillance and the career: employment on the Great Western Railway 1833–1914', in *Foucault, management and organization theory: from panopticon to technologies of self*, A. McKinlay and K. Starkey, eds, Sage, London, pp. 65–94.

Scapens, R. W. 1978, 'A neoclassical measure of profit', *Accounting Review*, vol. 53, no. 2, pp. 448–469.

—— 1984, 'Management accounting: a survey', in *Management accounting, organizational behaviour and capital budgeting*, R. W. Scapens, D. T. Otley and R. J. Lister, eds, Macmillan, London, pp. 15–95.

—— 1994, 'Never mind the gap: towards an institutional perspective on management accounting practice', *Management Accounting Research*, vol. 5, nos. 3–4, pp. 301–321.

—— 2006, 'Understanding management accounting practices: a personal journey', *British Accounting Review*, vol. 38, no. 1, pp. 1–30.

Scapens, R. W. and Jazayeri, M. 2003, 'ERP systems and management accounting change: opportunities or impacts? A research note', *European Accounting Review*, vol. 12, no. 1, pp. 201–233.

Scapens, R. W. and Roberts, J. 1993, 'Accounting and control: a case study of resistance to accounting change', *Management Accounting Research*, vol. 4, no. 1, pp. 1–32.

Schutz, A. 1967, *The phenomenology of the social world* Northwestern University Press, Evanston, IL.

Scorgie, M. E. 1997, 'Progenitors of modern management accounting concepts and mensurations in pre-industrial England', *Accounting, Business and Financial History*, vol. 7, no. 1, pp. 31–59.

Scott, W. R. 1995, *Institutions and organizations* Sage, Thousand Oaks, CA.

—— 2001, *Institutions and organizations*, 2nd edn, Sage, Thousand Oaks, CA.

Seal, W. 2006, 'Management accounting and corporate governance: an institutional interpretation of the agency problem', *Management Accounting Research*, vol. 17, no. 4, pp. 389–408.

Seal, W. and Vincent-Jones, P. 1997, 'Accounting and trust in the enabling of long-term relation', *Accounting, Auditing and Accountability Journal*, vol. 10, no. 3, pp. 406–431.

Seal, W., Berry, A. and Cullen, J. 2004, 'Disembedding the supply chain: institutionalized reflexivity and inter-firm accounting', *Accounting, Organizations and Society*, vol. 29, no. 1, pp. 73–92.

Seal, W., Cullen, J., Dunlop, A., Berry, T. and Ahmed, M. 1999, 'Enacting a European supply chain: a case study on the role of management accounting', *Management Accounting Research*, vol. 10, no. 3, pp. 303–322.

Selznick, P. 1949, *TVA and the grass roots: a study in the sociology of formal organization* University of California Press, Berkeley.

Senge, P. M. 1990, *The fifth discipline: the art and practice of the learning organization* Doubleday/Currency, New York.

Shalin, D. N. 1986, 'Pragmatism and social interactionism', *American Sociological Review*, vol. 51, no. 1, pp. 9–29.

Shank, J. K. 1989, 'Strategic cost management: new wine, or just new bottles?', *Journals of Management Accounting Research*, vol. 1, Fall, pp. 47–65.

—— 1996, 'Analysing technology investments – from NPV to strategic cost management (SCM)', *Management Accounting Research*, vol. 7, no. 2, pp. 185–197.

—— 2001, *Cases in cost management: a strategic emphasis*, 2nd edn, South-Western College, Australia/UK.

Shank, J. K. and Govindarajan, V. 1989, *Strategic cost analysis: the evolution from managerial to strategic accounting* Irwin, Homewood, IL.

—— 1993, *Strategic cost management: the new tool for competitive advantage* Free Press/Maxwell Macmillan, New York/Toronto.

Sharma, A. 1997, 'Professional as agent: knowledge asymmetry in agency exchange', *Academy of Management Review*, vol. 22, no. 3, pp. 758–798.

Shillinglaw, G. 1977, *Managerial cost accounting*, 4th edn, Irwin, Homewood, IL.

Simon, H. 1961, *Administrative behaviour*, 2nd edn, Macmillan, New York.

—— 1964, 'On the concept of organizational goal', *Administrative Science Quarterly*, vol. 9, no. 1, pp. 1–22.

Simons, R. 1987, 'Accounting control systems and business strategy: an empirical analysis', *Accounting, Organizations and Society*, vol. 12, no. 4, pp. 357–374.

Skinner, W. I. C. K. 1974, 'The focused factory', *Harvard Business Review*, vol. 52, no. 3, pp. 113–121.

Slack, N., Chambers, S. and Johnston, R. 2004, *Operations management*, 4th edn, Financial Times/Prentice-Hall, Harlow.

Smith, D. 1990, 'Organisation and class: Burawoy in Birmingham', in *Organisation theory and class analysis*, S. R. Clegg, ed., Walter de Gruyter, Berlin, pp. 367–388.

Soin, K., Seal, W. and Cullen, J. 2002, 'ABC and organizational change: an institutional perspective', *Management Accounting Research*, vol. 13, no. 2, pp. 249–271.

Solomons, D. 1952, *Studies in costing* Sweet & Maxwell, London.

Sombart, W. 1953, 'Medieval and modern commercial enterprise', in *Enterprise in secular change: readings in economics history*, F. C. Lane and J. C. Riemersma, eds, Allen & Unwin, London.

Sowell, E. M. 1973, *The evolution of the theories and techniques of standard costs* University of Alabama Press, Tuscaloosa.

Spekle, R. F. 2001, 'Explaining management control structure variety: a transaction cost economics perspective', *Accounting, Organizations and Society*, vol. 26, nos. 4–5, pp. 419–441.

Spencer, D. A. 2000, 'The demise of radical political economics? An essay on the evolution of a theory of capitalist production', *Cambridge Journal of Economics*, vol. 24, pp. 543–564.

Spicer, B. H. 1988, 'Towards an organizational theory of the transfer pricing process', *Accounting, Organizations and Society*, vol. 13, no. 3, pp. 303–322.

Spicer, B. H. and Ballew, V. 1983, 'Management accounting systems and the economics of internal organization', *Accounting, Organizations and Society*, vol. 8, no. 1, pp. 73–96.

Sproull, L. and Kiesler, S. 1986, 'Reducing social context cues: electronic mail in organizational communication', *Management Science*, vol. 32, no. 11, pp. 1492–1512.

Star, S. L. and Griesemer, J. R. 1989, 'Institutional ecology, "translations" and boundary objects: amateurs and professionals in Berkeley's Museum of Vertebrate Zoology, 1907–39', *Social Studies of Science*, vol. 19, no. 3, pp. 387–420.

Storey, J. 1983, *Managerial prerogative and the question of control* Routledge & Kegan Paul, London.

—— 1985, 'Management control as a bridging concept', *Journal of Management Studies*, vol. 22, no. 3, pp. 269–291.

—— 1986, 'The Phoney War? New office technology: organisation and control', in *Managing the labour process*, D. Knights and H. Willmott, eds, Gower, Aldershot, pp. 44–66.

Sward, K. 1948, *The legend of Henry Ford* Rinehart, New York.

Swieringa, R. J. and Waterhouse, J. H. 1982, 'Organizational views of transfer pricing', *Accounting, Organizations and Society*, vol. 7, no. 2, pp. 149–165.

Tangen, S. 2004, 'Performance measurement: from philosophy to practice', *International Journal of Productivity and Performance*, vol. 53, no. 8, pp. 726–737.

Taylor, F. W. 1964, *Scientific management: comprising Shop management, The principles of scientific management, Testimony before the Special House Committee* Harper & Row, London.

—— 1967, *The principles of scientific management* Norton, New York.

Teulings, A. W. M. 1986, 'Managerial labour process in the organised capitalism; the power of corporate management and the powerlessness of the manager', in *Managing the Labour Process*, D. Knights and H. Willmott, eds, Gower, Aldershot, pp. 142–165.

Theiss, E. L. 1932, 'Budgetory procedures as a means of administrative control', *Accounting Review*, vol. 7, no. 1, pp. 11–21.

Thompson, G. F. 1998, 'Encountering economics and accounting: some skirmishes and engagements', *Accounting, Organizations and Society*, vol. 23, no. 3, pp. 283–323.

Thompson, J. B. 1983, 'Rationality and social rationalization: an assessment of Habermas's *Theory of Communicative Action*', *Sociology*, vol. 17, no. 2, pp. 278–294.

Thompson, P. 1990, 'Crawling from the wreckage: the labour process and the politics of production', in *Labour process theory*, D. Knights and H. Willmott, eds, Macmillan, London, pp. 95–124.

Thompson, P. and McHugh, D. 2002, *Work organisations: a critical introduction*, 3rd edn, Palgrave, Basingstoke.

Thompson, P. and Smith, C. 2001, 'Follow the redbrick road: reflections on pathways in and out of the labour process debate', *International Studies of Management and Organization*, vol. 30, no. 4, pp. 40–67.

Tiessen, P. and Waterhouse, J. H. 1983, 'Towards a descriptive theory of management accounting', *Accounting, Organizations and Society*, vol. 8, no. 2/3, pp. 251–267.

Tillema, S. 2005, 'Towards an integrated contingency framework for MAS sophistication: case studies on the scope of accounting instruments in Dutch power and gas companies', *Management Accounting Research*, vol. 16, no. 1, pp. 101–129.

Tinker, A. M. 1980, 'Towards a political economy of accounting: an empirical illustration of the Cambridge controversies', *Accounting, Organizations and Society*, vol. 5, no. 1, pp. 147–160.

Tinker, A. M., Merino, B. D. and Neimark, M. D. 1982, 'The normative origins of positive theories: ideology and accounting thought', *Accounting, Organizations and Society*, vol. 7, no. 2, pp. 167–200.

Tinker, T. 1991, 'The accountant as partisan', *Accounting, Organizations and Society*, vol. 16, no. 3, pp. 297–310.

Tomkins, C. 2001, 'Interdependencies, trust and information in relationships, alliances and networks', *Accounting, Organizations and Society*, vol. 26, no. 2, pp. 161–191.

Tomkins, C. and Groves, R. 1983, '"The everyday accountant and researching his reality": further thoughts', *Accounting, Organizations and Society*, vol. 8, no. 4, pp. 407–415.

Towry, K. L. 2003, 'Control in a teamwork environment: the impact of social ties on the effectiveness of mutual monitoring contracts', *Accounting Review*, vol. 78, no. 4, pp. 1069–1095.

Tyson, T. 1988, 'The nature and function of cost-keeping in a later 19th-century small business', *Accounting Historians Journal*, vol. 15, no. 1, pp. 29–44.

Uddin, S. and Hopper, T. 2001, 'A Bangladesh soap opera: privatisation, accounting, and regimes of control in a less developed country', *Accounting, Organizations and Society*, vol. 26, nos. 7–8, pp. 643–672.

Urry, J. 1988, 'Disorganised capitalism', *Marxism Today*, October, pp. 30–33.

Utterback, J. M. and Abernathy, W. J. 1975, 'A dynamic model of process and product innovation', *Omega*, vol. 3, no. 6, pp. 639–656.

van den Bogaard, M. A. and Spekle, R. F. 2003, 'Reinventing the hierarchy: strategy and control in the Shell Chemicals carve-out', *Management Accounting Research*, vol. 14, no. 2, pp. 79–93.

Veblen, T. 1994, *The place of science in modern civilisation and other essays*, reprint of 1st edn, Routledge/Thoemmes Press, London.

Vickers, C. G. 1967, *Towards a sociology of management* Chapman and Hall, London.

—— 1972, *Freedom in a rocking boat: changing values in an unstable society* Penguin, Harmondsworth.

Walker, M. 1989, 'Agency theory: a falsificationist perspective', *Accounting, Organizations and Society*, vol. 14, nos. 5–6, pp. 433–453.

Ward, T. and Patel, K. 1990, 'ABC – a framework for improving shareholder value', *Management Accounting (UK)*, July, pp. 34–36.

Warhust, C. 1998, 'Recognizing the possible: the organization and control of socialist labour process', *Administrative Science Quarterly*, vol. 43, pp. 470–497.

Waterhouse, J. H. and Tiessen, P. 1978, 'A contingency framework for management accounting systems research', *Accounting, Organizations and Society*, vol. 3, no. 1, pp. 65–76.

Watkins, A. L. and Arrington, C. E. 2007, 'Accounting, new public management and American politics: theoretical insights into the national performance review', *Critical Perspectives on Accounting*, vol. 18, no. 1, pp. 33–58.

Watson, T. J. 2003, *Sociology, work and industry*, 4th edn, Routledge, London.

Weber, M. 1930, *The Protestant ethic and the spirit of capitalism* Allen & Unwin, London.

—— 1949, *The methodology of social sciences* Free Press, New York.

—— 1958, *From Max Weber: essays in sociology* Oxford University Press, New York.

—— 1961, *General economic history* Collier, New York.

—— 1964, *The theory of social and economic organization* Free Press, New York.

—— 1968, *Economy and society*, 3 vols, Bedminster Press, Totowa, NJ.

—— 1978, *Economy and society: an outline of interpretive sociology* University of California Press, Berkeley.

Wickramasinghe, D. and Hopper, T. 2005, 'A cultural political economy of management accounting controls: a case study of a textile mill in a traditional Sinhalese village', *Critical Perspectives on Accounting*, vol. 16, no. 4, pp. 473–503.

Wickramasinghe, D., Gunarathne, T. and Jayakody, J. A. S. K. Forthcoming, 'Interest lost: the rise and fall of a balanced scorecard project in Sri Lanka', *Advances in Public Interest in Accounting*.

Wickramasinghe, D., Hopper, T. and Rathnasiri, C. 2004, 'Japanese cost management meet Sri Lankan politics: disappearance and reappearance of bureaucratic management controls in a privatised utility', *Accounting, Auditing and Accountability Journal*, vol. 17, no. 1, pp. 85–120.

Wiener, N. 1948, *Cybernetics: or control and communication in the animal and the machine* MIT Press, Cambridge, MA.

Williams, K., Haslam, C. and Williams, J. 1992, 'Ford versus "Fordism": the beginning of mass production?', *Work, Employment and Society*, vol. 6, no. 4, pp. 517–555.

Williamson, O. E. 1970, *Corporate control and business behavior: an inquiry into the effects of organization form on enterprise behavior* Prentice-Hall, Englewood Cliffs, NJ.

—— 1975, *Markets and hierarchies: analysis and antitrust implications: a study in the economics of internal organization* Free Press/Collier-Macmillan, New York/London.

—— 1988, 'The logic of economic organization', *Journal of Law, Economics, and Organization*, vol. 4, no. 1, pp. 65–93.

—— 1991, 'Comparative economic organization: the analysis of discrete structural alternatives', *Administrative Science Quarterly*, vol. 36, no. 2, pp. 269–296.

Williamson, O. E. and Winter, S. G. 1988, 'Introduction', *Journal of Law, Economics, and Organization*, vol. 4, no. 1, pp. 1–2.

Willmott, H., Puxty, A. G. and Sikka, P. 1993, 'Losing one's reason: on the integrity of accounting academics', *Accounting, Auditing and Accountability Journal*, vol. 6, no. 2, pp. 98–110.

Willmott, H., Puxty, A. G., Cooper, D. J., Lowe, E. A. and Robson, K. 1992, 'Regulation of accountancy and accountants: a comparative analysis of accounting for research and development in four advanced capitalist countries', *Accounting, Auditing and Accountability Journal*, vol. 5, no. 2, pp. 32–56.

Wilson, R. M. S. and Chua, W. F. 1993, *Managerial accounting: method and meaning*, teachers' guide edn, Chapman and Hall, London.

Wood, S. 1979, 'A reappraisal of the contingency approach to organization', *Journal of Management Studies*, vol. 16, no. 3, pp. 334–355.

Woodward, J. 1965, *Industrial organization: theory and practice* Oxford University Press, London.

Yahikawa, T., Innes, J. and Mitchell, F. 1994, 'Functional analysis of activity-based cost information', *Journal of Cost Management*, Spring, pp. 40–48.

Yamey, B. S. 1964, 'Accounting and the rise of capitalism: further notes on a theme by Sombart', *Journal of Accounting Research*, vol. 2, no. 2, pp. 117–136.

Yates, M. D. 1999, 'Braverman and the class struggle', *Monthly Review*, January, pp. 2–11.

Young, D. W. 1979, 'Administrative theory and administrative systems: a synthesis among diverging fields of inquiry', *Accounting, Organizations and Society*, vol. 4, no. 3, pp. 235–244.

Zack, M. H. and McKenney, J. L. 1995, 'Social context and interaction in ongoing computer-supported management groups', *Organization Science*, vol. 6, no. 4, pp. 394–422.

Zimbalist, A. 1976, 'Technology and the labour process in the printing industry', in *Case studies on the labour process*, A. Zimbalist, ed., Monthly Review Press, New York, pp. 103–126.

Zucker, L. G. 1987, 'Institutional theories of organization', *Annual Review of Sociology*, vol. 13, pp. 443–464.

Index

541